T0250620

Lecture Notes in Computer Science 1192
Edited by G. Goos, J. Hartmanis and J. van Leeuwen

Advisory Board: W. Brauer D. Gries J. Stoer

Springer
Berlin
Heidelberg
New York
Barcelona
Budapest
Hong Kong
London
Milan
Paris
Santa Clara
Singapore
Tokyo

Mads Dam (Ed.)

Analysis and Verification of Multiple-Agent Languages

5th LOMAPS Workshop
Stockholm, Sweden, June 24-26, 1996
Selected Papers

Springer

Series Editors

Gerhard Goos, Karlsruhe University, Germany

Juris Hartmanis, Cornell University, NY, USA

Jan van Leeuwen, Utrecht University, The Netherlands

Volume Editor

Mads Dam
Swedish Institute of Computer Science
Box 1263, S-164 28 Kista, Sweden
E-mail: mfd@sics.se

Cataloging-in-Publication data applied for

Die Deutsche Bibliothek - CIP-Einheitsaufnahme

Analysis and verification of multiple agent languages : selected papers / 5th LOMAPS Workshop, Stockholm, Sweden, June 24 - 26, 1996 / Mads Dam (ed.). - Berlin ; Heidelberg ; New York ; Barcelona ; Budapest ; Hong Kong ; London ; Milan ; Paris ; Santa Clara ; Singapore ; Tokyo : Springer, 1997
(Lecture notes in computer science ; Vol. 1192)
ISBN 3-540-62503-8

NE: Dam, Mads [Hrsg.]; LOMAPS <5, 1996, Stockholm>; GT

CR Subject Classification (1991): F.3.1, D.1.3, D.3, D.2.4, C.2.4

ISSN 0302-9743
ISBN 3-540-62503-8 Springer-Verlag Berlin Heidelberg New York

This work is subject to copyright. All rights are reserved, whether the whole or part of the material is concerned, specifically the rights of translation, reprinting, re-use of illustrations, recitation, broadcasting, reproduction on microfilms or in any other way, and storage in data banks. Duplication of this publication or parts thereof is permitted only under the provisions of the German Copyright Law of September 9, 1965, in its current version, and permission for use must always be obtained from Springer-Verlag. Violations are liable for prosecution under the German Copyright Law.

© Springer-Verlag Berlin Heidelberg 1997
Printed in Germany

Typesetting: Camera-ready by author
SPIN 10549852 06/3142 – 5 4 3 2 1 0 Printed on acid-free paper

Preface

The present volume is the proceedings of the 5th LOMAPS workshop on Analysis and Verification of Multiple-Agent Languages held June 24–26 1996 on the island of Långholmen in Stockholm, Sweden. LOMAPS is an Esprit project started in December 1993 with the objective of investigating program analysis and verification techniques applicable to emerging multi-paradigm programming languages such as CML, Facile, Erlang, PICT and Oz, to name but a few of many recent examples. The project has held biannual internal progress workshops. With this workshop, the fifth in the series, we (the LOMAPS site leaders) wished to examine the status of the research area after the first two years of the LOMAPS project, and to expand the scope of discussion to other prominent researchers in our field.

The workshop included five invited presentations by *Giorgio Levi* (Pisa), *Fritz Knabe* (Santiago, Chile), *D. Le Metayer* (IRISA, Rennes), *Mike Williams* (Ericsson, Stockholm), and *R. Wilhelm* (Saarbrücken). In addition the workshop had 20 submitted presentations. A post-workshop call for papers resulted in 16 paper submissions of which, after a review process, 14 were selected to appear in these proceedings along with invited papers by Levi, Knabe, Le Metayer, and Wilhelm.

I am grateful to the other LOMAPS site leaders, and in particular to the project coordinator Flemming Nielson of DAIMI, Aarhus, for producing the introductory section on logical and operational methods in the analysis of programs and systems, surveying the state of the art of the area, and putting the proceedings papers into this context. Thanks are due also to Fredrik Orava for helping to organise the workshop.

The selection committee for these proceedings consisted of Mads Dam (SICS, Stockholm, chair), Pierpaolo Degano (Pisa), Pierre Jouvelot (Ecole des Mines, Paris), Alan Mycroft (Cambridge), Flemming Nielson (Aarhus), and Bent Thomsen (ICL/IC-PARC).

In addition to the selection committee members I wish to thank also Torben Amtoft, Anindya Banerjee, GianLuigi Ferrari, Nicoletta De Francesco, Lars-Åke Fredlund, Chris Hankin, Paola Inverardi, Lone Leth, Fredrik Orava, Joachim Parrow, Marco Pistore, Davide Sangiorgi and Jean-Pierre Talpin for their help with refereeing.

Stockholm, November 1996

Mads Dam
Selection Committee Chair

Contents

Logical and Operational Methods in the Analysis of Programs and Systems

F. Nielson

together with P. Cousot, M. Dam, P. Degano, P. Jouvelot, A. Mycroft, and B. Thomsen

The **LOMAPS** project studies the use of *Logical and Operational Methods in the Analysis of Programs and Systems* and is sponsored by ESPRIT Basic Research[1]. It has been fostered by the realisation that each of the existing programming paradigms (further discussed below) have their own strengths and weaknesses, and that the reliable construction of computer systems may benefit from a combination of paradigms, and hence the use of multiparadigmatic languages, in order to obtain the modularity, reactivity, and concurrency required. Since each programming paradigm typically has its own set of methods and techniques, this calls for general methods and techniques available over a spectrum of programming paradigms.

The main scientific aims of the project therefore are to conduct basic research into methods and techniques for the analysis of performance and reliability of high-level programs with emphasis on multiparadigmatic languages. This involves hybrid systems that exhibit one or more of the following characteristics: physical distribution, massive parallelism, combinations of computational paradigms (like functional programming and concurrency), higher order communication, and multiple agents with dynamically evolving interconnection topology.

The main technological objectives are the development of advanced analysis and verification techniques for software development. Of particular interest are their application in compilers and programming environments for multiparadigmatic programming languages implemented in a distributed setting. This is important because the market place is already beginning to see the arrival of "end-user" applications that require a multiparadigmatic approach: to handle multiple co-operating agents and to exploit the availability of massively parallel computing systems; examples include multi-media/multi-user systems and real-time process control systems. This development is likely to increase rapidly as access to the internet becomes available to the ordinary consumer, perhaps through dedicated web-browsing hardware to be placed side-by-side with the television and video recorder.

---

[1] Project number 8130 running from December 1993 to May 1997; for further information consult `http://www.daimi.aau.dk/~bra8130/LOMAPS.html`.

The present proceedings attempts to take a "snapshot" of the current state of affairs within five themes central to the LOMAPS project: Integration of Programming Paradigms [61], Annotated Type and Effect Systems [66], Abstract Interpretation [25], Modalities in Analysis and Verification [30], and Enhanced Operational Semantics [35]. Each section below begins with a presentation of our view of the state of affairs within the area, and ends with a brief explanation of how the papers in this volume enhance our knowledge of the area.

Integration of Programming Paradigms

Programming notions can be expressed in many different paradigms—imperative, object-oriented, concurrent, functional, logic-programming, constraint, etc. It is widely agreed that each programming paradigm has its own merits and is particularly appropriate for expressing certain classes of computation, thus the choice of paradigm can greatly affect the ease of programming.

Traditionally, when constructing large scale systems, in particular distributed systems, it is often necessary to use multiple programming styles with disparate programming models, and very often it is necessary to resolve conflicts by low level methods reverting to the lowest common denominator. Choosing locally optimal paradigms for each subsystem creates the problem of how to integrate the resulting modules into a coherent whole. The mathematical idea that we could choose a single globally optimal paradigm for expressing the whole system fails to take account of issues like maintenance and the desire for software re-use.

Historically, application developers split their system so that application-specific subsystems depend upon the operating system directly. However, this often causes difficulties with applications not being portable because each operating system has its own distinct application programming interface, and hence different versions of applications may wish to employ different subsystem architectures due to the fact that distinct operating systems provide services that differ in kind and semantics.

Current technology is working to solve these historical problems by introducing a concept called "middleware". Here, an application interfaces with the middleware and normally does not access the underlying operating system directly. One rapidly developing strand in this direction is the tendency of various GUI's (Graphical User Interfaces) such as X-Windows, Windows-95 and Windows-NT to be seen as a low-level interface; instead of providing X over a network one provides (for example) a Java API library. Thus one can see tools which started life as mere web browsers becoming, in effect, a higher level user interface for many systems.

Middleware suppliers strive to present the user with a collection of useful features whose interfaces can be neatly expressed in the various programming languages used for constructing large scale systems. However, little or no attention is paid to integrating these constructs into the programming environment.

To repair this situation several research teams and even a few commercial systems have proposed the notion of coordination languages (e.g. Linda [14], Gamma [6] and LO [4, 5]). The languages are usually not full programming languages, but rather limited to constructs for coordinating communication between component subsystems. Clearly coordination languages solve many of the problems found in the construction of large scale systems by unifying the level of coordination and communication. However, the application programmer is still faced with different programming models for the various modules in the system.

More recently languages that strive to combine several programming paradigms in a single system both for sequential and for distributed computing have been put forward, such as Facile [39, 80], Oz [77], and PICT [69, 70]. A language which supports multiple programming paradigms often enables a more direct expression of the design, since many problems and solutions consist of various components that are more natural and easier when viewed in different ways. Allowing the implementation to exploit a more direct expression of the design helps in avoiding unnecessary encodings that often are great sources of software errors and maintenance complication.

With the emergence on the internet of mobile agents [87, 81] or [41] applets, i.e. chunks of programs that can be sent around a network of computers and execute in different locations, the need for multiple programming paradigms has been further stressed.

It is important however, not to believe that multiparadigmatic programming gives us something for free. There are foundational issues concerned with the ability to express adequately the interface for a subsystem written in one paradigm to another subsystem written in another paradigm. One apposite example is to observe that calls to side-effecting sub-systems cannot directly be expressed in a lazy functional language without risk of losing the reasoning which the functional programmer tacitly assumed. Much work has been done on using "monads" which allow locally side-effecting code to be encapsulated in a manner which preserves functional properties like referential transparency. However, the general question of how the coordination language represents views of interfaces appropriate to each paradigm seems unresolved.

In this volume several papers address, at various levels, the issue of integration of programming paradigms:

Analysis of FACILE programs: a case study (by P. Degano, C. Priami, L. Leth and B. Thomsen) presents a method for analysing mobile agents built in the Facile language which integrates several programming paradigms. Since mobile agents may carry communication links with them as they move across the network, they create very dynamic interconnection structures that can be extremely complex to analyse. However, since the various paradigms have been integrated carefully with the support of formal semantics, Facile programs may be subjected to formal reasoning. This paper presents a non-interleaving semantics for Facile by looking only at the labels of transitions and then uses the new Facile semantics to debug an agent-based system.

Formalising and prototyping a concurrent object-based language (by L. Fredlund, J. Koistinen and F. Orava) presents a semantics for (a core of) a concurrent object-oriented language by encoding of the language into the polyadic π-calculus. Experimental implementation has been done in Facile. The main concern of the paper is adding constructs for concurrency and distribution to an existing object-oriented language used by Ericsson. The language design and prototype implementation is based on formal semantics to allow for easy experimentation with how the object-oriented paradigm interacts with concurrency and distribution.

Parallel implementation of functional languages (by R. Wilhelm) discusses using a high level lazy functional language to program parallel distributed memory machines. Such machines are difficult to program since they offer a bad ratio of computation speed versus communication speed. Disappointing results on implementing lazy functional languages by parallel graph reductions motivate the design of parallel functional languages (i.e. integration of the concurrent and functional programming paradigms) to facilitate the efficient programming of such machines.

An overview of mobile agent programming (by F. Knabe) presents an overview of mobile agents and an extension of Facile which supports agent programming. The extension takes a step towards making agent programming safer via strong static typing, but many challenges remain. Languages with first-class functions provide a good starting point for agent programming, as they make it easy to express the construction, transmission, receipt, and subsequent execution of agents. However, for developing real agent-based systems, a language implementation must handle architectural heterogeneity between communicating machines and provide sufficient performance for applications based on agents. In addition, agents need to be able to access resources on remote execution sites yet remain in a framework that provides sufficient security. An additional foundational problem is that higher order mechanisms for process (and the paradigm-varying notion of procedure) transmission provide very small-grain interplay between paradigms in contrast to the presumed much larger grained interplay offered by a coordination language.

Annotated Type and Effect Systems

Program analysis offers static techniques for predicting safe and computable approximations to the set of values or behaviours arising dynamically during computation. Traditionally this has been used to enable the application of program transformations and to allow compilers to generate more efficient code. This goes beyond merely validating the correctness of the modification; the profitability of performing the modification is also a key issue, and sometimes the modification is profitable only because it opens up for a host of other modifications that more directly improve performance. The presence of higher-order and distributed constructs gives this problem a completely new dimension. Examples include the use of program analysis to assist in documenting the software to be placed in a library of modules, thus helping the programmer in choosing the right module for the task at hand. To fully achieve these goals calls for more research into the theoretical foundations of program analysis as well as their algorithmic (or even decidability) properties.

One of the approaches to program analysis is that of annotated type and effect systems: it requires that a typed programming language be given [76, 45]. The type system is then modified with additional annotations (called effects) that expose further intensional or extensional properties of the semantics of the programs. The literature has seen a great variation in the annotations and effects used. Example effects are: collecting the set of procedures or functions called, collecting the set of storage cells written or read during execution [79], collecting the regions in which evaluation takes place [82]. Other classes of annotations are more ambitious in trying to identify the causality among various operations: that input takes place before output, that communication satisfies protocols as expressed by terms of a process algebra [65]. The interplay between types and effects is brought out when formulating the introduction and elimination rules for the various syntactic constructs (for example function abstraction and function application). Some aspects of a general methodology have emerged but a full understanding of the interplay remains an important research challenge.

The methodology of annotated type and effect systems consists of: *(i)* expressing a program analysis by means of an annotated type or effect system, *(ii)* showing the semantic correctness of the analysis, *(iii)* developing an inference algorithm and proving it syntactically sound and complete. Each of these phases have their own challenges and open problems.

(i) Much research concerns how to incorporate the flow based considerations of context dependent analysis: polyvariance (as opposed to monovariance), *k*-CFA, "polymorphic" splitting etc.; similarly for the model based considerations of relational (as opposed to independent attribute) analyses and more advanced notions of designing combined property spaces. Although the simple instances of monovariant *0*-CFA analyses in independent attribute form

can be expressed as annotated type and effect systems, it is still unclear how to achieve the more advanced possibilities. Current research suggests that the use of polymorphic recursion (for the annotations, not the types) may be essential and still decidable [82], but the interplay between the use of polymorphism and sub-typing and sub-effecting is still not fully understood [79] and is an important area of further research.

(ii) The techniques needed for establishing semantic soundness are mostly standard. For operational semantics the statement of correctness may be a subject reduction result and the method of proof may benefit from the use of co-induction; when the use of denotational semantics is possible one may benefit from the use of Kripke-logical relations[64].

(iii) Algorithmic techniques often involve the generation of constraint systems in a program independent representation. Sometimes efficient techniques developed for flow based analyses can be used to solve the constraint problems; in other cases the problems take the form of semi-unification problems and then even decidability becomes an issue [82]; furthermore, some applications demand general techniques for algebraic unification. An important area of further research is how to identify those features of the annotated type and effect systems that lead to algorithmic intractability.

In summary, program analysis by means of annotated type and effect systems seems a promising area. The main strength lies in the ability to interact with the user: clarifying what the analysis is about (and when it may fail to be of any help) and in propagating the results back to the user in an understable way (which is not always possible for approaches working on intermediate representations). It will generally be the case that the actual techniques used to obtain efficient implementations require a reformulation of the inference system in more algorithmic terms; however, it is the inference system that focuses on the key properties of the analysis, and hence the implementation must be able to provide feed-back in a form that the user can understand: expressed in terms of the inference system. This is still an area for further research as is the study of the expressiveness of the inference based specifications and the complexity and decidability of the algorithmic realisations.

In these proceedings there are several papers that address goals central to annotated type and effect systems:

The trilogy of papers *Polymorphic Subtyping for Effect Analysis: the Static Semantics* (by H. R. Nielson, F. Nielson, and T. Amtoft), *Polymorphic Subtyping for Effect Analysis: the Dynamic Semantics* (by T. Amtoft, F. Nielson, H. R. Nielson, and J. Ammann), and *Polymorphic Subtyping for Effect Analysis: the Algorithm* (by F. Nielson, H. R. Nielson, and T. Amtoft) all deal with supporting subtyping in polymorphic type and effect systems. This has been the goal of many researchers for quite some time now. Even though some success had been previously reported, in particular via the notion of "subeffecting", which however limited the static order relationship to the effect domain, the full generality of subtyping was still a challenge. This is what the trilogy of papers addresses and solves. While the first paper presents a general overview of the integration process, the two subsequent ones address more technical, though equally important, questions.

The *Static Semantics* paper describes a new static semantics that approximates some aspects of the behavior of Concurrent ML programs. In particular, for any expression, this semantics specifies a polymorphic ML-like type and an effect that gives an upper-approximation on what kind of channels are allocated during the expression evaluation. This annotated type system supports polymorphism, effects and subtyping and is the first to integrate these three aspects in a rigorous and compatible way. Applications of the presented approach to other effect systems, in particular memory effects, should pose no major problems. Effect systems could thus be used to cleanly specify the type generalization process in ML-like languages without restricting it in odd ways imposed by the effect system technology.

The *Dynamic Semantics* paper shows that the static semantics, which approximates some aspects of the behavior of Concurrent ML programs (and which is described in "the Static Semantics" paper), is sound with respect to an operational concurrent semantics. The main theorem is akin to a subject reduction one and expresses that evaluation preserves, in a sense made precise in the paper, types and behaviors, thus ensuring the semantic soundness of the static type and effect system.

The *Algorithm* paper is the last in this trilogy, and describes a Milner's W-like reconstruction algorithm for the new static semantics introduced in the two companion papers. This algorithm is inspired by previous techniques published in the literature but introduces a couple of new ideas, in particular the notion of closures over a set of constraints. It is proved sound (but not complete) with respect to the static semantics described above.

Polyvariance, Polymorphism and Flow Analysis (by K.-F. Faxén) considers determining an approximation of the set of possible values (mainly functions) expressions can have. This kind of analysis is of paramount importance in optimizing implementations of functional languages, since environment management for closures requires rather heavy machinery. Using ideas taken from the theory of type systems, control-flow analysis, set-based analysis, constraint systems, and polyvariant analysis, the paper suggests a family of heuristics for performing such flow analysis for untyped languages. Although the system is not yet implemented, examples are provided to support the claim that such analyses could be used for performing useful optimizations.

Type inference for a multiset rewriting language (by P. Fradet and D. Le Métayer) considers the multiset rewriting language Gamma extended with a notion of addresses and contents of addresses. This allows to code structured multisets corresponding to algebraic data structures and enhances the ease with which programming can be performed in Gamma. Context-free graph grammars are then used to define the shape that the structured multisets are supposed to have. The paper then develops a sound (but not complete) type checking algorithm for ensuring that each rewrite (allowed by the Gamma program) does in fact maintain the invariant expressed by the graph grammar.

Abstract Interpretation

Abstract interpretation aims at gathering information about programs by approximation of their runtime behavior. The point of view is that to automatically answer questions about programs one cannot only consider a single semantics but better a hierarchy of semantics each one adapted to a category of program properties. Abstract interpretation is a formalization of the relationships between these semantics and their combinations. In particular the abstraction, and its inverse, the refinement of a semantics are essential concepts used to partially order semantics in this hierarchy [24].

These ideas of discrete approximation are involved in formal semantics [18]. For example an operational trace semantics can be approximated by a denotational semantics by forgetting about intermediate states. A further approximation into a big step operational semantics essentially consists in forgetting about nontermination and in reformulating fixpoint definitions in equivalent rule-based form [23].

These ideas of discrete approximation are involved in proof methods [17]. For example the Floyd/Hoare/Owicki/Lamport proof method essentially consists in approximating sets of execution traces by sets of states, such invariants being adequate for safety but essentially incomplete for liveness properties.

These ideas of discrete approximation are central to program analysis methods [19]. A considerable number of program analysis methods have been designed (dataflow analysis, strictness analysis, termination analysis, closure analysis, projection analysis, binding-time analysis, set-based analysis, type inference, effect systems, lazy types, etc., to cite a few finitary methods). The purpose of abstract interpretation is to unify these superficially different methods in a single mathematical framework by understanding all of them as approximations of semantics using specific abstract domains to encode approximate program properties. This point of view often leads to cross-fertilization. For example understanding set-based analysis as an abstract interpretation yields a powerful generalization based upon context-sensitive tree grammars [22]. Formalization by abstract interpretation often leads to simplifications. For example, several independent analyses can be combined within the same abstract framework such as comportment analyses [21, 60, 84], the combination being more precise than the individual analyses. An important recent contribution has been the understanding of type inference as abstract interpretation [26, 56, 58, 57]. Another recurrent theme in abstract interpretation is the design of general approximation methods independently of a particular application. Essentially two classical methods are used, static ones, often based on Galois connections, where the approximation is fixed while defining the abstract properties for a programming language and dynamic ones, often based on widening operators, where the ultimate approximation is performed during the analysis process [20]. The Galois connection based abstract interpretation framework has been extended to higher-order functional languages [13, 67], by a clear separation of the computational and approximation ordering, both at the concrete and abstract level [21, 62, 59, 46]. The dynamic approximation is essentially more powerful than the static one, since it allows for infinite abstract domains, expressing non-uniform properties. The design of such very expressive infinite abstract domains with their associated widening operators is a continuous research topic in abstract interpretation, because they leads to extremely powerful program analyses [55, 51, 85], hardly achievable by the above mentioned finitary methods. Another application is the analysis of parallel, centralized [27] or distributed programs [42] e.g. for model-checking [27] or to automatically generate schedulers [42] by abstract interpretation of a truly-concurrent semantics using Higher-Dimensional Automata, in which the level of concurrency is specified by the dimension of the transitions that can be fired. Applications range from verification of protocols for distributed systems on a given architecture to the dual problem of parallelizing programs.

Proving Properties of Logic Programs by Abstract Diagnosis (by M. Comini, G. Levi, M.-C. Meo, and G. Vitiello) explore the verification of logic programs by comparison of an abstract semantics with an abstract specification, thus generalizing declarative diagnosis where the declarative semantics of a program is compared to a specification of its intended behavior. In particular, when they differ, the program components which are sources of errors must be determined. The paper introduces several abstract semantics and identifies corresponding conditions for the abstract diagnosis to be complete. In general however, the specification is infinite and some approximation is necessary. In this case, partial results are obtained. For example uncovered elements always correspond to a program bug while incorrect clauses provide a hint to locate possible bugs. Several useful abstractions are proposed.

Implementing a Static Analyzer of Concurrent Programs: Problems and Perspectives (by R. Cridlig) discusses the implementation of a prototype analyser of asynchronous shared-memory Concurrent Pascal programs. The truly parallel semantics using Higher Dimensional Automata is approximated into finite abstract automata by foldings by means of data-dependent widenings. The experiments show an important state space reduction of over 90%; only in one case is model-checking not feasible due to loss of information (in which case the concrete transition system explodes anyway).

Abstract Interpretation of Small-Step Semantics (by D.A. Schmidt) considers the analysis of CCS (and extensions such as channel creation): model-checking on a conservative approximation of the program semantics. Besides the use of small-step environment semantics, a characteristic of the analysis is the regular-expression-like abstract interpretation of the syntactic encoding of the program configurations (including the control and communication components), which is of general use for analysing programs with SOS semantics [71] (Structural Operational Semantics).

Abstract Interpretation of the π-Calculus (by A. Venet) is concerned with the analysis of the distribution of processes and the channel communication topology for systems of mobile processes. The analysis is based on a refinement of the classical operational semantics given by a structural congruence and a process reduction relation. This refined semantics allows for a direct way to compute the internal communication topology associated to a configuration, whereas, in the standard semantics, it is indirectly encoded within a process algebra. The abstraction uses an infinite abstract cofibrated domain with widening, originally introduced by the author for alias analysis. This abstract domain allows for tractable although undecidable analyses, with precise non-uniform distinction between instances of recursively spawned and untyped processes.

Modalities in Analysis and Verification

Typically, modal and temporal operators are used in program logics and types to express properties relating to dynamic behaviour, i.e. state change capabilities. Modal operators are used for local properties, for instance the fact that a transition leading to some desired state is enabled at the present state. Temporal operators describe properties of complete computations, for instance the existence of future states with some desired properties (like being terminal). Models are transition systems determined, for instance, by an SOS semantics. States are transition system states with a control component (typically the abstract program currently under evaluation) and maybe a store determining bindings of values to identifiers. Transitions may carry information relevant for synchronisation and parameter passing as in CCS, CSP or the π-calculus, and they may carry finer information as they do in proved transition systems [33].

A direct strategy for verifying programs against their modal and temporal specifications is thus to explore the transition graph or computation tree that programs give rise to by means of their operational semantics when started in a given initial state. If this graph is finite then most temporal queries can be answered by traversing and marking the graph using model checking. Alternatively, in an axiomatic setting, for each reachable control point of the program under consideration a unique constant is introduced to axiomatise the one-step computation relation. To a limited extent these approaches can be extended to infinite state programs. For model checking this is possible when the property under consideration depends only on a finite portion of an otherwise infinite state graph (cf. [3]), or where infinite domains can be given finite representations as in the π-calculus [29, 2]. Axiomatic approaches can permit infinite data domains in more general terms, as long as the number of control points remain bounded (c.f. [75]).

Even though these approaches work extremely well in many circumstances, a basic problem is that state spaces only rarely stay small enough for exhaustive traversal to be computationally feasible, or at all possible. One difficulty is the well-known state explosion problem that n parallel processes each with 2 states have 2^n global states. This problem has received much attention over the past years, in the LOMAPS project and elsewhere (c.f [36, 83, 88]). Related problems concern value-passing processes. Even for finite domains the state spaces can quickly become too large to be manageable. Options for addressing this issue is to use symbolic methods [29] or techniques based on abstract interpretation [19].

Not only value passing and combinatorial state explosion are sources of problems, however. A great many control constructs give rise to unbounded growth of state spaces. In a few cases (cf. [12, 86]) this growth can be checked by algorithmic means. Even for very simple parallel programs, however, decidability is lost [38]. This problem needs attention in particular for multiparadigmatic languages that combine concurrency and distribution with a "first-class" treatment of abstraction and communication. At the heart of the problem is the ability to dynamically create and communicate new processes. Furthermore, in many modern modelling and programming languages the distinction between data and control is becoming blurred: π-calculus is one example, and higher-order process communication is another.

Many approaches are being explored to deal algorithmically with large and infinite state spaces, including techniques based on BDDs (Binary Decision Diagrams) and their successors [11], techniques that exploit process symmetries (cf. [37]), and partial order techniques (cf. [88]). Further state space reduction may be obtained by resorting to approximate techniques such as abstract interpretation. This is not only a formal activity: Preceding a formal analysis is often an "abstraction" phase in which the problem at hand is modelled and simplified, for instance to make automatic analysis feasible (by limiting attention to, say, a finite value domain, or for protocol analysis to the case of a single sender and a single receiver). Once a formal model is obtained, further abstractions may be possible, for instance by collapsing "similar" states as in techniques based on abstract interpretation in the papers by Cridlig, Schmidt, and Venet (in the present volume), or, say, state space hashing as in Holzmann's SPIN system [43].

While fully automated, state space exploration-based approaches have the very important virtue that they require no user intervention (up to the modelling and abstraction phase referred to above), they also face some serious problems:

- Limited scope: Fundamentally the scope of these techniques is limited. Language constructs such as dynamic process creation and higher-order communication can not in general be accomodated if exact analyses are called for.
- Code verification: As a result of the previous point much emphasis needs to be put on an initial, informal modelling and abstraction phase, to force problems into a tractable framework. Thus code- (as opposed to model-) verification will often be difficult to accomodate.
- Scalability/feasibility: Even with very smart state space compression techniques the state space explosion problem quickly makes its presence felt as parallel components are added, or as the size of value domains is increased.
- Modularity/reusability: Often actual systems are constructed from reusable building blocks, or modules, and it is really properties of modules rather than actual system configurations that are of interest. However, even though actual configurations may well be finite-state, modules are not easily so represented: They are really *open* systems, designed to operate in environments that are not yet fully instantiated.
- Approximate analysis: The use of approximate techniques comes with a cost, namely that it may be difficult to interpret analysis results.

An alternative, then, is to accept undecidability and resort instead to some sort of theorem proving. Many frameworks have been proposed for this: Tableaux [53], Hoare-style proof systems based on the rely-guarantee paradigm (cf. [15]), embeddings into a higher-order type theory as in the PVS system [68]. The scope of deductive techniques is certainly in principle greater than that of algorithmic ones. However it is also clear that, state explosion will remain a problem, and certainly even in an interactive framework one will still need automated procedures to deal with the large amounts of trivia that verification of "real" systems gives rise to. Indeed the combination of deductive and automatic techniques is currently receiving considerable attention in the literature (c.f. [68, 75]). To deal with features like openness, dynamic process creation, and higher-order communication a compositional approach to verification seems indispensable. In [28] an approach was introduced with the scope, in principle, of addressing systems with such features. In this work general proof principles were identified for a proof-based compositional handling of temporal properties of dynamic process networks. The approach is based on a kind of "internalised abstraction" originating with Stirling [78]: Instead of proving directly an assertion such as $p \parallel q : \phi$, abstractions of p and q are provided as properties ψ and γ, and proof obligations are created to show the abstractions correct (to show $p : \psi$, $q : \gamma$, and that $x \parallel y : \phi$ whenever $x : \psi$ and $y : \gamma$). The difficulty is dealing in an adequate way with temporal properties. The work has been extended to the π-calculus (c.f. [2, 31]) and, at least partially, to higher-order processes [1]. However, much work remains to be done before we can truly claim that verification of open, dynamic, and higher-order process networks is feasible, theoretically as well as practically. It is certainly clear that both automated and interactive techniques must be brought to bear if this goal is to be realised.

Enhanced Operational Semantics

Since the very beginning of computer science, the behaviour of machines has been given through an operational approach which describes the transitions between states that a machine performs while computing. A graphical representation of behaviours as oriented graphs, usually called *transition systems*, is quite easy: nodes represent the set of states that the machine can pass through, and arcs, possibly labelled, denote the transitions between states.

The term operational semantics appeared in the literature during the sixties due to [52, 48]. A program is seen as a sequence of atomic instructions that operate on the states of the machine. States consists of the program itself and some auxiliary data which can represent the store or the data structure on which the program works. Then, a function from states to states indicates the moves from one given configuration to another. These transitions may be labelled by additional information on the activity performed. Finally, a run of a program (or computation) is represented through a sequence of states where each state is connected to the next one through the transition function. The last state of the sequence, if any, is the final configuration of the machine after the execution of the program. But we need also in some situations to be able to describe infinite computations. Operating systems, and some reactive systems should precisely never terminate, and we should be able to describe their infinite computations at least under some fairness conditions. Interesting infinite computations also appear in (interleaving) concurrency when a non-bounded number of processes can be put in parallel. Lazy functional languages also exhibit natural infinite computations (to deal with lazy infinite lists for instance).

A renewed interest in operational semantics is due to Plotkin, and to his formal method, called SOS for *Structural Operational Semantics* [71, 63]. The key idea is to deduce transitions by inducing on the syntactic structure of the machine itself. States are essentially programs expressed according to the abstract syntax of the considered language defined through a *BNF*-like grammar. In this way, one exploits the duality between languages and abstract machines. Transitions are then defined by a set of rules that induce on the abstract syntax. The inference rules have the following form

$$Premises \Longrightarrow Conclusion.$$

Its meaning is that when the premises are satisfied, the conclusion is satisfied as well. Operationally, the above rule says that when the computational steps corresponding to the premises occurred, the one corresponding to the conclusion is enabled.

Operational semantics is mathematically simple and is close to intuition, thus it gives guidelines to implementations. In fact, it describes the essential features that any computing device has. So also untrained people can grasp the meaning of a definition on the basis of their experience with their own machine. The inductive definition of transitions naturally suggests to use induction for proving properties of programs. This approach is better suited than others to cope with programming languages that include heterogeneous features. In fact, it has been successfully used to describe imperative, functional, logic, object-oriented, concurrent and distributed languages.

Within the LOMAPS project we study enhancements of structural operational semantics along several lines. The first relies on the observation that the labels of transitions can give an expressive and detailed description of the behaviour of complex systems; so we proposed to decorate transitions with structured, rich information. The second main line of research takes advantage of the structure of states; then, the transitions themselves maintain this structure, or rather, only the part of it relevant to the aspects of a system to be described. A third topic concerns the specification of infinite computations; for that purpose, $G_{\infty}SOS$ combines the inductive definition of finite behaviors and the simultaneous co-inductive definition of infinite behaviors within a unique bi-inductive interpretation of inference rules [18], which is preserved by abstract interpretation [23].

We start illustrating our first line, mainly discussing its applications to concurrency. Essentially, we propose a general, structural operational approach to semantics that can be easily instantiated to cover the various aspects relevant to build concurrent and distributed systems. More generally, we think that semantics offers firm grounds to the many distinct activities for producing software. The logical nature of structural operational semantics, and specifically the proofs of transitions, gather (almost) all the information needed in the various phases of system development, e.g. design, implementation, quality control, management, etc. This information can be roughly grouped in two. The first concerns the *behavioural* or *qualitative* aspects of systems, i.e. in *what* they do, regardless of how. The other kind of information has to do with the *quantitative* aspects of systems, i.e. *how* efficiently they perform.

Different views of the same system originated many different semantics that must be related to one another via a strict correspondence among them all.

For example, concurrent and distributed processes have been given descriptions that take care of aspects like causality and locality (so-called *true concurrency*), as well as priorities, time, probabilities. These descriptions, together with the classic interleaving ones, help improving the quality and robustness of code and efficient runtime management of systems. We think that there is no need of many semantic models defined ad hoc: a single *parametric* model can capture all aspects of interest, both qualitative and quantitative. The main semantics presented in the literature can be retrieved, by simply projecting the parametric model on the properties under investigation. The connections among different semantics are now easy to establish: comparison of projections suffice.

We implement the motto TRANSITIONS AS PROOFS through *proved transition systems* [32, 10]. Their transitions are labelled by encodings of their proofs. Then, suitable relabellings yield the wanted models, that are related to each other by comparing their relabelling functions [33, 34, 73, 9]. Also, proved transition systems can originate a hierarchy of semantic descriptions of the same process that are closer and closer to actual implementations. The parallel structure of processes, i.e. the network topology, made explicit by in the proofs of transitions, is exploited in [8] for transforming global environments of mobile processes into local ones.

Performance evaluation and other quantitative analysis should start already at the design level. Besides robustness and reliability of the design, these early measures may save efforts. Indeed, if the design meets all behavioural requirements but leads to inefficient implementations, the system must be re-designed. This calls for the integration of qualitative and quantitative analysis of systems in a single methodology. Proved transition systems are detailed enough to express these quantitative aspects; see [72, 74] for descriptions that include probabilistic aspects of concurrent systems, and these proceedings for a model that takes time into account.

In most timed operational models, time is assumed to be discrete, i.e. to be a multiple of some base time. This discrete approach cannot certainly account for continuous phenomena arising in hybrid systems, and runs into a complexity problem when put at work in a program analysis context when the base time is chosen as the greatest common divisor of the execution times of all actions considered in the semantics. When taking the refinement process up to its limit, dense time abstracts all possible base times. We have introduced dense time in the context of Higher-Dimensional Automata, a truly-concurrent model of computations [40] in which transitions are made up of several concurrent activities. Time is measured as the length of traces using some metric (defined locally by the norm of tangent vectors). The timed semantics can be defined compositionally (using constructors much alike those of timed process algebras). A SOS-like format has also been proposed and proved correct with respect to the underlying timed Higher-Dimensional Automata.

Our "economic" long-run goal is the realization of (semi-) automatic verification tools to be integrated in a programming environment for concurrency [16]. Again parametricity saves efforts. In fact, the implementation of verification tools is complex and expensive. If the tool is highly specialized, its cost may not be justified. Instead, parametric tools support many different semantics at the cost of a single one. Its specializations simply require to implement relabelling functions [44]. Indeed, the kernel of a parametric tool coincides with the construction of the proved transition system. It has the same shape and the same space and time complexity of the interleaving case. Then, model checking and (bisimulation-based) equivalence verifications are completely standard. We implemented a prototype of an equivalence checker based on proved transition systems [7]. It has also been used to support the debugging of *Facile* code [9] (and below).

Semantics expressed by means of transition systems and sets of rules to construct them have been proposed also for Statecharts, a formalism for the specification of systems consisting of concurrent components which react to signals from an environment and interact with each other by broadcast. Due to the complexity of specifications compositionality of semantic descriptions, concepts of equivalence of behaviours, composability of proof methods are mandatory ([49, 50, 47]).

In these proceedings there are several papers that address goals central to annotated type and effect systems:

A non-standard semantics for generating reduced transition systems (by N. De Francesco, A. Santone and G. Vaglini) proposes a new non-standard operational semantics for CCS that gives a transition system with much less transitions and states than the original one. The authors apply abstract interpretation to obtain their non-standard operational semantics, and prove that the new transition system of a process is deadlock free if and only if the standard one is. The key point is that the reachability relation of the standard transition system is preserved by the abstract interpretation they define.

Mobile processes with local clocks (by P. Degano, J.-V. Loddo, and C. Priami) defines a structural timed operational semantics for mobile processes. A distinguishing feature is that the time that actions consume depends on the basic operations needed for firing them. In this way, both the run-time support and the architecture of the system affect the estimate of time. Their proposal is truly concurrent, because any sequential component of a system has its own clock. A preorder is then defined that considers a process more efficient than another if it performs better from a given point on.

Testing semantics of asynchronous distributed programs (by R. De Nicola and R. Pugliese) carries over an existing language some important notions and concepts developped mainly for theoretical process calculi. It defines a structural operational semantics to IPAL, an imperative subset of the coordination language Linda. Essentially, this subset is a CSP-like process calculus. The main results of the paper are that assignment and Linda communication, based on tuples, are given a transitional semantics. Also, testing equivalence is extended to cover IPAL, a proof system is given, and a full abstraction theorem is proved.

The last two two papers address semantic and expressivity issues of Statecharts.

A process language for statecharts (by F. Levi) proposes a compositional labelled transition system for Statecharts. This new semantics is obtained via a translation of Statecharts into a process algebra, which can be seen as the counterpart of Statecharts. Notably, the process algebra used has an operator of process refinement that represents the hierarchical structure Statecharts have. The semantics proposed is shown correct with respect to Pnueli and Shalev's.

Priorities in Statecharts (by A. Maggiolo-Schettini and M. Merro) deals with the capability of the formalism to express notions of priority between transitions that are enabled and are mutually exclusive. A version of Statecharts without priority is introduced, and then is extended with various syntactic and semantic notions of priority. These are examined and classified according to their expressive power.

References

1. R. Amadio and M. Dam. Reasoning about higher-order processes. In *Proc. CAAP'94,* Lecture Notes in Computer Science, 915:202–217, 1995.
2. R. Amadio and M. Dam. A modal theory of types for the π-calculus. In *Proc. FTRTFT'96,* Lecture Notes in Computer Science, 1135:347–365, 1996.
3. H. Andersen, C. Stirling, and G. Winskel. A compositional proof system for the modal μ-calculus. In Proc. LICS'94, 1994.
4. J.-M Andreoli and R. Pareschi: "Linear objects: Logical processes with built-in inheritance". In D.H.D. Warren and P. Szeredi, editors, 7th Int. Conf. Logic Programming. MIT Press, 1990.
5. J.-M Andreoli, R. Pareschi, L. Leth and B. Thomsen: "True Concurrency Semantics for a Linear Logic Programming Language with Broadcast Communication". In proc. Conf. on Theory and Practice of Software Development (TAPSOFT'93), vol 668 of LNCS, pp. 182-198. Springer Verlag, 1993.
6. J.-P. Banatre and D. Le Metayer. "Programming by multiset transformations. CACM, 36(1):98, 1993
7. A. Bianchi, S. Coluccini, P. Degano, and C. Priami. An efficient verifier of truly concurrent properties. In V. Malyshkin, editor, *Proceedings of PaCT'95, LNCS 964,* pages 36–50. Springer-Verlag, 1995.
8. C. Bodei, P. Degano, and C. Priami. Mobile processes with a distributed environment. In *Proceedings of ICALP'96, LNCS 1099,* pages 490–501. Springer-Verlag, 1996.
9. Roberta Borgia, Pierpaolo Degano, Corrado Priami, Lone Leth, and Bent Thomsen. Understanding mobile agents via a non-interleaving semantics for Facile. In

R. Cousot and D.A. Schmidt, editors, *Proceedings of SAS'96*, LNCS 1145, pages 98–112. Springer-Verlag, 1996. Extended version in European Computer-Industry Research Center Tech. Rep. ECRC-96-4, 1996.

10. G. Boudol and I. Castellani. A non-interleaving semantics for CCS based on proved transitions. *Fundamenta Informaticae*, XI(4):433–452, 1988.
11. J. R. Burch, E. M. Clarke, K. L. McMillan, D. L. Dill, and J. Hwang. Symbolic model checking: 10^{20} states and beyond. *Proc. LICS'90*, 1990.
12. O. Burkart and B. Steffen. Model checking for context-free processes. In *Proc. CONCUR'92*, Lecture Notes in Computer Science, 630:123–137, 1992.
13. G. L. Burn, C. Hankin, and S. Abramsky. Strictness Analysis for Higher-Order Functions. *Science of Computer Programming*, 7:249–278, 1986.
14. N. Carriero, D. Gelernter, T. Mattson and A. Sherman. "The Linda alternative to message passing systems". Parallel Computing 20(4):633-655, April 1994.
15. A. Cau and P. Collette. Parallel composition of assumption-commitment specifications. *Acta Informatica*, 33:153–176, 1996.
16. R. Cleaveland, J. Parrow, and B. Steffen. The concurrency workbench: A semantics-based tool for the verification of concurrent systems. *ACM Transaction on Programming Languages and Systems*, pages 36–72, 1993.
17. P. Cousot. Methods and logics for proving programs. In J. van Leeuwen, editor, *Formal Models and Semantics*, volume B of *Handbook of Theoretical Computer Science*, chapter 15, pages 843–993. Elsevier, 1990.
18. P. Cousot and R. Cousot. Inductive definitions, semantics and abstract interpretation. In *19th POPL*, pages 83–94. ACM Press, 1992.
19. P. Cousot and R. Cousot. Abstract interpretation frameworks. *J. Logic and Comp.*, 2(4):511–547, 1992.
20. P. Cousot and R. Cousot. Comparing the Galois connection and widening/narrowing approaches to abstract interpretation, invited paper. In M. Bruynooghe and M. Wirsing, editors, *Proc. Int. Work. PLILP '92*. LNCS 631, pages 269–295. Springer-Verlag, 1992.
21. P. Cousot and R. Cousot. Higher-order abstract interpretation (and application to comportment analysis generalizing strictness, termination, projection and PER analysis of functional languages), invited paper. In *Proc. 1994 ICCL*, pages 95–112. IEEE Comp. Soc. Press, 1994.
22. P. Cousot and R. Cousot. Formal language, grammar and set-constraint-based program analysis by abstract interpretation. In *Proc. 7th FPCA*, pages 170–181. ACM Press, 1995.
23. P. Cousot and R. Cousot. Compositional and inductive semantic definitions in fixpoint, equational, constraint, closure-condition, rule-based and game-theoretic form, invited paper. In P. Wolper, editor, *Proc. 7th Int. Conf. CAV '95*. LNCS 939, pages 293–308. Springer-Verlag, 1995.
24. P. Cousot, R. Cousot, and A. Mycroft. Report on a Dagsthul seminar on abstract interpretation, 1995.
25. P. Cousot: Abstract Interpretation. *Computing Surveys* **28** *2*, pages 324–328, ACM Press, 1996.
26. P. Cousot. Types as abstract interpretation. In *24th POPL*. ACM Press, 1997.
27. R. Cridlig. Semantic analysis of shared-memory concurrent languages using abstract model-checking. In *Proc. PEPM '95*. ACM Press, 1995.
28. M. Dam. Compositional proof systems for model checking infinite state processes. In *Proc. CONCUR'95*, Lecture Notes in Computer Science, 962:12–26, 1995.

29. M. Dam. Model checking mobile processes. *Information and Computation*, 129:35–51, 1996.
30. M. Dam: Modalities in Analysis and Verification. *ACM Computing Surveys* **28** *2*, pages 346–348, ACM Press, 1996.
31. M. Dam. Compositional verification of mobile process networks. In preparation, 1997.
32. P. Degano, R. De Nicola, and U. Montanari. Partial ordering derivations for CCS. In *Proceedings of FCT, LNCS 199*, pages 520–533. Springer-Verlag, 1985.
33. P. Degano and C. Priami. Proved trees. In *Proceedings of ICALP'92, LNCS 623*, pages 629–640. Springer-Verlag, 1992.
34. P. Degano and C. Priami. Causality for mobile processes. In *Proceedings of ICALP'95, LNCS 944*, pages 660–671. Springer-Verlag, 1995.
35. P. Degano and C. Priami: Enhanced Operational Semantics. *Computing Surveys* **28** *2*, pages 352–354, ACM Press, 1996.
36. P. Degano and C. Priami: A Compact Representation of Finite State Processes. Report available via `http://www.daimi.aau.dk/~bra8130/LOMAPS_papers.html` by selection of LOMAPS-DIPISA-2.
37. E. A. Emerson and A.P. Sistla. Symmetry and model checking. *Formal Methods in System Design*, 9:105–131, 1996.
38. J. Esparza. Decidability of model checking for infinite-state concurrent systems. *Acta Informatica*, 1996. (to appear).
39. A. Giacalone, P. Mishra, and S. Prasad. Facile: A symmetric integration of concurrent and functional programming. *International Journal of Parallel Programming*, 18:121–160, 1989.
40. E. Goubault. Durations for truly-concurrent actions. In *Proceedings of ESOP'96, LNCS, 1058*, pages 173–187. Springer-Verlag, 1996.
41. J. Gosling and H. McGilton. The Java language environment. White paper, May 1995. Sun Microsystems, 2550 Garcia Avenue, Mountain View, CA 94043, USA.
42. E. Goubault. Schedulers as abstract interpretations of higher-dimensional automata. In *Proc. PEPM '95*, La Jolla, Calif., 21–23 jun 1995, pages 134–145. ACM Press, jun 1995.
43. G. J. Holzmann. An analysis of bitstate hashing. In *Proc. PSTV'95,* Chapman and Hall, pages 301–314, 1995.
44. P. Inverardi, C. Priami, and D. Yankelevich. Automatizing parametric reasoning on distributed concurrent systems. *Formal Aspects of Computing*, 6(6):676–695, 1994.
45. M. P. Jones. A theory of qualified types. In *Proc. ESOP '92*, pages 287–306, Springer Lecture Notes in Computer Science **582**, 1992.
46. N. D. Jones and F. Nielson. Abstract Interpretation: a Semantics-Based Tool for Program Analysis. In *Handbook of Logic in Computer Science volume 4*. Oxford University Press, 1995.
47. F. Levi. Verification of Temporal and Real-Time Properties of Statecharts. PhD Thesis in Computer Science, University of Pisa, to be discussed in January 1997.
48. P. Lucas. Formal definition of programming languages and systems. In Springer Verlag, editor, *Proceedings of IFIP'71*, 1971.
49. A. Maggiolo-Schettini and A. Peron Retiming Techniques for Statecharts In Proc. FTRTFT '96, LNCS 1135, pages 55–71. Springer-Verlag, 1996.
50. A. Maggiolo-Schettini, A. Peron and S. Tini Equivalences of Statecharts In Proc. CONCUR '96, LNCS 1119, pages 687–702. Springer-Verlag, 1996.

51. L. Mauborgne. Abstract interpretation using TDGs. In B. Le Charlier, editor, *Proc. SAS '94*, Namur, 20–22 sep 1994, LNCS 864, pages 363–379. Springer-Verlag, 1994.
52. J. McCarthy. Towards a mathematical science of computation. In C.M. Popplewell, editor, *Information Processing 1962*, pages 21–28, 1963.
53. Z. Manna and A. Pnueli. *Temporal Verification of Reactive Systems: Safety.* Springer-Verlag, 1995.
54. R. Milner, J. Parrow, and D. Walker. A calculus of mobile processes (I and II). *Information and Computation*, 100(1):1–77, 1992.
55. B. Monsuez. Polymorphic types and widening operators. In P. Cousot, M. Falaschi, G. Filé, and A. Rauzy, editors, *Proc. 3rd Int. Work. WSA '93 on Static Analysis.* LNCS 724, pages 267–281. Springer-Verlag, 1993.
56. B. Monsuez. Polymorphic typing for call-by-name semantics. In D. Bjørner, M. Broy, and I.V. Pottosin, editors, *Proc. FMPA.* LNCS 735, pages 156–169. Springer-Verlag, 1993.
57. B. Monsuez. System F and abstract interpretation. In A. Mycroft, editor, *Proc. SAS '95.* LNCS 983, pages 279–295. Springer-Verlag, 1995.
58. B. Monsuez. Using abstract interpretation to define a strictness type inference system. In *Proc. PEPM '95*, pages 122–133. ACM Press, 1995.
59. A. Mycroft and F. Nielson. Strong Abstract Interpretation using Power Domains. In *Proc. ICALP '83*, volume 154, pages 536–547. SLNCS, 1983.
60. A. Mycroft and K.L. Solberg. Uniform PERs and comportment analysis. PLILP'95, 1995.
61. A. Mycroft: On Integration of Programming Paradigms. *ACM Computing Surveys* **28** *2*, pages 309–311, ACM Press, 1996.
62. F. Nielson. Two-Level Semantics and Abstract Interpretation. *Theoretical Computer Science — Fundamental Studies*, 69:117–242, 1989.
63. F. Nielson and H.R. Nielson. *Semantics with applications: a formal introduction.* Wiley, 1992.
64. F Nielson and H.R. Nielson. Layered Predicates. In *Proc. REX'92 workshop on "Semantics—foundations and applications"*, pages 425–456, Springer Lecture Notes in Computer Science **666**, 1993.
65. H. R. Nielson and F. Nielson. Higher-Order Concurrent Programs with Finite Communication Topology. In *Proc. POPL '94*, pages 84–97, ACM Press, 1994.
66. F. Nielson: Annotated Type and Effect Systems. *ACM Computing Surveys* **28** *2*, pages 344–345, ACM Press, 1996.
67. F Nielson. Semantics-Directed Program Analysis: A Tool-Maker's Perspective. In *Proc. SAS'96*, pages 2–21, Springer Lecture Notes in Computer Science **1145**, 1996.
68. S. Owre, S. Rajan, J. M. Rushby, N. Shankar, and M. K. Srivas. PVS: Combining specification, proof checking, and model checking. In *Proc. CAV'96,* Lecture Notes in Computer Science, 1102:411–414, 1996.
69. B. Pierce and D. Turner. PICT Language Definition. University of Indiana, December 1995.
70. B. C. Pierce and D. N. Turner. Concurrent objects in a process calculus. In Theory and Practice of Parallel Programming, volume 907 of Lecture Notes in Computer Science. Springer-Verlag, April 1995.
71. G. Plotkin. A structural approach to operational semantics. Technical Report DAIMI FN-19, Aarhus University, Denmark, 1981.
72. C. Priami. Stochastic π-calculus. *The Computer Journal*, 38(6):578–589, 1995.

73. C. Priami. *Enhanced Operational Semantics for Concurrency*. PhD thesis, Dipartimento di Informatica, Università di Pisa, March 1996. Available as Tech. Rep. TD-08/96.
74. C. Priami. Integrating behavioural and performance analysis with topology information. In *Proceedings of 29th Hawaian International Conference on System Sciences*, volume 1, pages 508–516, Maui, Hawaii, 1996. IEEE.
75. H. B. Sipma, T. E. Uribe, and Z. Manna. Deductive model checking. In *Proc. CAV'96*, Lecture Notes in Computer Science, 1102:208–219, 1996.
76. G. S. Smith. Principal Type Schemes for Functional Programs with Overloading and Subtyping. *Science of Computer Programming* **23**, pages 197-226, 1994.
77. G. Smolka. The definition of kernal Oz, in Constraints: Basic and Trends, Lecture Notes in Computer Science 910. Springer Verlag, 1995.
78. C. Stirling. Modal logics for communicating systems. *Theoretical Computer Science*, 49:311–347, 1987.
79. J.-P. Talpin and P. Jouvelot. The type and effect discipline. *Information and Computation* **111**, pages 245–296, 1994.
80. B. Thomsen, L. Leth, and T.-M. Kuo. A Facile tutorial. In Proceedings of CONCUR'96 - Seventh Intl. Conf. on Concurrency Theory, volume 1119 of Lecture Notes in Computer Science, pages 278-298. Springer-Verlag, 1996.
81. B. Thomsen, F. Knabe, L. Leth and P.-Y. Chevalier. Mobile Agents Set to Work, In Communications International, July, 1995.
82. M. Tofte and J.-P. Talpin: Implementation of the Typed Call-by-Value λ-Calculus using a Stack of Regions. In *Proc. POPL '94*, pages 188–210, ACM Press, 1994.
83. A. Valmari. A stubborn attack on state explosion. *Formal Methods in System Design*, 1:297–322, 1992.
84. F. Védrine. Binding-time analysis and strictness analysis by abstract interpretation. In A. Mycroft, editor, *Proc. SAS'95*. LNCS 983, pages 400–417. Springer-Verlag, 1995.
85. A. Venet. Abstract cofibred domains: Application to the alias analysis of untyped programs. In R. Cousot and D.A. Schmidt, editors, *Proc. SAS'96*. LNCS 1145, pages 368–382. Springer-Verlag, 1996.
86. I. Walukiewicz. Pushdown processes: Games and model checking. In *Proc. CAV'96*, Lecture Notes in Computer Science, 1102:62–74, 1996.
87. J. E. White. "Telescript technology: The foundation for the electronic marketplace". General Magic white paper, 2465 Latham Street, Mountain View, CA 94040, 1994.
88. P. Wolper and P. Godefroid. Partial-order methods for temporal verification. In *Proc. CONCUR'93*, Lecture Notes in Computer Science, **715**:233–246, 1993.

Proving Properties of Logic Programs by Abstract Diagnosis

Marco Comini[1], Giorgio Levi[1], Maria Chiara Meo[2], and Giuliana Vitiello[3]

[1] Dipartimento di Informatica, Università di Pisa, Corso Italia 40, 56125 Pisa, Italy, {comini, levi}@di.unipi.it
[2] Dipartimento di Matematica Pura ed Applicata, Università di L'Aquila, via Vetoio, località Coppito, 67010 L'Aquila, Italy, meo@univaq.it
[3] Dipartimento di Informatica ed Applicazioni, Università di Salerno, Baronissi (Salerno), Italy, giuvit@dia.unisa.it

Abstract. We show how declarative diagnosis techniques can be extended to cope with verification of operational properties, such as computed answers, and of abstract properties, such as types and groundness dependencies. The extension is achieved by using a simple semantic framework, based on abstract interpretation. The resulting technique (abstract diagnosis) leads to elegant bottom-up and top-down verification methods, which do not require to determine the symptoms in advance, and which are effective in the case of abstract properties described by finite domains.

Keywords: Logic Programming, Declarative diagnosis, Verification, Semantics, Debugging

1 Introduction

Declarative diagnosis (debugging) can formally be defined as follows. Let P be a program, $\mathcal{S}[\![P]\!]$ be the (declarative) semantics of P, and $\mathcal{I}$ be the specification of the *intended* semantics of P. Declarative diagnosis [45,43,38,30] is a method to prove the correctness and completeness of P w.r.t. $\mathcal{I}$, and to determine the "errors" and the program components which are sources of errors, whenever $\mathcal{S}[\![P]\!] \neq \mathcal{I}$. Declarative diagnosis is concerned with model-theoretic properties. The related declarative semantics is the least Herbrand model in [45], the set of program completion models in [38] and the set of atomic logical consequences in [30].

Abstract diagnosis [16,18] is a generalization of declarative diagnosis, where we consider operational properties, i.e., *observables*, which are properties which can be extracted from a goal computation, i.e., *observables are abstractions of SLD-trees.*

Let $\mathcal{S}_\alpha[\![P]\!]$ be the behavior of P w.r.t. the observable property α, and $\mathcal{I}_\alpha$ be the specification of the *intended* behavior of P w.r.t. α. Abstract diagnosis consists of comparing $\mathcal{S}_\alpha[\![P]\!]$ and $\mathcal{I}_\alpha$ and determining the wrong program components, when $\mathcal{S}_\alpha[\![P]\!] \neq \mathcal{I}_\alpha$. The formulation is parametric w.r.t. the property (α) considered in the specification $\mathcal{I}_\alpha$ and in the actual behavior $\mathcal{S}_\alpha[\![P]\!]$.

Examples of useful observables are *computed answers* and *call patterns* (i.e., procedure calls selected in an *SLD*-derivation). Other examples come from program analysis, e.g. *depth(l)-answers* (i.e., answers containing terms whose depth is $\leq l$), *types*, *modes* and *ground dependencies*.

The most natural observable for the abstract diagnosis of positive logic programs is computed answers, which leads to a more precise verification than the declarative diagnoses in [45] and [30], which can be reconstructed in terms of the more abstract observables *ground instances of computed answers* and *correct answers*.

Less abstract observables, such as call patterns, can be useful to verify the control and data flow between different procedures, as we usually do in interactive debugging. For example, the intended behavior that we specify might be a set of assertions of the form "the execution of the procedure call $p(t_1, \ldots, t_n)$ leads to the procedure call $q(s_1, \ldots, s_m)$".

Observables coming from program analysis are useful

- to make the diagnosis effective, as in the case of depth(l)-answers, which are finite approximations of computed answers,
- to verify partial program properties, such as modes, types and groundness. For example, if $\mathcal{I}_\alpha$ specifies the intended program behavior w.r.t. types, abstract diagnosis boils down to type checking.

Declarative diagnosis is based on the preliminary detection of *symptoms*, which are deviations from the expected behavior, which have to be determined by using other techniques, e.g. testing techniques. Our formalization of abstract diagnosis does not require to determine symptoms in advance. The systematic derivation of all the errors in the program is possible because the semantics we use exhibit several useful properties (such as existence of a goal-independent top-down denotation equivalent to the fixpoint semantics, AND-compositionality, etc.). The same properties allow us to naturally relate bottom-up and top-down diagnosis algorithms.

The theory of abstract diagnosis is built on an algebraic semantic framework for positive logic programs [13,14], based on the formalization of observables as Galois insertions. The collecting semantics [19] is a "traces semantics", defined in terms of *SLD*-derivations. In this paper we are mainly concerned with observables which are abstractions of the computed answers semantics. We will therefore use a simplified version of the semantic framework, where the collecting semantics is the s-semantics [28,29,8], defined in Section 3 for a CLP-like version of positive logic programs. The abstraction framework is defined in Section 4. We then consider in Sections 5 and 6 two classes of observables, *denotational* and *semi-denotational* observables, for which several interesting semantic properties hold, namely

- existence of a goal-independent abstract top-down denotation (defined by means of a transition system), which is *AND*-compositional (or condensing).
- existence of an abstract bottom-up (fixpoint) denotation (defined by means of a denotational semantics definition), which is equivalent to the top-down one.

- the abstract transition system and the abstract denotational definition are systematically derived from the collecting semantics.

The difference between denotational and semi-denotational observables is related to precision. Namely, the abstract semantics coincides with the abstraction of the collecting semantics, in the case of denotational observables, while it is just a correct approximation, in the case of semi-denotational observables. We show that the class of denotational observables includes computed answers and the observables which allow us to reconstruct the traditional declarative semantics, i.e., the least Herbrand model and the least term model (atomic logical consequences or c-semantics). On the other hand, the class of semi-denotational observables includes several domains proposed for type, mode and groundness analysis. We will just consider the domain $\mathcal{POS}$ [7].

In Section 7 we give the basic definitions of abstract diagnosis, which are a straightforward adaptation of those given for declarative diagnosis, and the theorems on which the abstract diagnosis algorithms are based, for the case of denotational and semi-denotational observables. The diagnosis is based on *incorrect clauses* and *uncovered elements*, which can be detected by means of very simple bottom-up (application of the "abstract immediate consequences operator" to the abstract specification) or top-down ("oracle simulation", see Section 8) algorithms, without actually computing the abstract semantics (e.g. no fixpoint computation is required). Rather strong results hold for denotational observables. Namely,

- absence of incorrect clauses implies partial correctness.
- absence of uncovered elements implies completeness, for a large class of interesting programs (acceptable programs).
- an incorrect clause always corresponds to a bug in the program.
- an uncovered element always corresponds to a bug in the program.

On the other hand, the diagnosis may be non-effective, since abstract specifications for denotational observables may be infinite. The diagnosis is instead effective in the case of semi-denotational observables, which usually are defined by finite abstract domains. However, the results are weaker, because of approximation. Namely,

- absence of incorrect clauses implies partial correctness.
- an incorrect clause does not always correspond to a bug in the program.
- an uncovered element always corresponds to a bug in the program.

A nice feature of abstract specifications for semi-denotational observables is that they look like post-conditions in program verification. Abstract diagnosis can then be compared to other techniques from program verification, such as those based on the definitions of well-typed or well-moded programs. The relation between the two approaches is discussed in Section 10.

2 Preliminaries

In the following sections, we assume familiarity with the standard notions of logic programming as introduced in [2] and [39].

2.1 Logic programming

Throughout the paper we assume programs and goals being defined on a first order language given by a signature Σ consisting of a finite set F of *function symbols*, a finite set Π of *predicate symbols* and a denumerable set V of *variable symbols*. T denotes the set of terms built on F and V.

A substitution is a mapping $\vartheta : V \to T$ such that the set $dom(\vartheta) = \{x \mid \vartheta(x) \neq x\}$ (*domain* of ϑ) is finite. A substitution ϑ is called *idempotent* if $\vartheta\vartheta = \vartheta$. A *renaming* is a (non idempotent) substitution ρ for which there exists the inverse ρ^{-1} such that $\rho\rho^{-1} = \rho^{-1}\rho = id$. The pre-ordering $\leq$ (more general than) on substitutions is such that $\vartheta \leq \sigma$ if and only if there exists ϑ' such that $\vartheta\vartheta' = \sigma$. The result of the application of a substitution ϑ to a term t is an *instance* of t and is denoted by $t\vartheta$. Two terms t and t' are *variants* ($t \equiv t'$) if there exists a renaming ρ such that $t = t'\rho$ (where $=$ denotes syntactic equality). A substitution ϑ is a *unifier* of terms t and t' if $t\vartheta = t'\vartheta$. If two terms are unifiable then they have an idempotent most general unifier which is unique up to renaming. Therefore $mgu(t_1, t_2)$ denotes such an idempotent most general unifier of t_1 and t_2. All the above definitions can be extended to other syntactic expressions in the obvious way.

An atom is an object of the form $p(t_1, \dots, t_n)$ where $p \in \Pi$, $t_1, \dots, t_n \in T$. A *goal* is a sequence of atoms $A_1, \dots, A_m$. The empty goal is denoted by $\Box$. We denote by $\boldsymbol{G}$ and $\boldsymbol{B}$ possibly empty sequences of atoms, by $\boldsymbol{t}, \boldsymbol{x}$ tuples of, respectively, terms and *distinct* variables. Moreover we denote by $\boldsymbol{t}$ both the tuple and the set of corresponding syntactic objects. $\boldsymbol{B}, \boldsymbol{B}'$ denotes the concatenation of $\boldsymbol{B}$ and $\boldsymbol{B}'$. An atom is called *pure* if it is in the form $p(\boldsymbol{x})$ while a goal is called *pure* if it contains only pure atoms which do not share variables.

A (definite) *clause* is a formula of the form $H :- A_1, \dots, A_n$ with $n \geq 0$, where H (the *head*) and $A_1, \dots, A_n$ (the *body*) are atoms. ":–" and ", " denote logical implication and conjunction respectively, and all variables are universally quantified. A *program* is a finite set of (definite) clauses.

In the paper we use standard results on the ordinal powers $\uparrow$ of continuous functions on complete lattices. Namely, given any monotonic operator T on $(C, \leq)$, $T \uparrow 0 = \bot_C$, $T \uparrow n+1 = T(T \uparrow n)$ for $n < \omega$, and $T \uparrow \omega = \sqcup_{n<\omega} T \uparrow n$, where $\bot_C$ denotes the least element of C. Moreover if T is continuous its least fixpoint is $T \uparrow \omega$. We denote the *least fixed point* of T by $lfp\, T$ and the *greatest fixed point* of T by $gfp\, T$, if they exist.

In order to use partial functions we use lambda notation by admitting not always defined expressions. Hence a lambda expression $\lambda x.E$ denotes a partial function which on input x assumes the value $E[x]$ if the expression $E[x]$ is defined, otherwise it is undefined. $\bot$ denotes the undefined element. For each set S we define $\bot \subseteq S$ and $\bot \cup S = S$. Note that $\emptyset \not\subseteq \bot$.

2.2 Properties of substitutions and equations

Given a set of equations $E = \{s_1 = t_1, \dots, s_n = t_n\}$, a (most general) unifier of E is a (most general) unifier of $(s_1, \dots, s_n)$ and $(t_1, \dots, t_n)$. A unifiable set of equations (terms) has an idempotent *mgu*. Any unifier ϑ for E is called ***solution*** if $E\vartheta$ is variable free. A set E is solvable if it has solutions. The pre-ordering $\leq_E$ on equation sets is such that $E \leq_E E'$ if and only if the solutions of E are also solutions of E'. Two sets E_1, E_2 are called *equivalent* if they have the same solutions.

An equation set (possibly empty) is *in solved form* if it has the form $\{ v_1 = t_1, \dots, v_n = t_n \}$ and the v_i's are distinct variable which do not occur in the right hand side of any equation. The variables v_i are said to be *eliminable.* The set $\{ v_1, \dots, v_n \}$ is denoted by $elim(E)$. In the following, given a set of solved form equation sets $\mathcal{E}$, by $elim(\mathcal{E})$ we denote $\bigcup_{E \in \mathcal{E}} elim(E)$. If a set E is solvable then it has an equivalent solved form which is unique up to renaming. There exists an algorithm [37] which transforms any solvable equation set into an equivalent solved form equation set.

The lattice structure on idempotent substitutions [27] is isomorphic to the lattice structure on equations introduced in [37]. Therefore we can indifferently use idempotent *mgus* or equations. An *equational goal* is an object of the form $\mathcal{E}, \boldsymbol{B}$ where $\boldsymbol{B}$ is a pure goal and $\mathcal{E}$ is a finite set of solved form equation sets such that $elim(\mathcal{E}) \subseteq var(\boldsymbol{B})$. $\emptyset, \boldsymbol{B}$ will be denoted simply by $\boldsymbol{B}$. An *equational clause* is a formula of the form $H :- E, \boldsymbol{B}$, where $H, \boldsymbol{B}$ is a pure goal and E is a solved form equation set such that $elim(E) \subseteq var(H, \boldsymbol{B})$. In the following, given any program clause $p(\boldsymbol{t}) :- p_1(\boldsymbol{t}_1), \dots, p_n(\boldsymbol{t}_n)$ we will *always* consider its equational form $p(\boldsymbol{x}) :- E, p_1(\boldsymbol{x}_1), \dots, p_n(\boldsymbol{x}_n)$ where $E = \{ \boldsymbol{x} = \boldsymbol{t}, \boldsymbol{x}_1 = \boldsymbol{t}_1, \dots, \boldsymbol{x}_n = \boldsymbol{t}_n \}$ ($\boldsymbol{x}, \boldsymbol{x}_1, \dots, \boldsymbol{x}_n$ are new distinct variables).

2.3 Galois insertions and abstract interpretation

Abstract interpretation [22,23] is a theory developed to reason about the abstraction relation between two different semantics. The theory requires the two semantics to be defined on domains which are complete lattices. $(C, \preceq)$ (the concrete domain) is the domain of the concrete semantics, while $(A, \leq)$ (the abstract domain) is the domain of the abstract semantics. The partial order relations reflect an approximation relation. The two domains are related by a pair of functions α (*abstraction*) and γ (*concretization*), which form a Galois insertion.

Galois insertions can be defined on preordered sets. However in this paper we restrict our attention to lattices.

Definition 1 (Galois insertion). Let $(C, \preceq)$ be the concrete domain and $(A, \leq)$ be the abstract domain. A *Galois insertion* $(\alpha, \gamma) : (C, \preceq) \rightleftharpoons (A, \leq)$ is a pair of maps $\alpha : C \to A$ and $\gamma : A \to C$ such that

1. α and γ are monotonic,
2. $\forall x \in C, x \preceq (\gamma \circ \alpha)(x)$ and
3. $\forall y \in A, (\alpha \circ \gamma)(y) = y$.

Given a concrete semantics and a Galois insertion between the concrete and the abstract domain, we want to define an abstract semantics. The concrete semantics is the least fixpoint of a semantic function $F : C \to C$. The abstract semantic function $\tilde{F} : A \to A$ is *correct* if $\forall x \in C$, $F(x) \preceq \gamma(\tilde{F}(\alpha(x)))$. The same property holds for the least fixpoints of F and $\tilde{F}$. F is in turn defined as composition of "primitive" operators. Let $f : C^n \to C$ be one such an operator and assume that $\tilde{f}$ is its abstract counterpart. Then $\tilde{f}$ is *(locally) correct* w.r.t. f if $\forall x_1, \ldots, x_n \in C$, $f(x_1, \ldots, x_n) \preceq \gamma(\tilde{f}(\alpha(x_1), \ldots, \alpha(x_n)))$. The local correctness of all the primitive operators implies the global correctness. Hence, we can define an abstract semantics by defining locally correct abstract primitive semantic functions. An abstract computation is then related to the concrete computation, simply by replacing the concrete operators by the corresponding abstract operators. According to the theory, for each operator f, there exists an optimal (most precise) locally correct abstract operator $\tilde{f}$ defined as $\tilde{f}(y_1, \ldots, y_n) = \alpha(f(\gamma(y_1), \ldots, \gamma(y_n)))$. However the composition of optimal operators is not necessarily optimal.

The abstract operator $\tilde{f}$ is *precise* if $\forall x_1, \ldots, x_n \in C, \alpha(f(x_1, \ldots, x_n)) = \tilde{f}(\alpha(x_1), \ldots, \alpha(x_n))$. Hence the optimal abstract operator $\tilde{f}$ is precise if and only if $\alpha(f(x_1, \ldots, x_n)) = \alpha(f((\gamma \circ \alpha)(x_1), \ldots, (\gamma \circ \alpha)(x_n)))$. The precision of the optimal abstract operators can be reformulated in terms of properties of α, γ and the corresponding concrete operator. The above definitions are naturally extended to "primitive" semantic operators from $\wp(C)$ to C.

Note that if $\sqcup$ is the *lub* operation over $(C, \preceq)$ and (α, γ) is a Galois insertion then $\tilde{\sqcup} = \alpha \circ \sqcup \circ \gamma$ is the lub of $(A, \leq)$ and moreover for each $S \subseteq C$ $\alpha(\sqcup S) = \alpha(\sqcup(\gamma \circ \alpha)S)$.

3 The concrete collecting semantics

We denote by $\mathbb{E}$ the complete lattice of sets of finite solved form equation sets, partially ordered by $\subseteq$. We define a variance equivalence on $\mathbb{E}$ as follows. For any $\mathcal{E}, \mathcal{E}' \in \mathbb{E}$ and for any tuple of variables x, $\mathcal{E} \equiv_{\mathbb{E},x} \mathcal{E}'$ if and only if $\forall E \in \mathcal{E}$, $\exists E' \in \mathcal{E}'$ such that $x\, mgu(E) \equiv x\, mgu(E')$ and vice versa[1]. A *collection* C is a partial function *Goals* $\to \mathbb{E}$ such that, for every $G \in$ *Goals*, if $C(G)$ is defined, then it is a relevant set of equations sets, i.e., $\forall E \in C(G)$, $elim(E) \subseteq var(G)$. A pure collection is a collection defined only for pure atomic goals. $\mathbb{C}$ is the domain of all the collections ordered by $\sqsubseteq$, where $C \sqsubseteq C'$ if and only if $\forall G$, $C(G) \subseteq C'(G)$. The partial order on $\mathbb{C}$ formalizes the evolution of the computation process. $(\mathbb{C}, \sqsubseteq)$ is a complete lattice. We denote by $\mathbb{PC}$ the sublattice of all pure collections.

[1] Note that for any solved form equation set E, $mgu(E)$ can be "trivially" computed. Moreover the definition of $\equiv_{\mathbb{E},x}$ is independent from the choice of the mgu, since this is unique up to renaming.

We define the *equivalence modulo enhanced variance* $\equiv_{\mathbb{C}}$ on collections as $C \equiv_{\mathbb{C}} C'$ if and only if, for any G, there exists a renaming ρ such that, if $C(G)$ is defined, then $C'(G\rho)$ is defined and $C(G) \equiv_{\mathbb{E},var(G)} (C'(G\rho))\rho^{-1}$ and vice versa. An interpretation $\mathcal{I}$ is a pure collection modulo enhanced variance. We denote by $\mathbb{I}_{\mathbb{C}}$ the set of interpretations. $(\mathbb{I}_{\mathbb{C}}, \sqsubseteq)$ is a complete lattice. The interpretation $C|_{\mathbb{I}}$ represents the (greatest) pure sub-collection of any $C \in \mathbb{C}$ modulo $\equiv_{\mathbb{C}}$. We denote the equivalence class (modulo enhanced variance) of a collection σ by σ itself. Moreover, any interpretation $\mathcal{I}$ of $\mathbb{I}_{\mathbb{C}}$ is implicitly considered also as an arbitrary collection obtained by choosing an arbitrary representative of $\mathcal{I}$. All the operators that we use on interpretations are independent from the choice of the representative. Therefore we can define any operator on $\mathbb{I}_{\mathbb{C}}$ in terms of its counterpart defined on $\mathbb{C}$, independently from the choice of the representative. All the definitions are independent from the choice of the syntactic object. To simplify the notation, we denote the corresponding operators on $\mathbb{I}_{\mathbb{C}}$ and $\mathbb{C}$ by the same name.

We define the denotational semantics by using some basic operations on equation sets.

1. Let $\mathcal{E}_1, \mathcal{E}_2 \in \mathbb{E}$. Then $\mathcal{E}_1 \otimes \mathcal{E}_2$ denotes the set

$$\{\, E \mid E_1 \in \mathcal{E}_1, E_2 \in \mathcal{E}_2, E_1 \cup E_2 \text{ is solvable and } \\ E \text{ is a solved form of } E_1 \cup E_2 \,\}.$$

   The $\otimes$ operation is associative (and commutative). Moreover note that for any choice of solved form the results are equivalent modulo variance.
2. Let E be a solved form equation set. Then $E|_{\boldsymbol{x}}$ denotes the set

$$\{\, x = t \in E \mid x \text{ occurs in } \boldsymbol{x} \,\}.$$

   The $|_{\boldsymbol{x}}$ operation can be trivially extended to any $\mathcal{E} \in \mathbb{E}$.

3.1 Denotational semantics

In the following, to simplify the notation, given the (equational) goal $\mathcal{E}, A_1, \ldots, A_n$ and an interpretation $\mathcal{I} \in \mathbb{I}_{\mathbb{C}}$, we assume that in expressions of the form $\mathcal{E} \otimes \mathcal{I}(A_1) \otimes \cdots \otimes \mathcal{I}(A_n)$, for any $i \neq j \in \{1, \ldots, n\}$, all the variables in $var(\mathcal{I}(A_i)) \setminus var(A_i)$ are renamed apart from $\mathcal{E}$ and $\mathcal{I}(A_j)$.

The denotational semantics of a program P is defined as the least fixed point of the following continuous "immediate consequences" operator $\mathcal{P}[\![P]\!] : \mathbb{I}_{\mathbb{C}} \longrightarrow \mathbb{I}_{\mathbb{C}}$, i.e., $\mathcal{F}[\![P]\!] = lfp\, \mathcal{P}[\![P]\!] = \mathcal{P}[\![P]\!] \uparrow \omega$.

$$\mathcal{P}[\![P]\!](\mathcal{I}) = \lambda p(\boldsymbol{x}). \bigcup \{\, \mathcal{E} \mid p(\boldsymbol{x}) \text{ :- } E, A_1, \ldots, A_n \text{ is a renamed clause of } P, \\ \mathcal{E} = (\{\, E \,\} \otimes \mathcal{I}(A_1) \otimes \cdots \otimes \mathcal{I}(A_n))|_{\boldsymbol{x}} \,\}.$$

Example 2. Consider the program P of Figure 1, which is a "sum" program. Its concrete denotational semantics (s-semantics) is

$$\mathcal{F}[\![P]\!](sum(x, y, z)) = \{\, \{\, x = 0, z = y \,\}, \{\, x = s(0), z = s(y) \,\}, \ldots, \\ \{\, x = s^n(0), z = s^n(y) \,\}, \ldots \}. \quad \blacksquare$$

```
c1:  sum(0, X, X).
c2:  sum(s(X), Y, s(Z)) :- sum(X, Y, Z).
```

Fig. 1. A sum program

3.2 Operational semantics

Definite clauses have a natural computational reading based on the resolution procedure. The specific resolution strategy (using the leftmost rule), called (equational) *SLD*-derivation, can be described as follows. Let $G = \mathcal{E}, p(\boldsymbol{x}), \boldsymbol{B}$ be an (equational) goal and $c = p(\boldsymbol{x}) \coloneq E, \boldsymbol{B}'$ be a renamed apart clause of a program P, such that $var(c) \cap var(G) = \boldsymbol{x}$ and $\mathcal{E} \otimes \{ E \} \neq \bot_{\mathbf{E}}$. Then we have an *(equational) derivation step*

$$G \underset{P}{\longrightarrow} \mathcal{E} \otimes \{ E \}, \boldsymbol{B}', \boldsymbol{B}.$$

The *behavior* (set of computed answers) of the goal $\mathcal{E}, \boldsymbol{B}$ in P is

$$\mathcal{B}[\![\mathcal{E}, \boldsymbol{B} \ in \ P]\!] = \bigcup \{ \mathcal{E}'|_{var(\boldsymbol{B})} \mid \mathcal{E}, \boldsymbol{B} \underset{P}{\longrightarrow}^* \mathcal{E}', \Box \}.$$

The *top-down (goal-independent) denotation* of a program P is the interpretation obtained by collecting the behaviors for all the most general (pure) atomic goals, i.e.,

$$\mathcal{O}[\![P]\!] = (\lambda p(\boldsymbol{x}).\mathcal{B}[\![p(\boldsymbol{x}) \ in \ P]\!])_{/\equiv_{\mathrm{C}}}.$$

The main properties of the *s*-semantics are summarized by the following theorem.

Theorem 3. *Let $\mathcal{E}, A_1, \ldots, A_n$ be a goal and P be a program. Then*

1. $\mathcal{B}[\![\mathcal{E}, A_1, \ldots, A_n \ in \ P]\!] = (\mathcal{E} \otimes \mathcal{O}[\![P]\!](A_1) \otimes \cdots \otimes \mathcal{O}[\![P]\!](A_n))|_{var(A_1, \ldots, A_n)}$,
2. $\mathcal{P}[\![P]\!]$ *is continuous on* $\mathbb{I}_{\mathrm{C}}$,
3. $\mathcal{F}[\![P]\!] = \mathcal{O}[\![P]\!]$.

Property 1 is usually called *AND-compositionality* and is sometimes referred to as *condensing* in the program analysis field. It essentially shows that the behavior of any (conjunctive) goal can be derived from the goal-independent denotation $\mathcal{O}[\![P]\!]$, i.e., from the behaviors of (finitely many) pure atomic goals. It is the property which allows us to take $\mathcal{O}[\![P]\!]$ as *the* semantics of a program, without being concerned with the behaviors for all possible goals. The validity of the condensing property is relevant to diagnosis, since it allows us to compare the expected and actual goal-independent behaviors, i.e., the specification is the intended $\mathcal{O}[\![P]\!]$.

Properties 2 and 3 show that the goal-independent denotation can equivalently be computed in a bottom-up way as least fixpoint of the immediate consequences operator. This is again very important for the diagnosis problem, since the basic diagnosis algorithm requires the existence of an immediate consequences operator (see Section 7). Moreover, the equivalence of the top-down and the bottom-up definitions of the denotation will allow us to define (see Section 8) equivalent top-down diagnosis algorithms, based on oracle simulation.

4 The observables and the abstract semantics

We will model the abstractions by using abstract interpretation theory [22,23]. As already mentioned, the resulting semantic framework is a simplification of the framework in [13–15].

An observable property domain is a set of properties of computed answers with an ordering relation which can be viewed as an approximation structure. An observation consists of looking at a computed answer (a relevant solved form equation set), and then extracting some property (abstraction).

Definition 4. Let $(\mathbb{D}, \leq)$ be a complete lattice. A function $\alpha : \mathbb{E} \rightarrow \mathbb{D}$ is an *observable* if there exists γ such that

1. $(\alpha, \gamma) : (\mathbb{E}, \subseteq) \rightleftharpoons (\mathbb{D}, \leq)$ is a Galois insertion,
2. $\forall \mathcal{E}, \mathcal{E}' \in \mathbb{E}$, $\forall$ finite x such that $elim(\mathcal{E}) \cup elim(\mathcal{E}') \subseteq x \subseteq var(\mathcal{E}) \cup var(\mathcal{E}')$, $\mathcal{E} \equiv_{\mathbb{E},x} \mathcal{E}' \Longrightarrow \gamma(\alpha(\mathcal{E})) \equiv_{\mathbb{E},x} \gamma(\alpha(\mathcal{E}'))$.

Once we have an observable $\alpha : \mathbb{E} \rightarrow \mathbb{D}$, we want to systematically derive the abstract semantics. The idea is to define the optimal abstract versions of the various semantic operators and then check under which conditions (on the observable) we obtain the optimal abstract semantics. This will allow us to identify some interesting classes of observables.

We start by defining the optimal abstract counterparts of the basic operators defined on $\mathbb{E}$. Then for any D, D_1, D_2, $D_i \in \mathbb{D}$.

1. $D_1 \tilde{\otimes} D_2 = \alpha(\gamma(D_1) \otimes \gamma(D_2))$,
2. $D\tilde{|}_x = \alpha((\gamma(D))|_x)$,
3. $\tilde{\bigcup}\{ D_i \}_{i \in I} = \alpha\,(\bigcup\{ \gamma(D_i) \}_{i \in I})$.

For all $C \in \mathbb{C}$ and $G \in Goals$, let $\alpha^*(C) = \lambda G.\alpha(C(G))\tilde{|}_{var(G)}$. Then $\mathbb{A} = \alpha^*(\mathbb{C}) \sqsubseteq [Goals \rightarrow \mathbb{D}]$ is a complete lattice of functions from *Goals* to the abstract domain $\mathbb{D}$, ordered with the trivial extension of $\leq$, that, by abuse of notation, we denote by $\leq$ itself. We call $\mathbb{A}$-collection any element of $\mathbb{A}$. The insertion (α, γ) can be lifted to $(\alpha^*, \gamma^*) : \mathbb{C} \rightleftharpoons \mathbb{A}$ by defining[2] for all $S \in \mathbb{A}$ and $G \in Goals$, $\gamma^*(S) = \lambda G.(\gamma(S(G)))|_{var(G)}$. From now on we will often abuse notation and denote α^* by α itself. Note that in the following if there exists a bijective Galois insertion between two domains, we identify them. A pure $\mathbb{A}$-collection is an element $S \in \mathbb{A}$ which is undefined for every non-pure atom.

Condition 2 of Definition 4 states that the observation does not depend on the choice of the hidden variable names and on the choice of the solved form of the

[2] Remember that if $C(G)$ is undefined then also $\alpha(C(G))$ is undefined.

equations used in the computation. Hence we can define an abstract enhanced variance relation $\equiv_{\mathbb{A}}$ on pure $\mathbb{A}$-collections as follows: for any pure $\mathbb{A}$-collection S, S', $S \equiv_{\mathbb{A}} S' \iff \gamma(S) \equiv_{\mathbb{C}} \gamma(S')$. An *$\mathbb{A}$-interpretation* is a pure $\mathbb{A}$-collection modulo $\equiv_{\mathbb{A}}$. We denote by $(\mathbb{I}_{\mathbb{A}}, \leq)$ the complete lattice of $\mathbb{A}$-interpretations. For any $S \in \mathbb{A}$, the $\mathbb{A}$-interpretation $S|_{\mathbb{I}}$ is the greatest pure sub-$\mathbb{A}$-collection of S modulo $\equiv_{\mathbb{A}}$.

Once we have the optimal abstract operators, we can define the corresponding abstract semantics, obtained from the denotational and operational semantics of computed answers by replacing the concrete collecting semantic operators by their optimal abstract versions.

4.1 Abstract denotational semantics

An abstract goal is an object of the form $D, \boldsymbol{B}$ where $\boldsymbol{B}$ is a pure goal and $D \in \mathbb{D}$ is an abstract constraint, such that $D\tilde{|}_{var(\boldsymbol{B})} = D$ (i.e., D is relevant for $\boldsymbol{B}$).

In the following, to simplify the notation, given an abstract interpretation $\mathcal{I}_\alpha \in \mathbb{I}_{\mathbb{A}}$ and the abstract goal $D, A_1, \ldots, A_n$, we assume that in expressions of the form $D \tilde{\otimes} \mathcal{I}_\alpha(A_1) \tilde{\otimes} \cdots \tilde{\otimes} \mathcal{I}_\alpha(A_n)$, for any $i \neq j \in \{1, \ldots, n\}$, all the variables in $var(\mathcal{I}_\alpha(A_i)) \setminus var(A_i)$ are renamed apart from D and $\mathcal{I}_\alpha(A_j)$.

The abstract denotational semantics of a program P is defined as the least fixed point of the following monotonic "abstract immediate consequences" operator $\mathcal{P}_\alpha[\![P]\!] : \mathbb{I}_{\mathbb{A}} \longrightarrow \mathbb{I}_{\mathbb{A}}$, i.e., $\mathcal{F}_\alpha[\![P]\!] = \mathit{lfp}\, \mathcal{P}_\alpha[\![P]\!]$.

$$\mathcal{P}_\alpha[\![P]\!](\mathcal{I}_\alpha) = \lambda p(\boldsymbol{x}). \tilde{\bigcup}\{ D \mid p(\boldsymbol{x}) :- E, A_1, \ldots, A_n \text{ is a renamed clause of } P,\ D = (\alpha(\{E\}) \tilde{\otimes} \mathcal{I}_\alpha(A_1) \tilde{\otimes} \cdots \tilde{\otimes} \mathcal{I}_\alpha(A_n))\tilde{|}_{\boldsymbol{x}} \}.$$

Note that $\mathcal{P}_\alpha[\![P]\!]$ is well defined, namely it is possible to show that if $\mathcal{I}_\alpha \equiv_{\mathbb{A}} \mathcal{I}'_\alpha$ then $\mathcal{P}_\alpha[\![P]\!](\mathcal{I}_\alpha) \equiv_{\mathbb{A}} \mathcal{P}_\alpha[\![P]\!](\mathcal{I}'_\alpha)$.

4.2 Abstract operational semantics

Let $\boldsymbol{G} = D, p(\boldsymbol{x}), \boldsymbol{B}$ be an abstract goal and $c = p(\boldsymbol{x}) :- E, \boldsymbol{B}'$ be a renamed apart clause of a program P, such that $var(c) \cap var(\boldsymbol{G}) = \boldsymbol{x}$ and $D \tilde{\otimes} \alpha(\{E\}) \neq \bot_{\mathbb{D}}$. Then we have an *abstract derivation step*

$$\boldsymbol{G} \xrightarrow[P]{\alpha} D \tilde{\otimes} \alpha(\{E\}), \boldsymbol{B}', \boldsymbol{B}.$$

The *abstract behavior* of the abstract goal $D, \boldsymbol{B}$ in P is

$$\mathcal{B}_\alpha[\![D, \boldsymbol{B} \text{ in } P]\!] = \tilde{\bigcup}\{ D'\tilde{|}_{var(\boldsymbol{B})} \mid D, \boldsymbol{B} \xrightarrow[P]{\alpha}{}^{*} D', \Box \}$$

and the *abstract top-down denotation* of a program P is the interpretation

$$\mathcal{O}_\alpha[\![P]\!] = (\lambda p(\boldsymbol{x}).\mathcal{B}_\alpha[\![p(\boldsymbol{x}) \text{ in } P]\!])_{/\equiv_{\mathbb{A}}}.$$

As already discussed at the end of Section 3, the semantic properties which are relevant to the diagnosis problem are the condensing property and the equivalence between the top-down and the bottom-up definitions of the denotation. An additional relevant issue is precision, i.e., the relation between the abstract semantics and the abstraction of the concrete semantics. We will then identify two interesting classes of observables (denotational and semi-denotational). All the observables in both classes are condensing and lead to equivalent top-down and the bottom-up definitions. Denotational observables are also precise, i.e., $\alpha(\mathcal{F}[\![P]\!]) = \mathcal{F}_\alpha[\![P]\!]$, while semi-denotational observables (intended to be used for program analysis) lead to approximated abstract semantics, i.e., $\alpha(\mathcal{F}[\![P]\!]) \leq \mathcal{F}_\alpha[\![P]\!]$. Note that there exist observables, which are interesting for program analysis and which are not even semi-denotational (for example, the domain *depth*(l) [44] and the domain of groundness dependencies $\mathcal{DEF}$ [7] are not condensing).

5 Denotational observables

First of all recall that any observable is precise w.r.t. the union operation since for any Galois insertion,

$$\alpha(\bigcup\{\,\mathcal{E}_i\,\}_{i\in I}) = \alpha(\bigcup\{\,(\gamma\circ\alpha)\mathcal{E}_i\,\}_{i\in I}).$$

Definition 5. Let $\alpha : \mathbb{E} \to \mathbb{D}$ be an observable. Then α is a *denotational observable* if

1. $\alpha(\mathcal{E}|_{\boldsymbol{x}}) = \alpha(((\gamma\circ\alpha)\mathcal{E})|_{\boldsymbol{x}})$,
2. $\alpha(\mathcal{E}_1 \otimes \mathcal{E}_2) = \alpha((\gamma\circ\alpha)\mathcal{E}_1 \otimes (\gamma\circ\alpha)\mathcal{E}_2)$.

Theorem 6. *Let $\alpha : \mathbb{E} \to \mathbb{D}$ be a denotational observable, $D, A_1, \ldots, A_n$ be an abstract goal and P be a program. Then*

1. $\alpha(\mathcal{O}[\![P]\!]) = \mathcal{O}_\alpha[\![P]\!]$,
2. $\mathcal{B}_\alpha[\![D, A_1, \ldots, A_n \text{ in } P]\!] = (D \mathbin{\tilde{\otimes}} \mathcal{O}_\alpha[\![P]\!](A_1) \mathbin{\tilde{\otimes}} \cdots \mathbin{\tilde{\otimes}} \mathcal{O}_\alpha[\![P]\!](A_n))\tilde{|}_{var(A_1,\ldots,A_n)}$,
3. $\alpha(\mathcal{P}[\![P]\!](\mathcal{I})) = \mathcal{P}_\alpha[\![P]\!](\alpha(\mathcal{I}))$,
4. *$\mathcal{P}_\alpha[\![P]\!]$ is continuous on $\mathbb{I}_{\mathbb{A}}$ ($\mathcal{F}_\alpha[\![P]\!] = \mathcal{P}_\alpha[\![P]\!] \uparrow \omega$),*
5. $\alpha(\mathcal{F}[\![P]\!]) = \mathcal{F}_\alpha[\![P]\!]$,
6. $\mathcal{F}_\alpha[\![P]\!] = \mathcal{O}_\alpha[\![P]\!]$.

Theorem 6 shows that denotational observables satisfy all the properties of the concrete semantics. In particular, they are condensing (Property 2) and the abstract top-down and bottom-up semantics are equivalent (Property 6). In addition, denotational observables are precise (Properties 1 and 5). The class of denotational observables includes computed answers (the *id* observable) and the observables correct answers and ground instances of computed answers, whose semantics are the atomic logical consequences observables (c-semantics) and the least Herbrand model, respectively.

5.1 The c-semantics

We show how to obtain a semantics which models correct answers [9,28]. Correct answers are closed under instantiation. This property corresponds to the downward closure of the corresponding equations sets. Any $\mathcal{E} \in \mathbb{E}$ is *downward closed* (w.r.t. $\leq_E$) if and only if, for any $E \in \mathcal{E}$, $E' \leq_E E$ implies $E' \in \mathcal{E}$. We denote by $\downarrow$ the downward closure operator, i.e., $\mathcal{E}\!\downarrow = \{ E' \mid E' \leq_E E, E \in \mathcal{E} \}$.

Let $\mathbb{D}_\psi = (\mathbb{E}\!\downarrow, \subseteq)$ denote the complete lattice of downward closed sets of finite solved form equation sets, partially ordered by $\subseteq$. The *correct answers observable* $\psi : \mathbb{E} \longrightarrow \mathbb{D}_\psi$ is

$$\psi(\mathcal{E}) = \mathcal{E}\!\downarrow.$$

By applying the definitions, the abstract operators are $\tilde{\otimes} = \cap$, $\tilde{\cup} = \cup$ and $\tilde{|}_{\boldsymbol{x}} = \downarrow \circ |_{\boldsymbol{x}}$.

ψ is a denotational observable and its immediate consequences operator is

$$\mathcal{P}_\psi[\![P]\!](\mathcal{I}_\psi) = \lambda p(\boldsymbol{x}). \bigcup \{ \mathcal{E}\!\downarrow \mid p(\boldsymbol{x}) :- E, A_1, \ldots, A_n \text{ is a renamed clause of } P,\ \mathcal{E} = (\psi(\{ E \}) \cap \textstyle\bigcap_{i=1}^{n} \mathcal{I}_\psi(A_i))|_{\boldsymbol{x}} \}.$$

5.2 The least Herbrand model

We show how to obtain the least Herbrand model semantics [47]. The least Herbrand model gives the ground correct answers. This corresponds to the solutions of the corresponding equations sets. Any $\mathcal{E} \in \mathbb{E}$ is *grounding* if and only if, for any $E \in \mathcal{E}$, $var(E) = elim(E)$. We denote by $\downarrow_g$ the grounding operator, i.e., $\mathcal{E}\!\downarrow_g = \{ E' \mid E' \text{ is grounding }, E' \in \mathcal{E}\!\downarrow \}$.

Let $\mathbb{D}_\varphi = (\mathbb{E}\!\downarrow_g, \subseteq)$ denote the complete lattice of grounding sets of finite solved form equation sets, partially ordered by $\subseteq$. The *ground answers observable* $\varphi : \mathbb{E} \longrightarrow \mathbb{D}_\varphi$ is

$$\varphi(\mathcal{E}) = \mathcal{E}\!\downarrow_g.$$

By applying the definitions, the abstract operators are $\tilde{\otimes} = \cap$, $\tilde{\cup} = \cup$ and $\tilde{|}_{\boldsymbol{x}} = \downarrow_g \circ |_{\boldsymbol{x}}$.

φ is a denotational observable and its immediate consequences operator is

$$\mathcal{P}_\varphi[\![P]\!](\mathcal{I}_\varphi) = \lambda p(\boldsymbol{x}). \bigcup \{ \mathcal{E}\!\downarrow_g \mid p(\boldsymbol{x}) :- E, A_1, \ldots, A_n \text{ is a renamed clause of } P,\ \mathcal{E} = (\varphi(\{ E \}) \cap \textstyle\bigcap_{i=1}^{n} \mathcal{I}_\varphi(A_i))|_{\boldsymbol{x}} \}.$$

It is worth noting that, both for the c-semantics and for the least Herbrand model, the abstract $\otimes$ operator is simply the *glb* operator in the abstract domain.

6 Semi-denotational observables

Semi-denotational observables are intended to model domains, where we cannot require the precision property. We therefore relax the axioms of denotational observables to admit non precise $\tilde{\otimes}$ and $\tilde{\rceil}$ operators. However we still want to guarantee that the condensing and equivalence properties are satisfied. This can be achieved by the following definition.

Definition 7. Let $\alpha : \mathbb{E} \to \mathbb{D}$ be an observable. Then α is a *semi-denotational observable* if

1. $\tilde{\rceil}$ and $\tilde{\otimes}$ are additive on $(\mathbb{D}, \leq)$,
2. $\tilde{\otimes}$ is associative,
3. $\forall D, D' \in \mathbb{D}$, $\forall \boldsymbol{x}, \boldsymbol{y}$, $var(D') \cap (var(D) \cup \boldsymbol{x}) \subseteq \boldsymbol{y} \subseteq \boldsymbol{x}$ implies $(D \tilde{\otimes} D'\tilde{\rceil}_{\boldsymbol{y}})\tilde{\rceil}_{\boldsymbol{x}} = (D \tilde{\otimes} D')\tilde{\rceil}_{\boldsymbol{x}}$.

Note that, differently form the case of denotational observables, the class of semi-denotational observables is characterized in terms of properties of the abstract operators. An equivalent characterization, given in terms of α, γ and the concrete operators, is possible, but would be harder to understand.

Theorem 8. *Let $\alpha : \mathbb{E} \to \mathbb{D}$ be a semi-denotational observable, $D, A_1, \ldots, A_n$ be an abstract goal and P be a program. Then*

1. $\alpha(\mathcal{O}[\![P]\!]) \leq \mathcal{O}_\alpha[\![P]\!]$,
2. $\mathcal{B}_\alpha[\![D, A_1, \ldots, A_n \text{ in } P]\!] = (D \tilde{\otimes} \mathcal{O}_\alpha[\![P]\!](A_1) \tilde{\otimes} \cdots \tilde{\otimes} \mathcal{O}_\alpha[\![P]\!](A_n))\tilde{\rceil}_{var(A_1,\ldots,A_n)}$,
3. $\mathcal{P}_\alpha[\![P]\!]$ *is continuous on* $\mathbb{I}_{\mathbb{A}}$ $(\mathcal{F}_\alpha[\![P]\!] = \mathcal{P}_\alpha[\![P]\!] \uparrow \omega)$,
4. $\mathcal{P}_\alpha[\![P]\!] \geq \alpha \circ \mathcal{P}[\![P]\!] \circ \gamma$,
5. $\alpha(\mathcal{F}[\![P]\!]) \leq \mathcal{F}_\alpha[\![P]\!]$,
6. $\mathcal{F}_\alpha[\![P]\!] = \mathcal{O}_\alpha[\![P]\!]$.

Theorem 8 shows that semi-denotational observables are condensing (Property 2) and that the abstract top-down and bottom-up semantics are equivalent (Property 6). However, the denotations are just correct approximations, yet they are not precise (Properties 1 and 5). Note that the above characterization of semi-denotational observables does only guarantee the correctness of the abstract immediate consequences operator and not its optimality (see Property 4). If the additional axiom

$$\alpha(\gamma\alpha(D) \otimes \gamma\alpha(D')) = \alpha(D \otimes \gamma\alpha(D'))$$

is satisfied, we get the optimality property of $\mathcal{P}_\alpha$, namely $\mathcal{P}_\alpha[\![P]\!] = \alpha \circ \mathcal{P}[\![P]\!] \circ \gamma$. The optimality, however, is not required for abstract diagnosis.

6.1 Groundness dependencies

We show now how to model the domain $\mathcal{POS}$, designed for the *groundness analysis* of logic programs [7,41,21]. $\mathcal{POS}$ is a domain of equivalence classes of propositional formulas, built using the logical connectives $\leftrightarrow$, $\wedge$ and $\vee$, and ordered by implication. The propositional formulas represent groundness dependencies among variables. The domain $\mathcal{POS}$ for two variables is shown in Figure 2.

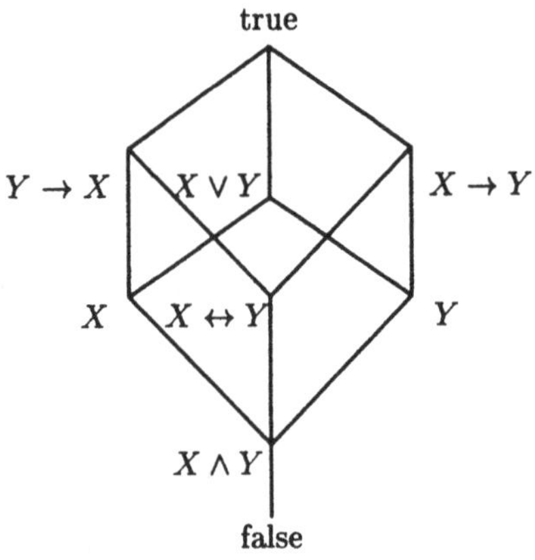

Fig. 2. The domain $\mathcal{POS}$

First of all we have to define the abstraction $\Gamma(t)$ of the concrete term t. If $var(t) = \{ x_1, \ldots, x_n \}$ then $\Gamma(t) = x_1 \wedge \ldots \wedge x_n$. The intuition is that, in order for t to be ground, all its variables $x_1, \ldots, x_n$ must be ground.

We can extend Γ to solved form equation sets to obtain abstract formulas as $\Gamma(E) = \bigwedge_{x=t \in E}(x \leftrightarrow \Gamma(t))$, where $\Gamma(\emptyset) = \mathit{true}$. Abstract formulas are propositional formulas which express the *groundness dependencies* among the eliminable variables and the other variables of the concrete solved form equation set.

By applying the definition, the abstract operators turn out to be

$$F_1 \tilde{\otimes} F_2 = F_1 \wedge F_2$$

$$\tilde{\bigcup}\{ F_i \}_{i \in I} = \bigvee_{i \in I} F_i$$

$$F \tilde{\rceil}_x = \begin{cases} F & \text{if } var(F) \subseteq \{ x \} \\ (F[y \mapsto \mathit{true}] \vee F[y \mapsto \mathit{false}])\tilde{\rceil}_x & \text{for some } y \in var(F) \setminus \{ x \} \end{cases}$$

where $F[y \mapsto E]$ is obtained by replacing each occurrence of the variable y in F by E. Note that the abstract notion of restriction of an abstract formula corresponds to *Schröder's elimination principle*.

The *groundness dependencies observable* $\alpha_\Gamma : \mathbb{E} \longrightarrow \mathcal{POS}$ is

$$\alpha_\Gamma(\mathcal{E}) = \bigvee_{E \in \mathcal{E}} \Gamma(E),$$

where $\alpha_\Gamma(\emptyset) = \mathit{false}$.

```
r(X,Y) :- p(X,Y), q(X,Y).
p(a,Y).
p(X,b).
q(X,X).
```

Fig. 3. The program in Example 9

It is easy to prove that this is a semi-denotational observable. The abstract immediate consequences operator $\mathcal{P}_{\alpha_\Gamma}[\![P]\!]$ (which turns out to be optimal) is

$$\mathcal{P}_{\alpha_\Gamma}[\![P]\!](\mathcal{I}_{\alpha_\Gamma}) = \lambda p(x). \bigvee_{\substack{p(x) :- E, A_1, \ldots, A_n \text{ is} \\ \text{a renamed clause of } P}} (\alpha_\Gamma(\{E\}) \wedge \bigwedge_{i=1}^{n} \mathcal{I}_{\alpha_\Gamma}(A_i)) \tilde{\restriction}_x$$

Note that $\mathcal{P}_{\alpha_\Gamma}[\![P]\!]$ is defined in terms of abstract restriction $\tilde{\restriction}$ and of the *lub* and *glb* operators on $\mathcal{POS}$ ($\wedge$ and $\vee$ respectively). Note also that (concrete) equations do occur within the expression $\alpha_\Gamma(E)$ only. This suggest that one can equivalently transform the program into an *abstract program*, by replacing equations by their abstractions [12,34].

Example 9. Consider the program P of Figure 3 and the groundness dependencies observable. The abstract denotation of P is

$$\begin{aligned}
\mathcal{F}_{\alpha_\Gamma}[\![P]\!](p(x,y)) &= x \vee y \\
\mathcal{F}_{\alpha_\Gamma}[\![P]\!](q(x,y)) &= x \leftrightarrow y \\
\mathcal{F}_{\alpha_\Gamma}[\![P]\!](r(x,y)) &= x \wedge y.
\end{aligned}$$

which turns out to be precise since $\mathcal{F}_{\alpha_\Gamma}[\![P]\!] = \alpha_\Gamma(\mathcal{F}[\![P]\!])$. Note that, if we choose to represent groundness dependencies by the domain $\mathcal{DEF}$, which does not contain disjunctive formulas (and which is not a semi-denotational observable), we would obtain a less precise abstract semantics, where the semantics of $p(x,y)$ would be *true* and the semantics of $r(x,y)$ would be $x \leftrightarrow y$. ∎

7 (Abstract) diagnosis w.r.t. (semi-)denotational observables

Let P be a program. If α is a semi-denotational observable, we know that the actual and the intended behaviors of P for all the goals are uniquely determined by the behaviors for most general goals. The following Definition 10 extends to abstract diagnosis the definitions given in [45,30,38] for declarative diagnosis. In the following $\mathcal{I}_\alpha$ is the specification of the intended behavior of program P for most general atomic goals w.r.t. the semi-denotational observable α.

Remember that denotational observables are also semi-denotational. Moreover the computed answers observable is also denotational. We will then define the theory for semi-denotational observables. Some stronger results will hold for denotational observables only. The diagnosis w.r.t. computed answers [17] is obtained as an instance of the scheme.

Definition 10. Let P be a program and α be a semi-denotational observable.

1. P is *partially correct* w.r.t. $\mathcal{I}_\alpha$ if $\alpha(\mathcal{F}[\![P]\!]) \leq \mathcal{I}_\alpha$.
2. P is *complete* w.r.t. $\mathcal{I}_\alpha$ if $\mathcal{I}_\alpha \leq \alpha(\mathcal{F}[\![P]\!])$.
3. P is *totally correct* w.r.t. $\mathcal{I}_\alpha$, if $\alpha(\mathcal{F}[\![P]\!]) = \mathcal{I}_\alpha$.

If $\alpha = id$ the previous definition reduces to: P is *partially correct* w.r.t. $\mathcal{I}$ if $\mathcal{F}[\![P]\!] \sqsubseteq \mathcal{I}$, P is *complete* w.r.t. $\mathcal{I}$ if $\mathcal{I} \sqsubseteq \mathcal{F}[\![P]\!]$, P is *totally correct* w.r.t. $\mathcal{I}$ if $\mathcal{F}[\![P]\!] = \mathcal{I}$.

Note that we do not address termination issues, since the concrete semantics we use is too abstract.

If P is not totally correct, we are left with the problem of determining the errors, which are related to the *symptoms*. Symptoms are $\mathbb{A}$-*elements*, according to the following definition.

Definition 11. An $\mathbb{A}$-*element* is an $\mathbb{A}$-interpretation defined for a pure atom only, which returns a singleton. We denote by $\sigma = A \mapsto D$ the $\mathbb{A}$-element σ such that $\sigma(A) = D$ (and is otherwise undefined).

Definition 12. Let P be a program and α be a semi-denotational observable. Then

1. An *incorrectness symptom* is an $\mathbb{A}$-element σ such that $\sigma \leq \alpha(\mathcal{F}[\![P]\!])$ and $\sigma \not\leq \mathcal{I}_\alpha$.
2. An *incompleteness symptom* is an $\mathbb{A}$-element σ such that $\sigma \leq \mathcal{I}_\alpha$ and $\sigma \not\leq \alpha(\mathcal{F}[\![P]\!])$.

If $\alpha = id$ the previous definition reduces to: an *incorrectness symptom* is an $\mathbb{A}$-element ϑ such that $\vartheta \sqsubseteq \mathcal{F}[\![P]\!]$ and $\vartheta \not\sqsubseteq \mathcal{I}$ and an *incompleteness symptom* is an $\mathbb{A}$-element ϑ such that $\vartheta \sqsubseteq \mathcal{I}$ and $\vartheta \not\sqsubseteq \mathcal{F}[\![P]\!]$.

Note that a totally correct program has no incorrectness and no incompleteness symptoms. Our incompleteness symptoms are related to the insufficiency symptoms in [30], which are defined by taking $gfp\ \mathcal{P}_\alpha[\![P]\!]$ instead of $\mathcal{F}_\alpha[\![P]\!] = lfp\ \mathcal{P}_\alpha[\![P]\!]$ as program semantics. The two definitions, even if different, turn out to be the same for the class of programs we are interested in (see Section 7). Ferrand's choice is motivated by the fact that $gfp\ \mathcal{P}_\alpha[\![P]\!]$ is related to finite failures. The approach of using two different semantics for reasoning about incorrectness and incompleteness has been pursued in [31], leading to an elegant uniform (yet non-effective) characterization of correctness and completeness.

It is straightforward to realize that an $\mathbb{A}$-element may sometimes be an incorrectness or incompleteness symptom, just because of another symptom.

Example 13. Consider the program P of Figure 4 and the specification

```
c1:  q(X) :- p(X).
c2:  p(a).
```

Fig. 4. The program of Example 13

$$\mathcal{I}_\alpha(p(x)) = \emptyset$$
$$\mathcal{I}_\alpha(q(x)) = \emptyset.$$

The s-semantics of P is

$$\mathcal{F}[\![P]\!](p(x)) = \{\{x = a\}\}$$
$$\mathcal{F}[\![P]\!](q(x)) = \{\{x = a\}\}.$$

Hence $\sigma_1 = p(x) \mapsto \{\{x = a\}\}$ and $\sigma_2 = q(x) \mapsto \{\{x = a\}\}$ are both incorrectness symptoms but σ_2 is just a consequence of σ_1.

Consider now the specification

$$\mathcal{I}_\alpha(q(x)) = \{\{x = a\}\}.$$

The s-semantics of P is

$$\mathcal{F}[\![P]\!](p(x)) = \{\{x = a\}\}$$
$$\mathcal{F}[\![P]\!](q(x)) = \{\{x = a\}\}.$$

There exists only an incorrectness symptom, i.e., $\sigma = p(x) \mapsto \{\{x = a\}\}$. If we fix this bug (by removing the second clause), we get an incompleteness symptom, since $\mathcal{F}[\![Q]\!](q(x)) = \emptyset$. ■

The *diagnosis* determines the "basic" symptoms, and, in the case of incorrectness, the relevant clause in the program. This is captured by the definitions of *incorrect clause* and *uncovered* $\mathbb{A}$*-element*, which are related to incorrectness and incompleteness symptoms, respectively.

Definition 14. If there exists an $\mathbb{A}$-element σ such that $\sigma \not\leq \mathcal{I}_\alpha$ and $\sigma \leq \mathcal{P}_\alpha[\![\{c\}]\!](\mathcal{I}_\alpha)$, then the clause $c \in P$ is *incorrect* on σ.

If $\alpha = id$ the previous definition reduces to: if there exists an $\mathbb{A}$-element ϑ such that $\vartheta \not\sqsubseteq \mathcal{I}$ and $\vartheta \sqsubseteq \mathcal{P}[\![\{c\}]\!](\mathcal{I})$, then the clause $c \in P$ is *incorrect* on ϑ.

Informally, c is incorrect on σ, if it derives a wrong $\mathbb{A}$-element from the intended semantics. $\mathcal{P}_\alpha[\![\{c\}]\!]$ is the operator associated to the program $\{c\}$, consisting of the clause c only.

Definition 15. An $\mathbb{A}$-element σ is *uncovered* if $\sigma \leq \mathcal{I}_\alpha$ and $\sigma \not\leq \mathcal{P}_\alpha[\![P]\!](\mathcal{I}_\alpha)$.

If $\alpha = id$ the previous definition reduces to: an $\mathbb{A}$-element ϑ is *uncovered* if $\vartheta \sqsubseteq \mathcal{I}$ and $\vartheta \not\sqsubseteq \mathcal{P}[\![P]\!](\mathcal{I})$.

Informally, σ is uncovered if there are no clauses deriving it from the intended semantics.

It is worth noting that checking the conditions of Definitions 14 and 15 requires one application of $\mathcal{P}_\alpha[\![P]\!]$ to $\mathcal{I}_\alpha$, while the detection of symptoms (Definition 12) would require the construction of $\mathcal{F}[\![P]\!]$ and therefore a fixpoint computation. As we will show in the following, the detection of bugs can be based on Definitions 14 and 15, while this is not the case for Definition 12.

The following theorem shows the relation between partial correctness (Definition 10) and absence of incorrect clauses (Definition 14).

Theorem 16. *If there are no incorrect clauses in P, then P is partially correct w.r.t. α. The converse does not hold.*

The theorem shows the feasibility of a diagnosis method for incorrectness based on the comparison between $\mathcal{I}_\alpha$ and $\mathcal{P}_\alpha[\![P]\!](\mathcal{I})$ and does not require to actually compute the denotation $\mathcal{F}_\alpha[\![P]\!]$ (i.e., the least fixpoint of $\mathcal{P}_\alpha[\![P]\!]$).

Example 17. Consider the program of Figure 3 and the following specification w.r.t. the α_Γ observable.

$$\begin{aligned}\mathcal{I}_{\alpha_\Gamma}(p(x,y)) &= \mathit{true}\\ \mathcal{I}_{\alpha_\Gamma}(q(x,y)) &= x \leftrightarrow y\\ \mathcal{I}_{\alpha_\Gamma}(r(x,y)) &= x \leftrightarrow y.\end{aligned}$$

By applying the $\mathcal{P}_{\alpha_\Gamma}[\![P]\!]$ operator to $\mathcal{I}_{\alpha_\Gamma}$ we have

$$\begin{aligned}\mathcal{P}_{\alpha_\Gamma}[\![P]\!](\mathcal{I}_{\alpha_\Gamma})(p(x,y)) &= x \vee y\\ \mathcal{P}_{\alpha_\Gamma}[\![P]\!](\mathcal{I}_{\alpha_\Gamma})(q(x,y)) &= x \leftrightarrow y\\ \mathcal{P}_{\alpha_\Gamma}[\![P]\!](\mathcal{I}_{\alpha_\Gamma})(r(x,y)) &= x \leftrightarrow y.\end{aligned}$$

Since $\mathcal{P}_{\alpha_\Gamma}[\![P]\!](\mathcal{I}_{\alpha_\Gamma}) \leq \mathcal{I}_{\alpha_\Gamma}$ there are no incorrect clauses. Then (by applying Theorem 16) P turns out to be partially correct w.r.t. $\mathcal{I}_{\alpha_\Gamma}$. ∎

Note that the second part of Theorem 16 asserts that there might be incorrect clauses even if there are no incorrectness symptoms. In other words, if we just look at the semantics of the program, some incorrectness bugs can be "hidden" (because of an incompleteness bug). However, if there are no incompleteness bugs, all the incorrect clauses identify incorrectness symptoms, as shown by the following theorem.

Theorem 18. *Let α be a denotational observable and P be a complete program w.r.t. $\mathcal{I}_\alpha$. If there exists an incorrect clause in P on the $\mathbb{A}$-element σ, then σ is an incorrectness symptom (and therefore P is not partially correct).*

Example 19. Consider the program of Figure 4 w.r.t. an empty specification $\mathcal{I}$. In Example 13 we showed that $\sigma_1 = p(x) \mapsto \{\{x = a\}\}$ and $\sigma_2 = q(x) \mapsto \{\{x = a\}\}$ are both incorrectness symptoms. By applying $\mathcal{P}$ to $\mathcal{I}$ we obtain

$$\mathcal{P}[\![P]\!](\mathcal{I})(p(x)) = \{\{x = a\}\}$$

```
c1:  p(f(X)) :- q(X).
c2:  q(a).
c3:  r(X) :- p(g(X)).
c4:  s(X,Y) :- r(X).
c5:  s(X,a).
```

Fig. 5. The program in Example 20

$$\mathcal{P}[\![P]\!](\mathcal{I})(q(x)) = \emptyset.$$

Hence the clause c2 is incorrect on σ_1. ∎

Theorem 18 does not hold for semi-denotational observables, because the abstract semantics may be not precise, as shown by Example 20. Absence of incorrect clauses implies partial correctness, any way, while the detection of an incorrect clause is just a hint about a possible source of errors.

Example 20. Consider the program P of Figure 5 and the following abstract specification w.r.t. the α_Γ observable.

$$\begin{aligned}\mathcal{I}_{\alpha_\Gamma}(p(x)) &= x\\ \mathcal{I}_{\alpha_\Gamma}(q(x)) &= x\\ \mathcal{I}_{\alpha_\Gamma}(r(x)) &= \mathit{false}\\ \mathcal{I}_{\alpha_\Gamma}(s(x,y)) &= y.\end{aligned}$$

The abstract semantics is

$$\begin{aligned}\mathcal{F}_{\alpha_\Gamma}[\![P]\!](p(x)) &= x\\ \mathcal{F}_{\alpha_\Gamma}[\![P]\!](q(x)) &= x\\ \mathcal{F}_{\alpha_\Gamma}[\![P]\!](r(x)) &= x\\ \mathcal{F}_{\alpha_\Gamma}[\![P]\!](s(x,y)) &= x \vee y,\end{aligned}$$

while the abstraction of the concrete denotational semantics is

$$\begin{aligned}\alpha_\Gamma(\mathcal{F}[\![P]\!])(p(x)) &= x\\ \alpha_\Gamma(\mathcal{F}[\![P]\!])(q(x)) &= x\\ \alpha_\Gamma(\mathcal{F}[\![P]\!])(r(x)) &= \mathit{false}\\ \alpha_\Gamma(\mathcal{F}[\![P]\!])(s(x,y)) &= y.\end{aligned}$$

The abstract semantics is not precise, i.e., $\mathcal{F}_{\alpha_\Gamma} \neq \alpha_\Gamma(\mathcal{F}[\![P]\!])$. The program P turns out to be totally correct w.r.t. $\mathcal{I}_{\alpha_\Gamma}$. However, since $\mathcal{P}_{\alpha_\Gamma}[\![\{\,\mathsf{c3}\,\}]\!](\mathcal{I}_{\alpha_\Gamma})(r(x)) = x$, the clause c3 turns out to be incorrect on the $\mathbb{A}$-element $\sigma = r(x) \mapsto x$. This is due to the approximation introduced by the $\mathcal{P}_{\alpha_\Gamma}$ operator. ∎

As in the case of declarative diagnosis, handling completeness turns out to be more complex, since some incompletnesses cannot be detected by comparing $\mathcal{I}_\alpha$ and $\mathcal{P}_\alpha[\![P]\!](\mathcal{I})$. The following example shows that we cannot base the diagnosis of incompleteness on the detection of uncovered $\mathbb{A}$-elements.

Example 21. Consider the program $P = \{$ `p :- p.` $\}$ and the specification $\mathcal{I} = \{p\}$ w.r.t. the *id* observable. Then $\mathcal{P}[\![P]\!](\mathcal{I}) = \mathcal{I}$, while $\mathcal{F}[\![P]\!] = \emptyset$. Hence

1. there are no uncovered $\mathbb{A}$-elements in P,
2. P is not complete w.r.t. $\mathcal{I}$ (i.e., there exist incompleteness symptoms). ∎

The problem shown by Example 21 is that $\mathcal{I}$ is a fixpoint of $\mathcal{P}[\![P]\!]$ different from the least fixpoint. The following theorem shows that the diagnosis of incompleteness can be based on Definition 15, if the operator $\mathcal{P}_\alpha[\![P]\!]$ has a unique fixpoint.

Theorem 22. *Let α be a denotational observable and assume $\mathcal{P}_\alpha[\![P]\!]$ has a unique fixpoint. If there are no uncovered elements, then P is complete w.r.t. $\mathcal{I}_\alpha$. The converse does not hold.*

Note that, if $\mathcal{P}[\![P]\!]$ has a unique fixpoint, $\mathit{lfp}\,\mathcal{P}[\![P]\!] = \mathit{gfp}\,\mathcal{P}[\![P]\!]$. Hence our incompleteness symptoms are exactly the insufficiency symptoms in [30].

The requirement on $\mathcal{P}_\alpha[\![P]\!]$ seems to be very strong. However, this property holds for a large class of programs, i.e., for *acceptable programs* as defined in [6]. Acceptable programs are the left-terminating programs, i.e., those programs for which the *SLD*-derivations of ground goals (via the leftmost selection rule) are finite. Most interesting programs are acceptable (all the pure PROLOG programs in [46] are reported in [6] to be acceptable). The same property holds for the wrong versions of acceptable programs provided that the errors do not affect the left-termination property. One relevant technical property of acceptable programs is that the ground immediate consequences operator has a unique fixpoint [6]. The same property holds for all the immediate consequences operators $\mathcal{P}_\alpha[\![P]\!]$, corresponding to denotational observables.

Theorem 23 (fixpoint uniqueness). *[16] Let P be an acceptable program and α be a denotational observable. Then $\mathit{lfp}\,\mathcal{P}_\alpha[\![P]\!]$ is the unique fixpoint of $\mathcal{P}_\alpha[\![P]\!]$.*

Note that this result applies to declarative diagnosis as well, since it is based on the least Herbrand model or on the *c*-semantics.

Example 24. The example is intended to show the relation among the various concepts involved in the diagnosis. Consider the acceptable program P of Figure 6, which is an "ancestor" program with a wrong clause (c2 instead of **`ancestor(X,Y):- parent(X,Y).`**) and missing database tuples. The intended interpretation w.r.t. the *id* observable is

$$\begin{aligned}\mathcal{I}(\mathit{parent}(x,y)) = \{\, & \{\, x = \mathit{terach}, y = \mathit{abraham} \,\},\\ & \{\, x = \mathit{abraham}, y = \mathit{isaac} \,\} \,\}\end{aligned}$$

```
c1:  ancestor(X,Y) :- parent(Z,Y), ancestor(X,Z).
c2:  ancestor(X,Y) :-  parent(Y,X).
```

Fig. 6. A wrong acceptable program

$$\begin{aligned}\mathcal{I}(ancestor(x,y)) = \{\, & \{\, x = terach, y = abraham \,\},\\ & \{\, x = terach, y = isaac \,\},\\ & \{\, x = abraham, y = isaac \,\} \,\},\end{aligned}$$

while

$$\begin{aligned}\mathcal{P}[\![P]\!](\mathcal{I})(ancestor(x,y)) = \{\, & \{\, x = abraham, y = terach \,\},\\ & \{\, x = terach, y = isaac \,\},\\ & \{\, x = isaac, y = abraham \,\} \,\}.\end{aligned}$$

The diagnosis delivers the following result.

- The clause `ancestor(X,Y):- parent(Y,X).` is incorrect on
  1. $ancestor(x,y) \mapsto \{\, x = abraham, y = terach \,\}$ and
  2. $ancestor(x,y) \mapsto \{\, x = isaac, y = abraham \,\}$.
- The following $\mathbb{A}$-elements are uncovered.
  1. $parent(x,y) \mapsto \{\, x = terach, y = abraham \,\}$,
  2. $parent(x,y) \mapsto \{\, x = abraham, y = isaac \,\}$,
  3. $ancestor(x,y) \mapsto \{\, x = terach, y = abraham \,\}$ and
  4. $ancestor(x,y) \mapsto \{\, x = abraham, y = isaac \,\}$.

Note that $\mathcal{F}[\![P]\!] = \lambda p(x).\emptyset$. Hence there are no incorrectness symptoms, even if there is an incorrect clause. Note also that the $\mathbb{A}$-element $ancestor(x,y) \mapsto \{\, x = terach, y = isaac \,\}$ is not uncovered, even if it is an incompleteness symptom. ∎

The following corollaries are a justification of the overall diagnosis method.

Corollary 25. *Let α be a denotational observable and assume $\mathcal{P}_\alpha[\![P]\!]$ has a unique fixpoint. Then P is totally correct w.r.t. $\mathcal{I}_\alpha$, if and only if there are no incorrect clauses and uncovered $\mathbb{A}$-elements.*

Corollary 26. *Assume P is an acceptable program and α is a denotational observable. Then P is totally correct w.r.t. $\mathcal{I}$, if and only if there are no incorrect clauses and uncovered $\mathbb{A}$-elements.*

Theorem 22 (together with its corollaries) does not hold for semi-denotational observables, because the absence of uncovered $\mathbb{A}$-elements, even under the unique fixpoint assumption, does not imply program completeness. Incompleteness bugs might be hidden by the approximation of the abstract semantics.

The detection of uncovered $\mathbb{A}$-elements is instead meaningful even in the case of semi-denotational observables, as shown by the following theorem.

Theorem 27. *Let α be a semi-denotational observable and P be partially correct w.r.t. $\mathcal{I}_\alpha$. If there exists an uncovered $\mathbb{A}$-element σ, then σ is an incompleteness symptom (and therefore P is not complete).*

Example 28. Consider the program of Figure 3 and the intended specification of Example 17. The incompleteness diagnosis delivers the following results.

1. The $\mathbb{A}$-element $\sigma_1 = p(x,y) \mapsto \mathit{true}$ is uncovered and therefore it is an incompleteness symptom.
2. The $\mathbb{A}$-element $\sigma_2 = r(x,y) \mapsto x \leftrightarrow y$ is also an incompleteness symptom but it is not uncovered. ∎

8 The oracle and the "top-down" diagnosis

The "bottom-up" diagnosis is based on Definitions 14 and 15 and requires the application of $\mathcal{P}_\alpha[\![P]\!]$ to the intended semantics $\mathcal{I}_\alpha$. Hence $\mathcal{I}_\alpha$ has to be specified in an extensional way. We are not concerned, for the time being, with the problem of effectivity (i.e., finiteness of $\mathcal{I}_\alpha$). Rather we are concerned with the problem of specifying $\mathcal{I}_\alpha$ by means of an *oracle*, as first suggested in [45]. The oracle is usually implemented by querying the user. Several oracles have been used in declarative debugging (see the discussion in [42]). We will use one oracle only, directly related to the property we are concerned with, namely abstractions of computed answers.

Definition 29. The *abstract oracle* $\mathcal{A}_\alpha$ is

$$\mathcal{A}_\alpha = \lambda p(\boldsymbol{x}).\, \tilde{\cup}\{\, D \mid D \text{ is an abstract answer of } p(\boldsymbol{x}) \text{ according to the intended semantics } \}.$$

Once we have the oracle, we can define the *abstract oracle simulation*, following [45]. The oracle simulation allows us to express in a compact way new top-down diagnosis conditions. The oracle simulation performs one step of abstract goal rewriting by using the program clauses and then gets the abstract answers for the resulting abstract goal from the oracle.

Definition 30. Let P be a program. Then the *abstract oracle simulation* $\mathcal{S}_\alpha$ of P is

$$\mathcal{S}_\alpha[\![P]\!] = \lambda p(\boldsymbol{x}).\, \tilde{\bigcup}\{\, D \mid p(\boldsymbol{x}) \xrightarrow[P]{\alpha} D', A_1, \ldots, A_n,\ D = (D' \,\tilde{\otimes}\, \mathcal{A}_\alpha(A_1) \,\tilde{\otimes} \cdots \tilde{\otimes}\, \mathcal{A}_\alpha(A_n))\tilde{\rceil}_{\boldsymbol{x}} \,\}.$$

Note that the elements of the sets computed by $\mathcal{A}$ and $\mathcal{S}_\alpha[\![P]\!]$ are equivalence classes w.r.t. variance, as was the case for the domain of our semantics. The following two theorems justify the top-down diagnosis.

Theorem 31. *The clause $c \in P$ is incorrect on the $\mathbb{A}$-element σ if and only if $\sigma \leq \mathcal{S}_\alpha[\![\{c\}]\!]$ and $\sigma \not\leq \mathcal{A}_\alpha$.*

Theorem 32. *The* $\mathbb{A}$*-element* σ *is uncovered if and only if* $\sigma \leq \mathcal{A}_\alpha$ *and* $\sigma \not\leq \mathcal{S}_\alpha[\![P]\!]$.

The proofs of Theorems 31 and 32 are based on the properties of our semantics, which relate fixpoint bottom-up computations to top-down refutations for pure atomic goals.

9 Abstract diagnosis: summary and discussion

We have defined a general diagnosis method based on incorrect clauses and uncovered $\mathbb{A}$-elements, which does not require to detect symptoms in advance. Incorrect clauses and uncovered $\mathbb{A}$-elements can be detected by means of very simple bottom-up and top-down algorithms, without actually computing the abstract semantics (e.g. no fixpoint computation is required).

Rather strong results hold for denotational observables, which allow us to handle the diagnosis w.r.t. computed answers [17] and to reconstruct the declarative diagnosis methods based on the least Herbrand model and on the *c*-semantics. Namely,

- absence of incorrect clauses implies partial correctness.
- absence of uncovered $\mathbb{A}$-elements implies completeness for a large class of interesting programs (acceptable programs).
- incorrect clauses and uncovered $\mathbb{A}$-elements always correspond to bugs in the program.

On the other hand, the diagnosis is non-effective, unless the specification is finite. In fact, if the specification is infinite (as it is usually the case for denotational observables), the bottom-up diagnosis is unfeasible and, in the top-down diagnosis, the oracle should return infinitely many answers to some queries. In order to make the diagnosis effective, we need finite approximations. A first solution was suggested in [17] for the diagnosis w.r.t. computed answers, by introducing ***partial specifications***. A more elegant solution can be found by handling approximation via abstract interpretation techniques, i.e., *widening* [25] or Galois insertions. The latter is exactly what we obtain by using semi-denotational observables, which are usually defined by finite (or noetherian) abstract domains. On one side, we make the diagnosis effective. On the other side, as one might expect, the results are weaker, just because of approximation. Namely,

- absence of incorrect clauses implies partial correctness.
- an uncovered $\mathbb{A}$-element always corresponds to a bug in the program.
- an incorrect clause is just a hint about a possible bug in the program, yet it does not always correspond to a bug.
- there exists no sufficient condition for completeness.

Several interesting abstract program properties can be handled by semi-denotational observables. In Section 6 we have considered groundness dependencies. Types and modes can be handled in a similar way. In particular, various notions of types (including polymorphic types) can be represented by semi-denotational observables. As a very simple example, $\mathcal{POS}$ itself can be viewed as a domain consisting of a single type (say natural numbers). We only need to redefine the abstraction function as follows. Let

$$\tau(t) = \begin{cases} t & \text{if } t \text{ is a variable} \\ \mathit{true} & \text{if } t = 0 \\ \tau(t') & \text{if } t = s(t') \\ \mathit{false} & \text{otherwise} \end{cases}$$

then

$$\alpha_{nat}(\mathcal{E}) = \bigvee_{E \in \mathcal{E}} \Big(\bigwedge_{x=t \in E} x \leftrightarrow \tau(t) \Big).$$

The abstract immediate consequences operator is exactly the one of Subsection 6.1 with α_Γ replaced by α_{nat}.

Example 33. Consider the program P of Figure 1 and the following specification w.r.t. the α_{nat} observable.

$$\mathcal{I}_{\alpha_{nat}}(sum(x, y, z)) = x \wedge y \wedge z.$$

The abstract denotation of P is

$$\alpha_{nat}(\mathcal{F}[\![P]\!])(sum(x, y, z)) = x \wedge y \leftrightarrow z.$$

By applying the $\mathcal{P}_{\alpha_{nat}}$ operator to $\mathcal{I}_{\alpha_{nat}}$ we have

$$\mathcal{P}_{\alpha_{nat}}[\![\{\, \mathtt{c1} \,\}]\!](\mathcal{I}_{\alpha_{nat}})(sum(x, y, z)) = x \wedge y \leftrightarrow z$$
$$\mathcal{P}_{\alpha_{nat}}[\![\{\, \mathtt{c2} \,\}]\!](\mathcal{I}_{\alpha_{nat}})(sum(x, y, z)) = x \wedge y \wedge z.$$

The abstract diagnosis shows that `c1` is an incorrect clause and that, therefore, there might be a bug, as it is actually the case.

10 Relation to verification techniques

Abstract diagnosis with respect to semi-denotational observables is clearly related to other techniques introduced for program verification, namely those based on the definition of *well-typed* and *well-moded* programs [3–5]. In the case of types, these techniques can be characterized as follows.

- a domain for types, which are usually sets closed under instantiation,
- a specification, given as a pair of pre- and post-conditions,
- a syntactic condition of persistency w.r.t. the specification (well-typedness).

The above notions are indeed introduced as a first step towards more general program verification, since, in the case of well-typed programs and queries, properties of computed answers can be verified on a "suitable" least Herbrand model, i.e., by using the declarative semantics. That's why, in the following discussion, we will call the above techniques verification techniques.

We can first note that abstract specifications for semi-denotational observables can simply be viewed as "specifications by means of post-conditions". For example, the specification of Example 33

$$\mathcal{I}_{\alpha_{nat}}(+(x,y,z)) = x \wedge y \wedge z$$

can be read as "every successful computation of a call of the procedure + binds x, y and z to natural numbers". We can then compare abstract diagnosis to verification techniques, from several viewpoints.

Aims: proving partial correctness versus bug detection. The goal of program verification is proving partial correctness w.r.t. the specification, while the main goal of abstract diagnosis is locating the sources of errors, when the program is not partial correct or not complete, by providing algorithms to locate incompleteness bugs and clauses which are possibly sources of incorrectness bugs. One might argue that abstract diagnosis provides more information, since it is based on property inference (computation of the abstract semantics) rather than on property checking.

Proving correctness. Verification techniques are stronger, since they provide a sufficient condition for partial correctness and completeness, while abstract diagnosis in general only provides a sufficient condition for partial correctness (because of approximation). However, the precision property $\alpha(\mathcal{F}[\![P]\!]) = \mathcal{F}_\alpha[\![P]\!]$ can be satisfied for some program P, even if α is semi-denotational. In such a case, all the properties valid for denotational observables would hold, and abstract diagnosis would be stronger, since it would provide a *necessary and sufficient* condition for partial correctness and completeness (absence of incorrect clauses and uncovered elements). We are currently investigating the problem of finding a characterization of classes of programs for which the precision property holds.

Pre- and post-conditions. Verification is performed w.r.t. a pair of pre- and post-conditions. The pre-condition specifies a class of abstract goals and the post-condition is guaranteed to be satisfied for that class of abstract goals only. On the other hand, abstract diagnosis uses a post-condition only and correctness is guaranteed for all the abstract goals (abstract goal-independence). The condensing property of semi-denotational observables allows us to derive the properties of any abstract goal from the goal-independent properties (e.g. from the properties of most general atomic goals), without introducing further approximations. The diagnosis method can anyway easily be adapted to cope with pre-conditions. We are currently investigating how our techniques can be extended to obtain the automatic generation of the weakest pre-condition from the post-condition.

Verification algorithms and design of property domains: the role of abstract interpretation theory in the systematic derivation. In abstract diagnosis, the diagnosis algorithms (i.e., the abstract immediate consequences operator and the abstract oracle simulation) are systematically derived from the concrete semantics and from the property domain (observable), using abstract interpretation techniques. Moreover, correctness w.r.t. the concrete semantics is guaranteed. The persistency conditions developed for verification techniques (see, for example the definitions of well-typedness and well-modedness [5]) have a similar structure, which looks like the application of an immediate consequences operator. However, they are different ad-hoc definitions, not explicitly related to the concrete semantics.

Abstract diagnosis can exploit several general-purpose techniques developed by abstract interpretation theory to improve the precision of the property domains (domain composition [23,24] and domain refinement operators [32]). Examples of useful operators are the *reduced product* [23,20,11,10], the *disjunctive completion* [26,33,36] and the *functional dependencies* [23,35]. For example, *directional types* [1] can systematically be derived from atomic types, by refining the domain by means of a functional dependencies operator. The above mentioned use of $\mathcal{POS}$ for handling the simple case of natural numbers does indeed model directional types. As another example, if we are interested in an observable, which does not satisfy a specific property relevant to diagnosis (such as condensing or precision), the operators can be used to refine it to a more concrete observable satisfying that property. We are currently investigating, within our semantic framework, the problem of characterizing the optimal (most abstract) refinements which derive denotational and semi-denotational observables.

A similar set of results to be used for the systematic design of property domains does not exist yet for verification techniques, even if some of the results in [40] are strongly related to this problem.

References

1. A. Aiken and T. K. Lakshman. Directional type checking of logic programs. In B. Le Charlier, editor, *Proc. Static Analysis Symposium, SAS'94*, volume 864 of *Lecture Notes in Computer Science*, pages 43–60. Springer-Verlag, 1994.
2. K. R. Apt. Introduction to Logic Programming. In J. van Leeuwen, editor, *Handbook of Theoretical Computer Science*, volume B: Formal Models and Semantics, pages 495–574. Elsevier and The MIT Press, 1990.
3. K. R. Apt. Program verification and Prolog. In E. Börger, editor, *Specification and validation methods for programming languages and systems*. Oxford University Press, 1994.
4. K. R. Apt, M. Gabbrielli, and D. Pedreschi. A closer look to declarative interpretations. *Journal of Logic Programming*, 28(2):147–180, 1996.
5. K. R. Apt and E. Marchiori. Reasoning about Prolog programs: from modes through types to assertions. *Formal Aspects of Computing*, 6(6A):743–765, 1994.
6. K. R. Apt and D. Pedreschi. Reasoning about termination of pure PROLOG programs. *Information and Computation*, 106(1):109–157, 1993.

7. T. Armstrong, K. Marriott, P. Schachte, and H. Søndergaard. Boolean functions for dependency analysis: Algebraic properties and efficient representation. In B. Le Charlier, editor, *Proc. Static Analysis Symposium, SAS'94*, volume 864 of *Lecture Notes in Computer Science*, pages 266–280. Springer-Verlag, 1994.
8. A. Bossi, M. Gabbrielli, G. Levi, and M. Martelli. The s-semantics approach: Theory and applications. *Journal of Logic Programming*, 19-20:149–197, 1994.
9. K. L. Clark. Predicate logic as a computational formalism. Res. Report DOC 79/59, Imperial College, Dept. of Computing, London, 1979.
10. C. Click and K. D. Cooper. Combining analyses, combining optimizations. *ACM Transactions on Programming Languages and Systems*, 17(2):181–196, 1995.
11. M. Codish, A. Mulkers, M. Bruynooghe, M. García de la Banda, and M. Hermenegildo. Improving abstract interpretations by combining domains. *ACM Transactions on Programming Languages and Systems*, 17(1):28–44, 1995.
12. P. Codognet and G. Filè. Computations, Abstractions and Constraints. In *Proc. Fourth IEEE Int'l Conference on Computer Languages*. IEEE Press, 1992.
13. M. Comini and G. Levi. An algebraic theory of observables. In M. Bruynooghe, editor, *Proceedings of the 1994 Int'l Symposium on Logic Programming*, pages 172–186. The MIT Press, 1994.
14. M. Comini, G. Levi, and M. C. Meo. Compositionality of *SLD*-derivations and their abstractions. In J. Lloyd, editor, *Proceedings of the 1995 Int'l Symposium on Logic Programming*, pages 561–575. The MIT Press, 1995.
15. M. Comini, G. Levi, and M. C. Meo. A theory of observables for logic programs. Submitted for publication, 1996.
16. M. Comini, G. Levi, and G. Vitiello. Abstract debugging of logic programs. In L. Fribourg and F. Turini, editors, *Proc. Logic Program Synthesis and Transformation and Metaprogramming in Logic 1994*, volume 883 of *Lecture Notes in Computer Science*, pages 440–450. Springer-Verlag, 1994.
17. M. Comini, G. Levi, and G. Vitiello. Declarative diagnosis revisited. In J. Lloyd, editor, *Proceedings of the 1995 Int'l Symposium on Logic Programming*, pages 275–287. The MIT Press, 1995.
18. M. Comini, G. Levi, and G. Vitiello. Efficient detection of incompleteness errors in the abstract debugging of logic programs. In M. Ducassé, editor, *Proc. 2nd International Workshop on Automated and Algorithmic Debugging, AADEBUG'95*, 1995.
19. M. Comini and M. C. Meo. Compositionality properties of *SLD*-derivations. Submitted for publication, 1996.
20. A. Cortesi, G. Filé, R. Giacobazzi, C. Palamidessi, and F. Ranzato. Complementation in abstract interpretation. In A. Mycroft, editor, *Proceedings of the 2nd International Static Analysis Symposium (SAS '95)*, volume 983 of *Lecture Notes in Computer Science*, pages 100–117. Springer-Verlag, 1995. To appear in *ACM Transactions on Programming Languages and Systems*.
21. A. Cortesi, G. Filè, and W. Winsborough. *Prop* revisited: Propositional Formula as Abstract Domain for Groundness Analysis. In *Proc. Sixth IEEE Symp. on Logic In Computer Science*, pages 322–327. IEEE Computer Society Press, 1991.
22. P. Cousot and R. Cousot. Abstract Interpretation: A Unified Lattice Model for Static Analysis of Programs by Construction or Approximation of Fixpoints. In *Proc. Fourth ACM Symp. Principles of Programming Languages*, pages 238–252, 1977.
23. P. Cousot and R. Cousot. Systematic Design of Program Analysis Frameworks. In *Proc. Sixth ACM Symp. Principles of Programming Languages*, pages 269–282, 1979.

24. P. Cousot and R. Cousot. Abstract Interpretation and Applications to Logic Programs. *Journal of Logic Programming*, 13(2 & 3):103–179, 1992.
25. P. Cousot and R. Cousot. Comparing the Galois Connection and Widening/Narrowing Approaches to Abstract Interpretation. In M. Bruynooghe and M. Wirsing, editors, *Proc. of PLILP'92*, volume 631 of *Lecture Notes in Computer Science*, pages 269–295. Springer-Verlag, 1992.
26. P. Cousot and R. Cousot. Higher-order abstract interpretation (and application to comportment analysis generalizing strictness, termination, projection and per analysis of functional languages). In *Proceedings of the IEEE International Conference on Computer Languages (ICCL '94)*, pages 95–112. IEEE Computer Society Press, 1994.
27. E. Eder. Properties of substitutions and unifications. *Journal of Symbolic Computation*, 1:31–46, 1985.
28. M. Falaschi, G. Levi, M. Martelli, and C. Palamidessi. Declarative Modeling of the Operational Behavior of Logic Languages. *Theoretical Computer Science*, 69(3):289–318, 1989.
29. M. Falaschi, G. Levi, M. Martelli, and C. Palamidessi. A Model-Theoretic Reconstruction of the Operational Semantics of Logic Programs. *Information and Computation*, 102(1):86–113, 1993.
30. G. Ferrand. Error Diagnosis in Logic Programming, an Adaptation of E. Y. Shapiro's Method. *Journal of Logic Programming*, 4:177–198, 1987.
31. G. Ferrand. The notions of symptom and error in declarative diagnosis of logic programs. In P. A. Fritzson, editor, *Automated and Algorithmic Debugging, Proc. AADEBUG '93*, volume 749 of *Lecture Notes in Computer Science*, pages 40–57. Springer-Verlag, 1993.
32. G. Filé, R. Giacobazzi, and F. Ranzato. A unifying view on abstract domain design. *ACM Computing Surveys*, 28(2):333–336, 1996.
33. G. Filé and F. Ranzato. Improving abstract interpretations by systematic lifting to the powerset. In M. Bruynooghe, editor, *Proceedings of the 1994 International Logic Programming Symposium (ILPS '94)*, pages 655–669. The MIT Press, 1994.
34. R. Giacobazzi, S.K. Debray, and G. Levi. Generalized Semantics and Abstract Interpretation for Constraint Logic Programs. *Journal of Logic Programming*, 25(3):191–247, 1995.
35. R. Giacobazzi and F. Ranzato. Functional dependencies and Moore-set completions of abstract interpretations and semantics. In J. Lloyd, editor, *Proceedings of the 1995 Interantional Symposium on Logic Programming (ILPS '95)*, pages 321–335. The MIT Press, 1995.
36. R. Giacobazzi and F. Ranzato. Compositional optimization of disjunctive abstract interpretations. In H.R. Nielson, editor, *Proc. of the 1996 European Symposium on Programming*, volume 1058 of *Lecture Notes in Computer Science*, pages 141–155. Springer-Verlag, 1996.
37. J. L. Lassez, M. J. Maher, and K. Marriott. Unification Revisited. In J. Minker, editor, *Foundations of Deductive Databases and Logic Programming*, pages 587–625. Morgan Kaufmann, Los Altos, Ca., 1988.
38. J. W. Lloyd. Declarative error diagnosis. *New Generation Computing*, 5(2):133–154, 1987.
39. J. W. Lloyd. *Foundations of Logic Programming*. Springer-Verlag, 1987. Second edition.
40. E. Marchiori. Prime factorizations of abstract domains using first order logic. In M. Hanus and M. Rodriguez-Artalejo, editors, *Algebraic and Logic Program-*

ming, volume 1139 of *Lecture Notes in Computer Science*, pages 209–223. Springer-Verlag, 1996.

41. K. Marriott and H. Søndergaard. Precise and efficient groundness analysis for logic programs. *ACM Letters on Programming Languages and Systems*, 2(1–4):181–196, 1993.
42. L. Naish. Declarative diagnosis of missing answers. *New Generation Computing*, 10:255–285, 1991.
43. L. M. Pereira. Rational debugging in logic programming. In E. Y. Shapiro, editor, *Proceedings of the 3rd International Conference on Logic Programming*, volume 225 of *Lecture Notes in Computer Science*, pages 203–210. Springer-Verlag, 1986.
44. T. Sato and H. Tamaki. Enumeration of Success Patterns in Logic Programs. *Theoretical Computer Science*, 34:227–240, 1984.
45. E. Y. Shapiro. Algorithmic program debugging. In *Proc. Ninth Annual ACM Symp. on Principles of Programming Languages*, pages 412–531. ACM Press, 1982.
46. L. Sterling and E. Y. Shapiro. *The Art of Prolog*. The MIT Press, 1986.
47. M. H. van Emden and R. A. Kowalski. The semantics of predicate logic as a programming language. *Journal of the ACM*, 23(4):733–742, 1976.

Abstract Interpretation of the π-Calculus

Arnaud Venet*

LIX, École Polytechnique, 91128 Palaiseau, France.
venet@lix.polytechnique.fr
http://lix.polytechnique.fr/~venet

Abstract. We are concerned with the static analysis of the communication topology for systems of mobile processes. For this purpose we construct an abstract interpretation of a large fragment of the π-calculus which can be used as a metalanguage to specify the behaviour of these systems. The abstract domain is expressive enough to give accurate descriptions of infinite and non-uniform distributions of processes and communication channels. We design appropriate widening operators for the automatic inference of such information.

1 Introduction

The static analysis of communicating processes with dynamically changing structure - commonly called *mobile processes* - has been mostly studied in the particular case of CML-like programs [NN94, Col95a, Col95b]. The design of these analyses heavily depends on type and control-flow information that is specific to CML. In this paper we propose an analysis of communications in the *π-calculus* [Mil91, MPW92]. Our choice is motivated by the fact that the π-calculus is a widely accepted model for describing mobile processes. It is fairly simple and yet very expressive, since it can encode data structures [Mil91], higher-order communication [Mil91, San94a] and various λ-calculi [Mil92].

Our purpose is to analyze the *communication topology* of a system of mobile processes, i.e. the distribution of processes and communication channels during the evolution of the system. In the standard semantics of the π-calculus this information is encoded within a process algebra. We construct a refinement of this semantics where an instance of a process at a certain stage of evolution of the system is represented by the sequence of internal computations that lead to it. The communication channels are represented in turn as the congruence classes of an equivalence relation over the communication ports of all process instances. This semantic model originated in the study of data structures [Jon81] and has been successfully applied to the alias analysis of ML-like programs by A. Deutsch [Deu92a, Deu92b, Deu94] who designed a powerful analysis based on Abstract Interpretation [CC77, CC92].

C. Colby [Col95b] further extended Deutsch's work and built an analysis for a subset of CML which can discover non-uniform descriptions of infinitely growing communication topologies. However, the whole framework relies on having a

* This work was partly supported by ESPRIT BRA 8130 LOMAPS.

good approximation of the control-flow of the program before doing the analysis of communications. Whereas a closure analysis can be used for higher-order CML programs, there is no realistic solution for the π-calculus where the *only* kind of computation is communication. Therefore we design a new abstract interpretation which gets rid of this problem and still ensures a comparable level of accuracy. We use the technique of ***cofibered domains*** introduced in [Ven96] which allows us to infer ***simultaneously*** an approximation of control-flow and communications.

The paper is organized as follows. In Sect. 2 we present the syntax and semantics of the π-calculus. The refined semantics is described in Sect. 3. In Sect. 4 we present the basic concepts of Abstract Interpretation. We construct an abstract domain for the analysis of the π-calculus in Sect. 5. The abstract semantics of the π-calculus is described in Sect. 6. In Sect. 7 we design widening operators in order to make the analysis effective.

2 The π-Calculus

The basic entities in the π-calculus are *names*, which are provided to represent communication channels. The key point is that computation is restricted to the transmission and reception of names along channels. There are various possibilities of defining processes in the π-calculus, depending on the way communication, recursion and nondeterminism are handled. Our presentation is based on a subset of the *polyadic π-calculus* [Mil91]. Let $\mathcal{X} = \{x, y, \ldots\}$ be an infinite set of names. The syntax of π-terms $\mathcal{P} = \{P, Q, \ldots\}$ is given by the following grammar:

$$
\begin{array}{lll}
P & ::= \sum_{i \in I} \pi_i . P_i & \text{guarded sum of finitely many processes} \\
 & \mid\ P \mid Q & \text{parallel composition} \\
 & \mid\ \nu x . P & \text{restriction} \\
 & \mid\ !\iota . P & \text{guarded replication} \\
\pi & ::= \iota \mid o & \text{atomic action} \\
\iota & ::= x(\mathbf{y}) & \text{input} \\
o & ::= \overline{x}[\mathbf{y}] & \text{output}
\end{array}
$$

where $\mathbf{y}$ is a (possibly empty) tuple $(y_1, \ldots, y_n)$ of pairwise distinct names. We denote by $\mathbf{0}$ the empty sum of processes (that is when $I = \emptyset$). We call a nonempty sum $\sum_{i \in I} \pi_i . P_i$ of processes an *agent*, and a replication[2] $!\iota . P$ a *server*. We use the common abbreviation that consists of omitting the trailing $.\mathbf{0}$ in π-terms. The restriction $\nu x . P$ binds the name x in P and an input guard $x(y_1, \ldots, y_n).P$ binds the names $y_1, \ldots, y_n$ in P. We denote by $\mathit{fn}(P)$ the set of names occurring free in a process P. If $\mathbf{x}$ and $\mathbf{y}$ are tuples of names of the same length, we denote by $\{\mathbf{y}/\mathbf{x}\}$ the substitution that maps any x_i to y_i. The standard operational semantics of the π-calculus is given by a structural congruence $\equiv$ and a reduction relation defined in Fig. 1 and Fig. 2.

[2] We use a restricted form of replication inspired from the one involved in the definition of PICT [Tur95]. Yet it is expressive enough to perform all major constructions in the π-calculus (data structures, higher-order communication, etc.).

Let $\equiv$ be the smallest congruence relation on $\mathcal{P}$ which satisfies the following axioms:

- $P \equiv Q$ if P and Q are α-convertible.
- $(\mathcal{P}/_{\equiv}, |, \mathbf{0})$ is a commutative monoid.
- $\nu x.\nu y.P \equiv \nu y.\nu x.P$.
- $\nu x.\mathbf{0} \equiv \mathbf{0}$.
- $\nu x.(P \mid Q) \equiv P \mid \nu x.Q$ whenever x is not free in P.

Fig. 1. Structural congruence

$$\frac{P \to P'}{P \mid Q \to P' \mid Q} \qquad\qquad \frac{P \to P'}{\nu x.P \to \nu x.P'}$$

$$(\cdots + x(\mathbf{y}).P + \cdots) \mid (\cdots + \overline{x}[\mathbf{z}].Q + \cdots) \to \{\mathbf{z}/\mathbf{y}\}P \mid Q$$

$$!x(\mathbf{y}).P \mid (\cdots + \overline{x}[\mathbf{z}].Q + \cdots) \to \{\mathbf{z}/\mathbf{y}\}P \mid !x(\mathbf{y}).P \mid Q$$

$$\frac{P \equiv P' \qquad P' \to Q' \qquad Q' \equiv Q}{P \to Q}$$

Fig. 2. Process reduction

We model a system S of mobile processes by a closed π-term. The evolution of the system is determined by the internal communications. The structural laws allow us to rewrite a π-term in order to bring communicands in juxtaposition. They are the analogue of the heating/cooling rules of the Chemical Abstract Machine [BB92]. In the chemical metaphore, a π-term is a syntactic encoding of a "solution of floating ions", i.e. a multiset of agents and servers, in which reaction is communication. The structural congruence identifies all encodings of the same solution. In particular, any closed process P is structurally equivalent to a term of the following form:

$$\nu x_1 \ldots \nu x_l.(A_1 \mid \cdots \mid A_m \mid S_1 \mid \cdots \mid S_n) \qquad (\star)$$

where the A_i are agents and the S_j are servers, such that each name occurring free in any one of the A_i or S_j lies in $\{x_1, \ldots, x_l\}$. Intuitively, this π-term exhibits the *communication topology* of P, i.e. all active agents and servers linked together by communication channels. Whereas the A_i and S_j are unique (up to permutation of the indices), the decomposition $(\star)$ is not, because of α-renaming and the possibility to add and remove useless channel names by structural rewriting[3].

[3] If $x \notin fn(P)$, $\nu x.P \equiv P$.

Hence, we will define this notion more formally and unambiguously using *hypergraphs*.

The notion of hypergraph is a generalization of that of graph where an edge can connect more than two vertices. More precisely, an undirected hypergraph H labelled over L is given by a set V of *vertices*, a set E of *hyperedges*, a *boundary* function $\partial : E \longrightarrow \wp(V)$, and a labelling function $\lambda : E \longrightarrow L$. We identify hypergraphs which only differ by a bijective renaming of their vertices and hyperedges, i.e. we consider *abstract* hypergraphs.

Definition 1 Communication Topology. Let P be a closed π-term and A_1, $\ldots, A_m, S_1, \ldots, S_n$ be the agents and servers appearing in decomposition $(\star)$. The *communication topology* $\mathcal{T}_c(P)$ of P is the undirected hypergraph $(V, E, \partial, \lambda)$ labelled over the set $\{\mathtt{a}, \mathtt{s}\}$ where:

1. $V = \bigcup_{i=1}^{m} fn(A_i) \cup \bigcup_{j=1}^{n} fn(S_j)$.
2. $E = \{(\mathtt{a}, 1), \ldots, (\mathtt{a}, m), (\mathtt{s}, 1), \ldots, (\mathtt{s}, n)\}$.
3. $\partial(\mathtt{a}, i) = fn(A_i)$, $\partial(\mathtt{s}, j) = fn(S_j)$.
4. $\forall (t, x) \in E : \lambda(t, x) = t$. □

Note that the definition is not ambiguous because we are working with abstract hypergraphs. Hyperedges represent processes that are "glued" together via vertices which are communication ports. The labelling of hyperedges represents the type of each process appearing in the communication topology, either agent (a) or server (s).

Given a system S of mobile processes represented as a closed term of the π-calculus, we are interested in the communication topology of the system at any stage of its evolution, that is in the following set of hypergraphs:

$$\mathcal{T}_c^*(S) \stackrel{\text{def}}{=} \{\mathcal{T}_c(P) \mid S \stackrel{*}{\to} P\}$$

Example 1. Let S be the closed π-term

$$\nu l.\nu c.\nu x.(\bar{l}[x] \mid !l(y).\nu z.(\bar{c}[y, z] \mid \bar{l}[z]))$$

After $n > 0$ computation steps, the system is structurally equivalent to the process

$$\nu l.\nu c.\nu x_0 \ldots \nu x_n.(\bar{c}[x_0, x_1] \mid \cdots \mid \bar{c}[x_{n-1}, x_n] \mid \bar{l}[x_n] \mid !l(y).\nu z.(\bar{c}[y, z] \mid \bar{l}[z]))$$

whose communication topology is given by the following hypergraph:

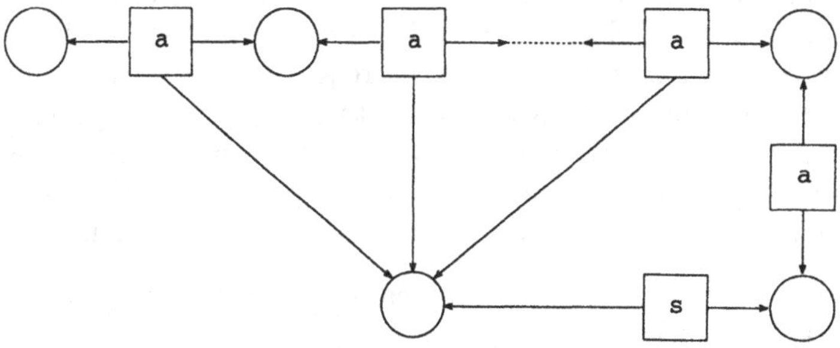

where boxes (resp. circles) represent hyperedges (resp. vertices). □

Our goal is to discover automatically a finitely representable superset of $\mathcal{T}_c^*(S)$. We will apply techniques coming from the area of alias analysis [Ven96], but this requires first to refine the standard semantics of the π-calculus.

3 Nonstandard Semantics of the π-Calculus

Let S be a closed π-term. A careful inspection of the reduction rules of Fig. 2 shows that any active agent or server of a process P such that $S \overset{*}{\to} P$, is a *residual* of a subprocess of S, i.e. a process sQ, where s is a substitution and Q is a subterm of S. In particular, several residuals of a same subprocess of S can only be obtained by repeated requests to a server via communication. Thereby, we can uniquely identify an active process in P with the sequence of requests to servers during the computation $S \overset{*}{\to} P$ that contributed to create the process, together with the subprocess of S from which it is a residual[4]. We use this idea to construct a new operational semantics of the system S of mobile processes.

In order to simplify the presentation of the semantics, we assume that S is in *normal form*, given by the following grammar:

$$\begin{array}{lcl} N & ::= & \mathbf{0} \mid \nu x_1 \ldots \nu x_m.(AS_1 \mid \cdots \mid AS_n) \\ AS & ::= & !\iota.N \mid \sum_{i \in I} \pi_i.N_i \end{array}$$

where $I \neq \emptyset$ and ι, π are the atomic actions of the π-calculus defined in Sect. 2. Moreover, we require that all variable bindings in S be pairwise distinct. Any process can always be brought into normal form by using the structural laws. We uniquely label each occurrence of an agent or a server in S. Let $\mathcal{L}(S)$ be the set of these labels, and $\mathcal{A}(S)$ be the subset corresponding to all labels of agents. For any $\ell \in \mathcal{L}(S)$, we denote by S_ℓ the process labelled by ℓ. A configuration in our operational semantics is a pair $(\Phi, \leftrightsquigarrow)$ where:

1. Φ is a function from $\mathcal{L}(S)$ into $\wp(\mathcal{A}(S)^*)$ such that, for each $\ell \in \mathcal{L}(S)$, $\Phi(\ell)$ is finite.
2. $\leftrightsquigarrow$ is an equivalence relation over the following set:

$$\mathit{Ports}(\Phi) \overset{\text{def}}{=} \{(\ell, L, x) \mid \ell \in \mathcal{L}(S), L \in \Phi(\ell), x \in \mathit{fn}(S_\ell)\}$$

The function Φ associates to each label ℓ the set of residuals of S_ℓ in the configuration. A residual is identified with the sequence of agent labels which were involved in the creation of the process via requests to servers. $\mathit{Ports}(\Phi)$ is the set of communication ports corresponding to the distribution of processes Φ. The communication channels are given by the congruence classes of the channel relation $\leftrightsquigarrow$ which expresses the links between ports. Note that since we use the $\leftrightsquigarrow$ relation, we get rid of problems of name generation and α-conversion

[4] This idea is somehow related to the notion of *locality* developed for process algebras [BCHK94, San94b].

as it is the case in the standard semantics. The nonstandard semantics gives more information than what is really needed to define the communication topology. However, this higher level of expressivity is required to design an accurate abstract interpretation, as we will see in Sect. 5.

We denote by $\mathcal{C}(S)$ the set of all configurations $(\Phi, \leftrightsquigarrow)$. If $\Phi \in \mathcal{L}(S) \longrightarrow \wp(\mathcal{A}(S)^*)$ and ρ is a binary relation over $Ports(\Phi)$, we denote by $[\rho]_\Phi$ the smallest equivalence relation over $Ports(\Phi)$ containing ρ. We denote by $\dot{\cup}$ the pointwise inclusion on $\mathcal{L}(S) \longrightarrow \wp(\mathcal{A}(S)^*)$. The nonstandard operational semantics of S is given by a transition relation $\Rightarrow$ on $\mathcal{C}(S)$ defined in Fig. 3 and Fig. 4. The semantic rules require a few explanations. In the case of communication between two agents (Fig. 3), the instances of S_{ℓ_i} and S_{ℓ_o} are removed from Φ and new instances of the $S_{\ell_i^j}$ and $S_{\ell_o^k}$ are created with the same residual as their parent process. The channel relation is defined on the process distribution $\Phi \dot{\cup} \Phi'$ including the communicands and the newly released processes. The relation $\leftrightsquigarrow_c$ implements communication, i.e. it links y_i and t_i in all spawned processes that involve these names. The rôle of $\leftrightsquigarrow_i$ and $\leftrightsquigarrow_o$ is to bind the free names in the $S_{\ell_i^j}$ and $S_{\ell_o^k}$ to the corresponding ones in the parent processes. Finally $\leftrightsquigarrow_\nu$ relates all occurrences of a newly created name among the processes spawned by the sender and the receiver. This information is then propagated to all other ports by the transitive closure involved in $[-]_{\Phi \dot{\cup} \Phi'}$. Once this has been done, the restriction of $\leftrightsquigarrow'$ to $Ports(\Phi')$ eliminates all information relative to the communicands. The situation is almost identical for a communication between an agent and a server (Fig. 4), except that the instance of the server is not deleted. The newly spawned instances of the S_i^j are assigned the residual $L_o.\ell_o$, thus formalizing our intuition about the meaning of residuals.

In our context, given a closed π-term S in normal form, we are interested in computing an upper-approximate of the *collecting semantics* [CC77] $\mathcal{S}_S$ of S, that is the set $\{P \mid S \xrightarrow{*} P\}$ of descendants of the initial configuration in the standard operational semantics. Thereby, we connect the nonstandard operational semantics with the standard one via a relation $\kappa \in \wp(\mathcal{P} \times \mathcal{C}(S))$ defined as follows. If $\mathcal{L}(S) = \{\ell_1, \dots, \ell_n\}$ and, for all $i \in \{1, \dots, n\}$, $\Phi(\ell_i) = \{L_{\ell_i,1}, \dots, L_{\ell_i,k_i}\}$, then

$$(p, (\Phi, \leftrightsquigarrow)) \in \kappa$$

whenever $p \equiv \nu x_1 \dots \nu x_m.(P_{\ell_1,1} \mid \cdots \mid P_{\ell_1,k_1} \mid \cdots \mid P_{\ell_n,1} \mid \cdots \mid P_{\ell_n,k_n})$ where:

- For all $i \in \{1, \dots, n\}$ and $j \in \{1, \dots, k_i\}$, $P_{\ell_i,j} = s_{i,j}S_{\ell_i}$, where $s_{i,j}$ is a substitution such that $s_{i,j}(fn(S_{\ell_i})) \subseteq \{x_1, \dots, x_m\}$.
- $\forall i,j \in \{1, \dots, n\} : \forall x \in fn(S_{\ell_i}) : \forall y \in fn(S_{\ell_j}) : \forall p \in \{1, \dots, k_i\} : \forall q \in \{1, \dots, k_j\} : s_{\ell_i,p}(x) = s_{\ell_j,q}(y) \iff (\ell_i, L_{\ell_i,p}, x) \leftrightsquigarrow (\ell_j, L_{\ell_j,q}, y)$.

If $S = \nu x_1 \dots \nu x_l.(S_{\ell_1} \mid \cdots \mid S_{\ell_n})$ we denote by c_S the nonstandard configuration $(\Phi_S, \leftrightsquigarrow_S)$ where

$$\Phi_S(\ell) = \begin{cases} \{\varepsilon\} & \text{if } \ell = \ell_i \text{ for } i \in \{1, \dots, n\} \\ \emptyset & \text{otherwise} \end{cases}$$

and $\leftrightsquigarrow_S = [\{((\ell_i, \varepsilon, x), (\ell_j, \varepsilon, x)) \mid 1 \leq i, j \leq n, x \in fn(S_{\ell_i}) \cap fn(S_{\ell_j})\}]_{\Phi_S}$. Note that $(S, c_S) \in \kappa$. The nonstandard collecting semantics $\mathcal{S}_S^\natural$ is given by $\{c \mid c_S \stackrel{*}{\Rightarrow} c\}$.

Theorem 2. *Let $\Gamma : \wp(\mathcal{C}(S)) \longrightarrow \wp(\mathcal{P})$ be the function that sends any set C of configurations to $\{p \mid \exists c \in C : (p, c) \in \kappa\}$. Then, $\mathcal{S}_S = \Gamma(\mathcal{S}_S^\natural)$.*

This means that the standard and nonstandard collecting semantics of the π-calculus are equivalent. Note that κ provides a direct way to compute the communication topology associated to a nonstandard configuration $(\Phi, \leftrightsquigarrow)$, the vertices being given by the congruence classes of $\leftrightsquigarrow$.

Example 2. Consider the π-term S of Example 1 (which is in normal form) that we label as follows:

$$\nu l.\nu c.\nu x.(\boxed{\ell_1 : \bar{l}[x]} \mid \boxed{\ell_2 :!l(y).\nu z.(\boxed{\ell_3 : \bar{c}[y, z]} \mid \boxed{\ell_4 : \bar{l}[z]})})$$

If $c_S \stackrel{n}{\Rightarrow} (\Phi, \leftrightsquigarrow)$, for $n > 0$, then

$$\Phi = \left\{\begin{array}{l} \ell_1 \mapsto \emptyset \\ \ell_2 \mapsto \{\varepsilon\} \\ \ell_3 \mapsto \{\ell_1.\ell_4^i \mid 0 \leq i < n\} \\ \ell_4 \mapsto \{\ell_1.\ell_4^{n-1}\} \end{array}\right\}$$

and $\leftrightsquigarrow$ is the smallest equivalence relation on $Ports(\Phi)$ such that:

- $(\ell_3, \ell_1.\ell_4^i, y) \leftrightsquigarrow (\ell_3, \ell_1.\ell_4^j, z) \iff i = j + 1$
- $(\ell_4, \ell_1.\ell_4^{n-1}, z) \leftrightsquigarrow (\ell_3, \ell_1.\ell_4^{n-1}, z)$
- $(\ell_4, \ell_1.\ell_4^{n-1}, l) \leftrightsquigarrow (\ell_2, \varepsilon, l)$
- $(\ell_3, \ell_1.\ell_4^i, c) \leftrightsquigarrow (\ell_2, \varepsilon, c)$, for all $i \in \{0, \ldots, n-1\}$ □

It now remains to build an abstract interpretation of the π-calculus based upon the nonstandard semantics.

4 Abstract Interpretation

Abstract Interpretation [CC77, CC92] provides general frameworks to reason about *semantic approximation*. Typically, this problem amounts to finding an upper-approximate of the least fixpoint $\mathcal{S}^\natural$ of a $\sqcup^\natural$-complete endomorphism $F^\natural$ over a complete lattice $(\mathcal{D}^\natural, \sqsubseteq^\natural, \perp^\natural, \sqcup^\natural, \top^\natural, \sqcap^\natural)$, the *concrete semantic function.*

Example 3. The nonstandard collecting semantics $\mathcal{S}_S^\natural$ of a system S of mobile processes can be shown to be equal to the least fixpoint of the $\cup$-complete morphism F_S defined over $(\wp(\mathcal{C}(S)), \subseteq, \emptyset, \cup, \mathcal{C}(S), \cap)$ as follows (see [CC77]):

$$F_S \stackrel{\text{def}}{=} \lambda X \cdot \{c_S\} \cup \{c \mid \exists c' \in X : c' \Rightarrow c\}$$

We can thereby apply an abstract interpretation framework to the analysis of the π-calculus. □

If

- $\ell_i, \ell_o \in \mathcal{L}(S)$,
- $L_i \in \Phi(\ell_i), L_o \in \Phi(\ell_o)$,
- $S_{\ell_i} = \cdots + x(y_1, \ldots, y_m).\nu v_1^i \ldots \nu v_{l_i}^i.(S_{\ell_i^1} \mid \cdots \mid S_{\ell_i^{n_i}}) + \cdots$,
- $S_{\ell_o} = \cdots + \overline{z}[t_1, \ldots, t_m].\nu v_1^o \ldots \nu v_{l_o}^o.(S_{\ell_o^1} \mid \cdots \mid S_{\ell_o^{n_o}}) + \cdots$,
- $(\ell_i, L_i, x) \leftrightsquigarrow (\ell_o, L_o, z)$,

then

$$(\Phi, \leftrightsquigarrow) \Rightarrow (\Phi', \leftrightsquigarrow')$$

where:

- If we put
$$\Phi^\dagger(\ell) = \begin{cases} \Phi(\ell) - \{L_\eta\} & \text{if } \ell = \ell_\eta \text{ for } \eta \in \{i, o\} \\ \Phi(\ell) & \text{otherwise} \end{cases}$$
then
$$\Phi'(\ell) = \begin{cases} \Phi^\dagger(\ell) \cup \{L_\eta\} & \text{if } \ell = \ell_\eta^k \text{ for } \eta \in \{i, o\},\ k \in \{1, \ldots, n_\eta\} \\ \Phi^\dagger(\ell) & \text{otherwise} \end{cases}$$
- $\leftrightsquigarrow' = [\leftrightsquigarrow \cup \leftrightsquigarrow_c \cup \leftrightsquigarrow_i \cup \leftrightsquigarrow_o \cup \leftrightsquigarrow_\nu]_{\Phi \dot\cup \Phi'} \cap (Ports(\Phi') \times Ports(\Phi'))$ where:
  - $\leftrightsquigarrow_c = \{((\ell_i^j, L_i, y_h), (\ell_o^k, L_o, t_h)) \mid 1 \le j \le n_i, 1 \le k \le n_o, 1 \le h \le m, y_h \in fn(S_{\ell_i^j}), t_h \in fn(S_{\ell_o^k})\}$.
  - $\leftrightsquigarrow_\eta = \{((\ell_\eta, L_\eta, u), (\ell_\eta^j, L_\eta, u)) \mid 1 \le j \le n_\eta, u \in fn(S_{\ell_\eta}) \cap fn(S_{\ell_\eta^j})\}$, for $\eta \in \{i, o\}$.
  - $\leftrightsquigarrow_\nu = \{((\ell_\eta^j, L_\eta, v_h^\eta), (\ell_\eta^k, L_\eta, v_h^\eta)) \mid j, k \in \{1, \ldots, n_\eta\}, h \in \{1, \ldots, l_\eta\}, v_h^\eta \in fn(S_{\ell_\eta^j}) \cap fn(S_{\ell_\eta^k})\}$, for $\eta \in \{i, o\}$.

Fig. 3. Interagent communication

Following [CC92], the semantic approximation is achieved via an *abstract semantic specification* given by a preordered set $(\mathcal{D}^\sharp, \preceq)$, the *abstract semantic domain*, related to $\mathcal{D}^\natural$ by a *concretization function* $\gamma : \mathcal{D}^\sharp \longrightarrow \mathcal{D}^\natural$, an *abstract basis* $\bot^\sharp \in \mathcal{D}^\sharp$, and an *abstract semantic function* $F^\sharp : \mathcal{D}^\sharp \longrightarrow \mathcal{D}^\sharp$, such that:

1. $\bot^\natural \sqsubseteq^\natural \gamma(\bot^\sharp)$.
2. $\forall x, y \in \mathcal{D}^\sharp : x \preceq y \Longrightarrow \gamma(x) \sqsubseteq^\natural \gamma(y)$.
3. $\forall x \in \mathcal{D}^\sharp : F^\natural \circ \gamma(x) \sqsubseteq^\natural \gamma \circ F^\sharp(x)$.

In order to compute effectively an approximation of $\mathcal{S}^\natural$, we introduce the notion of *widening operator*.

Definition 3 Widening Operator [CC77, CC92]. A *widening* on $(\mathcal{D}^\sharp, \preceq)$ is a binary operator $\nabla : \mathcal{D}^\sharp \times \mathcal{D}^\sharp \longrightarrow \mathcal{D}^\sharp$ which satisfies the following properties:

1. $\forall x, y \in \mathcal{D}^\sharp : x \preceq x \nabla y$.

If

- $\ell_i, \ell_o \in \mathcal{L}(S)$,
- $L_i \in \Phi(\ell_i), L_o \in \Phi(\ell_o)$,
- $S_{\ell_i} = !x(y_1, \ldots, y_m).\nu v_1^i \ldots \nu v_{l_i}^i.(S_{\ell_i^1} \mid \cdots \mid S_{\ell_i^{n_i}})$,
- $S_{\ell_o} = \cdots + \overline{z}[t_1, \ldots, t_m].\nu v_1^o \ldots \nu v_{l_o}^o.(S_{\ell_o^1} \mid \cdots \mid S_{\ell_o^{n_o}}) + \cdots$,
- $(\ell_i, L_i, x) \leftrightsquigarrow (\ell_o, L_o, z)$,

then

$$(\Phi, \leftrightsquigarrow) \Rightarrow (\Phi', \leftrightsquigarrow')$$

where:

- If we put

$$\Phi^\dagger(\ell) = \begin{cases} \Phi(\ell) - \{L_o\} & \text{if } \ell = \ell_o \\ \Phi(\ell) & \text{otherwise} \end{cases}$$

  then

$$\Phi'(\ell) = \begin{cases} \Phi^\dagger(\ell) \cup \{L_o\} & \text{if } \ell = \ell_o^k \text{ for } k \in \{1, \ldots, n_o\} \\ \Phi^\dagger(\ell) \cup \{L_o.\ell_o\} & \text{if } \ell = \ell_i^k \text{ for } k \in \{1, \ldots, n_i\} \\ \Phi^\dagger(\ell) & \text{otherwise} \end{cases}$$

- $\leftrightsquigarrow' = [\leftrightsquigarrow \cup \leftrightsquigarrow_c \cup \leftrightsquigarrow_i \cup \leftrightsquigarrow_o \cup \leftrightsquigarrow_\nu]_{\Phi \cup \Phi'} \cap (Ports(\Phi') \times Ports(\Phi'))$ where:
  - $\leftrightsquigarrow_c = \{((\ell_i^j, L_o.\ell_o, y_h), (\ell_o^k, L_o, t_h)) \mid 1 \leq j \leq n_i, 1 \leq k \leq n_o, 1 \leq h \leq m, y_h \in fn(S_{\ell_i^j}), t_h \in fn(S_{\ell_o^k})\}$.
  - $\leftrightsquigarrow_i = \{((\ell_i, L_i, u), (\ell_i^j, L_o.\ell_o, u)) \mid 1 \leq j \leq n_i, u \in fn(S_{\ell_i}) \cap fn(S_{\ell_i^j})\}$.
  - $\leftrightsquigarrow_o = \{((\ell_o, L_o, u), (\ell_o^j, L_o, u)) \mid 1 \leq j \leq n_o, u \in fn(S_{\ell_o}) \cap fn(S_{\ell_o^j})\}$.
  - $\leftrightsquigarrow_\nu = \{((\ell_o^j, L_o, v_h^o), (\ell_o^k, L_o, v_h^o)) \mid j, k \in \{1, \ldots, n_o\}, h \in \{1, \ldots, l_o\}, v_h^o \in fn(S_{\ell_o^j}) \cap fn(S_{\ell_o^k})\} \cup \{((\ell_i^j, L_o.\ell_o, v_h^i), (\ell_i^k, L_o.\ell_o, v_h^i)) \mid j, k \in \{1, \ldots, n_i\}, h \in \{1, \ldots, l_i\}, v_h^i \in fn(S_{\ell_i^j}) \cap fn(S_{\ell_i^k})\}$.

Fig. 4. Agent-server communication

2. $\forall x, y \in \mathcal{D}^\sharp : y \preceq x \nabla y$.
3. For every sequence $(x_n)_{n \geq 0}$ of elements of $\mathcal{D}^\sharp$, the sequence $(x_n^\nabla)_{n \geq 0}$ inductively defined as follows:

$$\begin{cases} x_0^\nabla &= x_0 \\ x_{n+1}^\nabla &= x_n^\nabla \nabla x_{n+1} \end{cases}$$

   is ultimately stationary. □

The approximation of the least fixpoint is obtained as the limit of an *abstract iteration sequence* with widening.

Theorem 4 Abstract Iterates [CC92]. *The iteration sequence* $(F_n^\nabla)_{n\geq 0}$ *defined as:*

$$\begin{cases} F_0^\nabla &= \bot^\sharp \\ F_{n+1}^\nabla = F_n^\nabla & \text{if } F(F_n^\nabla) \preceq F_n^\nabla \\ \quad\quad = F_n^\nabla \nabla F(F_n^\nabla) & \text{otherwise} \end{cases}$$

is ultimately stationary and its limit $S^\sharp$ *satisfies* $S^\natural \sqsubseteq^\natural \gamma(S^\sharp)$. *Moreover, if* $N \geq 0$ *is such that* $F_N^\nabla = F_{N+1}^\nabla$, *then* $\forall n \geq N : F_n^\nabla = F_N^\nabla$.

We now have to construct an abstract domain $(\mathcal{D}^\sharp, \preceq)$ approximating $\mathcal{C}(S)$ via a concretization function $\gamma : \mathcal{D}^\sharp \longrightarrow \mathcal{C}(S)$.

5 Abstract Semantic Domain

We construct $\mathcal{D}^\sharp$ as a set of abstract configurations $(\Phi^\sharp, \leftrightsquigarrow^\sharp)$ defined as follows. We represent a set of residuals of a process S_ℓ by a rational language. More precisely, let $\mathbb{A}$ be the set of automata (Q, I, T, τ), where Q is a finite set of states, $I, T \subseteq Q$ are the initial and final states, and $\tau \in \wp(Q \times \mathcal{A}(S) \times Q)$ is the transition relation. In order to keep $\mathbb{A}$ small and representable, we suppose that all states come from an infinite recursive set $\mathcal{Q}$. For any automaton $\mathcal{A}$ in $\mathbb{A}$, we denote by *Paths*$(\mathcal{A})$ the set of successful paths of $\mathcal{A}$, and by $\tau(\mathcal{A})$ the set of transitions of $\mathcal{A}$. An abstract distribution of processes $\Phi^\sharp$ is a function from $\mathcal{L}(S)$ into $\mathbb{A}$. An abstract communication port is a tuple (ℓ, i, t, x) where $\ell \in \mathcal{L}(S)$, $x \in fn(S_\ell)$, i and t being respectively initial and final states of the automaton $\Phi^\sharp(\ell)$. It describes all concrete ports (ℓ, L, x) where L is a word labelling a path[5] from i to t in $\Phi^\sharp(\ell)$. We denote by *Ports*$^\sharp(\Phi^\sharp)$ the set of all abstract communication ports associated to $\Phi^\sharp$.

Our representation of the abstract channel relation is based upon a numerical encoding of paths. The aim of this construction is to be able to represent *non-uniform channel relations*, i.e. to distinguish instances of a process which is recursively spawned. Intuitively, if ℓ is the label of such a process, the automaton $\Phi^\sharp(\ell)$, which is an approximation of the residuals of S_ℓ, certainly contains cycles (since there is potentially an infinity of instances of S_ℓ). The encoding amounts to assigning a counter to each of these cycles and to identify a residual L of S_ℓ by the number of times a path labelled by L runs through each cycle, i.e. by a tuple of counter values. This idea was first introduced by A. Deutsch [Deu92a, Deu92b] in the context of alias analysis, with a different formulation though. In order to avoid having to find cycles and also to ensure a better precision, we will actually assign a counter to each arrow of the automaton. We now give a formal definition of this construction.

If p is a successful path in (Q, I, T, τ), we denote by p° its *commutative image*, that is the function from τ into the set of integers $\mathbb{N}$, which maps any transition of the automaton to the number of times it occurs in p. If $\ell_1, \ell_2 \in \mathcal{L}(S)$ and

[5] We can reduce the number of abstract ports to consider by requiring that there be at least one path in $\Phi^\sharp(\ell)$ from i to t.

$\Phi^\sharp(\ell_i) = (Q_i, I_i, T_i, \tau_i)$ for $i \in \{1, 2\}$, the channel relation between abstract ports is given by a set of tuples $(\ell_1, i_1, t_1, x) \overset{\nu}{\leftrightsquigarrow}^\sharp (\ell_2, i_2, t_2, y)$ where $\nu \in (\tau_1 \longrightarrow \mathbb{N}) \times (\tau_2 \longrightarrow \mathbb{N})$. If we denote by $i(p)$ (resp. $t(p)$) the initial (resp. final) state of a successful path p of an automaton, this abstract channel relation denotes all pairs $(\ell_1, L_1, x) \leftrightsquigarrow (\ell_2, L_2, y)$ for which there exists a successful path p_j in $\Phi^\sharp(\ell_j)$ labelled by L_j, such that $i(p_j) = i_j$ and $t(p_j) = t_j$, for each $j \in \{1, 2\}$, and $\nu = (p_1^\circ, p_2^\circ)$. Considering commutative images of paths instead of tuples of counter values alleviates us from introducing explicit counter variables which would have led to intricate problems of renaming when it had come to defining the abstract semantics. In the following we will tacitly use the isomorphism:

$$(\tau_1 \longrightarrow \mathbb{N}) \times (\tau_2 \longrightarrow \mathbb{N}) \cong (\tau_1 \oplus \tau_2) \longrightarrow \mathbb{N}$$

where $\oplus$ denotes the coproduct in the category **Sets** of sets and functions (i.e. the disjoint union).

In order to guarantee finite representability for the abstract configurations, we require that the set:

$$(\ell_1, i_1, t_1, x) \leftrightsquigarrow^\sharp (\ell_1, i_2, t_2, y) \overset{\text{def}}{=} \{\nu \mid (\ell_1, i_1, t_1, x) \overset{\nu}{\leftrightsquigarrow}^\sharp (\ell_1, i_2, t_2, y)\}$$

be effectively given. This can be achieved by considering an *abstract numerical domain*, that is a representable class of subsets of $(\tau_1 \oplus \tau_2) \longrightarrow \mathbb{N}$. Several numerical domains have already been developed for abstract interpretation using various kinds of representations: *intervals* [CC76], *arithmetic congruences* [Gra89], *affine equalities* [Kar76], *convex polyhedra* [CH78] or *congruence equalities* [Gra91]. They all can be described in an abstract way. Let **FinSets** be the category of finite sets and functions. If $f : V \longrightarrow W$ is a function between finite sets, we define $\mathcal{V}f : \wp(V \longrightarrow \mathbb{N}) \longrightarrow \wp(W \longrightarrow \mathbb{N})$ to be the function that maps any $X \in \wp(V \longrightarrow \mathbb{N})$ to the set:

$$\{\mu : W \longrightarrow \mathbb{N} \mid \exists \nu \in X : \mu = \lambda w \cdot \sum_{v \in f^{-1}(w)} \nu(v)\}$$

Definition 5 Abstract Numerical Domain. An abstract numerical domain is a functor $\mathcal{V}^\sharp$: **FinSets** $\longrightarrow$ **PoSets** that sends any finite set V to a poset that comes with the structure of a lattice $(\mathcal{V}^\sharp V, \subseteq^\sharp, \sqcup_V^\sharp, \emptyset_V^\sharp, \sqcap_V^\sharp, \top_V^\sharp)$ and a monotone map $\gamma_V : (\mathcal{V}^\sharp V, \subseteq^\sharp) \longrightarrow (\wp(V \longrightarrow \mathbb{N}), \subseteq)$. We will omit the subscript V whenever it will be clear from the context. Moreover, if $V \longrightarrow W$ is an arrow in **FinSets**, then $\mathcal{V}f \circ \gamma_V \subseteq \gamma_W \circ \mathcal{V}^\sharp f$. □

Example 4. We denote by $\mathbb{Q}$ the field of rational numbers. Karr's abstract numerical domain [Kar76] associates to each finite set V the set of all affine subspaces of $V \longrightarrow \mathbb{Q}$ endowed with its canonical affine structure[6]. γ_V sends any element

[6] An affine subspace of $V \longrightarrow \mathbb{Q}$ is a set $\{p + \lambda_1.e_1 + \cdots + \lambda_n.e_n \mid \lambda_1, \ldots, \lambda_n \in \mathbb{Q}\}$ where p, e_1, ..., e_n are elements of $V \longrightarrow \mathbb{Q}$, addition and multiplication by a scalar being defined componentwise.

$X^\sharp$ of $\mathcal{V}^\sharp V$ to $X^\sharp \cap (V \longrightarrow \mathbb{N})$, whereas $\sqcap^\sharp_V$ is the intersection and $\sqcup^\sharp_V$ the sum of affine subspaces. An affine subspace of $V \longrightarrow \mathbb{Q}$ can equivalently be seen as the set of solutions **Sol(S)** of a system **S** of affine equations $a_1.v_1 + \cdots + a_n.v_n = c$ over the variables $V = \{v_1, \ldots, v_n\}$. □

Thereby, an abstract channel relation $\leftrightsquigarrow^\sharp$ can equivalently be seen as a function of domain $Ports^\sharp(\Phi^\sharp) \times Ports^\sharp(\Phi^\sharp)$ that maps any pair $((\ell_1, i_1, t_1, x), (\ell_2, i_2, t_2, y))$ of abstract ports to the element $(\ell_1, i_1, t_1, x) \leftrightsquigarrow^\sharp (\ell_2, i_2, t_2, y)$ of $\mathcal{V}^\sharp(\tau_1 \oplus \tau_2)$. We leave the choice of the abstract numerical domain $\mathcal{V}^\sharp$ as a parameter of our analysis.

Following [Ven96], we provide $\mathcal{D}^\sharp$ with the structure of a *cofibered domain.* Given two automata $\mathcal{A}_1 = (Q_1, I_1, T_1, \tau_1)$ and $\mathcal{A}_2 = (Q_2, I_2, T_2, \tau_2)$, we define a morphism $\mathcal{A}_1 \xrightarrow{f} \mathcal{A}_2$ as a pair of functions $f_1 : Q_1 \longrightarrow Q_2$ and $f_2 : \tau_1 \longrightarrow \tau_2$ satisfying the following conditions:

1. $f_1(I_1) \subseteq I_2$.
2. $f_1(T_1) \subseteq T_2$.
3. $\forall (q, \ell, q') \in \tau_1 : f_2(q, \ell, q') = (f_1(q), \ell, f_1(q'))$.

$\mathbb{A}$ can thereby be turned into a category. We denote by $\Phi^\sharp(S)$ the product category $\prod_{\ell \in \mathcal{L}(S)} \mathbb{A}$. An object of $\Phi^\sharp(S)$ is an abstract distribution of processes previously defined. We now construct a functor Δ from $\Phi^\sharp(S)$ into the category **PoSets** of partially ordered sets and monotone maps. The image of an object $\Phi^\sharp$ in $\Phi^\sharp(S)$ is the set of all abstract channel relations $\leftrightsquigarrow^\sharp$ over $\Phi^\sharp$ ordered by inclusion. We call $\Delta\Phi^\sharp$ the *fiber* of Δ over $\Phi^\sharp$. Now let $\Phi^\sharp_1 \xrightarrow{\mathcal{F}} \Phi^\sharp_2$ be a morphism[7] in $\Phi^\sharp(S)$. $\Delta\mathcal{F}$ maps any abstract channel relation $\leftrightsquigarrow^\sharp_1$ in $\Phi^\sharp_1$ to the relation $\leftrightsquigarrow^\sharp_2$ such that, for all $(\ell_1, i'_1, t'_1, x), (\ell_2, i'_2, t'_2, y) \in Ports^\sharp(\Phi^\sharp_2)$, the set $(\ell_1, i'_1, t'_1, x) \leftrightsquigarrow^\sharp_2 (\ell_2, i'_2, t'_2, y)$ is defined as:

$$\sqcup^\sharp_{\tau_1 \oplus \tau_2} \{\mathcal{V}^\sharp(\mathcal{F}(\ell_1)_2 \oplus \mathcal{F}(\ell_2)_2)((\ell_1, i_1, t_1, x) \leftrightsquigarrow^\sharp_1 (\ell_2, i_2, t_2, y)) \mid \begin{array}{l} \mathcal{F}(\ell_j)_1(i_j) = i'_j, \\ \mathcal{F}(\ell_j)_1(t_j) = t'_j, \\ 1 \leq j \leq 2\} \end{array}$$

where $\Phi^\sharp_2(\ell_i) = (Q_j, I_j, T_j, \tau_j)$, for $j \in \{1, 2\}$. We define the preorder $\preceq$ on $\mathcal{D}^\sharp$ from the *Grothendieck construction* [BW90] applied to Δ, i.e. $(\Phi^\sharp_1, \leftrightsquigarrow^\sharp_1) \preceq (\Phi^\sharp_2, \leftrightsquigarrow^\sharp_2)$ iff there exists a morphism $\Phi^\sharp_1 \xrightarrow{\mathcal{F}} \Phi^\sharp_2$ such that $\Delta\mathcal{F}(\leftrightsquigarrow^\sharp_1) \subseteq \leftrightsquigarrow^\sharp_2$. We call Δ the *display* associated to the cofibered domain $(\mathcal{D}^\sharp, \preceq)$. Intuitively, $\mathcal{D}^\sharp$ consists of a category of posets "glued" together. The cofibered structure will play a major rôle in the definition of the abstract semantics and widening operators.

The concretization function $\gamma : \mathcal{D}^\sharp \longrightarrow \mathcal{C}(S)$ sends any abstract configuration $(\Phi^\sharp, \leftrightsquigarrow^\sharp)$ to the set of concrete configurations $(\Phi, \leftrightsquigarrow)$ for which there exists a family of functions $(\Lambda_\ell : \Phi(\ell) \longrightarrow Paths(\Phi^\sharp(\ell)))_{\ell \in \mathcal{L}(S)}$ satisfying the following conditions:

[7] For each $\ell \in \mathcal{L}(S)$, $\mathcal{F}(\ell) : \Phi^\sharp_1(\ell) \longrightarrow \Phi^\sharp_2(\ell)$ is a morphism of automata.

1. For all $\ell \in \mathcal{L}(S)$ and $L \in \Phi(\ell)$, the path $\Lambda_\ell(L)$ is labelled by L.
2. Let (ℓ_1, L_1, x), (ℓ_2, L_2, y) be distinct[8] ports of Φ, and p_j be the path $\Lambda_{\ell_j}(L_j)$, for $j \in \{1,2\}$. We denote by τ_j, $j \in \{1,2\}$, the set of transitions of $\Phi^\sharp(\ell_j)$. Then, $(\ell_1, L_1, x) \leftrightsquigarrow (\ell_2, L_2, y)$ implies that

$$(p_1^\circ, p_2^\circ) \in \gamma_{\tau_1 \oplus \tau_2}((\ell_1, i(p_1), t(p_1), x) \leftrightsquigarrow^\sharp (\ell_2, i(p_2), t(p_2), y))$$

Proposition 6. $\forall c_1^\sharp, c_2^\sharp \in \mathcal{D}^\sharp : c_1^\sharp \preceq c_2^\sharp \Longrightarrow \gamma(c_1^\sharp) \subseteq \gamma(c_2^\sharp)$.

Example 5. We carry on with Example 2. Let $\Phi^\sharp \in \Phi^\sharp(S)$ be the abstract distribution of processes defined by the following automata:

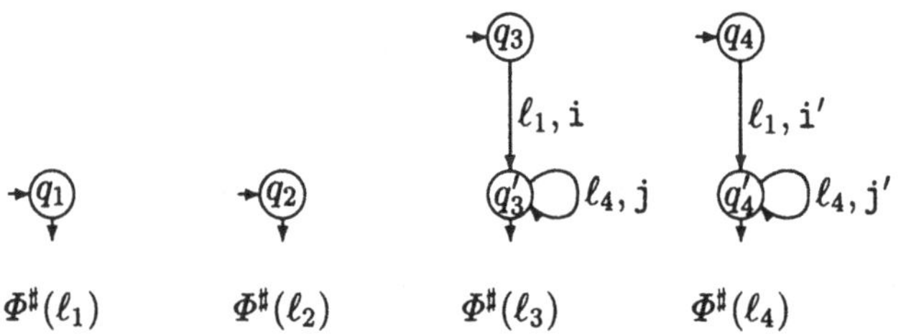

where we associate distinct counter variables $\{\mathtt{i}, \mathtt{j}, \mathtt{i}', \mathtt{j}'\}$ to each transition of the automata. If $\ell_1, \ell_2 \in \mathcal{L}(S)$, and $\mathtt{c}$ is a counter variable associated to a transition $\sigma \in \tau(\Phi^\sharp(\ell_i))$, for $i \in \{1,2\}$, we denote by $\mathtt{c}_i$ a counter variable associated to the canonical image of σ into $\tau(\Phi^\sharp(\ell_1)) \oplus \tau(\Phi^\sharp(\ell_2))$. We use Karr's abstract numerical domain, hence systems of affine equations represent the abstract values. Now let $\leftrightsquigarrow^\sharp$ be the abstract channel relation of $\Delta\Phi^\sharp$ that satisfies:

$$\left\{\begin{array}{ll}
(\ell_1, q_1, q_1, l) \leftrightsquigarrow^\sharp (\ell_2, q_2, q_2, l) & = \top^\sharp \\
(\ell_1, q_1, q_1, l) \leftrightsquigarrow^\sharp (\ell_4, q_4, q_4', l) & = \top^\sharp \\
(\ell_2, q_2, q_2, l) \leftrightsquigarrow^\sharp (\ell_4, q_4, q_4', l) & = \top^\sharp \\
(\ell_3, q_3, q_3', c) \leftrightsquigarrow^\sharp (\ell_3, q_3, q_3', c) & = \top^\sharp \\
(\ell_3, q_3, q_3', c) \leftrightsquigarrow^\sharp (\ell_2, q_2, q_2', c) & = \top^\sharp \\
(\ell_3, q_3, q_3', y) \leftrightsquigarrow^\sharp (\ell_3, q_3, q_3', z) & = \left\{\begin{array}{l} \mathtt{i}_1 = \mathtt{i}_2 = 1 \\ \mathtt{j}_1 = \mathtt{j}_2 + 1 \end{array}\right\} \\
(\ell_4, q_4, q_4', z) \leftrightsquigarrow^\sharp (\ell_3, q_3, q_3', z) & = \left\{\begin{array}{l} \mathtt{i}'_1 = \mathtt{i}_2 \\ \mathtt{j}'_1 = \mathtt{j}_2 \end{array}\right\}
\end{array}\right.$$

the other components being defined symmetrically. Thus $\leftrightsquigarrow^\sharp$ denotes *exactly* all communication channels that may be created during the evolution of S. □

---

[8] We do not require the channel relation to denote reflexivity since this information can be extracted from Φ.

6 Abstract Semantics of the π-Calculus

Before defining the abstract semantics, we need some additional properties of abstract numerical domains. Let $V \overset{f}{\rightarrowtail} W$ be an injective map in **FinSets**. Any abstract numerical domain $\mathcal{V}^\sharp$: **FinSets** $\longrightarrow$ **PoSets** provides two computable functions, an *embedding* $\overrightarrow{f} : \mathcal{V}^\sharp V \longrightarrow \mathcal{V}^\sharp W$, and a *projection* $\overleftarrow{f} : \mathcal{V}^\sharp W \longrightarrow \mathcal{V}^\sharp V$, satisfying the following conditions:

1. $\forall X^\sharp \in \mathcal{V}^\sharp V : \forall \nu \in \gamma_V(X^\sharp) : \{\mu \in W \longrightarrow \mathbb{N} \mid \mu \circ f = \nu\} \subseteq \gamma_W(\overrightarrow{f}(X^\sharp))$.
2. $\forall Y^\sharp \in \mathcal{V}^\sharp W : \forall \nu \in \gamma_W(Y^\sharp) : \nu \circ f \in \gamma_V(\overleftarrow{f}(Y^\sharp))$.

If **S** is a system of linear equations over the set of variables V, there is a computable element $\mathbf{Sol}^\sharp_V(\mathbf{S})$ of $\mathcal{V}^\sharp V$ which upper-approximates the set of variable assignments in $V \longrightarrow \mathbb{N}$ that are solutions of **S**. We will omit the subscript V whenever it will be clear from the context. Moreover, the lattice $\mathcal{V}^\sharp V$ is provided with a widening operator.

Example 6. For Karr's abstract numerical domain, $\overleftarrow{f}(Y^\sharp)$ amounts to the elimination of the coordinates corresponding to the variables $W - f(V)$ from a system of a point and vectors describing $Y^\sharp$. $\overrightarrow{f}(X^\sharp)$ is described by the same system of affine equations as $X^\sharp$. $\mathbf{Sol}^\sharp_V(S)$ is of course directly expressible in $\mathcal{V}^\sharp V$. Since $\mathcal{V}^\sharp V$ satisfies the ascending chain condition, a widening is provided by the join $\sqcup^\sharp_V$. □

We first construct the abstract counterpart of the closure operator $[-]_\Phi$ that maps any binary relation ρ over $Ports(\Phi)$ to the smallest equivalence relation containing ρ. This closure operation can be expressed by the following inductive rules:

$$\frac{x \in Ports(\Phi)}{(x,x) \in \rho} \qquad \frac{(x,y) \in \rho \quad (y,z) \in \rho}{(x,z) \in \rho} \qquad \frac{(x,y) \in \rho}{(y,x) \in \rho}$$

The computation of $[\rho]_\Phi$ amounts to calculating a least fixpoint in $(\wp(Ports(\Phi) \times Ports(\Phi)), \subseteq)$ (see [CC95]). Thereby, we define the corresponding abstract operation as the limit of an abstract iteration sequence[9] on a fiber of $\mathcal{D}^\sharp$ using Theorem 4. For this purpose, we introduce a closure relation $\triangleright$ on abstract channel relations which mimics the inductive rules for $[-]_\Phi$. Let $\Phi^\sharp$ be an abstract distribution of processes. We define $\triangleright$ on $\Delta\Phi^\sharp$ as follows:

1. If $pt'_1, pt'_2 \in Ports^\sharp(\Phi^\sharp)$ and $\leftrightsquigarrow^\sharp_1 \in \Delta\Phi^\sharp$, then $\leftrightsquigarrow^\sharp_1 \triangleright \leftrightsquigarrow^\sharp_2$ where, for all $pt_1, pt_2 \in Ports^\sharp(\Phi^\sharp)$:

$$pt_1 \leftrightsquigarrow^\sharp_2 pt_2 = \begin{cases} pt_1 \leftrightsquigarrow^\sharp_1 pt_2 & \text{if } pt_1 = pt'_2 \text{ and } pt_2 = pt'_1 \\ \emptyset^\sharp & \text{otherwise} \end{cases}$$

[9] Note that we only have to cope with the symmetry and transitivity rules (cf. the definition of γ).

2. Let $\ell_1, \ell_2, \ell_3 \in \mathcal{L}(S)$ and $pt'_j = (\ell_j, i_j, t_j, x_j) \in Ports^\sharp(\Phi^\sharp)$, for $j \in \{1,2,3\}$. We denote by (Q_j, I_j, T_j, τ_j) the automaton $\Phi^\sharp(\ell_j)$, for $j \in \{1,2,3\}$. Let $\tau = \tau_1 \oplus \tau_2 \oplus \tau_3$ and $\tau_1 \oplus \tau_2 \overset{f_1}{\rightarrowtail} \tau$, $\tau_2 \oplus \tau_3 \overset{f_2}{\rightarrowtail} \tau$, $\tau_1 \oplus \tau_3 \overset{f_3}{\rightarrowtail} \tau$ be the canonical inclusion maps in **FinSets**. Now let $\leftrightsquigarrow^\sharp{}_1 \in \Delta\Phi^\sharp$ and $X_j = (\ell_j, i_j, t_j, x_j) \leftrightsquigarrow^\sharp{}_1 (\ell_{j+1}, i_{j+1}, t_{j+1}, x_{j+1})$, for $j \in \{1,2\}$. Then, $\leftrightsquigarrow^\sharp{}_1 \triangleright \leftrightsquigarrow^\sharp{}_2$ where, for all $pt_1, pt_2 \in Ports^\sharp(\Phi^\sharp)$,

$$pt_1 \leftrightsquigarrow^\sharp{}_2\, pt_2 = \begin{cases} \overleftarrow{f_3}(\overrightarrow{f_1}(X_1) \sqcap^\sharp_\tau \overrightarrow{f_2}(X_2)) & \text{if } pt_1 = pt'_1 \text{ and } pt_2 = pt'_3 \\ \emptyset^\sharp & \text{otherwise} \end{cases}$$

The fiber $\Delta\Phi^\sharp$ can be endowed with a lattice structure, the join $\sqcup_{\Phi^\sharp}$ and the meet $\sqcap_{\Phi^\sharp}$ being defined by componentwise application of $\sqcup^\sharp$ and $\sqcap^\sharp$. We define similarly an operator $\nabla_{\Phi^\sharp}$ on $\Delta\Phi^\sharp$ by componentwise application of the widening operators provided by the abstract numerical domain.

Proposition 7. *$\nabla_{\Phi^\sharp}$ is a widening operator on $\Delta\Phi^\sharp$.*

We define an endomorphism $F_\triangleright$ on the fiber $\Delta\Phi^\sharp$ as:

$$F_\triangleright \overset{\text{def}}{=} \lambda(\leftrightsquigarrow^\sharp) \cdot \bigsqcup_{\Phi^\sharp} \{\leftrightsquigarrow^\sharp{}_\bullet \mid \leftrightsquigarrow^\sharp \triangleright \leftrightsquigarrow^\sharp{}_\bullet\}$$

Definition 8 Abstract Closure. Let $\Phi^\sharp$ be an abstract distribution of processes and $\leftrightsquigarrow^\sharp$ an element of $\Delta\Phi^\sharp$. The abstract closure $[\leftrightsquigarrow^\sharp]_{\Phi^\sharp}$ of $\leftrightsquigarrow^\sharp$ is given by the limit of the abstract iteration sequence of Theorem 4 applied to the function $F_\triangleright$ on the domain $\Delta\Phi^\sharp$, with $\leftrightsquigarrow^\sharp$ as abstract basis and $\nabla_{\Phi^\sharp}$ as widening operator. □

Note that this closure operation enforces transitivity on an abstract channel relation $\leftrightsquigarrow^\sharp$. It may cause an important loss of accuracy, since the union of transitive relations (which is what is denoted by $\leftrightsquigarrow^\sharp$) is in general not transitive. In fact, as we will see when we will define the abstract semantics, we only need to perform this closure operation on a relation $\leftrightsquigarrow^\sharp = \leftrightsquigarrow^\sharp{}_1 \cup \leftrightsquigarrow^\sharp{}_2$ where $\leftrightsquigarrow^\sharp{}_1$ denotes concrete channel relations and $\leftrightsquigarrow^\sharp{}_2$ contains additional relations between ports in the domain of $\leftrightsquigarrow^\sharp{}_1$ and some newly created ports. Therefore, it is possible to modify the rules defining $\triangleright$ so that they can only be applied to pairs involving a new port, leaving the relation $\leftrightsquigarrow^\sharp{}_1$ unchanged[10]. In order to keep the presentation simple, we do not detail this improvement of the analysis.

We define the abstract semantics of the π-calculus by a transition relation $\Rightarrow^\sharp$ on $\mathcal{D}^\sharp$ which mimics $\Rightarrow$. Let $(\Phi^\sharp, \leftrightsquigarrow^\sharp)$ be an abstract configuration and $\ell_o \in \mathcal{L}(S)$ such that:

$$S_{\ell_o} = \cdots + \overline{z}[t_1, \ldots, t_m].\nu v_1^o \ldots \nu v_{l_o}^o.(S_{\ell_o^1} \mid \cdots \mid S_{\ell_o^{n_o}}) + \cdots$$

We have a transition $(\Phi^\sharp, \leftrightsquigarrow^\sharp) \Rightarrow^\sharp (\Phi^\sharp_\bullet, \leftrightsquigarrow^\sharp{}_\bullet)$ whenever there is $\ell_i \in \mathcal{L}(S)$, such that S_{ℓ_i} is one of the following processes:

[10] This was pointed out to us by Alain Deutsch.

- $\cdots + x(y_1, \ldots, y_m).\nu v^i_1 \ldots \nu v^i_{l_i}.(S_{\ell^1_i} \mid \cdots \mid S_{\ell^{n_i}_i}) + \cdots$
- $!x(y_1, \ldots, y_m).\nu v^i_1 \ldots \nu v^i_{l_i}.(S_{\ell^1_i} \mid \cdots \mid S_{\ell^{n_i}_i})$

and

$$(\ell_i, s_i, t_i, x) \leftrightsquigarrow^\sharp (\ell_o, s_o, t_o, z) \neq \emptyset^\sharp$$

for two abstract ports (ℓ_i, s_i, t_i, x) and (ℓ_o, s_o, t_o, z). In other words, there is the possibility of a communication between two residuals of S_{ℓ_i} and S_{ℓ_o} in a concrete configuration abstracted by $(\Phi^\sharp, \leftrightsquigarrow^\sharp)$. We denote by $X^\sharp_c$ the abstract value $(\ell_i, s_i, t_i, x) \leftrightsquigarrow^\sharp (\ell_o, s_o, t_o, z)$.

We define $\Phi^\sharp_\bullet$ as follows:

$$\Phi^\sharp_\bullet(\ell) \stackrel{\text{def}}{=} \begin{cases} \Phi^\sharp(\ell) \oplus \mathcal{A}_\eta & \text{if } \ell = \ell^k_\eta, \text{ for } \eta \in \{i, o\},\ k \in \{1, \ldots, n_\eta\} \\ \Phi^\sharp(\ell) & \text{otherwise} \end{cases}$$

where $\mathcal{A}_i$ and $\mathcal{A}_o$ are automata representing the residuals of the newly spawned processes, and $\oplus$ denotes the coproduct in $\mathbb{A}$. Whatever S_{ℓ_i} may be, agent or server, $\mathcal{A}_o$ is always defined as the automaton $(Q_o, \{s_o\}, \{t_o\}, \tau_o)$, where, for $\eta \in \{i, o\}$, Q_η (resp. τ_η) is the set of states (resp. transitions) of $\Phi^\sharp(\ell_\eta)$. Indeed, in the nonstandard semantics the residuals of the processes spawned by the sender are always inherited from their parent agent. For $\mathcal{A}_i$ there are two different cases depending on the type of S_{ℓ_i}:

1. S_{ℓ_i} is an agent. Then we put
$$\mathcal{A}_i \stackrel{\text{def}}{=} (Q_i, \{s_i\}, \{t_i\}, \tau_i)$$
2. S_{ℓ_i} is a server. We suppose that we are provided with a distinguished element Ω in the set $\mathcal{Q}$ of all states of the automata in $\mathbb{A}$. Let $Q_o \xrightarrow{\xi_1} Q_o \oplus \{\Omega\}$ and $\{\Omega\} \xrightarrow{\xi_2} Q_o \oplus \{\Omega\}$ be the canonical inclusion maps in **FinSets**. We denote by $\tau_o \xrightarrow{\Xi} \tau'_o$ the function that maps any transition (q, ℓ, q') to $(\xi_1(q), \ell, \xi_1(q'))$. Then we put
$$\mathcal{A}_i \stackrel{\text{def}}{=} (Q_o \oplus \{\Omega\}, \{\xi_1(s_o)\}, \{\xi_2(\Omega)\}, \tau'_o)$$
where $\tau'_o \stackrel{\text{def}}{=} \{(\xi_1(q), \ell, \xi_1(q')) \mid (q, \ell, q') \in \tau_o\} \cup \{(\xi_1(t_o), \ell_o, \xi_2(\Omega))\}$. This is the abstract counterpart of assigning the residual $L_o.\ell_o$ to the processes created by the server in the concrete semantics.

We denote by $\mathcal{A}_\eta \xrightarrow{\iota^l_\eta} \Phi^\sharp_\bullet(\ell^l_\eta)$ the canonical inclusion morphism in $\mathbb{A}$, for $\eta \in \{i, o\}$, $l \in \{1, \ldots, n_\eta\}$. Note that the sets of residuals denoted by $\Phi^\sharp_\bullet$ are larger than the ones denoted by $\Phi^\sharp$. Indeed, we are not allowed to remove anything since we have lost all information about the number of residuals of each S_ℓ.

The abstract channel relation $\leftrightsquigarrow^\sharp_\bullet$ mimics the concrete one:

$$\leftrightsquigarrow^\sharp_\bullet \stackrel{\text{def}}{=} [\Delta\mathcal{F}(\leftrightsquigarrow^\sharp) \sqcup_{\Phi^\sharp_\bullet} \leftrightsquigarrow^\sharp_c \sqcup_{\Phi^\sharp_\bullet} \leftrightsquigarrow^\sharp_i \sqcup_{\Phi^\sharp_\bullet} \leftrightsquigarrow^\sharp_o \sqcup_{\Phi^\sharp_\bullet} \leftrightsquigarrow^\sharp_\nu]_{\Phi^\sharp_\bullet}$$

where, for all $\ell \in \mathcal{L}(S)$, $\Phi^\sharp(\ell) \xrightarrow{\mathcal{F}(\ell)} \Phi^\sharp_\bullet(\ell)$ is the canonical inclusion morphism in $\mathbb{A}$. The definitions of $\leftrightsquigarrow^\sharp_c$, $\leftrightsquigarrow^\sharp_i$, $\leftrightsquigarrow^\sharp_o$ and $\leftrightsquigarrow^\sharp_\nu$ follow the lines of their concrete counterparts in Fig. 3 and Fig. 4. We distinguish two cases, depending on the type of S_{ℓ_i}.

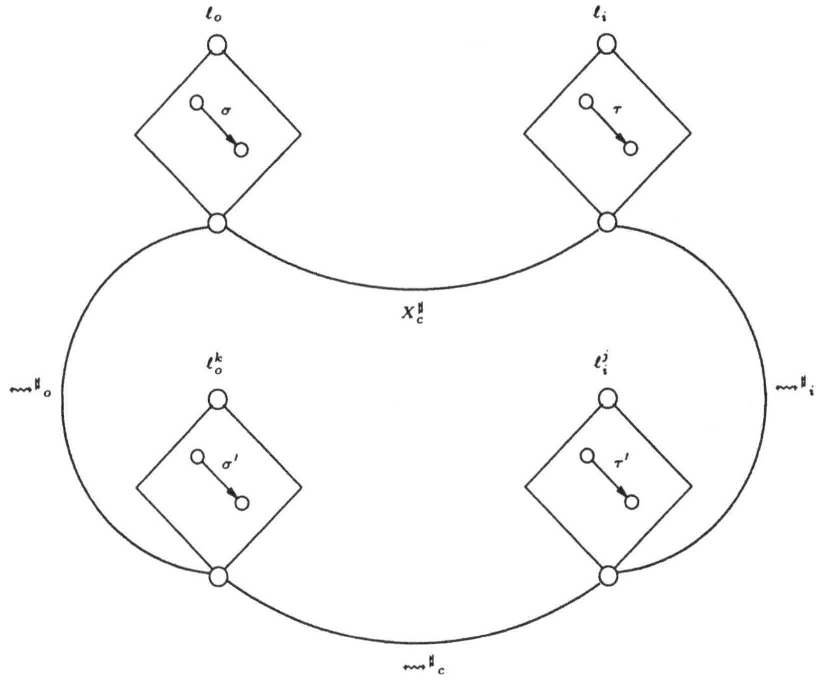

Fig. 5. Abstract interagent communication

Interagent Communication. If S_{ℓ_i} is an agent, the abstract semantics of communication is summarized in Fig. 5. We have represented the automata corresponding to the residuals of S_{ℓ_i}, S_{ℓ_o}, $S_{\ell_i^j}$ and $S_{\ell_o^k}$, the latter being two processes spawned by the sender and the receiver after the communication occurred.

The abstract channel relation $\leftrightsquigarrow^\sharp{}_c$ performs the binding between the names y_h and t_h involved in the communication. Since $X_c^\sharp$ denotes residuals of S_{ℓ_i} and S_{ℓ_o} that may communicate, we use this same abstract numerical value to denote all possible channels between the ports associated to y_h and t_h. This can be stated formally as follows. For all $j \in \{1, \ldots, n_i\}$, $k \in \{1, \ldots, n_o\}$, $h \in \{1, \ldots, m\}$, $y_h \in fn(S_{\ell_i^j})$ and $t_h \in fn(S_{\ell_o^k})$, we put

$$(\ell_i^j, (\iota_i^j)_1(s_i), (\iota_i^j)_1(t_i), y_h) \leftrightsquigarrow^\sharp{}_c (\ell_o^k, (\iota_o^k)_1(s_o), (\iota_o^k)_1(t_o), t_h) \stackrel{\text{def}}{=} \mathcal{V}^\sharp((\iota_i^j)_2 \oplus (\iota_o^k)_2)(X_c^\sharp)$$

For any other abstract ports $pt_1, pt_2 \in Ports^\sharp(\Phi_\bullet^\sharp)$, we put $pt_1 \leftrightsquigarrow^\sharp{}_c pt_2 \stackrel{\text{def}}{=} \emptyset^\sharp$.

The abstract channel relations $\leftrightsquigarrow^\sharp{}_i$ and $\leftrightsquigarrow^\sharp{}_o$ bind the free names in the instances of S_{ℓ_i} and S_{ℓ_o} to the corresponding ones in the processes released after the communication. Their rôle is thereby to propagate the scope of free names. The abstract numerical value associated to the relation $\leftrightsquigarrow^\sharp{}_i$, for example, is the

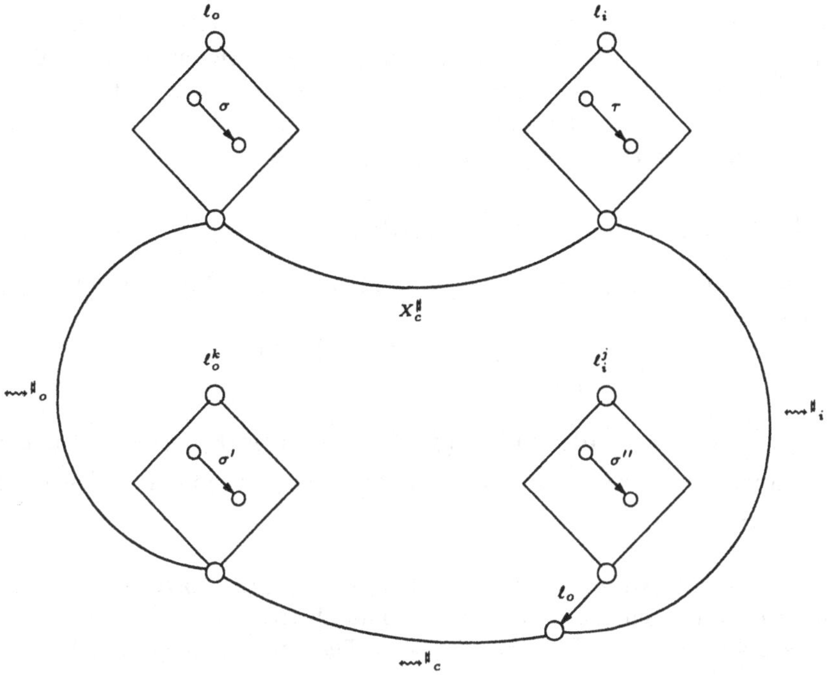

Fig. 6. Abstract agent-server communication

solution in the abstract numerical domain of the system of equations $\tau = \tau'$, where τ is any transition in the automaton corresponding to S_{ℓ_i} and τ' is the copy of τ in the automaton associated to the newly created process $S_{\ell^j_i}$, as shown in Fig. 5. The definition of $\leftrightsquigarrow^\sharp{}_o$ is similar. The meaning of these operations at the concrete level is to bind pairs of ports with the same residuals. Since we abstract a residual by the number of times a path labelled by this residual runs through each transition of the automaton, our definition is quite natural. This can be stated more formally as follows. For all $\eta \in \{i, o\}$, $k \in \{1, \dots, n_\eta\}$ and $u \in fn(S_{\ell_\eta}) \cap fn(S_{\ell^k_\eta})$, we put

$$(\ell_\eta, \mathcal{F}(\ell_\eta)_1(s_\eta), \mathcal{F}(\ell_\eta)_1(t_\eta), u) \leftrightsquigarrow^\sharp{}_\eta (\ell^k_\eta, (\iota^k_\eta)_1(s_\eta), (\iota^k_\eta)_1(t_\eta), u) \stackrel{\text{def}}{=} \mathbf{Sol}^\sharp(\mathbf{S}^k_\eta)$$

where $\mathbf{S}^k_\eta$ is the system of affine equations over $\tau(\Phi^\sharp_\bullet(\ell_\eta)) \oplus \tau(\Phi^\sharp_\bullet(\ell^k_\eta))$ defined as follows:

$$\begin{cases} \zeta_1 \circ \mathcal{F}(\ell_\eta)_2(\sigma) = \zeta_2 \circ (\iota^k_\eta)_2(\sigma) \\ \sigma \in \tau_\eta \end{cases}$$

where $\tau(\Phi^\sharp_\bullet(\ell_\eta)) \xrightarrow{\zeta_1} \tau(\Phi^\sharp_\bullet(\ell_\eta)) \oplus \tau(\Phi^\sharp_\bullet(\ell^k_\eta)) \xleftarrow{\zeta_2} \tau(\Phi^\sharp_\bullet(\ell^k_\eta))$ are the canonical inclusion maps in **FinSets**. For any other abstract ports $pt_1, pt_2 \in Ports^\sharp(\Phi^\sharp_\bullet)$, we put $pt_1 \leftrightsquigarrow^\sharp{}_\eta pt_2 \stackrel{\text{def}}{=} \emptyset^\sharp$.

The abstract channel relation $\leftrightsquigarrow^\sharp_\nu$ binds the new ports created by the communication in the spawned processes. Since all processes released during a communication by either the sender or the receiver have the same residuals, we define $\leftrightsquigarrow^\sharp_\nu$ similarly to $\leftrightsquigarrow^\sharp_i$ and $\leftrightsquigarrow^\sharp_o$ as the abstract solution of a system of linear equations. That is, for all $\eta \in \{i, o\}$, $j, k \in \{1, \ldots, n_\eta\}$, with $j \neq k$[11], and $j \in \{1, \ldots, l_\eta\}$ such that $v^j_\eta \in fn(S_{\ell^j_\eta}) \cap fn(S_{\ell^k_\eta})$, we put

$$(\ell^j_\eta, (\iota^j_\eta)_1(s_\eta), (\iota^j_\eta)_1(t_\eta), u) \leftrightsquigarrow^\sharp_\nu (\ell^k_\eta, (\iota^k_\eta)_1(s_\eta), (\iota^k_\eta)_1(t_\eta), u) \stackrel{\text{def}}{=} \mathbf{Sol}^\sharp(\mathbf{S}^{j,k}_\eta)$$

where $\mathbf{S}^{j,k}_\eta$ is the system of affine equations over $\tau(\Phi^\sharp_\bullet(\ell^j_\eta)) \oplus \tau(\Phi^\sharp_\bullet(\ell^k_\eta))$ defined as follows:

$$\begin{cases} \theta_1 \circ (\iota^j_\eta)_2(\sigma) = \theta_2 \circ (\iota^k_\eta)_2(\sigma) \\ \sigma \in \tau_\eta \end{cases}$$

where $\tau(\Phi^\sharp_\bullet(\ell^j_\eta)) \xrightarrow{\theta_1} \tau(\Phi^\sharp_\bullet(\ell^j_\eta)) \oplus \tau(\Phi^\sharp_\bullet(\ell^k_\eta)) \xleftarrow{\theta_2} \tau(\Phi^\sharp_\bullet(\ell^k_\eta))$ are the canonical inclusion maps in **FinSets**. For any other abstract ports $pt_1, pt_2 \in Ports^\sharp(\Phi^\sharp_\bullet)$, we put $pt_1 \leftrightsquigarrow^\sharp_\nu pt_2 \stackrel{\text{def}}{=} \emptyset^\sharp$.

Agent-Server Communication. If S_{ℓ_i} is a server, the abstract semantics of communication is summarized in Fig. 6. The abstract channel relations $\leftrightsquigarrow^\sharp_o$ and $\leftrightsquigarrow^\sharp_\nu$ are constructed exactly as above. The situation is quite different for $\leftrightsquigarrow^\sharp_i$ and $\leftrightsquigarrow^\sharp_c$, because the automata corresponding to the processes spawned by S_{ℓ_i} are copies of the automaton associated to S_{ℓ_o} suffixed with a transition labelled by ℓ_o.

The definition of $\leftrightsquigarrow^\sharp_c$ is very similar to the definition of $\leftrightsquigarrow^\sharp_i$ in the previous case. The binding between the names involved in the communication is performed by taking the solution of the system of equations $\sigma' = \sigma''$ in the abstract numerical domain, as illustrated in Fig. 6. Since residuals of the processes released by the receiver are suffixed with ℓ_o, we furthermore require that the corresponding transition be crossed exactly once. This operation can be formalized as follows. For all $j \in \{1, \ldots, n_i\}$, $k \in \{1, \ldots, n_o\}$, $h \in \{1, \ldots, m\}$, $y_h \in fn(S_{\ell^j_i})$ and $t_h \in fn(S_{\ell^k_o})$, we put

$$(\ell^j_i, (\iota^j_i)_1 \circ \xi_1(s_o), (\iota^j_i)_1 \circ \xi_2(\Omega), y_h) \leftrightsquigarrow^\sharp_c (\ell^k_o, (\iota^k_o)_1(s_o), (\iota^k_o)_1(t_o), t_h) \stackrel{\text{def}}{=} \mathbf{Sol}^\sharp(\mathbf{S}^{j,k}_c)$$

where $\mathbf{S}^{j,k}_c$ is the system of affine equations over $\tau(\Phi^\sharp_\bullet(\ell^j_i)) \oplus \tau(\Phi^\sharp_\bullet(\ell^k_o))$ defined as follows:

$$\begin{cases} \zeta_1 \circ (\iota^j_i)_2(\xi_1(t_o), \ell_o, \xi_2(\Omega)) = 1 \\ \zeta_1 \circ (\iota^j_i)_2 \circ \Xi(\sigma) = \zeta_2 \circ (\iota^k_o)_2(\sigma) \\ \sigma \in \tau_o \end{cases}$$

where $\tau(\Phi^\sharp_\bullet(\ell^j_i)) \xrightarrow{\zeta_1} \tau(\Phi^\sharp_\bullet(\ell^j_i)) \oplus \tau(\Phi^\sharp_\bullet(\ell^k_o)) \xleftarrow{\zeta_2} \tau(\Phi^\sharp_\bullet(\ell^k_o))$ are the canonical inclusion maps in **FinSets**. For any other abstract ports $pt_1, pt_2 \in Ports^\sharp(\Phi^\sharp_\bullet)$, we put $pt_1 \leftrightsquigarrow^\sharp_c pt_2 \stackrel{\text{def}}{=} \emptyset^\sharp$.

[11] Reflexivity is implicit by definition of γ.

The definition of $\leftrightsquigarrow^{\sharp}_i$ is slightly more delicate. The residuals of the processes spawned by the server are represented by a copy of the automaton associated to the sender and $\leftrightsquigarrow^{\sharp}_i$ relates the instances of S_{ℓ_i} which may communicate with S_{ℓ_o} to the instances of $S_{\ell_i^j}$ which have been effectively spawned by the communication. Thereby, the abstract numerical value associated to $\leftrightsquigarrow^{\sharp}_i$ consists of $X_c^{\sharp}$ for which each σ has been mapped to its copy σ'' in the automaton corresponding to $S_{\ell_i^j}$ (see Fig. 6), together with the constraint that the additional transition labelled by ℓ_o must be crossed once. This can be stated formally as follows. Let $\tau_i' \stackrel{\text{def}}{=} \tau_i \oplus \tau_o'$ and $\tau_i \stackrel{\chi_1}{\rightarrowtail} \tau_i'$, $\tau_o' \stackrel{\chi_2}{\rightarrowtail} \tau_i'$ be the canonical inclusion maps in **FinSets**. For all $k \in \{1, \dots, n_i\}$ and $u \in fn(S_{\ell_i}) \cap fn(S_{\ell_i^k})$, we put

$$(\ell_i, \mathcal{F}(\ell_i)_1(s_i), \mathcal{F}(\ell_i)_1(t_i), u) \leftrightsquigarrow^{\sharp}_i (\ell_i^k, (\iota_i^k)_1 \circ \xi_1(s_o), (\iota_i^k)_1 \circ \xi_2(\Omega), u) \stackrel{\text{def}}{=}$$
$$\mathcal{V}^{\sharp}(\mathcal{F}(\ell_i)_2 \oplus (\iota_i^k)_2) \left(\overrightarrow{[\chi_1 \oplus (\chi_2 \circ \Xi)]}(X_c^{\sharp}) \sqcap^{\sharp}_{\tau_i'} \mathbf{Sol}^{\sharp}_{\tau_i'}(\{\chi_2(\xi_1(t_o), \ell_o, \xi_2(\Omega)) = 1\})\right)$$

For any other abstract ports $pt_1, pt_2 \in Ports^{\sharp}(\Phi_\bullet^{\sharp})$, we put $pt_1 \leftrightsquigarrow^{\sharp}_i pt_2 \stackrel{\text{def}}{=} \emptyset^{\sharp}$.

Definition 9 Abstract Semantic Function. Let $c^{\sharp} = (\Phi^{\sharp}, \leftrightsquigarrow^{\sharp})$ be an abstract configuration. For any configuration $(\Phi_\bullet^{\sharp}, \leftrightsquigarrow^{\sharp}_\bullet)$ such that $c^{\sharp} \Rightarrow^{\sharp} (\Phi_\bullet^{\sharp}, \leftrightsquigarrow^{\sharp}_\bullet)$, we denote by $\mathcal{F}[\Phi_\bullet^{\sharp}, \leftrightsquigarrow^{\sharp}_\bullet] : \Phi^{\sharp} \longrightarrow \Phi_\bullet^{\sharp}$ the canonical inclusion morphism. Let $\Phi_\dagger^{\sharp}$ be the colimit in $\Phi^{\sharp}(S)$ of the diagram $\{\mathcal{F}[\Phi_\bullet^{\sharp}, \leftrightsquigarrow^{\sharp}_\bullet] : \Phi^{\sharp} \longrightarrow \Phi_\bullet^{\sharp} \mid c^{\sharp} \Rightarrow^{\sharp} (\Phi_\bullet^{\sharp}, \leftrightsquigarrow^{\sharp}_\bullet)\}$ and $\{\mathcal{F}^{\dagger}[\Phi_\bullet^{\sharp}, \leftrightsquigarrow^{\sharp}_\bullet] : \Phi_\bullet^{\sharp} \longrightarrow \Phi_\dagger^{\sharp} \mid c^{\sharp} \Rightarrow^{\sharp} (\Phi_\bullet^{\sharp}, \leftrightsquigarrow^{\sharp}_\bullet)\}$ be the colimiting cocone. We define the abstract semantic function $F^{\sharp} : \mathcal{D}^{\sharp} \longrightarrow \mathcal{D}^{\sharp}$ as follows:

$$F^{\sharp}(c^{\sharp}) \stackrel{\text{def}}{=} \bigsqcup_{\Phi_\dagger^{\sharp}} \{\Delta\mathcal{F}^{\dagger}[\Phi_\bullet^{\sharp}, \leftrightsquigarrow^{\sharp}_\bullet](\leftrightsquigarrow^{\sharp}_\bullet) \mid c^{\sharp} \Rightarrow^{\sharp} (\Phi_\bullet^{\sharp}, \leftrightsquigarrow^{\sharp}_\bullet)\}$$

□

Theorem 10 Soundness of the Abstract Semantics.

$$F_S \circ \gamma \subseteq \gamma \circ F^{\sharp}$$

It now remains to define a widening operator on $\mathcal{D}^{\sharp}$ in order to make the abstract semantics of S computable.

7 Widening Operators

There is a generic method to construct widening operators on cofibered domains by combining the widenings defined locally on each fiber [Ven96]. This requires to extend the notion of widening to categories.

Definition 11 Widening on a Category. Let $\mathbb{C}$ be a category. A *widening operator* ∇ on $\mathbb{C}$ associates to any two objects X, Y of $\mathbb{C}$ two arrows:

$$X \xrightarrow{\quad X \overrightarrow{\nabla}_1 Y \quad} X \nabla Y \xleftarrow{\quad X \overrightarrow{\nabla}_2 Y \quad} Y$$

such that for any sequence of objects $(X_n)_{n \geq 0}$, the sequence of arrows $(X_n^\nabla \xrightarrow{f_n^\nabla} X_{n+1}^\nabla)_{n \geq 0}$ in $\mathbb{C}$ defined by:

$$\begin{cases} X_0^\nabla = X_0 \\ X_{n+1}^\nabla = X_n^\nabla \nabla X_{n+1} \\ f_n^\nabla = X_n^\nabla \overrightarrow{\nabla}_1 X_{n+1} \end{cases}$$

is ultimately pseudo-stationary, i.e. there exists N such that, for all $n \geq N$, f_n^∇ is an isomorphism. Moreover we require ∇ to be stable under isomorphism, that is, whenever $X \cong X'$ and $Y \cong Y'$, then $X \nabla Y \cong X' \nabla Y'$. $\qquad\square$

Assuming that $\Phi^\sharp(S)$ is provided with a widening ∇, we construct a widening operator $\nabla^\sharp$ on $\mathcal{D}^\sharp$ as follows. Let $(\Phi_1^\sharp, \rightsquigarrow^\sharp_1)$ and $(\Phi_2^\sharp, \rightsquigarrow^\sharp_2)$ be abstract configurations, $(\Phi_1^\sharp, \rightsquigarrow^\sharp_1) \nabla^\sharp (\Phi_2^\sharp, \rightsquigarrow^\sharp_2)$ is given by:

- $(\Phi_1^\sharp, \rightsquigarrow^\sharp_1 \nabla_{\Phi_1^\sharp} \Delta((\Phi_1^\sharp \overrightarrow{\nabla}_1 \Phi_2^\sharp)^{-1} \circ (\Phi_1^\sharp \overrightarrow{\nabla}_2 \Phi_2^\sharp))(\rightsquigarrow^\sharp_2))$ when $\Phi_1^\sharp \overrightarrow{\nabla}_1 \Phi_2^\sharp$ is an isomorphism,

- $(\Phi_1^\sharp \nabla \Phi_2^\sharp, \Delta(\Phi_1^\sharp \overrightarrow{\nabla}_1 \Phi_2^\sharp)(\rightsquigarrow^\sharp_1) \nabla_{\Phi_1^\sharp \nabla \Phi_2^\sharp} \Delta(\Phi_1^\sharp \overrightarrow{\nabla}_2 \Phi_2^\sharp)(\rightsquigarrow^\sharp_2))$ otherwise.

Intuitively the first case means that when the fiber is "stable", i.e. $\Phi_1^\sharp \overrightarrow{\nabla}_1 \Phi_2^\sharp$ is an isomorphism, we "transfer" the abstract channel relation $\rightsquigarrow^\sharp_2$ into the fiber and we make the widening with $\rightsquigarrow^\sharp_1$:

$$\Phi_1^\sharp \xleftarrow{\quad (\Phi_1^\sharp \overrightarrow{\nabla}_1 \Phi_2^\sharp)^{-1} \quad} \Phi_1^\sharp \nabla \Phi_2^\sharp \xleftarrow{\quad \Phi_1^\sharp \overrightarrow{\nabla}_2 \Phi_2^\sharp \quad} \Phi_2^\sharp$$

$$\nabla_{\Phi_1^\sharp} \begin{cases} \rightsquigarrow^\sharp_1 \\ \Delta((\Phi_1^\sharp \overrightarrow{\nabla}_1 \Phi_2^\sharp)^{-1} \circ (\Phi_1^\sharp \overrightarrow{\nabla}_2 \Phi_2^\sharp))(\rightsquigarrow^\sharp_2) \end{cases} \qquad \dashleftarrow \rightsquigarrow^\sharp_2$$

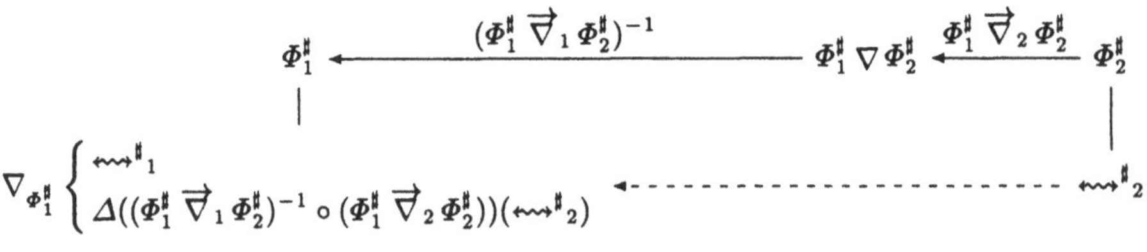

Otherwise we transfer $\rightsquigarrow^\sharp_1$ and $\rightsquigarrow^\sharp_2$ into the fiber over $\Phi_1^\sharp \nabla \Phi_2^\sharp$ and we make the widening in this fiber:

$$\Phi_1^\sharp \xrightarrow{\quad \Phi_1^\sharp \overrightarrow{\nabla}_1 \Phi_2^\sharp \quad} \Phi_1^\sharp \nabla \Phi_2^\sharp \xleftarrow{\quad \Phi_1^\sharp \overrightarrow{\nabla}_2 \Phi_2^\sharp \quad} \Phi_2^\sharp$$

$$\rightsquigarrow^\sharp_1 \dashrightarrow \Delta(\Phi_1^\sharp \overrightarrow{\nabla}_1 \Phi_2^\sharp)(\rightsquigarrow^\sharp_1) \nabla_{\Phi_1^\sharp \nabla \Phi_2^\sharp} \Delta(\Phi_1^\sharp \overrightarrow{\nabla}_2 \Phi_2^\sharp)(\rightsquigarrow^\sharp_2) \dashleftarrow \rightsquigarrow^\sharp_2$$

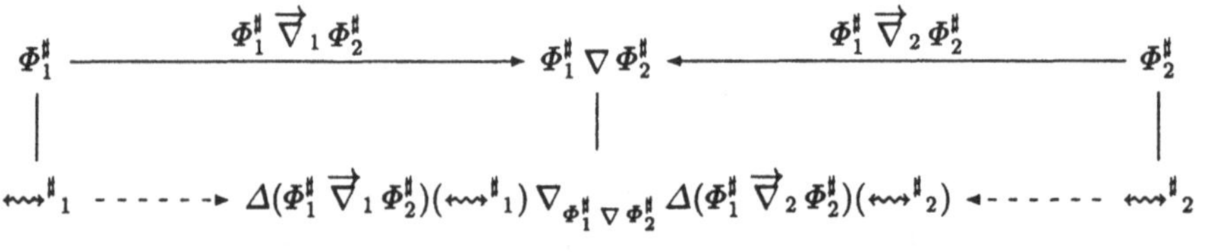

Theorem 12. $\nabla^\sharp$ *is a widening operator on* $(\mathcal{D}^\sharp, \preceq)$.

We now define a widening ∇ on $\Phi^\sharp(S)$ by componentwise application of a widening $\nabla_{\mathbb{A}}$ on $\mathbb{A}$. The idea is to fold states in an automaton $\mathcal{A} = (Q, I, T, \tau)$ with respect to some "similarity" criterion which is represented by an equivalence relation $\equiv^{\nabla}_{\mathcal{A}}$ on Q. The folding operation is achieved by quotienting the automaton with respect to this relation.

Example 7. Let k be a nonnegative integer. For any $q \in Q$, we denote by $L_{\leq k}(q)$ the set of words labelling a path in $\mathcal{A}$ originating from q and of length bounded by k. We define $\equiv^{\nabla}_{\mathcal{A}}$ as follows:

$$q \equiv^{\nabla}_{\mathcal{A}} q' \iff L_{\leq k}(q) = L_{\leq k}(q')$$

This folding criterion is inspired by the *k-limiting* approximation of [JM81]. □

Definition 13 Quotient of an Automaton. Let $\mathcal{A} = (Q, I, T, \tau)$ be an automaton of $\mathbb{A}$ and $\sim$ be an equivalence relation on Q. We denote by $\pi_\sim : Q \longrightarrow Q/_\sim$ the canonical projection onto the quotient set[12]. The quotient $\mathcal{A}/_\sim$ of $\mathcal{A}$ by $\sim$ is then defined as

$$\mathcal{A}/_\sim \stackrel{\text{def}}{=} (Q/_\sim, \pi_\sim(I), \pi_\sim(T), \{(\pi_\sim(q), \ell, \pi_\sim(q')) \mid (q, \ell, q') \in \tau\})$$

□

Example 8. Let $\equiv_\delta$ be the smallest equivalence relation on Q such that:

1. $\forall i, i' \in I : i \equiv_\delta i'$.
2. $\forall (q, \ell, r), (q', \ell', r') \in \tau : q \equiv_\delta q' \wedge \ell = \ell' \Longrightarrow r \equiv_\delta r'$.

Then it is obvious that the quotient automaton $\mathcal{A}/_{\equiv_\delta}$ is deterministic. This is an approximate[13] procedure to make an automaton deterministic. □

Let $\mathcal{A}_1$, $\mathcal{A}_2$ be two automata. We denote by $\mathcal{A}_i \xrightarrow{e_i} \mathcal{A}_1 \oplus \mathcal{A}_2$, $i \in \{1, 2\}$, the canonical inclusion morphisms in $\mathbb{A}$. If for each automaton $\mathcal{A}$ in $\mathbb{A}$ we have a computable equivalence relation $\equiv^{\nabla}_{\mathcal{A}}$ on the states of $\mathcal{A}$, we put

$$\mathcal{A}_1 \nabla_{\mathbb{A}} \mathcal{A}_2 \stackrel{\text{def}}{=} (\mathcal{A}_1 \oplus \mathcal{A}_2)/_{\equiv^{\nabla}_{\mathcal{A}_1 \oplus \mathcal{A}_2}}$$

If $\mathcal{A}_1 \oplus \mathcal{A}_2 \xrightarrow{\pi} (\mathcal{A}_1 \oplus \mathcal{A}_2)/_{\equiv^{\nabla}_{\mathcal{A}_1 \oplus \mathcal{A}_2}}$ is the morphism of automata induced by the canonical projection $\pi_{\equiv^{\nabla}_{\mathcal{A}_1 \oplus \mathcal{A}_2}}$, we put $\mathcal{A}_1 \overrightarrow{\nabla}_i \mathcal{A}_2 \stackrel{\text{def}}{=} \pi \circ e_i$, for $i \in \{1, 2\}$.

We cannot say much about $\nabla_{\mathbb{A}}$ in whole generality. We have to check by hand that each operator defined in this way satisfies the properties of Definition 11.

Proposition 14. *The operator $\nabla_{\mathbb{A}}$ defined from the equivalence relations $\equiv^{\nabla}_{\mathcal{A}}$ of Example 7 is a widening on $\mathbb{A}$.*

---

[12] Strictly speaking $Q/_\sim$ is a representative of the quotient set in $\mathcal{Q}$.

[13] The language recognized by the quotient automaton can be larger than the original one.

It only remains to define the abstract basis $\bot^\sharp = (\Phi^\sharp_\bot, \leftsquigarrow\!\!\rightsquigarrow^\sharp_\bot)$ in order to compute the iteration sequence. If S is the labelled π-term $\nu x_1 \dots \nu x_m.(\ell_1 : AS_1 \mid \cdots \mid \ell_n : AS_n)$, where the AS_i are either agents or servers, $\Phi^\sharp_\bot$ is defined as follows:

$$\Phi^\sharp_\bot(\ell) \stackrel{\text{def}}{=} \begin{cases} (\{\Omega\}, \{\Omega\}, \{\Omega\}, \emptyset) & \text{if } \ell \in \{\ell_1, \dots, \ell_n\} \\ (\emptyset, \emptyset, \emptyset, \emptyset) & \text{otherwise} \end{cases}$$

For all distinct $\ell, \ell' \in \{\ell_1, \dots, \ell_n\}$ and all $x \in fn(S_\ell) \cap fn(S_{\ell'})$, we put

$$(\ell, \Omega, \Omega, x) \leftsquigarrow\!\!\rightsquigarrow^\sharp_\bot (\ell', \Omega, \Omega, x) \stackrel{\text{def}}{=} \top^\sharp$$

Example 9. If we use the widening of Example 7 and enforce the automata to be deterministic with the procedure of Example 8, the limit of the abstract iteration sequence corresponding to the π-term S of Example 2 is given by the abstract configuration defined in Example 5. Our analysis is thus able to infer non-uniform communication topologies. □

8 Conclusion

We have presented an analysis of communications in the π-calculus based on Abstract Interpretation. This analysis is able to infer accurate descriptions of the communication topology of a system S of mobile processes, since it can distinguish instances of recursively spawned processes, as illustrated by Examples 5 and 9. This can be applied in particular to problems of security in distributed systems, where this kind of information is required to ensure that confidential data cannot be accessed by unauthorized elements of the system. Another possible application would be to use the information about the communication topology to statically derive an allocation strategy of the processes on a multiprocessor architecture which optimizes the communication cost. Future work will focus on the implementation of the analysis and the experimental study of its usefulness for these applications.

Further extensions to the abstract interpretation of the π-calculus are to be investigated. One can enrich the abstract domain to take into account the number of instances of a process. This may improve the analysis and give interesting information for compilation (channels used only once, finite communication topologies, etc.). However the major extension is to consider π-terms with free variables in order to achieve modular analysis. This requires to modify the non-standard semantics in order to model interaction with the environment. Finally, other directions for the approximation of the communication topology should be studied, like hypergraph grammars in the style of [Hab92].

Acknowledgements: I am grateful to Torben Amtoft, Radhia Cousot, Patrick Cousot and Ian Mackie for helpful comments on first versions of this paper. All diagrams have been designed using Paul Taylor's and Paul Gastin's LaTeX packages.

References

[BB92] G. Berry and G. Boudol. The chemical abstract machine. *Theoretical Computer Science*, 96:217–248, 1992.

[BCHK94] G. Boudol, I. Castellani, M. Hennessy, and A Kiehn. A theory of processes with localities. *Formal Aspects of Computing*, 6(2):165–200, 1994.

[BW90] M. Barr and C. Wells. *Category Theory for Computing Science.* Prentice Hall, 1990.

[CC76] P. Cousot and R. Cousot. Static determination of dynamic properties of programs. In *Proceedings of the 2nd International Symposium on Programming*, pages 106–130, Paris, 1976. Dunod.

[CC77] P. Cousot and R. Cousot. Abstract interpretation : a unified lattice model for static analysis of programs by construction or approximation of fixpoints. In *Conference Record of the 4th ACM Symposium on Principles of Programming Languages*, pages 238–252, Los Angeles, California, U.S.A., 1977.

[CC92] P. Cousot and R. Cousot. Abstract interpretation frameworks. *Journal of logic and computation*, 2(4):511–547, August 1992.

[CC95] P. Cousot and R. Cousot. Compositional and inductive semantic definitions in fixpoint, equational, constraint, closure-condition, rule-based and game theoretic form. In *Conference on Computer-Aided Verification, 7th International Conference, CAV'95*, volume 939 of *Lecture Notes in Computer Science*, pages 293–308. Springer-Verlag, 1995. Invited paper.

[CH78] P. Cousot and N. Halbwachs. Automatic discovery of linear restraints among variables of a program. In 5th *POPL*. ACM Press, 1978.

[Col95a] C. Colby. Analyzing the communication topology of concurrent programs. In *Symposium on Partial Evaluation and Program Manipulation*, 1995.

[Col95b] C. Colby. Determining storage properties of sequential and concurrent programs with assignment and structured data. In *Proceedings of the Second International Static Analysis Symposium*, volume 983 of *Lecture Notes in Computer Science*, pages 64–81. Springer-Verlag, 1995.

[Deu92a] A. Deutsch. *Operational models of programming languages and representations of relations on regular languages with application to the static determination of dynamic aliasing properties of data.* PhD thesis, University Paris VI (France), 1992.

[Deu92b] A. Deutsch. A storeless model of aliasing and its abstraction using finite representations of right-regular equivalence relations. In *Proceedings of the 1992 International Conference on Computer Languages*, pages 2–13. IEEE Computer Society Press, Los Alamitos, California, U.S.A., 1992.

[Deu94] A. Deutsch. Interprocedural may-alias analysis for pointers : beyond k-limiting. In *ACM SIGPLAN'94 Conference on Programming Language Design and Implementation.* ACM Press, 1994.

[Gra89] P. Granger. Static analysis of arithmetical congruences. *International Journal of Computer Mathematics*, 30:165–190, 1989.

[Gra91] P. Granger. Static analysis of linear congruence equalities among variables of a program. In *TAPSOFT'91*, volume 493. Lecture Notes in Computer Science, 1991.

[Hab92] A. Habel. *Hyperedge replacement: grammars and languages*, volume 643 of *Lecture Notes in Computer Science.* Springer-Verlag, 1992.

[JM81] N. Jones and S. Muchnick. Flow analysis and optimization of lisp-like structures. In *Program Flow Analysis: Theory and Applications*, pages 102–131. Prentice Hall, 1981.

[Jon81] H.B.M Jonkers. Abstract storage structures. In De Bakker and Van Vliet, editors, *Algorithmic languages*, pages 321–343. IFIP, 1981.

[Kar76] M. Karr. Affine relationships among variables of a program. *Acta Informatica*, pages 133–151, 1976.

[Mil91] R. Milner. The polyadic π-calculus: a tutorial. In *Proceedings of the International Summer School on Logic and Algebra of Specification*. Springer Verlag, 1991.

[Mil92] R. Milner. Functions as processes. *Journal of Mathematical Structures in Computer Science*, 2, 1992.

[MPW92] R. Milner, J. Parrow, and D. Walker. A calculus of mobile processes. *Information and Computation*, 100:1 - 77, 1992.

[NN94] H. R. Nielson and F. Nielson. Higher-order concurrent programs with finite communication topology. In 21st *ACM Symposium on Principles of Programming Languages*, 1994.

[San94a] D. Sangiorgi. *Expressing mobility in process algebras: first-order and higher-order paradigms*. PhD thesis, University of Edinburgh, 1994.

[San94b] D. Sangiorgi. Locality and true-concurrency in calculi for mobile processes. In *International Symposium on Theoretical Aspects of Computer Software*, Lecture Notes in Computer Science, 1994.

[Tur95] D. N. Turner. *The Polymorphic Pi-Calculus: Theory and Implementation*. PhD thesis, Edinburgh University, 1995.

[Ven96] A. Venet. Abstract cofibered domains: Application to the alias analysis of untyped programs. In *Proc. of the Third International Static Analysis Symposium SAS'96*, volume 1145 of *Lecture Notes in Computer Science*, pages 366–382. Springer-Verlag, 1996.

Abstract Interpretation of Small-Step Semantics

David A. Schmidt
Kansas State University[1]

Abstract. The techniques of classical abstract interpretation are extended to the big- and small-step operational semantics of higher-order and communicative languages: Well-known techniques, such as memoization, and lesser-known ones, such as abstraction on program syntax, are employed to generate finite abstract interpretations of source programs based on their formal operational semantic definitions. The result is a clear methodology for generating semantically safe (and live) abstract, regular trees for programs that do not possess obvious, finite, state-transition diagram depictions. The primary application of the research is to the validation of program properties; in particular, the application of model checking to validate safety properties in the box-mu calculus and liveness properties in the diamond-mu calculus is discussed.

1 Introduction

Two motivations triggered the research in this paper: *(i)* A desire to generalize the elegant abstract intepretation techniques of Cousot and Cousot [8] from flowchart languages to higher-order and communicative languages by abstractly interpreting big-step and small-step operational semantics; *(ii)* Application of the results of (i) to model checking infinite-state systems for safety and liveness properties.

The emphasis of this paper lies upon Topic (i), since it is crucial that semantically correct abstract interpretations exist before analysis techniques like model checking are employed. Nonetheless, a discussion of Topic (ii) and related research is presented once (i) has been achieved.

For Topic (i), the abstract interpretation methodology is an extension of earlier research on abstract interpretation of big-step (natural) semantics [25]. As we will see, a distinguishing feature of small-step semantics is the generation of new program syntax during the calculation of a source program's semantics. (This can happen when a concurrent program spawns new processes, for example.) This complicates convergence of the abstract interpretation but can be handled by abstractly interpreting the source language syntax itself, using techniques from analysis of logic programs [5, 6].

For Topic (ii), we see that abstract interpretation techniques are ideally suited for safety checking, where the box-mu-calculus (that is, the modal-mu-calculus less the diamond modality [30]), can be used as the safety specification language. Liveness checking of properties encoded in the diamond-mu-calculus can also be performed on an abstract interpretation, but the abstractions used for liveness

[1] Computing and Information Sciences Department, 234 Nichols Hall, Manhattan, KS 66506 USA. schmidt@cis.ksu.edu. Supported by NSF CCR-9302962 and ONR N00014-94-1-0866.

tend to be different than those used for safety, and this presents challenges for practical application. Some suggestions for future research will be made.

The paper is organized as follows: a review of the abstract interpretation methodology for big-step semantics comes first, then an adaption of the methodology for small-step semantics follows. Next, the methodology is applied to a CCS-subset and a π-calculus subset. Safety and liveness issues are discussed. Finally, related work is examined and future developments are suggested.

2 Analysis of Big-Step Semantics

The classic example of safety checking is the calculation of the input domains of program points by a data-flow analyzer. In abstract interpretation theory, the input domain sets for a program's phrases is called the program's *collecting semantics*. Property checking depends crucially on the collecting semantics, so we focus initially upon it.

We begin with abstract interpretation of big-step (natural) semantics. The methodology proceeds in three stages:

- Given a concrete, environment-based semantics,[2] define the concrete operational semantics of a program as the (possibly infinite) derivation tree drawn with the semantics rules; next, define the program's concrete collecting semantics as the set of (environment, program subphrase) pairs attached to the nodes of the tree.

- Replace the concrete value sets by abstract value sets and define the abstract operational semantics of the program as the (probably infinite) derivation tree drawn with the semantics rules. Define the abstract collecting semantics as the collecting semantics of the tree.

- Finitely approximate the program's abstract operational semantics as a regular tree; define the data-flow analysis of the program as the collecting semantics of the regular tree.

Since the technical details are available in [10, 25], the methodology is presented here via an example.

Figure 1 shows two of the rules that might be found in a big-step semantics of a functional programming language with recursive definitions, and Figure 2 shows the concrete, operational semantics of the program `(rec f x.f(x+1)+1)2`, which is an infinite derivation tree. In the derivation, a box at a node represents an unknown value to be supplied by a result from a child node; as noted in [25], a least-fixed point interpretation of derivation tree construction would insert $\perp$ into all boxes in the figure.

[2] Identifier bindings are represented by an environment rather than by syntactic substitution.

$$\rho \vdash \mathbf{rec}\ f\ x.e \Downarrow \mu_f\langle x,\ e,\ \rho\rangle$$

$$\frac{\rho \vdash e_1 \Downarrow \mu_f\langle x',\ e',\ \rho'\rangle \quad \rho \vdash e_2 \Downarrow v \quad \rho' \oplus \{f = \mu_f\langle x',\ e',\ \rho'\rangle\} \oplus \{x' = v\} \vdash e' \Downarrow v'}{\rho \vdash e_1\ e_2 \Downarrow v'}$$

Figure 1: Sample big-step semantics rules

Let $\rho_i = \rho \oplus \{f = cl\} \oplus \{x = i\}$ and $cl = \mu_f\langle$`x, f(x+1)+1`$, \rho\rangle$ in

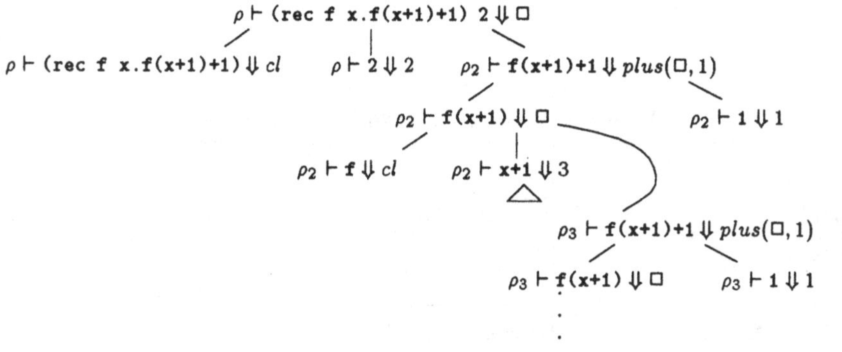

Figure 2: Concrete semantics derivation

The concrete collecting semantics of the program is depicted as follows:

Subphrase	*Environments*
`(rec f x.f(x+1)+1) 2`	$\{\rho\}$
`rec f x.f(x+1)+1`	$\{\rho\}$
`2`	$\{\rho\}$
`f(x+1)+1`	$\{\rho_i \mid i \geq 2\}$
`f`	$\{\rho_i \mid i \geq 2\}$
...	...

Next, say that the program is to be abstractly interpreted for sign properties: the concrete value set of integers, *Int*, is replaced by the set $\{neg, zero, pos\}_{\bot}^{\top}$; the semantics rules are revised to calculate upon sign properties, most notably,

$$\frac{\rho \vdash e_1 \Downarrow v_1 \quad \rho \vdash e_2 \Downarrow v_2}{\rho \vdash e_1 + e_2 \Downarrow plus(v_1, v_2)} \quad \text{becomes} \quad \frac{\alpha \vdash e_1 \Downarrow a_1 \quad \alpha \vdash e_2 \Downarrow a_2}{\alpha \vdash e_1 + e_2 \Downarrow absplus(a_1, a_2)}$$

where α is the abstract environment argument, which maps identifiers to signs, and *absplus* is addition on signs (e.g., $absplus(pos, pos) = pos$, $absplus(pos, neg) = \top$, etc.). The abstract semantics is calculated as the infinite derivation tree in Figure 3, and the abstract collecting semantics goes as follows:

Let $\alpha_{pos} = \rho \oplus \{f = cl\} \oplus \{x = pos\}$ and $cl = \mu_f\langle$x, f(x+1)+1, $\alpha\rangle$ in

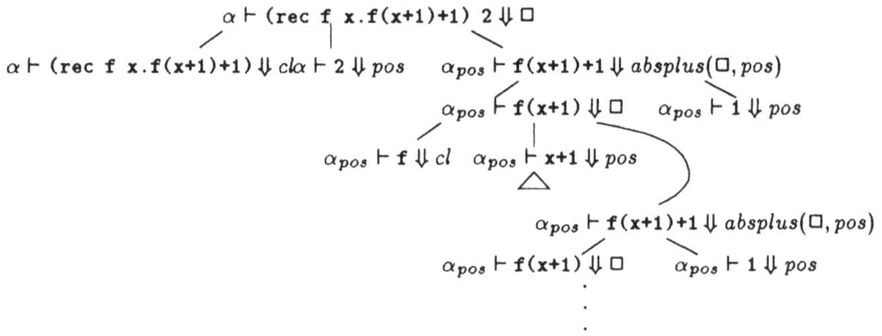

Figure 3: Abstract semantics derivation

Subphrase	*Environments*
(rec f x.f(x+1)+1) 2	$\{\alpha\}$
...	...
f(x+1)+1	$\{\alpha_{pos}\}$
f	$\{\alpha_{pos}\}$
...	...

Of course, a data flow analysis does not have the luxury of drawing the infinite abstract tree, so one must ensure that one can always draw a finitely presented tree that contains the collecting information in the infinite derivation. In the example in Figure 3, one notes immediately that the tree is *regular*, that is, every infinite path contains a node that repeats. Therefore, one can terminate the unfolding of the infinite path at the "repetition node." In the example, the repetition node is $\alpha_{pos} \vdash$ f(x+1)+1 $\Downarrow$ *absplus*$(\Box, pos)$. Indeed, once the repetition node appears, one can calculate the values that should be inserted into the boxes in the tree by a least-fixed-point calculation: whatever value, v, should appear at the repeating node, $\alpha_{pos} \vdash$ f(x+1)+1 $\Downarrow v$, it must be the case that $v = absplus(v, pos)$. The least such value that satisfies this equality is $\perp$, so $\perp$ fills the boxes in the figure.

In the general case, one is not guaranteed that an abstract derivation tree will be regular—sometimes one must "force" it to happen. As an example, consider a constant propagation analysis of the program in Figure 2, where the integer value set, *Int*, is replaced by $Int_\perp^\top$; the "abstract" derivation of the program looks exactly like Figure 2, and it is not a regular tree.

To force the issue, we apply the well-known technique from iterative data-flow analysis of memoizing the environments that appear with the subphrases of the program at the nodes of the derivation tree. When a subphrase, e, repeats in a path of the tree, the values of the environments that appeared with the earlier occurrences of e are joined to the current value of the environment that

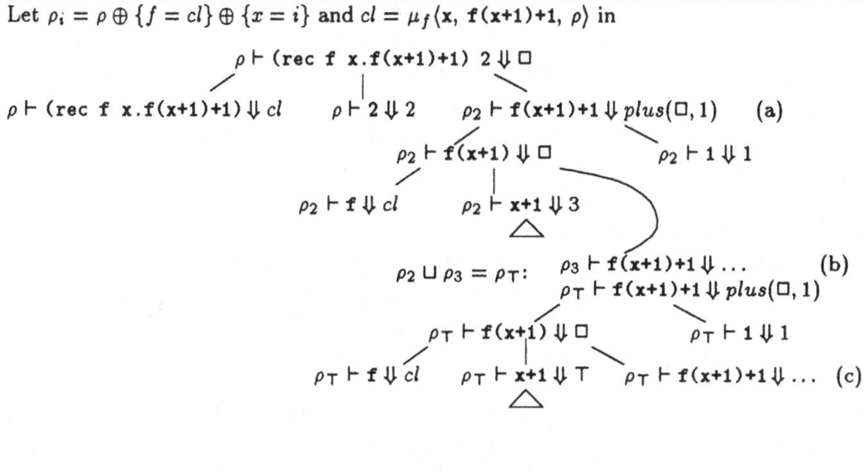

Figure 4: Abstract, regular tree derivation

appears with the repeated occurrence of e.[3] Because of the finite chain property of the abstract value sets, this forces a repetition node to appear in the path, and a regular tree results.

Figure 4 shows this technique applied to the constant propagation analysis of the program in Figure 2. The syntax phrase `f(x+1)+1` at node (a) repeats at (b), so the environment ρ_2 at (a) is joined to the environment ρ_3 at (b), giving $\rho_2 \sqcup \rho_3 = \rho_\top$, which is used to continue the derivation. This quickly produces a repetition node at (c). Now, we can determine the values that should be inserted into the boxes in the tree. The value to calculate first is the one for node (c): since node (c) is a repetition of node (b), we must find the least value, v, such that $v = plus(v, 1)$ holds. The answer is $\bot$, and substituting $\bot$ for the box at node (c) fills the rest of the boxes with $\bot$ also.

The collecting semantics of the regular tree is

Subphrase	*Environments*
`(rec f x.f(x+1)+1) 2`	ρ
...	...
`f(x+1)+1`	$\rho_\top$
`f`	$\rho_\top$
...	...

This is a safe approximation of the abstract collecting semantics and is the information calculated by a classic iterative data-flow analysis.

A crucial feature of the environment-based, big-step semantics that ensures the construction of regular trees is that the semantics is *semicompositional*,[4] that is, all syntax phrases that are analyzed in the calculation of the program's semantics are subphrases of the original source program. Thus, there are at

[3] This technique can be formalized as a *widening* of the least-fixed point calculation of the abstract semantics tree[8].

[4] This term is due to Neil Jones.

most a finite number of subphrases that can appear at nodes of the derivation tree.[5] This, plus the finite chain property of the abstract value sets, ensures that regular trees must result from the memoization construction.

The correctness criterion for the methodology is straightforward: To relate the concrete semantics derivation tree to the abstract tree, define a safety relation rel_{Tree} as follows: for concrete tree, t, and abstract tree, u,

$$
\begin{aligned}
& t\ rel_{Tree}\ u \text{ iff } root(t)\ rel_{Node}\ root(q) \\
& \quad \text{and for every subtree}, t_i, \text{ there exists a subtree}, u_j, \text{ such that } t_i\ rel_{Tree}\ u_j \\
& \text{where } (\rho \vdash e \Downarrow v)\ rel_{Node}\ (\alpha \vdash e \Downarrow a) \text{ iff } \rho\ rel_{Env}\ \alpha \text{ and } v\ rel_{Value}\ a \\
& \text{and } \rho\ rel_{Env}\ \alpha \text{ iff } domain(\rho) = domain(\alpha) \\
& \qquad \text{and for all } i \in domain(\rho), \rho(i)\ rel_{Value}\ \alpha(i)
\end{aligned}
$$

The definition of rel_{Value} depends on the particular application area, e.g., for sign analysis, $-n\ rel_{Value}\ neg$, $+n\ rel_{Value}\ pos$, etc.[6]

The safety relation rel_{Tree} states that every path in the concrete derivation tree is approximated by a path in the abstract derivation tree. Since rel_{Tree} is defined recursively and infinite trees are involved, one wants the largest such relation satisfying the definition (that is, the greatest-fixed-point interpretation), and the related coinductive proof techniques prove the main safety result, namely: for all expressions, e, and environments ρ and α such that $\rho\ rel_{Env}\ \alpha$, $t\ rel_{Tree}\ u$ must hold, where t is the concrete derivation tree whose root is $\rho \vdash e \Downarrow v$ and u is the abstract derivation tree with root $\alpha \vdash e \Downarrow a$. A corollary of the safety result is that the collecting semantics of the abstract tree safely approximates the collecting semantics of the concrete tree.

Once the safety of the abstract interpretation is established, one notes that the regular tree built with the memoization technique safely approximates the abstract semantics derivation tree.[7] This result implies that the concrete tree is safely approximated by the regular tree.[8]

Of course, the pragmatics of data-flow analysis demands an implementation technique that is more efficient than the regular-tree-building methodology described in this section. Nonetheless, the methodology is important because it produces simple correctness proofs [10, 25] and separates design concerns from implementation concerns. For this reason, we pursue its application to small-step semantics.

---

[5] In contrast, a substitution-based semantics would not have this property. For example, the substitution semantics rule for **rec** would be $\dfrac{e_1 \Downarrow rec\ f\ x.e \quad e_2 \Downarrow v \quad [rec\ f\ x.e/f][v/x]e \Downarrow v'}{e_1\ e_2 \Downarrow v'}$.

[6] For closure values, there are two possibilities for rel_{Value} : the simpler definition is $\langle x, e, \rho\rangle\ rel_{Value}\ \langle x, e, \alpha\rangle$ iff $\rho\ rel_{Env}\ \alpha$. In a simply typed language, a more complex definition can be helpful: $\langle x, e, \rho\rangle\ rel_{Value}\ \langle x', e', \alpha\rangle$ iff for all v, a such that $v\ rel_{Value}\ a$, $apply_{con}(\langle x, e, \rho\rangle, v)\ rel_{Tree}\ apply_{abs}(\langle x', e', \alpha\rangle, a)$, where $apply_{con}$ and $apply_{abs}$ are the tree-building operations for concrete and abstract function application, respectively.

[7] This is formalized like above: for abstract tree, u, and regular tree, r, $u\ rel_{Atree}\ r$ iff $root(u)\ rel_{Anode}\ root(r)$ and for every subtree, u_i, there exists a subtree r_j, such that $u_i\ rel_{Atree}\ r_j$. Next, $(\alpha \vdash e \Downarrow a)\ rel_{Anode}\ (\alpha' \vdash e \Downarrow a')$ iff $\alpha \sqsubseteq \alpha'$ and $a \sqsubseteq a'$.

[8] We must require, however, that rel_{Value} is *U-closed*, that is, $v\ rel_{Value}\ a_1$ and $a_1 \sqsubseteq a_2$ imply $v\ rel_{Value}\ a_2$ [25].

$$e ::= 0 \mid \alpha.e \mid e_1 \,||\, e_2 \mid \mu p\,(e) \mid p$$

$$\alpha.e \stackrel{\alpha}{\to} e \qquad \frac{e_1 \stackrel{\alpha}{\to} e_1'}{e_1 \,||\, e_2 \stackrel{\alpha}{\to} e_1' \,||\, e_2} \qquad \frac{e \stackrel{\alpha}{\to} e'}{\mu p(e) \stackrel{\alpha}{\to} [\mu p(e)/p]e'} \qquad etc.$$

plus usual symmetric monoidal laws: $0 \,||\, e \equiv e$, $e_1 \,||\, e_2 \equiv e_2 \,||\, e_1$, etc.

Figure 5: Subset of CCS-like language

Let $P = \mu x(\alpha.(\beta.x \,||\, x))$ in

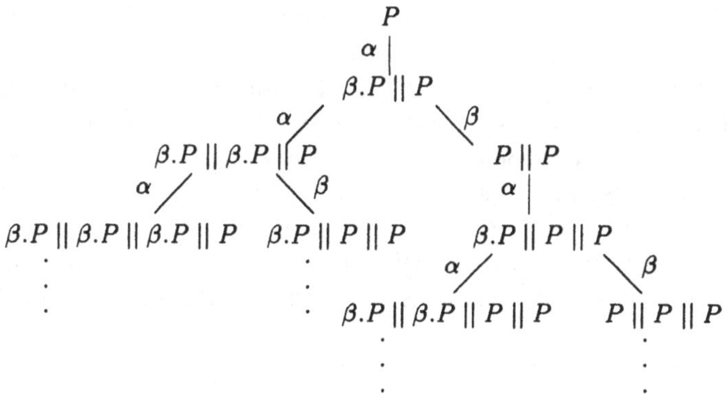

Figure 6: Example operational semantics

3 A CCS Subset and its Analysis

A Plotkin-style structural operational semantics [23] and a term rewriting system [18] are two examples of small-step semantics definitions—both rewrite a program configuration, step by step, to an answer or normal form. If a configuration contains multiple redexes so that there exist multiple possible next stages, we will draw the rewriting as a *behavior tree*, with one path for each of the contracted redexes. Figure 5 shows a CCS-like notation [20] whose small-step semantics spawns processes via unfolding of a recursion constructor, μ.[9] Because the μ-rules generates new program syntax, the semantics derivations will not be semicompositional. Figure 6 displays a simple example that shows how the operational semantics of the program $\mu x.(\alpha.(\beta.x \,||\, x))$ generates new processes, that is, new program syntax. All paths in the behavior tree are infinite, and the newly generated processes make impossible a regular tree representation. Clearly, to undertake an abstract interpretation, some means must be found to

[9] The rule for μ in the figure unfolds a μ-process exactly once when it makes a communication step. This differs from the bisimular rule often used: $\frac{[\mu p(e)/p]e \stackrel{\alpha}{\to} e'}{\mu p(e) \stackrel{\alpha}{\to} e'}$, which operates on closed terms only but allows unbounded unfolding.

approximate finitely the dynamically generated processes.

An abstract interpretation must approximate the program configurations that arise during execution. To do this, we abstractly interpret the source program syntax itself.[10] To set the stage for the abstract interpretation, it is helpful to view a program configuration as a "process pool" [21, 22], that is, as a bag of processes. For example, the configuration $\beta.P \parallel \beta.P \parallel P$ is written as the bag $\{\beta.P, \beta.P, P\}$.

Next, as is common to abstract interpretation applications, assume that the subphrases of the original source program are indexed by "labels," ℓ_i, e.g.,

$$P = \ell_0\colon \mu x\ (\ell_1\colon \alpha.\ell_2\colon (\ell_3\colon \beta.\ \ell_4\colon x \parallel \ell_5\colon x))$$

Then a process pool is coded by a function of the form $Label \rightarrow Nat$, e.g., the bag just above is encoded by the function $[\ell_3 \mapsto 2][\ell_0 \mapsto 1](\lambda\ell.0)$.[11]

To perform an abstract interpretation, one must define a finite-height, sup-semilattice of abstract process pools. For the current example, we define an abstract process pool to be a function of the form $Label \rightarrow \{0, 1, \omega\}$. Since both domain and codomain of this function space are finite, there exist a finite number of abstract process pools, that is, program configurations. The concrete process pool above is abstracted by $[\ell_3 \mapsto \omega][\ell_0 \mapsto 1](\lambda\ell.0)$, and the logical relationship between concrete and abstract process pools is of course: for $cp \in Pool$, $ap \in AbsPool$,

$$cp\ rel_{Pool}\ ap \text{ iff for all } \ell \in Label, cp(\ell) \leq ap(\ell)$$

The bag union operation, $\uplus$, is interpreted abstractly in the expected way: $ap_1 \uplus ap_2 = \lambda\ell.ap_1(\ell) \oplus ap_2(\ell)$, where $1 \oplus 1 = \omega$, and $m \oplus n = \max\{m, n\}$ otherwise.[12]

Figure 7 shows the abstract interpretation of the derivation in Figure 6. For simplicity, an abstract process pool is written as a kind of regular expression, where a "+" marks a process whose count is ω. This reveals our abstraction technique to be the "star abstraction" of Codish, Falaschi, and Marriott [6, 5]. Using this representation of abstract process pools, the semantics rules in Figure 5 can be used as the abstract semantics rules along with one new rule which accounts for processes whose count is ω:

$$\frac{e \stackrel{\alpha}{\rightarrow} e'}{e^+ \stackrel{\alpha}{\rightarrow} e^+ \parallel e'}$$

Since there are a finite number of abstract process pools, that is, syntax configurations, the abstract behavior tree must be regular.

[10] Indeed, the purpose of a *closure analysis* [24, 26, 27] of a functional program is to abstractly interpret syntax phrases—lambda abstractions, in particular—that are passed about and evaluated during execution of the program. Both closure analysis and the analysis in this section are "control flow analysis," and additional work is planned to demonstrate the relationship between the two.

[11] In the example, ℓ_3 labels $\beta.x$ rather than $\beta.P$. The discrepency is due to the substitution semantics of μ-process unfolding. This is tolerated for now—treat x and P as "the same"—but will be repaired in the next section with an environment semantics.

[12] That is, let $[\![e]\!]$ denote e's process pool representation. Then, $[\![e_1 \parallel e_2]\!] = [\![e_1]\!] \uplus [\![e_2]\!]$.

Let $P = \mu x(\alpha.(\beta.x \parallel x))$ in

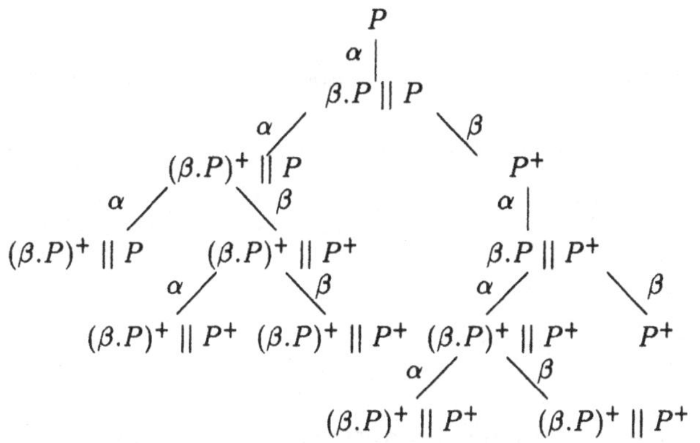

Figure 7: Abstract interpretation of process creation

The safety proof for the abstract interpretation goes the same way as the one for big-step semantics: one must show that every path in the concrete behavior tree is approximated by a path in the abstract behavior tree. This can be proved in terms of a relation, rel_{Tree}, defined like the one in the previous section:

> $t\ rel_{Tree}\ u$ iff $root(t)\ rel_{Pool}\ root(q)$
> and for every transition, $root(t) \overset{\alpha}{\rightarrow} t_i$, there exists a transition, $root(u) \overset{\alpha}{\rightarrow} u_j$, such that $t_i\ rel_{Tree}\ u_j$

If one can prove the following simulation property

$$cp\ rel_{Pool}\ ap \text{ and } cp \overset{\alpha}{\rightarrow} cp' \text{ imply there exists } ap' \text{ such that } ap \overset{\alpha}{\rightarrow} ap' \text{ and } cp'\ rel_{Pool}\ ap'$$

then one obtains by coinduction the corollary that the concrete behavior tree is related to the abstract tree. The simulation property is easy to prove for the semantics rules used here.

3.1 Safety Analysis and Liveness Analysis

Once an abstract, regular tree has been constructed, an analysis of the tree can proceed. Compiler code improvement is usually based upon properties of the tree's collecting semantics, but Steffen [28, 29] has noted that collecting-semantics techniques can be encoded as model-checking problems, so we focus on the latter.

Say that the interesting properties of derivation tree nodes are defined by a language, $\mathcal{P}$, of atomic propositions; we write $n \models p$ when property p holds true at node n.

To use the results of an abstract interpretation to check propositions in $\mathcal{P}$, one needs this consistency property for concrete tree nodes, c, and abstract tree nodes. a:

$$c\ rel_{Node}\ a \text{ implies, for all } p \in \mathcal{P}, \text{ that } a \models p \text{ implies } c \models p$$

Ideally, the first implication in the line above should be an equivalence [9], so that the abstract interpretation computes directly upon propositions, but this is not essential.

The examples developed so far in this paper are oriented towards safety properties: for concrete tree, t, and abstract tree, u, $t\ rel_{Tree}\ u$ iff every computation path in t is safely approximated by a path in u. Thus, one can model check such abstract trees with the box-mu-calculus [30]:

$$\begin{array}{l} p \in \mathcal{P}, \quad \alpha \in \text{Channel}, \quad \phi \in \text{State-formula} \\ \quad \phi \ ::= \ p \ \mid \ \neg p \ \mid \ [\alpha]\phi \ \mid \ \phi_1 \wedge \phi_2 \ \mid \ \phi_1 \vee \phi_2 \ \mid \ \mu x.\phi \ \mid \ \nu x.\phi \end{array}$$

Using the consistency property on atomic propositions, it is easy to prove that the property lifts to the box-mu-calculus: $t\ rel_{Tree}\ u$ and $root(u) \models \phi$ imply $root(t) \models \phi$.

A liveness analysis can be undertaken in a similar fashion: starting from a consistent relation, rel_{Node}, one must generate abstract trees that satisfy this liveness relation:

$$\begin{array}{l} t\ live_{Tree}\ u \text{ iff } root(t)\ rel_{Node}\ root(q) \\ \qquad \text{and for every transition, } root(u) \stackrel{\alpha}{\rightarrow} u_i, \text{ there exists a transition,} \\ \qquad root(t) \stackrel{\alpha}{\rightarrow} t_j, \text{ such that } t_j\ live_{Tree}\ u_i \end{array}$$

That is, existence of an α-transition in the abstract tree implies that all related concrete trees must be capable of making α-transitions to related nodes.

A liveness analysis for the CCS-notation defined in the previous section requires a different abstraction of a process pool: an abstract pool is a mapping in $Label \rightarrow \{0, 1, \ldots, n\}$, for fixed $n \geq 0$. For example, for $n = 2$, the abstract pool representation of $\beta.0 \parallel \beta.0 \parallel \alpha.0 \parallel \beta.0$ is $(\beta.0)^2 \parallel \alpha.0$.

The relation between concrete pools and the new form of abstract pool is

$$cp\ rel_{Pool}\ ap \text{ iff for all } \ell \in Label, cp(\ell) \geq ap(\ell)$$

and the abstract semantics rules are the concrete rules along with

$$\frac{e \stackrel{\alpha}{\rightarrow} e'}{e^n \stackrel{\alpha}{\rightarrow} e^{n-1} \parallel e'} \text{ for } n > 0, \text{ where } e^1 \equiv e \text{ and } e^0 \equiv 0$$

It is straightforward to prove that the above relation and rule generate abstract trees that are live-related to concrete ones.

The natural language for checking liveness properties is the diamond-mu-calculus:

$$\phi \ ::= \ p \ \mid \ \neg p \ \mid \ \langle\alpha\rangle\phi \ \mid \ \phi_1 \wedge \phi_2 \ \mid \ \phi_1 \vee \phi_2 \ \mid \ \mu x.\phi \ \mid \ \nu x.\phi$$

We have that consistency holds for the diamond-mu-calculus: $t\ live_{Tree}\ u$ and $root(u) \models \phi$ imply $root(t) \models \phi$.

As noted by Dams [12], the set of abstract nodes/pools for the safety and liveness analyses should be the same, as should be the relation, rel_{Node} , because this lets one model check the full mu-calculus, but this appears to be difficult to ensure in practice.

3.2 Argument Transmission via Channels

Now that the basic analysis method is in place, we consider value passing along CCS channels. The syntax is altered to read

$$e \ ::= \ 0 \ \mid \ \alpha?x.e \ \mid \ \alpha!n.e \ \mid \ e_1 \,||\, e_2 \ \mid \ \mu p(e) \ \mid \ p$$

where $\alpha?x.e$ inputs a value on channel α and binds it to identifier x within scope e, and $\alpha!n.e$ outputs (the value of) numeric expression n on channel α and proceeds with e. The relevant semantics rules are

$$\alpha?x.e \stackrel{\alpha?v}{\rightarrow} [v/x]e \qquad \alpha!x.v \stackrel{\alpha!v}{\rightarrow} e \qquad \frac{e_1 \stackrel{\alpha?v}{\rightarrow} e_1' \quad e_2 \stackrel{\alpha!v}{\rightarrow} e_2'}{e_1 \,||\, e_2 \stackrel{\tau}{\rightarrow} e_1' \,||\, e_2'}$$

where v is a numeral and τ represents an internal step, a "tau move." To keep the examples small, we will present from here on examples containing only tau moves. But the techniques apply with no restriction to behavior trees with non-tau moves as well.

The above semantics rules define argument transmission via substitution, but substitutions generate new program syntax, which hampers an abstract interpretation. For this reason, we revise the semantics rules into an environment semantics: each process, e, owns a local environment, ρ, that holds bindings of identifiers to numerals, and we write a process configuration $\rho \vdash e$. Further, assume that the evaluation of arithmetic expressions will be performed by an orthogonal set of semantics rules: for environment, ρ, and numeric expression, n, we write $\rho \vdash n \Downarrow v$ to assert that numeric expression n evaluates to numeral value v in environment ρ. Although it is not essential, we eliminate the substitution semantics for $\mu p(e)$ by saving a "closure" of $\mu p(e)$ in the environment of the unfolded process, e.

Figure 8 shows the resulting semantics. To simplify matters, we assume that argument identifiers are distinct from process indentifiers; also, each recursive process, $\mu p(e)$, uses a unique process identifier, p. Environments hold bindings of argument identifiers to numbers and process identifiers to local environments.

The computation rules are kept simple by employing the usual symmetric, monoidal congruences plus three more: the first additional congruence explains how an environment is copied to component processes of a system; the second shows how the semantics rules for numeric-expression evaluation interact with process configurations; and the third describes recursive process unfolding in terms of process-identifier lookup. The computation rules themselves are as

$c \in$ Expression-configuration $\quad \rho \in$ Environment
$e \in$ Expression $\quad n \in$ Arithmetic-expression
$x \in$ Argument-identifier $\quad v \in$ Numeral
$p \in$ Process-identifier $\quad \alpha \in$ Channel

$$\begin{array}{lcl} e & ::= & 0 \mid \alpha?x.e \mid \alpha!n.e \mid e_1 \,||\, e_2 \mid \mu p(e) \mid p \\ c & ::= & \rho \vdash e \mid c_1 \,||\, c_2 \\ \rho & ::= & \{x_i = v_i\} \cup \{p_j \mapsto \rho_j\} \end{array}$$

Congruences: usual symmetric, monoidal rules, plus:

$$\rho \vdash (e_1 \,||\, e_2) \equiv (\rho \vdash e_1) \,||\, (\rho \vdash e_2) \qquad \frac{\rho \vdash n \Downarrow v}{\rho \vdash \alpha!n.e \equiv \rho \vdash \alpha!v.e} \qquad \frac{(p \mapsto \rho) \in \rho'}{\rho' \vdash p \equiv \rho \vdash \mu p(e)}$$

Computation rules:

$$\rho \vdash \alpha?x.e \xrightarrow{\alpha?v} \rho \oplus \{x = v\} \vdash e \qquad \rho \vdash \alpha!v.e \xrightarrow{\alpha!v} \rho \vdash e \qquad \frac{\rho \vdash e \xrightarrow{\Delta} \rho' \vdash e'}{\rho \vdash \mu p(e) \xrightarrow{\Delta} \rho' \oplus \{p \mapsto \rho\} \vdash e'}$$

$$\frac{c_1 \xrightarrow{\alpha?v} c_1' \quad c_2 \xrightarrow{\alpha!v} c_2'}{c_1 \,||\, c_2 \xrightarrow{\tau} c_1' \,||\, c_2'} \qquad \frac{c_1 \xrightarrow{\Delta} c_1'}{c_1 \,||\, c_2 \xrightarrow{\Delta} c_1' \,||\, c_2} \qquad \frac{c_2 \xrightarrow{\Delta} c_2'}{c_1 \,||\, c_2 \xrightarrow{\Delta} c_1 \,||\, c_2'}$$

Figure 8: Semantics for value passing

expected; the only novel rule is the one for recursive processes: it creates a closure, $\{p \mapsto \rho\}$, when the recursively defined process, $\rho \vdash \mu p(e)$, is evaluated.

Figure 9 displays an example behavior tree.

In order to perform an abstract interpretation, it is helpful to use again the concepts of concrete and abstract process pool. Here, a concrete process pool is a bag of (environment,process) pairs. Assuming that processes are labelled, one can represent a process pool as a function of form $Label \rightarrow Bag(Environment)$, where $Environment = (ArgumentId \rightarrow Nat) \times (ProcessId \rightarrow Environment)$.[13] This suggests that an an abstract process pool is a function of form $Label \rightarrow (AbstractEnv \times \{0, 1, \omega\})$, where $AbstractEnv = (ArgumentId \rightarrow AbstractNat) \times (ProcessId \rightarrow AbstractEnv)$.[14] That is, multiple occurrences of the same process are combined, which means their environments must be joined into one. For example, for the labelling

$$P = \ell_0\colon \mu p\, \ell_1\colon (\ell_2\colon \alpha?x.\ell_3\colon \alpha!x + 1.\ell_4\colon p \,||\, \ell_5\colon p)$$

the configuration $\rho_2 \vdash P \,||\, \rho_3 \vdash \alpha!x + 1.p \,||\, \rho_4 \vdash P$ is encoded as the process pool $[\ell_0 \mapsto \{\rho_2, \rho_4\}][\ell_3 \mapsto \{\rho_3\}](\lambda\ell.\emptyset)$. For the purposes of constant

[13] We work only with well-founded, that is, inductively defined, environments.

[14] Since the sets *ArgumentId* and *ProcessId* are finite, and the language is first order and statically scoped, if *AbstractNat* has the finite chain property, so must *AbstractEnv*.

Let $P = \mu p(\alpha?x.(\beta!x.0 \,||\, \alpha!x + 1.0 \,||\, p))$ and $\rho_i = \{x = i, p \mapsto \emptyset\}$ in

$$\emptyset \vdash (\alpha!3.0 \,||\, P) \quad \equiv \emptyset \vdash \alpha!3.0 \,||\, \emptyset \vdash P$$

$$\Big|\ \tau\ (\alpha!3)$$

$$\rho_3 \vdash (\beta!x.0 \,||\, \alpha!x + 1.0 \,||\, p) \quad \equiv \rho_3 \vdash \beta!x.0 \,||\, \rho_3 \vdash \alpha!x + 1.0 \,||\, \rho_3 \vdash p$$

$$\equiv \rho_3 \vdash \beta!x.0 \,||\, \rho_3 \vdash \alpha!x + 1.0 \,||\, \emptyset \vdash P \quad \equiv \rho_3 \vdash \beta!3.0 \,||\, \rho_3 \vdash \alpha!4.0 \,||\, \emptyset \vdash P$$

$$\Big|\ \tau\ (\alpha!4)$$

$$\rho_3 \vdash \beta!3.0 \,||\, \rho_4 \vdash \beta!x.0 \,||\, \rho_4 \vdash \alpha!x + 1.0 \,||\, \rho_4 \vdash p$$

$$\equiv \rho_3 \vdash \beta!3.0 \,||\, \rho_4 \vdash \beta!4.0 \,||\, \rho_4 \vdash \alpha!5.0 \,||\, \emptyset \vdash P$$

$$\Big|\ \tau\ (\alpha!5)$$

$$\rho_3 \vdash \beta!3.0 \,||\, \rho_4 \vdash \beta!4.0 \,||\, \rho_5 \vdash \beta!x.0 \,||\, \rho_5 \vdash \alpha!x + 1.0 \,||\, \rho_5 \vdash p$$

$$\vdots$$

Figure 9: Program with value passing

propagation analysis, the corresponding abstract process pool would appear $[\ell_0 \mapsto (\rho_\top, \omega)][\ell_3 \mapsto (\rho_3, 1)](\lambda\ell.(\bot, 0))$.

The relation between concrete and abstract pools is again a safety relation:

$$\begin{array}{c} cp\ rel_{Pool}\ ap \text{ iff for all } \ell \in Label, |cp(\ell)| \leq ap(\ell) \downarrow 2 \\ \text{and for all } \rho \in cp(\ell), \rho\ rel_{Env}\ ap(\ell) \downarrow 1 \end{array}$$

where concrete and abstract environments are related in the expected way:[15]

$$\begin{array}{l} (\{x_i = v_i\}, \{p_j \mapsto \rho_j\})\ rel_{Env}\ (\{x_i = a_i\}, \{p_j \mapsto \rho'_j\} \\ \text{ iff } (i) \text{ for all } x_i, v_i\ rel_{Nat}\ a_i, \text{ and } (ii) \text{ for all } p_j, \rho_j\ rel_{Env}\ \rho'_j \end{array}$$

As in the previous section, a new computation rule is needed for the abstract interpretation:

$$\frac{\rho \vdash e \overset{\Delta}{\rightarrow} \rho' \vdash e'}{\rho \vdash e^+ \overset{\Delta}{\rightarrow} \rho \vdash e^+ \,||\, \rho' \vdash e'}$$

Figure 10 shows the constant propagation analysis of the example in the previous figure. Nodes of interest are labelled: node (a) is an unfolding equivalence that can be enacted by the analysis, but node (b) is placed in parentheses because it is for exposition only—the analysis does *not* generate new source program syntax.[16] The transition from (a) must be a τ-step, transmitting $\alpha!4$; The

[15] Although the relation rel_{Env} is defined recusively, the syntax definitions of concrete and abstract environments are defined inductively, so the least relation satisfying the recursive definition can be used.

[16] Nonetheless, an implementation would of course calculate that the x in $\beta!x$ and the $x + 1$ in $\alpha!x + 1$ evaluate to 3 and 4 respectively.

Let $P = \mu p(\alpha?x.(\beta!x.0 \,||\, \alpha!x + 1.0 \,||\, p))$ and $\rho_i = \{x = i, p \mapsto \emptyset\}$ in

$$\emptyset \vdash \alpha!3.0 \,||\, \emptyset \vdash P$$

$$\Big|\ \tau\ (\alpha!3)$$

$$\rho_3 \vdash \beta!x.0 \,||\, \rho_3 \vdash \alpha!x + 1.0 \,||\, \rho_3 \vdash p$$

(a) $\equiv \rho_3 \vdash \beta!x.0 \,||\, \rho_3 \vdash \alpha!x + 1.0 \,||\, \emptyset \vdash P$

(b) $(\equiv \rho_3 \vdash \beta!3.0 \,||\, \rho_3 \vdash \alpha!4.0 \,||\, \emptyset \vdash P)$

$$\Big|\ \tau\ (\alpha!4)$$

(c) $\rho_\top \vdash (\beta!x.0)^+ \,||\, \rho_4 \vdash \alpha!x + 1.0 \,||\, \rho_4 \vdash p$

$\equiv \rho_\top \vdash (\beta!x.0)^+ \,||\, \rho_4 \vdash \alpha!x + 1.0 \,||\, \emptyset \vdash P$

(d) $(\equiv \rho_\top \vdash (\beta!\top.0)^+ \,||\, \rho_4 \vdash \alpha!5.0 \,||\, \emptyset \vdash P)$

$$\Big|\ \tau\ (\alpha!5)$$

(e) $\rho_\top \vdash (\beta!x.0)^+ \,||\, \rho_5 \vdash \alpha!x + 1.0 \,||\, \rho_5 \vdash p$

(f) $\rho_\top \vdash (\beta!x.0)^+ \,||\, \rho_\top \vdash \alpha!x + 1.0 \,||\, \rho_\top \vdash p$

$\equiv \rho_\top \vdash (\beta!x.0)^+ \,||\, \rho_\top \vdash \alpha!x + 1.0 \,||\, \emptyset \vdash P$

$(\equiv \rho_\top \vdash (\beta!\top.0)^+ \,||\, \rho_\top \vdash \alpha!\top.0 \,||\, \emptyset \vdash P)$

$$\Big|\ \tau\ (\alpha!\top)$$

(g) $\rho_\top \vdash (\beta!x.0)^+ \,||\, \rho_\top \vdash \alpha!x + 1.0 \,||\, \rho_\top \vdash p$

Figure 10: Constant propagation analysis

resulting configuration reads $\rho_3 \vdash \beta!x.0 \,||\, \rho_4 \vdash \beta!x.0 \,||\, \rho_4 \vdash \alpha!x + 1.0 \,||\, \rho_4 \vdash p$, but the two occurrences of process $\beta!x.0$ must be combined, producing the abstract process configuration at node (c)—note that $\rho_3 \sqcup \rho_4 = \rho_\top$. Node (d), also parenthesized, states that the x in $\beta!x.0$ evaluates to $\top$. Node (d) is coded as it is because, if $\rho \vdash n \Downarrow v$ holds, then $\rho \vdash (\alpha!n.e)^+$ is bisimular to $\rho \vdash (\alpha!v.e)^+$. Following the transition to node (e), the memoization process notes that the syntax configuration at (e) appeared earlier at (c); this forces the respective environments at nodes (c) and (e) to be joined and produces node (f). Finally, node (f) repeats at node (g), making the tree regular.

The abstract interpretation of the source syntax plus the usual finite chain property of the abstract environment set ensure that the abstract behavior trees must be regular. Because environments hold the numerical values of the argument identifiers, no new source program syntax is generated.

4 Channels as Arguments

It is straightforward to adapt the CCS-variant in the previous section to use channels as arguments; the relevant changes are presented in Figure 11. An

$c \in$ Expression-configuration	$p \in$ Process-identifier
$e \in$ Expression	$\rho \in$ Environment
$g \in$ Guard	$v \in$ Channel-expression
$x \in$ Argument-identifier	$\alpha \in$ Channel

$$\begin{array}{lcl} c & ::= & \rho \vdash e \mid c_1 \,||\, c_2 \\ e & ::= & 0 \mid g.e \mid e_1 \,||\, e_2 \mid \mu p(e) \mid p \\ g & ::= & v?x \mid v_1!v_2 \\ v & ::= & \alpha \mid x \\ \rho & ::= & \{x_i = \alpha_i\} \cup \{p_j \mapsto \rho_j\} \end{array}$$

Congruences: like Figure 8, but replace second congruence by:

$$\frac{(x = \alpha) \in \rho}{\rho \vdash g.e \equiv \rho \vdash ([\alpha/x]g).e}$$

Computation rules: like Figure 8, but replace first two rules by:

$$\rho \vdash \alpha?x.e \stackrel{\alpha?\alpha'}{\to} \rho \oplus \{x = \alpha'\} \vdash e \qquad \rho \vdash \alpha!\alpha'.e \stackrel{\alpha!\alpha'}{\to} \rho \vdash e$$

Figure 11: Semantics for channels as arguments

example computation is given in Figure 12.

As before, think of a program as a concrete process pool, that is, a function of the form *Label* $\to$ *Bag*(*Environment*), where *Environment* $=$ (*ArgumentId* $\to$ *Channel*) $\times$ (*ProcessId* $\to$ *Environment*). A useful abstract interpretation defines an abstract process pool to be a function of the form *Label* $\to$ *AbstractEnv* $\times \{0, 1, \omega\}$, where *AbstractEnv* $=$ (*ArgumentId* $\to$ $\wp$(*Channel*)) $\times$ (*ProcessId* $\to$ *AbstractEnv*). That is, in the abstract interpretation, an abstract environment must associate an argument identifier with a set of possible channels that the identifier might denote. Since the set of channels that appear in a given program is finite, $\wp$(*Channel*) has the finite chain property.

The relation between concrete and abstract process pools is as before:

$$\begin{array}{c} cp\ rel_{Pool}\ ap \text{ iff for all } \ell \in Label, |cp(\ell)| \leq ap(\ell) \downarrow 2 \\ \text{and for all } \rho \in cp(\ell), \rho\ rel_{Env}\ ap(\ell) \downarrow 1 \end{array}$$

where concrete and abstract environments are related like before:

$$\begin{array}{c} (\{x_i = \alpha_i\}, \{p_j \mapsto \rho_j\})\ rel_{Env}\ (\{x_i = S_i\}, \{p_j \mapsto \rho'_j\}) \\ \text{iff } (i) \text{ for all } x_i, \alpha_i \in S_i, \text{ and } (ii) \text{ for all } p_j, \rho_j\ rel_{Env}\ \rho'_j \end{array}$$

Based on the above definitions, it is easy to see, for example, that for concrete pool $\{x = \alpha\} \vdash x!x.0 \,||\, \{x = \beta\} \vdash x!x.0 \,||\, \emptyset \vdash \alpha?y.0$ the abstract pool that best describes it is $\{x = \{\alpha, \beta\}\} \vdash (x!x.0)^+ \,||\, \emptyset \vdash \alpha?y.0$.

Let $P = \mu p(\alpha?x.(x!x.0 \parallel p))$ and $\rho_a = \{x = a, p \mapsto \emptyset\}$ in

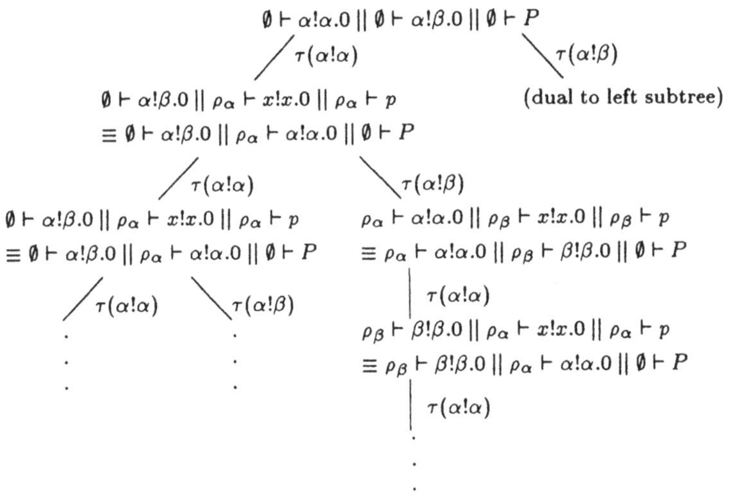

Figure 12: Program with channel arguments

If we use the congruence rule in Figure 11 to define substitution in the abstract interpretation, then a set of channels is substituted for a channel identifier, e.g., $\{x = \{\alpha,\beta\}\} \vdash x!x.0 \equiv \{x = \{\alpha,\beta\}\} \vdash \{\alpha,\beta\}!\{\alpha,\beta\}.0$. This implies that we should use the following safe, simple, but inexact abstract computation rules for communication:

$$\rho \vdash S?x.e \overset{\alpha?S'}{\rightarrow} \rho \oplus \{x = S'\} \vdash e \text{ for } \alpha \in S \qquad \rho \vdash S!S'.e \overset{\alpha!S'}{\rightarrow} \rho \vdash e \text{ for } \alpha \in S$$

That is, the entire set of channels, S, is transmitted along any $\alpha \in S$. This is a form of "independent attribute" analysis of channel flow.

In contrast, a "relational analysis" would keep distinct the channels in S; we can formalize this idea with the following congruence rule:

$$\frac{(x = S) \in \rho}{\rho \vdash g.e \equiv \sum_{\alpha \in S} \rho \vdash ([\alpha/x]g).e}$$

That is, the substitution of the elements of a set, S, into $g.e$ generates not one but a set of new abstract processes to choose from. For example, $\{x = \{\alpha,\beta\}\} \vdash x!x.0 \equiv (\{x = \{\alpha,\beta\}\} \vdash \alpha!\alpha.0) + (\{x = \{\alpha,\beta\}\} \vdash \beta!\beta.0)$.[17] But more importantly, we have, if $(x = S) \in \rho$, then $\rho \vdash (g.e)^+$ is bisimilar to $\|_{\alpha \in S}\, \rho \vdash (([\alpha/x]g).e)^+$. This result ensures that a process configuration can be understood still as a process pool.

[17] The "+" operator is external choice, and the usual computation rules for it would be required. We will not develop this concept further in this paper.

Let $P = \mu p(\alpha?x.(x!x.0 \,||\, p))$ and $\rho_S = \{x = S, p \mapsto \emptyset\}$ in

$$\emptyset \vdash \alpha!\alpha.0 \,||\, \emptyset \vdash \alpha!\beta.0 \,||\, \emptyset \vdash P$$

$\swarrow \tau(\alpha!\alpha)$ $\qquad\qquad$ $\searrow \tau(\alpha!\beta)$ (dual to left subtree)

$\emptyset \vdash \alpha!\beta.0 \,||\, \rho_\alpha \vdash x!x.0 \,||\, \rho_\alpha \vdash p$

$\equiv \emptyset \vdash \alpha!\beta.0 \,||\, \rho_\alpha \vdash x!x.0 \,||\, \emptyset \vdash P$

$(\equiv \emptyset \vdash \alpha!\beta.0 \,||\, \rho_\alpha \vdash \alpha!\alpha.0 \,||\, \emptyset \vdash P)$

$\swarrow \tau(\alpha!\alpha)$ $\qquad\qquad$ $\searrow \tau(\alpha!\beta)$

$\emptyset \vdash \alpha!\beta.0 \,||\, \rho_\alpha \vdash x!x.0 \,||\, \rho_\alpha \vdash p$

(a) $\rho_{\{\alpha,\beta\}} \vdash (x!x.0)^+ \,||\, \rho_\beta \vdash p$

(b) $\equiv \rho_{\{\alpha,\beta\}} \vdash (x!x.0)^+ \,||\, \emptyset \vdash P$

(c) $(\equiv \rho_{\{\alpha,\beta\}} \vdash (\alpha!\alpha.0)^+ \,||\, \rho_{\{\alpha,\beta\}} \vdash (\beta!\beta.0)^+ \,||\, \emptyset \vdash P)$

$|\ \tau(\alpha!\alpha)$

(d) $\rho_{\{\alpha,\beta\}} \vdash (x!x.0)^+ \,||\, \rho_\alpha \vdash p$

(e) $\rho_{\{\alpha,\beta\}} \vdash (x!x.0)^+ \,||\, \rho_{\{\alpha,\beta\}} \vdash p$

(f) $\equiv \rho_{\{\alpha,\beta\}} \vdash (x!x.0)^+ \,||\, \emptyset \vdash P$

Figure 13: Abstract interpretation of channel-argument passing

Of course, the price paid for the extra precision of the relational analysis is a slower convergence of construction of the regular tree.

Figure 13 shows the regular tree that results from the relational analysis of the program in Figure 12. The interesting stages in the analysis are lettered (a)-(f). The transition into node (a), that is, the transmission of $\alpha!\beta$, generates the configuration $\rho_\alpha \vdash x!x.0 \,||\, \rho_\beta \vdash x!x.0 \,||\, \rho_\beta \vdash p$, which has as its abstract representation node (a). The equivalence for process identifier lookup gives node (b); and the equivalence for argument identifier lookup gives (c), which is parenthesized to emphasize that node (c) is not actually generated—the analysis does not generate new source program syntax. (As just stated, $\rho_{\{\alpha,\beta\}} \vdash (x!x.0)^+$ is bisimilar to $\rho_{\{\alpha,\beta\}} \vdash (\alpha!\alpha.0)^+ \,||\, \rho_{\{\alpha,\beta\}} \vdash (\beta!\beta.0)^+$.) The next transition, caused by $\alpha!\alpha$, generates node (d), which is a syntax configuration that appeared earlier at (a); so, node (e) is a result of the memoization process, which joins the respective environments of (a) and (d). The substitution for p uncovers node (f), which is a repetition of (b).

4.1 Channel Creation

In the π-calculus [19], new channels can be created on the fly by using a new construction, $\nu x.e$, where a new channel is created and used for all references to x in e. In this paper, we treat channel creation as an observable action, and we write a substitution semantics for it as follows:

$$\nu x.e \stackrel{\nu\alpha}{\rightarrow} [\alpha/x]e \quad \text{where } \alpha \text{ is globally fresh}$$

$$e ::= \ldots \mid \nu x.e \mid (\mu p\ x)(e)$$

Congruences: like Figures 8 and 11, plus:

$$\frac{(y = \alpha,\ p \mapsto \rho) \in \rho'}{\rho' \vdash p(y) \equiv \rho \vdash ((\mu p\ x)(e))(\alpha)}$$

Computation rules: like Figures 8 and 11, but add:

$$\rho \vdash \nu x.e \overset{\nu\alpha}{\rightarrow} \rho \oplus \{x = \alpha\} \vdash e, \quad \text{where } \alpha \text{ is globally fresh}$$

$$\frac{\rho \oplus \{x = \alpha\} \vdash e \overset{\Delta}{\rightarrow} \rho' \vdash e'}{\rho \vdash (\mu p\ x)(e)(\alpha) \overset{\Delta}{\rightarrow} \rho' \oplus \{p \mapsto \rho\} \vdash e'}$$

Figure 14: Channel creation and parameterized recursive processes

By "globally fresh," we mean that α is new to the entire program. (To define this precisely, we should employ a "channel environment" [22], but we use the informal definition here.) To integrate the semantics of channel creation into the environment semantics of Figures 8 and 11, we present the environment-semantics rule for channel creation in Figure 14. For ease in stating the examples in this section, we parameterize recursive processes, $\mu p(e)$, on a single channel argument, x, giving $(\mu p\ x)(e)$. The congruences and computation rules for parameterized processes are presented in Figure 14 as well. Figure 15 gives an example computation. The example computation shows how multiple new channels can be created in the course of the computation. Say that the *origin* of a channel is the νx that created it. (Global channels have themselves as their "origins.") Since we work with labelled expressions, we use the label, ℓ, of $\ell\colon \nu x.e$ to denote the origin of the channel(s) created by the νx.

Our abstract interpretation of channel creation cannot track precisely the number of channels created, but it can trace the paths of communications formed by those channels created by the νx constructions. When the labelled expression, $\ell\colon \nu x.e$ is abstractly interpreted, the origin, ℓ, is used to represent the created channel. Of course, this means that subsequent executions of the same $\nu x.e$ generate a new channel named by the same origin, ℓ, causing a loss of precision of the number of channels created and the control paths within the program.[18] But this simplistic analysis has a simple and natural correctness criterion:

$$\begin{array}{c} cp\ rel_{Pool}\ ap \text{ iff for all } \ell \in Label, |cp(\ell)| \leq ap(\ell) \downarrow 2 \\ \text{and for all } \rho \in cp(\ell), \rho\ rel_{Env}\ ap(\ell) \downarrow 1 \end{array}$$

[18] Alternatively, one can name the newly created channel with the computation path in the behavior tree which led to the channel's creation [31].

Let $P = (\mu p\ x)(x!x.0 \mid\mid \nu y.(p(y) \mid\mid y?a.0))$
Let $\rho_\gamma = \{x = \delta, p \mapsto \emptyset\}$ and $\rho_{\gamma\delta} = \{x = \gamma, y = \delta, p \mapsto \emptyset\}$ in

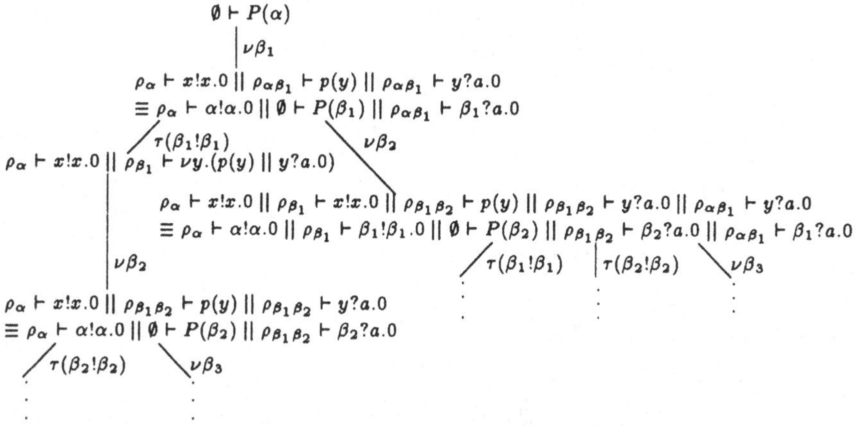

Figure 15: Computation with channel creation

where concrete and abstract environments are related as follows:

$$(\{x_i = \alpha_i\}, \{p_j \mapsto \rho_j\})\ rel_{Env}\ (\{x_i = S_i\}, \{p_j \mapsto \rho'_j\})$$
$$\text{iff } (i) \text{ for all } x_i, origin(\alpha_i) \in S_i, \text{ and } (ii) \text{ for all } p_j, \rho_j\ rel_{Env}\ \rho'_j$$

Given our simplistic abstract interpretation of syntax, where a process can occur 0, 1, or ω times, the above modelling suffices.

Figure 16 gives the abstract interpretation of the example in Figure 15, where ℓ is used as the label of the ν-expression in the example.

5 Related Work

The direct antecedent of the syntax abstraction technique in this paper is the "star abstraction" technique of Codish, Falaschi, and Marriott [5, 6], where the size of an unfolded logic program is controlled by using what is essentially the "+" operator shown in the examples of this paper. It is important to note that the regular-expression-like abstraction of syntax in this paper was chosen primarily for ease of exposition. A natural extension would use a context-free grammar to abstract a program's syntax.[19] Indeed, a similar approach was undertaken by Giannotti and Latella [16], where the concrete semantics of an equationally-defined program is taken to be the Herbrand universe of its terms, and the abstract semantics is a finite subset of "partial terms," e.g., the program $add(0, y) = y \mid add(s(x), y) = s(add(x, y)$ is abstractly interpreted over the set of partial terms $\{0, s(0), \top, s(\top)\}$, where the partial terms were extracted from the definition of add.

[19] This suggestion is due to Patrick Cousot.

Let $P = (\mu p\ x)(x!x.0 \parallel \nu y.(p(y) \parallel y?a.0))$
Let $\rho_\gamma = \{x = \delta, p \mapsto \emptyset\}$ and $\rho'_{\gamma\delta} = \{x = \gamma, y = \delta, p \mapsto \emptyset\}$ in

$$\emptyset \vdash P(\alpha)$$

$$\Big| \nu\ell$$

$$\rho_\alpha \vdash x!x.0 \parallel \rho'_{\alpha\ell} \vdash p(y) \parallel \rho'_{\alpha\ell} \vdash y?a.0$$
$$(\equiv \rho_\alpha \vdash \alpha!\alpha.0 \parallel \emptyset \vdash P(\ell) \parallel \rho'_{\alpha\ell} \vdash \ell?a.0)$$

$\tau(\ell!\ell)$ $\nu\ell$

$\rho_\alpha \vdash x!x.0 \parallel \rho_\ell \vdash \nu y.(p(y) \parallel y?a.0)$ $\rho_{\{\alpha,\ell\}} \vdash (x!x.0)^+ \parallel \rho'_{\ell\ell} \vdash p(y) \parallel \rho'_{\{\alpha,\emptyset\}\ell} \vdash (y?a.0)^+$

$\Big| \nu\ell$ (similar to left lower subtree)

$\rho_\alpha \vdash x!x.0 \parallel \rho'_{\ell\ell} \vdash p(y) \parallel \rho'_{\ell\ell} \vdash y?a.0$
$(\equiv \rho_\alpha \vdash \alpha!\alpha.0 \parallel \emptyset \vdash P(\ell) \parallel \rho'_{\ell\ell} \vdash \ell?a.0)$

$\tau(\ell!\ell)$

$\rho_\alpha \vdash x!x.0 \parallel \rho_\ell \vdash \nu y.(p(y) \parallel y?a.0)$

     $\nu\ell$

$\rho_{\{\alpha,\ell\}} \vdash (x!x.0)^+ \parallel \rho'_{\ell\ell} \vdash p(y) \parallel \rho'_{\ell\ell} \vdash (y?a.0)^+$
$(\equiv \rho_{\{\alpha,\ell\}} \vdash (\alpha!\alpha.0)^+ \parallel \rho_{\{\alpha,\ell\}} \vdash (\ell!\ell.0)^+ \parallel \emptyset \vdash P(\ell) \parallel \rho'_{\ell\ell} \vdash (\ell?a.0)^+)$

$\tau(\ell!\ell)$ $\nu\ell$

$\rho_{\{\alpha,\ell\}} \vdash (x!x.0)^+ \parallel \rho_\ell \vdash p(y) \parallel \rho'_{\ell\ell} \vdash (y?a.0)^+$ $\rho_{\{\alpha,\ell\}} \vdash (x!x.0)^+ \parallel \rho'_{\ell\ell} \vdash p(y) \parallel \rho'_{\ell\ell} \vdash (y?a.0)^+$

        $\Big| \tau(\ell!\ell)$

$\rho_{\{\alpha,\ell\}} \vdash (x!x.0)^+ \parallel \rho_\ell \vdash \nu y.(p(y) \parallel y?a.0) \parallel \rho'_{\ell\ell} \vdash (y?a.0)^+$

         $\nu\ell$

$\rho_{\{\alpha,\ell\}} \vdash (x!x.0)^+ \parallel \rho'_{\ell\ell} \vdash p(y) \parallel \rho'_{\ell\ell} \vdash (y?a.0)^+$

$\tau(\ell!\ell)$

$\rho_{\{\alpha,\ell\}} \vdash (x!x.0)^+ \parallel \rho_\ell \vdash \nu y.(p(y) \parallel y?a.0) \parallel \rho'_{\ell\ell} \vdash (y?a.0)^+$

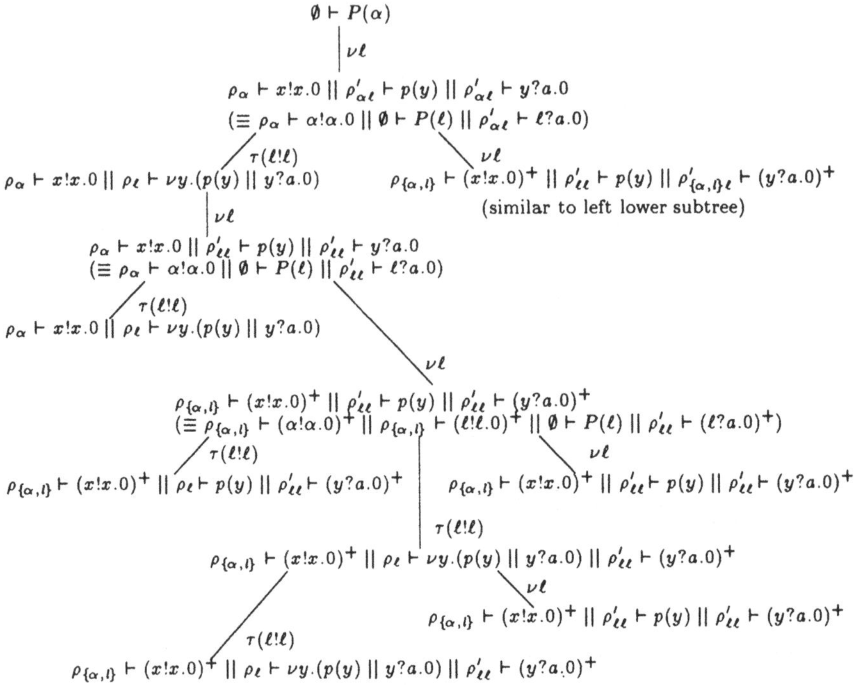

Figure 16: Abstract interpretation of channel creation

The papers of Colby [7] and Dwyer [15] on analysis of concurrent programs are also relevant; in particular, Colby applies both abstraction and partitioning techniques on program trees.

The primary application of the techniques in this paper is calculation of the abstract collecting semantics of a program; such information is essential for code improvement. But collecting-semantics-based code improvement is subsumed by model checking [28, 29], so we briefly review relevant research in applying abstract interpretation to model checking and in model checking processes with infinite state spaces.

The canonical work in abstract interpretation of models for model checking is that of Clarke, Grumberg, and Long [3]. Starting with a (possibly infinite) set of concrete states, C, and a concrete state transition relation, $R_C \subseteq C \times C$, one proposes a finite set of abstract states, A, and a surjective map, $\beta : C \to A$; one obtains the abstract transition relation, $R_A(a, a')$ iff there exist $c, c' \in C$ such that $\beta(c) = a, \beta(c') = a'$, and $R_C(c, c')$. Thus, R_A is a simulation of R_C, and properties in $\forall$CTL* can be checked on the abstract model. It is crucial that the abstract state set is finite, because no memoization techniques are used to force regular tree creation.

This basic approach is examined by Bensalem, Bouajjani, Loiseaux, and Sifakis [1] and Dams, Grumberg, and Gerth [13], where Galois connection machinery is used in place of the β map.

All these lines of work note that the dual of the usual simulation gives a technique for liveness property checking with ∃CTL*, and a bisimulation allows one to check full CTL*. Dams [12] notes that a bisimulation is not essential for checking CTL*: one needs only simulations in both directions where the same abstract state set is used for both simulations. Cleaveland, Iyer, and Yankelevich [4] formalize this idea.

Models with infinite state spaces are handled directly by Hungar and Steffen [17], where a process is a context free grammar, or equivalently, a finite state automaton with "subroutine calls" to other automata. Such processes define the context free languages. Both iterative [2] and tableau-based [17] model-checking algorithms are given for this format; the algorithms are complete for the alternation-free mu-calculus. Note that Hungar and Steffen are *not* concerned with discovering a context-free representation (if any) for an arbitrary CCS-specification.

Another representative direction of research is that of De Francesco, Fantechi, Gnesi, and Inverardi [14], where arbitrary CCS-specifications (including those that define non-context-free languages) with infinite state spaces are handled directly with least-fixed point theory: for a CCS program, p, its infinite state transition system, $SS(p)$, is the limit of its finite approximations (unfoldings), $SS_i(p)$, $i \geq 0$. One can do model checking directly upon the $SS_i(p)$, for $i = 0, 1, \ldots$, and verify a useful subset of (a variant of) CTL*. For practical use, it is crucial that repetition nodes are located as quickly as possible in the generation of the $SS_i(p)$s.

5.1 Conclusions, Applications, and Future Work

As stated in the Introduction, the primary goal of this paper was to extend simply and elegantly abstract interpretation techniques to modern programming languages defined by structured operational semantics. The net result is a clear methodology for generating semantically safe (and live) abstract, regular trees for programs that do not possess obvious state-transition diagram depictions. This widens the application of the work of Steffen [28], for example. A new insight is that one can employ memoization on abstract interpretations with infinite data sets to generate finite structures for model checking; this has not been attempted in earlier research. Also, the work here makes clear that the abstraction of program syntax can play a central role in classical abstract interpretation.

The primary application of this research is to the validation of safety properties of programs, whether these properties are validated by collecting-semantics techniques or by model checking. An implementation of techniques similar to the ones described in this paper is already underway by Cridlig [11].

It is a greater challenge to formulate useful liveness checking techniques for modern languages defined with structured operational semantics: Since liveness is the abstract interpretive dual of safety, semantic joins of abstract data at control-flow join points (e.g., the arms of a conditional) must be replaced by semantic meets. This requires a rethinking of the classical abstract data sets used with data-flow analyses and is certainly deserving of future work.

It is also planned to apply the techniques in this paper to model checking linkage specifications of statically typed, modular systems.

6 Acknowledgements

I must first thank Ed Clarke for his interest in this work and his comments on related research. Patrick Cousot, Mads Dam, Rocco De Nicola, and Giorgio Levi also provided helpful comments and pointers to the literature. The anonymous referee is thanked for his insightful commentary.

References

[1] S. Bensalem, A. Bouajjani, C. Loiseaux, and J. Sifakis. Property preserving simulations. In G. vanBochman and D. Probst, editors, *Computer Aided Verification: CAV'92*, number 663 in Lecture Notes in Computer Science, pages 260–273. Springer-Verlag, 1992.

[2] O. Burkart and B. Steffen. Model checking for context-free processes. In *Proc. CONCUR92*, Lecture Notes in Computer Science 630, pages 123–137. Springer, 1992.

[3] E.M. Clarke, O. Grumberg, and D.E. Long. Model checking and abstraction. *ACM Transactions on Programming Languages and Systems*, 16(5):1512–1542, 1994.

[4] R. Cleaveland, P. Iyer, and D. Yankelevich. Optimality in abstractions of model checking. In *SAS'95: Proc. 2d. Static Analysis Symposium*, Lecture Notes in Computer Science 983, pages 51–63. Springer, 1995.

[5] M. Codish, S. Debray, and R. Giacobazzi. Compositional analysis of modular logic programs. In *Proc. 20th ACM Symp. on Principles of Programming Languages*, pages 451–464. ACM Press, 1993.

[6] M. Codish, M. Falaschi, and K. Marriott. Suspension analysis for concurrent logic programs. In *Proc. 8th Int'l. Conf. on Logic Programming*, pages 331–345. MIT Press, 1991.

[7] C. Colby. Analyzing the communication topology of concurrent programs. In *ACM Symp. on Partial Evaluation and Semantics-Based Program Manipulation (PEPM'95)*, pages 202–214, 1995.

[8] P. Cousot and R. Cousot. Abstract interpretation: a unified lattice model for static analysis of programs. In *Proc. 4th ACM Symp. on Principles of Programming Languages*, pages 238–252. ACM Press, 1977.

[9] P. Cousot and R. Cousot. Abstract interpretation frameworks. *Journal of Logic and Computation*, 2(4):511–547, 1992.

[10] P. Cousot and R. Cousot. Inductive definitions, semantics, and abstract interpretation. In *Proc. 19th ACM Symp. on Principles of Programming Languages*, pages 83–94. ACM Press, 1992.

[11] R. Cridlig. Implementing a static analyzer of concurrent programs: problems and perspectives. In M. Dam and F. Orava, editors, *Proc. LOMAPS Workshop on Analysis and Verification of Multiple-Agent Languages*, Lecture Notes in Computer Science. Springer, 1996.

[12] D. Dams. *Abstract interpretation and partition refinement for model checking.* PhD thesis, Technische Universiteit Eindhoven, The Netherlands, 1996.

[13] D. Dams, O. Grumberg, and R. Gerth. Abstract intepretation of reactive systems. In E.-R. Olderog, editor, *Proc. IFIP Working Conference on Programming Concepts, Methods, and Calculi.* North-Holland, 1994.

[14] N. DeFrancesco, A. Fantechi, S. Gnesi, and P. Inverardi. Model checking of non-finite state processes by finite approximations. In *Proc. Tools and Algorithms for the Construction and Analysis of Systems (TACAS'95)*, Lecture Notes in Computer Science 1019, pages 195–215. Springer, 1995.

[15] M. Dwyer and L. Clark. Data flow analysis for verifying properties of concurrent programs. In *Proc. 2d ACM SIGSOFT Symposium on Foundations of Software Engineering*, pages 62–75. ACM Press, 1994.

[16] F. Giannotti and D. Latella. Gate splitting in LOTOS specifications using abstract interpretation. In M.-C. Gaudel and J.-P. Jouannaud, editors, *TAPSOFT'93*, number 668 in Lecture Notes in Computer Science, pages 437–452. Springer-Verlag, 1993.

[17] H. Hungar and B. Steffen. Local model checking for context-free processes. In *Proc. ICALP93*, Lecture Notes in Computer Science 700, pages 593–605. Springer, 1993.

[18] J.W. Klop. Term rewriting systems. In S. Abramsky, D. Gabbay, and T. Maibaum, editors, *Handbook of Logic in Computer Science*, volume 2, pages 2–117. Oxford University Press, 1992.

[19] R. Milner. The polyadic π-calculus: a tutorial. Technical Report ECS-LFCS-91-180, Lab. for Foundations of Computer Science, University of Edinburgh, 1991. Also in Logic and Algebra of Specification, F.L.Bauer, ed., Springer, 1993.

[20] Robin Milner. *Communication and Concurrency.* Prentice-Hall, 1989.

[21] F. Nielson and H. R. Nielson. Higher-order concurrent programs with finite communication topology. In *Proc. ACM POPL'94*, pages 84–97, 1994.

[22] F. Nielson and H. R. Nielson. From CML to its process algebra. *Theoretical Computer Science*, 155(1):179–220, 1996.

[23] H. R. Nielson and F. Nielson. *Semantics with Applications, a formal introduction.* Wiley Professional Computing. John Wiley and Sons, 1992.

[24] J. Palsberg. Global program analysis in constraint form. In M. P. Fourman, P. T. Johnstone, and A. M. Pitts, editors, *Proc. CAAP'94*, Lecture Notes in Computer Science, pages 258–269. Springer-Verlag, 1994.

[25] D.A. Schmidt. Natural-semantics-based abstract interpretation. In A. Mycroft, editor, *Static Analysis Symposium*, number 983 in Lecture Notes in Computer Science, pages 1–18. Springer-Verlag, 1995.

[26] P. Sestoft. *Analysis and Efficient Implementation of Functional Programs.* PhD thesis, Copenhagen University, 1991.

[27] O. Shivers. Control-flow analysis in Scheme. In *Proc. SIGPLAN88 Conf. on Prog. Language Design and Implementation*, pages 164–174, 1988.

[28] B. Steffen. Generating data-flow analysis algorithms for modal specifications. *Science of Computer Programming*, 21:115–139, 1993.

[29] B. Steffen. Property-oriented expansion. In R. Cousot and D. Schmidt, editors, *Static Analysis Symposium: SAS'96*, volume 1145 of *Lecture Notes in Computer Science*, pages 22–41. Springer-Verlag, 1996.

[30] C. Stirling. Modal and temporal logics. In S. Abramsky, D. Gabbay, and T.S.E. Maibaum, editors, *Handbook of Logic in Computer Science*, volume 2, pages 477–563. Oxford University Press, 1992.

[31] A. Venet. Abstract interpretation of the pi-calculus. In M. Dam and F. Orava, editors, *Proc. LOMAPS Workshop on Analysis and Verification of Multiple-Agent Languages*, Lecture Notes in Computer Science. Springer, 1996.

An Overview of Mobile Agent Programming

Frederick Knabe*

P. Universidad Católica de Chile, Casilla 306, Santiago 22, Chile

Abstract. Mobile agents are code-containing objects that may be transmitted between communicating participants in a distributed system. Compared to systems that only allow the exchange of nonexecutable data, those incorporating mobile agents can achieve significant gains in performance and functionality.
Languages with first-class functions provide a good starting point for agent programming, as they make it easy to express the construction, transmission, receipt, and subsequent execution of agents. However, for developing real agent-based systems, a language implementation must handle architectural heterogeneity between communicating machines and provide sufficient performance for applications based on agents. In addition, agents need to be able to access resources on remote execution sites yet remain in a framework that provides sufficient security.
In this paper we consider the uses of mobile agents and how a distributed functional language can be extended to support them. We review other agent languages and present several observations on how further work in this area may proceed.

1 Mobile Agents

The recent and dramatic growth of the Internet is a clear sign that computing has entered a new era. Networking has changed computers from isolated data processors into powerful communication devices. Users now have access to a vast, expanding array of information and services that range from stock trading to football scores. The computer in its new role is steadily permeating and transforming society, much as the telephone did 100 years ago.

The existence of widespread distributed application infrastructures, in particular the World Wide Web, has enabled the quick spread of new services. These infrastructures permit computers and users to communicate and interact via standardized interfaces. Each interface determines such characteristics as how resources at network nodes can be accessed, what information can be exchanged, how control flow in an application can be distributed over the network, and what connectivity must be maintained between interacting partners.

As interfaces incorporate richer data formats and communication protocols, more possibilities for innovative applications emerge. In the World Wide Web, the drive for increased functionality has led many service providers to make their own piecemeal extensions to the interface. For example, there are now dozens of plug-in modules for Netscape's popular Navigator browser, with each plug-in specialized to yet another kind of multimedia content. However, these many individual extensions break down

* Author's e-mail address: `knabe@ing.puc.cl`.

the common standard and lead to a lack of interoperability. If a user has not previously downloaded and installed a particular plug-in (or worse, if it is not available for his machine), those parts of the Web that depend on that plug-in become unusable.

This sort of problem suggests that the common interface fundamentally must incorporate the capability for defining and implementing new extensions to itself. These new interface extensions can then support specialized tasks. For example, a service provider may want to use a custom protocol to broadcast information to subscribers. A client may need to run a special terminal emulator for interacting with a central legacy database. A scientist may want to distribute a computation-intensive task to colleagues who volunteer CPU cycles. In each case, a common interface is needed initially so that parties can begin communicating, but then those parties must be able to extend that interface to suit a specialized purpose.

The means to provide such extensibility is for the interface to support *the transmission and execution of mobile agents.* By sending mobile agents through the network to execute at remote nodes, servers and clients can install these special-purpose interfaces with whatever properties they require. The agents can embody anything from communication protocols to data filters to complete applications.

Not surprisingly, the agent approach to structuring distributed computation places its own demands on programming languages. Conventional languages and their implementations are poorly suited to those demands. One approach that I have explored and implemented is to extend a distributed functional programming language to support agent programming [8]. The motivation for starting with a functional language is that transmissible, first-class functions provide a natural model for the creation and use of agents. However, other features are also necessary to support agent programming.

The next section presents potential applications for mobile agents in more detail. Section 3 then details a set of requirements for agent programming languages, and Section 4 continues with several additional desirable properties. Using the requirements as a guide, Section 5 describes Facile, a distributed functional language, and how it was modified to support agent programming. Section 6 presents related work and is followed in Section 7 by conclusions and observations on agent programming languages.

2 Applications

Mobile agents offer solutions to a range of problems frequently encountered in distributed applications. At the same time, they make possible new kinds of applications with novel functionalities. In the following we discuss a sampling of these uses.

Heterogeneous Communication. Although networking offers many potential benefits, it can raise just as many challenges when existing centralized systems must be retrofitted for communication and distribution. Tying together two systems quickly reveals incompatibilities in command languages and data formats, and as more systems are added the incompatibilities multiply.

Mobile agents can solve these kinds of problems by serving as a lingua franca that many systems can share. Because they include code, agents can be used to map between complex interfaces on heterogeneous systems. The one requirement is for the agent language primitives to be executable by each type of system.

This idea is not new, and it dates back to the very founding of the Internet. In 1968, the original ARPANET designers were already considering the problem of emulating the terminals for one timesharing system on the terminals of another. Their solution was the Decode–Encode Language, or DEL [12]. On connecting to a remote system, the appropriate terminal emulator would be sent back to the client as DEL code. The client would execute the emulator using its local implementation of DEL. Unfortunately, this innovative work was set aside before it could be fully developed.

Falcone [3] also faced the problem of providing common views of several centralized services across a heterogeneous distributed environment. These services and their clients were located on a variety of machines running different operating systems. Service interfaces generally consisted of a set of system calls, but each operating system, and thus the clients running on it, had its own view of what those calls should be. The different views were resolved by having each server support a generic interface consisting of many simple routines. A system call from a client on any of the operating systems could then be broken down into an agent program. The agent, written in a variant of Lisp, would be transmitted to the appropriate server for execution, where it would use the simpler calls to recreate the behavior of the original one.

Reduced Communication. A key advantage of agents is that they can decrease communication costs. In a client–server system structured around agents, part of the client or the server can move to the other side of the communications link. Once the client or server has moved, interactions between the two can bypass the network.

Falcone's system also demonstrated this use of agents. In principle, system calls made by clients could have been translated into multiple RPCs made to generic interface routines on the appropriate servers. However, the resulting overhead from communication latencies would have been unacceptable. By sending agents to make the calls, these latencies were avoided.

The NeWS window system [6] provides another example. In NeWS, clients communicate with the display server by sending PostScript programs. Instead of drawing a grid by sending several thousand messages for individual points, it is possible to send one brief program that will compute and draw the entire grid. The code sent by the client can also be used to extend the server, so that complex actions can be carried out in the future using a single message.

By reducing communication needs, agents can make interactivity possible even in cases where the network connection is poor. When Ever Systems developed a home banking system for Unibanco in Brazil, they reduced the need for data transmissions over slow, noisy phone lines by downloading application agents onto customers' personal computers [9]. In the Wit project [16], portable palmtop computers can access applications on Unix servers via an infrared link. To overcome the weaknesses of the link (low bandwidth and frequent interruptions during movement), the user interface components of an application are moved to the palmtop when the application is first accessed.

Communication can also be reduced by moving the client to the server. In a wireless networked environment, even if agents are used for service interfaces, communication costs may still be too high for a user to navigate the network and to find the resources and services of interest to her. Instead of only receiving agents from services, it might be possible for a user to upload her own agent to the wired network where it can search for information and services and carry out other tasks on her behalf. The only communications that the user's computer must make are the initial upload followed by the eventual receipt of the agent's results.

Specialized Protocols. Mobile agents allow servers to use custom communication protocols with clients. To receive an agent initially, the client and server must share some standard protocol. Once the agent is running, though, it can use a specialized protocol for communication back to its home server. Furthermore, an executing agent can communicate repeatedly with the server without intervention from the user, allowing the construction of dynamic services. As an example of both these concepts, a weather server or stock ticker might transmit regular updates to agents on scattered clients by using a special multicast protocol.

Reduced Server Loads. One of the challenges in providing services on the Internet today is that the computational components of a service must reside on the server machine. Because commonly used application protocols such as HTTP, Gopher, and Telnet only provide for the exchange of nonexecutable data, servers must take complete responsibility for performing any service-related computation for clients.

For example, a number of services now provide historical financial data. Providing this data in a simple textual format is straightforward and requires little computation by the server. However, many users prefer to see the data formatted as a graph. The service provider can add value by plotting the data and then transmitting an image of the resulting graph for display by the client. Note that the service provider cannot assume that the client has any plotting software itself.

The addition of graph plotting has a number of consequences. First, the computational demands on the server are increased. Popular servers are overloaded, so more and more resources must be dedicated by the service provider to ensure adequate performance. Second, plotting the data on the server means the server must send an image of a graph rather than a numeric data set. The image will almost certainly be many times larger than the original data set, so more packets have to be transmitted to the user. Larger data transmissions drive up bandwidth requirements on the network and mean the user must wait longer for the service to deliver its results. Finally, the user only receives an image, and therefore cannot locally apply useful plotting operations (such as adding a grid). Any modifications to the graph involve requests to the server, adding communication latency to the other problems. On a global network, such latency may be noticeable to a large number of potential users.

Structuring a service with agents can solve or reduce all of these problems. The most important characteristic of agents is that they allow computation to move. A server can off-load work onto a client by sending it an agent. The client presumably is willing to dedicate resources such as CPU time to the service interaction, and these resources can be used directly by the agent. In our example, the transmitted agent could do the plotting of received numeric data itself, while also providing a user interface to the plotting parameters. The user gains better performance while the load on the server and network is lessened.

The same effect can be achieved without mobile agents. If the client already has specialized software installed for interactions with a particular service (e.g., a plug-in), there is no need for agents to be transmitted over the network. However, there are thousands of publicly available services on the Internet today. Their success largely depends on *ease of access* from a wide range of potential clients. It will often be too much to require a first-time client to install manually special software for accessing a service. Mobile agents provide a sufficiently general and transparent means of moving computation from servers to clients.

Enriched Interfaces. Agents permit servers to present more sophisticated interfaces to the user. For example, a virtual reality interface would normally require far too much computation and network communication for a server to provide it remotely. Even if the CPU time and bandwidth were available, communication latency would make interactivity difficult. But by sending an agent containing the interface to the client, the server can sidestep these problems.

Temporary Applications. An agent need not be part of a larger distributed application; it may be self-contained and have no communication needs at all. For example, an agent could consist of the data and manipulation code for a simple model of the globe. Downloading such an agent from a server is no different from downloading an application from an FTP site. However, the agent has the advantage that it can leverage off the client's existing agent infrastructure. The infrastructure (i.e., the program on the client that receives and executes agents) allows the user to download and run the agent without the steps of creating source directories, configuring, compiling, and installing binaries. This simplicity makes it much easier to download applications temporarily; the user can retrieve an application with little effort and discard it later.

Agents that can function in a stand-alone mode are suitable for portable computers that have no wireless connections. Before disconnecting from the network at her home location, a user might download an agent with train schedules and a route planner. Such an agent may have no need for communication and can be thrown away after the trip. If the user periodically reconnects to the network, the agent may be able to take advantage of these moments to retrieve updates silently.

As a user moves into a new environment such as a city, company, or conference site, she may want to access special services that are particular to the environment. In addition to services that are only usable while some connectivity can be maintained, an environment may provide stand-alone agents with domain-specific information. A simple example is an agent that contains a local guide book along with software to search and scan it in various ways.

The HotJava browser [5] for the World Wide Web encourages this style of agent programming. With HotJava (and now with browsers from Netscape and Microsoft),

Web pages may contain *applets* written in the Java language. These applets are self-contained programs that start execution once they have been downloaded. Java applets range from games and simulations to interactive proofs, and many more are being developed.

Intelligent Data. Associating agents with data provides a way for the data to "know" how to process itself. An example is provided by the MPEG 4 compression standard for video [7], where the decompression algorithm is bundled with the data. This approach makes the standard highly flexible and adaptable to different needs.

In the SOFTNET packet radio system [11, 18], each network packet is an agent written in FORTH. The code for how to process a packet is included in the packet itself; routers simply execute the packets they receive. Once again, flexibility is one of the primary advantages of the system.

3 Requirements for an Agent Programming Language

Mobile agents offer compelling advantages for constructing flexible and adaptable distributed systems. However, the transmission of code places new demands on programming languages and run-time systems. We can distill those demands into the following four requirements, which together form a bare minimum for building mobile agent applications in real distributed environments.

Code Manipulation. The construction and use of mobile agents requires that the language support several basic ways to manipulate code:

- *Identify.* The language must provide a means to identify the code of an agent, allowing it to be distinguished from other agents and program code. For example, if an agent consists of a number of functions, one designated function (its main entry point) may serve to identify it.
- *Transmit.* There must be suitable language primitives or library functions with which the programmer can express that an agent should be transmitted.
- *Receive and execute.* The language run-time environment must be able to execute received agents *within the existing address space of the recipient.* This condition is an important assumption underlying many of the possible applications for agents and the potential performance gains.

Languages may support these requirements to different degrees. At the highest level the language may provide constructs and abstractions that allow code to be manipulated completely within the language. For example, a language might provide a construct that allows blocks of code to be identified as agents. Special operators might then be used to transmit, receive, and execute these blocks.

At the lowest level, a language might require that agents be developed as separate programs that are placed in files managed by the operating system; the language might then provide a means to transmit such a file, to load its contents dynamically into an address space, and to start executing the new code. This approach is more awkward to program than when all parts of code manipulation are integrated into the language.

Heterogeneity. Distributed systems are characterized by heterogeneity in machine architectures and operating systems. In open networks such as the Internet, users may access services from hundreds of different machine environments. For agent technology to be widely useful, it must be possible for agents built on one machine to execute on other machines. Though homogeneous implementations of agents are certainly easier to build, they are not as general and are unrealistic for real distributed applications.

The heterogeneity problem is not restricted to agent programming; in conventional distributed programming, nonexecutable data must be transmissible between different machine architectures.

Performance. An agent language implementation should minimize the performance overhead of using agents. Agents incur space and time costs through their size, transmission time, time to convert to an executable form, speed of execution, etc. These costs must be kept low enough to meet the needs of applications.

Because this requirement is by nature application dependent, it can be difficult to determine if an implementation meets it. Comparing applications based on agents with those based on standard techniques may be misleading. As a simple example, the time to transmit a million consecutive integers is almost surely longer than the time to transmit and execute an agent that generates those integers, but this difference tells us very little about whether agents have been efficiently implemented.

In the absence of a standard suite of agent benchmarks, implementors should report the performance of their languages on real applications.

Security. Agent languages make it easy for systems to receive and execute code off the network. Though this feature offers great flexibility to agent-based applications, it also makes them an ideal route for attacks on a system. A user of an application may have no idea that it is based on agents and that it may introduce foreign code into her system. Using agents to create worms and viruses is trivial.

An agent language for open distributed systems should either provide its own run-time security model or be coupled with some external model that provides system security. As an example of the former approach, the run-time system might only execute agents written in a restricted language that does not include system calls and does not permit the examination or modification of arbitrary memory locations. In the latter approach, agent-based applications might be required to execute behind internal firewalls provided by the operating system.

4 Desirable Properties of an Agent Language

In addition to the preceding requirements, an agent language may also support several *desirable* properties. For example, strong typing and automatic memory management are desirable because they eliminate or reduce certain classes of hard-to-find bugs that can occur in distributed applications. Other properties are less obvious and are due to the particular characteristics of agent programming. In the following we examine the most important of these properties.

Stand-Alone Execution. Agents should not require a connection to their originating site to execute unless the requirement arises from the application. In Section 2 we pointed out the usefulness of agents in cases where connections back to a service may not be available, such as mobile computing. The agent programming environment should make agents stand-alone unless the programmer explicitly programs them otherwise.

Supporting stand-alone execution rules out the use of *implicit callbacks* in the language. A callback is a communication back to the originating site to retrieve a value or to call a function. Implicit callbacks are those that are not directly obvious from the program code; they are inserted by the compiler or initiated by the run-time system.

Implicit callbacks may be used to hide the distributed nature of applications, the argument being that hiding distribution simplifies programming. The problem is that dependencies and the costs of access are hidden as well, leaving programs fragile and prone to serious flaws.[1]

The counterargument is that implicit callbacks may improve performance. Rather than transmitting all the components making up an agent, the system only transmits some subset. The remaining components are only retrieved when they are needed by the executing agent. However, each retrieval incurs the latency associated with the original agent transmission; these costs may outweigh any benefits from an initially smaller transmission. Moreover, if in the meantime the connection to the originating site has been lost, then the callbacks fail and the agent does as well. Callbacks should only be programmed explicitly, leaving the programmer to evaluate their appropriateness.

Remote Resource Access. Agents should be able to interact with locally available services and resources in their eventual execution environments. An agent may need to access library routines, system data, and other values to accomplish its tasks.

The agent language should provide a means for specifying and controlling these accesses. The access mechanism should be specific enough that the programmer can indicate particular resources for an agent to use.

Independent Compilation. In providing any other properties (particularly strong static typing), the agent language should not require that all components of a distributed application using agents be compiled together. In open distributed systems, servers and clients are frequently developed and maintained separately. It is unrealistic to require that entire systems pass through a single compilation at a single site.

5 Extended Facile

Conventional languages and compilers do not satisfy the preceding requirements. All the code in a program is assumed to stay in a single address space. To maximize performance, the compiler strives to make the code as machine-specific as possible. Ad

[1] Waldo et al. [15] argue that trying to hide the distinction between local and remote resources and the communication in a distributed system is doomed to failure. They discredit the "unified view" that hides the distinction because of its inability to handle the problems of latency, memory access, partial failures, and concurrency.

hoc approaches to supporting mobile agents, such as transmitting source files and compiling them on receipt, suffer from poor performance and lack of integration with the language.

In an attempt to solve these problems, I designed and implemented an extended version of Facile. Facile [4, 14] is a higher-order, mostly functional programming language that integrates support for concurrency and distribution. Building an agent language by modifying Facile allowed me to reuse large parts of a design and implementation and to focus on the features specific to agent programming.

Facile made a good starting point for an agent language because it already supported all of the code manipulation requirements for agent programming, including integration of code manipulation into the language. The natural representation for an agent in Facile is simply a function. Functions in Facile are first-class values, so they can be created at run time, applied to arguments, passed to and from functions, and transmitted over channels.

5.1 Agents in Facile

Because the clean representation of agents in Facile is one of the language's strongest points as an agent programming language, it is worth examining in more detail.

A function in Facile consists of the function's code and the bindings from its lexical environment. An agent can therefore be structured as many functions with one of them designated as the main entry point; all of the other functions will be part of the main function's environment.

An example will show how in principle an agent could be programmed in the original version of Facile. We will consider an agent that transmits the local time in seconds back to its sender. First we write a function for getting the time:

```
fun getTimeSeconds () =
    let val TIME{sec=seconds,...} = gettimeofday()
    in seconds
    end
```

We next create a channel called `answerChannel` for sending the time back. A main agent function named `reportTimeAgent` calls `getTimeSeconds` and sends the result over `answerChannel`. Because they are free inside `reportTimeAgent`, both `answerChannel` and `getTimeSeconds` are part of its environment:

```
val answerChannel : int channel = channel()

fun reportTimeAgent () =          (* Main agent function *)
    send(answerChannel, getTimeSeconds())
```

Because main agent functions look the same as other functions, the programmer may want to distinguish them using a naming convention (such as appending `Agent` to their names).

On the sender side we transmit `reportTimeAgent` through a preexisting channel named `clientChannel` and await the result. The value transmitted for `reportTime-`

`Agent` consists of a *closure* record that contains both `reportTimeAgent`'s code and the components of its environment.

```
val remoteTime =
    (send(clientChannel, reportTimeAgent);
     receive(answerChannel))
```

The remote host receives the agent from `clientChannel` and executes it by applying it to a null argument:

```
let val agent = receive clientChannel
in agent()
end
```

The point of this example is that using lexically scoped functions makes agent programming straightforward. Any function can be an agent; we simply create one and transmit it.

The implementation of functions as closures is not a feature of Facile oriented specifically towards agents; rather, closures are generally necessary to implement higher-order functions. A closure encapsulates a function and allows it to be executed in a different environment while still preserving static scoping. The different environment can be in another part of the program or it can be on a different machine.

When the `send` communication primitive is passed an argument, it recursively descends through the components of the argument and prepares it for transmission. Closures in Facile are simply records consisting of a code string and the values free in that code, and they are treated like any other values by `send`. When a function closure is passed to the `send` primitive, all the components of the closure record are prepared for transmission, including components that are themselves closures. The `send` primitive can therefore easily transmit the entire set of functions making up an agent when passed just the main function of the set.

During its recursive descent, the `send` primitive makes a complete copy of its argument's components, which is then transmitted to the remote site. The important implication for agents is that a transmitted closure contains all the values it needs from the sending site. Reference cells pointed to by the transmitted argument are also copied. They do not provide an implicit means to share state with the sending site. (For cases when state must be shared, Facile provides a separate library for distributed references that is implemented using channels and explicit communication.) Thus Facile supports stand-alone execution; there are no implicit callbacks.

Facile also supports strong static typing and automatic memory management, two further desirable properties.

5.2 Extensions for Agent Programming

In [8] I describe how I extended Facile to satisfy the properties of heterogeneity, remote resource access, independent compilation, and performance. At the same time I preserved the agent language properties it supported already. I did not address security in the extensions; deferring the problems of security allowed me to concentrate on satisfying the other properties.

The extensions fell into four major groups, which we now briefly examine.

Transmissible Code Representations. Although unmodified Facile permitted the transmission of functions between hosts, the code component of those functions was sent in native compiled format. A transmitted function could only be executed on hosts with the same architecture as the one where it was compiled. Facile therefore did not support the heterogeneity requirement for agents.

For extended Facile, I implemented a code transmission scheme that supports more than one transmissible representation and also allows several representations to be transmitted *together.* The transmissible representations are derived from architecture-independent representations used during compilation. Support for more than one representation makes it possible to achieve different balances between the execution speed of received code and the latency before that code begins executing. For example, interpreting received code allows execution to start immediately but execution then proceeds at relatively slow speeds. Compilation produces faster native code but adds a latency penalty. The second feature, sending more than one representation at a time, permits senders to use optimistic strategies that balance increased transmission times with the capability to include machine-specific representations with machine-independent ones. The former offer the highest performance, but only if the recipient has the right architecture.

Typed Remote Resource Access. Extending Facile's strong static typing to remote resource access by agents presents several problems. The programmer of an agent needs a way to specify which remote resources the agent will access. The compiler of the agent needs to know the types of those remote resources so that it can type-check the agent code. Finally, the run-time system must be able to link a received agent with the resources that the agent needs.

For flexibility, we want a naming and linking scheme that allows an agent to be linked and executed on multiple sites. That is, the name of a resource should not be tied to a particular implementation on a particular machine. An agent should be able to move around the network and to use the local implementation of the resource wherever it is.

At the same time, we want to preserve strong typing across the distributed environment. Although an agent may use different implementations of a resource, that resource should have the same type on every site. The type should be the same as the one assigned to the resource when the agent code was type-checked.

To accomplish these goals, I introduced a new language construct, *proxy structures,* that can be used to specify remote resources by their types and names. In Facile, values can be grouped into modules (called *structures*) with associated interface specifications (called *signatures*). An agent writer who wants to program an access to a remote resource first obtains a copy of the advertised signature that serves as the specification for remote structures providing the resource. The programmer then uses the signature to create a proxy structure; the proxy introduces a placeholder name that represents all remote structures matching the signature. Acceses in the program to members of the proxy structure then look like normal structure accesses, but at execution time they will become accesses to remote resources. Because the advertised signature describes the types of the resources, the compiler can also type-check the uses of the resources in the agent program.

On transmission to a remote site, an agent carries with it the signatures for the structures containing needed resources. At the site, the agent is linked to the local structures that match those signatures. (In the implementation the signatures are not actually transmitted; see [8].) On retransmission, the agent is conceptually unlinked from these local structures and relinked at the next site.

Proxy structures represent a balance between several competing goals. Their key advantage is that they permit strong typing and also independent compilation. The cost is that the use of abstract types is restricted and that certain assumptions must be maintained (for example, that the built-in, primitives types such as integers and strings are universally the same at all sites).

Ubiquitous Values. Extended Facile also supports *ubiquitous values* as an efficiency optimization. Ubiquitous values are values that exist at multiple sites; the values are all assumed to be equivalent, although they may have different implementations. A library function such as the `gettimeofday` function in our previous example is a typical ubiquitous value. A ubiquitous value that appears in the closure of an agent can and should be removed from the closure before transmission. It does not need to be transmitted because the agent can be linked with and use the local implementation of the value wherever it is executed. The process of removing these values before transmission is known as *closure trimming.*

Performance studies [8] show that closure trimming can markedly reduce the transmission times and latencies associated with using agent applications.

Lazy Run-Time Compilation. A further efficiency measure introduced into Facile makes run-time compilation *lazy*. Before a received agent can be run, it must be converted to an executable form, normally via compilation. Compilation can be explicit or implicit. In the former case, the programmer must explicitly call the compiler on the received object to convert it into an executable agent. In the latter, an agent is received as an agent (i.e., a function) and compilation is handled automatically.

Implicit compilation simplifies the burden on the programmer, and this option is the one I chose for extended Facile. A second choice that then must be made is when to perform the automatic compilation. The *eager* strategy is to compile a function as soon as it is received. The *lazy* strategy is to defer compilation until the function is called.

The eager strategy is easier to implement, but the lazy one offers a potential performance benefit. If an agent is never used at a site, perhaps because it will simply be forwarded to another destination, we save the work of compiling it.

This argument is not the only one for lazy compilation. An agent will typically consist of many functions, which are used at different times and in response to different events. Some of these functions may not be used at all during a run, and some may be used for the first time only late in the run. By compiling each function in the agent separately and on demand, we can further eliminate unnecessary compilation and also amortize the compilation that does occur over the run of an agent. Amortization may be particularly attractive for interactive applications, where it decreases the start-up delay.

Extended Facile uses lazy compilation in this way. This feature was complex to implement, but once again performance studies showed that it significantly eliminated needless compilation.

6 Related Work

Although the area of mobile agents has only recently begun to attract widespread interest, there are a number of languages and systems that support agent programming in various ways. We will not try to make a comprehensive list here but will rather highlight several systems.

REV. The REV system [13] provides code transmission in an RPC context (REV stands for *remote evaluation*). A client can relocate a procedure call $P(x,y,z)$ to a server S with the language construct **at** S **eval** $P(x,y,z)$. P and its arguments are transmitted to S for execution, and any results are returned to the client via a reply message.

A transmitted procedure may access resources on the server. REV is the only code transmission system other than extended Facile that provides strong static typing for these accesses. *Service interfaces* specify the names of abstract types and their associated operations. Interfaces are assumed to have globally unique names and to exist in some global database available to the compiler. An REV procedure can access the operations in an interface, and these uses are statically checked. At run time, the procedure can only be transmitted to servers that implement an instance of the interface.

A prototype REV implementation was developed that used transmission of source code, but REV's real contribution is its design.

Obliq. Obliq [2] is a distributed object-oriented programming language. The language is lexically scoped and untyped. Obliq supports first-class functions, and functions as well as other values may be transmitted over the network. Heterogeneity is handled by sending function code as abstract syntax trees, though at the cost of large transmissible representations.

Obliq distinguishes between values that embody state (such as arrays) and those that do not. The former values are transmitted as *network references,* while the latter are simply copied. On a remote site, use of a network reference invokes an implicit callback to retrieve or update the value. A transmitted function closure may contain both kinds of values.

Because of its strict lexical scoping, Obliq functions cannot access remote resources directly. For a function to use any values local to a recipient, those values must be passed explicitly to it as arguments. One drawback to this approach is that in a loosely coupled distributed system, fixing the set of resources available to received functions creates problems of extensibility and backwards compatibility.

The use of implicit callbacks is another important distinction between Facile and Obliq. An Obliq programmer can create a stand-alone function, but she must take care not to refer to any nontransmissible values. In Facile there is never a danger of agents including implicit callbacks because all values are copied on transmission, including state-containing ones.

Safe-Tcl. The emphasis in Safe-Tcl [1] is on the agent language properties of heterogeneity and security. Tcl interpreters are widely available for many platforms, making it easy to send Tcl programs between different machine architectures. Security is provided by executing normal Tcl code in one interpreter while untrusted Tcl programs received off the network are executed in a second interpreter. The two interpreters share one address space, but the interpreter for untrusted code is deliberately crippled. Certain library calls and functions are not available within it, so untrusted code is effectively encapsulated and cannot access or modify the larger environment.

Although Safe-Tcl allows transmitted code to execute within an existing address space, other support for code manipulation is not integrated into the language model. Safe-Tcl's original application domain was as a means to add safe executable content to electronic mail, but it continues to draw interest for agent programming.

Java. The Java language [5] has attracted significant attention since its announcement in 1995. Java is an object-oriented language that in many ways is similar to C++, but its type system is stronger and it uses automatic memory management.

The most interesting use of Java is in *applets.* As mentioned previously, applets are self-contained mobile agents that constitute complete applications. Popular World Wide Web browsers allow applets to run within Web pages, providing a means to add animation and interactivity to the content.

Java supports applets through several features. Heterogeneity is addressed by transmitting Java programs in machine-independent virtual machine code. Java programs are compiled to this representation, which is then interpreted on receipt. Interpretation is relatively slow, and to improve performance just-in-time compilers for Java virtual machine code are being developed for various platforms.

Security in Java is provided by carefully controlling what received applets can do. Before virtual machine code is executed, it is checked for a variety of potential faults including type errors, illegal instructions, and possible stack overflows. Furthermore, applets may only access a restricted subset of "safe" libraries.

In addition to satisfying these requirements for agent programming, Java also supports independent compilation, remote resource access, and stand-alone execution. However, Java's weak point is in code manipulation. Although new code can be received into an existing address space and executed there, there is no language support for identifying and transmitting agents from within a larger program. Each agent must be in a separate file, and agents are transmitted via file transfer.

The poor support for code manipulation is not surprising given Java's C++ background. The language also does not contain built-in communication primitives. These two aspects of Java limit the types of agent applications for which it can be used.

Telescript. One language designed and implemented specifically for agent programming is General Magic's Telescript [17]. Telescript contains many language constructs for creating, transmitting, and manipulating agents. An executing agent can choose to move itself to a new location with the *go* primitive, and once there can access local resources. In turn, the recipient of an agent can call procedures inside the agent. Telescript is strongly object oriented, and the entry points into an agent are its public methods.

To provide security, Telescript uses capabilities (called *permits*) and authentication. The capabilities define what actions an agent is allowed to perform, while authentication allows sites to accept only certain agents. Telescript code is executed within a virtual machine that checks for illegal instructions and other violations. Within agents themselves, exception handling allows recovery from various errors. Telescript also provides persistent storage for agents, protecting them against loss in the event of a machine crash.

Telescript appears to fulfill all of the agent language requirements as well as the desirable properties (however, we should note that remote resource access in Telescript is not *statically* typed). Unfortunately, the language is proprietary and no free implementations exist. These restrictions have severely limited its use.

7 Conclusions

Mobile agents offer many advantages for structuring distributed applications. Given the need to implement mobile agents, the challenge is to develop programming languages that effectively support the new requirements that they impose.

Functional programming languages have an important contribution to make in this area. First-class functions and lexical scoping provide a natural way to create and manipulate agents. Unlike other styles of programming languages, functional languages inherently provide the means to work with code-containing values. In other kinds of languages, clean manipulation of code within the language is often not possible.

As our work with Facile shows, this easy mapping between functions and agents can be translated into a real implementation that supports the agent language requirements. At the same time, many desirable properties of advanced functional languages can be retained and incorporated into the agent programming model. Strong static typing is a key example.

Even given these advantages, however, most of the mobile agent market is now focused on Java. Though it is far from an ideal agent language, Java supports enough agent language properties to be useful. Most significantly, its incorporation into popular World Wide Web browsers gives it an enormous installed base. In the medium term, most code transmission that happens in real applications will involve Java.

Fortunately, there is still room for functional languages to have an effect. First, extended versions of Java that incorporate functional language features can be developed that use plain Java as their compilation target. The Pizza project [10] takes this approach. Another possibility is to sidestep the Java language altogether and instead to compile functional languages directly to Java virtual machine code (it is this code, after all, that is actually transmitted over the network).

In whatever work that follows, designers of agent programming languages should take care to support the requirements we have described. Security is very important for real agent programming but is often ignored (extended Facile makes this mistake). Similarly, as the number of agent applications increases, good performance will become more important. Innovative run-time compilation techniques and new transmissible representations will need to be developed. Combining these features with more sophisticated language models will lead to better, more powerful agent languages.

References

1. Nathaniel S. Borenstein. Email with a mind of its own: The Safe-Tcl language for enabled mail. In *Proceedings of the 1994 IFIP WG6.5 Conference on Upper Layer Protocols, Architectures, and Applications*, Barcelona, May 1994. North-Holland.
2. Luca Cardelli. *Obliq: A Language with Distributed Scope*. DEC Systems Research Center, May 1994.
3. Joseph R. Falcone. A programmable interface language for heterogeneous distributed systems. *ACM Transactions on Computer Systems*, 5(4):330–351, November 1987.
4. Alessandro Giacalone, Prateek Mishra, and Sanjiva Prasad. Facile: A symmetric integration of concurrent and functional programming. *International Journal of Parallel Programming*, 18(2):121–160, April 1989.
5. James Gosling and Henry McGilton. The Java language environment. White paper, May 1995. Sun Microsystems, 2550 Garcia Avenue, Mountain View, CA 94043, USA. Available at `http://java.sun.com/`.
6. James Gosling, David S. H. Rosenthal, and Michelle J. Arden. *The NeWS Book: An Introduction to the Network/extensible Window System*. Springer-Verlag, New York, 1989.
7. MPEG-4 Proposal Package Description (PPD) — Revision 3 (Tokyo Revision). International Organisation for Standardisation document ISO/IEC JTC1/SC29/WG11 N0998, July 1995. Produced by the working group on Coding of Moving Pictures and Associated Audio Information.
8. Frederick C. Knabe. *Language Support for Mobile Agents*. PhD thesis, School of Computer Science, Carnegie Mellon University, Pittsburgh, Pennsylvania 15213, December 1995. Technical report CMU-CS-95-223.
9. Scott McCartney and Jonathan Friedland. Computer sales hot as poorer nations try to string PC gap. *The Wall Street Journal*, 29 June 1995.
10. Martin Odersky and Philip Wadler. Evolving Java. Outline for the Pizza research project. More information can be found at `http://wwwipd.ira.uka.de/~espresso/Project/`. February 1996.
11. Birger Olofsson. *SOFTNET Programming Guide (Linköping Implementation)*. Department of Electrical Engineering, Linköping University, S-581 83 Linköping, Sweden, March 1985.
12. Jeff Rulifson. DEL. ARPANET Request For Comments 5, available at `ftp://ds.internic.net/rfc/rfc5.txt`, June 1969.
13. James W. Stamos and David K. Gifford. Remote evaluation. *ACM Transactions on Programming Languages and Systems*, 12(4):537–565, October 1990.
14. Bent Thomsen, Lone Leth, Sanjiva Prasad, Tsung-Min Kuo, André Kramer, Fritz Knabe, and Alessandro Giacalone. Facile Antigua Release programming guide. Technical Report ECRC-93-20, European Computer-Industry Research Centre, Arabellastr. 17, 81925 Munich, Germany, December 1993. Available at `http://www.ecrc.de/`.
15. Jim Waldo, Geoff Wyant, Ann Wollrath, and Sam Kendall. A note on distributed computing. Technical Report SMLI TR-94-29, Sun Microsystems Laboratories, 2550 Garcia Avenue, Mountain View, California 94043, USA, November 1994.
16. Terri Watson. Effective wireless communication through application partitioning. In *Proceedings of the Fifth Workshop on Hot Topics in Operating Systems (HotOS-V)*, May 1995.
17. James E. White. Telescript technology: Mobile agents. General Magic white paper, 2465 Latham Street, Mountain View, CA 94040, 1996. Available from `http://www.genmagic.com/`.
18. Jens Zander and Robert Forchheimer. High-level packet communication. *FORTH Dimensions*, 6(5):32–33, 1984.

Formalising and Prototyping a Concurrent Object-Based Language

Lars-åke Fredlund*[1], Jari Koistinen**[2] and Fredrik Orava[1]

[1] Swedish Institute of Computer Science, P.O. Box 1263, S-164 28 Kista, Sweden
[2] Ericsson AB

Abstract. This document aims to provide a formal semantics for an object-oriented language with constructs for concurrency and distribution. The semantics is defined via a translation into the π-calculus process algebra. As is (perhaps regrettably) standard when giving the semantics of a language in such a way, we concentrate on faithfully capturing the program dynamics while abstracting away from many important aspects of object-oriented languages, most notably inheritance.

1 Introduction

The piece of work reported here originates from the design of a real concurrent and distributed object-oriented design language (Delos) developed within Ericsson [KW95]. Originally constructs for distribution and concurrency were missing from the language, making it necessary to call on operating system services to implement distributed applications. A project was set up to remedy this shortcoming by including support for concurrency and distribution in the language itself, thereby facilitating implementations on different operating system platforms. One central activity of the project was the prototyping of new language constructs using formal methods. In this paper we concentrate on the formal definition of a small core fraction of the design language, which we name Erken, and on some simulation and prototyping activities based on the formal definition.

In our opinion the foremost motive to formally define the semantics of a programming language is to enable language proposals to be stated precisely at an early design phase. This facilitates discussions about language design by reducing the potential for confusion due to unclear ideas and specifications. Forcing design decisions to be stated precisely generally leads to clear and well structured designs, and in many cases potential problems can be discovered early so that remedies are more likely not to influence large parts of the design. Finally, in addition to providing a basis for formalised analysis, a formally defined semantics

* The first and third authors were supported in part by the ESPRIT project LOMAPS and the HCM project EXPRESS.

** Current affiliation is Hewlett-Packard Laboratories, 1501 Page Mill Road, MS 1U3, Palo Alto, CA, USA.

also enables simulators to be easily built and thus opens up for experimentation with alternative language proposals.

In this paper we define the Erken semantics by translating its language constructs into the polyadic π-calculus [MPW92, Mil91]. To enable experimentation with the semantics, the translation was implemented in the form of a compiler from Erken to the concurrent functional programming language Facile [TLP+93].

The π-calculus has previously been used in giving semantics to object-oriented programming and design languages [Jon93, Wal95]. The existence of these previous works was indeed a compelling argument for defining the semantics of Erken in such a way. Our work differs from [Jon93, Wal95] in mainly two aspects: (i) the defined language permits intra-object concurrency, i.e., several execution threads are allowed to co-exist in the same object, and (ii) our focus and motivation is on prototyping language constructs, via an implementation of the translation function, rather formally proving properties about the semantics. Other process algebras have also been used in the definition of language semantics. For instance, Milner defined the semantics of the concurrent and imperative language $\mathcal{M}$ using CCS [Mil89] while Vaandrager [Vaa90] and Papathomas [Pap92] use ACP [BW90] and CCS respectively, to provide semantics for object-oriented languages. Alternative implementation languages besides Facile are PICT [PT95] and CML [Rep91]; however, only Facile has built-in support for distribution.

2 The Erken Language

The syntax of the Erken language is defined in Fig. 1. The set of expressions are generated by E while the syntax for method definitions is given by Mth (M ranges over method names). Classes are defined by Ot (O ranges over class names) and X ranges over the attributes (variables). In order to concentrate on program dynamics, the semantics abstracts away from many important aspect of object-oriented languages, most notably inheritance; however, these aspects are present in the original language.

An Erken class defines templates for creation of object instances. An object instance is a container for a number of attributes local to the object and a set of methods which can be called by other objects or by the object itself. The signature of a method $M(X_1 : O_1, \ldots, X_n : O_n)) : O$ defines its name, number and types of parameters, as well as the type of the return value. The method body consists of an expression which defines the value the method returns upon invocation. Expressions invariably evaluate to object references, and have the following behaviour: **new** O creates a new object of class O and returns a reference to that object. **self** returns a reference to the object within which the expression is evaluated. Evaluating an attribute X returns its stored value. A method call is written $E \rightarrow M(E_1, \ldots, E_k)$ and returns the result of executing method M, with actual parameters $E_1, \ldots, E_k$, in the object referenced by the expression E. The assignment $X := E$ returns the value of E and, as a side effect, updates the attribute X. Sequential composition, $E_1; E_2$, evaluates E_1 followed by E_2 and returns the value of the latter. The expression **asynch** E introduces

$$
\begin{aligned}
Ot \ &::= \textbf{class } O \textbf{ is} \\
&\qquad \textbf{attributes } X_1 : O_1, \ldots, X_n : O_n \\
&\qquad Mth_1 \cdots Mth_j \\
&\quad \textbf{end}
\end{aligned}
$$

$$
Mth ::= \textbf{method } M(X_1 : O_1, \ldots, X_k : O_k) : O \textbf{ is } E
$$

$$
\begin{aligned}
E \ ::= \ & \textbf{new } O \\
| \ & \textbf{self} \\
| \ & X \\
| \ & E \rightarrow M(E_1, \ldots, E_k) \\
| \ & X := E \\
| \ & E_1 ; E_2 \\
| \ & \textbf{asynch } E \\
| \ & \textbf{if } E_1 = E_2 \textbf{ then } E_t \textbf{ else } E_e
\end{aligned}
$$

Fig. 1. The syntax of Erken

concurrency into the language. Upon evaluation of **asynch** E a reference to a new object is immediately returned, concurrently with the evaluation of E. The new object has a single method *retrieve* by which the result of the evaluation of E can be retrieved. A call to *retrieve* will block until E has been evaluated. These "return objects" are similar to *futures* which are found in, for example, Concurrent Smalltalk [YT87]. The type of the return object is $\hat{}O$ if the type (class) of expression E is O. Finally, the conditional returns the value of E_t if E_1 and E_2 evaluate to the same object reference, otherwise the value of E_e is returned.

The semantics of method calls is defined by *method call schedulers*. Each object has its own method call scheduler[3], these control the amount of concurrent activity within an object, i.e., the number of execution threads that can be concurrently active within the object. In addition a scheduler determines in which order incoming method calls to the object are serviced, for example, using FIFO order or perhaps an ordering based on some notion of call priorities. Method call schedulers are specified on a class basis and are "user programmable"[4]. That is, they can take method names as well as values of parameters and attributes into account when making scheduling decisions. The translation of Erken given in this paper uses only simple schedulers that non-deterministically select the next method call to service.

Figure 2 shows the definition of a simple bag class in Erken, inspired by [Wal93, Jon93].

[3] Schedulers are similar to *capsules*, as introduced in [Geh93].

[4] The syntax for specifying schedulers is not given in this paper.

```
class Store is
  attributes v : Elem, l : Store

  method init(null : Store) : Store is
    l := null; self
  end

  method insert(null : Store, x : Elem) : Store is
    ( if l = null then v := x; l := (new Store) → init(null)
      else l → insert(null, x) );
    self
  end

  method test(null : Store, x : Elem, t : Bool, f : Bool) : Bool is
    if l = null then f
    else if x = v then t
    else l → test(null, x, t, f)
  end
end
```

Fig. 2. An Erken bag class

3 The Translation into π-Calculus

3.1 An Overview of the π-Calculus

In this section we give the syntax and informal semantics of the particular variant of polyadic π-calculus that is used in the translation. The syntax is summarised in Fig. 3.

Let $x, y, z, u, v, \ldots$ range over the set of *names*, $\mathcal{N}$ and assume a set of *agent identifiers* ranged over by $A, B, \ldots$. We let $P, Q, \ldots$ range over the *agents*, which are of the following kinds: $\mathbf{0}$ is an agent which can do nothing. The output prefix, $x!\langle y_1, \ldots, y_n\rangle . P$, is an agent whose first action will be to output the names $y_1, \ldots, y_n$ on x; thereafter it behaves as P. The input prefix, $x?\langle y_1, \ldots, y_n\rangle . P$, is an agent whose first action is to receive a tuple of names on x; thereafter it behaves as P but with the newly received names in place of $\langle y_1, \ldots, y_n\rangle$; these names are just place holders for new names to be received. $P + Q$ is an agent which behaves like either P or Q. The parallel composition of P and Q, written $P|Q$, is an agent that can do anything P or Q can do, and moreover a communication between P and Q can occur if one agent outputs a tuple of names and the other inputs an equally long tuple on the same name. $(\nu\ x)\ P$ is an agent which acts like P but the name x is *restricted*, i.e., it cannot be used for communications with the environment of the agent. An *abstraction*, $(\lambda\ e)\ P$, is an agent that must be applied to a name a before it can perform any action. The *application* $((\lambda\ e)\ P)a$ behaves like P with a substituted for the abstracted name e. The conditional $P[x = y]Q$ is an agent which behaves like P if x and y are the

$$
\begin{array}{llr}
P ::= & \mathbf{0} & \text{(inaction)} \\
\mid & \pi\,.\,P & \text{(prefix)} \\
\mid & P[x=y]Q & \text{(conditional)} \\
\mid & P+Q & \text{(summation)} \\
\mid & P|Q & \text{(composition)} \\
\mid & \downarrow P & \text{(replication)} \\
\mid & (\nu\ x)\,P & \text{(restriction)} \\
\mid & (\lambda\ x)\,P & \text{(abstraction)} \\
\mid & P(x) & \text{(application)} \\
\mid & \text{let } A_0 \stackrel{\text{def}}{=} P_0 \cdots A_n \stackrel{\text{def}}{=} P_n \text{ in } P & \text{(agent definition)} \\
\mid & A & \text{(agent reference)} \\
\\
\pi ::= & x!\langle y_1,\ldots,y_n\rangle & \text{(output)} \\
\mid & x?\langle y_n,\ldots,y_n\rangle & \text{(input)}
\end{array}
$$

Fig. 3. The syntax of polyadic π-calculus

same name; otherwise it behaves as Q. The agent $\downarrow P$ represents an unbounded number of parallel copies of P, that is, $P|P|\cdots$. The identifier A behaves like the agent P if there is a *defining equation* $A \stackrel{\text{def}}{=} P$; agent identifiers provide recursion since the defining equation for A may contain A itself. Such defining equations may be global to an agent or local, i.e., occur in the agent itself using the *let* construct:

$$\textit{let } A_0 \stackrel{\text{def}}{=} P_0 \cdots A_n \stackrel{\text{def}}{=} P_n \textit{ in } P$$

The formal operational semantics of agents is defined in the papers [MPW92, Mil91]; hopefully this paper can be understood without it.

The following abbreviations are used in the paper. An agent $\pi.\mathbf{0}$ can be written π. The output prefix $x!\langle y\rangle$ can be abbreviated as $x!y$ and the prefix $x!\langle\rangle$ as $x!$. Analogous abbreviations are introduced for input prefixes. Repeated abstractions or restrictions can be concatenated, that is, $(\lambda\ x_1,\ldots,x_n)\ P$ is equivalent to $(\lambda\ x_1)\cdots(\lambda\ x_n)\ P$ and $(\nu\ x_1,\ldots,x_n)\ P$ is equivalent to $(\nu\ x_1)\cdots(\nu\ x_n)\ P$. Defining equations $A \stackrel{\text{def}}{=} (\lambda\ y_1,\ldots,y_n)\ P$ can be written in the equivalent form $A(y_1,\ldots,y_n) \stackrel{\text{def}}{=} P$. The symbol "$\equiv$" will be used to denote syntactic equality between agents.

3.2 The Translation

This section describes the systematic translation of Erken classes into the polyadic π-calculus. The translation function (denoted by $[\![\,]\!]$) is defined over the syntactic structure of Erken classes, method definitions and expressions. Although the translation defines the sort of every generated agent, we omit the sortings here to make the presentation more concise[5].

[5] Such sorting information is required for the translation from the π-calculus to Facile.

The Translation of a Class. The definition of a class with name O, attributes $X_1 \cdots X_n$ and methods $Mth_1 \cdots Mth_j$ is translated into a π-calculus agent that is continuously prepared to synchronise over the name O, thereby receiving the name of a new object instance *self*.

$$\downarrow O?self\,.\,(\nu\ s, x_1, \ldots, x_n, m_1, \ldots, m_j)\begin{pmatrix} \downarrow self!\langle m_1, \ldots, m_j\rangle \\ \mid Scheduler(s) \\ \mid MH_1(s, m_1) \mid \cdots \mid MH_j(s, m_j) \\ \mid Attr(x_1) \mid \cdots \mid Attr(x_n) \end{pmatrix}$$

After receiving *self*, a new agent is located at *self*, representing the new object instance. The new agent continuously offers the tuple $\langle m_1, \ldots, m_j\rangle$, thereby providing access to the methods of the object. The agents $Scheduler(s)$ (a method call scheduler), and $MH_i(s, m_i)$ (the representation of a method definition) will be explained below.

An attribute is represented by an agent that offers to receive two names $\langle r_p, w_p\rangle$ on x, and then synchronises on either of the names, thus reading or writing the value of the attribute.

$$Attr \equiv (\lambda\ x)\begin{pmatrix} let\ A \stackrel{\text{def}}{=} (\lambda\ v)\ x?\langle r_p, w_p\rangle\,.\,(r_p!v\,.\,A(v) + w_p?v'\,.\,A(v')) \\ in\ x?\langle r_p, w_p\rangle\,.\,w_p?v'\,.\,A(v') \end{pmatrix}$$

The Translation of a Method. The agent MH_i, representing a method definition, is defined

$$MH_i \equiv \\ (\lambda\ s, m_i)\begin{pmatrix} \downarrow m_i?\langle a, r\rangle\,.\,a?\langle v_{i1}, \ldots, v_{ik}\rangle\,.\,(\nu\ rls)\ s!rls\,. \\ (\nu\ e)\ ([\![Mth_i]\!](v_{i1}, \ldots, v_{ik}, e) \mid e?v\,.\,rls!\,.\,r!v) \end{pmatrix}$$

The above agent is continuously prepared to synchronise over m_i (the name of method M_i), receiving names a and r over which the arguments in the method call and the return value of the method call are communicated. First the actual parameters of the method call are retrieved $a?\langle v_{i1}, \ldots, v_{ik}\rangle$, after which the *method call scheduler* is informed of the new method call $(\nu\ rls)\ s!rls$. The translation of the method definition itself $[\![Mth_i]\!](v_{i1}, \ldots, v_{ik}, e)$, with suitable arguments, is then put in parallel with an agent $e?v\,.\,rls!\,.\,r!v$ that receives the result of the method call via the name e, and then informs the scheduler that the method call has terminated. Finally the agent offers the value of the method call over the r name. The above protocol for handling method calls may appear cumbersome; much of the apparent complexity is a result of the rather limited sorting discipline available in the standard polyadic π-calculus [Mil91]. By switching to a more expressive type language (see for example [San96]) we expect to improve the clarity of the translation.

The coding of Mth_i is straightforward:

$$
\begin{array}{l}
(\lambda\ v_{i1},\ldots,v_{ik},r) \\
(\nu\ x_{i1},\ldots,x_{ik}) \\
\left(\begin{array}{l}
\quad Attr(x_{i1}) \mid \ldots \mid Attr(x_{ik}) \\
\mid (\nu\ r_p, w_p)\ x_{i1}!\langle r_p, w_p\rangle . w_p!v_{i1} . \ \ldots\ . x_{ik}!\langle r_p, w_p\rangle . w_p!v_{ik} . [\![E]\!](r)
\end{array}\right)
\end{array}
$$

The method call scheduler (*Scheduler*) controls the execution of methods. Two rather simplistic schedulers are shown below. The leftmost one does not impose any restrictions on the execution of method calls, while the rightmost scheduler guarantees that at most one method call in a given object is active at any time.

$$
Scheduler_a(s) \stackrel{\mathrm{def}}{=} \downarrow s?rls\,.\,rls? \qquad Scheduler_b(s) \stackrel{\mathrm{def}}{=} s?rls\,.\,rls?\,.\,Scheduler_b(s)
$$

In the definitions above, neither the method names nor the arguments of the calls are submitted to the scheduler. In the full language it is possible to base the decision on when to start executing a method call on the values of the actual parameters in the method call, as well as the attributes of the called object.

The Translation of an Expression. An expression is translated into an agent abstracted on the name parameter e (a continuation). Such an agent computes the value of the expression and then communicates it over the name e. As an example, the translation of the **new** expression is shown below:

$$
[\![\mathbf{new}\ O]\!] \equiv (\lambda\ e)\ (\nu\ o)\ O!o\,.\,e!o
$$

When the above agent is applied to a return address e a new object is allocated by synchronising with the translation of the class definition (see above) over the O name, offering the fresh name o as the name of the new object instance. Finally the name of the new object instance is signaled over the return name e.

A call to a method M_i in an object referenced by the expression E is translated:

$$
\begin{array}{l}
[\![E \rightarrow M_i(E_1,\ldots,E_m)]\!] \equiv \\
\quad (\lambda\ e)\ (\nu\ e', e_1, \ldots e_n) \\
\quad \left(\begin{array}{l}
\quad [\![E]\!](e') \mid [\![E_1]\!](e_1) \mid \ldots [\![E_n]\!](e_n) \\
\mid e'?o\,.\,e_1?f_1\,.\ \ldots\ .\,e_n?f_n\,. \\
\quad o?\langle m_1,\ldots,m_j\rangle\,.\,(\nu\ x)\ m_i!\langle x, e\rangle\,.\,x!\langle f_1,\ldots,f_n\rangle
\end{array}\right)
\end{array}
$$

According to the definition above, arguments to method calls (E_1 to E_m) and E are evaluated in parallel. Method calls are strict; that is, a method call cannot return a result until all arguments have been evaluated (this observation holds for all expression forms except the **if** and **asynch** expressions).

The translation of **asynch** E essentially creates a new object with a single method *retrieve*. Upon calling this method (using a normal method call) the caller will block until the expression E has been evaluated. As specified, at most one call to the *retrieve* method can be made.

$$
\begin{array}{l}
[\![\textbf{asynch } E]\!] \equiv \\
\quad (\lambda\, e)\ (\nu\ \mathit{self}', \mathit{retrieve}, e') \\
\quad \left(\begin{array}{l}
\downarrow \mathit{self}'!\mathit{retrieve} \\
\mid [\![E]\!](e') \\
\mid e!\mathit{self}' \\
\mid e'?v\,.\,\mathit{retrieve}?\langle a, r\rangle\,.\,a?\,.\,r!v
\end{array}\right)
\end{array}
$$

The problem with the semantics of **asynch** above is the potential for uncoordinated concurrent activity. That is, the evaluation of E in (**asynch** E); S will proceed concurrently with the evaluation of S. Unfortunately, the amount of concurrency in the object cannot be controlled by the method call scheduler unless E is a method call $E \to M(E_1, \ldots, E_k)$. Even then the evaluation of actual parameters $E_1, \ldots, E_k$ can proceed in parallel with S.

In an alternative semantics we restrict **asynch** to method call arguments, as in **asynch** $E \to M(E_1, \ldots, E_k)$. The translation of the new construct is as shown above except for the following changes:

1. $(\nu\ \mathit{self}', \mathit{retrieve}, e')$ is replaced by $(\nu\ \mathit{self}', \mathit{retrieve}, e', c)$.
2. $e!\mathit{self}'$ is replaced by $c?\,.\,e!\mathit{self}'$.
3. $[\![E]\!](e')$ is replaced by the following non-standard encoding of a method call:

$$
\left(\begin{array}{l}
(\lambda\, e)\ (\nu\ e', e_1, \ldots e_n) \\
\quad \left(\begin{array}{l}
[\![E]\!](e') \mid [\![E_1]\!](e_1) \mid \ldots [\![E_n]\!](e_n) \\
\mid e'?o\,.\,e_1?f_1\,.\ \ldots\ .\,e_n?f_n\,. \\
\quad o?\langle m_1, \ldots, m_j\rangle\,.\,(\nu\ x)\ m_i!\langle x, e\rangle\,.\,x!\langle f_1, \ldots, f_n\rangle\,.\,c!
\end{array}\right)
\end{array}\right) e'
$$

The above encoding ensures that **asynch** $E \to M(E_1, \ldots, E_k)$ returns a new object (that encapsulates the value of the method call) only after the arguments $E_1, \ldots, E_k$ have been evaluated.

In the translation of the **if** expression shown below, the mismatching operator $P[x = y]Q$ is used:

$$
\begin{array}{l}
[\![\textbf{if } E_1 = E_2 \textbf{ then } E_t \textbf{ else } E_e]\!] \equiv \\
\quad (\lambda\, e)\ (\nu\ e_1, e_2) \left(\begin{array}{l}
[\![E_1]\!](e_1) \mid [\![E_2]\!](e_2) \\
\mid e_1?v_1\,.\,e_2?v_2\,.\ ([\![E_t]\!](e)[v_1 = v_2][\![E_e]\!](e))
\end{array}\right)
\end{array}
$$

The translation of the rest of the constructs of the Erken language are relatively straightforward. For completeness they are given below:

$$
\begin{array}{ll}
[\![\textbf{self}]\!] & \equiv (\lambda\, e)\ e!\mathit{self} \\
[\![X]\!] & \equiv (\lambda\, e)\ (\nu\ r_p, w_p)\ x!\langle r_p, w_p\rangle\,.\,r_p?v\,.\,e!v \\
[\![X := E]\!] & \equiv (\lambda\, e)\ (\nu\ e')\ ([\![E]\!](e') \mid e'?v\,.\,(\nu\ r_p, w_p)\ x!\langle r_p, w_p\rangle\,.\,w_p!v\,.\,e!v) \\
[\![E_1; E_2]\!] & \equiv (\lambda\, e)\ (\nu\ e')\ ([\![E_1]\!](e') \mid e'?v\,.\,[\![E_2]\!](e))
\end{array}
$$

Note that, in the above scheme, we assume that the translation of each attribute X is located at x.

There are, however, some subtle issues that concerns concurrency. Consider for instance the translation of $X := E$. The coding above tries to synchronise with the attribute X as late as possible, i.e., only after receiving the value of E. An alternative would be to first send the read and write ports to X and then wait for the evaluation of E:

$$[\![X := E]\!] \equiv (\lambda\, e)\ (\nu\, e')\ ([\![E]\!](e') \mid (\nu\, r_p, w_p)\ x!\langle r_p, w_p\rangle \,.\, e'?v \,.\, w_p!v \,.\, e!v)$$

This alternative translation has the unfortunate consequence of preventing further accesses to X until E is evaluated, possibly even causing a deadlock if X is referred to in E. Our guiding principle is to make reads and writes to attributes as "atomic" as possible.

4 Prototyping Activities

At the time of writing we have finished a first version of the compiler, without support for interprocess method calls, written in Standard ML. The compilation of an Erken class is performed in two phases: the first step generates sorted polyadic π-calculus agents which are then translated into Facile. The compilation of Erken into the π-calculus follows closely the translation function defined in this paper.

The resulting code makes use of the Facile constructs for concurrency and communication. For example, a π-calculus name is translated to a tuple consisting of a Facile channel and a global identity[6]. Communication in the π-calculus is simply mapped to communication in Facile.

To provide further support for experimentation "native" Facile code, i.e, not resulting from the compilation process, can easily interact with the compiled code, through automatically generated interfaces.

The compiler does put a few restrictions on the syntax of π-calculus agents: (i) summands P and Q in $P + Q$ must be guarded, and (ii) an argument P to a replication $\downarrow P$ must also be guarded. By guarded we mean that $P \equiv \pi.P'$ for some π and P', although π may be preceded by restrictions $(\nu\, x)$ or conditionals $P[x = y]Q$.

Acknowledgment

The authors wants to thank Martin Bostrm and Einar Wennmyr of Ericsson AB for fruitful discussions on the topics of this paper.

[6] The identity (an integer) is required since Facile does not allow the comparison of channels.

References

[BW90] J.C.M. Baeten and W.P. Weijland. *Process algebra*, volume 18 of *Cambridge Tracts in Theoretical Computer Science*. Cambridge University Press, 1990.

[Geh93] N. H. Gehani. Capsules: A shared memory access mechanism for concurrent C/C++. *IEEE Transactions on Parallel and Distributed Systems*, 4(7):795–811, July 1993.

[Jon93] C.B. Jones. A pi-calculus semantics for an object based design notation. In E. Best, editor, *Proc. CONCUR'93 4th International Conference on Concurrency Theory*, volume 715 of *Lecture Notes in Computer Science*, pages 158–172. Springer Verlag, 1993.

[KW95] J. Koistinen and E. Wennmyr. Delos/SM: A language for structuring of coarse-grained modules, specifications and interfaces. In *Proc. 1995 International Switching Symposium*, Berlin, 1995.

[Mil89] R. Milner. *Communication and Concurrency*. Prentice Hall, 1989.

[Mil91] R. Milner. The polyadic π-calculus: a tutorial. Technical Report ECS-LFCS-91-180, LFCS, Dept. of Computer Science, University of Edinburgh, 1991. Also available in *Proc. of the International Summer School on Logic and Algebra of Specification*, Marktoberdorf, August 1991.

[MPW92] R. Milner, J. Parrow, and D. Walker. A calculus of mobile processes, part I and II. *Information and Computation*, 100(1):1–77, 1992.

[Pap92] M. Papathomas. *Language design rationale and semantic framework for concurrent object-oriented programming*. PhD thesis, University of Geneva, 1992.

[PT95] B.C. Pierce and D.N. Turner. Concurrent objects in a process calculus. In Takayasu Ito and Akinori Yonezawa, editors, *Theory and Practice of Parallel Programming (TPPP), Sendai, Japan (Nov. 1994)*, number 907 in Lecture Notes in Computer Science, pages 187–215. Springer-Verlag, 1995.

[Rep91] J. Reppy. CML: A higher-order concurrent language. In *Programming Language Design and Implementation*, pages 293–259. SIGPLAN, ACM, 1991.

[San96] D. Sangiorgi. An interpretation of typed objects into typed π-calculus. Manuscript, July 1996.

[TLP+93] B. Thomsen, L. Leth, S. Prasad, T.-S. Kuo, A. Kramer, F. Knabe, and A. Giacalone. Facile antigua release — programming guide. Technical Report ECRS–93–20, ECRC, 1993.

[Vaa90] F.W. Vaandrager. Process algebra semantics of POOL. In J.C.M. Baeten, editor, *Applications of Process Algebra*, pages 173–236. Cambridge University Press, 1990.

[Wal93] D. Walker. Process calculus and parallel object-oriented programming languages. In P. Tvrdik, T. Casavant, and F. Plasil, editors, *Parallel Computers: Theory and Practice*, pages 369–390. Computer Society Press, 1993. Available as Research Report CS-RR-242, Department of Computer Science, University of Warwick.

[Wal95] D. Walker. Objects in the π-calculus. *Journal of Information and Computation*, 116(2):253–271, 1995.

[YT87] Y. Yokote and M. Tokoro. Concurrent programming in Concurrent Smalltalk. In M. Tokoro, editor, *Object-oriented concurrent programming*, pages 129–158. MIT Press, 1987.

Type Checking for a Multiset Rewriting Language

Pascal Fradet and Daniel Le Métayer
IRISA/INRIA
Campus de Beaulieu,
35042 Rennes, France
[fradet,lemetayer]@irisa.fr

Abstract. We enhance Gamma, a multiset rewriting language, with a notion of ***structured multiset***. A structured multiset is a set of addresses satisfying specific relations which can be used in the rewriting rules of the program. A type is defined by a context-free graph grammar and a structured multiset belongs to a type T if its underlying set of addresses satisfies the invariant expressed by the grammar defining T. We define a type checking algorithm which allows us to prove mechanically that a program maintains its data structure invariant.

Keywords: multiset rewriting, graph grammars, type checking, invariant, verification.

1 Gamma: motivations and limitations

Gamma is a kernel language which can be introduced intuitively through the chemical reaction metaphor [2, 3]. The unique data structure is the multiset which can be seen as a chemical solution. A simple program is a pair (*Condition*, *Action*) called a reaction. Execution proceeds by replacing in the multiset elements satisfying the condition by the products of the action. The result is obtained when a stable state is reached, that is to say when no more reactions can take place. The following is an example of a Gamma program computing the maximum element of a non-empty set.

$$max \; : \; x \; , \; y \; , \; x \leq y \; \Rightarrow \; y$$

$x \leq y$ specifies a property to be satisfied by the selected elements x and y. These elements are replaced in the set by the value y. Nothing is said in this definition about the order of evaluation of the comparisons. If several disjoint pairs of elements satisfy the condition, the reactions can be performed in parallel. Let us consider as another introductory example, a sorting program. We represent a sequence as a set of pairs $(index, value)$ and the program exchanges ill-ordered values until a stable state is reached and all values are well-ordered.

$$sort \; : \; (i,x) \; , \; (j,y) \; , \; (i<j) \; , \; (x>y) \; \Rightarrow \; (i,y) \; , \; (j,x)$$

The interested reader may find in [2] a longer series of examples (string processing problems, graph problems, geometry problems, ...) illustrating the Gamma style of programming and in [3] a review of contributions related to the chemical reaction model. The fundamental quality of the language is the possibility of writing programs without any artificial sequentiality (sequentiality which is not imposed by the logic of the program). This makes program derivation easier [1] and naturally leads to the construction of programs suitable for execution on parallel machines. But our experience with Gamma has also highlighted some weaknesses of the language. In particular, the language does not make it easy to structure data or to specify particular control strategies. An unfortunate consequence is that the programmer sometimes has to resort to tricky encodings to express his algorithm. For instance, the exchange sort algorithm shown above is expressed in terms of multisets of pairs (*index,value*). Also, it is difficult to reach a decent level of efficiency in any general purpose implementation of Gamma, partly because the underlying structure of the data (and control) is not exposed to the compiler. Such information could be exploited to improve the implementation [5] but it can usually not be recovered by an automatic analysis of the program. So, the lack of structuring facility is detrimental both for reasoning about programs and for implementing them. In this paper, we propose a solution to this problem which does not jeopardize the basic qualities of the language. Our proposal is based on a notion of *structured multiset* which is a set of addresses satisfying specific relations and associated with values. The relations express a form of neighborhood between the molecules of the solution; they can be used in the reaction condition of a program or transformed by the action. In our framework, a type is defined in terms of rewrite rules on the relations of a multiset. A structured multiset belongs to a type T if its underlying set of addresses satisfies the invariant expressed by the rewrite system defining T. The paper defines a type checking algorithm which allows us to prove mechanically that a program maintains its data structure invariant.

We define the notion of structured multiset and structured program in section 2. The notion of structuring types is introduced in section 3 with a collection of examples illustrating the programming style of Structured Gamma. In section 4, we describe a checking algorithm and illustrate it with several examples. The conclusion presents several applications built upon the ideas developed in this paper.

2 Syntax and semantics of Structured Gamma

A structured multiset is a set of addresses satisfying specific relations. As an example, the list [5; 2; 7] can be represented by a structured multiset whose set of addresses is $\{a_1,\ a_2,\ a_3\}$ and associated values are $Val(a_1) = 5$, $Val(a_2) = 2$, $Val(a_3) = 7$. Let **succ** be a binary relation and **end** a unary relation; the addresses satisfy

$$\mathbf{succ}\ a_1\ a_2\ ,\ \mathbf{succ}\ a_2\ a_3\ ,\ \mathbf{end}\ a_3$$

A Structured Gamma program is defined in terms of pairs of a condition and an action which can:

- test/modify the relations on addresses,
- test/modify the values associated with addresses.

As an illustration, an exchange sort for lists can be written in Structured Gamma as:

$$Sort = \mathbf{succ}\ x\ y\ ,\ \overline{x} > \overline{y} \ \Rightarrow\ \mathbf{succ}\ x\ y\ ,\ x\ :=\ \overline{y}\ ,\ y\ :=\ \overline{x}$$

The two selected addresses x and y must satisfy the relation $\mathbf{succ}\ x\ y$ and their values $\overline{x}$ and $\overline{y}$ are such that $\overline{x} > \overline{y}$. The action exchanges their values and leaves the relation unchanged.

In order to define the syntax and semantics of Structured Gamma, we consider three basic domains:

- $\mathbf{R}$: set of relation symbols,
- $\mathbf{A}$: set of addresses,
- $\mathbf{V}$: set of values.

We note $\mathbf{A}(M)$ the set of addresses occurring in the multiset M.

Syntax The syntax of Structured Gamma programs is described by the following grammar:

$< Program >$ ::= ProgName = $[< Reaction >]^*$
$< Reaction >$ ::= $< Condition > \Rightarrow < Action >$
$< Condition >$ ::= $\mathbf{r}\ x_1 \ldots x_n \mid f^{\mathrm{Bool}}(\overline{x_1}, \ldots, \overline{x_n}) \mid < Condition >, < Condition >$
$< Action >$ ::= $\mathbf{r}\ x_1 \ldots x_n \mid x := f^{\mathbf{V}}(\overline{x_1}, \ldots, \overline{x_n}) \mid < Action >, < Action >$

where $\mathbf{r}$ ($\in \mathbf{R}$) denotes a n-ary relation, x_i is an address variable, $\overline{x_i}$ is the value at address x_i and $f^{\mathbf{X}}$ is a function from $\mathbf{V}^n$ to $\mathbf{X}$.

As can be seen in the *Sort* example, $\overline{x}$ refers to the value of address x when it is selected in the multiset. The evaluation order of the basic operations of an action (in particular, assignments) is not semantically relevant. In order to fit with this design choice, a valid Structured Gamma program must satisfy two additional syntactic conditions:

- If $\overline{x}$ occurs in the reaction then x occurs in the condition.
- An action may not include two assignments to the same variable.

Semantics A structured multiset M can be seen as $M = Rel + Val$ where

- *Rel* is a *multiset* of relations represented as tuples $(\mathbf{r}, a_1, \ldots, a_n)$ $(\mathbf{r} \in \mathbf{R}, a_i \in \mathbf{A})$
- *Val* is a *set* of values represented by triplets of the form $(\mathbf{val}, a, v)$ $(a \in \mathbf{A}, v \in \mathbf{V})$

For example, the structured multiset shown at the beginning of this section can be noted:

$$\{(\mathbf{succ}, a_1, a_2), (\mathbf{succ}, a_2, a_3), (\mathbf{end}, a_3), (\mathbf{val}, a_1, 5), (\mathbf{val}, a_2, 2), (\mathbf{val}, a_3, 7)\}$$

A valid structured multiset is such that an address x does not have more than one value (i.e. x occurs at most once in Val). On the other hand, there may be several occurrences of the same tuple in Rel. Also, we do not enforce that

$$\mathbf{A}(Rel) \subseteq \mathbf{A}(Val) \text{ nor that } \mathbf{A}(Val) \subseteq \mathbf{A}(Rel)$$

So, allocated addresses may not to possess a value or may have a value but not occur in any relation (although, in this case, they cannot be accessed by a Structured Gamma program and may be garbage collected).

In order to define the semantics of programs, we associate three functions with each reaction $C \Rightarrow A$:

- a boolean function $\mathcal{T}(C)$ representing the condition of application of a reaction:
$\mathcal{T}(C)(a_1, \ldots, a_i, b_1, \ldots, b_j) = (\mathbf{val}, a_1, \overline{a_1}) \in Val \ \wedge \ldots \wedge \ (\mathbf{val}, a_i, \overline{a_i}) \in Val$
$\wedge \ (\mathbf{val}, b_1, \overline{b_1}) \in Val \ \wedge \ldots \wedge \ (\mathbf{val}, b_j, \overline{b_j}) \in Val \ \wedge \lfloor C \rfloor$
- A function $\mathcal{C}(C)$ representing the tuples selected by the condition (i.e. the relations and values occurring in C):
$\mathcal{C}(C)(a_1, \ldots, a_i, b_1, \ldots, b_j) = \{(\mathbf{val}, a_1, \overline{a_1}), \ldots, (\mathbf{val}, a_i, \overline{a_i}),$
$(\mathbf{val}, b_1, \overline{b_1}), \ldots, (\mathbf{val}, b_j, \overline{b_j})\} + \lceil C \rceil$
- A function $\mathcal{A}(A)$ representing the tuples added by the action (i.e. the relations occurring in A, the values selected but unchanged by the reaction and assigned values):

$$\mathcal{A}(A)(a_1, \ldots, a_i, b_1, \ldots, b_j, c_1, \ldots, c_k) = \{(\mathbf{val}, a_1, \overline{a_1}), \ldots, (\mathbf{val}, a_i, \overline{a_i})\} + \lceil A \rceil$$

where

- $(a_1, \ldots, a_i)$ denotes the set of non-assigned variables whose value occurs in the reaction,
- $(b_1, \ldots, b_j)$ denotes the set of assigned variables occurring in the condition C,
- $(c_1, \ldots, c_k)$ denotes the set of variables occurring only in the action A.

and $\lceil \ \rceil$ and $\lfloor \ \rfloor$ are defined by:

$$\begin{array}{ll} \lceil X_1, X_2 \rceil = \lceil X_1 \rceil + \lceil X_2 \rceil & \lfloor X_1, X_2 \rfloor = \lfloor X_1 \rfloor \wedge \lfloor X_2 \rfloor \\ \lceil \mathbf{r}\ x_1 \ldots x_n \rceil = \{(\mathbf{r},\ x_1, \ldots, x_n)\} & \lfloor \mathbf{r}\ x_1 \ldots x_n \rfloor = (\mathbf{r},\ x_1, \ldots, x_n) \in Rel \\ \lceil f(\overline{x_1}, \ldots, \overline{x_n}) \rceil = \emptyset & \lfloor f(\overline{x_1}, \ldots, \overline{x_n}) \rfloor = f(\overline{x_1}, \ldots, \overline{x_n}) \\ \lceil x := f(\overline{x_1}, \ldots, \overline{x_n}) \rceil = \{(\mathbf{val}, x, f(\overline{x_1}, \ldots, \overline{x_n}))\} & \end{array}$$

The semantics of a Structured Gamma program $P = C_1 \Rightarrow A_1, \ldots, C_m \Rightarrow A_m$ applied to a multiset M is defined as the set of normal forms of the following rewrite system:

$$M \longrightarrow_P \mathcal{GC}(M) \quad \text{if } \forall \{x_1, \ldots, x_n\} \subseteq \mathbf{A}(M) \quad \forall i \in [1 \ldots m] \quad \neg \mathcal{T}(C_i)(x_1, \ldots, x_n)$$

$$M \longrightarrow_P M - \mathcal{C}(C_i)(x_1, \ldots, x_n) + \mathcal{A}(A_i)(x_1, \ldots, x_n, y_1, \ldots, y_k) \text{ (with } y_i \notin \mathbf{A}(M))$$

$$\text{if } \exists \{x_1, \ldots, x_n\} \subseteq \mathbf{A}(M) \text{ and } \exists i \in [1 \ldots m] \text{ such that } \mathcal{T}(C_i)(x_1, \ldots, x_n)$$

If no tuple of addresses satisfies any condition then a normal form is found. The result is the accessible structure described by the relations. Addresses which do not occur in *Rel* are removed from *Val*. More precisely:

$$\mathcal{GC}(Rel + Val) = Rel + \{(\mathbf{val}, a, v) \mid (\mathbf{val}, a, v) \in Val \ \wedge \ a \in \mathbf{A}(Rel)\}$$

Otherwise, a tuple of addresses $(x_1, \ldots, x_n)$ and a pair (C_i, A_i) such that $\mathcal{T}(C_i)(x_1, \ldots, x_n)$ are non-deterministically chosen. The multiset is transformed by removing $\mathcal{C}(C_i)(x_1, \ldots, x_n)$, allocating fresh addresses $y_1, \ldots, y_k$ and adding $\mathcal{A}(A_i)(x_1, \ldots, x_n, y_1, \ldots, y_k)$.

Correspondence between Structured Gamma and original Gamma Compared to the original Gamma formalism, the basic model of computation remains unchanged. It still consists in repeated applications of local actions in a global data structure. Actually, our way to define the semantics of Structured Gamma programs is very close to a translation into equivalent pure Gamma programs.

Rather than providing a formal definition of the translation, we illustrate it with the exchange sort program which is defined as follows in Structured Gamma:

$$Sort = \mathbf{succ}\ x\ y\ ,\ \overline{x} > \overline{y} \quad \Rightarrow \mathbf{succ}\ x\ y\ ,\ x\ := \ \overline{y}\ ,\ y\ :=\ \overline{x}$$

and can be rewritten in pure Gamma as:

$$\begin{aligned} Sort = {} & (\mathbf{val}, x, \overline{x})\ ,\ (\mathbf{val}, y, \overline{y})\ ,\ (\mathbf{succ}, x, y)\ ,\ \overline{x} > \overline{y} \\ & \Rightarrow\ (\mathbf{succ}, x, y)\ ,\ (\mathbf{val}, x, \overline{y})\ ,\ (\mathbf{val}, y, \overline{x}) \end{aligned}$$

3 Structuring types

Structured multisets can be seen as a syntactic facility allowing the programmer to make the organization of the data explicit. We are now in a position to introduce a new notion of type which characterizes the structure of a multiset. We provide a formal definition of types and we illustrate them with a collection of examples.

3.1 Syntax and semantics of structuring types

Syntax The syntax of types is defined by the following grammar:

<*TypeDeclaration*> ::= TypeName = <*Prod*> , [<*NonTerminal*> = <*Prod*>]*
<*NonTerminal*> ::= NTName $x_1 \ldots x_n$
<*Prod*> ::= **r** $x_1 \ldots x_n$ | <*NonTerminal*> | <*Prod*> , <*Prod*>

where **r** ($\in \mathbf{R}$) is an n-ary relation ($n > 0$), and x_i is a variable denoting an address.

A type definition resembles a context-free graph grammar. For example, lists can be defined as

$$\begin{array}{lll} List & = & L\ x \\ L\ x & = & \mathbf{succ}\ x\ y\ ,\ L\ y \\ L\ x & = & \mathbf{end}\ x \end{array}$$

The definition of a type T can be associated with a rewrite system (noted bc_T) which can fold any multiset of type T in the start symbol T. It amounts to reverse the grammar rules and to consider '=' symbols as '$\rightsquigarrow_T$' and nonterminal names N as relations. We keep the same notation $NTx_1 \ldots x_p$ to denote a nonterminal in a type definition or a relation in the rewrite system associated with a type. The correct interpretation is usually clear from the context. For example, the rewrite system associated with the type *List* is noted:

$$\begin{array}{ll} L\ x & \rightsquigarrow_{List}\ List \\ \mathbf{succ}\ x\ y\ ,\ L\ y & \rightsquigarrow_{List}\ L\ x \\ \mathbf{end}\ x & \rightsquigarrow_{List}\ L\ x \end{array}$$

This system rewrites any multiset of type List into the atom *List*.

We note $\mid M \mid$ the multiset restricted to relations ($\mid Rel + Val \mid = Rel$).

Definition 1 *A multiset M has type T (noted M:T) iff* $\mid M \mid \overset{*}{\rightsquigarrow}_T \{T\}$.

Let us point out that $\rightsquigarrow_T$ reductions must enforce that if a variable of the *lhs* does not occur in the *rhs* it does not occurs in the rest of the multiset. This is a global operation and such rewriting systems are clearly not Structured Gamma programs. This global condition is induced by the semantics of Structured Gamma programs which enforces variables of the *rhs* not occurring in the *lhs* to be fresh.

3.2 Examples of types

Abstract types found in functional languages such as ML can be defined in a natural way in Structured Gamma. For example, the type corresponding to binary trees is

$$\begin{array}{lll} Bintree & = & B\ x \\ B\ x & = & \mathbf{node}\ x\ y\ z\ ,\ B\ y\ ,\ B\ z \\ B\ x & = & \mathbf{leaf}\ x \end{array}$$

However, structuring types make it possible to define not only tree shaped but also graph structures. Actually, the main blessing of the framework is to allow concise definitions of complicated pointer-like structures. To give a few examples, it quite easy to define common imperative structures such as

- doubly-linked lists:

$$\begin{aligned} Doubly &= L\ x \\ L\ x &= \textbf{succ}\ x\ y\ ,\ \textbf{pred}\ y\ x\ ,\ L\ y \\ L\ x &= \textbf{end}\ x \end{aligned}$$

- lists with connections to the last element:

$$\begin{aligned} Last &= L\ x\ z \\ L\ x\ z &= \textbf{succ}\ x\ y\ ,\ \textbf{last}\ x\ z\ ,\ L\ y\ z \\ L\ x\ z &= \textbf{succ}\ x\ z\ ,\ \textbf{last}\ x\ z\ ,\ \textbf{end}\ z \end{aligned}$$

- circular lists:

$$\begin{aligned} Circular &= L\ x \\ L\ x &= L'\ x\ z\ ,\ L'\ z\ x \\ L\ x &= \textbf{succ}\ x\ x \\ L'\ x\ y &= L'\ x\ z\ ,\ L'\ z\ y \\ L'\ x\ y &= \textbf{succ}\ x\ y \end{aligned}$$

- binary trees with linked leaves:

$$\begin{aligned} Binlinked &= L\ x\ y\ z \\ L\ x\ y\ z &= \textbf{left}\ x\ u\ ,\ L\ u\ y\ v\ ,\ R\ x\ v\ z \\ L\ x\ y\ z &= \textbf{left}\ x\ y\ ,\ R\ x\ y\ z \\ R\ x\ y\ z &= \textbf{right}\ x\ u\ ,\ \textbf{succ}\ y\ v\ ,\ L\ u\ v\ z \\ R\ x\ y\ z &= \textbf{right}\ x\ z\ ,\ \textbf{succ}\ y\ z \end{aligned}$$

3.3 Programming using structuring types

Many programs are expressed more naturally in Structured Gamma than in pure Gamma. The underlying structure of the multiset can be described by a type whereas in pure Gamma we had to encode it using tuples and tags. Let us give a few examples of Structured Gamma programs whose description in pure Gamma is cumbersome. Note that the syntax of programs is extended to account for typed programs (ProgName : TypeName = ...).

Iota takes a singleton $[a]$ and yields the list $[\overline{a}; \overline{a-1}; \ldots; 1]$.

$$Iota\ :\ List = \textbf{end}\ a\ ,\ \overline{a} > 1 \quad \Rightarrow \quad \textbf{succ}\ a\ b\ ,\ \textbf{end}\ b\ ,\ b\ :=\ \overline{a} - 1$$

MultB takes a binary tree and yields a leaf whose value is the product of all the nodes and leaves values of the original tree.

$$MultB\ :\ Bintree = \textbf{node}\ a\ b\ c\ ,\ \textbf{leaf}\ b\ ,\ \textbf{leaf}\ c \quad \Rightarrow \quad \textbf{leaf}\ a\ ,\ a\ :=\ \overline{a} * \overline{b} * \overline{c}$$

In order to get more potential parallelism, we may also add the rules

$$\textbf{node}\; a\; b\; c\;,\; \textbf{node}\; b\; d\; e,\; \textbf{leaf}\; c \;\Rightarrow\; \textbf{node}\; a\; d\; e,\; a := \overline{a} * \overline{b} * \overline{c}$$
$$\textbf{node}\; a\; b\; c\;,\; \textbf{leaf}\; b\;,\; \textbf{node}\; c\; d\; e \;\Rightarrow\; \textbf{node}\; a\; d\; e,\; a := \overline{a} * \overline{b} * \overline{c}$$

Types can also be used to express precise control constraints. For example, lists can be defined with two identified elements used as pointers to enforce a specific reduction strategy.

$$\begin{aligned}
List_m &= L_0\; x \\
L_0\; x &= \textbf{m1}\; x\;,\; \textbf{succ}\; x\; y\;,\; L_1\; y \\
L_0\; x &= \textbf{succ}\; x\; y\;,\; L_0\; y \\
L_1\; x &= \textbf{m2}\; x\;,\; L_2\; x \\
L_1\; x &= \textbf{succ}\; x\; y\;,\; L_1\; y \\
L_2\; x &= \textbf{succ}\; x\; y\;,\; L_2\; y \\
L_2\; x &= \textbf{end}\; x
\end{aligned}$$

The type definition enforces that **m1** identifies a list element located before the list element marked by **m2**. Assuming an initial list where **m1** marks the first element and **m2** the second one, we can describe a sequential sort.

$$\begin{aligned}
&SeqSort\; :\; List_m = \\
&\textbf{m1}\; a\;,\; \textbf{m2}\; b\;,\; \overline{a} > \overline{b} \;\Rightarrow\; \textbf{m1}\; a\;,\; \textbf{m2}\; b\;,\; a := \overline{b}\;,\; b := \overline{a} \\
&\textbf{m1}\; a\;,\; \textbf{m2}\; b\;,\; \textbf{succ}\; b\; c\;,\; \overline{a} \leq \overline{b} \Rightarrow \textbf{m1}\; a\;,\; \textbf{m2}\; c\;,\; \textbf{succ}\; b\; c \\
&\textbf{m1}\; a\;,\; \textbf{m2}\; b\;,\; \textbf{end}\; b\;, \\
&\textbf{succ}\; a\; c\;,\; \textbf{succ}\; c\; d\;,\; \overline{a} \leq \overline{b} \;\Rightarrow\; \textbf{m1}\; c\;,\; \textbf{m2}\; d\;,\; \textbf{end}\; b\;,\; \textbf{succ}\; a\; c\;,\; \textbf{succ}\; c\; d
\end{aligned}$$

In fact, $List_m$ can be shown more precisely to be a refinement of *List*. We come back to this issue in the conclusion.

To summarize, Structured Gamma retains the spirit of Gamma while providing means to declare data structures and to enforce specific reduction strategies (e.g. for efficiency purposes).

4 Static type checking

The natural question following the introduction of a new type system concerns the design of an associated type checking algorithm. In the context of Structured Gamma, type checking must ensure that a program maintains the underlying structure defined by a type. It amounts to the proof of an invariant property. We propose a checking algorithm based on the construction of an abstract reduction graph which summarizes all possible reduction chains from a condition C to a unique nonterminal. We describe its application to some examples, suggesting that the algorithm is precise enough to tackle most common cases.

4.1 The basic idea

First, let us note that values and assignments are not relevant for type checking. So, we may consider multisets and rewriting rules restricted to relations. Also, we assume that checking is done relatively to a given type T.

A reduction step of a multiset by a Structured Gamma program is of the form $M + C \longrightarrow_P M + A$ where C and A represent multisets of relations matching a reaction of the program. The algorithm has to check that the application of every reaction of the program leaves the type of the multiset unchanged. In other terms, for any reaction $C \Rightarrow A$ and multiset $M + C$ of type T it checks that $M + A$ is of type T (i.e. $M + A \overset{*}{\leadsto}_T \{T\}$).

The checking algorithm is based on the observation that if $M + C$ has type T, there must be a context X ($X \subseteq M$) such that $C + X$ reduces by $\leadsto_T$ to a unique nonterminal $NT\ x_1 \ldots x_p$ (possibly T). The reduction of a term $C (= C_0)$ to a nonterminal $NT\ x_1\ \ldots\ x_p$ can be described as

$$C_0 + X_0 \leadsto_T C_1 \quad C_1 + X_1 \leadsto_T C_2 \quad \ldots \quad C_n + X_n \leadsto_T \{NT\ x_1\ \ldots\ x_p\}$$

Each step is an application of a $\leadsto_T$ rule which reduces at least a component of C_i and X_i is a *basic context*. Basic contexts are the smallest (possibly empty) multisets of relations needed to match the *lhs* of a reduction rule. They are therefore completely reduced by the reduction rule.

The context $X = X_0 + \ldots + X_n$ must be produced by the reduction of M, that is

$$M \overset{*}{\leadsto}_T M' + X$$

and the $\leadsto_T$ reduction of the multiset $M + C$ can then be described as

$$M + C \overset{*}{\leadsto}_T M' + X + C \overset{*}{\leadsto}_T M' + \{NTx_1 \ldots x_p\} \overset{*}{\leadsto}_T \{T\}$$

Now, if $A + X$ reduces to the same unique nonterminal $NTx_1 \ldots x_p$, then

$$M + A \overset{*}{\leadsto}_T M' + X + A \overset{*}{\leadsto}_T M' + \{NTx_1 \ldots x_p\} \overset{*}{\leadsto}_T \{T\}^1$$

and the type of the multiset is maintained.

It is sufficient to check the property $A + X \overset{*}{\leadsto}_T \{NTx_1 \ldots x_p\}$ for every possible reduction chain from C to a nonterminal $NTx_1 \ldots x_p$ with context X. To get round the problem posed by the unbounded length of such chains, we consider residuals C_i up to renaming of variables.

4.2 A checking algorithm

The type checking algorithm consists in examining in turn each reaction of the program.

$$\mathsf{TypeCheck}\ (P, T) = \forall (C, A) \text{ of } P.\ \mathsf{Check}\ (A, T, \mathsf{Build}\ (C, \{C\}, T))$$

[1] The global conditions on this reduction are ensured by the validity of the reduction of $M + C$ and the fact that variables of A are either variables of C or fresh variables.

For each reaction $C \Rightarrow A$, a reduction graph summarizing all possible reduction chains from C to a nonterminal is built by Build. Then, Check verifies that for any reduction chain and context X of the graph from C to a nonterminal, $A+X$ reduces to the same nonterminal. These functions are described in Figure 1.

Build takes an initial graph made of the root C. The reduction graph is such that nodes are residuals C_i which are all different (even up to renaming of variables) and edges are of the form $C_i \stackrel{X,\sigma}{\longrightarrow} C_j$. This notation indicates that $C_i + X \leadsto_T \sigma C_j$ where X is a basic context and σ is a variable renaming.

Build (C, G, T)
if C is a nonterminal then return G else
let $CX = \{(C_i, X_i) \mid C + X_i \leadsto_T C_i\}$ in   *CX is a finite set (up to fresh variable renaming)*
for each (C_i, X_i) in CX do
    if $\exists C_j \in G$ and σ_j such that $C_i = \sigma_j C_j$ then $G := G + C \stackrel{X_i,\sigma_j}{\longrightarrow} C_j$
    else $G := G + C_i + C \stackrel{X_i,id}{\longrightarrow} C_i$; $G :=$ Build(C_i, G, T)
od
return G

Check (A, T, G)
let $\mathcal{S} = \{(X_0 + \sigma_1 X_1 + \ldots + \sigma_1 \circ \ldots \circ \sigma_n\ X_n, \sigma_1 \circ \ldots \circ \sigma_{n+1}\ \{NT\ x_1 \ldots x_p\})$
    $\mid C_0 \stackrel{X_0,\sigma_1}{\longrightarrow} C_1 \stackrel{X_1,\sigma_2}{\longrightarrow} \ldots C_n \stackrel{X_n,\sigma_{n+1}}{\longrightarrow} \{NT\ x_1 \ldots x_p\} \in G\}$
and $\mathcal{C} = \{(X_0 + \sigma_1 X_1 + \ldots + \sigma_1 \circ \ldots \circ \sigma_{i-1}\ X_{i-1}, \sigma_1 \circ \ldots \circ \sigma_i\ C_i)$
    $\mid C_0 \stackrel{X_0,\sigma_1}{\longrightarrow} \ldots \stackrel{X_{i-1},\sigma_i}{\longrightarrow} C_i \in G$ and $\exists C_i \stackrel{X,\sigma_x}{\longrightarrow} \ldots C_i \in G$
        and $\exists C_i \stackrel{Y,\sigma_y}{\longrightarrow} \ldots N \in G$ (N a nonterminal)
        and $\nexists\ j < i \mid C_j \stackrel{Z,\sigma_z}{\longrightarrow} \ldots C_j \in G\}$
in $\forall (X, Y) \in \mathcal{S} \cup \mathcal{C}$. Reduces_to $(A + X, Y, T)$

Reduces_to (X, Y, T)
if X=Y then True
else if X is irreducible then False
else let {X$_1$, ..., X$_n$} the set of all possible residuals of X by a $\leadsto_T$ reduction
    in $\bigvee_{i=1}^{n}$ Reduces_to (X$_i$, Y, T)

Fig. 1. Type checking functions

The structure of Build is a depth first traversal of all possible reduction chains. The recursion stops when C is a nonterminal or is already present in the graph. CX is the set of basic contexts and residuals denoting all the different $\leadsto_T$ reductions of C. If a residual C_i in already present in the graph, that is, there is already a node C_j such that $C_i = \sigma_j C_j$, then the edge $C \stackrel{X_i,\sigma_j}{\longrightarrow} C_j$ is added to the graph. Otherwise, a new node C_i is created and the edge $C \xrightarrow{X_i, id} C_i$ is added.

The function Check takes the graph as argument and performs the following verifications:

- For every simple path from the root to a nonterminal N with context X, it checks that $A + X \overset{*}{\leadsto}_T N$.
  Let us focus on the meaning of a path $C_0 \xrightarrow{X_0, \sigma_1} C_1 \ldots \xrightarrow{X_n, \sigma_{n+1}} \{NT\ x_1 \ldots x_p\}$. By definition, we have

  $$C_0 + X_0 \leadsto_T \sigma_1 C_1, \ldots, C_n + X_n \leadsto_T \sigma_{n+1}\{NT\ x_1 \ldots x_p\}$$

  thus

  $$C_0 + X_0 + \sigma_1 X_1 + \ldots + \sigma_1 \circ \ldots \circ \sigma_n\ X_n \overset{*}{\leadsto}_T \sigma_1 \circ \ldots \circ \sigma_{n+1}\{NT\ x_1 \ldots x_p\}$$

  So, the context and nonterminal (X, N) associated with the above path are $X = X_0 + \sigma_1 X_1 + \ldots + \sigma_1 \circ \ldots \circ \sigma_n\ X_n$ and $N = \sigma_1 \circ \ldots \circ \sigma_n \circ \sigma_{n+1}\ \{NT\ x_1 \ldots x_p\}$.
- For every simple path with context X from the root to a residual C_i belonging to a cycle, it checks that $A + X \overset{*}{\leadsto}_T C_i$. In fact, it is sufficient to check this property for the first residual belonging to a cycle occurring on the path from the root and only for cycles which may lead to a nonterminal.

The verifications that the action A with context X can be reduced to Y are implemented by function Reduces_to$(A + X, Y, T)$. It simply tries all the $\leadsto_T$ reductions on the term $A+X$ using a depth first strategy. If a path leading to Y is found then True is returned. If Reduces_to finds out that all the normal forms of $A+X$ by "$\leadsto_T$" are different from Y, it returns False which entails the failure of the verification (TypeCheck(P, T) = False).

The termination of TypeCheck is ensured by the following observations:

- The reduction graph is finite. Using the context-free nature of types and equality up to renaming, it is easy to show that the number of nodes and edges is bounded.
- It is possible to find a well-founded decreasing ordering for $\leadsto_T$ reductions ensuring the termination of Reduces_to.

The type checking is correct if it ensures that the type of a program is invariant throughout the reduction. The proof amounts to showing a subject reduction property.

Property 1 *$\forall P$, $M_1 : T$ $M_1 \longrightarrow_P M_2$ and* TypeCheck$(P, T) \Rightarrow M_2 : T$

The proof of this property and a more detailed presentation of the algorithm can be found in a companion paper [6].

4.3 Examples

Even if the theoretical complexity of the algorithm is prohibitive, the cost seems reasonable in practice. We take here a few examples to illustrate the type checking process at work.

Example 1. Let us take the *Iota* program working on type *List*. The program is

$$Iota \;:\; List = \mathbf{end}\ a\ ,\ \overline{a} > 1 \quad \Rightarrow \quad \mathbf{succ}\ a\ b\ ,\ \mathbf{end}\ b\ ,\ b\ :=\ \overline{a} - 1$$

Operations on values are not relevant for type checking and we consider the single reduction rule

$$\mathbf{end}\ a \quad \Rightarrow \quad \mathbf{succ}\ a\ b\ ,\ \mathbf{end}\ b$$

The type definition and associated rewriting system are:

$$\begin{array}{ll} List = L\ x & \\ L\ x\ = \mathbf{succ}\ x\ y\ ,\ L\ y & \\ L\ x\ = \mathbf{end}\ x & \end{array} \qquad \begin{array}{ll} L\ x & \rightsquigarrow_{List} List \\ \mathbf{succ}\ x\ y\ ,\ L\ y & \rightsquigarrow_{List} L\ x \\ \mathbf{end}\ x & \rightsquigarrow_{List} L\ x \end{array}$$

The type checking amounts to the call

$$\mathsf{Check}((\mathbf{succ}\ a\ b,\ \mathbf{end}\ b),\ List,\ \mathsf{Build}(\mathbf{end}\ a,\ \{\mathbf{end}\ a\},\ List))$$

There is a single $\rightsquigarrow_{List}$ reduction of $\mathbf{end}\ a + X$ (with X a basic context), namely

$$\mathbf{end}\ a \rightsquigarrow_{List} L\ a$$

So, $CX = \{(L\ a, \emptyset)\}$ and, since $L\ a$ is a nonterminal, the reduction graph is

$$\mathbf{end}\ a \xrightarrow{\emptyset,id} L\ a$$

There is a single simple path and we are left with checking
$\mathsf{Reduces\_to}\ ((\mathbf{succ}\ a\ b\ ,\ \mathbf{end}\ b), L\ a, List)$
The set of possible residuals of $(\mathbf{succ}\ a\ b\ ,\ \mathbf{end}\ b)$ is $\{(\mathbf{succ}\ a\ b\ ,\ L\ b)\}$, so $\mathsf{Reduces\_to}\ ((\mathbf{succ}\ a\ b\ ,\ L\ b),\ L\ a\ ,\ List)$ is recursively called. The set of possible residuals of $(\mathbf{succ}\ a\ b\ ,\ L\ b)$ by a $\rightsquigarrow_{List}$ reduction is $\{L\ a\}$ and $\mathsf{Reduces\_to}$ $(L\ a, L\ a, List) = \mathsf{True}$. So, $\mathsf{TypeCheck}(Iota, List) = \mathsf{True}$ and we conclude that the "List" invariant is maintained.

Example 2. Let us consider a program performing an insertion at the end of a list of type *Last*.
Wrong : Last =
$\mathbf{succ}\ x\ z\ ,\ \mathbf{last}\ x\ z\ ,\ \mathbf{end}\ z\ \Rightarrow \mathbf{succ}\ x\ z\ ,\ \mathbf{succ}\ z\ t\ ,\ \mathbf{last}\ x\ t\ ,\ \mathbf{last}\ z\ t\ ,\ \mathbf{end}\ t$

Obviously this program is ill-typed. If the list has more than two elements, the first elements would still point to z whereas t is the new last element. The definition of the rewriting system of *Last* is:

$$\begin{array}{ll} L\ x\ z & \leadsto_{Last}\ Last \\ \mathbf{succ}\ x\ y\ ,\ \mathbf{last}\ x\ z\ ,\ L\ y\ z & \leadsto_{Last}\ L\ x\ z \\ \mathbf{succ}\ x\ z\ ,\ \mathbf{last}\ x\ z\ ,\ \mathbf{end}\ z & \leadsto_{Last}\ L\ x\ z \end{array}$$

There is a single reduction sequence from the condition to a nonterminal:

$$\mathbf{succ}\ x\ z\ ,\ \mathbf{last}\ x\ z\ ,\ \mathbf{end}\ z\ \leadsto_{Last}\ L\ x\ z$$

but,

$$\mathbf{succ}\ x\ z\ ,\ \mathbf{succ}\ z\ t\ ,\ \mathbf{last}\ x\ t\ ,\ \mathbf{last}\ z\ t\ ,\ \mathbf{end}\ t\ \not\leadsto_{Last}\ L\ x\ z$$

and the "Last" invariant is not maintained.

However, if we consider the insertion program:

$$Add : Last\ = \mathbf{succ}\ x\ y,\ \mathbf{last}\ x\ z\ \Rightarrow \mathbf{succ}\ x\ t,\ \mathbf{succ}\ t\ y,\ \mathbf{last}\ x\ z,\ \mathbf{last}\ t\ z$$

There is one reduction sequence from the condition to a nonterminal:

$$\mathbf{succ}\ x\ y\ ,\ \mathbf{last}\ x\ z\ ,\ L\ y\ z\ \leadsto_{Last}\ L\ x\ z$$

and it is easy to check that

$$\begin{array}{rl} \mathbf{succ}\ x\ t,\ \mathbf{succ}\ t\ y,\ \mathbf{last}\ x\ z,\ \mathbf{last}\ t\ z,\ L\ y\ z & \leadsto_{Last}\ \mathbf{succ}\ x\ t,\ \mathbf{last}\ x\ z,\ L\ t\ z \\ & \leadsto_{Last}\ L\ x\ z \end{array}$$

and the "Last" invariant is maintained.

5 Conclusion

We have applied the framework developed in this paper in three different areas: program refinement, coordination and type systems for imperative languages. We sketch these applications in turn.

- Structured Gamma can serve as a basis for program refinements leading to efficient implementations. The basic source of inefficiency of any "naïve" implementation of Gamma is the combinatorial explosion entailed by the semantics of the language for the selection of reacting elements. As pointed out in [5], most of the refinements leading to efficient optimizations of Gamma programs can be expressed as specific selection orderings. Several refinements are introduced in [5] which shows that they often lead to efficient well-known implementations of the corresponding algorithms. This result is quite satisfactory from a formal point of view because it shows that there is a continuum from specifications written in Gamma to lower-level and efficient program descriptions. These refinements, however, had to be checked manually. Using Structured Gamma as a basis, we can provide general conditions ensuring the correctness of program refinements [6]. The basic idea, which was already alluded to in section 3.3, consists in considering multiset (and type) refinements as the addition of extra relations between addresses. These relations are used as further constraints on the control in order to impose a specific ordering for the selection of elements.

- Coordination languages [4, 9], software architecture languages [8] and configuration languages [12] were proposed as a way to make large applications more manageable and more amenable to formal verifications. They are based on the principle that the definition of a software application should make a clear distinction between individual components and their interaction in the overall software organization. We have used Structured Gamma as a coordination language by interpreting the addresses in the multisets as names of individual entities to be coordinated [13]. Their associated value defines their behavior (in a given programming language which is independent of the coordination language) and the relations correspond to communication links. A structuring type provides a description of the shape of the overall architecture. An important advantage of our approach is that coordinators can be checked statically (using the algorithm of section 4) to ensure that they preserve the style of the architecture.
- The type systems currently available for imperative languages are too weak to detect a significant class of programming errors. For example, they cannot express the property that a list is doubly-linked or circular. Such structures can be specified naturally using a subset of structuring types that we call "shape types". We have proposed a syntax for a smooth integration of shape types in C [7]. Shapes are manipulated by reactions which can be statically checked and translated in pure C. The programmer can still express pointer manipulations with the expected constant time execution and benefit from the additional guarantee that the property specified by the structuring type is an invariant of the program. The graph types approach [11] shares the same concern. In their framework, a graph is defined using a canonical spanning tree (called the backbone) and auxiliary pointers. Only the backbone can be manipulated by programs and some simple operations may implicitly involve non-constant updates of the auxiliary pointers. In contrast, shape types do not privilege any part of the graph and all operations on the structure appear explicitly in the rewrite rules.

Directions for further research include other application areas such as the specification of networks of processors and various extensions like the use of context-sensitive grammars to describe structuring types.

Acknowledgments. This work was supported by Esprit Basic Research project 9102 *Coordination*.

References

1. J.-P. Banâtre and D. Le Métayer, *The Gamma model and its discipline of programming*, Science of Computer Programming, Vol. 15, pp. 55-77, 1990.
2. J.-P. Banâtre and D. Le Métayer. Programming by multiset transformation, *Communications of the ACM*, Vol. 36-1, pp. 98-111, January 1993.

3. J.-P. Banâtre and D. Le Métayer. Gamma and the chemical reaction model: ten years after, *Coordination programming: mechanisms, models and semantics*, Imperial College Press, 1996.
4. N. Carriero and D. Gelernter, Linda in context, *Communications of the ACM*, Vol. 32-4, pp. 444-458, April 1989.
5. C. Creveuil. *Techniques d'analyse et de mise en œuvre des programmes Gamma*, Thesis, University of Rennes I, 1991.
6. P. Fradet and D. Le Métayer, Structured Gamma, *Irisa Research Report PI-989*, March 1996.
7. P. Fradet and D. Le Métayer, Shape types, In *Proc. of the 24rd ACM SIGPLAN-SIGACT Symposium on Principles of Programming Languages*, January 1997.
8. D. Garlan and D. Perry, Editor's Introduction, *IEEE Transactions on Software Engineering, Special Issue on Software Architectures*, 1995.
9. A. A. Holzbacher, A software environment for concurrent coordinated programming, *Proc. First int. Conf. on Coordination Models, Languages and Applications*, Springer Verlag, LNCS 1061, pp. 249-266, April 1996.
10. P. Inverardi and A. Wolf. Formal specification and analysis of software architectures using the chemical abstract machine model, *IEEE Transactions on Software Engineering*, Vol. 21, No. 4, pp. 373-386, April 1995.
11. N. Klarlund and M. Schwartzbach. Graph types. In *Proc. 20th Symp. on Princ. of Prog. Lang.*, pp. 196-205. ACM, 1993.
12. J. Kramer, Configuration programming. A framework for the development of distributable systems, *Proc. COMPEURO'90*, IEEE, pp. 374-384, 1990.
13. D. Le Métayer, Software architecture styles as graph grammars, in *Proc. of the ACM SIGSOFT'96 4th Symposium on the Foundations of Software Engineering*, 1996, pp. 15-23.

Polymorphic Subtyping for Effect Analysis: The Static Semantics

Hanne Riis Nielson & Flemming Nielson & Torben Amtoft

Computer Science Department, Aarhus University, Denmark

e-mail: {hrnielson,fnielson,tamtoft}@daimi.aau.dk

Abstract. The integration of polymorphism (in the style of the ML `let`-construct), subtyping, and effects (modelling assignment or communication) into one common type system has proved remarkably difficult. One line of research has succeeded in integrating polymorphism and subtyping; adding effects in a straightforward way results in a semantically unsound system. Another line of research has succeeded in integrating polymorphism, effects, and subeffecting; adding subtyping in a straightforward way invalidates the construction of the inference algorithm. This paper integrates all of polymorphism, effects, and subtyping into an annotated type and effect system for Concurrent ML and shows that the resulting system is a conservative extension of the ML type system.

1 Introduction

Motivation. The last decade has seen a number of papers addressing the difficult task of developing type systems for languages that admit polymorphism in the style of the ML `let`-construct, that admit subtyping, and that admit effects as may arise from assignment or communication.

This is a problem of practical importance. The programming language Standard ML has been joined by a number of other high-level languages demonstrating the power of polymorphism for large scale software development. Already Standard ML contains imperative effects in the form of `ref`-types that can be used for assignment; closely related languages like Concurrent ML or Facile further admit primitives for synchronous communication. Finally, the trend towards integrating aspects of object orientation into these languages necessitates a study of subtyping.

Apart from the need to type such languages we see a need for type systems integrating polymorphism, subtyping, and effects in order to be able to continue the present development of annotated type and effect systems for a number of static program analyses; example analyses include control flow analysis, binding time analysis and communication analysis. This will facilitate modular proofs of correctness while at the same time allowing the inference algorithms to generate syntax-free constraints that can be solved efficiently.

State of the art. One of the pioneering papers in the area is [10] that developed the first polymorphic type inference and algorithm for the applicative fragment of ML; a shorter presentation for the typed λ-calculus with `let` is given in [3].

Since then many papers have studied how to integrate subtyping. A number of early papers did so by mainly focusing on the typed λ-calculus and only briefly dealing with `let` [11, 5]. Later papers have treated polymorphism in full generality [18, 8]. A key ingredient in these approaches is the simplification of the enormous set of constraints into something manageable [4, 18].

Already ML necessitates an incorporation of imperative effects due to the presence of `ref`-types. A pioneering paper in the area is [21] that develops a distinction between imperative and applicative type variables: for *creation* of a reference cell we demand that its type contain imperative variables only; and one is not allowed to generalise over imperative variables unless the expression in question is *non-expansive* (i.e. does not expand the store) which will be the case if it is an identifier or a function abstraction.

The problem of typing ML with references (but without subtyping) has lead to a number of attempts to improve upon [21]; this includes the following:

- [23] is similar in spirit to [21] in that one is not allowed to generalise over a type variable if a reference cell has been *created* with a type containing this variable; to trace such variables the type system is augmented with *effects*. Effects may be approximated by larger effects, that is the system employs *subeffecting*.
- [19] can be considered a refinement of [23] in that effects also record the *region* in which a reference cell is created (or a read/write operation performed); this information enables one to "mask" effects which have taken place in "inaccessible" regions.
- [9] presents a somewhat alternative view: here focus is not on detecting *creation* of reference cells but rather to detect their *use*; this means that if an identifier occurs free in a function closure then all variables in its type have to be "examined". This method is quite powerful but unfortunately it fails to be a conservative extension of ML (cf. Sect. 2.6): some purely applicative programs which are typeable in ML may be untypeable in this system.

The surveys in [19, section 11] and in [23, section 5] show that many of these systems are incomparable, in the sense that for any two approaches it will often be the case that there are programs which are accepted by one of them but not by the other, and vice versa. Our approach (which will be illustrated by a fragment of Concurrent ML but is equally applicable to Standard ML with references) involves subtyping which is strictly more powerful than subeffecting (as shown in Example 4); apart from this we do not attempt to measure its strength relative to other approaches.

In the area of static program analysis, annotated type and effect systems have been used as the basis for control flow analysis [20] and binding time analysis [14, 7]. These papers typically make use of a polymorphic type system with subtyping and no effects, or a non-polymorphic type system with effects and subtyping. A more ambitious analysis is the approach of [15] to let annotated type and effect systems extract terms of a process algebra from programs with communication; this involves polymorphism and subeffecting but the algorithmic issues are non-trivial [12] (presumably because the inference system is expressed without using constraints); [1] presents an algorithm that is sound as well as complete, but which generates constraints that are not guaranteed to have best solutions. Finally we should mention [22] where effects are incorporated into ML types in order to deal with *region inference.*

A step forward. In this paper we take an important step towards integrating polymorphism, subtyping, and effects into one common type system. As far as the annotated type and effect system is concerned this involves the following key idea:

- Carefully taking effects into account when deciding the set of variables over which to generalise in the rule for `let`; this involves taking upwards closure with respect to a constraint set and is essential for maintaining semantic soundness and a number of substitution properties.

This presents a major step forward in generalising the subeffecting approach of [19] and in admitting effects into the subtyping approaches of [18, 8]. The development is not only applicable to Concurrent ML (with communication) but also Standard ML (with references) and similar settings.

The essence of Concurrent ML. In this paper we study a fragment of Concurrent ML (CML) that as ML includes the λ-calculus and `let`-polymorphism, but which also includes five primitives for synchronous communication:

The constant `channel` allocates a new communication channel when applied to `()`.

The function `fork` spawns a new process e when applied to the expression `fn` dummy $\Rightarrow$ e; this process will then execute concurrently with the other processes, one of which is the program itself.

The constant `sync` activates and synchronises a delayed communication created by either `send` or `receive`. Thus one process can send the value of e to another process by the expression `sync(send(ch,`e`))` where communication takes place along the channel `ch`; similarly a process can receive a value from another process by the expression `sync(receive(ch))`.

The following program illustrates some of the essential features: it is a version of the well-known *map* function except that a process is forked for each tail while the forking process itself works on the head.

```
rec map2 f =>
   fn xs =>
     if isnil(xs) then []
     else let ch = channel ()
          in fork (fn d =>
                    (sync (send (ch, map2 f (tl xs)))));
             cons (f (hd xs))
                  (sync (receive ch))
```

That is, when applied to some function `f` and say the list `[x1,x2,x3]` the initial process p_0 will wait for a new process p_1 to send the value of `[f x2,f x3]` over a new channel ch_1 and in the meantime p_0 computes `f x1` such that it can finally return the value of `[f x1,f x2,f x3]`; p_1 will do its job by waiting for a new process p_2 to communicate the value of `[f x3]` over a new channel ch_2 and in the meantime p_1 computes `f x2`; etc.

Overview. We develop an annotated type and effect system in which a simple notion of behaviours is used to keep track of the types of channels created; unlike previous approaches by some of the authors no attempt is made to model any causality among the individual behaviours. Finally, we show that the system is a "conservative extension" of the usual type system for Standard ML.

The formal demonstration of semantic soundness, as well as the construction of the inference algorithm, are dealt with in companion papers [2, 13].

2 Inference System

The fragment of Concurrent ML [17, 16] we have chosen for illustrating our approach has *expressions* ($e \in Exp$) and *constants* ($c \in Con$) given by the following syntax:

$$\begin{aligned} e ::= {} & c \mid x \mid \texttt{fn}\ x \Rightarrow e \mid e_1\, e_2 \mid \texttt{let}\ x = e_1\ \texttt{in}\ e_2 \\ \mid {} & \texttt{rec}\ f\ x \Rightarrow e \mid \texttt{if}\ e\ \texttt{then}\ e_1\ \texttt{else}\ e_2 \end{aligned}$$

$$\begin{aligned} c ::= {} & \texttt{()} \mid \texttt{true} \mid \texttt{false} \mid n \mid \texttt{+} \mid \texttt{*} \mid \texttt{=} \mid \cdots \\ \mid {} & \texttt{pair} \mid \texttt{fst} \mid \texttt{snd} \mid \texttt{nil} \mid \texttt{cons} \mid \texttt{hd} \mid \texttt{tl} \mid \texttt{isnil} \\ \mid {} & \texttt{send} \mid \texttt{receive} \mid \texttt{sync} \mid \texttt{channel} \mid \texttt{fork} \end{aligned}$$

For expressions this includes constants, identifiers, function abstraction, application, polymorphic `let`-expressions, recursive functions, and conditionals; a *program* is an expression without any free identifiers.

Constants can be divided into four classes, according to whether they are *sequential* or *non-sequential* and according to whether they are *constructors* or *base functions*.

The sequential constructors include the unique element `()` of the unit type, the two booleans, numbers ($n \in Num$), `pair` for constructing pairs, and `nil` and `cons` for constructing lists.

The sequential base functions include a selection of arithmetic operations, `fst` and `snd` for decomposing a pair, and `hd`, `tl` and `isnil` for decomposing and inspecting a list.

We shall allow to write (e_1,e_2) for $\texttt{pair}\, e_1\, e_2$, to write `[]` for `nil` and $[e_1 \cdots e_n]$ for $\texttt{cons}\,(e_1,\texttt{cons}(\cdots,\texttt{nil})\cdots)$. Additionally we shall write $e_1;e_2$ for $\texttt{snd}\,(e_1,e_2)$; to motivate this notice that since the language is call-by-value, evaluation of the latter expression will give rise to evaluation of e_1 followed by evaluation of e_2, the value of which will be the final result.

The unique flavour of Concurrent ML is due to the non-sequential constants which are the primitives for communication; we include five of these but more (in particular `choose` and `wrap`) can be added. The non-sequential constructors are **send** and **receive**: rather than actually enabling a communication they create *delayed communications* which are first-class entities that can be passed around freely. This leads to a very powerful programming discipline (in particular in the presence of `choose` and `wrap`) as is discussed in [17]. The non-sequential base functions are `channel` for allocating new communication channels, `fork` for spawning new processes, and `sync` for synchronising delayed communications; examples of their use are given in the Introduction.

Remark. We stated in the Introduction that our development is widely applicable. To this end it is worth pointing out the similarities between the `ref`-types of Standard ML and the delayed communications of Concurrent ML. In particular `ref` e corresponds to `channel ()`, e_1`:=`e_2 corresponds to `sync (send (`e_1`,`e_2`))`, and `!`e corresponds to `sync (receive` e`)`. Looking slightly ahead the Standard ML type t `ref` will correspond to the Concurrent ML type t `chan`. □

Example 1. Consider the program

```
fn f => let id = fn y =>
                  (if true
                   then f
                   else fn x =>
                         (sync (send (channel (), y));
                          x));
                  y
        in id id
```

that takes a function `f` as argument, defines an identity function `id`, and then applies `id` to itself. The identity function contains a conditional whose sole purpose is to force `f` and a locally defined function to have the same type. The locally defined function is yet another identity function except that it attempts to send the argument to `id` over a newly created channel. (To be able to execute one would need to fork a process that could read over the same channel.)

This program is of interest because it will be rejected by a system using subeffecting only, whereas it will be accepted in the systems of [19] and [21]. We shall see that we will be able to type this program in our system as well! □

2.1 Annotated Types

To prepare for the type inference system we must clarify the syntax of types, effects, type schemes, and constraints. The syntax of *types* ($t \in Typ$) is given by:

$$\begin{aligned} t ::= {} & \alpha \mid \texttt{unit} \mid \texttt{int} \mid \texttt{bool} \mid t_1 \times t_2 \mid t\ \texttt{list} \\ \mid {} & t_1 \rightarrow^{b} t_2 \mid t\ \texttt{chan} \mid t\ \texttt{com}\ b \end{aligned}$$

Here we have base types for the unit type, booleans and integers; type variables are denoted α; composite types include the product type, the function type and the list type; finally we have the type t `chan` for a typed channel allowing values of type t to be transmitted, and the type t `com` b for a delayed communication that will eventually result in a value of type t.

Except for the presence of a b-component in $t_1 \rightarrow^b t_2$ and t `com` b this is much the same type structure that is actually used in Concurrent ML [17]. The role of the b-component is to express the dynamic effect that takes place when the function is applied or the delayed communication synchronised. Motivated by [19] and (a simplified version of) [15] the syntax of *effects*, or *behaviours*, ($b \in Beh$) is given by:

$$b ::= \{t \text{ CHAN}\} \mid \beta \mid \emptyset \mid b_1 \cup b_2$$

Apart from the presence of behaviour variables (denoted β) a behaviour can thus be viewed as a set of "atomic" behaviours each of form $\{t \text{ CHAN}\}$, recording the allocation of a channel of type t `chan`. The definition of types and behaviours is of course mutually recursive.

A *constraint set* C is a finite set of type $(t_1 \subseteq t_2)$ and behaviour inclusions $(b_1 \subseteq b_2)$. A *type scheme* ($ts \in TSch$) is given by

$$ts ::= \forall(\vec{\alpha}\vec{\beta} : C).\ t$$

where $\vec{\alpha}\vec{\beta}$ is the list of quantified type and behaviour variables, C is a constraint set, and t is the type. We regard type schemes as equivalent up to alpha-renaming of bound variables. There is a natural injection from types into type schemes which takes the type t into the type scheme $\forall(() : \emptyset).\ t$.

We list in Figure 1 the type schemes of a few selected constants. For those constants also to be found in Standard ML the constraint set is empty and the type is as in Standard ML except that the empty behaviour has been placed on all function types. The type of `sync` interacts closely with the types of `send` and `receive`: if `ch` is a channel of type t `chan`, the expression `receive ch` is going to have type t `com` $\emptyset$, and the expression `sync (receive ch)` is going to have type t; similarly for `send`. The type of `channel` (indirectly) records the type of the created channel in the behaviour labelling the function type. Finally[1] the type of `fork` indicates that the argument may have any behaviour whatsoever, in particular this means that e in `fork (fn` dummy $\Rightarrow e$) may create new channels without this being recorded in the overall effect[2].

Following the approach of [18, 8] we will incorporate the effects of [19, 15] by defining a type inference system with judgements of the form

$$C, A \vdash e : \sigma \,\&\, b$$

where C is a constraint set, A is an environment i.e. a list $[x_1 : \sigma_1, \cdots, x_n : \sigma_n]$ of typing assumptions for identifiers, σ is a type t or a type scheme ts, and b is an

[1] As discussed previously one might add `wrap` to the language: this constant transforms delayed communications of type t `com` b into delayed communications of type t' `com` b'; here b' (and thus also b) may be non-trivial.

[2] To repair this one could add behaviours of form FORK b.

c	TypeOf(c)
+	$\mathtt{int} \times \mathtt{int} \rightarrow^{\emptyset} \mathtt{int}$
pair	$\forall(\alpha_1\alpha_2 : \emptyset).\ \alpha_1 \rightarrow^{\emptyset} \alpha_2 \rightarrow^{\emptyset} \alpha_1 \times \alpha_2$
fst	$\forall(\alpha_1\alpha_2 : \emptyset).\ \alpha_1 \times \alpha_2 \rightarrow^{\emptyset} \alpha_1$
snd	$\forall(\alpha_1\alpha_2 : \emptyset).\ \alpha_1 \times \alpha_2 \rightarrow^{\emptyset} \alpha_2$
send	$\forall(\alpha : \emptyset).\ (\alpha\ \mathbf{chan}) \times \alpha \rightarrow^{\emptyset} (\alpha\ \mathbf{com}\ \emptyset)$
receive	$\forall(\alpha : \emptyset).\ (\alpha\ \mathbf{chan}) \rightarrow^{\emptyset} (\alpha\ \mathbf{com}\ \emptyset)$
sync	$\forall(\alpha\beta : \emptyset).\ (\alpha\ \mathbf{com}\ \beta) \rightarrow^{\beta} \alpha$
channel	$\forall(\alpha\beta : \{\{\alpha\ \mathrm{CHAN}\} \subseteq \beta\}).\ \mathbf{unit} \rightarrow^{\beta} (\alpha\ \mathbf{chan})$
fork	$\forall(\alpha\beta : \emptyset).\ (\mathbf{unit} \rightarrow^{\beta} \alpha) \rightarrow^{\emptyset} \mathbf{unit}$

Fig. 1. Type schemes for selected constants.

effect. This means that e has type or type scheme σ, and that its execution will result in a behaviour described by b, assuming that free identifiers have types as specified by A and that all type and behaviour variables are related as described by C.

The overall structure of the type inference system of Figure 2 is very close to those of [18, 8] with a few components from [19, 15] thrown in; the novel ideas of our approach only show up as carefully constructed side conditions for some of the rules. Concentrating on the "overall picture" we thus have rather straightforward axioms for constants and identifiers; here $A(x)$ denotes the rightmost entry for x in A. The rules for abstraction and application are as usual in effect systems: the latent behaviour of the body of a function abstraction is placed on the arrow of the function type, and once the function is applied the latent behaviour is added to the effect of evaluating the function and its argument (reflecting that the language is call-by-value). The rule for `let` is straightforward given that both the `let`-bound expression and the body needs to be evaluated. The rule for recursion makes use of function abstraction to concisely represent the "fixed point requirement" of typing recursive functions; note that we do not admit polymorphic recursion[3]. The rule for conditional is unable to keep track of which branch is chosen, therefore an upper approximation of the branches is taken. We then have separate rules for subtyping, instantiation and generalisation and we shall explain their side conditions shortly.

[3] Even though this is undecidable in general [6] one might allow polymorphic recursion in the annotations as in [7] or [22].

(con) $C, A \vdash c : \text{TypeOf(c)} \,\&\, \emptyset$

(id) $C, A \vdash x : A(x) \,\&\, \emptyset$

(abs) $$\frac{C, A[x : t_1] \vdash e : t_2 \,\&\, b}{C, A \vdash \mathtt{fn}\ x \Rightarrow e : (t_1 \to^{b} t_2) \,\&\, \emptyset}$$

(app) $$\frac{C_1, A \vdash e_1 : (t_2 \to^{b} t_1) \,\&\, b_1 \qquad C_2, A \vdash e_2 : t_2 \,\&\, b_2}{(C_1 \cup C_2), A \vdash e_1\, e_2 : t_1 \,\&\, (b_1 \cup b_2 \cup b)}$$

(let) $$\frac{C_1, A \vdash e_1 : ts_1 \,\&\, b_1 \qquad C_2, A[x : ts_1] \vdash e_2 : t_2 \,\&\, b_2}{(C_1 \cup C_2), A \vdash \mathtt{let}\ x = e_1\ \mathtt{in}\ e_2 : t_2 \,\&\, (b_1 \cup b_2)}$$

(rec) $$\frac{C, A[f : t] \vdash \mathtt{fn}\ x \Rightarrow e : t \,\&\, b}{C, A \vdash \mathtt{rec}\ f\ x \Rightarrow e : t \,\&\, b}$$

(if) $$\frac{C_0, A \vdash e_0 : \mathtt{bool} \,\&\, b_0 \qquad C_1, A \vdash e_1 : t \,\&\, b_1 \qquad C_2, A \vdash e_2 : t \,\&\, b_2}{(C_0 \cup C_1 \cup C_2), A \vdash \mathtt{if}\ e_0\ \mathtt{then}\ e_1\ \mathtt{else}\ e_2 : t \,\&\, (b_0 \cup b_1 \cup b_2)}$$

(sub) $$\frac{C, A \vdash e : t \,\&\, b}{C, A \vdash e : t' \,\&\, b'}$$ if $C \vdash t \subseteq t'$ and $C \vdash b \subseteq b'$

(ins) $$\frac{C, A \vdash e : \forall(\vec{\alpha}\vec{\beta} : C_0).\ t_0 \,\&\, b}{C, A \vdash e : S_0\, t_0 \,\&\, b}$$ if $\forall(\vec{\alpha}\vec{\beta} : C_0).\ t_0$ is solvable from C by S_0

(gen) $$\frac{C \cup C_0, A \vdash e : t_0 \,\&\, b}{C, A \vdash e : \forall(\vec{\alpha}\vec{\beta} : C_0).\ t_0 \,\&\, b}$$ if $\forall(\vec{\alpha}\vec{\beta} : C_0).\ t_0$ is both well-formed, solvable from C, and satisfies $\{\vec{\alpha}\vec{\beta}\} \cap FV(C, A, b) = \emptyset$

Fig. 2. The type inference system.

2.2 Subtyping

Rule (sub) generalises the subeffecting rule of [19] by incorporating subtyping and extends the subtyping rule of [18] to deal with effects. To do this we associate two kinds of judgements with a constraint set: the relations $C \vdash b_1 \subseteq b_2$ and $C \vdash t_1 \subseteq t_2$ are defined by the rules and axioms of Figure 3. In all cases we write $\equiv$ for the equivalence induced by the orderings. We shall also write $C \vdash C'$ to mean that $C \vdash b_1 \subseteq b_2$ for all $(b_1 \subseteq b_2)$ in C' and that $C \vdash t_1 \subseteq t_2$ for all $(t_1 \subseteq t_2)$ in C'.

The relation $C \vdash t_1 \subseteq t_2$ expresses the usual notion of subtyping, in particular it is contravariant in the argument position of a function type but there

Ordering on behaviours

(axiom) $C \vdash b_1 \subseteq b_2$ if $(b_1 \subseteq b_2) \in C$

(refl) $C \vdash b \subseteq b$

(trans) $$\frac{C \vdash b_1 \subseteq b_2 \quad C \vdash b_2 \subseteq b_3}{C \vdash b_1 \subseteq b_3}$$

(CHAN) $$\frac{C \vdash t \equiv t'}{C \vdash \{t\ \text{CHAN}\} \subseteq \{t'\ \text{CHAN}\}}$$

($\emptyset$) $C \vdash \emptyset \subseteq b$

($\cup$) $C \vdash b_i \subseteq (b_1 \cup b_2)$ for $i = 1, 2$

(lub) $$\frac{C \vdash b_1 \subseteq b \quad C \vdash b_2 \subseteq b}{C \vdash (b_1 \cup b_2) \subseteq b}$$

Ordering on types

(axiom) $C \vdash t_1 \subseteq t_2$ if $(t_1 \subseteq t_2) \in C$

(refl) $C \vdash t \subseteq t$

(trans) $$\frac{C \vdash t_1 \subseteq t_2 \quad C \vdash t_2 \subseteq t_3}{C \vdash t_1 \subseteq t_3}$$

($\rightarrow$) $$\frac{C \vdash t_1' \subseteq t_1 \quad C \vdash t_2 \subseteq t_2' \quad C \vdash b \subseteq b'}{C \vdash (t_1 \rightarrow^{b} t_2) \subseteq (t_1' \rightarrow^{b'} t_2')}$$

($\times$) $$\frac{C \vdash t_1 \subseteq t_1' \quad C \vdash t_2 \subseteq t_2'}{C \vdash (t_1 \times t_2) \subseteq (t_1' \times t_2')}$$

(`list`) $$\frac{C \vdash t \subseteq t'}{C \vdash (t\ \mathtt{list}) \subseteq (t'\ \mathtt{list})}$$

(`chan`) $$\frac{C \vdash t \equiv t'}{C \vdash (t\ \mathtt{chan}) \subseteq (t'\ \mathtt{chan})}$$

(`com`) $$\frac{C \vdash t \subseteq t' \quad C \vdash b \subseteq b'}{C \vdash (t\ \mathtt{com}\ b) \subseteq (t'\ \mathtt{com}\ b')}$$

Fig. 3. Subtyping and subeffecting.

is no inclusion between base types. In the case of **chan** note that the type t of t **chan** essentially occurs covariantly (when used in `receive`) as well as contravariantly (when used in **send**); hence we must require that $C \vdash t \equiv t'$ in order for $C \vdash t$ **chan** $\subseteq t'$ **chan** to hold.

The definition of $C \vdash b_1 \subseteq b_2$ is a fairly straightforward axiomatisation of set inclusion upon behaviours; note that the premise for $C \vdash \{t_1 \text{ CHAN}\} \subseteq \{t_2 \text{ CHAN}\}$ is that $C \vdash t_1 \equiv t_2$.

2.3 Generalisation

We now explain some of the side conditions for the rules (ins) and (gen). This involves the notion of substitution: a mapping from type variables to types and from behaviour variables to behaviours[4] such that the domain is finite. Here the domain of a substitution S is $Dom(S) = \{\gamma \mid S\,\gamma \neq \gamma\}$ and the range is $Ran(S) = \bigcup \{FV(S\,\gamma) \mid \gamma \in Dom(S)\}$ where the concept of free variables, denoted $FV(\cdots)$, is standard. The identity substitution is denoted Id and we sometimes write $Inv(S) = Dom(S) \cup Ran(S)$ for the set of variables that are involved in the substitution S.

Rule (ins) is much as in [18] and merely says that to take an instance of a type scheme we must ensure that the constraints are satisfied; this is expressed using the notion of *solvability*:

Definition 1. The type scheme $\forall(\vec{\alpha}\vec{\beta} : C_0).\ t_0$ is *solvable* from C by the substitution S_0 if $Dom(S_0) \subseteq \{\vec{\alpha}\vec{\beta}\}$ and if $C \vdash S_0\,C_0$.

A type t is trivially solvable from C, and an environment A is solvable from C if for all x in $Dom(A)$ it holds that $A(x)$ is solvable from C.

Except for the well-formedness requirement (explained later), rule (gen) seems close to the corresponding rule in [18]: clearly we cannot generalise over variables free in the global type assumptions or global constraint set, and as in effect systems (e.g. [19]) we cannot generalise over variables visible in the effect. Furthermore, as in [18] solvability is imposed to ensure that we do not create type schemes that have no instances; this condition ensures that the expressions `let x =` e_1 `in` e_2 and `let x =` e_1 `in (x;`e_2`)` are going to be equivalent in the type system.

Example 2. Without an additional notion of well-formedness this does not give a semantically sound rule (gen); as an example consider the expression e given by

```
let ch = channel ()
in  ...
    (sync(send(ch,7)))
    (sync(send(ch,true)))
```

[4] We use γ to range over α's and β's as appropriate and use g range over t's and b's as appropriate.

and note that it is semantically unsound (at least if "$\cdots$" forked some process receiving twice over **ch** and adding the results). Writing $C = \{\{\alpha\ \text{CHAN}\} \subseteq \beta,$ $\{\{\texttt{int}\ \text{CHAN}\}\} \subseteq \beta,\ \{\{\texttt{bool}\ \text{CHAN}\}\} \subseteq \beta\}$ and $C' = \{\{\alpha'\ \text{CHAN}\} \subseteq \beta\}$ then gives

$$C \cup C', [\,] \vdash \texttt{channel ()} \ : \ \alpha'\ \texttt{chan} \,\&\, \beta$$

and, without taking well-formedness into account, rule (gen) would give

$$C, [\,] \vdash \texttt{channel ()} \ : \ (\forall(\alpha' : C').\ \alpha'\ \texttt{chan}) \,\&\, \beta$$

because $\alpha' \notin FV(C, \beta)$ and $\forall(\alpha' : C').\ \alpha'\ \texttt{chan}$ is solvable from C by either of the substitutions $[\alpha' \mapsto \alpha]$, $[\alpha' \mapsto \texttt{int}]$ and $[\alpha' \mapsto \texttt{bool}]$. This then would give

$$C, [\texttt{ch} : \forall(\alpha' : C').\ \alpha'\ \texttt{chan}] \vdash \texttt{ch} \ : \ \texttt{int chan} \,\&\, \emptyset$$
$$C, [\texttt{ch} : \forall(\alpha' : C').\ \alpha'\ \texttt{chan}] \vdash \texttt{ch} \ : \ \texttt{bool chan} \,\&\, \emptyset$$

so that

$$C, [\,] \vdash e \ : \ t \,\&\, b$$

for suitable t and b. As it is easy to find S such that $\emptyset \vdash S\,C$, we shall see (by Lemma 10 and Lemma 11) that we even have

$$\emptyset, [\,] \vdash e \ : \ t' \,\&\, b'$$

for suitable t' and b'. This shows that some notion of well-formedness is essential for semantic soundness; actually the example suggests that if there is a constraint $(\{\alpha'\ \text{CHAN}\} \subseteq \beta)$ then one should not generalise over α' if it is impossible to generalise over β. □

The arrow relation

In order to formalise the notion of well-formedness we next associate a third kind of judgement and three kinds of closure with a constraint set. Motivated by the concluding remark of Example 2 we establish a relation between the left hand side variables and the right hand side variables of a constraint:

Definition 2. The judgement $C \vdash \gamma_1 \leftarrow \gamma_2$ holds if there exists $(g_1 \subseteq g_2)$ in C such that $\gamma_i \in FV(g_i)$ for $i = 1, 2$.

From this relation we define a number of other relations: $\rightarrow$ is the inverse of $\leftarrow$, i.e. $C \vdash \gamma_1 \rightarrow \gamma_2$ holds iff $C \vdash \gamma_2 \leftarrow \gamma_1$ holds, and $\leftrightarrow$ is the *union* of $\leftarrow$ and $\rightarrow$, i.e. $C \vdash \gamma_1 \leftrightarrow \gamma_2$ holds iff either $C \vdash \gamma_1 \leftarrow \gamma_2$ or $C \vdash \gamma_1 \rightarrow \gamma_2$ holds. As usual $\leftarrow^*$ (respectively $\rightarrow^*$, $\leftrightarrow^*$) denotes the reflexive and transitive closure of the relation.

For a set X of variables we then define the downwards closure $X^{C\downarrow}$, the upwards closure $X^{C\uparrow}$ and the bidirectional closure $X^{C\updownarrow}$ by:

$$X^{C\downarrow} = \{\gamma_1 \mid \exists \gamma_2 \in X : C \vdash \gamma_1 \leftarrow^* \gamma_2\}$$

$$X^{C\uparrow} = \{\gamma_1 \mid \exists \gamma_2 \in X : C \vdash \gamma_1 \rightarrow^* \gamma_2\}$$

$$X^{C\updownarrow} = \{\gamma_1 \mid \exists \gamma_2 \in X : C \vdash \gamma_1 \leftrightarrow^* \gamma_2\}$$

It is instructive to think of $C \vdash \gamma_1 \leftarrow \gamma_2$ as defining a directed graph structure upon $FV(C)$; then $X^{C\downarrow}$ is the reachability closure of X, $X^{C\uparrow}$ is the reachability closure in the graph where all edges are reversed, and $X^{C\updownarrow}$ is the reachability closure in the corresponding undirected graph.

Well-formedness

We can now define the notion of well-formedness for constraints and for type schemes; for the latter we make use of the arrow relations defined above.

Definition 3. *Well-formed constraint sets*

A constraint set C is *well-formed* if all right hand sides of $(g_1 \subseteq g_2)$ in C have g_2 to be a variable; in other words all inclusions of C have the form $t \subseteq \alpha$ or $b \subseteq \beta$.

The well-formedness assumption on constraint sets is motivated by the desire to be able to use the subtyping rules "backwards" (as spelled out in Lemma 4 below) and in ensuring that subtyping interacts well with the arrow relation (see Lemma 5 below).

Lemma 4. Suppose C is well-formed and that $C \vdash t \subseteq t'$.

- If $t' = t'_1 \rightarrow^{b'} t'_2$ there exist t_1, t_2 and b such that $t = t_1 \rightarrow^{b} t_2$ and such that $C \vdash t'_1 \subseteq t_1$, $C \vdash t_2 \subseteq t'_2$ and $C \vdash b \subseteq b'$.
- If $t' = t'_1$ $\texttt{com}$ b' there exist t_1 and b such that $t = t_1$ $\texttt{com}$ b and such that $C \vdash t_1 \subseteq t'_1$ and $C \vdash b \subseteq b'$.
- If $t' = t'_1 \times t'_2$ there exist t_1 and t_2 such that $t = t_1 \times t_2$ and such that $C \vdash t_1 \subseteq t'_1$ and $C \vdash t_2 \subseteq t'_2$.
- If $t' = t'_1$ $\texttt{chan}$ there exists t_1 such that $t = t_1$ $\texttt{chan}$ and such that $C \vdash t_1 \equiv t'_1$.
- If $t' = t'_1$ $\texttt{list}$ there exists t_1 such that $t = t_1$ $\texttt{list}$ and such that $C \vdash t_1 \subseteq t'_1$.
- If $t' = \texttt{int}$ (respectively $\texttt{bool}$, $\texttt{unit}$) then $t = \texttt{int}$ (respectively $\texttt{bool}$, $\texttt{unit}$).

Proof. See Appendix A.

Lemma 5. Suppose C is well-formed:

$$\text{if } C \vdash b \subseteq b' \text{ then } FV(b)^{C\downarrow} \subseteq FV(b')^{C\downarrow}.$$

Proof. See Appendix A.

We now turn to well-formedness of type schemes where we ensure that the embedded constraints are themselves well-formed. Additionally we shall wish to ensure that the set of variables over which we generalise, is sensibly related to the constraints (unlike the situation in Example 2). The key idea is that if $C \vdash \gamma_1 \leftarrow \gamma_2$ then we do not generalise over γ_1 unless we also generalise over γ_2. These considerations lead to:

Definition 6. *Well-formed type schemes*

A type scheme $\forall(\vec{\alpha}\vec{\beta} : C_0).\ t_0$ is *well-formed* if C_0 is well-formed, if all $(g \subseteq \gamma)$ in C_0 contain at least one variable among $\{\vec{\alpha}\vec{\beta}\}$, and if $\{\vec{\alpha}\vec{\beta}\} = \{\vec{\alpha}\vec{\beta}\}^{C_0\uparrow}$.

A type t is trivially well-formed.

Notice that if $C = \emptyset$ then $\forall(\vec{\alpha}\vec{\beta} : C).\ t$ is well-formed. It is essential for our development that the following property holds:

Fact 7. *Well-formedness and Substitutions*

If $\forall(\vec{\alpha}\vec{\beta} : C).\ t$ is well-formed then also $S\,(\forall(\vec{\alpha}\vec{\beta} : C).\ t)$ is well-formed (for all substitutions S).

Proof. We can, without loss of generality, assume that $(Dom(S) \cup Ran(S)) \cap \{\vec{\alpha}\vec{\beta}\} = \emptyset$. Then $S\,(\forall(\vec{\alpha}\vec{\beta} : C).\ t) = \forall(\vec{\alpha}\vec{\beta} : S\,C).\ S\,t$. Consider $(g_1' \subseteq g_2')$ in $S\,C$; it is easy to see that it suffices to show that g_2' is a variable in $\{\vec{\alpha}\vec{\beta}\}$.

Let $g_1' = S\,g_1$ and $g_2' = S\,g_2$ where $(g_1 \subseteq g_2) \in C$. Since C is well-formed it holds that g_2 is a variable, and since $FV(g_1, g_2) \cap \{\vec{\alpha}\vec{\beta}\} \neq \emptyset$ and since $\{\vec{\alpha}\vec{\beta}\} = \{\vec{\alpha}\vec{\beta}\}^{C\uparrow}$ it holds that $g_2 \in \{\vec{\alpha}\vec{\beta}\}$. Therefore $g_2' = S\,g_2 = g_2$ so g_2' is a variable in $\{\vec{\alpha}\vec{\beta}\}$.

Example 3. Continuing Example 2 note that $\{\alpha'\}^{C'\uparrow} = \{\alpha', \beta\}$ showing that our current notion of well-formedness prevents the erroneous typing. □

Example 4. Continuing Example 1 we shall now briefly explain why it is accepted by our system. For this let us assume that `y` will have type α_y and that `x` will have type α_x. Then the locally defined function

```
fn x => (sync (send (channel (), y)); x)
```

will have type $\alpha_x \rightarrow^b \alpha_x$ for $b = \{\alpha_y\ \text{CHAN}\}$. Due to our rule for subtyping we may let `f` have the type $\alpha_x \rightarrow^\emptyset \alpha_x$ and still be able to type the conditional. Clearly the expression defining `id` may be given the type $\alpha_y \rightarrow^\emptyset \alpha_y$ and the effect $\emptyset$. Since α_y is not free in the type of `f` we may use generalisation to give `id` the type scheme $\forall(\alpha_y : \emptyset).\ \alpha_y \rightarrow^\emptyset \alpha_y$. This then suffices for typing the application of `id` to itself.

Now consider a system with subeffecting only (as in [23]): then for the type of `f` to match that of the locally defined function we have to give `f` the type $\alpha_x \rightarrow^b \alpha_x$ where $b = \{\alpha_y\ \text{CHAN}\}$. This then means that while the defining expression for `id` still has the type $\alpha_y \rightarrow^\emptyset \alpha_y$ we are unable to generalise it to $\forall(\alpha_y : \emptyset).\ \alpha_y \rightarrow^\emptyset \alpha_y$ because α_y is now free in the type of `f`. Consequently the application of `id` to itself cannot be typed. (It is interesting to point out that if one changed the applied occurrence of `f` in the program to the expression `fn z => f z` then subeffecting would suffice for generalising over α_y and hence would allow to type the self-application of `id`.)

The system of [19] does not have subtyping but nevertheless the application of `id` to itself is typeable [19, section 11, the case (`id4 id4`)]. This is due to the presence of *regions* and *masking* (cf. the discussion in the Introduction): with ρ the region in which the new channel is allocated, the expression `sync (send (channel (), y))` does not contain ρ in its type α_y and neither is ρ present in the environment, so it is possible to discard the effect $\{\alpha_y \text{ CHAN}\}_\rho$ (recording that a channel carrying values of type α_y has been allocated in region ρ). Thus the two branches of the conditional can both be given type $\alpha_x \rightarrow^{\emptyset} \alpha_x$.

Also in the approach of [21] one can generalise over α_y and hence type the self-application of `id`. To see this, first note that α_y is classified as an imperative type variable (rather than an applicative type variable which would directly have allowed the generalisation) because α_y is used in the channel construct and thus has a side effect. Despite of this, next note that the defining expression for the `id` function is classified as non-expansive (rather as expansive which would directly have prohibited the generalisation of imperative type variables) because all side effects occurring in the definition of `id` are "protected" by a function abstraction and hence not "dangerous". We refer to [21] for the details. □

2.4 Properties of the Inference System

We now list a few basic properties of the inference system that we shall use later.

Fact 8. For all constants c of Figure 1, the type scheme TypeOf(c) is closed, well-formed and solvable from $\emptyset$.

Fact 9. If $C, A \vdash e : \sigma \,\&\, b$ and A is well-formed and solvable from C then σ is well-formed and solvable from C.

Proof. A straightforward case analysis on the last rule applied; for constants we make use of Fact 8.

Lemma 10. *Substitution Lemma*

For all substitutions S:

(a) If $C \vdash C'$ then $S\,C \vdash S\,C'$.
(b) If $C, A \vdash e : \sigma \,\&\, b$ then $S\,C, S\,A \vdash e : S\sigma \,\&\, S\,b$ (and has the same shape).

Proof. See Appendix A.

Lemma 11. *Entailment Lemma*

For all sets C' of constraints satisfying $C' \vdash C$:

(a) If $C \vdash C_0$ then $C' \vdash C_0$;
(b) If $C, A \vdash e : \sigma \,\&\, b$ then $C', A \vdash e : \sigma \,\&\, b$ (and has the same shape).

Proof. See Appendix A.

2.5 Proof Normalisation

It turns out that the proof of semantic soundness [2] is complicated by the presence of the non-syntax directed rules (sub), (gen) and (ins) of Figure 2. This motivates trying to normalise general inference trees into a more manageable shape[5]; to this end we define the notions of "normalised" and "strongly normalised" inference trees. But first we define an auxiliary concept:

Definition 12. An inference for $C, A \vdash e : \sigma \,\&\, b$ is constraint-saturated, written $C, A \vdash_c e : \sigma \,\&\, b$, if and only if all occurrences of the rules (app), (let), and (if) have the same constraints in their premises; in the notation of Figure 2 this means that $C_1 = C_2$ for (app) and (let) and that $C_0 = C_1 = C_2$ for (if).

Fact 13. Given an inference tree for $C, A \vdash e : \sigma \,\&\, b$ there exists a constraint-saturated inference tree $C, A \vdash_c e : \sigma \,\&\, b$ (that has the same shape).

Proof. A straightforward induction in the shape of the inference tree using Lemma 11 in the cases (app), (let) and (if).

We now define the central concepts of T- and TS-normalised inference trees.

Definition 14. *Normalisation*

An inference tree for $C, A \vdash e : t \,\&\, b$ is *T-normalised* if it is created by:

- (con) or (id); or
- (ins) applied to (con) or (id); or
- (abs), (app), (rec), (if) or (sub) applied to T-normalised inference trees; or
- (let) applied to a TS-normalised inference tree and a T-normalised inference tree.

An inference tree for $C, A \vdash e : ts \,\&\, b$ is *TS-normalised* if it is created by:

- (gen) applied to a T-normalised inference tree.

We shall write $C, A \vdash_n e : \sigma \,\&\, b$ if the inference tree is T-normalised (if σ is a type) or TS-normalised (if σ is a type scheme).

Notice that if $jdg = C, A \vdash e : \sigma \,\&\, b$ occurs in a normalised inference tree then we in fact have $jdg = C, A \vdash_n e : \sigma \,\&\, b$, unless jdg is created by (con) or (id) and σ is a type scheme. Next consider the result of applying (ins) to a normalised inference tree; even though the resulting inference tree is not normalised the resulting judgement in fact has a normalised inference:

Lemma 15. Suppose that

$$jdg = C, A \vdash e : S\, t_0 \,\&\, b$$

follows by an application of (ins) to the normalised judgement

[5] This will also facilitate proving the completeness of an inference algorithm.

$$jdg' = C, A \vdash_n e : \forall(\vec{\alpha}\vec{\beta} : C_0).\ t_0 \,\&\, b$$

where $Dom(S) \subseteq \{\vec{\alpha}\vec{\beta}\}$ and $C \vdash S\,C_0$. Then also jdg has a normalised inference:

$$C, A \vdash_n e : S\,t_0 \,\&\, b.$$

Proof. The normalised judgement jdg' follows by an application of (gen) to the normalised judgement

$$C \cup C_0, A \vdash_n e : t_0 \,\&\, b$$

where $\{\vec{\alpha}\vec{\beta}\} \cap FV(C, A, b) = \emptyset$. From Lemma 10 we therefore get

$$C \cup S\,C_0, A \vdash_n e : S\,t_0 \,\&\, b$$

and using Lemma 11 we get $C, A \vdash_n e : S\,t_0 \,\&\, b$ as desired.

It is not a severe restriction to work with normalised inferences only:

Lemma 16. *Normalisation Lemma*

If A is well-formed and solvable from C then an inference tree $C, A \vdash e : \sigma \,\&\, b$ can be transformed into one $C, A \vdash_n e : \sigma \,\&\, b$ that is normalised.

Proof. See Appendix A.

A somewhat stronger property is the following:

Definition 17. An inference tree for $C, A \vdash e : \sigma \,\&\, b$ is strongly normalised if it is normalised as well as constraint-saturated. We write $C, A \vdash_s e : \sigma \,\&\, b$ when this is the case.

By Fact 13 we have:

Fact 18. A normalised inference tree $C, A \vdash_n e : \sigma \,\&\, b$ can be transformed into one that is strongly normalised.

2.6 Conservative Extension

We finally show that our inference system is a conservative extension of the system for ML type inference. For this purpose we restrict ourselves to consider *sequential* expressions only, that is expressions without the non-sequential constants `channel`, `fork`, `sync`, `send`, and `receive`.

An ML type u (as opposed to a CML type t, in the following just denoted type) is either a type variable α, a base type like `int`, a function type $u_1 \to u_2$, a product type $u_1 \times u_2$, or a list type u_1 `list`. An ML type scheme is of the form $\forall\vec{\alpha}.u$.

From a type t we can in a natural way construct an ML type $\epsilon(t)$: $\epsilon(\alpha) = \alpha$, $\epsilon(\texttt{int}) = \texttt{int}$, $\epsilon(t_1 \to^b t_2) = \epsilon(t_1) \to \epsilon(t_2)$, $\epsilon(t_1 \times t_2) = \epsilon(t_1) \times \epsilon(t_2)$, $\epsilon(t_1\ \texttt{list}) = \epsilon(t_1)\ \texttt{list}$, and $\epsilon(t\ \texttt{com}\ b) = \epsilon(t\ \texttt{chan}) = \epsilon(t)$.

From an ML type u we can construct a type $\iota(u)$ by annotating all arrows with $\emptyset$: $\iota(\alpha) = \alpha$, $\iota(\mathtt{int}) = \mathtt{int}$, $\iota(u_1 \rightarrow u_2) = \iota(u_1) \rightarrow^{\emptyset} \iota(u_2)$, $\iota(u_1 \times u_2) = \iota(u_1) \times \iota(u_2)$, $\iota(u_1\ \mathtt{list}) = \iota(u_1)\ \mathtt{list}$.

We say that a type scheme $ts = \forall(\vec{\alpha}\vec{\beta} : C).\ t$ is *sequential* if C is empty. From a sequential type scheme $ts = \forall(\vec{\alpha}\vec{\beta} : \emptyset).\ t$ we construct an ML type scheme $\epsilon(ts)$ as follows: $\epsilon(ts) = \forall\vec{\alpha}.\epsilon(t)$. (We shall dispense with defining $\epsilon(ts)$ on non-sequential type schemes for reasons to be discussed in Appendix A.) From an ML type scheme $us = \forall\vec{\alpha}.u$ we construct a (sequential) type scheme $\iota(us)$ as follows: $\iota(us) = \forall(\vec{\alpha} : \emptyset).\ \iota(u)$.

Fact 19. Let u be an ML type, then $\epsilon(\iota(u)) = u$. Similarly for ML type schemes.

The core of the ML type inference system is depicted in Figure 4. It employs a function MLTypeOf which to each sequential constant assigns either an ML type or an ML type scheme; as an example we have MLTypeOf(**pair**) $= \forall\alpha_1\alpha_2.\alpha_1 \rightarrow \alpha_2 \rightarrow \alpha_1 \times \alpha_2$.

Assumption 20. For all sequential constants c: $\iota(\text{MLTypeOf}(c)) = \text{TypeOf}(c)$ (so by Fact 19: $\text{MLTypeOf}(c) = \epsilon(\text{TypeOf}(c))$).

$$\text{(con)}\quad A \vdash_{\text{ML}} c : \text{MLTypeOf}(c)$$

$$\text{(id)}\quad A \vdash_{\text{ML}} x : A(x)$$

$$\text{(abs)}\quad \frac{A[x : u_1] \vdash_{\text{ML}} e : u_2}{A \vdash_{\text{ML}} \mathbf{fn}\ x \Rightarrow e : u_1 \rightarrow u_2}$$

$$\text{(app)}\quad \frac{A \vdash_{\text{ML}} e_1 : u_2 \rightarrow u_1,\ A \vdash_{\text{ML}} e_2 : u_2}{A \vdash_{\text{ML}} e_1\, e_2 : u_1}$$

$$\text{(let)}\quad \frac{A \vdash_{\text{ML}} e_1 : us_1,\ A[x : us_1] \vdash_{\text{ML}} e_2 : u_2}{A \vdash_{\text{ML}} \mathbf{let}\ x = e_1\ \mathbf{in}\ e_2 : u_2}$$

$$\text{(ins)}\quad \frac{A \vdash_{\text{ML}} e : \forall\vec{\alpha}.u}{A \vdash_{\text{ML}} e : Ru} \qquad \text{if } Dom(R) \subseteq \{\vec{\alpha}\}$$

$$\text{(gen)}\quad \frac{A \vdash_{\text{ML}} e : u}{A \vdash_{\text{ML}} e : \forall\vec{\alpha}.u} \qquad \text{if } FV(A) \cap \{\vec{\alpha}\} = \emptyset$$

Fig. 4. The core of the ML type inference system.

We are now ready to state that our system conservatively extends ML.

Theorem 21. Let e be a sequential expression:

- if $[\,] \vdash_{\text{ML}} e : u$ then $\emptyset, [\,] \vdash e : \iota(u)\ \&\ \emptyset$;
- if $C, [\,] \vdash e : t\ \&\ b$ where C contains no type constraints then $[\,] \vdash_{\text{ML}} e : \epsilon(t)$.

Proof: See Appendix A.

3 Conclusion

We have extended previous work on integrating polymorphism, subtyping and effects into a combined annotated type and effect system. The development was illustrated for a fragment of Concurrent ML but is equally applicable to Standard ML with references. A main ingredient of the approach was the notion of constraint closure, in particular the notion of upwards closure. We hope that this system will provide a useful basis for developing a variety of program analyses; in particular closure, binding-time and communication analyses for languages with imperative or concurrent effects.

The system developed here includes no causality concerning the temporal order of effects; in the future we hope to incorporate aspects of the causality information for the communication structure of Concurrent ML [15]. Another (and harder) goal is to incorporate decidable fragments of polymorphic recursion. Finally, it should prove interesting to apply these ideas also to strongly typed languages with object-oriented features.

Acknowledgement. This work has been supported in part by the *DART* project (Danish Natural Science Research Council) and the *LOMAPS* project (ESPRIT BRA project 8130); it represents joint work among the authors.

References

1. T. Amtoft, F. Nielson, H.R. Nielson: Type and behaviour reconstruction for higher-order concurrent programs. To appear in *Journal of Functional Programming*, 1997.
2. T. Amtoft, F. Nielson, H.R. Nielson, J. Ammann: Polymorphic subtypes for effect analysis: the dynamic semantics. This volume of SLNCS, 1997.
3. L. Damas and R. Milner: Principal type-schemes for functional programs. In *Proc. of POPL '82*. ACM Press, 1982.
4. Y.-C. Fuh and P. Mishra: Polymorphic subtype inference: closing the theory-practice gap. In *Proc. TAPSOFT '89*. SLNCS 352, 1989.
5. Y.-C. Fuh and P. Mishra: Type inference with subtypes. *Theoretical Computer Science*, 73, 1990.
6. F. Henglein: Type inference with polymorphic recursion. *ACM Transactions on Programming Languages and Systems*, 15(2):253-289, 1993.
7. F. Henglein and C. Mossin: Polymorphic binding-time analysis. In *Proc. ESOP '94*, pages 287–301. SLNCS 788, 1994.
8. M.P. Jones: A theory of qualified types. In *Proc. ESOP '92*, pages 287–306. SLNCS 582, 1992.
9. X. Leroy and P. Weis: Polymorphic type inference and assignment. In *Proc. POPL '91*, pages 291–302. ACM Press, 1991.
10. R. Milner: A theory of type polymorphism in programming. *Journal of Computer Systems*, 17:348–375, 1978.
11. J.C. Mitchell: Type inference with simple subtypes. *Journal of Functional Programming*, 1(3), 1991.

12. F. Nielson and H.R. Nielson: Constraints for polymorphic behaviours for Concurrent ML. In *Proc. CCL'94*. SLNCS 845, 1994.
13. F. Nielson, H.R. Nielson, T. Amtoft: Polymorphic subtypes for effect analysis: the algorithm. This volume of SLNCS, 1997.
14. H.R. Nielson and F. Nielson: Automatic binding analysis for a typed λ-calculus. *Science of Computer Programming*, 10:139–176, 1988.
15. H.R. Nielson and F. Nielson: Higher-order concurrent programs with finite communication topology. In *Proc. POPL'94*, pages 84–97. ACM Press, 1994.
16. P. Panangaden and J.H. Reppy: The essence of Concurrent ML. In *ML with Concurrency: Design, Analysis, Implementation and Application* (editor: Flemming Nielson), Springer-Verlag, 1996.
17. J.H. Reppy: Concurrent ML: Design, application and semantics. In *Proc. Functional Programming, Concurrency, Simulation and Automated Reasoning*, pages 165–198. SLNCS 693, 1993.
18. G.S. Smith: Polymorphic inference with overloading and subtyping. In SLNCS 668, *Proc. TAPSOFT '93*, 1993. Also see: Principal Type Schemes for Functional Programs with Overloading and Subtyping: *Science of Computer Programming* 23, pp. 197-226, 1994.
19. J.P. Talpin and P. Jouvelot: The type and effect discipline. *Information and Computation*, 111, 1994.
20. Y.-M. Tang: Control flow analysis by effect systems and abstract interpretation. PhD thesis, Ecoles des Mines de Paris, 1994.
21. M. Tofte. Type inference for polymorphic references. *Information and Computation*, 89:1–34, 1990.
22. M. Tofte and L. Birkedal: Region-annotated types and type schemes, 1996. Submitted for publication.
23. A.K. Wright: Typing references by effect inference. In *Proc. ESOP '92*, pages 473–491. SLNCS 582, 1992.

A Proofs of Main Results

Well-formedness

Lemma 4 Suppose C is well-formed and that $C \vdash t \subseteq t'$.

- If $t' = t'_1 \rightarrow^{b'} t'_2$ there exist t_1, t_2 and b such that $t = t_1 \rightarrow^{b} t_2$ and such that $C \vdash t'_1 \subseteq t_1$, $C \vdash t_2 \subseteq t'_2$ and $C \vdash b \subseteq b'$.
- If $t' = t'_1 \texttt{ com } b'$ there exist t_1 and b such that $t = t_1 \texttt{ com } b$ and such that $C \vdash t_1 \subseteq t'_1$ and $C \vdash b \subseteq b'$.
- If $t' = t'_1 \times t'_2$ there exist t_1 and t_2 such that $t = t_1 \times t_2$ and such that $C \vdash t_1 \subseteq t'_1$ and $C \vdash t_2 \subseteq t'_2$.
- If $t' = t'_1 \texttt{ chan}$ there exists t_1 such that $t = t_1 \texttt{ chan}$ and such that $C \vdash t_1 \equiv t'_1$.
- If $t' = t'_1 \texttt{ list}$ there exists t_1 such that $t = t_1 \texttt{ list}$ and such that $C \vdash t_1 \subseteq t'_1$.
- If $t' = \texttt{int}$ (respectively $\texttt{bool}$, $\texttt{unit}$) then $t = \texttt{int}$ (respectively $\texttt{bool}$, $\texttt{unit}$).

In addition we are going to prove that the size of each of the latter inference trees is strictly less than the size of the inference tree for $C \vdash t \subseteq t'$. Here the size of an inference tree is defined as the number of (not necessarily different) symbols occurring in the tree, except that occurrences in C do not count.

Proof. We only consider the case $t' = t_1' \rightarrow^{b'} t_2'$, as the others are similar. The proof is carried out by induction in the inference tree, and since C is well-formed the last rule applied must be either (refl), (trans) or $(\rightarrow)$.

(refl): the claim is trivial[6].

(trans): assume that $C \vdash t \subseteq t'$ by means of a tree of size n because $C \vdash t \subseteq t''$ by means of a tree of size n'' and because $C \vdash t'' \subseteq t'$ by means of a tree of size n'. Here $n = n' + n'' + |t| + |t'| + 2$. By applying the induction hypothesis on the latter inference we find t_1'', t_2'' and b'' such that $t'' = t_1'' \rightarrow^{b''} t_2''$ and such that $C \vdash t_1' \subseteq t_1''$ and $C \vdash t_2'' \subseteq t_2'$ and $C \vdash b'' \subseteq b'$, each judgement by means of an inference tree of size $< n'$. By applying the induction hypothesis on the former inference ($C \vdash t \subseteq t''$) we find t_1, t_2 and b such that $t = t_1 \rightarrow^{b} t_2$ and such that $C \vdash t_1'' \subseteq t_1$ and $C \vdash t_2 \subseteq t_2''$ and $C \vdash b \subseteq b''$, each judgement by means of an inference tree of size $< n''$. We thus have $C \vdash t_1' \subseteq t_1$, by means of an inference tree of size $< n' + n'' + |t_1'| + |t_1| + 2 < n' + n'' + |t'| + |t| + 2 = n$. By similar reasoning we infer that $C \vdash t_2 \subseteq t_2'$ and $C \vdash b \subseteq b'$, each judgement by means of an inference tree of size $< n$.

$(\rightarrow)$: the claim is trivial. □

For variables we need a different kind of lemma:

Lemma 22. Suppose $C \vdash \alpha \subseteq \alpha'$ with C well-formed. Then $\alpha \in \{\alpha'\}^{C\downarrow}$.

Proof. Induction in the proof tree, performing case analysis on the last rule applied:

(axiom): then $(\alpha \subseteq \alpha') \in C$ so the claim is trivial.

(refl): the claim is trivial.

(trans): assume that $C \vdash \alpha \subseteq \alpha'$ because $C \vdash \alpha \subseteq t''$ and $C \vdash t'' \subseteq \alpha'$. By using Lemma 4 on the inference $C \vdash \alpha \subseteq t''$ we infer that t'' is a variable α''. By applying the induction hypothesis we infer that $\alpha \in \{\alpha''\}^{C\downarrow}$ and that $\alpha'' \in \{\alpha'\}^{C\downarrow}$, from which we conclude that $\alpha \in \{\alpha'\}^{C\downarrow}$. □

Lemma 5 Suppose C is well-formed:

if $C \vdash b \subseteq b'$ then $FV(b)^{C\downarrow} \subseteq FV(b')^{C\downarrow}$, and

if $C \vdash t \equiv t'$ then $FV(t)^{C\downarrow} = FV(t')^{C\downarrow}$.

Proof. Induction in the size of the inference tree, where we define the size of the inference tree for $C \vdash t \equiv t'$ as the sum of the size of the inference tree for $C \vdash t \subseteq t'$ and the size of the inference tree for $C \vdash t' \subseteq t$.

First we consider the part concerning behaviours, performing case analysis on the last inference rule applied:

(axiom): then $(b \subseteq b') \in C$ so since C is well-formed b' is a variable; hence the claim.

(refl): the claim is trivial.

[6] This case is the reason for not defining the size of a tree as the number of inferences.

(trans): assume that $C \vdash b \subseteq b'$ because $C \vdash b \subseteq b''$ and $C \vdash b'' \subseteq b'$. The induction hypothesis tells us that $FV(b)^{C\downarrow} \subseteq FV(b'')^{C\downarrow}$ and that $FV(b'')^{C\downarrow} \subseteq FV(b')^{C\downarrow}$; hence the claim.

(CHAN): assume that $C \vdash \{t \text{ CHAN}\} \subseteq \{t' \text{ CHAN}\}$ because $C \vdash t \equiv t'$. The induction hypothesis tells us that $FV(t)^{C\downarrow} = FV(t')^{C\downarrow}$; hence the claim.

($\emptyset$): the claim is trivial.

($\cup$): the claim is trivial.

(lub): assume that $C \vdash b_1 \cup b_2 \subseteq b'$ because $C \vdash b_1 \subseteq b'$ and $C \vdash b_2 \subseteq b'$. The induction hypothesis tells us that $FV(b_1)^{C\downarrow} \subseteq FV(b')^{C\downarrow}$ and that $FV(b_2)^{C\downarrow} \subseteq FV(b')^{C\downarrow}$, from which we infer that $FV(b_1 \cup b_2)^{C\downarrow} = FV(b_1)^{C\downarrow} \cup FV(b_2)^{C\downarrow} \subseteq FV(b')^{C\downarrow}$.

Next we consider the part concerning types, where we perform case analysis on the form of t':

$t' = t_1' \rightarrow^{b'} t_2'$: Let n_1 be the size of the inference tree for $C \vdash t \subseteq t'$ and let n_2 be the size of the inference tree for $C \vdash t' \subseteq t$. Lemma 4 (applied to the former inference) tells us that there exist t_1, b and t_2 such that $t = t_1 \rightarrow^{b} t_2$ and such that $C \vdash t_1' \subseteq t_1$, $C \vdash b \subseteq b'$ and $C \vdash t_2 \subseteq t_2'$, where each inference tree is of size $< n_1$ (due to the remark prior to the proof). Lemma 4 (applied to the latter inference, i.e. $C \vdash t' \subseteq t$) tells us that $C \vdash t_1 \subseteq t_1'$, $C \vdash b' \subseteq b$ and $C \vdash t_2' \subseteq t_2$, where each inference tree is of size $< n_2$.

Thus $C \vdash t_1 \equiv t_1'$ and $C \vdash t_2 \equiv t_2'$, where each inference tree has size $< n_1 + n_2$. We can thus apply the induction hypothesis to infer that $FV(t_1)^{C\downarrow} = FV(t_1')^{C\downarrow}$ and that $FV(t_2)^{C\downarrow} = FV(t_2')^{C\downarrow}$; and similarly we can infer that $FV(b)^{C\downarrow} \subseteq FV(b')^{C\downarrow}$ and that $FV(b')^{C\downarrow} \subseteq FV(b)^{C\downarrow}$. This enables us to concluce that $FV(t)^{C\downarrow} = FV(t')^{C\downarrow}$.

t' has a topmost type constructor other than $\rightarrow$: we can proceed as above.

t' is a variable: Since $C \vdash t' \subseteq t$ we can use Lemma 4 to infer that t is a variable; then we use Lemma 22 to infer that $FV(t') \subseteq FV(t)^{C\downarrow}$. Similarly we can infer $FV(t) \subseteq FV(t')^{C\downarrow}$. This implies the desired relation $FV(t)^{C\downarrow} = FV(t')^{C\downarrow}$.
□

Properties of the inference system

Lemma 10 For all substitutions S:

(a) If $C \vdash C'$ then $S\,C \vdash S\,C'$.
(b) If $C, A \vdash e : \sigma \;\&\; b$ then $S\,C, S\,A \vdash e : S\,\sigma \;\&\; S\,b$ (and has the same shape).

Proof. The claim (a) is straight-forward by induction on the inference $C \vdash g_1 \subseteq g_2$ for each $(g_1 \subseteq g_2) \in C'$. For the claim (b) we proceed by induction on the inference.

For the case (con) we use that the type schemes of Fig. 1 are closed (Fact 8). For the case (id) the claim is immediate, and for the cases (abs), (app), (let), (rec), (if) it follows directly using the induction hypothesis. For the case (sub) we use (a) together with the induction hypothesis.

The case (ins). Then $C, A \vdash e : S_0\, t_0 \,\&\, b$ because $C, A \vdash e : \forall(\vec{\alpha}\vec{\beta} : C_0).\ t_0 \,\&\, b$ where $C \vdash S_0\, C_0$ and $Dom(S_0) \subseteq \{\vec{\alpha}\vec{\beta}\}$, and wlog. we can assume that $\{\vec{\alpha}\vec{\beta}\}$ is disjoint from $Inv(S)$. The induction hypothesis gives

$$S\,C, S\,A \vdash e : \forall(\vec{\alpha}\vec{\beta} : S\,C_0).\ S\,t_0 \,\&\, S\,b. \tag{1}$$

From (a) we get $S\,C \vdash S\,S_0\,C_0$. Let $S_0' = [\vec{\alpha}\vec{\beta} \mapsto S\,S_0\,(\vec{\alpha}\vec{\beta})]$, then on $FV(t_0, C_0)$ it holds that $S_0'\,S = S\,S_0$. Therefore $S\,C \vdash S_0'\,S\,C_0$, so we can apply (ins) on (1) with S_0' as the "instance substitution" to get $S\,C, S\,A \vdash e : S_0'\,S\,t_0 \,\&\, S\,b$. Since $S_0'\,S\,t_0 = S\,S_0\,t_0$ this is the required result.

The case (gen). Then $C, A \vdash e : \forall(\vec{\alpha}\vec{\beta} : C_0).\ t_0 \,\&\, b$ because $C \cup C_0, A \vdash e : t_0 \,\&\, b$, and

$$\forall(\vec{\alpha}\vec{\beta} : C_0).\ t_0 \text{ is well-formed} \tag{2}$$

$$\text{there exists } S_0 \text{ with } Dom(S_0) \subseteq \{\vec{\alpha}\vec{\beta}\} \text{ such that } C \vdash S_0\,C_0 \tag{3}$$

$$\{\vec{\alpha}\vec{\beta}\} \cap FV(C, A, b) = \emptyset \tag{4}$$

Define $R = [\vec{\alpha}\vec{\beta} \mapsto \vec{\alpha}'\vec{\beta}']$ with $\{\vec{\alpha}'\vec{\beta}'\}$ fresh. We then apply the induction hypothesis (with $S\,R$) and due to (4) this gives us $S\,C \cup S\,R\,C_0, S\,A \vdash e : S\,R\,t_0 \,\&\, S\,b$. Below we prove

$$\forall(\vec{\alpha}'\vec{\beta}' : S\,R\,C_0).\ S\,R\,t_0\ (= S\,(\forall(\vec{\alpha}\vec{\beta} : C_0).\ t_0)) \text{ is well-formed,} \tag{5}$$

$$\text{there exists } S' \text{ with } Dom(S') \subseteq \{\vec{\alpha}'\vec{\beta}'\} \text{ such that } S\,C \vdash S'\,S\,R\,C_0, \text{ and} \tag{6}$$

$$\{\vec{\alpha}'\vec{\beta}'\} \cap FV(S\,C, S\,A, S\,b) = \emptyset \tag{7}$$

It then follows that $S\,C, S\,A \vdash e : S\,(\forall(\vec{\alpha}\vec{\beta} : C_0).\ t_0) \,\&\, S\,b$ as required. Clearly the inference has the same shape.

First we observe that (5) follows from (2) and Fact 7. For (6) define $S' = [\vec{\alpha}'\vec{\beta}' \mapsto S\,S_0\,(\vec{\alpha}\vec{\beta})]$. From $C \vdash S_0\,C_0$ and (a) we get $S\,C \vdash S\,S_0\,C_0$. Since $S'\,S\,R = S\,S_0$ on $FV(C_0)$ the result follows. Finally (7) holds trivially by choice of $\vec{\alpha}'\vec{\beta}'$.
□

Lemma 11 For all sets C' of constraints satisfying $C' \vdash C$:

(a) If $C \vdash C_0$ then $C' \vdash C_0$.
(b) If $C, A \vdash e : \sigma \,\&\, b$ then $C', A \vdash e : \sigma \,\&\, b$ (and has the same shape).

Proof. The claim (a) is straight-forward by induction on the inference $C \vdash g_1 \subseteq g_2$ for each $(g_1 \subseteq g_2) \in C_0$. For the claim (b) we proceed by induction on the inference.

For the cases (con), (id) the claim is immediate, and for the cases (abs), (app), (let), (rec), (if) it follows directly using the induction hypothesis. For the cases (sub) and (ins) we use (a) together with the induction hypothesis.

The case (gen). Then $C, A \vdash e : \forall(\vec{\alpha}\vec{\beta} : C_0).\ t_0 \,\&\, b$ because $C \cup C_0, A \vdash e : t_0 \,\&\, b$ and

$$\forall(\vec{\alpha}\vec{\beta} : C_0).\ t_0 \text{ is well-formed} \tag{8}$$

$$\text{there exists } S \text{ with } Dom(S) \subseteq \{\vec{\alpha}\vec{\beta}\} \text{ such that } C \vdash S\,C_0 \tag{9}$$

$$\{\vec{\alpha}\vec{\beta}\} \cap FV(C, A, b) = \emptyset \tag{10}$$

We now use a small trick: let R be a renaming of the variables of $\{\vec{\alpha}\vec{\beta}\} \cap FV(C')$ to fresh variables. From $C' \vdash C$ and Lemma 10(a) we get $R\,C' \vdash R\,C$ and using (10) we get $R\,C = C$ so $R\,C' \vdash C$. Clearly $R\,C' \cup C_0 \vdash C \cup C_0$ so the induction hypothesis gives $R\,C' \cup C_0, A \vdash e : t_0 \,\&\, b$. Below we verify that

$$\text{there exists } S' \text{ with } Dom(S') \subseteq \{\vec{\alpha}\vec{\beta}\} \text{ such that } R\,C' \vdash S'\,C_0 \tag{11}$$

$$\{\vec{\alpha}\vec{\beta}\} \cap FV(R\,C', A, b) = \emptyset \tag{12}$$

and we then have $R\,C', A \vdash e : \forall(\vec{\alpha}\vec{\beta} : C_0).\ t_0 \,\&\, b$. Now define the substitution R' such that $Dom(R') = Ran(R)$ and $R'\,\gamma' = \gamma$ if $R\,\gamma = \gamma'$ and $\gamma' \in Dom(R')$. Using Lemma 10(b) with the substitution R' we get $C', A \vdash e : \forall(\vec{\alpha}\vec{\beta} : C_0).\ t_0 \,\&\, b$ as required. Clearly the inference has the same shape.

To prove (11) define $S' = S$. Above we showed that $R\,C' \vdash C$ so using (9) and (a) we get $R\,C' \vdash S'\,C_0$ as required. Finally (12) follows trivially from $\{\vec{\alpha}\vec{\beta}\} \cap FV(R\,C') = \emptyset$. □

Proof normalisation

Lemma 16 If A is well-formed and solvable from C then an inference tree $C, A \vdash e : \sigma \,\&\, b$ can be transformed into one $C, A \vdash_n e : \sigma \,\&\, b$ that is normalised.

Proof. Using Fact 13, we can, without loss of generality, assume that we have a constraint-saturated inference tree for $C, A \vdash e : \sigma \,\&\, b$. We proceed by induction on the inference.

The case (con). We assume $C, A \vdash_c c : \mathrm{TypeOf}(c) \,\&\, \emptyset$. If TypeOf($c$) is a type then we already have a T-normalised inference. So assume TypeOf(c) is a type scheme $\forall(\vec{\alpha}\vec{\beta} : C_0).\ t_0$ and let R be a renaming of $\vec{\alpha}\vec{\beta}$ to fresh variables $\vec{\alpha'}\vec{\beta'}$. We can then construct the following TS-normalised inference tree:

$$\dfrac{\dfrac{\dfrac{}{C \cup R\,C_0, A \vdash c : \forall(\vec{\alpha}\vec{\beta} : C_0).\ t_0 \,\&\, \emptyset}\,(\text{con})}{C \cup R\,C_0, A \vdash c : R\,t_0 \,\&\, \emptyset}\,(\text{ins})}{C, A \vdash c : \forall(\vec{\alpha'}\vec{\beta'} : R\,C_0).\ R\,t_0 \,\&\, \emptyset}\,(\text{gen})$$

The rule (ins) is applicable since $Dom(R) \subseteq \{\vec{\alpha}\vec{\beta}\}$ and $C \cup R\,C_0 \vdash R\,C_0$. The rule (gen) is applicable because $\forall(\vec{\alpha}\vec{\beta} : C_0).\ t_0 = \forall(\vec{\alpha'}\vec{\beta'} : R\,C_0).\ R\,t_0$ (up to alpha-renaming) is well-formed and solvable from C (Fact 8), and furthermore $\{\vec{\alpha'}\vec{\beta'}\} \cap FV(C, A, \emptyset) = \emptyset$ holds by choice of $\vec{\alpha'}\vec{\beta'}$.

The case (id). We assume $C, A \vdash_c x : A(x) \,\&\, \emptyset$. If $A(x)$ is a type then we already have a T-normalised inference. So assume $A(x) = \forall(\vec{\alpha}\vec{\beta} : C_0).\ t_0$ and let R be a renaming of $\vec{\alpha}\vec{\beta}$ to fresh variables $\vec{\alpha'}\vec{\beta'}$. We can then construct the following TS-normalised inference tree:

$$\dfrac{\dfrac{\dfrac{}{C \cup RC_0, A \vdash x : \forall(\vec{\alpha}\vec{\beta} : C_0).\ t_0 \,\&\, \emptyset}\ (\text{id})}{C \cup RC_0, A \vdash x : Rt_0 \,\&\, \emptyset}\ (\text{ins})}{C, A \vdash x : \forall(\vec{\alpha'}\vec{\beta'} : RC_0).\ Rt_0 \,\&\, \emptyset}\ (\text{gen})$$

The rule (ins) is applicable since $Dom(R) \subseteq \{\vec{\alpha}\vec{\beta}\}$ and $C \cup RC_0 \vdash RC_0$. The rule (gen) is applicable because $\forall(\vec{\alpha}\vec{\beta} : C_0).\ t_0 = \forall(\vec{\alpha'}\vec{\beta'} : RC_0).\ Rt_0$ (up to alpha-renaming) by assumption is well-formed and solvable from C, and furthermore $\{\vec{\alpha'}\vec{\beta'}\} \cap FV(C, A, \emptyset) = \emptyset$ holds by choice of $\vec{\alpha'}\vec{\beta'}$.

The case (abs). Then we have $C, A \vdash_c \texttt{fn}\ x \Rightarrow e : t_1 \to^b t_2 \,\&\, \emptyset$ because $C, A[x : t_1] \vdash_c e : t_2 \,\&\, b$. Since t_1 is well-formed and solvable from C we can apply the induction hypothesis and get $C, A[x : t_1] \vdash_n e : t_2 \,\&\, b$ from which we infer $C, A \vdash_n \texttt{fn}\ x \Rightarrow e : t_1 \to^b t_2 \,\&\, \emptyset$.

The case (app). Then we have $C, A \vdash_c e_1\, e_2 : t_1 \,\&\, (b_1 \cup b_2 \cup b)$ because $C, A \vdash_c e_1 : t_2 \to^b t_1 \,\&\, b_1$ and $C, A \vdash_c e_2 : t_2 \,\&\, b_2$. Then the induction hypothesis gives $C, A \vdash_n e_1 : t_2 \to^b t_1 \,\&\, b_1$ and $C, A \vdash_n e_2 : t_2 \,\&\, b_2$. We thus can infer the desired $C, A \vdash_n e_1\, e_2 : t_1 \,\&\, (b_1 \cup b_2 \cup b)$.

The case (let). Then we have $C, A \vdash_c \texttt{let}\ x = e_1\ \texttt{in}\ e_2 : t_2 \,\&\, (b_1 \cup b_2)$ because $C, A \vdash_c e_1 : ts_1 \,\&\, b_1$ and $C, A[x : ts_1] \vdash_c e_2 : t_2 \,\&\, b_2$. Then the induction hypothesis gives $C, A \vdash_n e_1 : ts_1 \,\&\, b_1$. From Fact 9 we get that ts_1 is well-formed and solvable from C, so we can apply the induction hypothesis to get $C, A[x : ts_1] \vdash_n e_2 : t_2 \,\&\, b_2$. This enables us to infer the desired $C, A \vdash_n \texttt{let}\ x = e_1\ \texttt{in}\ e_2 : t_2 \,\&\, (b_1 \cup b_2)$.

The cases (rec), (if), (sub): Analogous to the above cases.

The case (ins). Then we have $C, A \vdash_c e : S\,t_0 \,\&\, b$ because $C, A \vdash_c e : \forall(\vec{\alpha}\vec{\beta} : C_0).\ t_0 \,\&\, b$ where $Dom(S) \subseteq \{\vec{\alpha}\vec{\beta}\}$ and $C \vdash S\,C_0$. By applying the induction hypothesis we get $C, A \vdash_n e : \forall(\vec{\alpha}\vec{\beta} : C_0).\ t_0 \,\&\, b$ so by Lemma 15 we get $C, A \vdash_n e : S\,t_0 \,\&\, b$ as desired.

The case (gen). Then we have $C, A \vdash_c e : \forall(\vec{\alpha}\vec{\beta} : C_0).\ t_0 \,\&\, b$ because $C \cup C_0, A \vdash_c e : t_0 \,\&\, b$ where $\forall(\vec{\alpha}\vec{\beta} : C_0).\ t_0$ is well-formed, solvable from C and satisfies $\{\vec{\alpha}\vec{\beta}\} \cap FV(C, A, b) = \emptyset$. Now A is well-formed and solvable from $C \cup C_0$ so the induction hypothesis gives $C \cup C_0, A \vdash_n e : t_0 \,\&\, b$. Therefore we have the TS-normalised inference tree $C, A \vdash_n e : \forall(\vec{\alpha}\vec{\beta} : C_0).\ t_0 \,\&\, b$. □

Conservative extension

Theorem 21 Let e be a sequential expression:

- if $[\,] \vdash_{ML} e : u$ then $\emptyset, [\,] \vdash e : \iota(u) \,\&\, \emptyset$;
- if $C, [\,] \vdash e : t \,\&\, b$ where C contains no type constraints then $[\,] \vdash_{ML} e : \epsilon(t)$.

Before embarking on the proof we need to extend $\epsilon()$ and $\iota()$ to work on substitutions: from a substitution S we construct an ML substitution $R = \epsilon(S)$ by stipulating $R\,\alpha = \epsilon(S\,\alpha)$; and from an ML substitution R we construct a substitution $S = \iota(R)$ by stipulating $S\,\alpha = \iota(R\,\alpha)$.

Fact 23. For all S and R and all t and u, we have $\epsilon(S\,t) = \epsilon(S)\,\epsilon(t)$ and $\iota(R\,u) = \iota(R)\,\iota(u)$.

Proof. The claims are proved by induction in t respectively in u. If $t = \alpha$ the first equation follows from the definition of $\epsilon(S)$, and if $u = \alpha$ the second equation follows from the definition of $\iota(R)$. If t (respectively u) is a base type like `int`, the equations are trivial. If t is a composite type like $t_1 \rightarrow^{b}\ t_2$, the first equation reads

$$\epsilon(S\,t_1) \rightarrow\ \epsilon(S\,t_2) = \epsilon(S)\,\epsilon(t_1) \rightarrow\ \epsilon(S)\,\epsilon(t_2)$$

and follows from the induction hypothesis. If u is a composite type like $u_1 \rightarrow\ u_2$, the second equation reads

$$\iota(R\,u_1) \rightarrow^{\emptyset}\ \iota(R\,u_2) = \iota(R)\,\iota(u_1) \rightarrow^{\emptyset}\ \iota(R)\,\iota(u_2)$$

and follows from the induction hypothesis. □

Proof of the first part of Theorem 21 The first part of the theorem follows from the following proposition which admits a proof by induction:

Proposition 24. Let e be sequential. If $A \vdash_{\mathrm{ML}} e : u$ then $\emptyset, \iota(A) \vdash e : \iota(u)\,\&\,\emptyset$. Similarly with us instead of u.

Proof. Induction in the proof tree for $A \vdash_{\mathrm{ML}} e : us$, where we perform case analysis on the definition in Fig. 4 (the clauses for conditionals and for recursion are omitted, as they present no further complications).

The case (con): Follows from Assumption 20.

The case (id): Follows trivially.

The case (abs): By induction we get

$$\emptyset, \iota(A)[x : \iota(u_1)] \vdash e : \iota(u_2)\,\&\,\emptyset$$

and by using (abs) we get

$$\emptyset, \iota(A) \vdash \mathbf{fn}\ x \Rightarrow e : \iota(u_1) \rightarrow^{\emptyset}\ \iota(u_2)\,\&\,\emptyset$$

which is as desired since $\iota(u_1 \rightarrow\ u_2) = \iota(u_1) \rightarrow^{\emptyset}\ \iota(u_2)$.

The case (app): We can apply the induction hypothesis twice to arrive at

$$\emptyset, \iota(A) \vdash e_1 : \iota(u_2 \to u_1) \,\&\, \emptyset$$
$$\emptyset, \iota(A) \vdash e_2 : \iota(u_2) \,\&\, \emptyset$$

so since $\iota(u_2 \to u_1) = \iota(u_2) \to^{\emptyset} \iota(u_1)$ we can apply (app) to get

$$\emptyset, \iota(A) \vdash e_1\, e_2 : \iota(u_1) \,\&\, \emptyset \cup \emptyset \cup \emptyset.$$

As $\emptyset \vdash \emptyset \cup \emptyset \cup \emptyset \subseteq \emptyset$ by (sub) we have the desired judgement

$$\emptyset, \iota(A) \vdash e_1\, e_2 : \iota(u_1) \,\&\, \emptyset.$$

The case (let): By applying the induction hypothesis twice we get

$$\emptyset, \iota(A) \vdash e_1 : \iota(us_1) \,\&\, \emptyset$$
$$\emptyset, \iota(A)[x : \iota(us_1)] \vdash e_2 : \iota(u_2) \,\&\, \emptyset$$

so by applying (let) and (sub) we get the desired judgement

$$\emptyset, \iota(A) \vdash \texttt{let } x = e_1 \texttt{ in } e_2 : \iota(u_2) \,\&\, \emptyset.$$

The case (ins): We can apply the induction hypothesis to get

$$\emptyset, \iota(A) \vdash e : \forall(\vec{\alpha} : \emptyset).\ \iota(u) \,\&\, \emptyset$$

so applying (ins) with the substitution $\iota(R)$ we arrive at

$$\emptyset, \iota(A) \vdash e : \iota(R)\, \iota(u) \,\&\, \emptyset$$

which is as desired since by Fact 23 we have $\iota(R)\, \iota(u) = \iota(R\, u)$.

The case (gen): We can apply the induction hypothesis to get

$$\emptyset, \iota(A) \vdash e : \iota(u) \,\&\, \emptyset$$

and the conclusion we want to arrive at is

$$\emptyset, \iota(A) \vdash e : \forall(\vec{\alpha} : \emptyset).\ \iota(u) \,\&\, \emptyset$$

which follows by using (gen) provided that (i) $\forall(\vec{\alpha} : \emptyset).\ \iota(u)$ is well-formed and solvable from $\emptyset$ and (ii) $\{\vec{\alpha}\} \cap FV(\iota(A)) = \emptyset$. Here (i) is trivial; and (ii) follows from $\{\vec{\alpha}\} \cap FV(A) = \emptyset$ since clearly $FV(\iota(A)) = FV(A)$. □

Auxiliary notions. Before embarking on the second part of Theorem 21 we need to develop some extra machinery.

ML type equations. ML type equations are of the form $u_1 = u_2$. With C_t a set of ML type equations and with R an ML substitution, we say that R satisfies (or unifies) C_t iff for all $(u_1 = u_2) \in C_t$ we have $R\,u_1 = R\,u_2$.

The following fact is well-known from unification theory:

Fact 25. Let C_t be a set of ML type equations. If there exists an ML substitution which satisfies C_t, then C_t has a "most general unifier": that is, an idempotent substitution R which satisfies C_t such that if R' also satisfies C_t then there exists R'' such that $R' = R''\,R$.

Lemma 26. Suppose R_0 with $Dom(R_0) \subseteq G$ satisfies a set of ML type equations C_t. Then C_t has a most general unifier R with $Dom(R) \subseteq G$.

Proof. From Fact 25 we know that C_t has a most general unifier R_1, and hence there exists R_2 such that $R_0 = R_2\,R_1$. Let $G_1 = Dom(R_1) \setminus Dom(R_0)$; for $\alpha \in G_1$ we have $R_2\,R_1\,\alpha = R_0\,\alpha = \alpha$ and hence R_1 maps the variables in G_1 into distinct variables G_2 (which by R_2 are mapped back again). Since R_1 is idempotent we have $G_2 \cap Dom(R_1) = \emptyset$, so R_0 equals R_2 on G_2 showing that $G_2 \subseteq Dom(R_0)$. Moreover, $G_1 \cap G_2 = \emptyset$.

Let ϕ map $\alpha \in G_1$ into $R_1\,\alpha$ and map $\alpha \in G_2$ into $R_2\,\alpha$ and behave as the identity otherwise. Then ϕ is its own inverse so that $\phi\,\phi = \mathrm{Id}$. Now define $R = \phi\,R_1$; clearly R unifies C_t and if R' also unifies C_t then (since R_1 is most general unifier) there exists R'' such that $R' = R''\,R_1 = R''\,\phi\,\phi\,R_1 = (R''\,\phi)\,R$.

We are left with showing (i) that R is idempotent and (ii) that $Dom(R) \subseteq G$. For (i), first observe that $R_1\,\phi$ equals Id except on $Dom(R_1)$. Since R_1 is idempotent we have $FV(R_1\,\alpha) \cap Dom(R_1) = \emptyset$ (for all α) and hence

$$R\,R = \phi\,R_1\,\phi\,R_1 = \phi\,\mathrm{Id}\,R_1 = R$$

For (ii), observe that R equals Id on G_1 so it will be sufficient to show that $R\alpha = \alpha$ if $\alpha \notin (G \cup G_1)$. But then $\alpha \notin Dom(R_0)$ and hence $\alpha \notin G_2$ and $\alpha \notin Dom(R_1)$ so $R\,\alpha = \phi\,\alpha = \alpha$. □

From a constraint set C we construct a set of ML type equations $\epsilon(C)$ as follows:

$$\epsilon(C) = \{(\epsilon(t_1) = \epsilon(t_2)) \mid (t_1 \subseteq t_2) \in C\}.$$

Fact 27. Suppose $C \vdash t_1 \subseteq t_2$. If R satisfies $\epsilon(C)$ then $R\,\epsilon(t_1) = R\,\epsilon(t_2)$.

So if $C \vdash C'$ and R satisfies $\epsilon(C)$ then R satisfies $\epsilon(C')$.

Proof. Induction in the proof tree. If $(t_1 \subseteq t_2) \in C$, the claim follows from the assumptions. The cases for reflexivity and transitivity are straight-forward. For the structural rules, assume e.g. that $C \vdash t_1 \to^{b} t_2 \subseteq t'_1 \to^{b'} t'_2$ because (among other things) $C \vdash t'_1 \subseteq t_1$ and $C \vdash t_2 \subseteq t'_2$. By using the induction hypothesis we get the desired equality

$$R\,\epsilon(t_1 \to^{b} t_2) = R\,\epsilon(t_1) \to R\,\epsilon(t_2) = R\,\epsilon(t'_1) \to R\,\epsilon(t'_2) = R\,\epsilon(t'_1 \to^{b'} t'_2).$$

Relating type schemes. For a type scheme $ts = \forall(\vec{\alpha}\,\vec{\beta} : C).\ t$ we shall not in general (when $C \neq \emptyset$) define any entity $\epsilon(ts)$; this is because one natural attempt, namely $\forall(\vec{\alpha} : \epsilon(C)).\ \epsilon(t)$, is not an ML type scheme and another natural attempt, $\forall\vec{\alpha}\,.\epsilon(t)$, causes loss of the information in $\epsilon(C)$. Rather we shall define some relations between ML types, types, ML type schemes and type schemes:

Definition 28. We write $u \prec_\epsilon^R ts$, where $ts = \forall(\vec{\alpha}\,\vec{\beta} : C_0).\ t_0$ and where R is an ML substitution, iff there exists R_0 which equals R on all variables except $\vec{\alpha}$ such that R_0 satisfies $\epsilon(C_0)$ and such that $u = R_0\,\epsilon(t_0)$.

Notice that instead of demanding R_0 to equal R on all variables but $\vec{\alpha}$, it is sufficient to demand that R_0 equals R on $FV(ts)$. (We have the expected property that if $u \prec_\epsilon^R ts$ and ts is alpha-equivalent to ts' then also $u \prec_\epsilon^R ts'$.)

Definition 29. We write $u {\prec} us$, where $us = \forall\vec{\alpha}\,.u_0$, iff there exists R_0 with $Dom(R_0) \subseteq \vec{\alpha}$ such that $u = R_0\,u_0$.

Definition 30. We write $us \cong_\epsilon^R ts$ to mean that (for all u) $u {\prec} us$ iff $u \prec_\epsilon^R ts$.

Fact 31. Suppose $us = \epsilon(ts)$, where $ts = \forall(\vec{\alpha}\,\vec{\beta} : \emptyset).\ t$ is sequential. Then $us \cong_\epsilon^{\mathrm{Id}} ts$.

Proof. We have $us = \forall\vec{\alpha}\,.\epsilon(t)$, so for any u it holds that $u {\prec} us \Leftrightarrow \exists\ R$ with $Dom(R) \subseteq \vec{\alpha}$ such that $u = R\,\epsilon(t) \Leftrightarrow u \prec_\epsilon^{\mathrm{Id}} ts$. □

Notice that $\forall().u \cong_\epsilon^R \forall(() : \emptyset).\ t$ holds iff $u = R\,\epsilon(t)$. We can thus consistently extend $\cong_\epsilon^R$ to relate not only type schemes but also types:

Definition 32. We write $u \cong_\epsilon^R t$ iff $u = R\,\epsilon(t)$.

Definition 33. We write $A' \cong_\epsilon^R A$ iff $Dom(A') = Dom(A)$ and $A'(x) \cong_\epsilon^R A(x)$ for all $x \in Dom(A)$.

Fact 34. Let R and S be such that $\epsilon(S) = R$ (this will for instance be the case if $S = \iota(R)$, cf. Fact 19). Then the relation $u \prec_\epsilon^R ts$ holds iff the relation $u \prec_\epsilon^{\mathrm{Id}} S\,ts$ holds.

Consequently, $us \cong_\epsilon^R ts$ holds iff $us \cong_\epsilon^{\mathrm{Id}} S\,ts$ holds.

Proof. Let $ts = \forall(\vec{\alpha}\,\vec{\beta} : C).\ t$. Due to the remark after Definition 28 we can assume that $\vec{\alpha}\,\vec{\beta}$ is disjoint from $Dom(S) \cup Ran(S)$, so $S\,ts = \forall(\vec{\alpha}\,\vec{\beta} : S\,C).\ S\,t$.

First we prove "if". For this suppose that R' equals Id except on $\vec{\alpha}$ and that R' satisfies $\epsilon(S\,C)$ and that $u = R'\,\epsilon(S\,t)$, which by straight-forward extensions of Fact 23 amounts to saying that R' satisfies $R\,\epsilon(C)$ and that $u = R'\,R\,\epsilon(t)$. Since $\{\vec{\alpha}\} \cap Ran(R) = \emptyset$ we conclude that $R'\,R$ equals R except on $\vec{\alpha}$, so we can use $R'\,R$ to show that $u \prec_\epsilon^R ts$.

Next we prove "only if". For this suppose that R' equals R except on $\vec{\alpha}$ and that R' satisfies $\epsilon(C)$ and that $u = R'\,\epsilon(t)$. Let R'' behave as R' on $\vec{\alpha}$ and behave as the identity otherwise. Our task is to show that R'' satisfies $\epsilon(S\,C)$ and that $u = R'' \epsilon(St)$, which as we saw above amounts to showing that R'' satisfies $R\epsilon(C)$ and that $u = R'' R\epsilon(t)$. This will follow if we can show that $R' = R'' R$. But if $\alpha \in \vec{\alpha}$ we have $R'' R\alpha = R'' \alpha = R' \alpha$ since $Dom(R) \cap \{\vec{\alpha}\} = \emptyset$, and if $\alpha \notin \vec{\alpha}$ we have $R'' R\alpha = R\alpha = R' \alpha$ where the first equality sign follows from $Ran(R) \cap \{\vec{\alpha}\} = \emptyset$ and $Dom(R'') \subseteq \vec{\alpha}$. □

Fact 35. If $us \cong_\epsilon^{\mathrm{Id}} ts$ then $FV(us) \subseteq FV(ts)$.

Proof. We assume $us \cong_\epsilon^{\mathrm{Id}} ts$ where $us = \forall \vec{\alpha}'.u$ and $ts = \forall(\vec{\alpha}\vec{\beta} : C).\ t$. Let α_1 be given such that $\alpha_1 \notin FV(ts)$, our task is to show that $\alpha_1 \notin FV(us)$.

Clearly $u \prec us$ so $u \prec_\epsilon^{\mathrm{Id}} ts$, that is there exists R with $Dom(R) \subseteq \vec{\alpha}$ such that R satisfies $\epsilon(C)$ and such that $u = R\epsilon(t)$. Now define a substitution R_1 which maps α_1 into a fresh variable and is the identity otherwise. Due to our assumption about α_1 it is easy to see that $R_1 R$ equals Id on $FV(ts)$, and as $R_1 R$ clearly satisfies $\epsilon(C)$ it holds that $R_1 u = R_1 R\epsilon(t) \prec_\epsilon^{\mathrm{Id}} ts$ and hence also $R_1 u \prec us$. As $\alpha_1 \notin FV(R_1 u)$ we can infer the desired $\alpha_1 \notin FV(us)$. □

Proof of the second part of Theorem 21 The second part of the theorem follows (by letting $R = \mathrm{Id}$ and $A = A' = [\,]$) from the following proposition, which admits a proof by induction.

Proposition 36. Let e be sequential, suppose $C, A \vdash e : ts \,\&\, b$, suppose R satisfies $\epsilon(C)$, and suppose $A' \cong_\epsilon^R A$; then there exists a us with $us \cong_\epsilon^R ts$ such that $A' \vdash_{\mathrm{ML}} e : us$. Similarly with t and u instead of ts and us (in which case $u = R\epsilon(t)$).

We perform induction in the proof tree of $C, A \vdash e : ts \,\&\, b$, using terminology from Fig. 2 (the clauses for conditionals and for recursion are omitted, as they present no further complications):

The case (con): Here $ts = \mathrm{TypeOf}(c)$ and we choose $us = \mathrm{MLTypeOf}(c)$. By Assumption 20 and by Fact 31 we know that $us \cong_\epsilon^{\mathrm{Id}} ts$. Since TypeOf($c$) is closed (cf. Fact 8) we have $us \cong_\epsilon^{\mathrm{Id}} \iota(R)\, ts$ so Fact 34 gives us the desired relation $us \cong_\epsilon^R ts$.

The case (id): Here $ts = A(x)$. Since $A' \cong_\epsilon^R A$ it holds that $A'(x) \cong_\epsilon^R A(x)$ and $A' \vdash_{\mathrm{ML}} x : A'(x)$, as desired.

The case (abs): Suppose R satisfies $\epsilon(C)$ and that $A' \cong_\epsilon^R A$. Then also $A'[x : R\epsilon(t_1)] \cong_\epsilon^R A[x : t_1]$, so the induction hypothesis can be applied to find u_2 such that $u_2 = R\epsilon(t_2)$ and such that $A'[x : R\epsilon(t_1)] \vdash_{\mathrm{ML}} e : u_2$. By using (abs) we get the judgement

$$A' \vdash_{\mathrm{ML}} \mathtt{fn}\ x \Rightarrow e : R\epsilon(t_1) \rightarrow u_2$$

which is as desired since $R\epsilon(t_1) \rightarrow u_2 = R\epsilon(t_1 \rightarrow^b t_2)$.

The case (app): Suppose R satisfies $\epsilon(C_1 \cup C_2)$ and that $A' \cong^R_\epsilon A$. Clearly R satisfies $\epsilon(C_1)$ as well as $\epsilon(C_2)$, so the induction hypothesis can be applied to infer that

$$A' \vdash_{\mathrm{ML}} e_1 : R\,\epsilon(t_2 \rightarrow^b t_1) \text{ and } A' \vdash_{\mathrm{ML}} e_2 : R\,\epsilon(t_2)$$

and since $R\,\epsilon(t_2 \rightarrow^b t_1) = R\,\epsilon(t_2) \rightarrow R\,\epsilon(t_1)$ we can apply (app) to arrive at the desired judgement $A' \vdash_{\mathrm{ML}} e_1\, e_2 : R\,\epsilon(t_1)$.

The case (let): Suppose R satisfies $\epsilon(C_1 \cup C_2)$ and that $A' \cong^R_\epsilon A$. Since R satisfies $\epsilon(C_1)$ we can apply the induction hypothesis to find us_1 such that $us_1 \cong^R_\epsilon ts_1$ and such that $A' \vdash_{\mathrm{ML}} e_1 : us_1$.

Since R satisfies $\epsilon(C_2)$ and since $A'[x : us_1] \cong^R_\epsilon A[x : ts_1]$ we can apply the induction hypothesis to infer that $A'[x : us_1] \vdash_{\mathrm{ML}} e_2 : R\,\epsilon(t_2)$. Now use (let) to arrive at the desired judgement $A' \vdash_{\mathrm{ML}} \texttt{let}\ x = e_1\ \texttt{in}\ e_2 : R\,\epsilon(t_2)$.

The case (sub): Suppose R satisfies $\epsilon(C)$ and that $A' \cong^R_\epsilon A$. By applying the induction hypothesis we infer that $A' \vdash_{\mathrm{ML}} e : R\,\epsilon(t)$ and since by Fact 27 we have $R\,\epsilon(t) = R\,\epsilon(t')$ this is as desired.

The case (ins): Suppose that R satisfies $\epsilon(C)$ and that $A' \cong^R_\epsilon A$. The induction hypothesis tells us that there exists us with $us \cong^R_\epsilon \forall(\vec{\alpha}\,\vec{\beta} : C_0).\ t_0$ such that $A' \vdash_{\mathrm{ML}} e : us$.

Since $C \vdash S_0\, C_0$ and R satisfies $\epsilon(C)$, Fact 27 tells us that R satisfies $\epsilon(S_0\, C_0)$ which by Fact 23 equals $\epsilon(S_0)\,\epsilon(C_0)$, thus $R\,\epsilon(S_0)$ satisfies $\epsilon(C_0)$. As $R\,\epsilon(S_0)$ equals R except on $\vec{\alpha}$, it holds that $R\,\epsilon(S_0)\,\epsilon(t_0) \prec^R_\epsilon \forall(\vec{\alpha}\,\vec{\beta} : C_0).\ t_0$ and since $us \cong^R_\epsilon \forall(\vec{\alpha}\,\vec{\beta} : C_0).\ t_0$ we have $R\,\epsilon(S_0)\,\epsilon(t_0) \prec us$. But this shows that we can use (ins) to arrive at the judgement $A' \vdash_{\mathrm{ML}} e : R\,\epsilon(S_0)\,\epsilon(t_0)$ which is as desired since $\epsilon(S_0)\,\epsilon(t_0) = \epsilon(S_0\, t_0)$ by Fact 23.

The case (gen): Suppose that R satisfies $\epsilon(C)$ and that $A' \cong^R_\epsilon A$. Our task is to find us such that $us \cong^R_\epsilon \forall(\vec{\alpha}\,\vec{\beta} : C_0).\ t_0$ and such that $A' \vdash_{\mathrm{ML}} e : us$. Below we will argue that we can assume that $\{\vec{\alpha}\} \cap (\mathit{Dom}(R) \cup \mathit{Ran}(R)) = \emptyset$.

> Let T be a renaming substitution mapping $\vec{\alpha}$ into fresh variables $\vec{\alpha}\,'$. By applying Lemma 10, by exploiting that $\mathit{FV}(C, A, b) \cap \{\vec{\alpha}\,\vec{\beta}\} = \emptyset$, and by using (gen) we can construct a proof tree whose last nodes are
>
> $$\frac{C \cup T\, C_0, A \vdash e : T\, t_0\ \&\ b}{C, A \vdash e : \forall(\vec{\alpha}\,'\vec{\beta} : T\, C_0).\ T\, t_0\ \&\ b}$$
>
> the conclusion of which is alpha-equivalent to the conclusion of the original proof tree, and the shape of which (by Lemma 10) is equal to the shape of the original proof tree.

There exists S_0 with $\mathit{Dom}(S_0) \subseteq \{\vec{\alpha}\,\vec{\beta}\}$ such that $C \vdash S_0\, C_0$. Fact 27 then tells us that R satisfies $\epsilon(S_0\, C_0)$ which by Fact 23 equals $\epsilon(S_0)\,\epsilon(C_0)$.

Now define R'_0 to be a substitution with $Dom(R'_0) \subseteq \{\vec{\alpha}\}$ which maps $\vec{\alpha}$ into $R\,\epsilon(S_0)\,\vec{\alpha}$. It is easy to see (since $\vec{\alpha}$ is disjoint from $Dom(R) \cup Ran(R)$) that $R'_0\,R = R\,\epsilon(S_0)$, implying that R'_0 satisfies $R\,\epsilon(C_0)$.

By Lemma 26 there exists R_0 with $Dom(R_0) \subseteq \{\vec{\alpha}\}$ which is a most general unifier of $R\,\epsilon(C_0)$. Hence with $R' = R_0\,R$ it holds not only that R' satisfies $\epsilon(C)$ but also that R' satisfies $\epsilon(C_0)$, so in order to apply the induction hypothesis on R' we just need to show that $A' \cong_\epsilon^{R'} A$. This can be done by showing that R equals R' on $FV(A)$, but this follows since our assumptions tell us that $Dom(R_0) \cap FV(R\,A) = \emptyset$.

The induction hypothesis thus tells us that $A' \vdash_{\mathrm{ML}} e : R'\,\epsilon(t_0)$. Let $S = \iota(R)$ (which by Fact 19 implies that $R = \epsilon(S)$); by Fact 34 and Fact 35 we infer that $FV(A') \subseteq FV(S\,A)$, so since $\{\vec{\alpha}\} \cap FV(A) = \emptyset$ and $\{\vec{\alpha}\} \cap Ran(S) = \emptyset$ we have $\{\vec{\alpha}\} \cap FV(A') = \emptyset$. We can thus use (gen) to arrive at the judgement $A' \vdash_{\mathrm{ML}} e : \forall\vec{\alpha}.R'\,\epsilon(t_0)$.

We are left with showing that $\forall\vec{\alpha}.R'\,\epsilon(t_0) \cong_\epsilon^R \forall(\vec{\alpha}\,\vec{\beta} : C_0).\ t_0$ but this follows from the following calculation (explained below):

$$
\begin{aligned}
& u \prec_\epsilon^R \forall(\vec{\alpha}\,\vec{\beta} : C_0).\ t_0 \\
\Leftrightarrow\ & u \prec_\epsilon^{\mathrm{Id}} \forall(\vec{\alpha}\,\vec{\beta} : S\,C_0).\ S\,t_0 \\
\Leftrightarrow\ & \exists R_1 \text{ with } Dom(R_1) \subseteq \{\vec{\alpha}\} \\
& \qquad \text{such that } R_1 \text{ satisfies } R\,\epsilon(C_0) \text{ and } u = R_1\,R\,\epsilon(t_0) \\
\Leftrightarrow\ & \exists R_1 \text{ with } Dom(R_1) \subseteq \{\vec{\alpha}\} \\
& \qquad \text{such that } \exists R_2 : R_1 = R_2\,R_0 \text{ and } u = R_1\,R\,\epsilon(t_0) \\
\Leftrightarrow\ & \exists R_2 \text{ with } Dom(R_2) \subseteq \{\vec{\alpha}\} \text{ such that } u = R_2\,R_0\,R\,\epsilon(t_0) \\
\Leftrightarrow\ & u \prec \forall\vec{\alpha}.R'\,\epsilon(t_0).
\end{aligned}
$$

The first $\Leftrightarrow$ follows from Fact 34 where we have exploited that $\{\vec{\alpha}\,\vec{\beta}\}$ is disjoint from $Dom(S) \cup Ran(S)$; the second $\Leftrightarrow$ follows from the definition of $\prec_\epsilon^{\mathrm{Id}}$ together with Fact 23; the third $\Leftrightarrow$ is a consequence of R_0 being the most general unifier of $R\,\epsilon(C_0)$; and the fourth $\Leftrightarrow$ is a consequence of $Dom(R_0) \subseteq \{\vec{\alpha}\}$ since then from $R_1 = R_2\,R_0$ we conclude that if $\alpha' \notin \{\vec{\alpha}\}$ then $R_1\,\alpha' = R_2\,\alpha'$ and hence $Dom(R_1) \subseteq \{\alpha\}$ iff $Dom(R_2) \subseteq \{\alpha\}$.

Polymorphic Subtyping for Effect Analysis: The Dynamic Semantics

Torben Amtoft & Flemming Nielson & Hanne Riis Nielson & Jürgen Ammann

Computer Science Department, Aarhus University, Denmark

e-mail: {tamtoft,fnielson,hrnielson}@daimi.aau.dk

Abstract. We study an annotated type and effect system that integrates `let`-polymorphism, effects, and subtyping into an annotated type and effect system for a fragment of Concurrent ML. First a small-step operational semantics is defined and next the annotated type and effect system is proved semantically sound. This provides insights into the rule for generalisation in the annotated type and effect system.

1 Introduction

In a recent paper [6] we developed an annotated type and effect system for a fragment of Concurrent ML. Judgements are of form

$$C, A \vdash e : \sigma \,\&\, b$$

with e an expression, σ a type or a type scheme, b a behaviour (recording channel allocations and thereby the set of "dangerous variables"), C a set of constraints among types and behaviours, and A an environment.

In this paper we address the soundness of the static semantics (i.e. the type system) wrt. a dynamic semantics. Statements of semantic soundness typically contain as premise that the inference system assigns a type t to e but the conclusion depends on the kind of dynamic semantics used: for a denotational semantics one may require (as in [4]) that the denotation of e "has type" t; for a big-step (natural) semantics one may require (as in [10, 3]) that if $e \rightarrow v$ then v "has type" t; for a small-step semantics [7] one requires (as in [11]) the following *subject reduction* property: if $e \rightarrow e'$ then the inference system also assigns e' the type t. In addition, in order to ensure that "well-typed programs do not go wrong" one must establish that "error configurations" (those which are "stuck") cannot be typed. This is in contrast to the development in [1] where the construction of a denotational semantics is *based on* an annotated type and effect system in that *only* well-typed programs are given a semantics.

We shall choose a small-step semantics as we consider this the most appropriate for concurrent languages; the configurations of the transition system will be process pools PP which map process identifiers into expressions. To get a flavour of how subject reduction is formulated in our setting consider the case where PP rewrites to PP' because process p allocates a fresh channel ch which is able to transmit values of type t', and suppose that

$$C, A \vdash PP(p) : t \,\&\, b$$

holds: then we must also have $C, A' \vdash PP'(p) : t \,\&\, b'$ where A' is as A except that ch is bound to t' **chan**, and where b is the "union" of the "current action" $\{t' \text{ CHAN}\}$ (allocating a t'-channel) and the "future action" b'. The general picture is much as in [5] that types are unchanged whereas the behaviours get "smaller" and the environments are "extended".

Extending the environment is a potential danger to semantic soundness, cf. the considerations in [10, section 5] where it was concluded that store operations in Standard ML are harmless unless they actually expand the store. In [6] it was demonstrated that channel allocations (the way our setting "expands the store") may be harmful unless one is very careful when deciding the set of variables over which to generalise in the rule for `let` in the inference system: not only should this set be disjoint from the set of variables occurring in the behaviour (as is standard in effect systems, e.g. [9]) but it should also be "upwards closed" with respect to a constraint set. The present paper provides the formal justification and the proof of Lemma 37 highlights how the judicious choice of generalisation strategy allows to extend the environment.

Overview. We define a dynamic semantics which employs one system for the sequential components (Sect. 2.2) and another for the concurrent components (Sect. 2.3). Next (Sect. 2.4) we extend the repertoire of techniques [6] for normalising and manipulating the inference trees of the annotated type and effect system. Finally (Sect. 3), we show that the system is indeed semantically sound with respect to the dynamic semantics: we establish a sequential subject reduction result (Theorem 36) as a preparation for a concurrent subject reduction result (Theorem 41) which also demonstrates that the actions performed by the system are in a certain sense as "predicted" by the effect information; in Sect. 3.2 we demonstrate (informally) that it is not possible to assign a type to the "error configurations" which have been characterised in Proposition 22.

2 Inference System and Semantics

We shall make use of a variant of Concurrent ML [8] where expressions and constants are given by

$$\begin{aligned} e ::= &\ c \mid x \mid \texttt{fn}\ x \Rightarrow e \mid e_1\, e_2 \mid \texttt{let}\ x = e_1\ \texttt{in}\ e_2 \\ \mid &\ \texttt{rec}\ f\ x \Rightarrow e \mid \texttt{if}\ e\ \texttt{then}\ e_1\ \texttt{else}\ e_2 \end{aligned}$$

$$\begin{aligned} c ::= &\ \texttt{()} \mid \texttt{true} \mid \texttt{false} \mid n \mid \texttt{pair} \mid \texttt{nil} \mid \texttt{cons} \\ \mid &\ \texttt{+} \mid \texttt{*} \mid \texttt{=} \mid \cdots \mid \texttt{fst} \mid \texttt{snd} \mid \texttt{hd} \mid \texttt{tl} \mid \texttt{isnil} \\ \mid &\ \texttt{send} \mid \texttt{receive} \\ \mid &\ \texttt{sync} \mid \texttt{channel} \mid \texttt{fork} \end{aligned}$$

where there are four kinds of constants: sequential constructors like `true` and `pair`, sequential base functions like `+` and `fst`, the non-sequential constructors `send` and `receive` for creating delayed output and input communications, and the non-sequential base functions **sync** (for synchronising a delayed communication), **channel** (for allocating a new communication channel) and **fork** (for spawning a new process).

Types and behaviours are given by

$$\begin{aligned} t &::= \alpha \mid \texttt{unit} \mid \texttt{int} \mid \texttt{bool} \mid t_1 \times t_2 \mid t\ \texttt{list} \\ &\mid\ t_1 \rightarrow^b t_2 \mid t\ \texttt{chan} \mid t\ \texttt{com}\ b \\ b &::= \{t\ \text{CHAN}\} \mid \beta \mid \emptyset \mid b_1 \cup b_2 \end{aligned}$$

where a type $t_1 \rightarrow^b t_2$ denotes a function which given a value of type t_1 computes a value of type t_2 with "side effect" b; where a type t **chan** denotes a channel allowing values of type t to be transmitted; and where a type t **com** b denotes a delayed communication that when synchronised will give rise to side effect b and result in a type t. A behaviour can (apart from the presence of behaviour variables) be viewed as a set of "atomic" behaviours which each record the creation of a channel.

Type schemes ts are of form $\forall(\vec{\alpha}\vec{\beta} : C).\ t$ with C a set of constraints, where a constraint is either of form $t_1 \subseteq t_2$ or of form $b_1 \subseteq b_2$. The type schemes of selected constants are given in Figure 1.

c	TypeOf(c)
`true`	$\texttt{bool}$
`pair`	$\forall(\alpha_1\alpha_2 : \emptyset).\ \alpha_1 \rightarrow^{\emptyset} \alpha_2 \rightarrow^{\emptyset} \alpha_1 \times \alpha_2$
`+`	$\texttt{int} \times \texttt{int} \rightarrow^{\emptyset} \texttt{int}$
`fst`	$\forall(\alpha_1\alpha_2 : \emptyset).\ \alpha_1 \times \alpha_2 \rightarrow^{\emptyset} \alpha_1$
`snd`	$\forall(\alpha_1\alpha_2 : \emptyset).\ \alpha_1 \times \alpha_2 \rightarrow^{\emptyset} \alpha_2$
`send`	$\forall(\alpha : \emptyset).\ (\alpha\ \texttt{chan}) \times \alpha \rightarrow^{\emptyset} (\alpha\ \texttt{com}\ \emptyset)$
`receive`	$\forall(\alpha : \emptyset).\ (\alpha\ \texttt{chan}) \rightarrow^{\emptyset} (\alpha\ \texttt{com}\ \emptyset)$
`sync`	$\forall(\alpha\beta : \emptyset).\ (\alpha\ \texttt{com}\ \beta) \rightarrow^{\beta} \alpha$
`channel`	$\forall(\alpha\beta : \{\{\alpha\ \text{CHAN}\} \subseteq \beta\}).\ \texttt{unit} \rightarrow^{\beta} (\alpha\ \texttt{chan})$
`fork`	$\forall(\alpha\beta : \emptyset).\ (\texttt{unit} \rightarrow^{\beta} \alpha) \rightarrow^{\emptyset} \texttt{unit}$

Fig. 1. Type schemes for selected constants.

Constructors actually construct something (that is, a composite type) and this construction takes place "silently":

Fact 1. Let c be a constructor (sequential or non-sequential), and let

$$t'_1 \rightarrow^{b'_1} \cdots t'_m \rightarrow^{b'_m} t' \text{ with } m \geq 0 \text{ and } t' \text{ not a function type}$$

be the unique "maximal decomposition" of (the type part of) TypeOf(c). Then

t' is not a type variable and $b'_i = \emptyset$ for all $i \in \{1 \ldots m\}$. □

The ordering among types and behaviours is defined in Figure 2; in particular notice that the ordering is contravariant in the argument position of a function type and that both t **chan** $\subseteq t'$ **chan** and $\{t \text{ CHAN}\} \subseteq \{t' \text{ CHAN}\}$ demand that $t \equiv t'$, i.e. $t \subseteq t'$ and $t' \subseteq t$, since t occurs covariantly when used in `receive` and contravariantly when used in **send**.

The inference system is defined in Figure 3. The rules for abstraction and application are as usual in effect systems: the latent behaviour of the body of a function abstraction is placed on the arrow of the function type, and once the function is applied the latent behaviour is added to the effect of evaluating the function and its argument, reflecting that the language is call-by-value. The rule for recursion makes use of function abstraction to concisely represent the "fixed point requirement" of typing recursive functions; note that we do not admit polymorphic recursion. The rule (sub) makes use of the subtyping and subeffecting relation defined in Fig. 2. The rule (ins) allows one to instantiate a type scheme and employs the notion of solvability: we say that the type scheme $\forall(\vec{\alpha}\vec{\beta} : C_0).\ t_0$ is *solvable* from C by S_0 if $Dom(S_0) \subseteq \{\vec{\alpha}\vec{\beta}\}$ and if $C \vdash S_0\, C_0$, where we write $C \vdash C'$ to mean that[1] $C \vdash g_1 \subseteq g_2$ for all $g_1 \subseteq g_2$ in C'. The generalisation rule (gen) employs the notion of well-formedness, to be explained below.

A constraint set is *well-formed* if all constraints are of form $t \subseteq \alpha$ or $b \subseteq \beta$; this is motivated by the desire to be able to use the subtyping rules "backwards" (as spelled out in Lemma 4 below) and in ensuring that subeffecting preserves certain relations between the variables (see Lemma 5 below).

In order to define well-formedness for type schemes we need several auxiliary concepts: the judgement $C \vdash \gamma_1 \leftarrow \gamma_2$ holds if there exists $(g_1 \subseteq g_2)$ in C such that $\gamma_i \in FV(g_i)$ for $i = 1, 2$; we use $\leftarrow^*$ for the reflexive and transitive closure of $\leftarrow$; and we define *upwards closure* and *downwards closure* as follows:

$$X^{C\uparrow} = \{\gamma \mid \exists \gamma' \in X : C \vdash \gamma' \leftarrow^* \gamma\}$$
$$X^{C\downarrow} = \{\gamma \mid \exists \gamma' \in X : C \vdash \gamma \leftarrow^* \gamma'\}$$

Definition 2. A type scheme $\forall(\vec{\alpha}\vec{\beta} : C_0).\ t_0$ is well-formed if C_0 is well-formed and if all constraints in C_0 contain at least one variable among $\{\vec{\alpha}\vec{\beta}\}$ and if it is *upwards closed*: that is $\{\vec{\alpha}\vec{\beta}\}^{C_0\uparrow} = \{\vec{\alpha}\vec{\beta}\}$.

Requiring a type scheme to be well-formed (in particular upwards closed) is a crucial feature in our approach to achieve a semantically sound system, cf. the discussion in the Introduction (and the proof of Lemma 37). The following trivial result proves useful:

Fact 3. Suppose $C \cup C_0 \vdash \gamma_1 \leftarrow \gamma_2$ with $\gamma_1 \notin FV(C)$. Then $C_0 \vdash \gamma_1 \leftarrow \gamma_2$.

[1] Following [6] we use g to stand for t or b and we use γ to stand for α or β and we use σ to stand for t or ts.

Ordering on behaviours

(axiom) $C \vdash b_1 \subseteq b_2$ if $(b_1 \subseteq b_2) \in C$

(refl) $C \vdash b \subseteq b$

(trans) $$\frac{C \vdash b_1 \subseteq b_2 \quad C \vdash b_2 \subseteq b_3}{C \vdash b_1 \subseteq b_3}$$

(CHAN) $$\frac{C \vdash t \equiv t'}{C \vdash \{t \text{ CHAN}\} \subseteq \{t' \text{ CHAN}\}}$$

($\emptyset$) $C \vdash \emptyset \subseteq b$

($\cup$) $C \vdash b_i \subseteq (b_1 \cup b_2)$ for $i = 1, 2$

(lub) $$\frac{C \vdash b_1 \subseteq b \quad C \vdash b_2 \subseteq b}{C \vdash (b_1 \cup b_2) \subseteq b}$$

Ordering on types

(axiom) $C \vdash t_1 \subseteq t_2$ if $(t_1 \subseteq t_2) \in C$

(refl) $C \vdash t \subseteq t$

(trans) $$\frac{C \vdash t_1 \subseteq t_2 \quad C \vdash t_2 \subseteq t_3}{C \vdash t_1 \subseteq t_3}$$

($\rightarrow$) $$\frac{C \vdash t_1' \subseteq t_1 \quad C \vdash t_2 \subseteq t_2' \quad C \vdash b \subseteq b'}{C \vdash (t_1 \rightarrow^{b} t_2) \subseteq (t_1' \rightarrow^{b'} t_2')}$$

($\times$) $$\frac{C \vdash t_1 \subseteq t_1' \quad C \vdash t_2 \subseteq t_2'}{C \vdash (t_1 \times t_2) \subseteq (t_1' \times t_2')}$$

(list) $$\frac{C \vdash t \subseteq t'}{C \vdash (t \ \mathtt{list}) \subseteq (t' \ \mathtt{list})}$$

(chan) $$\frac{C \vdash t \equiv t'}{C \vdash (t \ \mathbf{chan}) \subseteq (t' \ \mathbf{chan})}$$

(com) $$\frac{C \vdash t \subseteq t' \quad C \vdash b \subseteq b'}{C \vdash (t \ \mathtt{com} \ b) \subseteq (t' \ \mathtt{com} \ b')}$$

Fig. 2. Subtyping and subeffecting.

(con) $C, A \vdash c : \text{TypeOf}(c) \,\&\, \emptyset$

(id) $C, A \vdash x : A(x) \,\&\, \emptyset$

$$\text{(abs)}\ \frac{C, A[x : t_1] \vdash e : t_2 \,\&\, b}{C, A \vdash \texttt{fn}\ x \Rightarrow e : (t_1 \rightarrow^{b} t_2) \,\&\, \emptyset}$$

$$\text{(app)}\ \frac{C_1, A \vdash e_1 : (t_2 \rightarrow^{b} t_1) \,\&\, b_1 \qquad C_2, A \vdash e_2 : t_2 \,\&\, b_2}{(C_1 \cup C_2), A \vdash e_1\, e_2 : t_1 \,\&\, (b_1 \cup b_2 \cup b)}$$

$$\text{(let)}\ \frac{C_1, A \vdash e_1 : ts_1 \,\&\, b_1 \qquad C_2, A[x : ts_1] \vdash e_2 : t_2 \,\&\, b_2}{(C_1 \cup C_2), A \vdash \texttt{let}\ x = e_1\ \texttt{in}\ e_2 : t_2 \,\&\, (b_1 \cup b_2)}$$

$$\text{(rec)}\ \frac{C, A[f : t] \vdash \texttt{fn}\ x \Rightarrow e : t \,\&\, b}{C, A \vdash \texttt{rec}\ f\ x \Rightarrow e : t \,\&\, b}$$

$$\text{(if)}\ \frac{C_0, A \vdash e_0 : \texttt{bool} \,\&\, b_0 \qquad C_1, A \vdash e_1 : t \,\&\, b_1 \qquad C_2, A \vdash e_2 : t \,\&\, b_2}{(C_0 \cup C_1 \cup C_2), A \vdash \texttt{if}\ e_0\ \texttt{then}\ e_1\ \texttt{else}\ e_2 : t \,\&\, (b_0 \cup b_1 \cup b_2)}$$

$$\text{(sub)}\ \frac{C, A \vdash e : t \,\&\, b}{C, A \vdash e : t' \,\&\, b'} \qquad \text{if } C \vdash t \subseteq t' \text{ and } C \vdash b \subseteq b'$$

$$\text{(ins)}\ \frac{C, A \vdash e : \forall(\vec{\alpha}\vec{\beta} : C_0).\ t_0 \,\&\, b}{C, A \vdash e : S_0\, t_0 \,\&\, b} \qquad \text{if } \forall(\vec{\alpha}\vec{\beta} : C_0).\ t_0 \text{ is solvable from } C \text{ by } S_0$$

$$\text{(gen)}\ \frac{C \cup C_0, A \vdash e : t_0 \,\&\, b}{C, A \vdash e : \forall(\vec{\alpha}\vec{\beta} : C_0).\ t_0 \,\&\, b}$$
if $\forall(\vec{\alpha}\vec{\beta} : C_0).\ t_0$ is both well-formed, solvable from C, and satisfies $\{\vec{\alpha}\vec{\beta}\} \cap FV(C, A, b) = \emptyset$

Fig. 3. The type inference system.

2.1 Properties of the Inference System

In this section we list some basic concepts and results which we shall use in the later development; except for Fact 8 and Fact 9 their proofs are given in [6].

The subtyping rules can be used "backwards" if the constraint set is well-formed:

Lemma 4. Suppose C is well-formed and that $C \vdash t \subseteq t'$.

- If $t' = t'_1 \rightarrow^{b'} t'_2$ there exist t_1, t_2 and b such that $t = t_1 \rightarrow^{b} t_2$ and such that $C \vdash t'_1 \subseteq t_1$, $C \vdash t_2 \subseteq t'_2$ and $C \vdash b \subseteq b'$.

- If $t' = t'_1$ $\texttt{com}$ b' there exist t_1 and b such that $t = t_1$ $\texttt{com}$ b and such that $C \vdash t_1 \subseteq t'_1$ and $C \vdash b \subseteq b'$.
- If $t' = t'_1 \times t'_2$ there exist t_1 and t_2 such that $t = t_1 \times t_2$ and such that $C \vdash t_1 \subseteq t'_1$ and $C \vdash t_2 \subseteq t'_2$.
- If $t' = t'_1$ $\texttt{chan}$ there exists t_1 such that $t = t_1$ $\texttt{chan}$ and such that $C \vdash t_1 \equiv t'_1$.
- If $t' = t'_1$ $\texttt{list}$ there exists t_1 such that $t = t_1$ $\texttt{list}$ and such that $C \vdash t_1 \subseteq t'_1$.
- If $t' = \texttt{int}$ ($\texttt{bool}$, $\texttt{unit}$) then $t = \texttt{int}$ ($\texttt{bool}$, $\texttt{unit}$).

Even if b is "less than" b' it does not necessarily hold that $FV(b) \subseteq FV(b')$, but taking downwards closure will establish the desired relation:

Lemma 5. Suppose that C is well-formed:

$$\text{if } C \vdash b \subseteq b' \text{ then } FV(b)^{C\downarrow} \subseteq FV(b')^{C\downarrow}.$$

We can apply a substitution to a judgement and still get a valid judgement (which even has the same shape, i.e. it is constructed using the same sequence of inference rules):

Lemma 6. For all substitutions S:

(a) If $C \vdash C'$ then $S\,C \vdash S\,C'$.
(b) If $C, A \vdash e : \sigma \,\&\, b$ then $S\,C, S\,A \vdash e : S\,\sigma \,\&\, S\,b$ (and has the same shape).

We can strengthen the constraint set and still get a valid judgement:

Lemma 7. For all sets C' of constraints satisfying $C' \vdash C$:

(a) If $C \vdash C_0$ then $C' \vdash C_0$.
(b) If $C, A \vdash e : \sigma \,\&\, b$ then $C', A \vdash e : \sigma \,\&\, b$ (and has the same shape).

We can swap distinct identifiers in the environment and still get a valid judgement:

Fact 8. Let x and y be distinct identifiers: if $C, A_1[x : \sigma_1][y : \sigma_2]A_2 \vdash e : \sigma \,\&\, b$ then $C, A_1[y : \sigma_2][x : \sigma_1]A_2 \vdash e : \sigma \,\&\, b$ (and has the same shape).

We can augment the environment with spurious identifiers and still get a valid judgement:

Fact 9. Let x be an identifier not occurring in e and let t be an arbitrary type. If $C, A \vdash e : \sigma \,\&\, b$ then $C, A[x : t] \vdash e : \sigma \,\&\, b$ (and has the same shape).

Proof. Let α be a fresh type variable. Then a straightforward induction in the proof tree (using Fact 8) tells us that $C, A[x : \alpha] \vdash e : \sigma \,\&\, b$ (and has the same shape). Now apply Lemma 6 with the substitution $[\alpha \mapsto t]$.

The proof of semantic soundness is complicated by the presence of the non-syntax directed rules (sub), (gen) and (ins) of Figure 3; this motivates considering inference trees having a more manageable shape.

Definition 10. An inference tree for $C, A \vdash e : t \,\&\, b$ is *T-normalised* if it is created by:

- (con) or (id); or
- (ins) applied to (con) or (id); or
- (abs), (app), (rec), (if) or (sub) applied to T-normalised inference trees; or
- (let) applied to a TS-normalised inference tree and a T-normalised inference.

An inference tree for $C, A \vdash e : ts \,\&\, b$ is *TS-normalised* if it is created by:

- (gen) applied to a T-normalised inference tree.

We shall write $C, A \vdash_n e : \sigma \,\&\, b$ if the inference tree is T-normalised (if σ is a type) or TS-normalised (if σ is a type scheme).

Notice that if $jdg = C, A \vdash e : \sigma \,\&\, b$ occurs in a normalised inference tree then jdg itself will be normalised, unless jdg is created by (con) or (id) and σ is a type scheme. By requiring an inference to be normalised one restricts the use of (ins), but the following result indicates that this is not a severe restriction.

Lemma 11. Suppose that

$$jdg = C, A \vdash e : S\,t_0 \,\&\, b$$

follows by an application of (ins) to the normalised judgement

$$jdg' = C, A \vdash_n e : \forall(\vec{\alpha}\vec{\beta} : C_0).\ t_0 \,\&\, b$$

where $Dom(S) \subseteq \{\vec{\alpha}\vec{\beta}\}$ and $C \vdash S\,C_0$. Then also jdg has a normalised inference:

$$C, A \vdash_n e : S\,t_0 \,\&\, b.$$

Definition 12. An inference is contraint-saturated (indicated by subscript c) whenever for all occurrences of the rules (app), (let), and (if) it holds that all constraint sets in the premises equal the constraint set in the conclusion.

An inference is strongly normalised (indicated by subscript s) if it is normalised as well as constraint-saturated.

Fact 13. Given an inference tree for $C, A \vdash e : \sigma \,\&\, b$ there exists a constraint-saturated inference tree $C, A \vdash_c e : \sigma \,\&\, b$ (that has the same shape).

In particular, a normalised inference tree $C, A \vdash_n e : \sigma \,\&\, b$ can be transformed into one that is strongly normalised.

2.2 The Sequential Semantics

We are now going to define a small-step semantics for the sequential part of the language. Transitions take the form $e \rightarrow e'$ where e and e' are expressions that are *essentially closed*: this means that they may contain free channel identifiers ch (created by previous channel allocations) but that they must not contain any free program identifiers.

We first stipulate the semantics of the sequential base functions (`+`, `fst` etc.) by means of an "evaluation function" δ:

Definition 14. The function δ is a partial mapping from expressions into expressions (preserving the property of being essentially closed); the domain of δ is a subset of the expressions of form $c\,e$ with c a sequential base function. It is defined by the (incomplete) Figure 4; notice that we encode "runtime errors" such as $\mathtt{hd}\,(\mathtt{nil})$ as loops whereas e.g. $\mathtt{hd}\,(7)$ is undefined.

c	e	$\delta(c\,e)$
`fst`	$\mathtt{pair}\,e_1\,e_2$	e_1
`snd`	$\mathtt{pair}\,e_1\,e_2$	e_2
`hd`	$\mathtt{cons}\,e_1\,e_2$	e_1
`hd`	`nil`	`hd nil`
`tl`	$\mathtt{cons}\,e_1\,e_2$	e_2
`tl`	`nil`	`tl nil`
`isnil`	`nil`	`true`
`isnil`	$\mathtt{cons}\,e_1\,e_2$	`false`
`+`	$\mathtt{pair}\,n_1\,n_2$	n where $n = n_1 + n_2$
⋮	⋮	
/	$\mathtt{pair}\,n\,0$	$/\,(\mathtt{pair}\,n\,0)$

Fig. 4. The evaluation function δ.

We next introduce the notion of *weakly evaluated expressions* ($w \in \mathit{WExp}$) that are the "terminal configurations" of the sequential semantics:

Definition 15. An expression w is a *weakly evaluated expression* provided that either

- w is a constant c; or
- w is a channel identifier ch; or
- w is a function abstraction $\mathbf{fn}\ x \Rightarrow e$; or
- w is of form $c\,w_1 \cdots w_n$, where $n \geq 1$, where $w_1, \cdots, w_n$ are weakly evaluated expressions, and where c is a constructor (sequential or non-sequential).

To formalise the call-by-value evaluation strategy we shall as in [8, 5] employ the notion of *evaluation contexts*[2].

Definition 16. Evaluation contexts E take the form

$$E ::= [\,] \mid E\,e \mid w\,E \mid \mathtt{let}\ x = E\ \mathtt{in}\ e \mid \mathtt{if}\ E\ \mathtt{then}\ e_1\ \mathtt{else}\ e_2$$

Notice that E is a context with exactly one hole in it, and that this hole is not inside the scope of any defining occurrence of a program identifier. We write $E[e]$ for the expression that has the hole in E replaced by e, and similarly $E[E']$ for the evalution context that results by replacing the hole in E with E'.

Fact 17. $(E_1[E_2])[e] = E_1[E_2[e]]$.

Proof. The proof is by induction in E_1. If $E_1 = [\,]$ the equation reads $E_2[e] = E_2[e]$, so assume that E_1 is a composite context and let us consider the case $E_1 = E\,e_2$ (the other cases are similar). By using the induction hypothesis for E we get the desired equation

$$E_1[E_2][e] = (E\,e_2)[E_2][e] = (E[E_2]\,e_2)[e] = E[E_2][e]\,e_2 = E[E_2[e]]\,e_2 = E_1[E_2[e]].$$

Now we are ready for:

Definition 18. *Sequential Evaluation*

The sequential transition relation $\rightarrow$ is defined by

$E[e]{\rightarrow}E[e']$ provided $e{\rightharpoonup}e'$ holds according to the following definition:

$$\begin{array}{rll}
\text{(apply)}\ (\texttt{fn}\ x \Rightarrow e)\,w & \rightharpoonup & e[w/x] \\
\text{(delta)}\ c\,w & \rightharpoonup & e' \text{ if } e' = \delta(c\,w) \\
\text{(let)}\ \texttt{let}\ x = w\ \texttt{in}\ e & \rightharpoonup & e[w/x] \\
\text{(rec)}\ \texttt{rec}\ f\ x \Rightarrow e & \rightharpoonup & (\texttt{fn}\ x \Rightarrow e)[(\texttt{rec}\ f\ x \Rightarrow e)/f] \\
\text{(branch)}\ \texttt{if}\ w\ \texttt{then}\ e_1\ \texttt{else}\ e_2 & \rightharpoonup & \begin{cases} e_1 & \text{if } w = \texttt{true} \\ e_2 & \text{if } w = \texttt{false} \end{cases}
\end{array}$$

Fact 19. If $e{\rightarrow}e'$ with e essentially closed then also e' is essentially closed.

Observe that $e_1\,e_2{\rightarrow}e'$ holds iff either (i) $e_1\,e_2{\rightharpoonup}e'$, or (ii) there exists e_1' such that $e_1{\rightarrow}e_1'$ and $e' = e_1'\,e_2$, or (iii) there exists e_2' such that $e_2{\rightarrow}e_2'$ and $e' = e_1\,e_2'$ (in which case e_1 is a weakly evaluated expression). Further observe that $\texttt{let}\ x = e_1\ \texttt{in}\ e_2{\rightarrow}e'$ holds iff either (i) $\texttt{let}\ x = e_1\ \texttt{in}\ e_2{\rightharpoonup}e'$, or (ii) there exists e_1' such that $e_1{\rightarrow}e_1'$ and $e' = \texttt{let}\ x = e_1'\ \texttt{in}\ e_2$. Finally observe that $\texttt{if}\ e_0\ \texttt{then}\ e_1\ \texttt{else}\ e_2{\rightarrow}e'$ holds iff either (i) $\texttt{if}\ e_0\ \texttt{then}\ e_1\ \texttt{else}\ e_2{\rightharpoonup}e'$, or (ii) there exists e_0' such that $e_0{\rightarrow}e_0'$ and $e' = \texttt{if}\ e_0'\ \texttt{then}\ e_1\ \texttt{else}\ e_2$.

As expected we have:

Fact 20. If w is a weakly evaluated expression then $w\not\rightarrow$.

Proof. It is easy to see that $w\not\rightharpoonup$; the result then follows by induction on w. □

We shall say that an essentially closed expression e is *exhausted* if it is not weakly evaluated and yet $e\not\rightarrow$. We shall say that an exhausted expression e is *top-level exhausted* if it cannot be written on the form $e = E[e']$ with $E \neq [\,]$ and with e' exhausted. It is easy to see (using Fact 17) that for any exhausted expression e there exists E and top-level exhausted e' such that $e = E[e']$.

Fact 21. Suppose that e is top-level exhausted; then either

- $e = c\,w$ with c a non-sequential base function; or
- $e = c\,w$ with c a sequential base function where $\delta(e)$ is undefined; or
- $e = ch\,w$ with ch a channel identifier; or

– $e = \texttt{if}\ w\ \texttt{then}\ e_1\ \texttt{else}\ e_2$ with $w \notin \{\texttt{true}, \texttt{false}\}$.

Proof. We perform a case analysis on e (which is essentially closed). If e is a constant, a channel identifier or an abstraction then e is weakly evaluated and hence not exhausted. If e is of form $\texttt{rec}\ f\ x \Rightarrow e$, then $e \rightharpoonup \cdots$ and hence e is not exhausted.

If e is of form $\texttt{let}\ x = e_1\ \texttt{in}\ e_2$ then e_1 is essentially closed and $e_1 \not\rightharpoonup$ (as otherwise $e \rightarrow$) but e_1 is not exhausted (as e is top-level exhausted). Hence we conclude that e_1 is weakly evaluated, but this is a contradiction since then $e \rightharpoonup \cdots$.

If e is of form $\texttt{if}\ e_0\ \texttt{then}\ e_1\ \texttt{else}\ e_2$ then e_0 is essentially closed and $e_0 \not\rightharpoonup$ (as otherwise $e \rightarrow$) but e_0 is not exhausted (as e is top-level exhausted). Hence we conclude that e_0 is weakly evaluated; and this yields the claim since if $e_0 = \texttt{true}$ or $e_0 = \texttt{false}$ then $e \rightharpoonup \cdots$.

If e is of form $e_1\, e_2$ we infer (using the same technique as in the above two cases) that e_1 is a weakly evaluated expression w_1 and subsequently that e_2 is a weakly evaluated expression w_2. Since e is not a weakly evaluated expression it cannot be the case that w_1 is of form $c\, w_1' \cdots w_n'$ with c a constructor and with $n \geq 0$; and since $e \not\rightharpoonup$ it cannot be the case that w_1 is of form $\texttt{fn}\ x \Rightarrow e_1'$ or a sequential base function such that $\delta(e)$ is defined. This yields the claim. □

From the preceding results we get:

Proposition 22. Suppose that e is essentially closed and that $e \rightarrow^* e' \not\rightharpoonup$. Then either

1. e' is a weakly evaluated expression; or
2. e' is of form $E[c\, w]$ with c a non-sequential base function; or
3. e' is either of form $E[c\, w]$ with c a sequential base function where $\delta(c\, w)$ is undefined (e.g. $\texttt{hd}\ 7$), or of form $E[ch\, w]$, or of form $E[\texttt{if}\ w\ \texttt{then}\ e_1\ \texttt{else}\ e_2]$ with $w \notin \{\texttt{true}, \texttt{false}\}$.

The configurations listed in case 3 can be thought of as error configurations, whereas in Section 2.3 we shall see that case 2 corresponds to a process that may be able to perform a concurrent action.

Fact 23. The rewriting relation $\rightarrow$ is deterministic.

Proof. We perform induction on e to show that if $e \rightarrow e'$ and $e \rightarrow e''$ then $e' = e''$. If e is a constant, a variable or a function abstraction then $e \not\rightharpoonup$ and if e is of form $\texttt{rec}\ f\ x \Rightarrow e$ determinism is obvious.

If e is of form $\texttt{let}\ x = w\ \texttt{in}\ e_2$ the claim follows from $w \not\rightharpoonup$. If e is of form $\texttt{let}\ x = e_1\ \texttt{in}\ e_2$ with e_1 not a weakly evaluated expression then e' takes the form $\texttt{let}\ x = e_1'\ \texttt{in}\ e_2$ where $e_1 \rightarrow e_1'$ and by the induction hypothesis this e_1' is unique.

If e is of form $\texttt{if}\ w\ \texttt{then}\ e_1\ \texttt{else}\ e_2$ the claim follows from $w \not\rightharpoonup$. If e is of form $\texttt{if}\ e_0\ \texttt{then}\ e_1\ \texttt{else}\ e_2$ with e_0 not a weakly evaluated expression then e' takes the form $\texttt{if}\ e_0'\ \texttt{then}\ e_1\ \texttt{else}\ e_2$ where $e_0 \rightarrow e_0'$ and by the induction hypothesis this e_0' is unique.

We are left with the case $e = e_1\, e_2$. First suppose that e_1 is not weakly evaluated. Then $e\not\hookrightarrow$ and we infer that e' takes the form $e'_1\, e_2$ where $e_1 \rightarrow e'_1$ so by the induction hypothesis this e'_1 is unique.

Next suppose that $e = w_1\, e_2$ with e_2 not weakly evaluated. Then $e\not\hookrightarrow$ and as $w_1\not\hookrightarrow$ we infer that e' takes the form $w_1\, e'_2$ where $e_2 \rightarrow e'_2$ so by the induction hypothesis this e'_2 is unique.

Finally assume that $e = w_1\, w_2$. Then $w_1\not\hookrightarrow$ and $w_2\not\hookrightarrow$ so it must hold that $e \rightarrow e'$. If w_1 is a function abstraction this e' is clearly unique; and if w_1 is a sequential base function uniqueness follows from δ being a function. □

2.3 The Concurrent Semantics

Next we are going to define a small-step semantics for the concurrent part of the language. Transitions take the form $PP \xrightarrow{a} PP'$, where PP as well as PP' is a *process pool* which is a finite mapping from process identifiers p into essentially closed expressions, and where a is a label describing what kind of action is taken.

Definition 24. *Concurrent Evaluation*

The concurrent transition relation $\xrightarrow{a}$ is defined by:

$$PP[p : e] \quad \xrightarrow{\mathtt{seq}} \quad PP[p : e'] \qquad \text{if } e \rightarrow e'$$

$$PP[p : E[\mathtt{channel}\,()]] \quad \xrightarrow{p\ \mathtt{chan}\ ch} \quad PP[p : E[ch]] \qquad \text{if } ch \text{ not in } PP \text{ or } E$$

$$PP[p : E[\mathtt{fork}\, w]] \quad \xrightarrow{p\ \mathtt{fork}\ p'} \quad PP[p : E[()]][p' : w\,()] \qquad \text{if } p' \notin Dom(PP) \cup \{p\}$$

$$\begin{array}{l} PP[p_1 : E_1[\mathtt{sync}\,(\mathtt{send}\,(\mathtt{pair}\, ch\, w))]] \\ \quad [p_2 : E_2[\mathtt{sync}\,(\mathtt{receive}\, ch)]] \end{array} \quad \xrightarrow{p_1\ \mathtt{comm}\ p_2} \quad PP[p_1 : E_1[w]][p_2 : E_2[w]] \qquad \text{if } p_1 \neq p_2$$

2.4 Reasoning about Proof Trees

In this section we present some auxiliary results which will eventually enable us to show that if there is a typing for e and if e gets "rewritten" into e' (sequentially or concurrently) then we can construct a typing for e'.

A common pattern will be that we have some judgement $C', A' \vdash E[e] : \sigma' \,\&\, b'$, but we want to reason about the typing of e rather than that of $E[e]$. To this end we need to be precise about what it means for a judgement to occur "at the address indicated by the hole in E":

Definition 25. The judgement $jdg = (C, A \vdash e : \sigma \,\&\, b)$ occurs at E (with depth n) in the inference tree for the judgement $jdg' = (C', A' \vdash e' : \sigma' \,\&\, b')$, provided that *either*

- $jdg = jdg'$ and $E = [\,]$ (and $n = 0$); *or*
- there exists a judgement jdg'' and an evaluation context E'' such that jdg occurs at E'' (with depth $n-1$) in the inference tree for jdg'', and such that the last rule applied in the inference tree for jdg' is *either*
  - (sub), (ins), or (gen), with jdg'' as premise and with $E = E''$; *or*
  - (app), with jdg'' as leftmost premise and with $E = E''\, e_2$ where e' is of form $e_1\, e_2$; *or*
  - (app), with jdg'' as rightmost premise and with $E = w_1\, E''$ where e' is of form $w_1\, e_2$; *or*
  - (let), with jdg'' as leftmost premise and with $E = \texttt{let}\ x = E''\ \texttt{in}\ e_2$ where e' is of form $\texttt{let}\ x = e_1\ \texttt{in}\ e_2$; *or*
  - (if), with jdg'' as leftmost premise and with $E = \texttt{if}\ E''\ \texttt{then}\ e_1\ \texttt{else}\ e_2$ where e' is of form $\texttt{if}\ e_0\ \texttt{then}\ e_1\ \texttt{else}\ e_2$.

This is well-defined in the size of the inference tree for jdg'. As expected we have the following results, the latter to be proved in Appendix A:

Fact 26. Suppose that $C, A \vdash e : \sigma \,\&\, b$ occurs at E in the inference tree for $C', A' \vdash e' : \sigma' \,\&\, b'$; then $e' = E[e]$.

Fact 27. Given $jdg' = (C', A' \vdash E[e] : \sigma' \,\&\, b')$; then there exists (at least one) judgement jdg of form $C, A \vdash e : \sigma \,\&\, b$ such that jdg occurs at E in the inference tree for jdg'. If jdg' is (strongly) normalised we can assume that jdg is (strongly) normalised.

The following result is convenient when performing induction in the depth of a judgement in an inference tree (as we shall do in the proof of Lemma 37):

Fact 28. Suppose the judgement jdg occurs at E with depth n in the inference tree for jdg', where $n \geq 2$. Then there exists a judgement jdg'' and evaluation contexts E_1 and E_2 such that

> jdg occurs at E_1 with depth $< n$ in the inference tree for jdg''; and
> jdg'' occurs at E_2 with depth $< n$ in the inference tree for jdg'; and
> $E = E_2[E_1]$.

Moreover, if jdg' is (strongly) normalised we can assume that also jdg'' is (strongly) normalised.

Proof. We can clearly use jdg'' as in Definition 25. □

Having set up the necessary machinery we are now ready for the first result, which states that "equivalent" expressions may be substituted for each other:

Fact 29. Suppose the judgement $C, A \vdash e : \sigma \,\&\, b$ occurs at E in the inference tree of $C', A' \vdash E[e] : \sigma' \,\&\, b'$. If e_n is such that $C, A \vdash e_n : \sigma \,\&\, b$ then also

$$C', A' \vdash E[e_n] \,:\, \sigma' \,\&\, b'$$

and this judgement is normalised if the abovementioned judgements are.

It proves useful to know something about the relationship between the root of an inference tree and the interior nodes of the tree; since the hole in an evaluation context is not inside the scope of any bound identifier we have:

Fact 30. Suppose the judgement $C, A \vdash e \,:\, \sigma \,\&\, b$ occurs at E in the inference tree of $C', A' \vdash e' \,:\, \sigma' \,\&\, b'$. Then

$A' = A$ and if C' is well-formed then also C is well-formed. □

The following lemma tells us something about the relationship between the type of an expression $c\, e_1 \cdots e_n$, the type of c, and the type of each e_i:

Lemma 31. Suppose that C is well-formed and that

$$C, A \vdash_n c\, e_1 \cdots e_n \,:\, t \,\&\, b \; (n \geq 0)$$

and that TypeOf(c) is of form

$$\forall(\vec{\alpha}\vec{\beta} : C_0).\ t'_1 \rightarrow^{b'_1} \cdots t'_m \rightarrow^{b'_m} t''$$

and that if c is a base function then $m \geq n$.
Then in all cases (i.e. also if c is a constructor) we can write

$$\text{TypeOf}(c) = \forall(\vec{\alpha}\vec{\beta} : C_0).\ t'_1 \rightarrow^{b'_1} \cdots t'_n \rightarrow^{b'_n} t'$$

and there exists S, $t_1 \cdots t_n$, and $b_1 \cdots b_n$, such that

$Dom(S) \subseteq \{\vec{\alpha}\vec{\beta}\}$ and $C \vdash S\, C_0$ and $C \vdash S\, t' \subseteq t$;

for all $i \in \{1 \cdots n\}$: $C, A \vdash_s e_i \,:\, t_i \,\&\, b_i$ and $C \vdash t_i \subseteq S\, t'_i$ and $C \vdash b_i \subseteq b$ and $C \vdash S\, b'_i \subseteq b$.

Similarly, if TypeOf(c) $= t'_1 \rightarrow^{b'_1} \cdots t'_m \rightarrow^{b'_m} t''$ in which case $\{\vec{\alpha}\vec{\beta}\} = \emptyset$ and $C_0 = \emptyset$ (so we have $S = \text{Id}$).

Proof. See Appendix A.

The following two lemmas, both to be proved in Appendix A, show

- that we can replace variables by expressions of the same type, provided these expressions have an empty behaviour; and
- that the latter condition can always be obtained for weakly evaluated expressions.

Lemma 32. Suppose that $C, A[x : \sigma'] \vdash_n e \,:\, \sigma \,\&\, b$ and $C, A \vdash_n e' \,:\, \sigma' \,\&\, \emptyset$; then $C, A \vdash_n e[e'/x] \,:\, \sigma \,\&\, b$.

Lemma 33. Suppose that $C, A \vdash_n w \,:\, \sigma \,\&\, b$ with C well-formed; then

$$C, A \vdash_n w \,:\, \sigma \,\&\, \emptyset.$$

3 Semantic Soundness

In this section we shall prove that the sequential as well as the concurrent transition relation "preserves types" and "decreases behaviours". First an auxiliary concept:

Definition 34. An environment A is a *channel environment* if $Dom(A)$ is a subset of the channel identifiers and for each $ch \in Dom(A)$ that $A(ch)$ takes the form t **chan**.

We then *impose* that the concurrent transition relation only operates on channel environments. This is going to hold for the initial environment which is empty, and we shall see that the concurrent soundness result (Theorem 41) guarantees that the assumption is maintained; thus our decision seems to be a benign one. To see that it is actually necessary to impose the condition, note that otherwise the type of the channel would be polymorphic and the sender and receiver of a transmitted value would then be allowed to disagree on its type; this is exactly where type insecurities would creep in.

3.1 Sequential Soundness

First we shall prove that "top-level" reduction is sound:

Lemma 35. Let C be well-formed and let A be a channel environment. If $e \rightharpoonup e'$ and

$$C, A \vdash_n e : \sigma \,\&\, b$$

then also

$$C, A \vdash_n e' : \sigma \,\&\, b.$$

Proof. By Fact 13 we can assume that we even have $C, A \vdash_s e : \sigma \,\&\, b$; we perform induction in the proof tree.

The rule (gen) has been applied: Then the situation is

$$\frac{C \cup C_0, A \vdash_s e : t_0 \,\&\, b}{C, A \vdash_s e : \forall(\vec{\alpha}\vec{\beta} : C_0).\ t_0 \,\&\, b}\ \text{(gen)}$$

and as C_0 is well-formed we can apply the induction hypothesis to get

$$C \cup C_0, A \vdash_n e' : t_0 \,\&\, b$$

from which we by (gen) arrive at the desired judgement

$$C, A \vdash_n e' : \forall(\vec{\alpha}\vec{\beta} : C_0).\ t_0 \,\&\, b.$$

<u>The rule (sub) has been applied:</u> Then the situation is

$$\frac{C, A \vdash_s e : t \,\&\, b}{C, A \vdash_s e : t' \,\&\, b'} \text{ (sub)}$$

and the induction hypothesis yields

$$C, A \vdash_n e' : t \,\&\, b$$

from which we by (sub) arrive at the desired judgement

$$C, A \vdash_n e' : t' \,\&\, b'.$$

<u>Otherwise</u> a "structural" rule has been applied (for if (ins) has been applied then e is a constant or an identifier and then $e \not\rightharpoonup$); we now perform case analysis on the transition $\rightharpoonup$:

The transition (let) has been applied: Then the situation is

$$\frac{C, A \vdash_s w : ts \,\&\, b_1 \qquad C, A[x : ts] \vdash_s e : t \,\&\, b_2}{C, A \vdash \texttt{let } x = w \texttt{ in } e : t \,\&\, b_1 \cup b_2} \text{ (let)}$$

and using Lemma 33 we have

$$C, A \vdash_n w : ts \,\&\, \emptyset$$

which by Lemma 32 can be combined with the second premise of the inference to yield

$$C, A \vdash_n e[w/x] : t \,\&\, b_2$$

and since $C \vdash b_2 \subseteq (b_1 \cup b_2)$ we can apply (sub) to get the desired result.

The transition (rec) has been applied: Then the situation is

$$\frac{C, A[f : t] \vdash_s \texttt{fn } x \Rightarrow e : t \,\&\, b}{C, A \vdash \texttt{rec } f\ x \Rightarrow e : t \,\&\, b} \text{ (rec)}$$

and using Lemma 33 we have

$$C, A[f : t] \vdash_n \texttt{fn } x \Rightarrow e : t \,\&\, \emptyset$$

so by applying (rec) we get the judgement

$$C, A \vdash_n \texttt{rec } f\ x \Rightarrow e : t \,\&\, \emptyset$$

which by Lemma 32 can be combined with the premise of the inference to yield

$$C, A \vdash_n (\texttt{fn } x \Rightarrow e)[(\texttt{rec } f\ x \Rightarrow e)/f] : t \,\&\, b$$

which is as desired.

The transition (branch) has been applied: Then the situation is

$$\frac{C, A \vdash_s w : \mathtt{bool}\,\&\, b_0 \qquad C, A \vdash_s e_1 : t\,\&\, b_1 \qquad C, A \vdash_s e_2 : t\,\&\, b_2}{C, A \vdash \mathtt{if}\ w\ \mathtt{then}\ e_1\ \mathtt{else}\ e_2 : t\,\&\, b_0 \cup (b_1 \cup b_2)}\ \text{(if)}$$

The claim now follows from the fact that for $i = 1, 2$ we have $C \vdash b_i \subseteq b_0 \cup (b_1 \cup b_2)$.

The transition (apply) has been applied: Then the situation is

$$\frac{\dfrac{C, A[x : t_2'] \vdash_s e : t'\,\&\, b_0'}{C, A \vdash_s \mathtt{fn}\ x \Rightarrow e : t_2 \rightarrow^{b_0} t\,\&\, b_1}\ \text{(abs) (sub)}^* \qquad C, A \vdash_s w : t_2\,\&\, b_2}{C, A \vdash (\mathtt{fn}\ x \Rightarrow e)\, w : t\,\&\, (b_1 \cup b_2 \cup b_0)}\ \text{(app)}$$

where $C \vdash t_2' \rightarrow^{b_0'} t' \subseteq t_2 \rightarrow^{b_0} t$ which by Lemma 4 implies that

$$C \vdash t_2 \subseteq t_2' \text{ and } C \vdash b_0' \subseteq b_0 \text{ and } C \vdash t' \subseteq t.$$

By Lemma 33 followed by an application of (sub) we get

$$C, A \vdash_n w : t_2'\,\&\, \emptyset$$

which by Lemma 32 can be combined with the upmost leftmost premise of the inference to yield

$$C, A \vdash_n e[w/x] : t'\,\&\, b_0'$$

and since $C \vdash t' \subseteq t$ and $C \vdash b_0' \subseteq b_0 \subseteq b_1 \cup b_2 \cup b_0$ we can apply (sub) to get the desired result.

The transition (delta) has been applied: The claim then follows from an examination of Figure 4; below we shall list a typical case only. In all cases we make use of Lemma 31 and Lemma 4 which can be applied since C is well-formed.

$e = \mathtt{fst}\,(\mathtt{pair}\, w_1\, w_2)$ and $\delta(e) = w_1$: Then the situation is that

$$C, A \vdash_s \mathtt{fst}\,(\mathtt{pair}\, w_1\, w_2) : t\,\&\, b$$

so since TypeOf($\mathtt{fst}$) $= \forall(\alpha_1\alpha_2 : \emptyset).\ \alpha_1 \times \alpha_2 \rightarrow^{\emptyset} \alpha_1$, Lemma 31 tells us that there exists t_0, b_0 and S_0 such that

$$C, A \vdash_s \mathtt{pair}\, w_1\, w_2 : t_0\,\&\, b_0 \text{ and}$$

$$C \vdash S_0\, \alpha_1 \subseteq t \text{ and } C \vdash t_0 \subseteq S_0\, (\alpha_1 \times \alpha_2) \text{ and } C \vdash b_0 \subseteq b.$$

Since TypeOf($\mathtt{pair}$) $= \forall(\alpha_1\alpha_2 : \emptyset).\ \alpha_1 \rightarrow^{\emptyset} \alpha_2 \rightarrow^{\emptyset} \alpha_1 \times \alpha_2$, Lemma 31 tells us that there exists t_1, b_1, t_2, b_2 and S such that

$$C, A \vdash_s w_1 : t_1 \,\&\, b_1 \text{ and } C, A \vdash_s w_2 : t_2 \,\&\, b_2;$$

$$C \vdash t_1 \subseteq S\, \alpha_1 \text{ and } C \vdash t_2 \subseteq S\, \alpha_2 \text{ and } C \vdash b_1 \cup b_2 \subseteq b_0;$$

$$C \vdash S\, (\alpha_1 \times \alpha_2) \subseteq t_0.$$

We thus have

$$C \vdash t_1 \times t_2 \subseteq S\, \alpha_1 \times S\, \alpha_2 \subseteq t_0 \subseteq S_0\, \alpha_1 \times S_0\, \alpha_2$$

so from Lemma 4 we deduce that

$$C \vdash t_1 \subseteq S_0\, \alpha_1 \subseteq t$$

and since $C \vdash b_1 \subseteq b_1 \cup b_2 \subseteq b_0 \subseteq b$ we from $C, A \vdash_s w_1 : t_1 \,\&\, b_1$ get

$$C, A \vdash_n w_1 : t \,\&\, b.$$

which is as desired. □

Theorem 36. *Sequential soundness*

Let C be well-formed and let A be a channel environment. If $e_1 \rightarrow e_2$ and

$$C, A \vdash_n e_1 : \sigma \,\&\, b$$

then also

$$C, A \vdash_n e_2 : \sigma \,\&\, b.$$

Proof. There exists E, e_1' and e_2' such that

$$e_1 = E[e_1'] \text{ and } e_2 = E[e_2'] \text{ and } e_1' \rightarrow e_2'.$$

By Fact 27 there exists C', A', σ' and b' such that $C', A' \vdash_n e_1' : \sigma' \,\&\, b'$ occurs at E in the inference tree of $C, A \vdash_n E[e_1'] : \sigma \,\&\, b$. By Fact 30 we infer that $A' = A$ and that C' is well-formed; this enables us to use Lemma 35 from which we get

$$C', A' \vdash_n e_2' : \sigma' \,\&\, b'$$

and by Fact 29 we get the desired judgement

$$C, A \vdash_n E[e_2'] : \sigma \,\&\, b.$$

This completes the proof.

3.2 Erroneous Programs cannot be Typed

The purpose of types is to detect certain kinds of errors at analysis time rather than at execution time. To this end one usually (cf. the methodical considerations in [11]) wants a result that guarantees that "error configurations are not typeable"; here we presuppose some well-formed constraint set C and some channel environment A. By Proposition 22 and the discussion after it (together with Fact 27 and Fact 30), it suffices to consider each of the error-configurations listed below, and to show that it is not typeable; for this we make use of Lemma 4.

$ch\,w$ with ch a channel identifier: since $A(ch)$ is of form t **chan** in order for $ch\,w$ to be typeable it must be the case that $C \vdash t\ \mathbf{chan} \subseteq t_1 \rightarrow^b t_2$ for some t_1,t_2; this conflicts with Lemma 4.

`if` w `then` e_1 `else` e_2 with $w \notin \{\mathtt{true}, \mathtt{false}\}$: for this to be typeable it must hold that

> w can be assigned the type `bool`.

From Lemma 4 we infer that w cannot be a channel identifier (as A is a channel environment); w cannot be a function abstraction; and an examination of Figure 1 (using Lemma 31) will reveal that w cannot be a constant apart from `true`, `false` or of form $c\,w_1 \cdots w_n$ $(n \geq 1)$ with c a constructor.

$c\,w$ with c a sequential base function with $\delta(c\,w)$ undefined: consider e.g. the expression `fst` w. For this to be typeable there must (cf. Lemma 31) exist t_1 and t_2 such that

> w can be assigned the type $t_1 \times t_2$.

From Lemma 4 we infer that w cannot be a channel identifier (as A is a channel environment); w cannot be a function abstraction; and an examination of Figure 1 (using Lemma 31) will reveal that w cannot be a constant and that w cannot be of form $c\,w_1 \cdots w_n$ with c a constructor apart from `pair`. Thus w is of form `pair` $w_1\,w_2$, but then $\delta(c\,w)$ is not undefined.

3.3 Concurrent Soundness

First a crucial result which generalises Fact 29 by allowing the "new" expression e_n to be typed using a channel environment which is an *extension* of the channel environment in which the old expression e was typed. Such an extension is a potential danger to semantic soundness, cf. the remarks made in the Introduction; in order to construct an inference tree with the new environment we must demand that the new environment variables are "present" in the behaviour.

Lemma 37. Suppose the judgement $jdg = (C, A \vdash e : \sigma \,\&\, b)$ occurs at E in the strongly normalised inference $jdg' = (C', A \vdash_s E[e] : \sigma' \,\&\, b')$ where C' (and by Fact 30 then also C) is well-formed.

Let b_n be a behaviour and let A_n be of form $A[x_1 : \sigma_1][\cdots][x_m : \sigma_m]$ with $m \geq 0$, such that $x_1 \cdots x_m$ do not occur in $E[e]$ and such that $FV(\sigma_1) \cup \cdots \cup FV(\sigma_m) \subseteq FV(b_n)$.

Let e_n be an expression and b_r a behaviour such that

$$C, A_n \vdash_n e_n : \sigma \,\&\, b_r \text{ and}$$

$$C \vdash b_n \cup b_r \subseteq b.$$

Then there exists b'_r such that

$$C', A_n \vdash_n E[e_n] : \sigma' \,\&\, b'_r \text{ and}$$

$$C' \vdash b_n \cup b'_r \subseteq b'.$$

Moreover, there exists S with $Dom(S) \cap FV(A, b_n) = \emptyset$ such that $C' \vdash S\,C$.

Proof. The full proof is given in Appendix A; here we only consider the crucial case where jdg' follows from jdg by an application of (gen). The situation is

$$\frac{jdg = (C \cup C_0, A \vdash e : t_0 \,\&\, b)}{jdg' = (C, A \vdash e : \forall(\vec{\alpha}\vec{\beta} : C_0).\, t_0 \,\&\, b)}$$

where $\forall(\vec{\alpha}\vec{\beta} : C_0).\, t_0$ is well-formed and where $\{\vec{\alpha}\vec{\beta}\} \cap FV(C, A, b) = \emptyset$ and where there exists S_0 with $Dom(S_0) \subseteq \{\vec{\alpha}\vec{\beta}\}$ such that $C \vdash S_0\, C_0$. Our assumptions are

$$C \cup C_0, A_n \vdash_n e_n : t_0 \,\&\, b_r \tag{1}$$

$$C \cup C_0 \vdash b_n \cup b_r \subseteq b \tag{2}$$

and we must show that there exists b'_r and S such that the following holds:

$$C, A_n \vdash_n e_n : \forall(\vec{\alpha}\vec{\beta} : C_0).\, t_0 \,\&\, b'_r \tag{3}$$

$$C \vdash b_n \cup b'_r \subseteq b \tag{4}$$

$$Dom(S) \cap FV(A, b_n) = \emptyset \text{ and } C \vdash S\,(C \cup C_0).$$

We choose $b'_r = b_r$ and $S = S_0$ and then it will suffice to prove

$$\{\vec{\alpha}\vec{\beta}\} \cap FV(b_n, b_r) = \emptyset \tag{5}$$

for then (2) and Lemma 6(a) give that $C \cup S\,C_0 \vdash b_n \cup b_r \subseteq b$ which (by Lemma 7) implies (4); and since $FV(A_n) \setminus FV(A) \subseteq FV(b_n)$ holds by assumption we will be able to use (gen) to arrive at (3) from (1).

So we are left with the task of proving (5). By the assumption $FV(b) \cap \{\vec{\alpha}\vec{\beta}\} = \emptyset$ this can be done by showing

$$\forall \gamma' \in FV(b_n, b_r) : \exists \gamma \in FV(b) : C \cup C_0 \vdash \gamma' \leftarrow^* \gamma \tag{6}$$

$$\forall \gamma' \in \{\vec{\alpha}\vec{\beta}\} : (C \cup C_0 \vdash \gamma' \leftarrow^* \gamma \text{ implies } \gamma \in \{\vec{\alpha}\vec{\beta}\}). \tag{7}$$

(6) follows from (2) by Lemma 5, since $C \cup C_0$ is well-formed. (7) follows from repeated application of the below argument: if $C \cup C_0 \vdash \gamma' \leftarrow \gamma$ with $\gamma' \in \{\vec{\alpha}\vec{\beta}\}$ then by Fact 3 we are able to infer (as $\{\vec{\alpha}\vec{\beta}\} \cap FV(C) = \emptyset$) that $C_0 \vdash \gamma' \leftarrow \gamma$ and since $\forall(\vec{\alpha}\vec{\beta} : C_0).\ t_0$ is well-formed (and thus $\{\vec{\alpha}\vec{\beta}\}^{C_0\uparrow} = \{\vec{\alpha}\vec{\beta}\}$) this implies $\gamma \in \{\vec{\alpha}\vec{\beta}\}$. □

Next some auxiliary results concerning the three kinds of concurrent transitions:

Lemma 38. Let C be well-formed and suppose that

$$C, A \vdash_s E[\texttt{channel ()}] : \sigma \,\&\, b.$$

Let ch be a channel identifier that does not occur in $E[\texttt{channel ()}]$; then there exists t_n and b_r such that

$$C \vdash \{t_n \text{ CHAN}\} \cup b_r \subseteq b \text{ and}$$

$$C, A[ch : t_n \textbf{ chan}] \vdash_n E[ch] : \sigma \,\&\, b_r.$$

Proof. The strongly normalised inference tree contains a judgement of form

$$C', A \vdash_s \texttt{channel ()} : t' \,\&\, b'$$

where C' is well-formed (Fact 30). Since

$$\text{TypeOf}(\texttt{channel}) = \forall(\alpha\beta : \{\{\alpha \text{ CHAN}\} \subseteq \beta\}).\ \texttt{unit} \rightarrow^{\beta} (\alpha \textbf{ chan})$$

we can use Lemma 31 to find S such that

$$C' \vdash \{S\,\alpha \text{ CHAN}\} \subseteq S\,\beta \text{ and } C' \vdash S\,\alpha \textbf{ chan} \subseteq t' \text{ and } C' \vdash S\,\beta \subseteq b'.$$

Now define $t_n = S\,\alpha$ and $b_n = \{t_n \text{ CHAN}\}$, then

$$C', A[ch : t_n \textbf{ chan}] \vdash_n ch : t' \,\&\, \emptyset \text{ and } C' \vdash \{t_n \text{ CHAN}\} \cup \emptyset \subseteq b'$$

so as $FV(t_n) \subseteq FV(b_n)$ Lemma 37 gives us b_r such that

$$C, A[ch : t_n \textbf{ chan}] \vdash_n E[ch] : \sigma \,\&\, b_r \text{ and } C \vdash \{t_n \text{ CHAN}\} \cup b_r \subseteq b.$$

This completes the proof.

Lemma 39. Let C be well-formed and suppose that

$$C, A \vdash_s E[\texttt{fork}\,w] : \sigma \,\&\, b.$$

Then there exists b_r, t'', b'' such that

(a) $C, A \vdash_n E[()] : \sigma \,\&\, b_r$;
(b) $C, A \vdash_n w\,() : t'' \,\&\, b''$;
(c) $C \vdash b_r \subseteq b$.

Proof. The strongly normalised inference tree contains a judgement of form

$$C', A \vdash_s \mathtt{fork}\, w \,:\, t' \,\&\, b'$$

where C' is well-formed (Fact 30). Since

$$\mathrm{TypeOf}(\mathtt{fork}) = \forall(\alpha\beta : \emptyset).\ (\mathtt{unit} \rightarrow^{\beta}\ \alpha) \rightarrow^{\emptyset}\ \mathtt{unit}$$

we from Lemma 31 get t_1, b_1 and S such that

$$C' \vdash \mathtt{unit} \subseteq t' \text{ and } C' \vdash b_1 \subseteq b' \tag{8}$$

$$C', A \vdash_s w \,:\, t_1 \,\&\, b_1 \text{ and } C' \vdash t_1 \subseteq \mathtt{unit} \rightarrow^{S\beta}\ S\alpha \tag{9}$$

and by Lemma 33 we infer that

$$C', A \vdash_n w \,:\, t_1 \,\&\, \emptyset. \tag{10}$$

From (8) we get

$$C', A \vdash_n () \,:\, t' \,\&\, \emptyset$$

and Lemma 37 (with $m = 0$ and $b_n = \emptyset$) then gives us a b_r such that

$$C, A \vdash_n E[()] \,:\, \sigma \,\&\, b_r \text{ and } C \vdash b_r \subseteq b$$

which yields the claims (a) and (c), and in addition an S' such that

$$\mathit{Dom}(S') \cap \mathit{FV}(A) = \emptyset \text{ and } C \vdash S'\, C'. \tag{11}$$

For the remaining claim (b), we from (9) and (10) infer that

$$C', A \vdash_n w\,() \,:\, S\,\alpha \,\&\, S\,\beta$$

so using (11) we (by Lemma 6 and Lemma 7) arrive at

$$C, A \vdash_n w\,() \,:\, t'' \,\&\, b''$$

for $t'' = S'\, S\,\alpha$ and $b'' = S'\, S\,\beta$, thus yielding the claim (b). □

Lemma 40. Let C be well-formed and let A be a channel environment and suppose that

$$C, A \vdash_s E_1[\mathrm{sync}\,(\mathrm{send}\,(\mathtt{pair}\, ch\, w))] \,:\, \sigma_1 \,\&\, b_1 \tag{12}$$

and suppose that

$$C, A \vdash_s E_2[\mathrm{sync}\,(\mathtt{receive}\, ch)] \,:\, \sigma_2 \,\&\, b_2. \tag{13}$$

Let $A(ch) = t$ chan, then there exists b_s and b_r such that

(a) $C, A \vdash_n E_1[w] \,:\, \sigma_1 \,\&\, b_s$ and $C \vdash b_s \subseteq b_1$;
(b) $C, A \vdash_n w \,:\, t \,\&\, \emptyset$;
(c) $C, A \vdash_n E_2[w] \,:\, \sigma_2 \,\&\, b_r$ and $C \vdash b_r \subseteq b_2$.

Proof. The tree (12) will contain a judgement of form

$$C_1, A \vdash_s \texttt{sync}\,(\texttt{send}\,(\texttt{pair}\,ch\,w)) \,:\, t_1 \,\&\, b_1' \tag{14}$$

where C_1 is well-formed (Fact 30). Since

$$\text{TypeOf}(\texttt{sync}) = \forall(\alpha\beta : \emptyset).\ (\alpha \;\texttt{com}\; \beta) \rightarrow^{\beta}\ \alpha,$$

Lemma 31 together with Lemma 33 tells us that there exists t_3 and S_3 such that

$$C_1, A \vdash_n \texttt{send}\,(\texttt{pair}\,ch\,w) \,:\, t_3 \,\&\, \emptyset;$$

$$C_1 \vdash S_3\,\alpha \subseteq t_1;$$

$$C_1 \vdash t_3 \subseteq (S_3\,\alpha) \;\texttt{com}\; (S_3\,\beta).$$

As $\text{TypeOf}(\texttt{send}) = \forall(\alpha : \emptyset).\ (\alpha \;\texttt{chan}) \times \alpha \rightarrow^{\emptyset}\ (\alpha \;\texttt{com}\; \emptyset)$, Lemma 31 (together with Lemma 33) tells us that there exists t_4 and S_4 such that

$$C_1, A \vdash_n \texttt{pair}\,ch\,w \,:\, t_4 \,\&\, \emptyset;$$

$$C_1 \vdash (S_4\,\alpha) \;\texttt{com}\; \emptyset \subseteq t_3;$$

$$C_1 \vdash t_4 \subseteq (S_4\,\alpha) \;\texttt{chan} \times (S_4\,\alpha).$$

Since $\text{TypeOf}(\texttt{pair}) = \forall(\alpha_1\alpha_2 : \emptyset).\ \alpha_1 \rightarrow^{\emptyset}\ \alpha_2 \rightarrow^{\emptyset}\ \alpha_1 \times \alpha_2$, Lemma 31 (together with Lemma 33) tells us that there exists t_5, t_6, and S_5 such that

$$C_1, A \vdash_n ch \,:\, t_5 \,\&\, \emptyset; \tag{15}$$

$$C_1, A \vdash_n w \,:\, t_6 \,\&\, \emptyset; \tag{16}$$

$$C_1 \vdash S_5\,\alpha_1 \times S_5\,\alpha_2 \subseteq t_4;$$

$$C_1 \vdash t_5 \subseteq S_5\,\alpha_1 \text{ and } C_1 \vdash t_6 \subseteq S_5\,\alpha_2.$$

Since $A(ch) = t$ **chan** we infer from (15) that

$$C_1 \vdash t \;\texttt{chan} \subseteq t_5.$$

We now apply Lemma 4 repeatedly: from

$$C_1 \vdash (S_4\,\alpha) \;\texttt{com}\; \emptyset \subseteq t_3 \subseteq (S_3\,\alpha) \;\texttt{com}\; (S_3\,\beta)$$

$$C_1 \vdash t_5 \times t_6 \subseteq S_5\,\alpha_1 \times S_5\,\alpha_2 \subseteq t_4 \subseteq (S_4\,\alpha) \;\texttt{chan} \times (S_4\,\alpha)$$

we deduce that

$$C_1 \vdash S_4\,\alpha \subseteq S_3\,\alpha \subseteq t_1$$

$$C_1 \vdash t \;\texttt{chan} \subseteq t_5 \subseteq (S_4\,\alpha) \;\texttt{chan}$$

$$C_1 \vdash t_6 \subseteq S_4\,\alpha$$

From (16) we therefore get

$$C_1, A \vdash_n w \,:\, t_1 \,\&\, \emptyset$$

so by Lemma 37 applied to (12) and (14) (with $m = 0$ and $b_n = \emptyset$) we find b_s and S_1 such that

$$C, A \vdash_n E_1[w] : \sigma_1 \,\&\, b_s \text{ and } C \vdash b_s \subseteq b_1;$$

$$Dom(S_1) \cap FV(A) = \emptyset \text{ and } C \vdash S_1\, C_1. \tag{17}$$

We have thus established (a). By exploiting the *contravariance*[2] of $\cdots$ **chan** (cf. the remarks concerning Figure 2), we get

$$C_1 \vdash t_6 \subseteq S_4\, \alpha \subseteq t \tag{18}$$

and from (16) therefore

$$C_1, A \vdash_n w : t \,\&\, \emptyset$$

which using (17) yields (as $FV(t) \subseteq FV(A)$)

$$C, A \vdash_n w : t \,\&\, \emptyset.$$

We have thus established (b).

Our remaining task is to show claim (c), where we first notice that the tree (13) will contain a judgement of form

$$C_2, A \vdash_s \texttt{sync}\,(\texttt{receive}\, ch) : t_2 \,\&\, b_2' \tag{19}$$

where C_2 is well-formed (Fact 30). Since

$$\text{TypeOf}(\texttt{sync}) = \forall(\alpha\beta : \emptyset).\ (\alpha \texttt{ com } \beta) \to^{\beta} \alpha$$

Lemma 31 (together with Lemma 33) tells us that there exists t_7 and S_7 such that

$$C_2, A \vdash_n \texttt{receive}\, ch : t_7 \,\&\, \emptyset;$$

$$C_2 \vdash S_7\, \alpha \subseteq t_2;$$

$$C_2 \vdash t_7 \subseteq (S_7\, \alpha) \texttt{ com } (S_7\, \beta).$$

Since TypeOf($\texttt{receive}$) $= \forall(\alpha : \emptyset).\ (\alpha \textbf{ chan}) \to^{\emptyset} (\alpha \texttt{ com } \emptyset)$, Lemma 31 tells us that there exists t_8 and S_8 such that

$$C_2, A \vdash_n ch : t_8 \,\&\, \emptyset; \tag{20}$$

$$C_2 \vdash (S_8\, \alpha) \texttt{ com } \emptyset \subseteq t_7;$$

$$C_2 \vdash t_8 \subseteq (S_8\, \alpha) \textbf{ chan}.$$

Since $A(ch) = t$ **chan** we infer from (20) that

$$C_2 \vdash t \textbf{ chan} \subseteq t_8.$$

We now apply Lemma 4 repeatedly: from

$$C_2 \vdash (S_8\, \alpha) \texttt{ com } \emptyset \subseteq t_7 \subseteq (S_7\, \alpha) \texttt{ com } (S_7\, \beta)$$

$$C_2 \vdash t \textbf{ chan} \subseteq t_8 \subseteq (S_8\, \alpha) \textbf{ chan}$$

[2] For later reference we note that if we were to use also the covariance of $\cdots$ **chan** we would additionally get that $C_1 \vdash t \subseteq S_4\, \alpha \subseteq t_1$.

we get, by exploiting the *covariance* of $\cdots$ **chan** (cf. the remarks concerning Figure 2),

$$C_2 \vdash t \subseteq S_8\, \alpha \subseteq S_7\, \alpha \subseteq t_2. \tag{21}$$

As the inference (13) is constraint saturated we have $C \subseteq C_2$ so by Lemma 7 we can deduce from claim (b) that

$$C_2, A \vdash_n w : t \,\&\, \emptyset$$

so by applying (sub) we arrive at

$$C_2, A \vdash_n w : t_2 \,\&\, \emptyset.$$

By applying Lemma 37 on (13) and (19) (with $m = 0$ and $b_n = \emptyset$) we find b_r such that

$$C, A \vdash_n E_2[w] : \sigma_2 \,\&\, b_r \text{ and } C \vdash b_r \subseteq b_2$$

which establishes (c) thus completing the proof. □

We are now able to formulate what it means for our system to be semantically sound. We write $C, A \vdash PP : PT \,\&\, PB$, where PT (respectively PB) is a mapping from process identifiers into types (respectively behaviours), if the domains of PP, PT and PB are equal and if for all $p \in Dom(PP)$ we have $C, A \vdash PP(p) : PT(p) \,\&\, PB(p)$.

Theorem 41. *Semantic (concurrent) soundness*

Let C be well-formed, let A be a channel environment, and suppose

$$C, A \vdash_n PP : PT \,\&\, PB.$$

If $PP \xrightarrow{a} PP'$ there exists PT', PB' and channel environment A' such that

$$C, A' \vdash_n PP' : PT' \,\&\, PB'$$

and such that if p is in the domain of PP then $PT'(p) = PT(p)$ and such that if ch occurs in PP then $A'(ch) = A(ch)$.

Furthermore we have the following property:

- If $a = \texttt{seq}$ then $PB'(p) = PB(p)$ for all p in the domain of PP.
- If $a = p_0$ **chan** ch then there exists t_0 such that $A'(ch) = t_0$ **chan**, such that
  $C \vdash \{t_0 \text{ CHAN}\} \cup PB'(p_0) \subseteq PB(p_0)$
  and such that $PB'(p) = PB(p)$ for $p \in Dom(PP) \setminus \{p_0\}$.
- If $a = p_0$ `fork` p' then
  $C \vdash PB'(p_0) \subseteq PB(p_0)$
  and $PB'(p) = PB(p)$ for $p \in Dom(PP) \setminus \{p_0\}$.
- If $a = p_1$ **comm** p_2 then
  $C \vdash PB'(p_1) \subseteq PB(p_1)$ and $C \vdash PB'(p_2) \subseteq PB(p_2)$
  and $PB'(p) = PB(p)$ for $p \in Dom(PP) \setminus \{p_1, p_2\}$.

Proof. By Fact 13 we can assume the inference trees in $C, A \vdash_n PP : PT \,\&\, PB$ to be strongly normalised. We perform case analysis on the action label a:

$a = \mathtt{seq}$: It follows from Theorem 36 that we can use $PT' = PT$, $PB' = PB$ and $A' = A$.

$a = p_0$ $\mathtt{chan}$ ch: It follows from Lemma 38 that there exists t_0 and b_r such that the claim follows with $PT' = PT$, $PB' = PB[p_0 : b_r]$ and $A' = A[ch : t_0\ \mathbf{chan}]$. (For $p \neq p_0$ ($\in Dom(PP)$) we must show that $C, A \vdash_n PP(p) : PT(p) \,\&\, PB(p)$ implies $C, A' \vdash_n PP(p) : PT(p) \,\&\, PB(p)$, but this follows from Fact 9.)

$a = p_0$ $\mathtt{fork}$ p': It follows from Lemma 39 that there exists t'', b'' and b_r such that that we can use $PT' = PT[p' : t'']$, $PB' = PB[p_0 : b_r][p' : b'']$ and $A' = A$.

$a = p_1$ $\mathtt{comm}$ p_2: It follows from Lemma 40 that there exists b_s and b_r such that we can use $PT' = PT$, $PB' = PB[p_1 : b_s][p_2 : b_r]$ and $A' = A$. □

Remark. Theorem 41 makes it explicit that the type of a channel does not change after it has been allocated. This should be compared with the subject reduction result in [11, lemma 5.2], the formulation of which allows one the possibility of assigning different types to the same location at various stages (although apparently it is always possible to choose the same type and still get subject reduction).

Remark. Theorem 41 says that if we start with a correctly typed program then we are never going to encounter programs that are not correctly typed. One consequence of this is that Lemma 40 will be applicable at all stages; this is a result that ensures that the value sent can always be given the type allowed on the channel on which it was sent, that having sent the value we still have a correctly typed sender, and that having received the value we still have a correctly typed receiver. However, the statement of Lemma 40 does not directly relate:

- the type t_6 of the value w actually communicated (see line 16),
- the type t of the entities allowed to be communicated over the channel,
- the type t_1 that the sender thinks was communicated (see line 14), and
- the type t_2 that the receiver thinks was communicated (see line 19).

However, by inspecting the proof of Lemma 40 one may note that the following relations are established (by (18), footnote 2 and (21)):

$$C_1 \vdash t_6 \subseteq t \qquad\qquad C_1 \vdash t \subseteq t_1 \qquad\qquad C_2 \vdash t \subseteq t_2$$

Here the constraint sets C_1 and C_2 are those corresponding to the point of sending and receiving, respectively. Thus we can be ensured that a value is always received with a type that is larger than the type it actually had when communicated. (It is possible for the sender to think that an even larger type was communicated, but this causes no harm.)

4 Conclusion

We have given a formal justification of the semantic soundness of a previously developed annotated type and effect system that integrates polymorphism, subtyping and effects [6]; in particular it was highlighted that the judicious choice of generalisation strategy in the system plays a crucial role, as witnessed by the proof of Lemma 37. Although the development was performed for a fragment of Concurrent ML we believe it equally possible for Standard ML with references; moreover we conjecture that the development can be extended to incorporate causality in the behaviours.

Acknowledgement. This work has been supported in part by the *DART* project (Danish Natural Science Research Council) and the *LOMAPS* project (ESPRIT BRA project 8130); it represents joint work among the authors. We would like to thank the anonymous referees for their thought-provoking comments on the preliminary version of this work.

References

1. M. Debbabi and D. Bolignano: A semantic theory for ML higher-order concurrency primitives. In *ML with Concurrency: Design, Analysis, Implementation and Application* (editor: Flemming Nielson), Springer-Verlag, 1996.
2. M. Felleisen and D.P. Friedman: Control operators, the SECD-Machine, and the λ-calculus. *Formal Descriptions of Programming Concepts III*, North-Holland, 1986.
3. X. Leroy and P. Weis: Polymorphic type inference and assignment. In *Proc. POPL '91*, pages 291–302. ACM Press, 1991.
4. R. Milner: A theory of type polymorphism in programming. *Journal of Computer and System Sciences*, 17:348–375, 1978.
5. H.R. Nielson and F. Nielson: Higher-order concurrent programs with finite communication topology. In *Proc. POPL'94*, pages 84–97. ACM Press, 1994.
6. H.R. Nielson, F. Nielson, T. Amtoft: Polymorphic subtypes for effect analysis: the static semantics. This volume of SLNCS, 1997.
7. G.D. Plotkin: A structural approach to operational semantics. Report DAIMI FN-19, Aarhus University, Denmark, 1981.
8. J. H. Reppy: Concurrent ML: Design, application and semantics. In *Proc. Functional Programming, Concurrency, Simulation and Automated Reasoning*, pages 165–198. SLNCS 693, 1993.
9. J. P. Talpin and P. Jouvelot: The type and effect discipline. *Information and Computation*, 111, 1994.
10. M. Tofte: Type inference for polymorphic references. *Information and Computation*, 89:1–34, 1990.
11. A.K. Wright and M. Felleisen: A syntactic approach to type soundness. *Information and Computation*, 115, pages 38–94, 1994.

A Proofs of Main Results

Reasoning about proof trees

Fact 27 Given $jdg' = C', A' \vdash E[e] : \sigma' \& b'$; then there exists (at least one) judgement jdg of form $C, A \vdash e : \sigma \& b$ such that jdg occurs at E in the inference tree for jdg'. If jdg' is (strongly) normalised we can assume that jdg is (strongly) normalised.

Proof. The proof is by induction in the inference tree for jdg'. If $E = []$ we can use $jdg = jdg'$, so assume $E \neq []$. Hence the last rule applied in the inference tree for jdg' is none of the following: (con), (id), (abs), or (rec). If (sub), (ins) or (gen) has been applied the induction hypothesis clearly yields the claim; notice that if jdg' is normalised then it cannot be the case that (ins) has been applied.

So we are left with (app), (let) and (if); we only consider (app) as the other cases are similar. Then E takes either the form $E_1\, e_2$ or the form $w_1\, E_2$; we consider the former only as the latter is similar.

The situation thus is that $E[e] = E_1[e]\, e_2$ so the left premise of jdg' is of form $C'', A'' \vdash E_1[e] : \sigma'' \& b''$ (abbreviated jdg''). Inductively we can assume that there exists jdg which occurs at E_1 in the inference tree for jdg''; but this shows that jdg occurs at E in the inference tree for jdg'. □

Lemma 31 Suppose that C is well-formed and that

$$C, A \vdash_n c\, e_1 \cdots e_n : t \& b \; (n \geq 0)$$

and that TypeOf(c) is of form

$$\forall(\vec{\alpha}\vec{\beta} : C_0).\; t'_1 \rightarrow^{b'_1} \cdots t'_m \rightarrow^{b'_m} t''$$

and that if c is a base function then $m \geq n$.

Then in all cases (i.e. also if c is a constructor) we can write

$$\text{TypeOf}(c) = \forall(\vec{\alpha}\vec{\beta} : C_0).\; t'_1 \rightarrow^{b'_1} \cdots t'_n \rightarrow^{b'_n} t' \tag{1}$$

and there exists S, $t_1 \cdots t_n$, and $b_1 \cdots b_n$, such that

$Dom(S) \subseteq \{\vec{\alpha}\vec{\beta}\}$ and $C \vdash S\, C_0$ and $C \vdash S\, t' \subseteq t$;

for all $i \in \{1 \cdots n\}$: $C, A \vdash_s e_i : t_i \& b_i$ and $C \vdash t_i \subseteq S\, t'_i$ and $C \vdash b_i \subseteq b$ and $C \vdash S\, b'_i \subseteq b$.

Similarly, if TypeOf(c) $= t'_1 \rightarrow^{b'_1} \cdots t'_m \rightarrow^{b'_m} t''$ in which case $\{\vec{\alpha}\vec{\beta}\} = \emptyset$ and $C_0 = \emptyset$ (so we have $S = \text{Id}$).

Proof. By Fact 13 we can assume that we in fact have $C, A \vdash_s c\, e_1 \cdots e_n : t \& b$. We perform induction in n. If $n = 0$ we can trivially always assume (1), i.e. that TypeOf(c) takes the form $\forall(\vec{\alpha}\vec{\beta} : C_0).\; t'$, and the claim is that if $C, A \vdash_s c : t \& b$ then there exists S with $Dom(S) \subseteq \{\vec{\alpha}\vec{\beta}\}$ and $C \vdash S\, C_0$ such that $C \vdash S\, t' \subseteq t$.

But since $C, A \vdash_s c : t \,\&\, b$ is constructed by an application of (con) followed by an application of (ins) followed by zero or more applications of (sub), this is immediate.

Next consider the inductive step. The situation is that there exists t_n, t^-, b_n, b' and b'' such that

$$\frac{C, A \vdash_s ce_1 \cdots e_{n-1} : t_n \to^{b''} t^- \,\&\, b' \qquad C, A \vdash_s e_n : t_n \,\&\, b_n}{C, A \vdash_s ce_1 \cdots e_n : t \,\&\, b} \text{(app)(sub)}^*$$

where $C \vdash t^- \subseteq t$ and $C \vdash b' \cup b_n \cup b'' \subseteq b$.

By the induction hypothesis we infer that in all cases it holds that

$$\text{TypeOf}(c) \text{ takes the form } \forall(\vec{\alpha}\vec{\beta} : C_0).\ t'_1 \to^{b'_1} \cdots t'_{n-1} \to^{b'_{n-1}} t'''$$

and that there exists S, $t_1 \cdots t_{n-1}$, and $b_1 \cdots b_{n-1}$, such that

$Dom(S) \subseteq \{\vec{\alpha}\vec{\beta}\}$ and $C \vdash S\, C_0$;

$$C \vdash S\, t''' \subseteq t_n \to^{b''} t^-; \tag{2}$$

for all $i \in \{1 \cdots n-1\}$: $C, A \vdash_s e_i : t_i \,\&\, b_i$ and $C \vdash t_i \subseteq S\, t'_i$ and $C \vdash b_i \subseteq b' \subseteq b$ and $C \vdash S\, b'_i \subseteq b' \subseteq b$.

Since C is well-formed we can apply Lemma 4 on (2) to infer that $S\, t'''$ is a function type. If c is a constructor Fact 1 tells us that t''' cannot be a variable; hence in all cases we can write $t''' = t'_n \to^{b'_n} t'$ which amounts to (1). Lemma 4 further tells us that $C \vdash t_n \subseteq S\, t'_n$ and that $C \vdash S\, b'_n \subseteq b'' \subseteq b$ and that $C \vdash S\, t' \subseteq t^- \subseteq t$. Thus all our proof obligations are fulfilled. □

Lemma 32 Suppose that $C, A[x : \sigma'] \vdash_n e : \sigma \,\&\, b$ and $C, A \vdash_n e' : \sigma' \,\&\, \emptyset$; then $C, A \vdash_n e[e'/x] : \sigma \,\&\, b$.

Proof. Induction in the shape of the proof tree for $C, A[x : \sigma'] \vdash_n e : \sigma \,\&\, b$; we perform case analysis on the way it is constructed (cf. Definition 10).

(con) or (con)(ins) has been applied: Then e is a constant, and $e[e'/x] = e$ so the claim is clear.

(id) or (id)(ins) has been applied: Then e is an identifier y. If $y \neq x$ then $e[e'/x] = e$ and the claim is clear since $A[x : \sigma'](y) = A(y)$.

If $y = x$ then the inference takes the form

$$\frac{C, A[x : \sigma'] \vdash x : \sigma' \,\&\, \emptyset}{C, A[x : \sigma'] \vdash x : t \,\&\, \emptyset}$$

where the last rule follows by zero or one application of (ins). We must show

$$C, A \vdash_n e' : t \,\&\, \emptyset$$

but this follows from the second part of the assumption, using Lemma 11.

(abs) has been applied: Here the inference takes the form

$$\frac{C, A[x:\sigma'][y:t_1] \vdash_n e : t_2 \,\&\, b}{C, A[x:\sigma'] \vdash_n \mathtt{fn}\; y \Rightarrow e : t_1 \rightarrow^b t_2 \,\&\, \emptyset}$$

where we can assume (by suitable alpha-renaming) that $y \neq x$ and that y does not occur in e'. Hence we can apply Fact 8 and Fact 9 to get

$C, A[y:t_1][x:\sigma'] \vdash_n e : t_2 \,\&\, b$ with the same shape as the premise
$C, A[y:t_1] \vdash_n e' : \sigma' \,\&\, \emptyset$.

We can thus apply the induction hypothesis and subsequently use (abs) to construct an inference tree whose last inference is

$$\frac{C, A[y:t_1] \vdash_n e[e'/x] : t_2 \,\&\, b}{C, A \vdash_n \mathtt{fn}\; y \Rightarrow e[e'/x] : t_1 \rightarrow^b t_2 \,\&\, \emptyset}$$

which is as desired since $(\mathtt{fn}\; y \Rightarrow e)[e'/x] = (\mathtt{fn}\; y \Rightarrow e[e'/x])$.

(app) has been applied: With $C = C_1 \cup C_2$ the inference takes the form

$$\frac{C_1, A[x:\sigma'] \vdash_n e_1 : t_2 \rightarrow^b t_1 \,\&\, b_1 \qquad C_2, A[x:\sigma'] \vdash_n e_2 : t_2 \,\&\, b_2}{C, A[x:\sigma'] \vdash_n e_1\, e_2 : t_1 \,\&\, (b_1 \cup b_2 \cup b)}$$

and by Lemma 7 we infer that

$$C, A[x:\sigma'] \vdash_n e_1 : t_2 \rightarrow^b t_1 \,\&\, b_1 \text{ and } C, A[x:\sigma'] \vdash_n e_2 : t_2 \,\&\, b_2$$

with the same shape as the premises; so we can apply the induction hypothesis twice and subsequently use (app) to construct an inference tree whose last inference is

$$\frac{C, A \vdash_n e_1[e'/x] : t_2 \rightarrow^b t_1 \,\&\, b_1 \qquad C, A \vdash_n e_2[e'/x] : t_2 \,\&\, b_2}{C, A \vdash_n e_1[e'/x]\, e_2[e'/x] : t_1 \,\&\, (b_1 \cup b_2 \cup b)}$$

which is as desired since $(e_1\, e_2)[e'/x] = e_1[e'/x]\, e_2[e'/x]$.

(let), (rec) or (if) has been applied: Similar to the above two cases, exploiting Fact 8 and Fact 9 and we only spell the case (rec) out in detail. Here the inference takes the form

$$\frac{C, A[x:\sigma'][f:t] \vdash_n \mathtt{fn}\; y \Rightarrow e : t \,\&\, b}{C, A[x:\sigma'] \vdash_n \mathtt{rec}\; f\; y \Rightarrow e : t \,\&\, b}$$

where we can assume that $y \neq x$, $f \neq x$ and that neither y nor f occurs in e'. Hence we can apply Fact 8 and Fact 9 to get

$C, A[f:t][x:\sigma'] \vdash_n \mathtt{fn}\; y \Rightarrow e : t \,\&\, b$
$C, A[f:t] \vdash_n e' : \sigma' \,\&\, \emptyset$

and as the former inference has the same shape as the premise we can apply the induction hypothesis to infer

$$C, A[f:t] \vdash_n (\texttt{fn}\ y \Rightarrow e)[e'/x] : t \,\&\, b$$

which since $y \neq x$ and y is not free in e' amounts to

$$C, A[f:t] \vdash_n \texttt{fn}\ y \Rightarrow e[e'/x] : t \,\&\, b.$$

By applying (rec) we get

$$C, A \vdash_n \texttt{rec}\ f\ y \Rightarrow e[e'/x] : t \,\&\, b$$

which is as desired since $(\texttt{rec}\ f\ y \Rightarrow e)[e'/x] = (\texttt{rec}\ f\ y \Rightarrow e[e'/x])$.

(sub) has been applied: Here the inference takes the form

$$\frac{C, A[x:\sigma'] \vdash_n e : t \,\&\, b}{C, A[x:\sigma'] \vdash_n e : t' \,\&\, b'}$$

with $C \vdash t \subseteq t'$ and $C \vdash b \subseteq b'$ so we can apply the induction hypothesis and subsequently use (sub) to construct an inference tree whose last inference is

$$\frac{C, A \vdash_n e[e'/x] : t \,\&\, b}{C, A \vdash_n e[e'/x] : t' \,\&\, b'}$$

(gen) has been applied: Here the inference takes the form

$$\frac{C \cup C_0, A[x:\sigma'] \vdash_n e : t_0 \,\&\, b}{C, A[x:\sigma'] \vdash_n e : ts \,\&\, b}$$

where $ts = \forall(\vec{\alpha}\vec{\beta} : C_0).\ t_0$ is well-formed, solvable from C, and satisfies $\{\vec{\alpha}\vec{\beta}\} \cap FV(C, A[x:\sigma'], b) = \emptyset$. By Lemma 7 we have

$$C \cup C_0, A \vdash_n e' : \sigma' \,\&\, \emptyset$$

so we can apply the induction hypothesis to get

$$C \cup C_0, A \vdash_n e[e'/x] : t_0 \,\&\, b.$$

We can then apply (gen) (since $\{\vec{\alpha}\vec{\beta}\} \cap FV(C, A, b) = \emptyset$) to arrive at the desired judgement $C, A \vdash_n e[e'/x] : ts \,\&\, b$. □

Lemma 33 Suppose that $C, A \vdash_n w : \sigma \,\&\, b$ with C well-formed; then

$$C, A \vdash_n w : \sigma \,\&\, \emptyset.$$

Proof. It is enough to consider the case where σ is a type t, for if the inference

$$\frac{C \cup C_0, A \vdash w : t_0 \,\&\, b}{C, A \vdash w : \forall(\vec{\alpha}\vec{\beta} : C_0).\ t_0 \,\&\, b}\ (\text{gen})$$

is valid it remains valid when b is replaced by $\emptyset$. We now prove the claim by induction in the size of w, and the only interesting case is where $w = c\, w_1 \cdots w_n$ for $n \geq 1$ and with c being a constructor.

Lemma 31 combined with Fact 1 tells us that

TypeOf(c) takes the form $\forall(\vec{\alpha}\vec{\beta} : C_0).\ t'_1 \rightarrow^{\emptyset} \cdots t'_n \rightarrow^{\emptyset} t'$

and Lemma 31 further tells us that there exists $t_1 \cdots t_n$, $b_1 \cdots b_n$, and S with $Dom(S) \subseteq \{\vec{\alpha}\vec{\beta}\}$ and $C \vdash S\,C_0$ such that

$C \vdash S\,t' \subseteq t$;

for all $i \in \{1 \cdots n\}$: $C, A \vdash_s w_i : t_i \,\&\, b_i$ and $C \vdash t_i \subseteq S\,t'_i$.

The induction hypothesis tells us that

for all $i \in \{1 \cdots n\}$: $C, A \vdash_n w_i : t_i \,\&\, \emptyset$

and by using (con), (ins) and (sub) we have

$C, A \vdash_n c : t_1 \rightarrow^{\emptyset} \cdots t_n \rightarrow^{\emptyset} t \,\&\, \emptyset$

so we can clearly construct the desired judgement $C, A \vdash_n c\,w_1 \cdots w_n : t \,\&\, \emptyset$. □

Concurrent soundness

Lemma 37 Suppose the judgement $jdg = (C, A \vdash e : \sigma \,\&\, b)$ occurs at E with depth n' in the strongly normalised inference $jdg' = (C', A \vdash_s E[e] : \sigma' \,\&\, b')$ where C' (and by Fact 30 then also C) is well-formed.

Let b_n be a behaviour and let A_n be of form $A[x_1 : \sigma_1][\cdots][x_m : \sigma_m]$ with $m \geq 0$, such that $x_1 \cdots x_m$ do not occur in $E[e]$ and such that $FV(\sigma_1) \cup \cdots \cup FV(\sigma_m) \subseteq FV(b_n)$.

Let e_n be an expression and b_r a behaviour such that

$C, A_n \vdash_n e_n : \sigma \,\&\, b_r$ and
$C \vdash b_n \cup b_r \subseteq b$.

Then there exists b'_r such that

$C', A_n \vdash_n E[e_n] : \sigma' \,\&\, b'_r$ and
$C' \vdash b_n \cup b'_r \subseteq b'$.

Moreover, there exists S with $Dom(S) \cap FV(A, b_n) = \emptyset$ such that $C' \vdash S\,C$.

Proof. We perform induction in n': if $n' = 0$ then $E = [\,]$, $C' = C$, $\sigma' = \sigma$, $b' = b$ and the claim is trivial as we can choose $b'_r = b_r$ and $S = \mathrm{Id}$.

If $n' > 1$ then by Fact 28 there exists evaluation contexts E_1 and E_2 with $E = E_2[E_1]$ and judgement $jdg'' = (C'', A \vdash_s e'' : \sigma'' \,\&\, b'')$ such that

jdg occurs at E_1 with depth $< n'$ in the inference tree for jdg''; and
jdg'' occurs at E_2 with depth $< n'$ in the inference tree for jdg'.

C'' is well-formed by Fact 30, so if $C, A_n \vdash_n e_n : \sigma \,\&\, b_r$ and $C \vdash b_n \cup b_r \subseteq b$ we can apply the induction hypothesis (with jdg and jdg'') to infer that there exists b''_r and S_1 such that $C'', A_n \vdash_n E_1[e_n] : \sigma'' \,\&\, b''_r$ and $C'' \vdash b_n \cup b''_r \subseteq b''$ and $Dom(S_1) \cap FV(A, b_n) = \emptyset$ and $C'' \vdash S_1\, C$. We can then apply the induction hypothesis once more (with jdg'' and jdg') to infer that there exists b'_r and S_2 such that $C', A_n \vdash_n E_2[E_1[e_n]] : \sigma' \,\&\, b'_r$ and $C' \vdash b_n \cup b'_r \subseteq b'$ and $Dom(S_2) \cap FV(A, b_n) = \emptyset$ and $C' \vdash S_2\, C''$. This is as desired, since with $S = S_2\, S_1$ we have $Dom(S) \cap FV(A, b_n) = \emptyset$ and (by Lemma 6 and 7) $C' \vdash S\, C$.

So we are left with the case $n' = 1$. We perform case analysis on E:

<u>$E = E_1\, e_2$:</u> Here $E_1 = [\,]$ and the situation is:

$$\frac{jdg = (C, A \vdash_n e_1 : (t_2 \to^{b_0} t_1) \,\&\, b_1) \qquad C, A \vdash_n e_2 : t_2 \,\&\, b_2}{jdg' = (C, A \vdash e_1\, e_2 : t_1 \,\&\, (b_1 \cup b_2 \cup b_0))}$$

and our assumptions are

$$C, A_n \vdash_n e_n : t_2 \to^{b_0} t_1 \,\&\, b_r \text{ and}$$
$$C \vdash b_n \cup b_r \subseteq b_1$$

and we must show that there exists b'_r and S such that

$$C, A_n \vdash_n e_n\, e_2 : t_1 \,\&\, b'_r \qquad (3)$$
$$C \vdash b_n \cup b'_r \subseteq b_1 \cup b_2 \cup b_0$$
$$Dom(S) \cap FV(A, b_n) = \emptyset \text{ and } C \vdash S\, C.$$

We can choose $b'_r = b_r \cup b_2 \cup b_0$ and $S = \mathrm{Id}$: then the only non-trivial claim is (3) which will follow provided we can show that

$$C, A_n \vdash_n e_2 : t_2 \,\&\, b_2$$

but this follows from Fact 9 since $x_1 \cdots x_m$ do not occur in e_2.

<u>$E = w\, E_2$:</u> Here $E_2 = [\,]$ and the situation is:

$$\frac{C, A \vdash_n w : (t_2 \to^{b_0} t_1) \,\&\, b_1 \qquad jdg = (C, A \vdash_n e_2 : t_2 \,\&\, b_2)}{jdg' = (C, A \vdash w\, e_2 : t_1 \,\&\, (b_1 \cup b_2 \cup b_0))}$$

and our assumptions are

$$C, A_n \vdash_n e_n : t_2 \,\&\, b_r \text{ and}$$
$$C \vdash b_n \cup b_r \subseteq b_2$$

and we must show that there exists b'_r and S such that

$$C, A_n \vdash_n w\, e_n : t_1 \,\&\, b'_r \text{ and}$$
$$C \vdash b_n \cup b'_r \subseteq b_1 \cup b_2 \cup b_0 \text{ and}$$
$$Dom(S) \cap FV(A, b_n) = \emptyset \text{ and } C \vdash S\, C.$$

By Lemma 33 and Fact 9 we infer that

$$C, A_n \vdash_n w : (t_2 \to^{b_0} t_1) \,\&\, \emptyset$$

which shows than we can use $b'_r = b_r \cup b_0$ and trivially $S = \mathrm{Id}$.

<u>$E = \texttt{let}\ x = E_1\ \texttt{in}\ e_2$:</u> Here $E_1 = [\,]$ and the situation is:

$$\frac{jdg = (C, A \vdash_n e_1 : ts_1 \,\&\, b_1) \qquad C, A[x : ts_1] \vdash_n e_2 : t_2 \,\&\, b_2}{jdg' = (C, A \vdash \texttt{let}\ x = e_1\ \texttt{in}\ e_2 : t_2 \,\&\, (b_1 \cup b_2))}$$

and our assumptions are

$C, A_n \vdash_n e_n : ts_1 \,\&\, b_r$ and
$C \vdash b_n \cup b_r \subseteq b_1$

and we must show that there exists b'_r and S such that

$$C, A_n \vdash_n \texttt{let}\ x = e_n\ \texttt{in}\ e_2 : t_2 \,\&\, b'_r \tag{4}$$
$C \vdash b_n \cup b'_r \subseteq b_1 \cup b_2$
$Dom(S) \cap FV(A, b_n) = \emptyset$ and $C \vdash S\,C$.

We can choose $b'_r = b_r \cup b_2$ and $S = \text{Id}$: then the only non-trivial claim is (4) which will follow provided we can show that

$$C, A_n[x : ts_1] \vdash_n e_2 : t_2 \,\&\, b_2.$$

But this follows from Fact 9 and Fact 8 since all of $x_1 \cdots x_m$ are $\neq x$ and do not occur in e_2.

<u>$E = \texttt{if}\ E_0\ \texttt{then}\ e_1\ \texttt{else}\ e_2$:</u> Here $E_0 = [\,]$ and the situation is:

$$\frac{jdg = (C, A \vdash_n e_0 : \texttt{bool} \,\&\, b_0) \qquad C, A \vdash_n e_1 : t \,\&\, b_1 \qquad C, A \vdash_n e_2 : t \,\&\, b_2}{jdg' = (C, A \vdash \texttt{if}\ e_0\ \texttt{then}\ e_1\ \texttt{else}\ e_2 : t \,\&\, b_0 \cup (b_1 \cup b_2))}$$

and our assumptions are

$C, A_n \vdash_n e_n : \texttt{bool} \,\&\, b_r$ and
$C \vdash b_n \cup b_r \subseteq b_0$

and we must show that there exists b'_r and S such that

$C, A_n \vdash_n \texttt{if}\ e_n\ \texttt{then}\ e_1\ \texttt{else}\ e_2 : t \,\&\, b'_r$ and
$C \vdash b_n \cup b'_r \subseteq b_0 \cup (b_1 \cup b_2)$ and
$Dom(S) \cap FV(A, b_n) = \emptyset$ and $C \vdash S\,C$.

We can choose $b'_r = b_r \cup (b_1 \cup b_2)$ and $S = \text{Id}$; then the claims will follow since by Fact 9 we have

$$C, A_n \vdash_n e_1 : t \,\&\, b_1 \text{ and } C, A_n \vdash_n e_2 : t \,\&\, b_2.$$

$E = [\,]$: In this case jdg' follows from jdg by one application of either (sub), (ins) or (gen).

(sub) has been applied: the situation is

$$\frac{jdg = (C, A \vdash_n e : t \,\&\, b)}{jdg' = (C, A \vdash e : t' \,\&\, b')}$$

where $C \vdash t \subseteq t'$ and $C \vdash b \subseteq b'$. Our assumptions are

$C, A_n \vdash_n e_n : t \,\&\, b_r$ and
$C \vdash b_n \cup b_r \subseteq b$.

and we must show that there exists b'_r and S such that

$C, A_n \vdash_n e_n : t' \,\&\, b'_r$ and
$C \vdash b_n \cup b'_r \subseteq b'$ and
$Dom(S) \cap FV(A, b_n) = \emptyset$ and $C \vdash S\,C$.

But we can clearly choose $b'_r = b_r$ and $S = \mathrm{Id}$.

(ins) has been applied: the situation is

$$\frac{jdg = (C, A \vdash e : \forall(\vec{\alpha}\vec{\beta} : C_0).\ t_0 \,\&\, b)}{jdg' = (C, A \vdash e : S_0\, t_0 \,\&\, b)}$$

where $\forall(\vec{\alpha}\vec{\beta} : C_0).\ t_0$ is solvable from C by S_0 (and where the premise is constructed by (con) or (id)). Our assumptions are

$C, A_n \vdash_n e_n : \forall(\vec{\alpha}\vec{\beta} : C_0).\ t_0 \,\&\, b_r$ and
$C \vdash b_n \cup b_r \subseteq b$.

and we must show that there exists b'_r and S such that

$C, A_n \vdash_n e_n : S_0\, t_0 \,\&\, b'_r$ and
$C \vdash b_n \cup b'_r \subseteq b$ and
$Dom(S) \cap FV(A, b_n) = \emptyset$ and $C \vdash S\,C$.

But we can clearly choose $b'_r = b_r$ and $S = \mathrm{Id}$, using Lemma 11.

(gen) has been applied: this case has been covered in the main text. □

Polymorphic Subtyping for Effect Analysis: The Algorithm

Flemming Nielson & Hanne Riis Nielson & Torben Amtoft

Computer Science Department, Aarhus University, Denmark

e-mail: {fnielson,hrnielson,tamtoft}@daimi.aau.dk

Abstract. We study an annotated type and effect system that integrates let-polymorphism, effects, and subtyping into an annotated type and effect system for a fragment of Concurrent ML. First we define a type inference algorithm and then construct procedures for constraint normalisation and simplification. Next these algorithms are proved syntactically sound with respect to the annotated type and effect system.

1 Introduction

In a recent paper [11] we developed an annotated type and effect system for a fragment of Concurrent ML [12]. Judgements are of form

$$C, A \vdash e : \sigma \,\&\, b$$

with e an expression, b a "behaviour", σ a type or a type scheme (to incorporate ML-style let-polymorphism), C a set of constraints among types and behaviours, and A an environment. Behaviours record channel allocations and thereby the set of "dangerous variables", cf. [19] (where these are called "imperative" variables) and [21]. A subtyping relation is defined using a subeffecting relation on behaviours, with the usual contravariant ordering for function space but there is no inclusion between base types.

In our approach types are annotated with behaviour information (for example the function type $t_1 \rightarrow^b t_2$). Compared with the literature we do not attempt to collect information about the *regions* in which communications take place [17, 20]; neither do we enable polymorphic recursion in the type annotations as in [4, 20]; on the other hand we *do* allow behaviours to contain annotated types.

In [11] it was demonstrated that one must be very careful when deciding the set of variables over which to generalise in the inference rule for let: not only should this set be disjoint from the set of variables occurring in the behaviour (as is standard in effect systems, e.g. [17]) but it should also be *upwards closed* with respect to a constraint set. The semantic soundness of the generalisation rule (and of the overall system) was proved in [1] and relied heavily on the upwards closure.

The goal of this paper is to produce a type reconstruction algorithm in the spirit of Milner's algorithm $\mathcal{W}$ [7]: given an expression e and an environment A, the recursively defined function $\mathcal{W}$ will produce a substitution S, a type t, and a behaviour b. The definition in [7] employs unification: if e_1 has been given type $t_0 \rightarrow t_1$ and e_2 has been given type t_2 then in order to type $e_1\, e_2$ one must unify t_0 and t_2. Unification works by decomposition: in order to unify $t_1 \rightarrow t_2$ and $t'_1 \rightarrow t'_2$ one recursively unifies t_1 with t'_1 and t_2 with t'_2. Decomposition is valid because types constitute a "free algebra": two types are equal if and only if they have the same top-level constructor and also their subcomponents are equal. However, this will not be the case for behaviours, and therefore $\mathcal{W}$ of [7] cannot immediately be generalised to work on annotated types.

We thus have to rethink the unification algorithm. As the behaviours of this paper satisfy certain associativity and commutativity properties one might adapt results from unification theory [13] to get a unification algorithm producing a set of unifiers from which all other unifiers can be derived; but as we shall aim at a theory which facilitates extension to more complex behaviours (such as those presented in [10]) where it seems unlikely that we can use results from unification theory, we shall refrain from such attempts and instead follow [6] and generate *behaviour constraints*: that is, in the process of unifing $t_1 \rightarrow^b t_2$ and $t'_1 \rightarrow^{b'} t'_2$ we generate constraints relating b and b'.

In order to incorporate subtyping we also need to generate *type constraints* as in [3, 15] (in these papers there may also be inclusions between base types such as $\texttt{int} \subseteq \texttt{real}$). The presence of type constraints as well as behaviour constraints is a consequence of our overall design: types and behaviours should be inferred simultaneously "from scratch", as is done by the algorithm $\mathcal{W}$ presented in Sect. 3. This should be compared with the approach in [18] where an effect system with subtyping but without polymorphism is presented; as the "underlying" types are given in advance it is sufficient to generate behaviour constraints.

The constraints generated by $\mathcal{W}$ have to be massaged so as to satisfy certain invariants ("atomicity" and "simplicity") and for this we devise the algorithm $\mathcal{F}$ (Sect. 4), inspired by [3]. Still the algorithm will produce a rather unwieldy number of constraints; to reduce this number dramatically we may apply an algorithm $\mathcal{R}$ (defined in Sect. 5) which adapts the techniques of [2, 15]. The resulting algorithm $\mathcal{W}$ (which uses $\mathcal{F}$ and $\mathcal{R}$) has been implemented, and in Sect. 6 we shall see that the output produced by our prototype is quite readable and informative.

Soundness. In Sect. 7 we shall prove that $\mathcal{W}$ is (syntactically) sound, that is if $\mathcal{W}(A, e) = (S, t, b, C)$ then $C, S\,A \vdash e : t \,\&\, b$; the completeness of $\mathcal{W}$ is still an open question and we do not attempt to estimate the complexity of the algorithm.

As the main distinguishing feature of our inference system (as mentioned above), essential for semantic soundness, was the choice of generalisation rule; so the distinguishing feature of our algorithm, essential for syntactic soundness (and which still leaves hope for completeness), is the choice of generalisation rule. This involves (much as in [21]) taking downwards closure of a set of variables with respect to a constraint set.

In Sect. 8 we shall see that the constraints generated by $\mathcal{W}$ can always be solved provided recursive behaviour systems are admitted. Alternatively recursive behaviour systems can be disallowed thus rejecting programs that implement recursion in an indirect way through communication; this is quite analogous to the way the absence of recursive types in the simply typed λ-calculi forbids defining the Y combinator and instead requires recursion to be an explicit primitive in the language.

2 Inference System

In this section we briefly recapitulate the inference system [11]. Expressions and constants are given by

$$\begin{aligned} e ::= {} & c \mid x \mid \texttt{fn}\ x \Rightarrow e \mid e_1\, e_2 \mid \texttt{let}\ x = e_1\ \texttt{in}\ e_2 \\ \mid {} & \texttt{rec}\ f\ x \Rightarrow e \mid \texttt{if}\ e\ \texttt{then}\ e_1\ \texttt{else}\ e_2 \end{aligned}$$

$$\begin{aligned} c ::= {} & () \mid \texttt{true} \mid \texttt{false} \mid n \mid \texttt{+} \mid \texttt{*} \mid \texttt{=} \mid \cdots \\ \mid {} & \texttt{pair} \mid \texttt{fst} \mid \texttt{snd} \mid \texttt{nil} \mid \texttt{cons} \mid \texttt{hd} \mid \texttt{tl} \mid \texttt{isnil} \\ \mid {} & \texttt{send} \mid \texttt{receive} \mid \texttt{sync} \mid \texttt{channel} \mid \texttt{fork} \end{aligned}$$

where there are four kinds of constants: sequential constructors like `true` and `pair`, sequential base functions like `+` and `fst`, the non-sequential constructors `send` and `receive` for creating delayed output and input communications, and the non-sequential base functions `sync` (for synchronising a delayed communication), `channel` (for allocating a new communication channel) and `fork` (for spawning a new process).

Types and behaviours are given by

$$\begin{aligned} t ::= {} & \alpha \mid \texttt{unit} \mid \texttt{int} \mid \texttt{bool} \mid t_1 \times t_2 \mid t\ \texttt{list} \\ \mid {} & t_1 \to^b t_2 \mid t\ \texttt{chan} \mid t\ \texttt{com}\ b \\ b ::= {} & \{t\ \text{CHAN}\} \mid \beta \mid \emptyset \mid b_1 \cup b_2 \end{aligned}$$

where a type $t_1 \to^b t_2$ denotes a function which given a value of type t_1 computes a value of type t_2 with "side effect" b; where a type t `chan` denotes a channel allowing values of type t to be transmitted; and where a type t `com` b denotes a delayed communication that when synchronised will give rise to side effect b and result in a type t. A behaviour can (apart from the presence of behaviour variables) be viewed as a set of "atomic" behaviours which each record the creation of a channel.

Type schemes ts are of form $\forall(\vec{\alpha}\vec{\beta} : C).\ t$ with C a set of constraints, where a constraint is either of form $t_1 \subseteq t_2$ or of form $b_1 \subseteq b_2$. The type schemes of selected constants are given in Figure 1.

The ordering among types and behaviours is depicted in Figure 2; in particular notice that the ordering is contravariant in the argument position of a function type and that in order for $t\ \texttt{chan} \subseteq t'\ \texttt{chan}$ and $\{t\ \text{CHAN}\} \subseteq \{t'\ \text{CHAN}\}$ to hold we must demand that $t \equiv t'$, i.e. $t \subseteq t'$ and $t' \subseteq t$, since t occurs covariantly when used in `receive` and contravariantly when used in `send`.

The inference system is defined in Figure 3. The rules for abstraction and application are as usual in effect systems: the latent behaviour of the body of

c	TypeOf(c)
+	$\texttt{int} \times \texttt{int} \rightarrow^{\emptyset} \texttt{int}$
pair	$\forall(\alpha_1\alpha_2 : \emptyset).\ \alpha_1 \rightarrow^{\emptyset} \alpha_2 \rightarrow^{\emptyset} \alpha_1 \times \alpha_2$
fst	$\forall(\alpha_1\alpha_2 : \emptyset).\ \alpha_1 \times \alpha_2 \rightarrow^{\emptyset} \alpha_1$
snd	$\forall(\alpha_1\alpha_2 : \emptyset).\ \alpha_1 \times \alpha_2 \rightarrow^{\emptyset} \alpha_2$
send	$\forall(\alpha : \emptyset).\ (\alpha\ \texttt{chan}) \times \alpha \rightarrow^{\emptyset} (\alpha\ \texttt{com}\ \emptyset)$
receive	$\forall(\alpha : \emptyset).\ (\alpha\ \texttt{chan}) \rightarrow^{\emptyset} (\alpha\ \texttt{com}\ \emptyset)$
sync	$\forall(\alpha\beta : \emptyset).\ (\alpha\ \texttt{com}\ \beta) \rightarrow^{\beta} \alpha$
channel	$\forall(\alpha\beta : \{\{\alpha\ \text{CHAN}\} \subseteq \beta\}).\ \texttt{unit} \rightarrow^{\beta} (\alpha\ \texttt{chan})$
fork	$\forall(\alpha\beta : \emptyset).\ (\texttt{unit} \rightarrow^{\beta} \alpha) \rightarrow^{\emptyset} \texttt{unit}$

Fig. 1. Type schemes for selected constants.

a function abstraction is placed on the arrow of the function type, and once the function is applied the latent behaviour is added to the effect of evaluating the function and its argument, reflecting that the language is call-by-value. The rule for recursion makes use of function abstraction to concisely represent the "fixed point requirement" of typing recursive functions; note that we do not admit polymorphic recursion. The rule (sub) makes use of the subtyping and subeffecting relation defined in Fig. 2. The rule (ins) allows one to instantiate a type scheme and employs the notion of solvability: we say that the type scheme $\forall(\vec{\alpha}\vec{\beta} : C_0).\ t_0$ is *solvable* from C by S_0 if $Dom(S_0) \subseteq \{\vec{\alpha}\vec{\beta}\}$ and if $C \vdash S_0\, C_0$, where we write $C \vdash C'$ to mean that[1] $C \vdash g_1 \subseteq g_2$ for all $g_1 \subseteq g_2$ in C'.

The generalisation rule (gen) employs the notion of *well-formedness* where we need several auxiliary concepts: the judgement $C \vdash \gamma_1 \leftarrow \gamma_2$ holds if there exists $(g_1 \subseteq g_2)$ in C such that $\gamma_i \in FV(g_i)$ for $i = 1, 2$; the relation $\rightarrow$ is the inverse of $\leftarrow$; the relation $\leftrightarrow$ is the *union* of $\leftarrow$ and $\rightarrow$; and as usual $\leftarrow^*$ (respectively $\rightarrow^*$ and $\leftrightarrow^*$) denotes the reflexive and transitive closure of these relations. We then define *upwards closure*, *downwards closure*, and *up-downwards closure*:

$$X^{C\uparrow} = \{\gamma \mid \exists \gamma' \in X : C \vdash \gamma' \leftarrow^* \gamma\}$$
$$X^{C\downarrow} = \{\gamma \mid \exists \gamma' \in X : C \vdash \gamma' \rightarrow^* \gamma\}$$
$$X^{C\updownarrow} = \{\gamma \mid \exists \gamma' \in X : C \vdash \gamma' \leftrightarrow^* \gamma\}$$

and are then ready to define well-formedness for constraints and for type schemes:

[1] We use g to range over t or b as appropriate and γ to range over α and β as appropriate and σ to range over t and ts as appropriate.

Ordering on behaviours

(axiom) $C \vdash b_1 \subseteq b_2$ if $(b_1 \subseteq b_2) \in C$

(refl) $C \vdash b \subseteq b$

(trans) $$\frac{C \vdash b_1 \subseteq b_2 \quad C \vdash b_2 \subseteq b_3}{C \vdash b_1 \subseteq b_3}$$

(CHAN) $$\frac{C \vdash t \equiv t'}{C \vdash \{t \text{ CHAN}\} \subseteq \{t' \text{ CHAN}\}}$$

($\emptyset$) $C \vdash \emptyset \subseteq b$

($\cup$) $C \vdash b_i \subseteq (b_1 \cup b_2)$ for $i = 1, 2$

(lub) $$\frac{C \vdash b_1 \subseteq b \quad C \vdash b_2 \subseteq b}{C \vdash (b_1 \cup b_2) \subseteq b}$$

Ordering on types

(axiom) $C \vdash t_1 \subseteq t_2$ if $(t_1 \subseteq t_2) \in C$

(refl) $C \vdash t \subseteq t$

(trans) $$\frac{C \vdash t_1 \subseteq t_2 \quad C \vdash t_2 \subseteq t_3}{C \vdash t_1 \subseteq t_3}$$

($\rightarrow$) $$\frac{C \vdash t_1' \subseteq t_1 \quad C \vdash t_2 \subseteq t_2' \quad C \vdash b \subseteq b'}{C \vdash (t_1 \rightarrow^{b} t_2) \subseteq (t_1' \rightarrow^{b'} t_2')}$$

($\times$) $$\frac{C \vdash t_1 \subseteq t_1' \quad C \vdash t_2 \subseteq t_2'}{C \vdash (t_1 \times t_2) \subseteq (t_1' \times t_2')}$$

(list) $$\frac{C \vdash t \subseteq t'}{C \vdash (t \ \mathtt{list}) \subseteq (t' \ \mathtt{list})}$$

(chan) $$\frac{C \vdash t \equiv t'}{C \vdash (t \ \mathtt{chan}) \subseteq (t' \ \mathtt{chan})}$$

(com) $$\frac{C \vdash t \subseteq t' \quad C \vdash b \subseteq b'}{C \vdash (t \ \mathtt{com}\ b) \subseteq (t' \ \mathtt{com}\ b')}$$

Fig. 2. Subtyping and subeffecting.

Definition 1. A constraint set is well-formed if all constraints are of form $t \subseteq \alpha$ or $b \subseteq \beta$.

A type scheme $\forall(\vec{\alpha}\vec{\beta} : C_0).\ t_0$ is well-formed if C_0 is well-formed and if all constraints in C_0 contain at least one variable among $\{\vec{\alpha}\vec{\beta}\}$ and if it is *upwards closed*: that is $\{\vec{\alpha}\vec{\beta}\}^{C_0\uparrow} = \{\vec{\alpha}\vec{\beta}\}$.

A type t is trivially well-formed. □

Requiring a type scheme to be well-formed (in particular upwards closed) is a crucial feature in the approach of [11], the semantic soundness of which was established in [1].

(con) $C, A \vdash c : \mathrm{TypeOf}(c)\ \&\ \emptyset$

(id) $C, A \vdash x : A(x)\ \&\ \emptyset$

(abs) $$\frac{C, A[x : t_1] \vdash e : t_2\ \&\ b}{C, A \vdash \mathtt{fn}\ x \Rightarrow e : (t_1 \rightarrow^{b} t_2)\ \&\ \emptyset}$$

(app) $$\frac{C_1, A \vdash e_1 : (t_2 \rightarrow^{b} t_1)\ \&\ b_1 \qquad C_2, A \vdash e_2 : t_2\ \&\ b_2}{(C_1 \cup C_2), A \vdash e_1\, e_2 : t_1\ \&\ (b_1 \cup b_2 \cup b)}$$

(let) $$\frac{C_1, A \vdash e_1 : ts_1\ \&\ b_1 \qquad C_2, A[x : ts_1] \vdash e_2 : t_2\ \&\ b_2}{(C_1 \cup C_2), A \vdash \mathtt{let}\ x = e_1\ \mathtt{in}\ e_2 : t_2\ \&\ (b_1 \cup b_2)}$$

(rec) $$\frac{C, A[f : t] \vdash \mathtt{fn}\ x \Rightarrow e : t\ \&\ b}{C, A \vdash \mathtt{rec}\ f\ x \Rightarrow e : t\ \&\ b}$$

(if) $$\frac{C_0, A \vdash e_0 : \mathtt{bool}\ \&\ b_0 \qquad C_1, A \vdash e_1 : t\ \&\ b_1 \qquad C_2, A \vdash e_2 : t\ \&\ b_2}{(C_0 \cup C_1 \cup C_2), A \vdash \mathtt{if}\ e_0\ \mathtt{then}\ e_1\ \mathtt{else}\ e_2 : t\ \&\ (b_0 \cup b_1 \cup b_2)}$$

(sub) $$\frac{C, A \vdash e : t\ \&\ b}{C, A \vdash e : t'\ \&\ b'}$$ if $C \vdash t \subseteq t'$ and $C \vdash b \subseteq b'$

(ins) $$\frac{C, A \vdash e : \forall(\vec{\alpha}\vec{\beta} : C_0).\ t_0\ \&\ b}{C, A \vdash e : S_0\, t_0\ \&\ b}$$ if $\forall(\vec{\alpha}\vec{\beta} : C_0).\ t_0$ is solvable from C by S_0

(gen) $$\frac{C \cup C_0, A \vdash e : t_0\ \&\ b}{C, A \vdash e : \forall(\vec{\alpha}\vec{\beta} : C_0).\ t_0\ \&\ b}$$ if $\forall(\vec{\alpha}\vec{\beta} : C_0).\ t_0$ is both well-formed, solvable from C, and satisfies $\{\vec{\alpha}\vec{\beta}\} \cap FV(C, A, b) = \emptyset$

Fig. 3. The type inference system.

As expected (and proved in [11]) we have the following results, crucial for showing soundness of our inference algorithm, saying that we can apply a substitution or strengthen the constraint set, and still get a valid judgement:

Lemma 2. *Substitution Lemma*

For all substitutions S:

(a) If $C \vdash C'$ then $S\,C \vdash S\,C'$.
(b) If $C, A \vdash e : \sigma \,\&\, b$ then $S\,C, S\,A \vdash e : S\,\sigma \,\&\, S\,b$ (and has the same shape).

Lemma 3. *Entailment Lemma*

For all sets C' of constraints satisfying $C' \vdash C$:

(a) If $C \vdash C_0$ then $C' \vdash C_0$.
(b) If $C, A \vdash e : \sigma \,\&\, b$ then $C', A \vdash e : \sigma \,\&\, b$ (and has the same shape).

3 The Inference Algorithm

In designing an inference algorithm $\mathcal{W}$ for the type inference system we are (cf. the Introduction) motivated by the overall approach of [15, 3]. One ingredient (called $\mathcal{W}'$) of this will be to perform a syntax-directed traversal of the expression in order to determine its type and behaviour; this will involve constructing a constraint set for expressing the required relationship between the type and behaviour variables. The second ingredient (called $\mathcal{F}$) will be to perform a decomposition of the constraint set into one that is well-formed. The third ingredient (called $\mathcal{R}$) amounts to reducing the constraint set; this is optional and a somewhat open ended endeavour.

3.1 Well-formedness, Simplicity and Atomicity

In Definition 1 we introduced the notion of well-formedness for constraint sets and type schemes; for use by the algorithm we shall in addition introduce the notions of *simplicity* and *atomicity*.

Simplicity. As we do not know how to solve general behaviour constraints (for example we have no techniques available for decomposing constraints of form $\beta_1 \subseteq \beta_2 \cup \beta_3$) we shall wish to maintain the invariant that all (behaviour) constraints which arise in the algorithm must be well-formed. In order to achieve this we must follow [16] and [21] and demand that all types in question are (what [9] calls) *simple*, that is all behaviour annotations are variables (as is the case for $\texttt{int} \rightarrow^{\beta} \texttt{int}$).

Definition 4. A type is simple if all its behaviour annotations are behaviour variables; a constraint set is simple if all type constraints are of form $(t_1 \subseteq t_2)$ with t_1 and t_2 simple and if all behaviour constraints are of form $(b \subseteq \beta)$; a type scheme is simple if the constraint set and the type both are; an environment is simple if all its type schemes are; finally a substitution is simple if it maps behaviour variables to behaviour *variables* and type variables to simple types.

That is, with *st* ranging over simple types we have

$$st ::= \cdots \mid st_1 \rightarrow^{\beta} st_2 \mid st_1 \times st_2 \mid \cdots st \text{ com } \beta$$

Fact 5. Let t be a simple type, C be a simple constraint set, ts be a simple type scheme, and S, S' be simple substitutions. Then $S\,t$ is a simple type, $S\,C$ is a simple constraint set, $S\,ts$ is a simple type scheme, and $S'\,S$ is a simple substitution.

There is a discrepancy between the inference system and the algorithm in the sense that non-simple types are allowed in the former, in order to increase expressibility, but disallowed in the latter. In [21] a "direct" as well as an "indirect" inference system is presented; the "indirect" is geared towards an algorithm and requires simplicity and employs constraints. A perhaps more uniform approach is given in [20] where arrows are annotated with pairs of form $\epsilon.\phi$ with ϵ an effect variable and with ϕ a set of region or effect variables; one can think of this as an arrow annotated by ϵ *together with* the constraint $\phi \subseteq \epsilon$.

Atomicity. As in [8, 3, 15] we shall want the type constraints to *match* and shall decompose them into *atomic* constraints; in our setting these will not contain base types as we have no ordering among those.

Definition 6. A constraint set is atomic if all type constraints are of form $\alpha_1 \subseteq \alpha_2$ and if all behaviour constraints are of form $\{t \text{ CHAN}\} \subseteq \beta$ or $\beta' \subseteq \beta$.

Fact 7. An atomic constraint set is also well-formed and simple.

Requiring a well-formed set of behaviour constraints to be atomic is unproblematic because a constraint $(\emptyset \subseteq \beta)$ can always be thrown away and a constraint $(b_1 \cup b_2 \subseteq \beta)$ can always be split to $(b_1 \subseteq \beta)$ and $(b_2 \subseteq \beta)$. Requiring atomicity of type constraints is responsible for transforming constraints like $(\texttt{int} \subseteq \alpha)$ and $(t_1 \times t_2 \subseteq \alpha)$ by forcing α to be replaced by a type expression that "matches" the left hand side, and for disallowing constraints like $(t_1 \times t_2 \subseteq t_1' \rightarrow^{b} t_2')$. This feature is responsible for making the algorithm a "conservative extension" of the way algorithm $\mathcal{W}$ for Standard ML would operate if effects were not taken into account: in particular our algorithm will fail, rather than produce an unsolvable constraint set, if the underlying type constraints of the effect-free system cannot be solved. (We shall make this point more precise at the end of Section 7.)

3.2 Algorithm $\mathcal{W}$

Our key algorithm $\mathcal{W}$ is described by

$$\mathcal{W}(A, e) = (S, t, b, C)$$

and we shall aim at defining it such that $C, S\,A \vdash e : t \,\&\, b$ holds (soundness) and such that we might hope for some notion of principality (completeness); here completeness might be taken to mean that if also $C', S''\,A \vdash e : t' \,\&\, b'$ then there exists S' such that $C' \vdash S'\, C$ and $C' \vdash S'\, t \subseteq t'$ and $C' \vdash S'\, b \subseteq b'$ and $S'\, S$ equals S'' on A. It is an open question whether such a principal typing exists and, if this is the case, whether our algorithm actually computes this principal typing.

We shall enforce throughout that if A is simple then all of S, t and C are simple and that C is atomic. Algorithm $\mathcal{W}$ is defined by the clause

$$\begin{aligned}\mathcal{W}(A, e) = {} & \text{let } (S_1, t_1, b_1, C_1) = \mathcal{W}'(A, e)\\ & \text{let } (S_2, C_2) = \mathcal{F}(C_1)\\ & \text{let } (C_3, t_3, b_3) = \mathcal{R}(C_2, S_2\, t_1, S_2\, b_1, S_2\, S_1\, A)\\ & \text{in } (S_2\, S_1, t_3, b_3, C_3)\end{aligned}$$

where the definitions of $\mathcal{W}'$ and $\mathcal{W}$ are mutually recursive; algorithm $\mathcal{W}'$ is responsible for the syntax-directed traversal of the argument expression e. In general, $\mathcal{W}'$ will fail to produce an atomic constraint set C, even when the environment A is well-formed and simple; it will be the case, however, that all of S_1, t_1, and C_1 are simple. This then motivates the need for a transformation $\mathcal{F}$ (Section 4) that maps a simple constraint set into an atomic (hence also well-formed and simple) constraint set; since this involves splitting variables we shall need to produce a simple substitution as well. The final transformation $\mathcal{R}$ merely attempts to get a smaller constraint set by removing variables that are not strictly needed. Its operation is not essential for the soundness of our algorithm and thus one might define it by $\mathcal{R}(C, t, b, A) = (C, t, b)$; in Section 5 we shall consider a more powerful version of $\mathcal{R}$.

Example 1. To make the intentions a bit clearer suppose $\mathcal{W}'(A, e) = (S_1, t_1, b_1, C_1)$ so that $C_1, S_1\, A \vdash e : t_1 \,\&\, b_1$ is a typing of e. If

$$C_1 = \{\alpha_1 \times \alpha_2 \subseteq \alpha_3,\ \mathtt{int} \subseteq \alpha_4,\ \{\alpha_5\ \text{CHAN}\} \cup \emptyset \subseteq \beta\}$$

then $(S_2, C_2) = \mathcal{F}(C_1)$ should give

$$C_2 = \{\alpha_1 \subseteq \alpha_{31},\ \alpha_2 \subseteq \alpha_{32},\ \{\alpha_5\ \text{CHAN}\} \subseteq \beta\}$$

$$S_2 = [\alpha_3 \mapsto \alpha_{31} \times \alpha_{32},\ \alpha_4 \mapsto \mathtt{int}]$$

Here we expand α_3 to $\alpha_{31} \times \alpha_{32}$ so that the resulting constraint $\alpha_1 \times \alpha_2 \subseteq \alpha_{31} \times \alpha_{32}$ can be "decomposed" into $\alpha_1 \subseteq \alpha_{31}$ and $\alpha_2 \subseteq \alpha_{32}$ that are both atomic. Furthermore we have expanded α_4 to $\mathtt{int}$ as it follows from Figure 2 that $\emptyset \vdash \mathtt{int} \subseteq t$ necessitates that t equals $\mathtt{int}$. Finally we have decomposed the constraint upon β into two and then removed the trivial $\emptyset \subseteq \beta$ constraint. The intention is that also $C_2, S_2\, S_1\, A \vdash e : S_2\, t_1 \,\&\, S_2\, b_1$ is a typing of e; additionally the constraint set is atomic (unlike what is the case for C_1); and we have not lost any principality when going from the former typing to the latter. □

3.3 Algorithm $\mathcal{W}'$

Algorithm $\mathcal{W}'$ is defined by the clauses in Figure 4 and calls $\mathcal{W}$ in a number of places. Actually it could call itself recursively, rather than calling $\mathcal{W}$, in all but one place[2]: the call to $\mathcal{W}$ immediately prior to the use of *GEN* to generalise the type of the `let`-bound identifier to a type scheme. The algorithm follows the overall approach of [15, 5] except that as in [3] there are no explicit unification steps; these all take place as part of the $\mathcal{F}$ transformation. The only novel ingredient of our approach shows up in the clause for `let` as we shall explain shortly. Concentrating on "the overall picture" we thus have clauses for identifiers and constants; both make use of the auxiliary function *INST* defined by

$$\begin{aligned} INST(\forall(\vec{\alpha}\vec{\beta} : C).\, t) &= \text{let } \vec{\alpha}'\vec{\beta}' \text{ be fresh} \\ &\quad\;\, \text{let } R = [\vec{\alpha}\vec{\beta} \mapsto \vec{\alpha}'\vec{\beta}'] \\ &\quad\;\, \text{in } (\text{Id}, Rt, \emptyset, RC) \\[1em] INST(t) &= (\text{Id}, t, \emptyset, \emptyset) \end{aligned}$$

in order to produce a fresh instance of the relevant type or type scheme (as determined from TypeOf or from A); in order to ensure that this instance is simple (as will be needed if it is determined from TypeOf) we also need the funktion *Mk-simple* which replaces all occurrences of $\emptyset$ in a type by fresh behaviour variables, for instance we have *Mk-simple*($\texttt{int} \to^{\emptyset} \texttt{int} \to^{\emptyset} \texttt{int}$) = $\texttt{int} \to^{\beta_1} \texttt{int} \to^{\beta_2} \texttt{int}$ with β_1 and β_2 fresh. As all behaviour annotations in Fig. 1 are either $\emptyset$ or variables, and as the former kind of annotation occurs only in top-level positive position (that is, not on the left hand side of a function arrow or inside some channel type), the following property holds:

Fact 8. Let c be a constant, and let *INST*(TypeOf(c)) = (S, t, b, C). Then C is a simple constraint set, *Mk-simple*(t) is a simple type and $\emptyset \vdash t \subseteq$ *Mk-simple*(t).

The clause for function abstraction is rather straightforward; note the use of a fresh behaviour variable in order to ensure that only simple types are produced; we then add a constraint to record the "meaning" of the behaviour variable. Also the clause for application is rather straightforward; note that instead of a unification step we record the desired connection between the operator and operand types by means of a constraint. The clauses for recursion and conditional follow the same pattern as the clauses for abstraction and application.

The only novelty in the clause for `let` is the function *GEN* used for generalisation:

$$\begin{aligned} GEN(A, b)(C, t) &= \text{let } \{\vec{\alpha}\vec{\beta}\} = (FV(t)^{C\uparrow}) \setminus (FV(A, b)^{C\downarrow}) \\ &\quad\;\, \text{let } C_0 = C \mid_{\{\vec{\alpha}\vec{\beta}\}} \\ &\quad\;\, \text{in } \forall(\vec{\alpha}\vec{\beta} : C_0).\, t \end{aligned}$$

where $C \mid_{\{\vec{\alpha}\vec{\beta}\}} = \{(g_1 \subseteq g_2) \in C \mid FV(g_1, g_2) \cap \{\vec{\alpha}\vec{\beta}\} \neq \emptyset\}$. The definition of C_0 thus establishes the part of the well-formedness condition that requires each constraint to involve at least one bound variable.

[2] Interestingly, this is exactly the place where the algorithm of [15] makes use of constraint simplification in the "*close*" function; however, our prototype implementation suggests that the choice embodied in the definition of $\mathcal{W}$ gives faster performance.

$$\begin{aligned}\mathcal{W}'(A,c) = {}& \text{if } c \in \mathit{Dom}(\text{TypeOf})\\ & \text{then let } (S,t,b,C) = \mathit{INST}(\text{TypeOf}(c))\\ & \qquad \text{in } (S, \mathit{Mk\text{-}simple}(t), b, C)\\ & \text{else } \mathit{fail}_{const}\end{aligned}$$

$$\mathcal{W}'(A,x) = \text{if } x \in \mathit{Dom}(A) \text{ then } \mathit{INST}(A(x)) \text{ else } \mathit{fail}_{ident}$$

$$\begin{aligned}&\mathcal{W}'(A,\mathtt{fn}\ x \Rightarrow e_0) =\\ &\qquad \text{let } \alpha \text{ be fresh}\\ &\qquad \text{let } (S_0,t_0,b_0,C_0) = \mathcal{W}(A[x:\alpha],e_0)\\ &\qquad \text{let } \beta \text{ be fresh}\\ &\qquad \text{in } (S_0, S_0\,\alpha \rightarrow^{\beta} t_0, \emptyset, C_0 \cup \{b_0 \subseteq \beta\})\end{aligned}$$

$$\begin{aligned}&\mathcal{W}'(A,e_1\,e_2) =\\ &\qquad \text{let } (S_1,t_1,b_1,C_1) = \mathcal{W}(A,e_1)\\ &\qquad \text{let } (S_2,t_2,b_2,C_2) = \mathcal{W}(S_1\,A,e_2)\\ &\qquad \text{let } \alpha,\beta \text{ be fresh}\\ &\qquad \text{in } (S_2\,S_1, \alpha, S_2\,b_1 \cup b_2 \cup \beta,\\ &\qquad\qquad S_2\,C_1 \cup C_2 \cup \{S_2\,t_1 \subseteq t_2 \rightarrow^{\beta} \alpha\})\end{aligned}$$

$$\begin{aligned}&\mathcal{W}'(A,\mathtt{let}\ x = e_1\ \mathtt{in}\ e_2) =\\ &\qquad \text{let } (S_1,t_1,b_1,C_1) = \mathcal{W}(A,e_1)\\ &\qquad \text{let } ts_1 = \mathit{GEN}(S_1\,A,b_1)(C_1,t_1)\\ &\qquad \text{let } (S_2,t_2,b_2,C_2) = \mathcal{W}((S_1\,A)[x:ts_1],e_2)\\ &\qquad \text{in } (S_2\,S_1, t_2, S_2\,b_1 \cup b_2, S_2\,C_1 \cup C_2)\end{aligned}$$

$$\begin{aligned}&\mathcal{W}'(A,\mathtt{rec}\ f\ x \Rightarrow e_0) =\\ &\qquad \text{let } \alpha_1,\beta,\alpha_2 \text{ be fresh}\\ &\qquad \text{let } (S_0,t_0,b_0,C_0) = \mathcal{W}(A[f:\alpha_1 \rightarrow^{\beta} \alpha_2][x:\alpha_1],e_0)\\ &\qquad \text{in } (S_0, S_0\,(\alpha_1 \rightarrow^{\beta} \alpha_2), \emptyset, C_0 \cup \{b_0 \subseteq S_0\,\beta,\ t_0 \subseteq S_0\,\alpha_2\})\end{aligned}$$

$$\begin{aligned}&\mathcal{W}'(A,\mathtt{if}\ e_0\ \mathtt{then}\ e_1\ \mathtt{else}\ e_2) =\\ &\qquad \text{let } (S_0,t_0,b_0,C_0) = \mathcal{W}(A,e_0)\\ &\qquad \text{let } (S_1,t_1,b_1,C_1) = \mathcal{W}(S_0\,A,e_1)\\ &\qquad \text{let } (S_2,t_2,b_2,C_2) = \mathcal{W}(S_1\,S_0\,A,e_2)\\ &\qquad \text{let } \alpha \text{ be fresh}\\ &\qquad \text{in } (S_2\,S_1\,S_0, \alpha, S_2\,S_1\,b_0 \cup S_2\,b_1 \cup b_2,\\ &\qquad\qquad S_2\,S_1\,C_0 \cup S_2\,C_1 \cup C_2 \cup \{S_2\,S_1\,t_0 \subseteq \mathtt{bool},\ S_2\,t_1 \subseteq \alpha,\ t_2 \subseteq \alpha\})\end{aligned}$$

Fig. 4. Syntax-directed constraint generation.

The exclusion of the set $FV(A,b)^{C\downarrow}$ (rather than just $FV(A,b)$) is necessary in order to ensure $\{\vec{\alpha}\vec{\beta}\}^{C_0\uparrow} = \{\vec{\alpha}\vec{\beta}\}$ which (cf. the remarks concerning Def. 1) is essential for semantic soundness; the computation of "Indirect Free Variables" of [21] is very similar to our notion of downwards closure. Finally we have chosen $FV(t)^{C\updownarrow}$ as the "universe" in which to perform the set difference; this universe must be large enough that we may still hope for syntactic completeness and all of $FV(t)$, $FV(t)^{C\downarrow}$ (similar to what is in fact taken in [21]) and $FV(t)^{C\uparrow}$ are apparently too small for this (except for the latter they are not even upwards closed).

Fact 9. Let $\sigma = GEN(A,b)(C,t)$; if C is well-formed then so is σ.

Proof. The only non-trivial task is to show that $\{\vec{\alpha}\vec{\beta}\}^{C_0\uparrow} \subseteq \{\vec{\alpha}\vec{\beta}\}$ where $\{\vec{\alpha}\vec{\beta}\}$ is as in the defining clause for *GEN*. So assume $C_0 \vdash \gamma_1 \leftarrow \gamma_2$ (and hence also $C \vdash \gamma_1 \leftarrow \gamma_2$) with $\gamma_1 \in \{\vec{\alpha}\vec{\beta}\}$; we must show that $\gamma_2 \in \{\vec{\alpha}\vec{\beta}\}$. Now $\gamma_1 \in FV(t)^{C\updownarrow}$ and $\gamma_1 \notin FV(A,b)^{C\downarrow}$, hence we infer $\gamma_2 \in FV(t)^{C\updownarrow}$ and $\gamma_2 \notin FV(A,b)^{C\downarrow}$ which amounts to the desired result. □

Remark. Note that $FV(t)^{C\updownarrow}$ is a subset of $FV(t,C)$ and that it may well be a proper subset; when this is the case it avoids to generalise over "purely internal" variables that are inconsequential for the overall type. If one were to regard `let` $x = e_1$ `in` e_2 as equivalent to $e_2[e_1/x]$ (which is sensible only if e_1 has an empty behaviour) this corresponds to forcing all "purely internal" variables in corresponding copies of e_1 to be equal. This is helpful for reducing the size of constraint sets and type schemes. □

4 Algorithm $\mathcal{F}$

We are now going to define the algorithm $\mathcal{F}$ which "forces type constraints to match" by transforming them into atomic constraints; the algorithm closely resembles [3, procedure MATCH].

The algorithm may be described as a non-deterministic rewriting process. It operates over triples of the form $(S, C, \sim)$ where S is a substitution, C is a constraint set, and $\sim$ is an equivalence relation among the finite set of type variables in C; we shall write Eq_C for the identity relation over type variables in C. We then define $\mathcal{F}$ by

$$\begin{aligned}\mathcal{F}(C) = {} & \text{let } (S', C', \sim') \text{ be given by } (\mathrm{Id}, C, \mathrm{Eq}_C) \longrightarrow^{*} (S', C', \sim') \not\longrightarrow \\ & \text{in if } C' \text{ is atomic} \\ & \quad \text{then } (S', C') \text{ else } \mathit{fail}_{\mathit{forcing}}\end{aligned}$$

The rewriting relation is defined by the axioms of Figure 6 and will be explained below; it makes use of an auxiliary rewriting relation, defined in Figure 5, which operates over constraint sets.

The axioms of Figure 5 are rather straightforward. For behaviours the axiom ($\emptyset$) simply throws away constraints of the form $\emptyset \subseteq b$ and the axiom ($\cup$) simply

$(\emptyset)\quad C\dot{\cup}\{\emptyset \subseteq b\} \rightharpoonup C$

$(\cup)\quad C\dot{\cup}\{b_1 \cup b_2 \subseteq b\} \rightharpoonup C \cup \{b_1 \subseteq b, b_2 \subseteq b\}$

$(\times)\quad C\dot{\cup}\{t_1 \times t_2 \subseteq t_3 \times t_4\} \rightharpoonup C \cup \{t_1 \subseteq t_3, t_2 \subseteq t_4\}$

$(\texttt{list})\ C\dot{\cup}\{t_1\ \texttt{list} \subseteq t_2\ \texttt{list}\} \rightharpoonup C \cup \{t_1 \subseteq t_2\}$

$(\texttt{chan})\ C\dot{\cup}\{t_1\ \texttt{chan} \subseteq t_2\ \texttt{chan}\} \rightharpoonup C \cup \{t_1 \subseteq t_2, t_2 \subseteq t_1\}$

$(\texttt{com})\ C\dot{\cup}\{t_1\ \texttt{com}\ b_1 \subseteq t_2\ \texttt{com}\ b_2\} \rightharpoonup C \cup \{t_1 \subseteq t_2, b_1 \subseteq b_2\}$

$(\rightarrow)\quad C\dot{\cup}\{t_1 \rightarrow^{b_1} t_2 \subseteq t_3 \rightarrow^{b_2} t_4\}$
$\quad\quad \rightharpoonup C \cup \{t_3 \subseteq t_1, b_1 \subseteq b_2, t_2 \subseteq t_4\}$

$$\left.\begin{array}{l}(\texttt{int})\ C\dot{\cup}\{\texttt{int} \subseteq \texttt{int}\}\\ (\texttt{bool})\ C\dot{\cup}\{\texttt{bool} \subseteq \texttt{bool}\}\\ (\texttt{unit})\ C\dot{\cup}\{\texttt{unit} \subseteq \texttt{unit}\}\end{array}\right\} \rightharpoonup C$$

Fig. 5. Decomposition of constraints.

$$(\texttt{dc})\ \frac{C \rightharpoonup C'}{(S, C, \sim) \longrightarrow (S, C', \sim)}$$

$(\texttt{mr})\ (S, C\dot{\cup}\{t \subseteq \alpha\}, \sim) \longrightarrow (R\,S, R\,C \cup \{R\,t \subseteq R\,\alpha\}, \sim')$
provided $\mathcal{M}(\alpha, t, \sim, R, \sim')$

$(\texttt{ml})\ (S, C\dot{\cup}\{\alpha \subseteq t\}, \sim) \longrightarrow (R\,S, R\,C \cup \{R\,\alpha \subseteq R\,t\}, \sim')$
provided $\mathcal{M}(\alpha, t, \sim, R, \sim')$

Fig. 6. Rewriting rules for $\mathcal{F}$: forcing well-formedness.

decomposes constraints of the form $b_1 \cup b_2 \subseteq b$ to the simpler constraints $b_1 \subseteq b$ and $b_2 \subseteq b$. (A small notational point: in Figure 5 and in Figure 6 we write $C\dot{\cup}C'$ for $C \cup C'$ in case $C \cap C' = \emptyset$.) For types the axioms ($\times$), (`list`), (`chan`), (`com`), and ($\rightarrow$) essentially run the inference system of Figure 2 in a backwards way and generate new constraints $t_1 \subseteq t_2$ and $t_2 \subseteq t_1$ whenever we had $t_1 \equiv t_2$ in Figure 2. Axioms (`int`), (`bool`) and (`unit`) are simple instances of reflexivity.

Fact 10. The rewriting relation $\rightharpoonup$ is confluent and if $C_1 \rightharpoonup C_2$ then $C_2 \vdash C_1$.

Proof. Confluence follows since each rewriting operates on a single element only, and for each element there is only one possible rewriting. □

We now turn to Figure 6. The axiom (dc) decomposes the constraint set but does not modify the substitution nor the equivalence relation among type variables. The axioms (mr) and (ml) force left and right hand sides of type constraints to match and produces a new substitution as a result; additionally it may modify the equivalence relation among type variables. The details require the predicate $\mathcal{M}$ (which performs an "occur check"), to be defined shortly. Before presenting the formal definition we consider an example.

Example 2. Consider the constraint $t_1 \subseteq \alpha_0$ where $t_1 = (\alpha_{11} \times \alpha_{12})\ \texttt{com}\ \beta_1$. Forcing the left and right hand sides to match means finding a substitution R such that $R\,t_1$ and $R\,\alpha_0$ have the same shape. A natural way to achieve this is by creating new type variables α_{21} and α_{22} and a new behaviour variable β_2 and by defining

$$R = [\alpha_0 \mapsto (\alpha_{21} \times \alpha_{22})\ \texttt{com}\ \beta_2].$$

Then $R\,t_1 = t_1 = (\alpha_{11} \times \alpha_{12})\ \texttt{com}\ \beta_1$ and $R\,\alpha_0 = (\alpha_{21} \times \alpha_{22})\ \texttt{com}\ \beta_2$ and these types intuitively have the same shape. Returning to Figure 6 we would thus expect $\mathcal{M}(\alpha_0, t_1, \sim, R, \sim)$.

If instead we had considered the constraint $(\alpha \times \alpha)\ \texttt{com}\ \beta \subseteq \alpha$ then the above procedure would not lead to a matching constraint. We would get

$$R = [\alpha \mapsto (\alpha' \times \alpha'')\ \texttt{com}\ \beta']$$

and the constraint $R\,((\alpha \times \alpha)\ \texttt{com}\ \beta) \subseteq R\,\alpha$ then is

$$(((\alpha' \times \alpha'')\ \texttt{com}\ \beta') \times ((\alpha' \times \alpha'')\ \texttt{com}\ \beta'))\ \texttt{com}\ \beta \subseteq (\alpha' \times \alpha'')\ \texttt{com}\ \beta'$$

which does not match. Indeed it would seem that matching could go on forever without ever producing a matching result. To detect this situation we have an "occur check": when $\mathcal{M}(\alpha, t, \sim, R, \sim')$ holds no variable in $Dom(R)$ must occur in t. This condition fails when $t = (\alpha \times \alpha)\ \texttt{com}\ \beta$.

However, there are more subtle ways in which termination may fail. Consider the constraint set

$$\{\alpha_1\ \texttt{com}\ \beta_1 \subseteq \alpha_0,\ \alpha_0 \subseteq \alpha_1\}$$

where only the first constraint does not match. Attempting a match we get

$$R_1 = [\alpha_0 \mapsto \alpha_2\ \texttt{com}\ \beta_2]$$

and note that the "occur check" succeeds. The resulting constraint set is

$$\{\alpha_1\ \texttt{com}\ \beta_1 \subseteq \alpha_2\ \texttt{com}\ \beta_2,\ \alpha_2\ \texttt{com}\ \beta_2 \subseteq \alpha_1\}$$

which may be reduced to

$$\{\alpha_1 \subseteq \alpha_2,\ \beta_1 \subseteq \beta_2,\ \alpha_2\ \texttt{com}\ \beta_2 \subseteq \alpha_1\}.$$

The type part is isomorphic to the initial constraints, so this process may continue forever: we perform a second match and produce a second substitution R_2, etc.

To detect this situation we follow [3] in making use of the equivalence relation $\sim$ and extend it with $\alpha_1 \sim \alpha_2$ after the first match that produced R_1; the intuition is that α_1 and α_2 eventually must be bound to types having the same shape. When performing the second match we then require R_2 not only to expand α_1 but also all α' satisfying $\alpha' \sim \alpha_1$; this means that R_2 must expand also α_2. Consequently the "extended occur check" $Dom(R_2) \cap FV(\alpha_2 \; \texttt{com} \; \beta_2) = \emptyset$ fails. □

Remark. Matching bears certain similarities to unification and can actually be defined in terms of unification. In [8] matching is performed by first doing unification and then the resulting substitution is transformed such that it "maps into fresh variables". In [14, Fig. 3.7] it is first checked whether it is possible to unify a certain set of equations, derived from the constraint set; if this is the case then the algorithm behaves similar to the one presented here except that the equivalence relation is no longer needed. □

To formalise the development of the example we need to be more precise about the shape of a type and when two types match.

Definition 11. A shape *sh* is a type with holes in it for all type variables and for all behaviours; it may be formally defined by:

$$\begin{aligned} sh ::= &\; [\,] \mid \texttt{unit} \mid \texttt{int} \mid \texttt{bool} \mid sh_1 \times sh_2 \mid sh_1 \rightarrow^{[\,]} sh_2 \mid sh \; \texttt{list} \\ &\mid sh \; \texttt{chan} \mid sh \; \texttt{com} \; [\,] \end{aligned}$$

We write $sh[\vec{t}, \vec{b}]$ for the type obtained by replacing all type holes with the relevant type in the list $\vec{t}$ and replacing all behaviour holes with the relevant behaviour in the list $\vec{b}$; we assume throughout that the lengths of the lists equal the number of holes and shall dispense with a formal definition. For each type t there clearly exists unique sh, $\vec{t}$ and $\vec{b}$ such that $t = sh[\vec{t}, \vec{b}]$, and t is simple if and only if all elements of $\vec{b}$ are variables.

Example 3. If $sh = ([\,] \times [\,]) \; \texttt{com} \; [\,]$ then $sh[\vec{t}, \vec{b}] = (t_1 \times t_2) \; \texttt{com} \; b_1$ if and only if $\vec{t} = t_1 t_2$ and $\vec{b} = b_1$. □

The axioms (mr) and (ml) force a type t to match a type variable α and employ the predicate $\mathcal{M}$ defined in Figure 7. This predicate may also be considered a partial function with its first three parameters being input and the last two being output; the "call" $\mathcal{M}(\alpha, t, \sim, R, \sim')$ produces the substitution R and modifies the equivalence relation $\sim$ (over the free type variables of a constraint set C') to another equivalence relation $\sim'$ (over the free type variables of the constraint set RC'). In axioms (mr) and (ml) the newly produced substitution R is composed with the previously produced substitution. Also note that the "extended occur check" in Figure 7 ensures that $Rt = t$. Using Fact 5 it is straightforward to establish:

$\mathcal{M}(\alpha, t, \sim, R, \sim')$ holds
if $\{\alpha_1, \cdots, \alpha_n\} \cap FV(t) = \emptyset$
and $R = [\alpha_1 \mapsto sh[\vec{\alpha}_1, \vec{\beta}_1], \ldots, \alpha_n \mapsto sh[\vec{\alpha}_n, \vec{\beta}_n]]$
and $\sim'$ is the least equivalence relation containing the pairs
$\{(\alpha', \alpha'') \mid \alpha' \sim \alpha'' \wedge \{\alpha', \alpha''\} \cap \{\alpha_1, \cdots, \alpha_n\} = \emptyset\} \bigcup$
$\{(\alpha_{0j}, \alpha_{ij}) \mid \vec{\alpha}_0 = \alpha_{01} \cdots \alpha_{0m}, \vec{\alpha}_i = \alpha_{i1} \cdots \alpha_{im}, 1 \leq i \leq n, 1 \leq j \leq m\}$
where $\{\alpha_1, \cdots, \alpha_n\} = \{\alpha' \mid \alpha' \sim \alpha\}$
and $sh[\vec{\alpha}_0, \vec{\beta}_0] = t$ with $\vec{\alpha}_0$ having length m
and $\vec{\alpha}_1, \cdots, \vec{\alpha}_n$ are vectors of fresh variables of length m
and $\vec{\beta}_1, \cdots, \vec{\beta}_n$ are vectors of fresh variables of the same length as $\vec{\beta}_0$

Fig. 7. Forced matching for simple types.

Fact 12. Suppose $(S, C, \sim) \longrightarrow (S', C', \sim')$. Then there exists simple R such that $S' = R\,S$ and such that $R\,C \rightharpoonup^* C'$. Moreover, if S and C are simple then also S' and C' are simple.

Remark: type cycles become behaviour cycles. To understand why $\mathcal{F}$ does not report failure in *more* cases than a "classical type checker", the following example is helpful. Consider the constraint set

$$C = \{\texttt{int} \to^{\{\alpha\ \text{CHAN}\}} \texttt{int} \subseteq \alpha\}$$

which will not cause a classical type checker to fail since α is simply unified with $\texttt{int} \to \texttt{int}$. Now let us see how $\mathcal{F}$ behaves on this constraint, encoded as a set of *simple* constraints:

$$\{\texttt{int} \to^{\beta} \texttt{int} \subseteq \alpha,\ \{\alpha\ \text{CHAN}\} \subseteq \beta\}.$$

Here case (mr) in Figure 6 is enabled, and consequentially a substitution which maps α into $\texttt{int} \to^{\beta'} \texttt{int}$ (with β' new) is applied to the constraints. The resulting constraint set is

$$\{\texttt{int} \to^{\beta} \texttt{int} \subseteq \texttt{int} \to^{\beta'} \texttt{int},\ \{(\texttt{int} \to^{\beta'} \texttt{int})\ \text{CHAN}\} \subseteq \beta\}$$

and after first applying case (dc) for $(\to)$ and then applying case (dc) for $(\texttt{int})$ we end up with the constraint set

$$C' = \{\beta \subseteq \beta',\ \{(\texttt{int} \to^{\beta'} \texttt{int})\ \text{CHAN}\} \subseteq \beta\}$$

which cannot be rewritten further. The set C' is atomic so Algorithm $\mathcal{F}$ succeeds on C. □

4.1 Termination and Soundness of $\mathcal{F}$

Having completed the definition of $\mathcal{M}$, $\longrightarrow$ and $\mathcal{F}$ we can state:

Lemma 13. $\mathcal{F}(C)$ always terminates (possibly with failure). If $\mathcal{F}(C) = (S', C')$ then

- if C is simple then S' is simple and C' is atomic;
- C' is determined from $S'\,C$ in the sense that $S'\,C \rightharpoonup^* C' \not\rightharpoonup$.

Proof. We first address termination and for this purpose we (much as in [3]) define an ordering on triples $(S, C, \sim)$ as follows: $(S', C', \sim')$ is less than $(S, C, \sim)$ if *either* the number of equivalence classes in $FV(C')$ wrt. $\sim'$ is less than the number of equivalence classes in $FV(C)$ wrt. $\sim$ *or* these numbers are equal but C' is less than C according to the following definition:

> for all $i \geq 0$ let s_i be the number of constraints in C containing i symbols and let s'_i be the number of constraints in C' containing i symbols; then C' is less than C if there exists a n such that $s'_n < s_n$ and such that $s'_i = s_i$ for all $i > n$.

This relation on constraint sets is clearly transitive and it is easy to see that it is also well-founded, hence the (lexicographically defined) ordering on triples is well-founded. Thus it suffices to show that if $(S, C, \sim) \longrightarrow (S', C', \sim')$ then $(S', C', \sim')$ is less than $(S, C, \sim)$. If the rule (dc) has been applied then C' is less than C (as n in the above definition we can use the number of symbols in the constraint being decomposed) and $\sim' = \sim$. If the rule (mr) or (ml) has been applied then the number of equivalence classes wrt. $\sim$ will decrease as can be seen from the definition of $\mathcal{M}$ in Fig. 7: the equivalence class containing α is removed (as this class equals $Dom(R)$ and $C' = R\,C$) and no new classes are added (as all type variables in $Ran(R)$ are put into some existing equivalence class).

We have thus proved termination; it is easy to see that the other claims will follow provided we can show that if

$$(\mathrm{Id}, C, \mathrm{Eq}_C) \longrightarrow^* (S_n, C_n, \sim_n)$$

then $S_n\,C \rightharpoonup^* C_n$ and if C is simple then S_n and C_n are simple. We do this by induction on the length of the derivation, where the base case as well as the part concerning simplicity (where we use Fact 12) is trivial. For the inductive step, suppose that

$$(\mathrm{Id}, C, \mathrm{Eq}_C) \longrightarrow^* (S_n, C_n, \sim_n) \longrightarrow (S_{n+1}, C_{n+1}, \sim_{n+1})$$

where the induction hypothesis ensures that $S_n\,C \rightharpoonup^* C_n$. By Fact 12 there exists R such that $S_{n+1} = R\,S_n$ and such that $R\,C_n \rightharpoonup^* C_{n+1}$. As it is easy to see that the relation $\rightharpoonup$ is closed under substitution it holds that $R\,S_n\,C \rightharpoonup^* R\,C_n$, hence the claim. □

Lemma 14. *$\mathcal{F}$ is sound*

If $\mathcal{F}(C) = (S', C')$ then $C' \vdash S'\,C$.

Proof. By Lemma 13 we have $S'\,C \rightharpoonup^* C'$, which yields the claim due to Fact 10.

Remark. By Fact 10 we know that $\rightharpoonup$ is confluent but this does not directly carry over to $\longrightarrow$ or $\mathcal{F}$: the constraint $\alpha_1 \subseteq \alpha_2$ may yield $([\alpha_1 \mapsto \alpha_0], \{\alpha_0 \subseteq \alpha_2\})$ as well as $([\alpha_2 \mapsto \alpha_0], \{\alpha_1 \subseteq \alpha_0\})$. However, Lemma 13 told us that $\mathcal{F}(C) = (S', C')$ ensures that C' is determined from $S'\,C$, and we conjecture that S' is determined (up to some notion of renaming) from C.

5 Algorithm $\mathcal{R}$

The purpose of algorithm $\mathcal{R}$ is to reduce the size of a constraint set which is already atomic. The techniques used are basically those of [15] and [2], adapted to our framework.

The transformation $\mathcal{R}$ may be described as a non-deterministic rewriting process, operating over triples of form (C, t, b), and with respect to a fixed environment A. We then define $\mathcal{R}$ by:

$$\begin{aligned}\mathcal{R}(C,t,b,A) = \text{let } & (C',t',b') \text{ be given by} \\ & A \vdash (C,t,b) \longrightarrow^* (C',t',b') \not\longrightarrow \\ \text{in } & (C',t',b')\end{aligned}$$

The rewriting relation is defined by the axioms of Figure 8 and will be explained below (recall that $\dot{\cup}$ means disjoint union). To understand the axioms, it is helpful to view the constraints as a directed graph where the nodes are type or behaviour variables or of form $\{t\ \text{CHAN}\}$, and the arrows cannot have a node of form $\{t\ \text{CHAN}\}$ as the source. To this end we define:

Definition 15. We write $C \vdash \gamma \Leftarrow^* \gamma'$ if there is a path from γ' to γ: that is there exists $\gamma_0 \cdots \gamma_n$ $(n \geq 0)$ such that $\gamma_0 = \gamma$ and $\gamma_n = \gamma'$ and $(\gamma_i \subseteq \gamma_{i+1}) \in C$ for all $i \in \{0 \ldots n-1\}$.

Notice that $C \vdash \gamma \Leftarrow^* \gamma$ holds also if $\gamma \notin FV(C)$. From reflexivity and transitivity of $\subseteq$ we have:

Fact 16. If $C \vdash \gamma \Leftarrow^* \gamma'$ then also $C \vdash \gamma \subseteq \gamma'$.

We have a substitution result similar to Lemma 2:

Fact 17. Let S be a substitution mapping variables into variables, and suppose $C \vdash \gamma \Leftarrow^* \gamma'$. Then also $S\,C \vdash S\,\gamma \Leftarrow^* S\,\gamma'$.

We say that C is cyclic if there exists $\gamma_1, \gamma_2 \in FV(C)$ with $\gamma_1 \neq \gamma_2$ such that $C \vdash \gamma_1 \Leftarrow^* \gamma_2$ and $C \vdash \gamma_2 \Leftarrow^* \gamma_1$.

We now explain the rules: (redund) removes constraints which are redundant due to the ordering $\subseteq$ being reflexive and transitive; applying this rule repeatedly is called "transitive reduction" in [15] and is essential for a compact representation of the constraints.

The remaining rules all replace some variable γ by another variable γ'. However, it is not the case that all substitutions that solve C can be written on the form $S'\,[\gamma \mapsto \gamma']$ and therefore we might lose completeness if the substitution

(redund) $A \vdash (C \dot{\cup} \{\gamma' \subseteq \gamma\}, t, b) \longrightarrow (C, t, b)$
provided $C \vdash \gamma' \Leftarrow^* \gamma$

(cycle) $A \vdash (C, t, b) \longrightarrow (S\,C, S\,t, S\,b)$
where $S = [\gamma \mapsto \gamma']$ with $\gamma \neq \gamma'$
provided $C \vdash \gamma \Leftarrow^* \gamma'$ and $C \vdash \gamma' \Leftarrow^* \gamma$ and
provided $\gamma \notin FV(A)$

(shrink) $A \vdash (C \dot{\cup} \{\gamma' \subseteq \gamma\}, t, b) \longrightarrow (S\,C, S\,t, S\,b)$
where $S = [\gamma \mapsto \gamma']$ with $\gamma \neq \gamma'$
provided $\gamma \notin FV(RHS(C), A)$ and
provided t, b, and each element in $LHS(C)$ is monotonic in γ

(boost) $A \vdash (C \dot{\cup} \{\gamma \subseteq \gamma'\}, t, b) \longrightarrow (S\,C, S\,t, S\,b)$
where $S = [\gamma \mapsto \gamma']$ with $\gamma \neq \gamma'$
provided $\gamma \notin FV(A)$ and
provided t, b and each element in $LHS(C)$ is anti-monotonic in γ

Fig. 8. Eliminating constraints.

$[\gamma \mapsto \gamma']$ was to be returned (in the style of $\mathcal{F}$) and subsequently applied to A. In order to maintain soundness we must therefore demand that $\gamma \notin FV(A)$.

The rule (cycle) collapses cycles in the graph; due to the remark above a cycle which involves *two* elements of $FV(A)$ cannot be eliminated. (In [14] it holds that $\emptyset \vdash t_1 \equiv t_2$ implies $t_1 = t_2$ so if γ and γ' belong to the same cycle in C then all substitutions that solve C can be written on the form $S'\,[\gamma \mapsto \gamma']$, hence cycle elimination can be part of the analogue of $\mathcal{F}$.)

The rule (shrink) expresses that a variable γ can be replaced by its "immediate predecessor" γ', and due to the ability to perform transitive reduction this can be strengthened to the requirement that γ' is the "only predecessor" of γ, which can be formalised as the side condition $\gamma \notin FV(RHS(C))$ where $RHS(C) = \{\gamma \mid \exists g : (g \subseteq \gamma) \in C\}$. We can allow γ to belong to t and b and $LHS(C)$, where $LHS(C) = \{g \mid \exists \gamma : (g \subseteq \gamma) \in C\}$, as long as we do not "lose instances", that is we must have that $S\,t \subseteq t$, $S\,b \subseteq b$, and $S\,g \subseteq g$ for each $g \in LHS(C)$. This will be the case provided t and b and each element of $LHS(C)$ are *monotonic* in γ, where for example $t = \alpha_1 \rightarrow^{\beta_1} \alpha_2 \rightarrow^{\beta_1} \alpha_1$ (recall that $\rightarrow$ is right-associative) is monotonic in γ for *all* $\gamma \notin \{\alpha_1, \alpha_2\}$. A more formal treatment of the concept of monotonicity will be given shortly, for now notice that if $\gamma \notin FV(g)$ or if $g = \gamma$ then g is monotonic in γ.

The rule (boost) expresses that a variable γ can be replaced by its "immediate successor" γ', and due to the ability to perform transitive reduction this can be strengthened to the requirement that γ' must be the "only successor" of γ. In addition we must demand that we do not "lose instances", that is we must have that $S\,t \subseteq t$, $S\,b \subseteq b$, and $S\,g \subseteq g$ for each $g \in$ *LHS*(C). This will be the case provided t and[3] b and each element of *LHS*(C) are *anti-monotonic* in γ, where for example $t = \alpha_1 \rightarrow^{\beta_1} \alpha_2 \rightarrow^{\beta_1} \alpha_1$ is anti-monotonic in γ for *all* $\gamma \notin \{\alpha_1, \beta_1\}$. Notice that if each element of *LHS*(C) is anti-monotonic in γ then γ' in fact is the only successor of γ.

Example 4. Let C and t be given by

$$C = \{\alpha_1 \subseteq \alpha_2\} \text{ and } t = \alpha_1 \rightarrow^{\beta} \alpha_2. \tag{1}$$

As t is monotonic in α_2, it is possible to apply (shrink) and get

$$C' = \emptyset \text{ and } t' = \alpha_1 \rightarrow^{\beta} \alpha_1. \tag{2}$$

The soundness and completeness of this transformation may informally be argued as follows: (1) "denotes" the set of types

$$\{t_1 \rightarrow^{b} t_2 \mid \emptyset \vdash t_1 \subseteq t_2\} \text{ and } b \text{ is a behaviour}$$

but this is also the set of types denoted by (2), due to the presence of subtyping.

Notice that since t is anti-monotonic in α_1, it is also possible to apply (boost) from (1) and arrive at

$$C' = \emptyset \text{ and } t' = \alpha_2 \rightarrow^{\beta} \alpha_2$$

which modulo renaming is equal to (2).

Example 5. Let C and t be given by

$$C = \{\alpha_2 \subseteq \alpha_1\} \text{ and } t = \alpha_1 \rightarrow^{\beta} \alpha_2.$$

Then neither (shrink) nor (boost) is applicable, as t is not monotonic in α_1 nor anti-monotonic in α_2.

Monotonicity

Definition 18. Given a constraint set C. We say that a substitution S is increasing (respectively decreasing) wrt. C if for all γ we have $C \vdash \gamma \subseteq S\,\gamma$ (respectively $C \vdash S\,\gamma \subseteq \gamma$).

We say that a substitution S increases (respectively decreases) g wrt. C whenever $C \vdash g \subseteq S\,g$ (respectively $C \vdash S\,g \subseteq g$).

We want to define the concepts of monotonicity and anti-monotonicity such that the following result holds:

---

[3] Actually, the condition that b is anti-monotonic in γ amounts to $\gamma \notin FV(b)$. Similarly with the requirement on *LHS*(C) (as C is atomic).

Lemma 19. Suppose that g is monotonic in all $\gamma \in \mathit{Dom}(S)$; then if S is increasing (respectively decreasing) wrt. C then S increases (respectively decreases) g wrt. C.

Suppose that g is anti-monotonic in all $\gamma \in \mathit{Dom}(S)$; then if S is increasing (respectively decreasing) wrt. C then S decreases (respectively increases) g wrt. C.

To this end we make the following recursive definition of sets $\mathit{NA}(g)$ and $\mathit{NM}(g)$ (for "Not Anti-monotonic" and "Not Monotonic"):

$\mathit{NA}(\gamma) = \{\gamma\}$ and $\mathit{NM}(\gamma) = \emptyset$;
$\mathit{NA}(\mathtt{unit}) = \mathit{NA}(\mathtt{int}) = \mathit{NA}(\mathtt{bool}) = \mathit{NA}(\emptyset) = \emptyset$;
$\mathit{NM}(\mathtt{unit}) = \mathit{NM}(\mathtt{int}) = \mathit{NM}(\mathtt{bool}) = \mathit{NM}(\emptyset) = \emptyset$;
$\mathit{NA}(t_1 \to^b t_2) = \mathit{NM}(t_1) \cup \mathit{NA}(b) \cup \mathit{NA}(t_2)$;
$\mathit{NM}(t_1 \to^b t_2) = \mathit{NA}(t_1) \cup \mathit{NM}(b) \cup \mathit{NM}(t_2)$;
$\mathit{NA}(t_1 \times t_2) = \mathit{NA}(t_1) \cup \mathit{NA}(t_2)$ and $\mathit{NM}(t_1 \times t_2) = \mathit{NM}(t_1) \cup \mathit{NM}(t_2)$;
$\mathit{NA}(t\ \mathtt{list}) = \mathit{NA}(t)$ and $\mathit{NM}(t\ \mathtt{list}) = \mathit{NM}(t)$;
$\mathit{NA}(t\ \mathbf{chan}) = \mathit{NM}(t\ \mathbf{chan}) = \mathit{FV}(t)$;
$\mathit{NA}(t\ \mathtt{com}\ b) = \mathit{NA}(t) \cup \mathit{NA}(b)$ and $\mathit{NM}(t\ \mathtt{com}\ b) = \mathit{NM}(t) \cup \mathit{NM}(b)$;
$\mathit{NA}(\{t\ \mathrm{CHAN}\}) = \mathit{NM}(\{t\ \mathrm{CHAN}\}) = \mathit{FV}(t)$;
$\mathit{NA}(b_1 \cup b_2) = \mathit{NA}(b_1) \cup \mathit{NA}(b_2)$ and $\mathit{NM}(b_1 \cup b_2) = \mathit{NM}(b_1) \cup \mathit{NM}(b_2)$.

We are now ready to define the concept "is monotonic in".

Definition 20. We say that g is monotonic in γ if $\gamma \notin \mathit{NM}(g)$; and we say that g is anti-monotonic in γ if $\gamma \notin \mathit{NA}(g)$.

Fact 21. For all types and behaviours g, it holds that $\mathit{NM}(g) \cup \mathit{NA}(g) = \mathit{FV}(g)$. (So if g is monotonic as well as anti-monotonic in γ, then $\gamma \notin \mathit{FV}(g)$.)

It does not necessarily hold that $\mathit{NM}(g)$ and $\mathit{NA}(g)$ are disjoint (we have e.g. $\alpha \in \mathit{NM}(\alpha\ \mathbf{chan}) \cap \mathit{NA}(\alpha\ \mathbf{chan})$). Now we can prove Lemma 19:

Proof. Induction on g, where there are two typical cases:

g is a variable: The claims follow from the fact that if g is anti-monotonic in all $\gamma \in \mathit{Dom}(S)$, then $g \notin \mathit{Dom}(S)$.

g is a function type $t_1 \to^b t_2$: First consider the sub-case where g is monotonic in all $\gamma \in \mathit{Dom}(S)$ and where S is increasing wrt. C. Then $\gamma \in \mathit{Dom}(S)$ gives $\gamma \notin \mathit{NM}(t_1 \to^b t_2)$, and we infer that $\gamma \notin \mathit{NA}(t_1)$, $\gamma \notin \mathit{NM}(b)$, and $\gamma \notin \mathit{NM}(t_2)$, so that t_1 is anti-monotonic in γ whereas t_2 and b are monotonic in γ. We can thus apply the induction hypothesis to infer that S decreases t_1 wrt. C and that S increases t_2 as well as b wrt. C. But then it is straightforward that S increases g wrt. C.

The other sub-cases are similar. □

5.1 Termination and Soundness of $\mathcal{R}$

Lemma 22. The algorithm $\mathcal{R}$ always terminates successfully. If $\mathcal{R}(C, t, b, A) = (C', t', b')$ where C is atomic and t is simple then also C' is atomic and t' is simple.

Proof. Termination is ensured since each rewriting step either decreases the number of constraints, or (as is the case for (cycle)) decreases the number of variables without increasing the number of constraints. Each rewriting step trivially preserves atomicity and simplicity. □

Turning to soundness, we first prove an auxiliary result about the rewriting relation:

Lemma 23. Suppose $A \vdash (C, t, b) \longrightarrow (C', t', b')$. Then there exists S such that $C' \vdash S\,C$, $t' = S\,t$, $b' = S\,b$, and $A = S\,A$.

Proof. For (redund) we can use $S = \mathrm{Id}$ and the claim follows from Fact 16. For (cycle) the claim is trivial; and for (shrink) and (boost) the claim follows from the fact that with $(\gamma_1 \subseteq \gamma_2)$ the "discarded" constraint it holds that $(S\,\gamma_1 \subseteq S\,\gamma_2)$ is an instance of reflexivity. □

Using Lemma 2 and Lemma 3 we then get:

Corollary 24. Suppose $A \vdash (C, t, b) \longrightarrow (C', t', b')$.
If $C, A \vdash e : t \,\&\, b$ then $C', A \vdash e : t' \,\&\, b'$.

By repeated application of this corollary we get the desired result:

Lemma 25. Suppose that $\mathcal{R}(C, t, b, A) = (C', t', b')$.
If $C, A \vdash e : t \,\&\, b$ then $C', A \vdash e : t' \,\&\, b'$.

5.2 Results concerning Confluence and Determinism

No new paths are introduced in the graph by applying $\longrightarrow$:

Lemma 26. Suppose $A \vdash (C', t', b') \longrightarrow (C'', t'', b'')$ and let $\gamma_1, \gamma_2 \in FV(C'')$. Then $C' \vdash \gamma_1 \Leftarrow^* \gamma_2$ holds iff $C'' \vdash \gamma_1 \Leftarrow^* \gamma_2$ holds.

Proof. See Appendix A.

Observation 27. Suppose $A \vdash (C, t, b) \longrightarrow (C', t', b')$ where the rule (cycle) is not applicable from the configuration (C, t, b). Then the rule (cycle) is not applicable from the configuration (C', t', b') either.

This suggests that an implementation could begin by collapsing all cycles once and for all, without having to worry about cycles again. On the other hand, it is not possible to perform transitive reduction in a separate phase as (redund) may become enabled after applying (shrink) or (boost): as an example consider the situation where C contains the constraints

$$\gamma_0 \subseteq \gamma, \ \gamma \subseteq \gamma_1,$$
$$\gamma_0 \subseteq \gamma', \ \gamma' \subseteq \gamma_1$$

and (redund) is not applicable. By applying (shrink) with the substitution $[\gamma \mapsto \gamma_0]$ we end up with the constraints

$$\gamma_0 \subseteq \gamma_1, \ \gamma_0 \subseteq \gamma', \ \gamma' \subseteq \gamma_1$$

of which the former can be eliminated by (redund).

Concerning confluency, one would like to show a "diamond property" but this cannot be done in the presence of cycles in the constraint set (especially if these contain multiple elements of $FV(A)$): as an example consider the constraints

$$\gamma_0 \subseteq \gamma, \ \gamma_0 \subseteq \gamma', \ \gamma \subseteq \gamma', \ \gamma' \subseteq \gamma$$

with $\gamma, \gamma' \in FV(A)$; here we can apply (redund) to eliminate either the first or the second constraint but then we are stuck as (cycle) is not applicable and therefore we cannot complete the diamond. As another example, consider the case where we have a cycle containing γ_0, γ_1 and γ_2 with $\gamma_0, \gamma_1 \in FV(A)$. Then we can apply (cycle) to map γ_2 into either γ_0 or γ_1 but then we are stuck and the graphs will be different (due to the arrows to or from γ_2) unless we devise some notion of graph equivalence.

On the other hand, we have the following result:

Proposition 28. Suppose that

$$A \vdash (C, t, b) \longrightarrow (C_1, t_1, b_1) \text{ and}$$
$$A \vdash (C, t, b) \longrightarrow (C_2, t_2, b_2)$$

where C is *acyclic* as well as atomic. Then there exists (C_1', t_1', b_1') and (C_2', t_2', b_2'), which are equal up to renaming, such that

$$A \vdash (C_1, t_1, b_1) \longrightarrow^{\leq 1} (C_1', t_1', b_1') \text{ and}$$
$$A \vdash (C_2, t_2, b_2) \longrightarrow^{\leq 1} (C_2', t_2', b_2')$$

(here $\longrightarrow^{\leq 1}$ denotes that either $\longrightarrow$ or $=$ holds).

Proof. See Appendix A.

5.3 Extensions of $\mathcal{R}$

In addition to the rewritings presented in Figure 8 one might introduce several other rules, some of which are listed in Figure 9.

The rule (lub-exists) allows us to dispense with constraints which state that some behaviours have an upper bound, as long as this upper bound does not occur elsewhere. Notice that a similar rule for types would be invalid, since two types do not necessarily possess an upper bound.

The rules (shrink-chan) and (shrink-empty) extend (shrink) in that they replace a variable β by its "immediate predecessor" b' even if b' is not a variable:

(lub-exists) $A \vdash (C \dot{\cup} \{b_1 \subseteq \beta\} \dot{\cup} \cdots \dot{\cup} \{b_n \subseteq \beta\}, t, b) \longrightarrow (C, t, b)$
provided $\beta \notin FV(C, t, b, A)$ and $\beta \notin FV(b_1, \cdots, b_n)$

(shrink-chan) $A \vdash (C \dot{\cup} \{\{t' \text{ CHAN}\} \subseteq \beta\}, t, b) \longrightarrow (S\,C, S\,t, S\,b)$
where $S = [\beta \mapsto \{t' \text{ CHAN}\}]$
provided $\beta \notin FV(RHS(C), A, t')$ and
provided t, b, and each element in $LHS(C)$ is monotonic in β and
provided that $S\,t$ is simple

(shrink-empty) $A \vdash (C, t, b) \longrightarrow (C', S\,t, S\,b)$
with $C' = \{(g_1 \subseteq g_2) \in S\,C \mid g_1 \neq \emptyset\}$
where $S = [\beta \mapsto \emptyset]$ with $\beta \in FV(C, t, b)$
provided $\beta \notin FV(RHS(C), A)$ and
provided t, b, and each element in $LHS(C)$ is monotonic in β and
provided that $S\,t$ is simple

Fig. 9. Additional simplifications.

for (shrink-chan) b' is a behaviour $\{t' \text{ CHAN}\}$ (where an "occur check" has to be performed), and for (shrink-empty) it is $\emptyset$ (which is a "trivial predecessor").

For the rules (shrink-chan) and (shrink-empty), we must preserve the simplicity of the type and we have explicit clauses for ensuring this; we also must preserve atomicity of the constraint set and therefore rule (shrink-empty) discards all constraints with $\emptyset$ on the left hand side.

Termination and soundness

Adding the rules in Figure 9 preserves termination and soundness, as it is easy to see that Lemma 22 and Lemma 23 still hold: for (shrink-chan) we employ the side condition $\beta \notin FV(t')$; for (shrink-empty) we employ that $\emptyset$ is the least behaviour; for (lub-exists) we use $S = [\beta \mapsto b_1 \cup \cdots \cup b_n]$ and then employ that $\cup$ is an upper bound operator, together with the side condition $\beta \notin FV(b_1, \cdots, b_n)$.

Notice, however, that it would no longer hold in general that the substitution S used in Lemma 23 is simple; so if we were to extend $\mathcal{R}$ with the rules in Figure 9 we would lose the property that the inference tree "constructed by" the inference algorithm is "simple".

6 Experimental Results

In [11] we considered the program

```
fn f => let id = fn y =>
                    (if true
```

```
                        then f
                        else fn x =>
                             (sync (send (channel (), y));
                             x));
                       y
        in id id
```

which demonstrated the power of our inference system relative to some other approaches. Analysing this program with $\mathcal{R}$ as described in Figure 8, our prototype implementation produces 4 type constraints and 7 behaviour constraints. The resulting simple type is

$$((\alpha_{44} \stackrel{\beta_{20}}{\rightarrow} \alpha_{45}) \stackrel{\beta_{34}}{\rightarrow} (\alpha_{54} \stackrel{\beta_{31}}{\rightarrow} \alpha_{54}))$$

the resulting behaviour is $\emptyset$ and the resulting type constraints are

$$\alpha_{44} \subseteq \alpha_{45},\ \alpha_{54} \subseteq \alpha_{49},\ \alpha_{58} \subseteq \alpha_{54},\ \alpha_{54} \subseteq \alpha_{59}$$

and the resulting behaviour constraints are

$$\begin{aligned}
&\beta_{20} \subseteq \beta_{23},\ \{\alpha_7\,\mathrm{CHAN}\} \subseteq \beta_{23},\\
&\beta_{20} \subseteq \beta_{25},\ \{(\alpha_{58} \stackrel{\beta_{33}}{\rightarrow} \alpha_{59})\,\mathrm{CHAN}\} \subseteq \beta_{25},\\
&\beta_{20} \subseteq \beta_{27},\ \{\alpha_{49}\,\mathrm{CHAN}\} \subseteq \beta_{27},\\
&\beta_{31} \subseteq \beta_{33}.
\end{aligned}$$

Remark. Analysing the program above with a version of $\mathcal{R}$ which uses only (redund) and (cycle) but not (shrink) or (boost), our implementation produces 71 type constraints and 88 behaviour constraints. This shows that it is essential to use a non-trivial version of $\mathcal{R}$ in order to get readable output. Alternatively, (shrink) and (boost) could be applied only in the top-level call to $\mathcal{W}$; then the implementation produces a result isomorphic to the one above (4 type constraints and 7 behaviour constraints), but is much slower (due to the need to carry around a large set of constraints). □

Additional simplifications. This is not quite as informative as we might wish, which suggests that $\mathcal{R}$ should be extended with the rules in Figure 9: by applying (lub-exists) repeatedly we can eliminate 6 of the behaviour constraints such that the remaining type and behaviour constraints are

$$\alpha_{44} \subseteq \alpha_{45},\ \alpha_{54} \subseteq \alpha_{49},\ \alpha_{58} \subseteq \alpha_{54},\ \alpha_{54} \subseteq \alpha_{59},\ \beta_{31} \subseteq \beta_{33}$$

and this makes it possible to shrink β_{33}, α_{49}, and α_{59} and to boost α_{58} such that we end up with one constraint only:

$$\begin{aligned}
&((\alpha_{44} \stackrel{\beta_{20}}{\rightarrow} \alpha_{45}) \stackrel{\beta_{34}}{\rightarrow} (\alpha_{54} \stackrel{\beta_{31}}{\rightarrow} \alpha_{54}))\\
&\text{where } \alpha_{44} \subseteq \alpha_{45}
\end{aligned}$$

This is small enough to be manageable and is actually more precise than the type

$$(\alpha \rightarrow^{\beta} \alpha) \rightarrow^{\emptyset} (\alpha' \rightarrow^{\emptyset} \alpha')$$

(and no constraints) that is perhaps closer to what the programmer might have expected.

7 Syntactic Soundness of Algorithm $\mathcal{W}$

A main technical property of algorithm $\mathcal{W}$ is that it always terminates:

Lemma 29. $\mathcal{W}(A, e)$ and $\mathcal{W}'(A, e)$ always terminate (possibly with failure). If A is simple then the following holds:

- if $\mathcal{W}(A, e) = (S, t, b, C)$ then t and S are simple and C is atomic;
- if $\mathcal{W}'(A, e) = (S, t, b, C)$ then t and S as well as C are simple;
- all subcalls to $\mathcal{W}$ and $\mathcal{W}'$ are made with a simple environment.

Proof. This result is proved by structural induction in e where for constants we employ Fact 8; to lift the results from $\mathcal{W}'$ to $\mathcal{W}$ we employ Lemma 13 and Lemma 22; and throughout we employ Fact 5. □

As a final preparation for establishing soundness of algorithm $\mathcal{W}$ we establish a result about our formula for generalisation.

Lemma 30. Let C be well-formed; then $C, A \vdash e : t \,\&\, b$ holds if and only if $C, A \vdash e : \mathit{GEN}(A, b)(C, t) \,\&\, b$.

Proof. See Appendix A.

Theorem 31. If $\mathcal{W}(A, e) = (S, t, b, C)$ with A simple then $C, S\,A \vdash e : t \,\&\, b$.

Proof. The result is shown by induction in e with a similar result for $\mathcal{W}'$. See Appendix A for the details.

Note that if the expression e only mentions identifiers in the domain of A (as when e is closed), and that if e only mentions constants for which TypeOf is defined, then the only possible form for failure is due to $\mathcal{F}$. We may hope (as a weak completeness property) that then also ML typing would have failed.

On the other hand, suppose that $\mathcal{W}$ succeeds on some program e; that is we have (with $[\,]$ the empty environment)

$$\mathcal{W}([\,], e) = (S, t, b, C)$$

which by Theorem 31 and Lemma 29 implies that

$$C, [\,] \vdash e : t \,\&\, b \text{ with } C \text{ atomic.}$$

We then have:

- **Semantic Soundness.** It is possible[4] to apply the subject reduction result [1, Theorem 41] which (loosely speaking) says:

  all configurations which arise during execution of e can be typed.

- **Conservative extension.** Let S' be a substitution which unifies all type variables and let C^b be the behaviour constraints of C; from Lemma 2 and Lemma 3 we get $S'\, C^b, [\,] \vdash e\, :\, S'\, t \,\&\, S'\, b$ so [11, Theorem 21] (loosely speaking) tells us that if e is a sequential ML-program then

  e can be assigned a type using the ML type system.

8 Solvability of the Constraints Generated

Typability of an expression e might be taken to mean

$$\exists t, b : \emptyset, [\,] \vdash e\, :\, t \,\&\, b$$

and to check for typability it is natural to perform a call $\mathcal{W}([\,], e)$ and to determine whether or not the call

$$\mathcal{W}([\,], e) \text{ terminates successfully} \qquad (1)$$

rather than with failure (recalling that by Lemma 29 the call $\mathcal{W}([\,], e)$ must terminate). As completeness issues are outside the scope of this paper we shall only ask whether (1) is a *sufficient* condition for typability.

If $\mathcal{W}([\,], e)$ terminates successfully producing (S, t, b, C) it follows from the Soundness Theorem 31 together with Lemma 29 that $C, [\,] \vdash e\, :\, t \,\&\, b$ with C atomic; but to achieve typability we must achieve an empty constraint set. Due to the substitution and entailment lemmas (2 and 3) it will suffice to find a substitution S' such that $\emptyset \vdash S'\, C$ for then we have a judgement of the desired form: $\emptyset, [\,] \vdash e\, :\, S'\, t \,\&\, S'\, b$. Our goal thus is:

$$\text{Given atomic } C\text{; find } S' \text{ such that } \emptyset \vdash S'\, C. \qquad (2)$$

This is a kind of simplification process and as this paper does not address completeness issues we shall not be concerned with principality (that $\emptyset \vdash S''\, C$ implies that S'' can be written as $S'''\, S'$).

We shall construct the S' mentioned in (2) by the formula $S' = S'_3\, S'_2\, S'_1$ where S'_1 solves the type constraints of form $(\alpha_1 \subseteq \alpha_2)$, where S'_2 solves the behaviour constraints of form $(\beta_1 \subseteq \beta_2)$, and S'_3 solves the behaviour constraints of form $(\{t \text{ CHAN}\} \subseteq \beta_2)$. By atomicity of C this takes care of all constraints of C (provided we demand that S'_1 and S'_2 preserve atomicity).

A crude approach to defining S'_1 is to select a unique type variable α_* and let S'_1 map all type variables of $FV(C)$ to α_*. Clearly this solves all type constraints of C in the sense that all type constraints of $S'_1\, C$ are of the form $(\alpha_* \subseteq \alpha_*)$ and

[4] As C is well-formed and $[\,]$ is a "channel environment", and as we can assume by [11, Lemma 16] that the inference is "normalised".

hence instances of the axiom of reflexivity. (A less crude approach would be to consider each $(\alpha_1 \subseteq \alpha_2)$ of C in turn and perform a most general unification of α_1 with α_2.)

A crude approach to defining S_2' is to select a unique behaviour variable β_* and to let S_2' map all behaviour variables of $FV(S_1'\ C)$ to β_*. Clearly this solves all behaviour constraints in C that were of the form $(\beta_1 \subseteq \beta_2)$ since in $S_2'\ S_1'\ C$ they appear as $(\beta_* \subseteq \beta_*)$. (A less crude approach would be to adopt the ideas of canonical solution from [17] but this is best combined with the construction of S_3' below.)

The remaining non-trivial constraints in $S_2'\ S_1'\ C$ are of form $\{t_i \text{ CHAN}\} \subseteq \beta_*$ with $i \in \{1 \ldots n\}$ and $n \geq 0$. If β_* does not occur in any of $t_1, \cdots, t_n$ we could follow [17] and define S_3' by letting it map β_* to $\beta_* \cup \{t_1 \text{ CHAN}\} \cup \cdots \cup \{t_n \text{ CHAN}\}$ and perhaps even dispense with the "$\beta_* \cup$". This situation corresponds to the scenario in [17] where the type inference algorithm enforces that β_* does not occur in $t_1, \cdots, t_n$ by terminating with failure if the condition is not met. Intuitively, failure to meet the condition means that the communication capabilities are used to code up recursion in "much the same way" that the Y combinator can be encoded in the λ-calculus with recursive types (or in the untyped λ-calculus). However, we shall take the view that it is too demanding to always forbid such use of the communication capabilities and we thus depart from [17].

It is important to note that a simple solution could be found if we *changed the representation* of constraints to record their free variables only: then a constraint $(\{t_i \text{ CHAN}\} \subseteq \beta_*)$ is replaced by $\{(\gamma \subseteq \beta_*) \mid \gamma \in FV(t_i)\}$. Even if β_* occurs in one of $t_1, \cdots, t_n$ one could still let S_3' map β_* to $\beta_* \cup \gamma_1 \cup \cdots \cup \gamma_m$ where $\{\gamma_1, \cdots, \gamma_m\} = FV(t_1, \cdots, t_n)$ and we could obtain a solution due to the axioms for $\cup$ in Figure 2. In many ways this would seem a sensible solution in that the actual structure of the type is of only minor importance.

Motivated by the goals of [10] of eventually incorporating more causal information also for behaviours, we shall favour another solution. This involves adding a new behaviour of form $REC\beta.b$. Formally we extend the syntax as in

$$b ::= \cdots \mid REC\beta.b$$

and extend the axiomatisation of Figure 2 with the axiom scheme

$$C \vdash (REC\beta.b) \equiv b[(REC\beta.b)/\beta]$$

With this new form of behaviour we can define S_3' by mapping β_* to

$$REC\beta_*.(\beta_* \cup \{t_1 \text{ CHAN}\} \cup \cdots \cup \{t_n \text{ CHAN}\}).$$

We then have $\emptyset \vdash S_3'\ S_2'\ S_1'\ C$ as desired.

9 Conclusion

We have developed an inference algorithm for an annotated type and effect system that integrates polymorphism, subtyping and effects [11]. Although the development was performed for a fragment of Concurrent ML we believe it equally applicable to Standard ML with references. The algorithm $\mathcal{W}$ involves the syntactically defined $\mathcal{W}'$ and the algorithm $\mathcal{F}$ for obtaining constraints that are well-formed; an optional component, algorithm $\mathcal{R}$ for reducing the size of constraint sets, is pragmatically very useful in reducing constraint sets to a manageable size, as is illustrated in our prototype implementation. In this paper we showed the syntactic soundness of these algorithms whereas the issue of completeness as well as of complexity is still open.

Acknowledgement. This work has been supported in part by the *DART* project (Danish Natural Science Research Council) and the *LOMAPS* project (ESPRIT BRA project 8130); it represents joint work among the authors. We would like to thank the anonymous referees for their thought-provoking comments on the preliminary version of this work.

References

1. T. Amtoft, F. Nielson, H.R. Nielson, J. Ammann: Polymorphic subtypes for effect analysis: the dynamic semantics. This volume of SLNCS, 1997.
2. Y.-C. Fuh and P. Mishra: Polymorphic subtype inference: closing the theory-practice gap. In *Proc. TAPSOFT '89*. SLNCS 352, 1989.
3. Y.-C. Fuh and P. Mishra: Type inference with subtypes. *Theoretical Computer Science*, 73, 1990.
4. F. Henglein and C. Mossin: Polymorphic binding-time analysis. In *Proc. ESOP '94*, pages 287–301. SLNCS 788, 1994.
5. M.P. Jones: A theory of qualified types. In *Proc. ESOP '92*, pages 287–306. SLNCS 582, 1992.
6. P. Jouvelot and D.K. Gifford: Algebraic reconstruction of types and effects. In *Proc. POPL'91*, pages 303–310. ACM Press, 1991.
7. R. Milner: A theory of type polymorphism in programming. *Journal of Computer Systems*, 17:348–375, 1978.
8. J.C. Mitchell: Type inference with simple subtypes. *Journal of Functional Programming*, 1(3), 1991.
9. F. Nielson and H.R. Nielson: Constraints for polymorphic behaviours for Concurrent ML. In *Proc. CCL'94*. SLNCS 845, 1994.
10. H.R. Nielson and F. Nielson: Higher-order concurrent programs with finite communication topology. In *Proc. POPL'94*, pages 84–97. ACM Press, 1994.
11. H.R. Nielson, F. Nielson, T. Amtoft: Polymorphic subtypes for effect analysis: the static semantics. This volume of SLNCS, 1997.
12. P. Panangaden and J.H. Reppy: The essence of Concurrent ML. In *ML with Concurrency: Design, Analysis, Implementation and Application* (editor: Flemming Nielson), Springer-Verlag, 1996.
13. J.H. Siekmann: Unification theory. *J. Symbolic Computation*, 7:207–274, 1989.
14. G.S. Smith: Polymorphic type inference for languages with overloading and subtyping. Ph.D thesis from Cornell, 1991.
15. G.S. Smith: Polymorphic inference with overloading and subtyping. In SLNCS 668, *Proc. TAPSOFT '93*, 1993. Also see: Principal type schemes for functional programs with overloading and subtyping: *Science of Computer Programming* 23, pp. 197-226, 1994.

16. J.P. Talpin and P. Jouvelot: Polymorphic type, region and effect inference. *Journal of Functional Programming*, 2(3), pages 245–271, 1992.
17. J.P. Talpin and P. Jouvelot: The type and effect discipline. *Information and Computation*, 111, 1994.
18. Y.-M. Tang: Control flow analysis by effect systems and abstract interpretation. PhD thesis, Ecoles des Mines de Paris, 1994.
19. M. Tofte. Type inference for polymorphic references. *Information and Computation*, 89:1–34, 1990.
20. M. Tofte and L. Birkedal: Region-annotated types and type schemes, 1996. Submitted for publication.
21. A.K. Wright: Typing references by effect inference. In *Proc. ESOP '92*, pages 473–491. SLNCS 582, 1992.

A Proofs of Main Results

Algorithm $\mathcal{R}$

Lemma 26 Suppose $A \vdash (C', t', b') \longrightarrow (C'', t'', b'')$ and let $\gamma_1, \gamma_2 \in FV(C'')$. Then $C' \vdash \gamma_1 \Leftarrow^* \gamma_2$ holds iff $C'' \vdash \gamma_1 \Leftarrow^* \gamma_2$ holds.

Proof. (We use the terminology from the relevant clauses in Figure 8, which does not conflict with the one used in the formulation of the lemma). For (redund) this is a straightforward consequence of the assumption $C \vdash \gamma' \Leftarrow^* \gamma$. For (cycle), (shrink) and (boost) the "only if"-part follows from Fact 17: if $C' \vdash \gamma_1 \Leftarrow^* \gamma_2$ then $S\,C' \vdash S\,\gamma_1 \Leftarrow^* S\,\gamma_2$ and as $\gamma_1, \gamma_2 \notin Dom(S)$ this amounts to $S\,C' \vdash \gamma_1 \Leftarrow^* \gamma_2$ which is clearly equivalent to $C'' \vdash \gamma_1 \Leftarrow^* \gamma_2$.

We are left with proving the "if"-part for (cycle), (shrink) and (boost); to do so it suffices to show that

$$(\gamma_1' \subseteq \gamma_2') \in C'' \text{ implies } C' \vdash \gamma_1' \Leftarrow^* \gamma_2'.$$

As $C'' = S\,C$ we can assume that there exists $(\gamma_1 \subseteq \gamma_2) \in C$ such that $\gamma_1' = S\,\gamma_1$ and $\gamma_2' = S\,\gamma_2$; then (since $C \subseteq C'$) our task can be accomplished by showing that

$$C' \vdash S\,\gamma_1 \Leftarrow^* \gamma_1 \text{ and } C' \vdash \gamma_2 \Leftarrow^* S\,\gamma_2.$$

This is trivial except if $\gamma_1 = \gamma$ or $\gamma_2 = \gamma$. The former is impossible in the case (boost) (as *LHS*(C) is anti-monotonic in γ) and otherwise the claim follows from the assumptions; the latter is impossible in the case (shrink) (as $\gamma \notin RHS(C)$) and otherwise the claim follows from the assumptions. □

Proposition 28 Suppose that

$$A \vdash (C, t, b) \longrightarrow (C_1, t_1, b_1) \text{ and}$$
$$A \vdash (C, t, b) \longrightarrow (C_2, t_2, b_2)$$

where C is *acyclic* as well as atomic. Then there exists (C_1', t_1', b_1') and (C_2', t_2', b_2'), which are equal up to renaming, such that

$$A \vdash (C_1, t_1, b_1) \longrightarrow^{\leq 1} (C_1', t_1', b_1') \text{ and}$$
$$A \vdash (C_2, t_2, b_2) \longrightarrow^{\leq 1} (C_2', t_2', b_2').$$

Proof. As (cycle) is not applicable, each of the two rewriting steps in the assumption can be of three kinds yielding six different combinations:

(redund) and (redund) eliminating $(\gamma_1' \subseteq \gamma_1)$ and $(\gamma_2' \subseteq \gamma_2)$ where we can assume that either $\gamma_1' \neq \gamma_2'$ or $\gamma_1 \neq \gamma_2$ as otherwise the claim is trivial. The situation thus is

$$A \vdash (C \dot\cup \{\gamma_1' \subseteq \gamma_1\} \dot\cup \{\gamma_2' \subseteq \gamma_2\}, t, b) \longrightarrow (C \dot\cup \{\gamma_2' \subseteq \gamma_2\}, t, b)$$
$$A \vdash (C \dot\cup \{\gamma_1' \subseteq \gamma_1\} \dot\cup \{\gamma_2' \subseteq \gamma_2\}, t, b) \longrightarrow (C \dot\cup \{\gamma_1' \subseteq \gamma_1\}, t, b)$$

where

$$C \dot\cup \{\gamma_2' \subseteq \gamma_2\} \vdash \gamma_1' \Leftarrow^* \gamma_1 \text{ and} \tag{1}$$
$$C \dot\cup \{\gamma_1' \subseteq \gamma_1\} \vdash \gamma_2' \Leftarrow^* \gamma_2. \tag{2}$$

It will suffice to show that

$$\text{either } C \vdash \gamma_1' \Leftarrow^* \gamma_1 \text{ or } C \vdash \gamma_2' \Leftarrow^* \gamma_2 \tag{3}$$

for if e.g. $C \vdash \gamma_1' \Leftarrow^* \gamma_1$ holds then by (2) also $C \vdash \gamma_2' \Leftarrow^* \gamma_2$ holds and we can apply (redund) twice to complete the diamond.

For the sake of arriving at a contradiction we now assume that (3) does not hold. Using (1) and (2) we see that the situation is that

$$C \vdash \gamma_1' \Leftarrow^* \gamma_2' \text{ and } C \vdash \gamma_2 \Leftarrow^* \gamma_1 \text{ and}$$
$$C \vdash \gamma_2' \Leftarrow^* \gamma_1' \text{ and } C \vdash \gamma_1 \Leftarrow^* \gamma_2$$

and this conflicts with the assumption about the graph being cycle-free.

(redund) and (shrink) eliminating $(\gamma_1' \subseteq \gamma_1)$ and shrinking γ_2 into γ_2' (with $\gamma_2' \neq \gamma_2$). First notice that it cannot be the case that $(\gamma_1' \subseteq \gamma_1) = (\gamma_2' \subseteq \gamma_2)$, for then (with C the remaining constraints) we would have $C \vdash \gamma_1' \Leftarrow^* \gamma_1$ as well as $\gamma_2 \notin \mathit{RHS}(C)$. The situation thus is

$$A \vdash (C \dot\cup \{\gamma_1' \subseteq \gamma_1\} \dot\cup \{\gamma_2' \subseteq \gamma_2\}, t, b) \longrightarrow (C \dot\cup \{\gamma_2' \subseteq \gamma_2\}, t, b)$$
$$A \vdash (C \dot\cup \{\gamma_1' \subseteq \gamma_1\} \dot\cup \{\gamma_2' \subseteq \gamma_2\}, t, b) \longrightarrow (S\,C \cup \{S\,\gamma_1' \subseteq S\,\gamma_1\}, S\,t, S\,b)$$

where $S = [\gamma_2 \mapsto \gamma_2']$ and where

$$C \cup \{\gamma_2' \subseteq \gamma_2\} \vdash \gamma_1' \Leftarrow^* \gamma_1 \text{ and}$$
$$\gamma_2 \notin \mathit{FV}(\mathit{RHS}(C), A) \text{ and } \gamma_2 \neq \gamma_1 \text{ and } t, b, \mathit{LHS}(C) \text{ is monotonic in } \gamma_2.$$

Applying Fact 17 we get $S\,C \vdash S\,\gamma_1' \Leftarrow^* S\,\gamma_1$ which shows that

$$A \vdash (S\,C \cup \{S\,\gamma_1' \subseteq S\,\gamma_1\}, S\,t, S\,b) \longrightarrow^{\leq 1} (S\,C, S\,t, S\,b)$$

(if $(S\,\gamma_1' \subseteq S\,\gamma_1) \in S\,C$ we have "=" otherwise "$\longrightarrow$"); it is also easy to see that the conditions are fulfilled for applying (shrink) to get

$$A \vdash (C \dot\cup \{\gamma_2' \subseteq \gamma_2\}, t, b) \longrightarrow (S\,C, S\,t, S\,b)$$

thus completing the diamond.

(redund) and (boost) eliminating $(\gamma_1 \subseteq \gamma_1')$ and boosting γ_2 into γ_2' (with $\gamma_2' \neq \gamma_2$). First notice that it cannot be the case that $(\gamma_1 \subseteq \gamma_1') = (\gamma_2 \subseteq \gamma_2')$, for then (with C the remaining constraints) we would have $C \vdash \gamma_1 \Leftarrow^* \gamma_1'$ showing that $\gamma_1 \in LHS(C)$, whereas a side condition for (boost) is that each element in $LHS(C)$ is anti-monotonic in γ_2.

Now we can proceed as in the case (redund),(shrink).

(shrink) and (shrink) shrinking γ_1 into γ_1' and shrinking γ_2 into γ_2' where we can assume that either $\gamma_1' \neq \gamma_2'$ or $\gamma_1 \neq \gamma_2$ as otherwise the claim is trivial. The situation thus is

$$A \vdash (C \dot{\cup} \{\gamma_1' \subseteq \gamma_1\} \dot{\cup} \{\gamma_2' \subseteq \gamma_2\}, t, b) \longrightarrow (S_1\, C \cup \{S_1\, \gamma_2' \subseteq S_1\, \gamma_2\}, S_1\, t, S_1\, b)$$
$$A \vdash (C \dot{\cup} \{\gamma_1' \subseteq \gamma_1\} \dot{\cup} \{\gamma_2' \subseteq \gamma_2\}, t, b) \longrightarrow (S_2\, C \cup \{S_2\, \gamma_1' \subseteq S_2\, \gamma_1\}, S_2\, t, S_2\, b)$$

where $S_1 = [\gamma_1 \mapsto \gamma_1']$ and $S_2 = [\gamma_2 \mapsto \gamma_2']$. Due to the side conditions for (shrink) we have $\gamma_1 \neq \gamma_2$ and $\gamma_1, \gamma_2 \notin RHS(C)$ implying $\gamma_1, \gamma_2 \notin RHS(S_1\, C)$ and $\gamma_1, \gamma_2 \notin RHS(S_2\, C)$, thus the "$\cup$" on the right hand sides is really "$\dot{\cup}$". Our goal then is to find S_1' and S_2' such that

$$S_2'\, S_1 = S_1'\, S_2 \text{ and}$$
$$A \vdash (S_1\, C \dot{\cup} \{S_1\, \gamma_2' \subseteq \gamma_2\}, S_1\, t, S_1\, b) \longrightarrow (S_2'\, S_1\, C, S_2'\, S_1\, t, S_2'\, S_1\, b) \text{ and}$$
$$A \vdash (S_2\, C \dot{\cup} \{S_2\, \gamma_1' \subseteq \gamma_1\}, S_2\, t, S_2\, b) \longrightarrow (S_1'\, S_2\, C, S_1'\, S_2\, t, S_1'\, S_2\, b).$$

We naturally define $S_1' = [\gamma_1 \mapsto S_2\, \gamma_1']$ and $S_2' = [\gamma_2 \mapsto S_1\, \gamma_2']$ with the purpose of using (shrink), and our proof obligations are:

$$S_2'\, S_1 = S_1'\, S_2; \tag{4}$$
$$S_2\, \gamma_1' \neq \gamma_1 \text{ and } S_1\, \gamma_2' \neq \gamma_2; \tag{5}$$
$$S_2\, t, S_2\, b, LHS(S_2\, C) \text{ is monotonic in } \gamma_1; \tag{6}$$
$$S_1\, t, S_1\, b, LHS(S_1\, C) \text{ is monotonic in } \gamma_2. \tag{7}$$

Here (4) and (5) amounts to proving that

$$S_2'\, \gamma_1' = S_2\, \gamma_1' \text{ and } S_1\, \gamma_2' = S_1'\, \gamma_2' \text{ and } S_2\, \gamma_1' \neq \gamma_1 \text{ and } S_1\, \gamma_2' \neq \gamma_2 \tag{8}$$

which is trivial if $\gamma_1' \neq \gamma_2$ and $\gamma_2' \neq \gamma_1$. If e.g. $\gamma_1' = \gamma_2$ then we from our assumption about the graph being cycle-free infer that $\gamma_2' \neq \gamma_1$ from which (8) easily follows.

The claims (6) and (7) are easy consequences of the fact that t, b and $LHS(C)$ are monotonic in γ_1 as well as in γ_2: for then we for instance have $\{\gamma_1, \gamma_2\} \cap NM(t) = \emptyset$ and hence $NM(S_1\, t) = NM(S_2\, t) = NM(t)$.

(boost) and (boost) where we proceed, *mutatis mutandis*, as in the case (shrink),(shrink).

(shrink) and (boost) shrinking γ_1 into γ_1' and boosting γ_2 into γ_2'. Let $S_1 = [\gamma_1 \mapsto \gamma_1']$ and $S_2 = [\gamma_2 \mapsto \gamma_2']$. Four cases:

$\underline{\gamma_1 = \gamma_2}$ (to be denoted γ). Then our assumption about the graph being cycle-free tells us that $\gamma_1' \neq \gamma_2'$, and the situation is

$$A \vdash (C \dot{\cup} \{\gamma_1' \subseteq \gamma\} \dot{\cup} \{\gamma \subseteq \gamma_2'\}, t, b) \longrightarrow (S_1\, C \cup \{\gamma_1' \subseteq \gamma_2'\}, S_1\, t, S_1\, b) \tag{9}$$
$$A \vdash (C \dot{\cup} \{\gamma_1' \subseteq \gamma\} \dot{\cup} \{\gamma \subseteq \gamma_2'\}, t, b) \longrightarrow (S_2\, C \cup \{\gamma_1' \subseteq \gamma_2'\}, S_2\, t, S_2\, b) \tag{10}$$

where (according to the side conditions for (shrink) and (boost)) it holds that $\gamma \notin RHS(C)$ and that t, b and each element in $LHS(C)$ is monotonic as well as anti-monotonic in γ. By Fact 21 and using that C is well-formed we infer that $\gamma \notin FV(C, t, b)$, thus the right hand sides of (9) and (10) are identical.

$\underline{\gamma_1 = \gamma_2'}$. By the side condition for (shrink) we then have $\gamma_2 = \gamma_1'$. The situation thus is

$$A \vdash (C \dot{\cup} \{\gamma_2 \subseteq \gamma_1\}, t, b) \longrightarrow (S_1\, C, S_1\, t, S_1\, b)$$
$$A \vdash (C \dot{\cup} \{\gamma_2 \subseteq \gamma_1\}, t, b) \longrightarrow (S_2\, C, S_2\, t, S_2\, b)$$

where the right hand sides are equal modulo renaming.

$\underline{\gamma_2 = \gamma_1'}$. By the side condition for (boost) we then have $\gamma_1 = \gamma_2'$ so we can proceed as in the previous case.

$\underline{\gamma_1 \notin \{\gamma_2, \gamma_2', \gamma_1'\} \text{ and } \gamma_2 \notin \{\gamma_1, \gamma_1', \gamma_2'\}}$ will hold in the remaining case. The situation thus is

$$A \vdash (C \dot{\cup} \{\gamma_1' \subseteq \gamma_1\} \dot{\cup} \{\gamma_2 \subseteq \gamma_2'\}, t, b) \longrightarrow (S_1\, C \cup \{\gamma_2 \subseteq \gamma_2'\}, S_1\, t, S_1\, b)$$
$$A \vdash (C \dot{\cup} \{\gamma_1' \subseteq \gamma_1\} \dot{\cup} \{\gamma_2 \subseteq \gamma_2'\}, t, b) \longrightarrow (S_2\, C \cup \{\gamma_1' \subseteq \gamma_1\}, S_2\, t, S_2\, b)$$

where $\gamma_1 \notin FV(RHS(C), A)$, where t and b and each element in $LHS(C)$ is monotonic in γ_1, where $\gamma_2 \notin FV(A)$, and where t and b and each element in $LHS(C)$ is anti-monotonic in γ_2.

As $\gamma_1 \neq \gamma_2'$ it is easy to see that $\gamma_1 \notin FV(RHS(S_2\, C), A)$ and that $S_2\, t$, $S_2\, b$ and $LHS(S_2\, C)$ is monotonic in γ_1; and as $\gamma_2 \neq \gamma_1'$ it is easy to see that $S_1\, t$, $S_1\, b$ and $LHS(S_1\, C)$ is anti-monotonic in γ_2. Hence we can apply (boost) and (shrink) to get

$$A \vdash (S_1\, C \dot{\cup} \{\gamma_2 \subseteq \gamma_2'\}, S_1\, t, S_1\, b) \longrightarrow (S_2\, S_1\, C, S_2\, S_1\, t, S_2\, S_1\, b)$$
$$A \vdash (S_2\, C \dot{\cup} \{\gamma_1' \subseteq \gamma_1\}, S_2\, t, S_2\, b) \longrightarrow (S_1\, S_2\, C, S_1\, S_2\, t, S_1\, S_2\, b)$$

which is as desired since clearly $S_2\, S_1 = S_1\, S_2$. □

Algorithm $\mathcal{W}$

Lemma 30 Let C be well-formed; then $C, A \vdash e : t \,\&\, b$ holds if and only if $C, A \vdash e : GEN(A, b)(C, t) \,\&\, b$.

Proof. For "if" simply use rule (ins) with $S_0 = Id$. Next consider "only if" and write

$$\{\vec{\gamma}\} = (FV(t)^{C\updownarrow}) \setminus (FV(A,b)^{C\downarrow})$$
$$C_0 = C\,|_{\{\vec{\gamma}\}} = \{(g_1 \subseteq g_2) \in C \mid FV(g_1, g_2) \cap \{\vec{\gamma}\} = \emptyset\}$$

so that $GEN(A,b)(C,t) = \forall(\vec{\gamma} : C_0).\ t$; this is well-formed by Fact 9.

Next let R be a renaming of $\{\vec{\gamma}\}$ into fresh variables. It is immediate that $\forall(\vec{\gamma} : C_0).\ t$ is solvable from $(C \setminus C_0) \cup R\,C_0$ by some S_0; simply take $S_0 = R$. Finally note that $\{\vec{\gamma}\} \cap FV((C \setminus C_0) \cup R\,C_0) = \emptyset$ by construction of C_0 and R, and that $\{\vec{\gamma}\} \cap FV(A,b) = \emptyset$ by construction of $\{\vec{\gamma}\}$.

We then have (using Lemma 3 on the assumption) that

$$((C \setminus C_0) \cup R\,C_0) \cup C_0, A \vdash e : t \,\&\, b$$

and (gen) gives

$$(C \setminus C_0) \cup R\,C_0, A \vdash e : \forall(\vec{\gamma} : C_0).\ t \,\&\, b$$

and finally Lemma 2 gives the desired result:

$$(C \setminus C_0) \cup C_0, A \vdash e : \forall(\vec{\gamma} : C_0).\ t \,\&\, b.$$

This completes the proof. □

Theorem 31 If $\mathcal{W}(A,e) = (S,t,b,C)$ with A simple then $C, S\,A \vdash e : t \,\&\, b$.

Proof. We proceed by structural induction on e; we first prove the result for $\mathcal{W}'$ (using the notation introduced in the defining clause for $\mathcal{W}'(A,e)$) and then in a joint final case extend the result to $\mathcal{W}$. Notice that by Lemma 29 the condition for applying the induction hypothesis will always be fulfilled.

The case $e ::= c$. By Fact 8 it will be sufficient to show that

$$C, A \vdash c : t \,\&\, \emptyset \tag{11}$$

with $INST(\text{TypeOf}(c)) = (\text{Id}, t, \emptyset, C)$, as we can then use (sub) to arrive at the desired judgement

$$C, A \vdash c : \textit{Mk-simple}(t) \,\&\, \emptyset.$$

If TypeOf(c) is a type then this type equals t so (11) follows by an application of (con). Otherwise write $\text{TypeOf}(c) = \forall(\vec{\alpha_0}\vec{\beta_0} : C_0).\ t_0$ such that $t = R\,t_0$ and $C = R\,C_0$ where R maps $\vec{\alpha_0}\vec{\beta_0}$ into fresh variables $\vec{\alpha'}\vec{\beta'}$; then (11) follows from the inference

$$\frac{R\,C_0, A \vdash c : \forall(\vec{\alpha_0}\vec{\beta_0} : C_0).\ t_0 \,\&\, \emptyset}{R\,C_0, A \vdash c : R\,t_0 \,\&\, \emptyset}\ \text{(ins)}$$

where the application of (ins) is justified since $R\,C_0 \vdash R\,C_0$.

The case $e ::= x$. If $A(x)$ is a type t_0 then the claim is that

$$\emptyset, A \vdash x \ : \ t_0 \,\&\, \emptyset$$

but this follows trivially by (id).

Otherwise write $A(x) = \forall(\vec{\alpha_0}\vec{\beta_0} : C_0).\ t_0$. The claim is that

$$R\,C_0, A \vdash x \ : \ R\,t_0 \,\&\, \emptyset$$

where R maps $\vec{\alpha_0}\vec{\beta_0}$ into fresh variables $\vec{\alpha'}\vec{\beta'}$. But this follows from the inference

$$\frac{R\,C_0, A \vdash x \ : \ \forall(\vec{\alpha_0}\vec{\beta_0} : C_0).\ t_0 \,\&\, \emptyset}{R\,C_0, A \vdash x \ : \ R\,t_0 \,\&\, \emptyset}\ \text{(ins)}$$

where the application of (ins) is justified since $R\,C_0 \vdash R\,C_0$.

The case $e ::= \mathtt{fn}\ x \Rightarrow e_0$. The induction hypothesis gives

$$C_0, S_0\,(A[x : \alpha]) \vdash e_0 \ : \ t_0 \,\&\, b_0$$

and using $C = C_0 \cup \{b_0 \subseteq \beta\}$ and $S = S_0$ we get

$$C, S\,(A[x : \alpha]) \vdash e_0 \ : \ t_0 \,\&\, b_0$$

$$C, (S\,A)[x : S\,\alpha] \vdash e_0 \ : \ t_0 \,\&\, \beta$$

$$C, S\,A \vdash \mathtt{fn}\ x \Rightarrow e_0 \ : \ S\,\alpha \rightarrow^{\beta}\ t_0 \,\&\, \emptyset$$

using first Lemma 3, then (sub) and finally (abs).

The case $e ::= e_1\,e_2$. Concerning e_1 the induction hypothesis gives

$$C_1, S_1\,A \vdash e_1 \ : \ t_1 \,\&\, b_1.$$

Using Lemmas 2 and 3 and then (sub) we get

$$S_2\,C_1, S_2\,S_1\,A \vdash e_1 \ : \ S_2\,t_1 \,\&\, S_2\,b_1$$

$$C, S\,A \vdash e_1 \ : \ S_2\,t_1 \,\&\, S_2\,b_1$$

$$C, S\,A \vdash e_1 \ : \ t_2 \rightarrow^{\beta}\ \alpha \,\&\, S_2\,b_1.$$

Turning to e_2 the induction hypothesis gives

$$C_2, S_2\,S_1\,A \vdash e_2 \ : \ t_2 \,\&\, b_2$$

and using Lemma 3 we get

$$C, S\,A \vdash e_2 \ : \ t_2 \,\&\, b_2.$$

Finally we get

$$C, S\,A \vdash e_1\,e_2 \ : \ \alpha \,\&\, S_2\,b_1 \cup b_2 \cup \beta$$

which is the desired result.

The case $e ::= \texttt{let}\ x = e_1\ \texttt{in}\ e_2$. Concerning e_1 the induction hypothesis gives

$$C_1, S_1\, A \vdash e_1 \,:\, t_1 \,\&\, b_1$$

and note that by Lemma 29 it holds that C_1 is atomic and hence well-formed. Next let $ts_1 = GEN(S_1\, A, b_1)(C_1, t_1)$ so that Lemmas 30, 2 and 3 give

$$C_1, S_1\, A \vdash e_1 \,:\, ts_1 \,\&\, b_1$$

$$S_2\, C_1, S\, A \vdash e_1 \,:\, S_2\, ts_1 \,\&\, S_2\, b_1$$

$$C, S\, A \vdash e_1 \,:\, S_2\, ts_1 \,\&\, S_2\, b_1.$$

Turning to e_2 the induction hypothesis gives

$$C_2, (S_2\, S_1\, A)[x : S_2\, ts_1] \vdash e_2 \,:\, t_2 \,\&\, b_2$$

and using Lemma 3 we get

$$C, S\, A[x : S_2\, ts_1] \vdash e_2 \,:\, t_2 \,\&\, b_2$$

and hence using (let)

$$C, S\, A \vdash \texttt{let}\ x = e_1\ \texttt{in}\ e_2 \,:\, t_2 \,\&\, S_2\, b_1 \cup b_2$$

and this is the desired result.

The case $e ::= \texttt{rec}\ f\ x \Rightarrow e_0$. Concerning e_0 the induction hypothesis gives

$$C_0, (S_0\, A)[f : S_0\, \alpha_1 \rightarrow^{S_0\, \beta}\ S_0\, \alpha_2][x : S_0\, \alpha_1] \vdash e_0 \,:\, t_0 \,\&\, b_0.$$

Using Lemma 3, (sub), (abs) and (rec) we then get

$$C, (S\, A)[f : S\, \alpha_1 \rightarrow^{S\, \beta}\ S\, \alpha_2][x : S\, \alpha_1] \vdash e_0 \,:\, t_0 \,\&\, b_0$$

$$C, (S\, A)[f : S\, \alpha_1 \rightarrow^{S\, \beta}\ S\, \alpha_2][x : S\, \alpha_1] \vdash e_0 \,:\, S\, \alpha_2 \,\&\, S\, \beta$$

$$C, (S\, A)[f : S\, \alpha_1 \rightarrow^{S\, \beta}\ S\, \alpha_2] \vdash \texttt{fn}\ x \Rightarrow e_0 \,:\, S\, \alpha_1 \rightarrow^{S\, \beta}\ S\, \alpha_2 \,\&\, \emptyset$$

$$C, S\, A \vdash \texttt{rec}\ f\ x \Rightarrow e_0 \,:\, S\, \alpha_1 \rightarrow^{S\, \beta}\ S\, \alpha_2 \,\&\, \emptyset$$

which is the desired result.

The case $e ::= \texttt{if}\ e_0\ \texttt{then}\ e_1\ \texttt{else}\ e_2$. The induction hypothesis, Lemmas 2 and 3 and rule (sub) give:

$$C, S\, A \vdash e_0 \,:\, \texttt{bool} \,\&\, S_2\, S_1\, b_0$$

$$C, S\, A \vdash e_1 \,:\, \alpha \,\&\, S_2\, b_1$$

$$C, S\, A \vdash e_2 \,:\, \alpha \,\&\, b_2$$

and rule (if) then gives

$$C, S\, A \vdash \texttt{if}\ e_0\ \texttt{then}\ e_1\ \texttt{else}\ e_2 \,:\, \alpha \,\&\, S_2\, S_1\, b_0 \cup (S_2\, b_1 \cup b_2)$$

which is the desired result.

Lifting the result from $\mathcal{W}'$ to $\mathcal{W}$. We have from the above that $\mathcal{W}'(A, e) = (S_1, t_1, b_1, C_1)$ and that

$$C_1, S_1\, A \vdash e : t_1 \,\&\, b_1.$$

Concerning $\mathcal{F}$ we have

$$(S_2, C_2) = \mathcal{F}(C_1)$$

where Lemma 14 ensures that $C_2 \vdash S_2\, C_1$. Using Lemmas 2 and 3 we get

$$C_2, S_2\, S_1\, A \vdash e : S_2\, t_1 \,\&\, S_2\, b_1.$$

Concerning $\mathcal{R}$ we have

$$(C_3, t_3, b_3) = \mathcal{R}(C_2, S_2\, t_1, S_2\, b_1, S_2\, S_1\, A)$$

so by Lemma 25 we get

$$C_3, S_2\, S_1\, A \vdash e : t_3 \,\&\, b_3$$

which is the desired result. □

Implementing a Static Analyzer of Concurrent Programs: Problems and Perspectives

Régis Cridlig

Laboratoire d'Informatique de l'Ecole Normale Supérieure*
(URA CNRS 1327)

Abstract. The aim of the paper is to share the design problems we experienced when we were implementing a prototype analyzer of an asynchronous concurrent language. This new kind of static analyzer is based on previous work about operational semantics of parallel languages that can express concurrency and non-determinism of actions: it constructs abstract automata reflecting all the possible execution behaviours of programs written in languages such as Parallel Pascal [Cri95] or Concurrent ML [Cri96].
We will also present some experimental results dealing with the size of the generated automata and the precision of the analysis. For instance some well-known mutual exclusion protocols have been automatically proven correct. The analyzer has been interfaced using the HTML markup language: this allows the user to ask for computed invariants at given program points.

1 Introduction

1.1 Motivation

Abstract interpretation is aimed at producing tools that automatically produce invariant properties of computer programs. Such tools have already been demonstrated for imperative languages (Syntox [Bou92]), functional and logical ones. Besides the intrinsic technical difficulties of program analysis these tools must provide useful information to be successful. One thing is to equip a compiler with a strictness analyzer, another thing is to build a interactive system for abstract debugging.

1.2 Theory behind the implementation

Abstract interpretation methods relate an approximate (abstract) semantics of programs with a standard (concrete) one by means of a correctness condition often expressed by a Galois connection [CC77]. Early application of the abstract interpretation framework to concurrent programs includes [CC80]. In an

* Address: Ecole Normale Supérieure - 45 rue d'Ulm, 75230 Paris Cedex 05, France. Electronic mail: Regis.Cridlig@ens.fr

operational semantic framework this means that concrete transition rules for operations that change the state of the program yield abstract transition rules that are interpreted on abstract states. In the case of concurrent languages the abstract state includes not only abstract data and control but has also to deal with abstract configurations of processes. We chose different solutions for different types of languages, i.e. graphs of abstract activation blocks for Parallel Pascal and a set of processes plus a global store of abstract locations in the case of Concurrent ML, to represent abstract configurations. As program semantics we chose automata or labelled transition systems. Our implementation can also deal with Higher Dimensional Automata [Gou95] that naturally express the true concurrency of actions.

In order to ensure computability one must be able to finitely represent abstract configurations. Abstract stack frames (or activation blocks) that refer to the same continuation are good candidates to be folded together because their structure is the same (i.e. they hold the same set of variables for instance). The folding of abstract configurations holding similar processes occurs in a second stage: this ensures that the set of abstract configurations remains finite.

1.3 Pragmatics of implementation

In order to test new ideas in a prototype the choice of a suited implementation language and of relevant data structures for programming the dynamic efficient construction of an automaton should be carefully considered. A functional language such as ML appears to be well-suited because the use of *purely functional* data structures for tables (e.g. AVL trees) permits an efficient sharing of all recurrent substructures in the related states of the automaton. Another worthy possibility would be to implement configurations as evolving objects...

For the purpose of abstract debugging a sensible interface has to be built: nowadays nobody would like to program a graphical interface in non-portable low-level environments such as X11 or Windows when standards for distributed environments such as HTML and Java have appeared. Distributed programming will enable the complete separation of the interface from the static analyzer itself, thus helping in the integration of the same tool inside a compiler, an abstract debugger, a verification environment, etc.

1.4 Abstract model-checking

Semi-verification aims at verifying behavioural properties on infinite systems (where it is undecidable in general) or on large finite-state systems (where it would take too much space or time to construct all states). Abstract model checking [Kel94] [DGG94] [CIY95] offers an alternative to exploit analysis results for semi-verification purposes. In [Cri95] and [Cri96] we have proposed to check modal logic formulae expressed in the μ-calculus on the abstract automaton automatically generated by the analyzer in a way that is consistent with the standard semantics of programs. But a good model-checker was not yet adapted to our implementation.

2 Application to Parallel Pascal

We define the abstract semantics of a concurrent language we shall call Parallel Pascal, according to the abstract interpretation framework we have presented in [Cri95]. We show how the abstract automaton can be finitely generated via abstract interpretation using folding of states and appropriate widening operators. An implementation of the standard semantics (called *Iconc*) and of this abstract semantics of upper approximation (*Iabs*) has been achieved using the CAML programming language.

Parallel Pascal is an extension of a fair subset of Pascal by two instructions, **Cobegin** and **Coend**, that control the creation and termination of concurrent subprocesses in a way similar to CSP [Hoa78]. Execution of **Cobegin** terminates only when execution of all subprocesses have terminated. This idea of marrying process definition and process synchronization originates from the **parbegin** statement of [Dij68].

Parallel Pascal is a stack-based language that can run on shared-memory computers. Communication between processes uses (shared) variables, although one could add message-passing primitives rather easily. Languages similar to Parallel Pascal are quite common in the industry for process control, system applications, etc., and are also used to specify low-level protocols for mutual exclusion or for consensus.

2.1 Concrete syntax

The syntax of programs, functions and procedures is standard [WJ78]. To simplify the semantic treatment, we will only consider call-by-value parameters in the following, while types will be restricted to basic types such as integers, strings, booleans. Here is the syntax of some instructions I and expressions E:

```
E ::= Const | Var | Func(E,..,E) | U_op E | E B_op E

I ::= Var := E
    | Proc(E,...,E)
    | If E Then I Else I
    | While E Do I
    | Read Var | Write E
    | Begin I ; ... ; I End
    | Cobegin I || ... || I Coend
```

Below are listed two valid Parallel Pascal programs:

1. Program **rw** is a short example where parallelism leads to non-determinism.
2. Program **dekker** implements a subtle mutual exclusion protocol [Ray84]. Inside the critical section the number of the executing process and the sum of **x** and **y** are displayed. This sum should remain constant as long as mutual exclusion is preserved.

```
Program rw;
Var x:integer;

Begin
  x := 10;
  Cobegin
    x := x+1
  ||
    x := x+5
  Coend;
  Write(x)
End.
```

```
Program dekker;

Var flag:array[0..1] of boolean;
Var turn:integer;
Var x:integer;
Var y:integer;

Procedure critic(i:integer);
Var temp:integer;
Var j:integer;

  Begin
    j:=1-i;
    flag[i]:=true;
    While flag[j] Do
      If turn=j Then
      Begin
        flag[i]:=false;
        While turn=j Do
          Begin
          End;
        flag[i]:=true
      End;
    { Critical Section }
    Write('Critical Section: ',i);
    temp:=x;  { Swap x and y }
    x:=y;
    y:=temp;
    Write('x+y=',x+y);
    { End of Critical Section }
    turn:=j;
    flag[i]:=false
  End;

Begin
  flag[0]:=false;
  flag[1]:=false;
  turn:=0;
  x:=22;
  y:=47;
  While true Do
    Cobegin
      critic(0)
    ||
      critic(1)
    Coend
End.
```

2.2 Intermediate operation graph

An operation graph, similar to a control-flow chart, is computed from the abstract syntax tree for each function, procedure and main block of the program. The graph of a function or procedure f is denoted by $Begin_f$. Thus each node of these graphs corresponds to a syntactic control point. The operation graph of Program **dekker** is presented on Fig. 1.

The operations have been chosen for the sake of simplicity of the operational semantics (each operation manipulates a small part of the stack), and they can be considered as atomic with respect to the analysis of concurrency.

While loops are converted into a loop of the operation graph with an `IF` node at the head of the loop.

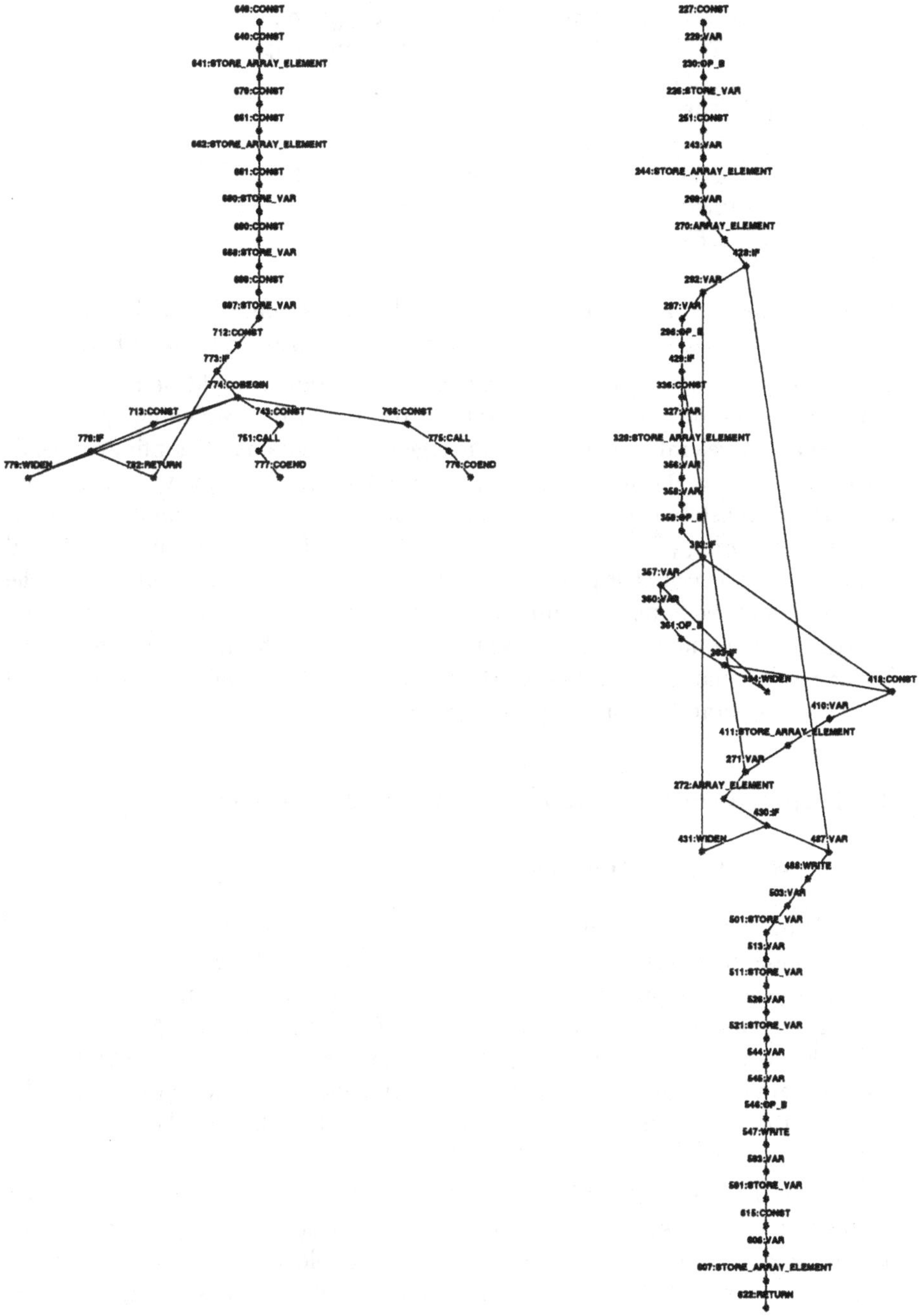

Fig. 1. Operation graph of Program **dekker**

```
op_graph = (CONST k | VAR v | OP o) * op_graph
         | (STORE v | WRITE | READ v) * op_graph
         | CALL f  * op_graph
         | RETURN
         | IF (op_graph, op_graph)
         | COBEGIN [op_graph list] * op_graph
         | COEND
         | WIDEN * op_graph
```

Except for **RETURN** and **COEND**, every node has a continuation node. **IF** nodes have two possible continuations, corresponding to a true and a false branch.

WIDEN are inserted in places where a widening operator should be used instead of the mere join of abstract configurations to be folded: a widening operator is necessary to accelerate the fixpoint convergence in domains with infinite ascending chains such as the well-known lattice of intervals of integer values. When a program is translated to a graph of operations by CPS transformation a static choice of widening points takes place at the head of loops and at the call and return points of recursive procedures. This choice is sufficient to guarantee the termination of the fixpoint computation that builds the automata. The iteration strategy for fixpoint computation we have chosen is depth-first: it generally gives better results than breadth-first or the linear one. But we have not investigated this point in detail for concurrent programs.

3 Implementation of the abstract semantics

3.1 Abstract activation blocks

A configuration or program state S is a set of stack activation blocks, some of them representing active processes. That is we distinguish between stack frames that are executing (noted $S^{\square}$) and other frames that are still waiting for the completion of processes (by operation **COEND**) or function calls (by **RETURN**) (noted $S^{\neg\square}$). Each activation block $A \in S$ refers to a syntactic control point cp of the program (actually, to a node of the intermediate operation graph) that determines the next action to be executed by this stack frame when it becomes active.

Sometimes the application of the abstract transition rules will lead to a pre-state S' in which two blocks of S' will have the same signature, i.e. they will have same activity and refer to the same control point. Both blocks in question have to be joined in order that states remain finite (the number of possible signatures is finite). The size of the local environment and the height of the local stack are uniquely determined by the control point. Local values have been abstracted using a lattice that represents sets of integer tuples. Our implementation uses integer intervals coupled with the relational lattice of Karr [Kar76] at the configuration level. The join of the two blocks consists in a new abstract block computed by taking the abstract join of the local environment and of the local stack and in taking the join of the static and dynamic links. The same kind of join of blocks will also happen when configurations will be folded.

```
type sig_block = Undef | Active of int*int | Inactive of int*int
  (* signature = control point of block and of its dynamic link *)
 and dyn_link  = sig_block list                (* sorted list *)
 and act_block = operation                     (* pc *)
               * (value env * sig_block)       (* env & static link *)
               * (value stack * dyn_link)      (* stack & dyn. link *)
```

Actually signatures of activation blocks also hold the control point of their return block: this is a refinement of the abstraction of dynamic stacks. They could as well hold a k-chain of return control points. Bourdoncle has shown that $k = 4$ is sufficient for every practical purpose.

3.2 Abstract configurations

Process configurations are sets of activation blocks:

```
type configuration = (sig_block,act_block) table   (* content   *)
                   * sig_block list                (* signature *)
```

As the transitions beginning from a state S directly depend on the actions executable by active blocks of S, it seems sensible to fold states that share the same set of active blocks. Thus, in the process of adding a state S to an abstract transition system, we will look for an already computed state T sharing the same set of active blocks: we therefore define configuration signatures to be equal to the sorted list of their active frame blocks. Comparing two configurations with respect to their signatures is very efficient. S and T will be joined, perhaps widening will occur. The fixpoint loop will continue with $S \sqcup T$.

3.3 Automata

An automaton is a set of transitions indexed on the signature of the source state:

```
type key = sig_block list              (* configuration signature *)

type result = State of configuration
            | Error of string

type transition = configuration * label * result

type automaton = (key,transition list) table
```

3.4 Abstract transition rules

Let S be an initial configuration, and A_{cp} an active block of $S^{\Box}$. The final configuration is computed by means of the abstract rules shown on Fig. 2, thus creating the transition $S \overset{\{cp\}}{\rightarrow} S'$[2]. Abstract rules are quite close to concrete ones (not shown here) except that abstract states are graphs of frames instead of trees, and that ground values (i.e., integers) are approximated. For instance, this means that a branching from S to S' and S'' occurs whenever it is impossible to decide at the abstract level between the two possible continuations of **IF** (see rule $\mathbf{IF}_{\top}$).

In the application of the abstract transition rules, we sometimes have to decide whether an activation block was already folded, that is whether it corresponds to different blocks in the standard configuration or not. This occurs in case of a **RETURN** or a **COBEGIN** when the block in question has to be removed. This problem is solved by a little trick. An auxiliary variable, *#folded*, is added to the environment of the join of two abstract blocks; its purpose is to count the number of times a block has been folded. So we can consider $S^{\Box}$ and $S^{\neg\Box}$ as abstract multisets of abstract activation blocks, where the (abstract) incrementation and decrementation of *#folded* provides the (abstract) addition and deletion of an element of a multiset.

Notice that the nature of the auxiliary variables *$sync* and *#folded* is completely different. The utility of *#folded* is to maintain a reasonable abstraction of an ordered (finite or infinite) set of blocks (concrete configuration) by an abstract multiset of a finite number of blocks (*#folded* is indeed modeled by an integer interval in the implementation), whereas *$sync* has a semantic purpose — to enable synchronization by counting the number of child processes to wait for in rules **COBEGIN** and **COEND** — and was already present in the concrete semantics.

3.5 Virtual coarsening

Virtual coarsening is a technique that allows the automaton generator to overlook states created by operations that are purely local to one concurrent process. It works by choosing to develop the trace of one particular active process. Transitions are still small-step, but represent the sequential execution of a finite number of atomic and local operations. Therefore, virtual coarsening is an abstraction enjoying the nice property that it does not imply any information loss, because the coarser transitions stored in the abstract automaton are still easily refinable.

There are two cases when one wants to store a configuration even though the operations involved are local:

- In order to preserve branchings, we shall store states that have different successors (because of a non-deterministic **IF** operation, for instance).

[2] If A_{cp} has been folded, the abstract transition represents several concrete transitions.

CONST $$\frac{A_{cp} = (\texttt{CONST}\, k, rest) * env * stack \in S^{\Box}}{A_{cp'} = rest * env * (k :: stack) \in S'^{\Box}}$$

READ $$\frac{A_{cp} = (\texttt{READ}\, v, rest) * env * stack \in S^{\Box}}{A_{cp'} = rest * env[v \leftarrow \top_{int}] * stack \in S'^{\Box}}$$

VAR $$\frac{A_{cp} = (\texttt{VAR}\, v, rest) * env[v \leftarrow x] * stack \in S^{\Box}}{A_{cp'} = rest * env * (x :: stack) \in S'^{\Box}}$$

OP $$\frac{A_{cp} = (b\_op, rest) * env * (x :: y :: stack) \in S^{\Box}}{A_{cp'} = rest * env * (b\_op(x, y) :: stack) \in S'^{\Box}}$$

$\texttt{IF}_{ff}$ $$\frac{A_{cp} = \texttt{IF}(op_t, op_f) * env * (ff :: stack) \in S^{\Box}}{A_{cp'} = op_t * env * stack \in S'^{\Box}}$$

$\texttt{IF}_{tt}$ $$\frac{A_{cp} = \texttt{IF}(op_t, op_f) * env * (tt :: stack) \in S^{\Box}}{A_{cp'} = op_t * env * stack \in S'^{\Box}}$$

$\texttt{IF}_{\top}$ $$\frac{A_{cp} = \texttt{IF}(op_t, op_f) * env * (\top_{bool} :: stack) \in S^{\Box}}{\begin{array}{c} A_{cp'} = op_t * env * stack \in S'^{\Box} \\ A_{cp''} = op_f * env * stack \in S''^{\Box} \end{array}}$$

CALL $$\frac{A_{cp} = (\texttt{CALL}\, f, ret) * env * (x_n :: \ldots :: x_1 :: stack) \in S^{\Box}}{\begin{array}{l} A_{cp'} = ret * env * stack \in S'^{\neg\Box} \text{ (no longer active)} \\ F_{cp''} = Begin_f * ([v_j \leftarrow x_j] + SL) * (void + A'_{cp}) \in S'^{\Box} \end{array}}$$

$\texttt{RETURN}_{void}$ $$\frac{A_{cp} = \texttt{RETURN} * env * (void + R_{cp'}) \in S^{\Box}}{\begin{array}{l} A_{cp} \text{ removed from } S'^{\Box} \\ R'_{cp} = R_{cp} \in S'^{\Box} \text{ (activated)} \end{array}}$$

$\texttt{RETURN}_{r}$ $$\frac{A_{cp} = \texttt{RETURN} * env * (r + (op * e * stack)) \in S^{\Box}}{\begin{array}{l} A_{cp} \text{ removed from } S'^{\Box} \\ R'_{cp} = (op * e * (r :: stack)) \in S'^{\Box} \end{array}}$$

COBEGIN $$\frac{A_{cp} = \texttt{COBEGIN}([op_1, \ldots, op_l], cont) * env * stack \in S^{\Box}}{\begin{array}{l} A'_{cp'} = cont * env[\$sync \leftarrow l] * stack \in S'^{\neg\Box} \text{ (no longer active)} \\ \forall j \in \{1, \ldots, l\},\ P'_j = (op_{cp_j} * (void, A'_{cp'}) * (void, NULL)) \in S'^{\Box} \end{array}}$$

COEND $$\frac{A_{cp} = \texttt{COEND} * (Q, \_) * stack \in S^{\Box}}{\begin{array}{l} A_{cp} \notin S'^{\Box}, \quad \$sync(Q) := \$sync(Q) - 1 \\ Q \text{ deleted from } S'^{\neg\Box} \text{ if } \gamma(\$sync) = \{0\}, \quad Q \in S'^{\Box} \text{ if } 0 \in \gamma(\$sync) \end{array}}$$

Fig. 2. Abstract transition rules of Parallel Pascal

– To ensure that the state generator will not loop, it is sufficient to store widening transitions.

Parallel Pascal has a number of constructs that act on one process only, so a program analyzer can benefit a lot from this technique. However, the abstract execution has to halt and store the global state after the execution of the following *critical* operations that are not local:

– a **Cobegin** or **Coend** construct;
– a **READ** or **STORE** to a *shared* variable.

It is easy to see that a variable or call-by-value parameter x is shared by other processes if there is a **Cobegin** but no corresponding **Coend** between the declaration of x and the **READ** or **STORE** operation in question. However, we would need some sort of *alias analysis* to decide whether a call-by-reference parameter is shared or not. Another optimization would consist in determining whether there is an actual risk of interference with another process q: this can be done on-the-fly if the execution of q has already been traced.

3.6 Example

Let us look again at Program **rw**. An operation graph suitable for abstract interpretation using virtual coarsening would be:

```
Begin_rw = (CONST 10) * (STORE x) * COBEGIN[1,2]
       1  = (VAR x) * 1'
       1' = (CONST 1) * (OP +) * (STORE x) * 3
       2  = (VAR x) * 2'
       2' = (CONST 5) * (OP +) * (STORE x) * 3
       3  = COEND * 4
       4  = (VAR x) * WRITE * RETURN
```

instead of

```
(CONST 10)*
(STORE x)*
COBEGIN[(VAR x)*(CONST 1)*(OP +)*(STORE x)*COEND,
        (VAR x)*(CONST 5)*(OP +)*(STORE x)*COEND]*
(VAR x)*
WRITE*
RETURN
```

The generated abstract automata are shown on Fig. 3, the left one without virtual coarsening and the right one optimized with virtual coarsening.

The standard semantics calculates the three possible results 11, 15 and 16.

If we choose to abstract the values of x by a lattice of intervals, then the folding of the states with control point **WRITE** gives an abstract state whose abstract

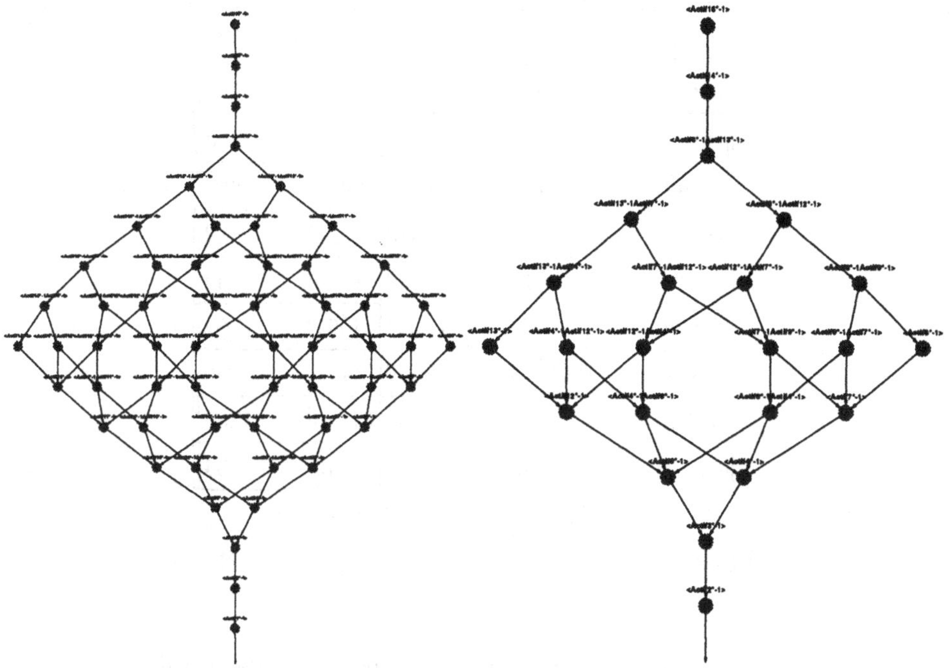

Fig. 3. Abstract automata computed for Program `rw`

value for variable x is $[11, 16]$. This kind of analysis is helpful for computing the range of integer values that a given variable or expression can take during the execution of the program.

4 Some results

Although the results shown on Fig. 4 are still preliminary, the number of states generated by the abstract interpreter is manageable in all the tested programs, while this number could not be measured in some cases for the concrete automaton generated by Iconc because the size was too large.

All presented test programs were concurrent programs with shared variables, except for Program **`eightqueens`** which sequentially computes the placement of eight queens on a chessboard. Some of them were mutual exclusion protocols: **`turn1`**, **`dekker`**, **`dijkstra2`**, ... The underlying graph of the abstract automaton computed for Program **`dekker`** is shown on Fig. 5 (only 2009 abstract states were computed instead of 111054 concrete ones). For all these programs the achieved state reduction was important. But were interesting properties preserved?

Analyzer	Iconc	Iconc+VC	Iabs	Iabs+VC
concur	18678	8571	659	294
turn1	7924	2791	728	265
turn2	n.a.	67684	2091	853
turn3	n.a.	43813	2131	812
turn4	18516	6309	1843	634
turn5	41844	14301	4097	1362
dekker	111054	45030	4441	2009
dijkstra2	n.a.	n.a.	13146	4235
eightqueens	n.a.	n.a.	149	64

Fig. 4. Analysis results: number of generated states

Except for Program **dijkstra2** mutual exclusion was automatically proved by the abstract interpreter when the protocol was correct. But a stronger version of the protocols (without the synchronization imposed by **COEND** in the main procedure) requires a relational lattice of numeric values. For this very purpose Karr's lattice of affine subspaces of $\mathbb{Z}^k$ was recently integrated into the analyzer.

5 User interface

It is important to design a sensible human interface if one wants to exploit the full potential of a program analyzer as an abstract debugging tool or as a semi-verification tool. This task is specially difficult in the case of a concurrent program analyzer because of the inherently non-deterministic and non-sequential dynamic behaviour. Our choice is two-fold:

1. By using the **graphplace** tool the computed automaton representing the approximate behaviour of the program to analyze can be visualized (see Fig. 5). Although this gives a nice global geometrical picture of the execution dynamics, this picture is usually too clumsy at first and should be refined (by marking selected paths and by masking non appropriate branches) to provide useful information.
2. At each control point static information can be computed by joining relevant information from all process configurations of the automaton. By use of Netscape's frames extension to HTML it is easy to develop an interactive graphical user interface to provide analysis results: the large top frame presents the program source where hypertext references have been inserted

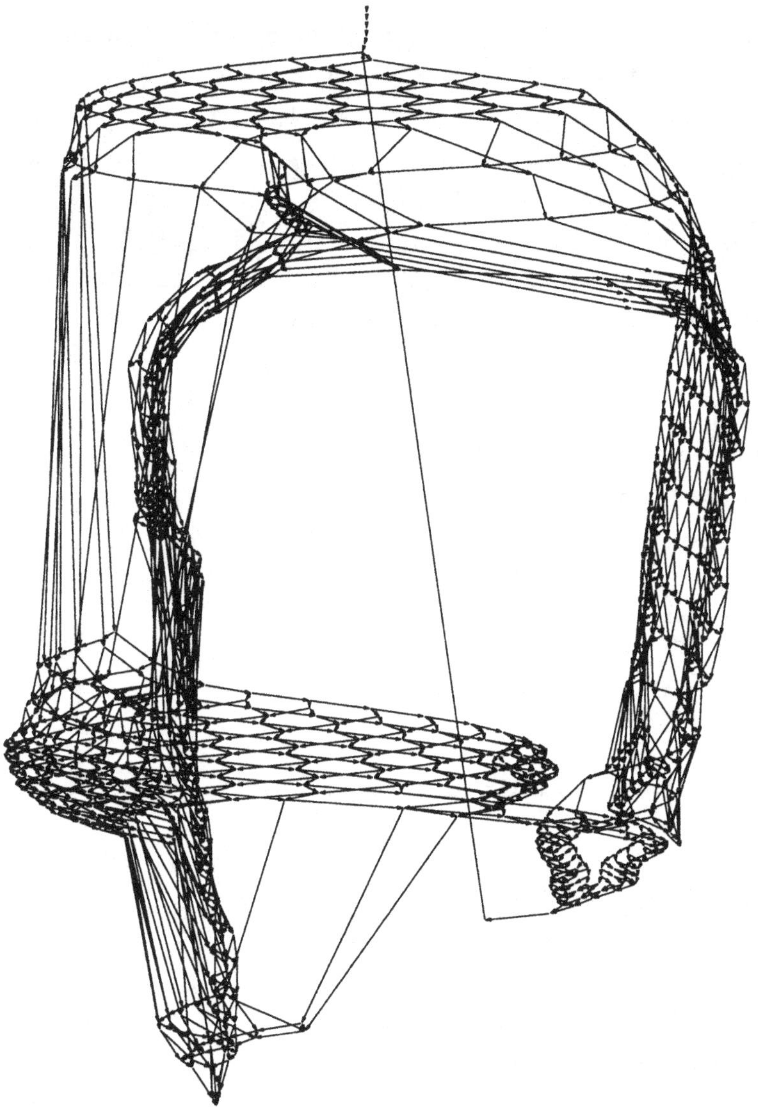

Fig. 5. Abstract automaton computed for Program `dekker`

at program points. When the user clicks on such a reference the computed information on variables (for instance) at this point is displayed within the bottom small frame. You can see at the bottom of Fig. 6 that variable `temp` keeps the constant value 69 at point 311. This means that mutual exclusion was preserved for this simple protocol `turn1`.

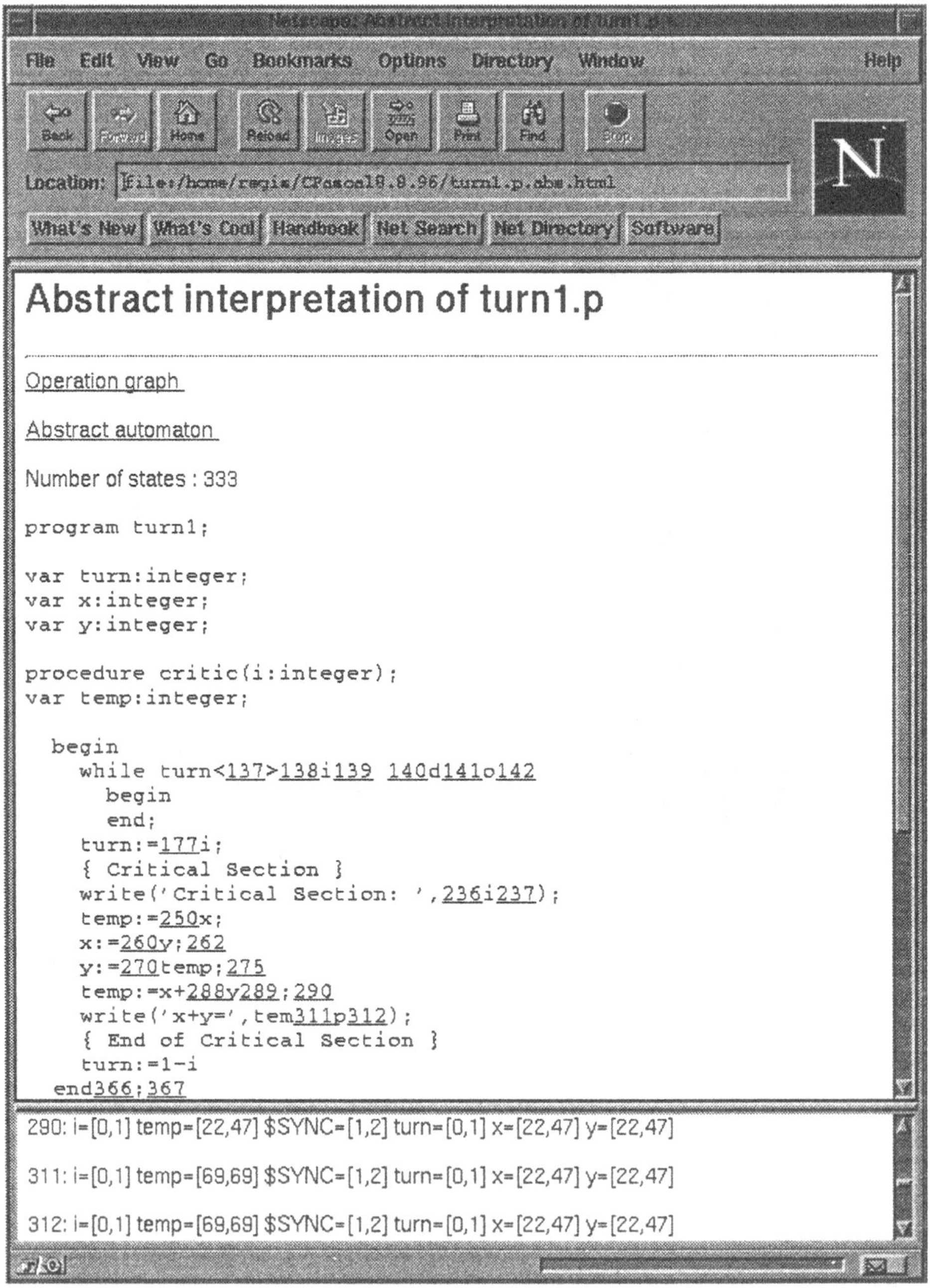

Fig. 6. Use of Netscape frames to present analysis results

6 Problems and perspectives

Concurrent programs can be statically analyzed by applying the methods of abstract interpretation. A prototype that computes the abstract automaton of Parallel Pascal programs has been developed. While many problems have been solved, difficult ones remain present.

Precision is always an issue with abstract interpretation. The standard and the abstract semantics should be able to express the process behaviour in a very precise way. This is the case with operational semantics and automata, although part of the history of computation is lost. It is still feasible to increase the precision of the abstract interpretation by alternating forward and backward iteration strategies while computing the abstract semantics.

An unexpected problem was the handling of tests: test predicates cannot be considered atomic in realistic concurrent languages. Most existing ways to reduce the tested state inside the **true** or the **false** branch do consider that the state was not altered since the beginning of the computation of the predicate. This property does not hold in Parallel Pascal! By clever use of a relational lattice only sound relations between members of the predicate will be propagated. As opposite relations $x = y$ and $x <> y$ cannot be easily maintained at the same place activation blocks whose stack or environment holds a different list of boolean values should have different signatures.

Some implementation (and semantic) techniques try to avoid the well-known state explosion problem by not generating the whole transition system, or at least by finding a compact representation of it [Val89]. Our implementation uses virtual coarsening of actions. Another idea would be to represent paved blocks of independent interleaving transitions by their contour only, which would save much space by *compacting* the size of automata. Partial order methods such as Valmari's stubborn sets try to generate transitions in a given order only. This maintains the traces of particular processes but forgets about the traces of the concurrent system.

Actually the complexity of the analysis depends on both the level of concurrency and the number of *critical* transitions, where communication can take place. There are many means to help lower this complexity, but will this kind of global automata construction remain feasible for large concurrent or distributed systems? Maybe only lazy generation methods combined with local model-checking will address this concern.

7 Acknowledgments

Many thanks to Patrick Cousot for discussions and support. Thanks to the anonymous referee who pointed a mistake in Program **dekker**: (s)he recalled us how easy it is to bug a concurrent protocol!

References

[Bou92] F. Bourdoncle. *Sémantique des langages impératifs d'ordre supérieur et interprétation abstraite*. PhD thesis, École polytechnique, 1992.

[CC77] P. Cousot and R. Cousot. Abstract Interpretation: A Unified Lattice Model for Static Analysis of Programs by Construction or Approximation of Fixpoints. In *Proc. 4th Annual ACM Symposium on Principles of Programming Languages*, 1977.

[CC80] P. Cousot and R. Cousot. Semantic analysis of communicating sequential processes. In *Proc. 7th International Colloquium on Automata, Languages and Programming*, Lecture Notes in Computer Science, 1980.

[CIY95] R. Cleaveland, S. Purushothaman Iyer, and D. Yankelevitch. Optimality in Abstractions of Model-Checking. In *Proc. of Static Analysis Symposium*, Lecture Notes in Computer Science. Springer-Verlag, September 1995.

[Cri95] R. Cridlig. Semantic Analysis of Shared-Memory Concurrent Languages using Abstract Model-Checking. In *Proc. ACM Symposium on Partial Evaluation and Program Manipulation*, June 1995.

[Cri96] R. Cridlig. Semantic Analysis of Concurrent ML by Abstract Model-Checking. In B. Steffen and T. Margaria, editors, *Proc. International Workshop on Verification of Infinite State Systems*, volume MIP-9614. Universität Passau, August 1996.

[DGG94] D. Dams, O. Grumberg, and R. Gerth. Abstract interpretation of reactive systems: Abstractions preserving $\forall$CTL*, $\exists$CTL* and CTL*. In E.-R. Olderog, editor, *Proc. IFIP WG2.1/WG2.2/WG2.3 Working Conference on Programming Concepts, Methods and Calculi (PROCOMET)*, IFIP Transactions, Amsterdam, June 1994. North-Holland/Elsevier.

[Dij68] E. W. Dijkstra. Cooperating sequential processes. In F. Genuys, editor, *Programming Languages*. Academic Press, 1968.

[Gou95] E. Goubault. *The Geometry of Concurrency*. PhD thesis, Ecole Polytechnique, Palaiseau, France, 1995.

[Hoa78] C. A. R. Hoare. Communicating Sequential Processes. *Communications of the ACM*, 21(8):667–677, 1978.

[Kar76] M. Karr. Affine relationships among variables of a program. *Acta Informatica*, 6:133–151, 1976.

[Kel94] P. Kelb. Model Checking and Abstraction: A Framework Approximating both Truth and Failure Information. Technical report, University of Oldenburg, 1994.

[Ray84] M. Raynal. *Algorithmique du parallélisme : le problème de l'exclusion mutuelle*. Dunod, 1984.

[Val89] A. Valmari. Eliminating redundant interleavings during concurrent program verification. In G. Goos and J. Hartmanis, editors, *PARLE '89*, volume 366 of *Lecture Notes in Computer Science*, pages 89–103, 1989.

[WJ78] N. Wirth and K. Jensen. *PASCAL user manual and report*. Springer-Verlag, second edition, 1978.

Polyvariance, Polymorphism and Flow Analysis

Karl-Filip Faxén

Dept. of Teleinformatics, Royal Institute of Technology
Electrum 204, S-164 40 Kista, tel: +46 8 752 13 78, fax: +46 8 751 17 93
kff@it.kth.se

Abstract. Flow analysis is a potentially very useful analysis for higher order functional languages, but its practical application has been slow in coming, partially hindered by shortcomings of the current analysis techniques. Among these are the limited precision, long analysis times, incompatibility with separate compilation, inapplicability to untyped languages and sensitivity to program structure associated with various earlier formulations.
We address these shortcomings with an approach based on a novel type system integrating recursive types, subtyping with liberal union types, and system F style polymorphism, in a constraint based formulation. The type system is "soft" in the sense that it does not reject programs. It is also not decidable, but there is a broad spectrum of sound and terminating, though incomplete, algorithms whose precision can be characterized by restricting the substitutions used for instantiation of type schemes.
We give an inference algorithm which simplifies constraints incrementally, rather than postponing all constraint solving until all of the constraints are generated. In this way we hope to avoid in practice the exponential growth in the size of constraint sets caused by repeated instantiation of unsimplified type schemes. Type schemes are also a suitable representation for communicationg the analysis result over module boundaries, making separate compilation feasible.
Keywords: Flow analysis, type systems, constraints, polymorphism, polyvariance, inference algorithms, functional languages.

1 Introduction

Flow analysis[1] of higher order functional languages determines, for each *program point* (or PP) which values this PP might take on during the execution of the program (in a functional language, the subexpressions of the program are typically considered PPs). The information gained is very useful for a number of important optimizations. For instance, the present author has achieved speed-ups of over a factor of three when compiling a lazy functional language [2].

Wide spread adoption of flow analysis has been slow in coming due to limitations in the current techniques. The problems include:

[1] What we call flow analysis, and very similar analyses, have been called different things by different authors. Examples include *set based analysis* [3], *closure analysis* [8, 9], or *control flow analysis* [10, 11].

Precision. Much of the early work on flow analysis of higher order languages is *monovariant*, i.e. based on finding a single approximation to the possible execution-time values of each PP (such approximations are often called *abstract values* since most of the work in flow analysis has been more or less based on abstract interpretation) such that certain consistency conditions are satisfied.
This means that, for each $\lambda x.e$ in a program, the abstract value of x approximates all arguments that $\lambda x.e$ may be applied to during execution, and the abstract value of every application where the function part may evaluate to $\lambda x.e$ includes the abstract value of e. This may lead to a severe loss of precision, especially in large programs where the same functions are applied in many places.

Performance. Increasing the precision of these early analyses by using more than one abstract value for each PP (generally called *polyvariance* as opposed to monovariance) has proved rather difficult because of combinatorial explosion. One popular approach is based on bounded length *call strings* which essentially capture the k topmost return addresses in the stack. The number of different call strings, and thus of different abstract values to keep track of for each PP, grows exponentially with the length k of the call strings. Also, call strings are of little help for recursive functions since they typically have statically unbounded depths in their recursion.
An alternative method is to *clone* (make several copies of) the functions in the program and run a monovariant analysis on the resulting program (see [3]). This approach has the same limitations with respect to combinatorial explosion as the previous one, but can be used to sidestep the problems with recursion (since clones are only made for nonrecursive calls).

Program structure. Both call string based and cloning based analyses are very sensitive to program structure. Adding just another layer of function calls can lead to a drastic reduction in precision.

Separate compilation. Most current techniques depend on the entire program being available for analysis. The root of this problem is related to the bad precision — since different calls to the same functions may share the same abstract value, the calls have to be analyzed simultaneously. Also, there is often no natural way to represent the result of analyzing part of a program.

Incompatibility. Type based approaches, which suffer less from the above problems, are restricted to typable programs, and thus to typed languages, and, since that is what one really wants to analyze, to typed intermediate languages. For this reason, type based analyses have not been immediately applicable to untyped languages such as Scheme and Erlang.

This paper reports on work in progress addressing these problems using a novel type-based analysis with the following features:

Subtypes. Subtype constraints are capable of capturing the direction of the flow of data in the program.

Soft typing. All programs are typable in our system. This means that well-typed programs (i.e. programs that can be successfully analyzed), can still go wrong. The analysis result is nevertheless valid—it simply states where the program may go wrong, rather than refusing to analyse (type) it. Thus the analysis can be used with untyped languages.

Higher order polymorphism. Rather than, as is done in the Hindley-Milner system, generalizing at let expressions and instantiating at occurrences of let-bound variables, our system generalizes at lambda abstractions and instantiates at applications. Together with subtyping, this gives roughly the same power as in subtyping extensions of System F. We also generalize over quantified types (type schemes) which can not be generalized over in the Hindley-Milner system. This power makes type inference in our system undecidable, but that is not a problem since there are still terminating analysis algorithms—they are not just guaranteed to find the "best" type of a program (because of softness, our system always finds *some* type).

Incremental constraint simplification. The key to the usefulness of the anaysis is the possibility of simplifying the constraints derived from a lambda abstraction before constructing a type scheme. In this way we hope to aviod combinatorial explosion while preserving good precision. The extent to which this will succeed must be determined experimentally, however, and we plan to implement the analysis in the near future.

Separate compilation. We believe that type schemes are a natural way to pass analysis results between modules.

While working on this type system, we defined a similar, but not type based, system closer to a conventional constraint based formulations such as [3] and which can be seen as forming a bridge between polyvariant constraint based formulations and polymorphic type based ones such as this. The work on relating these two is very tentative, however.

As this is work in progress, we do not present a fully fledged analyzer. The main omissions are:

- We deal with a very small language (call-by-value lambda calculus with constants).
- The analysis only yields information about the result of the program, rather than about all of the intermediate results which is what is needed for optimization purposes.
- No proofs. We are currently working on semantic and syntactic soundness proofs, but they are still not fit for publishing.

The rest of the paper is organized as follows. The rest of the Introduction presents the analyzed language and recalls monovariant flow analysis. This is included for presentational purposes, serving as a place to introduce some important concepts in a simple setting. Section 2 introduces the polyvariant analysis and Section 3 finally presents the polymorphic system.

1.1 The Language

Figure 1 gives the syntax and semantics of a flattened version of the untyped call-by-value lambda calculus. The (nonrecursive) let construct can be used to

$$e \in \text{Expr} \to x \mid c \mid x_1\, x_2 \mid \lambda x.e \mid \texttt{let}\ x\ \texttt{=}\ e_1\ \texttt{in}\ e_2$$

The syntax of the flattened lambda calculus

$$\rho \vdash x \to \rho(x) \quad \text{E-VAR} \qquad\qquad \rho \vdash c \to c \quad \text{E-CON}$$

$$\frac{\rho(x_1) = (\rho', \lambda x.e) \qquad \rho'[x \mapsto \rho(x_2)] \vdash e \to v}{\rho \vdash x_1\, x_2 \to v} \quad \text{E-APP}$$

$$\rho \vdash \lambda x.e \to (\rho, \lambda x.e) \quad \text{E-ABS} \qquad \frac{\rho \vdash e_1 \to v_1 \qquad \rho[x \mapsto v_1] \vdash e_2 \to v_2}{\rho \vdash \texttt{let}\ x\ \texttt{=}\ e_1\ \texttt{in}\ e_2 \to v_2} \quad \text{E-LET}$$

The semantics

Fig. 1. The language

translate arbitrary lambda terms into this syntax. The right hand side of the binding in a let expression may be another let expression.

We give this language an environment-based big step operational semantics. A *value* v is a *constant* c or a *closure* $(\rho, \lambda x.e)$ consisting of an *environment* mapping variables to values and a lambda abstraction. The inference rules allow us to prove judgements of the form $\rho \vdash e \to v$ where ρ is an environment and v a value.

For the purpose of generating names of flow variables later on, we will assume that every (sub)expression e in a program has a unique label $\mathsf{Label}(e)$, but to reduce clutter we will not write these out, but only use them in the specifications of the algorithms.

In the rest of the paper, we will use the following program as a running example:

```
let id = λx.x in
let n = 1 in
let f = id id in
  f n
```

1.2 Monovariant Constraint Based Flow Analysis

In this framework,[2] we associate each program point (subexpression or variable in the program) with a unique *flow variable* (ranged over by α). We will write the flow variable associated with the subexpression e or the variable x as $[\![e]\!]$ and

[2] This section is included for presentational reasons; the material is basically a reformulation of [3] with a different notation.

$[\![x]\!]$. The analyzer constructs a *constraint system* over these variables and some constants. We will let the flow variables range over sets of *flow values*, which are lambda abstractions or constants occurring in the program.

We then wish to find, for each flow variable, a set of flow values such that all of the constraints are satisfied. We call such an assignment a *model* of the constraint set, and we express it as a function Φ from flow variables to sets of flow values.

Among the constraints generated are some which link the formal parameter of a function to the actual parameters of all calls to this function, and the body of the function to the results of these applications. In a higher order language, it is in general very difficult to determine where functions are applied, so it is not obvious which such constraints to generate. In our example, which function is called in the application `f n`?

We solve this problem by generating, for each application $x_1\,x_2$, an *application constraint* of the form

$$[\![x_2]\!] \rightarrow [\![x_1\,x_2]\!] \supseteq [\![x_1]\!]$$

which is satisfied if, for every $\lambda x.e \in \Phi([\![x_1]\!])$, $[\![x]\!] \supseteq [\![x_2]\!]$ and $[\![x_1\,x_2]\!] \supseteq [\![e]\!]$ are satisfied. We thus arrive at the following definition of a model of a set of constraints:

Definition 1 (Model of a constraint set) *We say that Φ is a model of S, written $\Phi \models S$, iff the following holds:*

- *If $\alpha \supseteq \lambda x.e \in S$ then $\lambda x.e \in \Phi(\alpha)$.*
- *If $\alpha \supseteq c \in S$ then $c \in \Phi(\alpha)$.*
- *If $\alpha_1 \supseteq \alpha_2 \in S$ then $\Phi(\alpha_2) \subseteq \Phi(\alpha_1)$.*
- *If $\alpha_1 \rightarrow \alpha_2 \supseteq \alpha_3 \in S$ and $\lambda x.e \in \Phi(\alpha_3)$ then $\Phi(\alpha_1) \subseteq \Phi([\![x]\!])$ and $\Phi([\![e]\!]) \subseteq \Phi(\alpha_2)$.*

There may be more than one Φ satisfying these conditions; the one we are interested in is the *smallest* one,[3] which always exists since if Φ_1 and Φ_2 are both models of S, then their pointwise intersection is also a model.

When it comes to computing the least model of a set of constraints, we use a class of constraint sets called *closed constraint sets.*

Definition 2 (Closed constraint sets) *A constraint set S is* closed *iff the following conditions hold:*

- *If $\{\alpha_1 \supseteq \alpha_2,\ \alpha_2 \supseteq \lambda x.e\} \subseteq S$ then $\alpha_1 \supseteq \lambda x.e \in S$.*
- *If $\{\alpha_1 \supseteq \alpha_2,\ \alpha_2 \supseteq c\} \subseteq S$ then $\alpha_1 \supseteq c \in S$.*
- *If $\{\alpha_1 \rightarrow \alpha_2 \supseteq \alpha_3,\ \alpha_3 \supseteq \lambda x.e\} \subseteq S$ then $\{[\![x]\!] \supseteq \alpha_1, \alpha_2 \supseteq [\![e]\!]\} \subseteq S$.*

---

[3] We say that Φ_1 is smaller than Φ_2 if $Dom(\Phi_1) \subseteq Dom(\Phi_2)$ and for every $\alpha \in Dom(\Phi_1)$ $\Phi_1(\alpha) \subseteq \Phi_2(\alpha)$.

Every constraint set can be extended to a closed constraint set by adding constraints according to the rules in the definition. Termination is ensured by the fact that the new constraints are bounded in size and built from pieces of existing constraints. Moreover, for every constraint set S, there is a unique least S' such that $S \subseteq S'$ and S' is closed. We denote this S', called the *closure* of S, by $close(S)$.

Definition 3 (Explicit constraint) *Constraints of the form* $\alpha \supseteq \lambda x.e$ *and* $\alpha \supseteq c$ *are called* explicit. *We write* $explicit(S)$ *for the explicit constraints in* S.

The interesting thing about closed constraint sets is that the least model of a constraint set S is equal to the least model of $close(S)$ and the interesting thing about explicit constraints is that the least model of a closed constraint set S is equal to the least model of $explicit(S)$ and is given by:

$$\Phi(\alpha) = \{\lambda x.e \mid \alpha \supseteq \lambda x.e \in S\} \cup \{c \mid \alpha \supseteq c \in S\}$$

A consequence of this is that every constraint set S has a finite least model.

1.3 Monovariant Flow Analysis of the Example

Using this strategy, we derive the following constraints from our example:

$$\begin{aligned}
[\![\texttt{let id = }\lambda\texttt{x.x in ...}]\!] &\supseteq [\![\texttt{let n = 1 in ...}]\!] \\
[\![\texttt{id}]\!] &\supseteq [\![\lambda\texttt{x.x}]\!] \\
[\![\lambda\texttt{x.x}]\!] &\supseteq \lambda\texttt{x.x} \\
[\![\texttt{let n = 1 in ...}]\!] &\supseteq [\![\texttt{let f = id id in f n}]\!] \\
[\![\texttt{n}]\!] &\supseteq [\![\texttt{1}]\!] \\
[\![\texttt{1}]\!] &\supseteq \texttt{1} \\
[\![\texttt{let f = id id in f n}]\!] &\supseteq [\![\texttt{f n}]\!] \\
[\![\texttt{f}]\!] &\supseteq [\![\texttt{id id}]\!] \\
[\![\texttt{id}]\!] \to [\![\texttt{id id}]\!] &\supseteq [\![\texttt{id}]\!] \\
[\![\texttt{n}]\!] \to [\![\texttt{f n}]\!] &\supseteq [\![\texttt{f}]\!]
\end{aligned}$$

The least model Φ of the constraints above is given by:

$$\begin{aligned}
\Phi([\![\texttt{let id ...}]\!]) = \Phi([\![\texttt{let n ...}]\!]) = \Phi([\![\texttt{let f ...}]\!]) &= \{\lambda\texttt{x.x},\ \texttt{1}\} \\
\Phi([\![\texttt{f n}]\!]) = \Phi([\![\texttt{id id}]\!]) = \Phi([\![\texttt{f}]\!]) = \Phi([\![\texttt{x}]\!]) &= \{\lambda\texttt{x.x},\ \texttt{1}\} \\
\Phi([\![\texttt{id}]\!]) = \Phi([\![\lambda\texttt{x.x}]\!]) &= \{\lambda\texttt{x.x}\} \\
\Phi([\![\texttt{n}]\!]) = \Phi([\![\texttt{1}]\!]) &= \{\texttt{1}\}
\end{aligned}$$

Unfortunately, both λ`x.x` and `1` turn up as values of the program in this model, rather than just `1`, as one might have hoped.

The root of the problem is the variable `x` which is bound to both λ`x.x` and `1`, since the function `id` is applied two times. Then $[\![\texttt{x}]\!]$ must contain both values. What we must have, then, is more than one abstract value for each program point. This is generally referred to as *polyvariance*.

$$\chi \in \text{Constraint} ::= \alpha_1 \supseteq \alpha_2 \mid \alpha \supseteq c \mid \alpha \supseteq (A, \lambda x.e) \mid \alpha_1 \rightarrow \alpha_2 \supseteq \alpha_3$$

(a) Syntax of constraints

$$\{\alpha \supseteq A(x)\},\ A \vdash x : \alpha \quad \text{V-VAR} \qquad \{\alpha \supseteq c\},\ A \vdash c : \alpha \quad \text{V-CON}$$

$$\{A(x_2) \rightarrow \alpha \supseteq A(x_1)\},\ A \vdash x_1\, x_2 : \alpha \ \text{V-APP} \quad \{\alpha \supseteq (A,\ \lambda x.e)\},\ A \vdash \lambda x.e : \alpha \ \text{V-ABS}$$

$$\frac{S_1,\ A \vdash e_1 : \alpha_1 \qquad S_2,\ A[x \mapsto \alpha_1] \vdash e_2 : \alpha_2}{S_1 \cup S_2,\ A \vdash \texttt{let}\ x = e_1\ \texttt{in}\ e_2 : \alpha_2} \quad \text{V-LET}$$

(b) The inference rules

$$\begin{array}{ll}
\Phi \models \alpha_1 \supseteq \alpha_2 & \text{iff } \Phi(\alpha_2) \subseteq \Phi(\alpha_1) \\
\Phi \models \alpha \supseteq (A,\ \lambda x.e) & \text{iff } (A,\ \lambda x.e) \in \Phi(\alpha) \\
\Phi \models \alpha \supseteq c & \text{iff } c \in \Phi(\alpha) \\
\Phi \models \alpha_1 \rightarrow \alpha_2 \supseteq \alpha & \text{iff } (A,\ \lambda x.e) \in \Phi(\alpha) \Rightarrow \\
& \quad \exists\, S, \alpha_3, \alpha_4 \,.\, S,\ A[x \mapsto \alpha_3] \vdash e : \alpha_4 \\
& \quad\quad \wedge\ \Phi \models S \cup \{\alpha_3 \supseteq \alpha_1,\ \alpha_2 \supseteq \alpha_4\}
\end{array}$$

(c) Models of constraints: $\mu \models S$ iff $\mu \models \chi$ for all $\chi \in S$

$$\begin{array}{l}
\{\alpha_1 \supseteq \alpha_2,\ \alpha_2 \supseteq (A, \lambda x.e)\} \subseteq S \Rightarrow \{\alpha_1 \supseteq (A, \lambda x.e)\} \subseteq S \\
\{\alpha_1 \supseteq \alpha_2,\ \alpha_2 \supseteq c\} \subseteq S \Rightarrow \{\alpha_1 \supseteq c\} \subseteq S \\
\{\alpha_1 \rightarrow \alpha_2 \supseteq \alpha_3,\ \alpha_3 \supseteq (A, \lambda x.e)\} \subseteq S \Rightarrow \\
\quad \exists\, S', \alpha_1', \alpha_2' \,.\, S',\ A[x \mapsto \alpha_1'] \vdash e : \alpha_2' \wedge \{\alpha_1' \supseteq \alpha_1, \alpha_2 \supseteq \alpha_2'\} \cup S' \subseteq S
\end{array}$$

(d) Closure of constraint sets: S is *closed* iff all of the implications hold

Fig. 2. Specification of the polyvariant analysis

2 A Polyvariant Analysis

Figure 2 gives a summary of our polyvariant analysis. Here, the constraint system corresponding to a program is defined in a context dependent manner using an inference system deriving judgements of the form $S,\ A \vdash e : \alpha$ where S is a constraint set and α the flow variable corresponding to the expression e in flow environment A. A *flow environment* A is a finite mapping from program variables to flow variables. Flow environments are used both in the constraint derivation rules and in *flow closures*, where they are paired with lambda abstractions in a way analoguous to the pairing of environments and lambda abstractions to form closures in the semantics.

2.1 Models, Closed Constraint Sets, and Explicit Constraints

These concepts carry over from the monovariant analysis and they play a similar role here, although they are defined somewhat differently and have somewhat different properties. We will now comment on the major differences.

Closures of application constraints. Consider a constraint set S such that $\alpha_1 \to \alpha_2 \supseteq \alpha_3$ and $\alpha_3 \supseteq (A, \lambda x.e)$ are in S. For S to be closed in the polyvariant system, there must be *some* flow variables α_1' and α_2' and constraint set S' such that $S', A[x \mapsto \alpha_1'] \vdash e : \alpha_2'$ is derivable and $S' \cup \{\alpha_1' \supseteq \alpha_1,\ \alpha_2 \supseteq \alpha_2'\}$ is included in S. The arbitrary choice of α_1', α_2', and S' is what distinguishes the polyvariant analysis from the monovariant, where α_1' is constrained to be $[\![x]\!]$ and α_2' is constrainted to be $[\![e]\!]$. As for S', note that the inference rules for the polyvariant analysis do not "look inside" lambda abstractions, wheras those for the monovariant analysis do. Thus in the monovariant case, the equivalent of S' is already contained in S by construction. This difference is motivated by the fact that the monovariant analysis only analyses the body of a lambda abstraction occurring in the program in a single context, wheras the number of contexts the polyvariant analysis uses is not known when the constraints are initially generated.

The issue is analogous in the definition of models of application constraints.

Least models. Just as in the monovariant case, we have that if S is a closed constraint set, then S has a least model which is equal to the least model of *explicit*(S). We do however no longer in general have minimal (most informative) finite closures of constraint sets, and consequently, we do not have finite least models of all constraint sets. Instead of a function *close* we have a relation "is a closure of", written as $\triangleright$, such that $S' \triangleright S$ if $S \subseteq S'$ and S' is closed. There is a number of possible algorithms which compute closures of a constraint set which represent different cost/precision tradeoffs.

2.2 The Example Revisited

Using the derivation rules, we can construct the following constraints

$$\alpha_{\mathtt{id}} \supseteq ([\,], \lambda \mathtt{x}.\mathtt{x})$$
$$\alpha_{\mathtt{n}} \supseteq 1$$
$$\alpha_{\mathtt{id}} \to \alpha_{\mathtt{f}} \supseteq \alpha_{\mathtt{id}}$$
$$\alpha_{\mathtt{n}} \to \alpha_{\mathtt{p}} \supseteq \alpha_{\mathtt{f}}$$

with $\alpha_{\mathtt{p}}$ corresponding to the result of the program. We now close

$$\alpha_{\mathtt{id}} \to \alpha_{\mathtt{f}} \supseteq \alpha_{\mathtt{id}},\ \alpha_{\mathtt{id}} \supseteq ([\,], \lambda \mathtt{x}.\mathtt{x})$$

by adding the following constraints:

$$\alpha_{\mathtt{x}} \supseteq \alpha_{\mathtt{id}},\ \alpha_{\mathtt{f}} \supseteq \alpha_{\mathtt{b}},\ \alpha_{\mathtt{b}} \supseteq \alpha_{\mathtt{x}}$$

The first constraints are the parameter and result connecting constraints and the last one is the constraint derived from the body of $\lambda\mathtt{x}.\mathtt{x}$. It is easy to verify that we have $\{\alpha_{\mathtt{b}} \supseteq \alpha_{\mathtt{x}}\}$, $[\mathtt{x} \mapsto \alpha_{\mathtt{x}}] \vdash \mathtt{x} : \alpha_{\mathtt{b}}$ as required. We next get a number of constraints from transitivity, propagating the closure of the identity function:

$$\alpha_{\mathtt{x}} \supseteq ([], \lambda\mathtt{x}.\mathtt{x}),\ \alpha_{\mathtt{b}} \supseteq ([], \lambda\mathtt{x}.\mathtt{x}),\ \alpha_{\mathtt{f}} \supseteq ([], \lambda\mathtt{x}.\mathtt{x})$$

At this point we have

$$\alpha_{\mathtt{n}} \to \alpha_{\mathtt{p}} \supseteq \alpha_{\mathtt{f}},\ \alpha_{\mathtt{f}} \supseteq ([], \lambda\mathtt{x}.\mathtt{x})$$

to deal with. We can now choose either to close this with a new copy of the constraints for the body of the identity function, or to reuse the same constraint as before (as we are forced to in a monovariant analysis). Let us choose a new copy, and add the following constraints

$$\alpha'_{\mathtt{x}} \supseteq \alpha_{\mathtt{n}},\ \alpha_{\mathtt{p}} \supseteq \alpha'_{\mathtt{b}},\ \alpha'_{\mathtt{b}} \supseteq \alpha'_{\mathtt{x}}$$

which by transitivity give

$$\alpha'_{\mathtt{x}} \supseteq \mathtt{1},\ \alpha'_{\mathtt{b}} \supseteq \mathtt{1},\ \alpha_{\mathtt{p}} \supseteq \mathtt{1}$$

which completes a polyvariant flow analysis of the example.

2.3 The Analysis Algorithm

One difference between the monovariant and the polyvariant analyses brought out by this example is that the closure of a set of constraints is no longer uniquely determined. At first sight it might look like we can define the closure of a set of constraints uniquely up to renaming of flow variables by always choosing to close applications with fresh copies of the constraints for the bodies of the applied functions. This strategy will unfortunately lead to nontermination for recursive programs since when closing an application constraint corresponding to a recursive call, we get a new, renamed copy of the same constraint.

Thus we must do something special to ensure termination of the analysis algorithm. One way of achieving this is to ensure that the constraints we add when closing applications only contain flow variables drawn from some finite set. There are several ways to accomplish this; one which is popular in the literature is to have the flow variable names be bounded length strings over a finite alphabet.

In the algorithm we present in Fig. 3 we have an abstract type of *name supplies* and the following four functions: getname maps a name supply and a label (see Sec. 1.1) or program variable to a name, $\hat{}$ takes a name supply and a label and returns a new name supply, and F_1 and F_2 combine two name supplies to a new one according to the particular model of polyvariance the algorithm is instantiated to. The constraint construction function Polyvar takes a name supply as argument and uses getname and $\hat{}$ to generate flow variables when needed. It also decorates constraints with name supplies which are used by the closure algorithm. The functions F_1 and F_2 are used by the closure algorithm to construct the name supply decorating the new constraints it generates (this involves passing name supplies to Polyvar).

We will now look at a few instantiations of the polyvariant analysis.

$\psi \in$ DecConstr $::= \delta : \ \alpha_1 \supseteq \alpha_2 \mid \delta : \ \alpha \supseteq c \mid \delta : \ \alpha \supseteq (A, \lambda x.e) \mid \delta : \alpha_1 \to \alpha_2 \supseteq \alpha_3$
$\delta \in$ NameSupply

(a) Syntax of decorated constraints

$$
\begin{aligned}
&\mathsf{Polyvar}(\delta, A, x) = (\{\delta\hat{\ }\mathsf{Label}(x) :\ \alpha \supseteq A(x)\},\ \alpha) \\
&\qquad \text{where } \alpha = \mathsf{getname}(\delta, \mathsf{Label}(x)) \\
&\mathsf{Polyvar}(\delta, A, c) = (\{\delta\hat{\ }\mathsf{Label}(c) :\ \alpha \supseteq c\},\ \alpha) \\
&\qquad \text{where } \alpha = \mathsf{getname}(\delta, \mathsf{Label}(c)) \\
&\mathsf{Polyvar}(\delta, A, x_1\, x_2) = (\{\delta\hat{\ }\mathsf{Label}(x_1\, x_2) :\ A(x_2) \to \alpha \supseteq A(x_1)\},\ \alpha) \\
&\qquad \text{where } \alpha = \mathsf{getname}(\delta, \mathsf{Label}(x_1\, x_2)) \\
&\mathsf{Polyvar}(\delta, A, \lambda x.e) = (\{\delta\hat{\ }\mathsf{Label}(\lambda x.e) :\ \alpha \supseteq (A, \lambda x.e)\},\ \alpha) \\
&\qquad \text{where } \alpha = \mathsf{getname}(\delta, \mathsf{Label}(\lambda x.e)) \\
&\mathsf{Polyvar}(\delta, A, \mathtt{let}\ x\ \mathtt{=}\ e_1\ \mathtt{in}\ e_2) = (S_1 \cup S_2, \alpha_2) \\
&\qquad \text{where } S_1, \alpha_1 = \mathsf{Polyvar}(\delta, A, e_1) \\
&\qquad\qquad\quad S_2, \alpha_2 = \mathsf{Polyvar}(\delta, A[x \mapsto \alpha_1], e_2)
\end{aligned}
$$

$$
\begin{aligned}
\mathsf{Close}(S) = {} & \text{while } S \text{ is not closed do} \\
& \quad \text{if } \{\delta_1 :\ \alpha \supseteq \alpha',\ \delta_2 :\ \alpha' \supseteq \tau\} \subseteq S \text{ and } \tau \in \mathit{Clos} \cup \mathit{Const} \\
& \qquad \text{then } S := S \cup \{F_1(\delta_1, \delta_2) :\ \alpha \supseteq \tau\} \\
& \quad \text{or if } \{\delta_1 :\ \alpha_1 \to \alpha_2 \supseteq \alpha_3,\ \delta_2 :\ \alpha_3 \supseteq (A, \lambda x.e)\} \subseteq S \\
& \qquad \text{then } S := S \cup S' \cup \{\delta_3 :\ \alpha_1' \supseteq \alpha_1,\ \delta_1 :\ \alpha_2 \supseteq \alpha_2'\} \\
& \qquad \text{where } S', \alpha_2' = \mathsf{Polyvar}(\delta_3, A[x \mapsto \alpha_1'], e) \\
& \qquad\qquad\ \ \delta_3 = F_2(\delta_1, \delta_2) \\
& \qquad\qquad\ \ \alpha_1' = \mathsf{getname}(\delta_3, x) \\
& \text{od} \\
& \text{return } S
\end{aligned}
$$

(b) Constraint generation and closure algorithms

Fig. 3. Implementation of the polyvariant analysis

Dynamic k-cfa. Here the name supplies are strings of labels of length at most k and flow variable names are strings of length at most $k+1$ where last symbol in the string might be a variable or a label and all the other are labels. We have $\mathsf{getname}(\langle l_1, \ldots, l_n\rangle, a) = \langle l_1, \ldots, l_n, a\rangle$ where a is a (program) variable or a label. We build name supplies using $\hat{\ }$ according to $\langle l_1, \ldots, l_n\rangle\hat{\ }l = \mathit{last}_k(\langle l_1, \ldots, l_n, l\rangle)$ where last_k is defined by

$$
\mathit{last}_k(\langle l_1, \ldots, l_n\rangle) = \begin{cases} \langle l_1, \ldots, l_n\rangle & \text{if } n \leq k \\ \langle l_{n-k+1}, \ldots, l_n\rangle & \text{otherwise} \end{cases}
$$

and we have $F_1(\delta_1, \delta_2) = \langle\,\rangle$ and $F_2(\delta_1, \delta_2) = \delta_1$.

Static k-cfa. Here the definitions of name supplies, flow variable names, **getname**, and $\hat{}$ are as for dynamic k-cfa. The only difference is in the definitions of F_1 and F_2, which are given below.

$$F_1(\delta_1, \delta_2) = \begin{cases} \delta_1 \text{ if } \delta_1 \text{ corresponds to an occurrence of a let-bound variable} \\ \delta_2 \text{ otherwise} \end{cases}$$

$$F_2(\delta_1, \delta_2) = \begin{cases} \delta_1 \text{ if } \delta_1 \text{ corresponds to an application of a let-bound variable} \\ \delta_2 \text{ otherwise} \end{cases}$$

3 The Polymorphic Analysis

Looking at the specification of the polyvariant analysis, it is clear that the derivation of constraints from an expression is unique modulo renaming of flow variables. Hence, it is possible to derive the constraints for the body of a lambda abstraction once and make fresh copies of them, rather than rederive them, in the definitions of $\models$ and closure. This is the idea behind the polymorphic analysis, which is summarized in Fig. 4. The inference rules given there allow us to prove judgements of the form $S, A \vdash e : \alpha$ which correspond to those in the polyvariant analysis except that the constraint language is different.

Here, the flow closures have aquired a third component, a type scheme of the form $\forall \overline{\alpha} . \alpha_1 \to \alpha_2 \mid S$ where $\overline{\alpha}$ is a sequence of flow variables which are generalized over, α_1 corresponds to the formal parameter and α_2 to the function result, and S are the constraints derived from the function body.

The concepts of model, closed constraint sets and explicit constraints carry over with a few changes: The definitions of $\models$ and closure do not refer to $\vdash$, but instead instantiate the constraints in a type scheme using a substitution θ required to be the identity for the free flow variables of the type scheme.

The properties are the same as in the polyvariant case; closed constraint sets have least models equal to the least models of the explicit constraints, but in general constraint sets lack least finite closures and finite least models.

This suggests that the two analyses have a lot in common, and in fact they can simulate each other precisely — either inference system can be used as an implementation of the other. We leave it as an exercise for the reader to write down an inference algorithm along the same line as the algorithm for the polyvariant analysis.

We will however explore a different sort of algorithm for this system.[4] The key idea for this algorithm is not only to derive the constraints for the body of a lambda abstraction once, but to try to do as much of the work of solving them at that time as well. Thus we want to transform the constraint set S derived from

[4] This algorithm is not in general equivalent to the polyvariant analysis algorithm—it is the inference systems which are equivalent.

$$\chi \in \text{Constraint} \quad ::= \alpha_1 \supseteq \alpha_2 \mid \alpha \supseteq c \mid \alpha \supseteq w \mid \alpha_1 \rightarrow \alpha_2 \supseteq \alpha_3$$
$$w \in \text{TypeScheme} ::= (A, \lambda x.e, \forall \overline{\alpha}\,.\,\alpha_1 \rightarrow \alpha_2 \mid S)$$

(a) Syntax of constraints

$$\{\alpha \supseteq A(x)\},\ A \vdash x : \alpha \ \text{M-VAR} \qquad \{\alpha \supseteq c\},\ A \vdash c : \alpha \ \text{M-CON}$$

$$\{A(x_2) \rightarrow \alpha \supseteq A(x_1)\},\ A \vdash x_1\, x_2 : \alpha \qquad \text{M-APP}$$

$$\frac{S,\ A[x \mapsto \alpha_1] \vdash e : \alpha_2 \qquad \overline{\alpha} \cap FV(A) = \emptyset}{\{\alpha \supseteq (A,\ \lambda x.e,\ \forall \overline{\alpha}\,.\,\alpha_1 \rightarrow \alpha_2 \mid S)\},\ A \vdash \lambda x.e : \alpha}\ \text{M-ABS}$$

$$\frac{S_1,\ A \vdash e_1 : \alpha_1 \qquad S_2,\ A[x \mapsto \alpha_1] \vdash e_2 : \alpha_2}{S_1 \cup S_2,\ A \vdash \texttt{let}\ x\ \texttt{=}\ e_1\ \texttt{in}\ e_2 : \alpha_2}\ \text{M-LET}$$

(b) Polymorphic inference rules

$$\begin{array}{ll} \mu \models \alpha_1 \supseteq \alpha_2 & \text{if } \mu(\alpha_2) \subseteq \mu(\alpha_1) \\ \mu \models \alpha \supseteq (A, e, \sigma) & \text{if } (A, e, \sigma) \in \mu(\alpha) \\ \mu \models \alpha \supseteq c & \text{if } c \in \mu(\alpha) \\ \mu \models \alpha_1 \rightarrow \alpha_2 \supseteq \alpha & \text{if } w \in \mu(\alpha) \Rightarrow \exists \theta\,.\,\mu \models \mathcal{I}(w, \alpha_1 \rightarrow \alpha_2, \theta) \end{array}$$

(c) Models of constraints

$$\{\alpha_1 \supseteq \alpha_2,\ \alpha_2 \supseteq w\} \subseteq S \Rightarrow \{\alpha_1 \supseteq w\} \subseteq S$$
$$\{\alpha_1 \supseteq \alpha_2,\ \alpha_2 \supseteq c\} \subseteq S \Rightarrow \{\alpha_1 \supseteq c\} \subseteq S$$
$$\{\alpha_1 \rightarrow \alpha_2 \supseteq \alpha_3,\ \alpha_3 \supseteq w\} \subseteq S \Rightarrow \exists \theta.\ \mathcal{I}(w, \alpha_1 \rightarrow \alpha_2, \theta) \subseteq S$$

(d) Closure of constraints

$$\begin{aligned} &\mathcal{I}((A,\ e,\ \forall \overline{\alpha}\,.\,\alpha_1' \rightarrow \alpha_2' \mid S'),\ \alpha_1 \rightarrow \alpha_2,\ \theta) \\ &\qquad = \begin{cases} \theta(S') \cup \{\theta(\alpha_1') \supseteq \alpha_1, \alpha_2 \supseteq \theta(\alpha_2')\} & \text{if } \alpha \notin \overline{\alpha} \Rightarrow \theta(\alpha) = \alpha \\ \text{undefined} & \text{otherwise} \end{cases} \end{aligned}$$

(e) Instantiation of type schemes

Fig. 4. Specification of the polymorphic analysis

$$
\begin{aligned}
&\mathsf{Infer}(A, S_{let}, x) &&= \{\delta : \alpha \supseteq A(x)\},\ \alpha\\
&\mathsf{Infer}(A, S_{let}, c) &&= \{\delta : \alpha \supseteq c\},\ \alpha\\
&\mathsf{Infer}(A, S_{let}, x_1\ x_2) &&= \{\delta : A(x_2) \to \alpha \supseteq A(x_1)\},\ \alpha\\
&\mathsf{Infer}(A, S_{let}, \lambda x.e) &&= \text{ let } S_e, \alpha_2 = \mathsf{Infer}(A[x \mapsto \alpha_1], S_{let}, e)\\
& && \qquad \overline{\alpha}, S_g = \mathsf{Gen}(A, S_{let}, S_e, \alpha_1 \to \alpha_2)\\
& && \quad \text{in } \{\delta : \alpha \supseteq (A, \lambda x.e, \forall \overline{\alpha}.\alpha_1 \to \alpha_2 \mid S_g)\},\ \alpha\\
&\mathsf{Infer}(A, S_{let}, \texttt{let } x = e_1 \texttt{ in } e_2) &&= \text{ let } S_1, \alpha_1 = \mathsf{Infer}(A, S_{let}, e_1)\\
& && \qquad S_2, \alpha_2 = \mathsf{Infer}(A[x \mapsto \alpha_1], S_{let} \cup exp(S_1), e_2)\\
& && \quad \text{in } S_1 \cup S_2,\ \alpha_2
\end{aligned}
$$

$$exp(S) = \{\delta : \alpha \supseteq rhs \mid \delta : \alpha \supseteq rhs \in S \wedge rhs \in Clos \cup Const\}$$

Fig. 5. The inference algorithm

the body of the abstraction to another constraint set S' which in some sense contains the same information as S (or possibly more conservative information, depending on how applications have been closed).

3.1 The Inference Algorithm

The inference algorithm is presented in Fig. 5 and 6. The functions used by Gen in Fig. 6 can be used to analyze a program (closed expression) e in the following way:

$$
\begin{aligned}
S, \alpha &= \mathsf{Infer}([\,], \emptyset, e)\\
S', \emptyset &= \mathsf{Close}(\emptyset, \emptyset, S)\\
S'' &= \mathsf{Explicit}(\emptyset, \{\alpha\}, S')
\end{aligned}
$$

Then S'', α is a representation for the flow information of e. We will now give a short overview of the different parts of the algorithm and how they fit together followed by an example.

The function Infer. Infer takes three arguments; a flow environment, a set of constraints and an expression. The first and last correspond to the flow environment and expression in the inference system, but the middle argument deserves some explanation. In short, S_{let} provides some information about the values of let-bound variables that are in scope at a certain point (and about some variables that are not in scope). In a conventional type system, the typing environment maps let bound variables to type schemes rather than type variables, but here this is not the case, so S_{let} is needed to carry that information. Note that this is only for the purpose of simplifying constraints during the inference; if that is postponed until all of the constraints are generated, S_{let} is not needed.

In contrast to Polyvar, Infer has no name supply argument. This is because which variables occur in constraints added during the closing of application constraints is determined by a substitution, not by invoking Infer. Hence, the variables and name supplies generated by Infer can be arbitrary fresh ones.

Infer uses the function Gen for constructing type schemes. There are many possible definitions of Gen; the simplest one is $\mathsf{Gen}(A, S_{let}, S, \alpha_1 \rightarrow \alpha_2) = FV(S) \setminus FV(A),\ S$. Using this version of Gen, it is clear that Infer would generate the same constraints as the inference system, making the syntactic soundness of Infer unproblematic. The definition we give in Fig. 6 is considerably more complicated, and the question arises as to what the relation between the type schemes manipulated by the algorithm and the inference system is. We will return to this issue below, although we will not give it any formal treatment in this paper.

The function Gen. The overall strategy of the simplification algorithm we use is the same as for the monolithic solution used in the polyvariant analysis; close and extract the explicit constraints. The differences are motivated by the fact that we previously had all of the constraints available; now we must deal with the fact that the constraints will be part of a type scheme that will be instantiated, so that renamed copies of the constraints we are working with will be added to other constraint sets, and we must take care of possible interactions.

Roughly, such interactions come in two forms. First, flow variables that occur to the right in the type scheme might also occur to the left later. An example of this is the flow variable to the left of the arrow, which by the definition of instantiation will be constrained to include the value of the argument to the application. In a similar way, we may find values for the free flow variables of the type scheme. These flow variables are intuitively concerned with the flow of values *into* the type scheme.

Second, flow variables that occur to the left in the type scheme may occur to the right outside. This is true for the flow variable to the right of the arrow which by instantiation will end up to the right of the result of an application. These represent the flow of values *out of* the type scheme.

These two sets of flow variables must be taken into account when defining closure and explicit constraints, and this is done by the functions Close and Explicit. The initialisation of the set L reflects the facts that the type schemes in S_{let} may be instantiated during the simplification, leaving their free variables in the new type scheme, and that there are no other possible values for the free variables occurring to the left in S_{let} (by construction, the type schemes in S_{let} have no free variables occurring to the left, so $FV^L(S_{let}) = \{\alpha \mid \delta : \alpha \supseteq rhs \in S_{let}\}$).

In order for the algorithm to correspond to a sound derivation, we must not quantify over variables which are free in the flow envionment, but these can by construction not occur to the left in the simplified constraints (because they do not occur to the constraints before simplification). Hence they need not be explicitly excluded.

$$
\begin{aligned}
\mathsf{Gen}(A, S_{let}, S_e, \alpha_1 \to \alpha_2) = \ & \mathsf{let}\ L = FV(A) \cup FV(S_{let}) \cup \{\alpha_1\} \setminus FV^L(S_{let}) \\
& \quad S_e^*, L^* = \mathsf{Close}(L, S_{let}, S_e) \\
& \quad S = \mathsf{Explicit}(L^*, \{\alpha_2\}, S_e^*) \\
& \quad \overline{\alpha} = FV^L(S) \cup \{\alpha_1\} \\
& \mathsf{in}\ \overline{\alpha},\ S
\end{aligned}
$$

$\mathsf{Close}(L, S_{let}, S)$

$= \mathsf{while}\ S_{let} \cup S$ is not closed and L can grow do

  if $\{\delta_1 : \alpha \supseteq \alpha',\ \delta_2 : \alpha' \supseteq \tau\} \subseteq S_{let} \cup S$ and $\tau \in Clos \cup Const \cup L$

    then $S := S \cup \{F_1(\delta_1, \delta_2) :\ \alpha \supseteq \tau\}$

  or if $\{\delta_1 : \alpha_1 \to \alpha_2 \supseteq \alpha_3,\ \delta_2 : \alpha_3 \supseteq w\} \subseteq S_{let} \cup S$

    then $S := S \cup \mathsf{Inst}(w, \alpha_1 \to \alpha_2, \delta_1, F_2(\delta_1, \delta_2))$

  or if $\{\delta : \alpha_1 \to \alpha_2 \supseteq \alpha_3\} \subseteq S_{let} \cup S$ and $S \vdash \alpha_3 \succeq^1 L$

    then $L := L \cup \{\alpha_2\}$

od

return S, L

$\mathsf{Explicit}(L^*, R, S_e^*)$

$=$ begin

  $S := \emptyset$

  repeat

    if $\{\delta : \alpha \supseteq \tau\} \subseteq S_e^*$ and $\alpha \in R$ and $\tau \in Clos \cup Const \cup L^*$

      then $S := S \cup \{\delta : \alpha \supseteq \tau\}$; $R := R \cup FV^+(\tau)$

    or if $\{\delta : \alpha_1 \to \alpha_2 \supseteq \alpha_3\} \subseteq S_e^*$ and $\alpha_2 \in R$ and $S_e^* \vdash \alpha_3 \succeq^1 L^*$

      then $S := S \cup \{\delta : \alpha_1 \to \alpha_2 \supseteq \alpha_3\}$; $R := R \cup \{\alpha_1, \alpha_3\}$

  until nothing more can be added

  return S

end

$\mathsf{Inst}((A,\ e,\ \forall \overline{\alpha} . \alpha_1' \to \alpha_2' \mid S'),\ \alpha_1 \to \alpha_2,\ \delta_1,\ \delta_2)$

$= \mathsf{let}\ \theta = id[\overline{\alpha} \mapsto \mathsf{get\text{-}names}(\delta_2, S')]$

  $S_\theta = \{\delta_2 \hat{}\, \delta :\ \theta(lhs) \supseteq \theta(rhs) \mid \delta : lhs \supseteq rhs \in S'\}$

$\mathsf{in}\ S_\theta \cup \{\delta_2 : \theta(\alpha_1') \supseteq \alpha_1,\ \delta_1 : \alpha_2 \supseteq \theta(\alpha_2')\}$

Fig. 6. The generalization algorithm

$$FV^L(lhs \supseteq rhs) = FV^+(lhs) \cup FV^-(rhs)$$
$$FV^-(\alpha) = \emptyset$$
$$FV^-(\alpha_1 \to \alpha_2) = \{\alpha_1\}$$
$$FV^-(c) = \emptyset$$
$$FV^-(A, e, \forall \overline{\alpha}\,.\,\alpha_1 \to \alpha_2 \mid S) = (\{\alpha_1\} \cup FV^-(S)) \setminus \overline{\alpha}$$

$$FV^R(lhs \supseteq rhs) = FV^-(lhs) \cup FV^+(rhs)$$
$$FV^+(\alpha) = \{\alpha\}$$
$$FV^+(\alpha_1 \to \alpha_2) = \{\alpha_2\}$$
$$FV^+(c) = \emptyset$$
$$FV^+(A, e, \forall \overline{\alpha}\,.\,\alpha_1 \to \alpha_2 \mid S) = FV^+(A) \cup (\{\alpha_2\} \cup FV^+(S)) \setminus \overline{\alpha}$$

$$S \vdash \alpha \succeq^1 L \quad \Leftrightarrow \quad \alpha \in L \ \vee\ \delta : \alpha \supseteq \alpha' \in S \wedge \alpha' \in L$$

Fig. 7. The generalization algorithm; auxilliary definitions

The function Close. The closure algorithm is rather similar to the closure algorithm for the polyvariant analysis. We will point out the major differences below.

First, not only closures and constants are propagated, but also the flow variables in L (which are those whose values might be affected from outside the type scheme).

Second, we have the update to L. Intuitively, this means that if we do not know the possible functions that may flow to an application, then we do not know the possible results.

Third, when closing application constraints, we use the function Inst to instantiate w. For the simplifications to be sound, we must have that the constraints S' from the type scheme w (not the parameter and result connecting constraints) either are already contained in S (the closed constraint set under construction) or any variables occuring to the left in them do not occur in S. Thus we arrange for the instantiating substitution to depend on S' in such a way that different S' will always get disjoint substitutions. The closure algorithm also uses name supplies to generate unique flow variables so that a type scheme can be instantiated differently in different applications. Thus Inst uses the function get-names which is particular to the choice of name supply structure but must satisfy that if $\delta_1 \neq \delta_2$ or $S'_1 \neq S'_2$ then

$$\textsf{get-names}(\delta_1, S'_1) \cap \textsf{get-names}(\delta_2, S'_2) = \emptyset.$$

While we are on the subject of Inst and name supplies, we should add that $\hat{}$ now combines two name supplies, rather than a name supply and a label. We still have the requirement that the set of name supplies be finite.

The definition of get-names makes termination of the simplification slightly less obvious than before, since we may get new type schemes from instantiations, and those type schemes may be distinct since some free variable might have been instantiated differently. So while the set of name supplies is still finite, what about the set of type schemes? In fact, it is finite. To see that this is the case, assign a *depth* to each type scheme occurring in the original constraints S (those passed to Close from Gen) such that a type scheme occurring in S has depth 0 and a type scheme occurring in the constraints in a type scheme of depth n has depth $n+1$, and let k be the number of name supplies. Then each depth 0 type scheme can be instantiated k times yielding k copies of each depth 1 type scheme and so on. Thus the simplified constraints may contain at most k^n copies of a depth n type scheme, so the simplified constraints contain a finite number of type schemes.

3.2 A Slightly Different Example

The example program from the previous section is too simple to exhibit any opportunities for incremental constraint solution, so here is a slightly larger program containing a rather dumb implementation of the K combinator.

```
let id = λx.x in
let k = λy.λz.id y in
let n = 1 in
let f = k n in
  f n
```

We will concentrate on the simplification of the constraints derived from the body of the $\lambda\mathtt{z}$ abstraction. To reduce clutter, we will ignore the manipulation of name supplies and simply choose new flow variable names informally. We start when Infer has already processed the binding of `id`, descended into the right hand side of the binding of `k`, derived the constraints from the body of the $\lambda\mathtt{z}$ abstraction and is calling Gen as follows:

$$\mathsf{Gen}(A, S_{let}, S_e, \alpha_{\mathtt{z}} \to \alpha_{\mathtt{zb}})$$

where

$$A = [\mathtt{id} \mapsto \alpha_{\mathtt{id}},\ \mathtt{y} \mapsto \alpha_{\mathtt{y}}]$$
$$S_{let} = \{\alpha_{\mathtt{id}} \supseteq ([],\ \lambda\mathtt{x}.\mathtt{x},\ \forall \alpha_{\mathtt{x}}, \alpha_{\mathtt{xb}} . \alpha_{\mathtt{x}} \to \alpha_{\mathtt{xb}} \mid \{\alpha_{\mathtt{xb}} \supseteq \alpha_{\mathtt{x}}\})\}$$
$$S_e = \{\alpha_{\mathtt{y}} \to \alpha_{\mathtt{zb}} \supseteq \alpha_{\mathtt{id}}\}$$

Gen computes the set L as $\{\alpha_{\mathtt{y}}, \alpha_{\mathtt{z}}\}$; these are the as yet unknown input to the computation in the abstraction body. Since we have the value of $\alpha_{\mathtt{id}}$ from S_{let}, $\alpha_{\mathtt{id}}$ is not considered an unknown input.

We use S_{let} when closing S_e, so we get the following application to close:

$$\alpha_{\mathtt{y}} \to \alpha_{\mathtt{zb}} \supseteq \alpha_{\mathtt{id}} \qquad \alpha_{\mathtt{id}} \supseteq ([],\ \lambda\mathtt{x}.\mathtt{x},\ \forall \alpha_{\mathtt{x}}, \alpha_{\mathtt{xb}} . \alpha_{\mathtt{x}} \to \alpha_{\mathtt{xb}} \mid \{\alpha_{\mathtt{xb}} \supseteq \alpha_{\mathtt{x}}\})$$

Instantiating with the substitution $\theta = id[\alpha_{\mathtt{x}} \mapsto \alpha'_{\mathtt{x}}, \alpha_{\mathtt{xb}} \mapsto \alpha'_{\mathtt{xb}}]$ gives the following new constraints:

$$\alpha'_{\mathtt{x}} \supseteq \alpha_{\mathtt{y}} \qquad \alpha_{\mathtt{zb}} \supseteq \alpha'_{\mathtt{xb}} \qquad \alpha'_{\mathtt{xb}} \supseteq \alpha'_{\mathtt{x}}$$

Since α_y is included in L, it needs to be propagated, which yields these:

$$\alpha'_{xb} \supseteq \alpha_y \qquad \alpha_{zb} \supseteq \alpha_y$$

At this point closing is complete and we get $L^* = L = \{\alpha_y, \alpha_z\}$ since there were no applications which could not be closed because the applied function was unknown (that is, included in or dependent on L).

We will now compute the explicit constraints, i.e. those that are important for the value of α_{zb}. In this case, the first explicit constraint we find is $\alpha_{zb} \supseteq \alpha_y$ since $\alpha_{zb} \in R$ and $\alpha_y \in L$. Since we have decided that this constraint is important, anything that contributes to the value of its right hand side is also important, so we add α_y to R, but this yields no more explicit constraints. Note especially that $\alpha_y \to \alpha_{zb} \supseteq \alpha_{id}$ is not important; since the function (α_{id}) is known, we have been able to find the value of this application and it need not concern us further.

After this it is plain sailing; the flow variables to quantify over are α_z and α_{zb} and the type scheme constructed becomes:

$$w_z = (A,\ \lambda\mathtt{z.id\ y},\ \forall \alpha_z, \alpha_{zb} \,.\, \alpha_z \to \alpha_{zb} \mid \{\alpha_{zb} \supseteq \alpha_y\})$$

This type scheme is then included in the type scheme for the enclosing $\lambda\mathtt{y}$ abstraction:

$$w_y = ([\mathtt{id} \mapsto \alpha_{id}],\ \lambda\mathtt{y}.\lambda\mathtt{z.id\ y},\ \forall \alpha_y, \alpha_{yb} \,.\, \alpha_y \to \alpha_{yb} \mid \{\alpha_{yb} \supseteq w_z\})$$

Which is applied twice yielding the unsurprising result `1` for the little program.

4 Acknowledgements

This work was carried out while the author was visiting Hanne and Flemming Nielson and Torben Amtoft in Aarhus and has benefited very much from the discussions during our twice-a-week T-day meetings.

Funding was provided by Esprit BRA 8130 LOMAPS.

References

1. A. V. Aho, R. Sethi, and J. D. Ullman. *Compilers principles, techniques, and tools.* Addison-Wesley, Reading, MA, 1986.
2. Karl-Filip Faxén. Optimizing lazy functional programs using flow inference. In Alan Mycroft, editor, *Proceedings of the Second International Symposium on Static Analysis*, pages 136–153, Glasgow, UK, September 1995. Springer-Verlag.
3. Nevin Heintze. Set-based analysis of ML programs. In *Proc. ACM Conference on LISP and Functional Programming*, 1994.
4. Suresh Jagannathan and Stephen Weeks. A unified treatment of flow analysis in higher-order languages. In *Principles of Programming Languages*, 1995.
5. Suresh Jagannathan and Andrew Wright. Effective flow analysis for avoiding runtime checks. Technical Report 95-3, NEC Research Institute, May 1995.

6. N. D. Jones and S. S. Muchnick. A flexible approach to interprocedural data flow analysis and programs with recursive data structures. In *Conference Record of the 9th Annual ACM Symposium on Principles of Programming Languages*, pages 66–74, Albuquerque, NM, January 1982.
7. Neil D. Jones and Steven S. Muchnick. Flow analysis and optimization of Lisp-like structures. In *Conference Record of the 6th Annual ACM Symposium on Principles of Programming Languages*, pages 244–256, January 1979.
8. Jens Palsberg. Closure analysis in constraint form. In *CAAP'94*, 1994.
9. Peter Sestoft. *Analysis and efficient implementation of functional programs*. PhD thesis, DIKU, University of Copenhagen, Denmark, October 1991.
10. O. Shivers. Control flow analysis in Scheme. In *Proceedings of the ACM SIGPLAN '88 Conference on Programming Language Design and Implementation*, volume 23, pages 164–174, Atlanta, GA, June 1988.
11. O. Shivers. The semantics of Scheme control-flow analysis. In *Proceedings of the Symposium on Partial Evaluation and Semantics-Based Program Manipulation*, volume 26, pages 190–198, New Haven, CN, June 1991.

Parallel Implementation of Functional Languages*

R. Wilhelm, M. Alt, F. Martin, M. Raber **

Fachbereich 14 Informatik
Universität des Saarlandes
Saarbrücken

Lazy evaluation is optimal (up to overhead). J. Niehren, POPL'96

Abstract. Great hopes in the exploitation of the (implicit) parallelism inherent in functional programs have driven a number of projects. General frustration resulted wherever implementations on distributed memory machines were attempted. The grain size of potentially parallel tasks is too small to amortize the enormous costs of the necessary communication. The management of the parallelism is expensive. Decision making in the network operating system suffers from the fact, that most parameters such as the number of potentially parallel tasks and their execution times are dynamic.
This article tries to summarise the state of the art in the parallel implementation of functional languages, to give reasons why attempts have failed to show performance, and argues why this will probably remain so. Similar arguments will hold for other declarative languages and mechanisms with implicit fine grain parallelism such as logic and constraint languages.

1 Introduction

Parallel architectures are a big promise for a further increase in computation power of computer systems. However, the exploitation of the parallelism offered by them is still a difficult task. The step from a sequential to a parallel program incurs the following overheads for managing the parallelism.

- Processes have to be managed; they have to be created, blocked, resumed, and terminated.
- Global scheduling of the processes usually requires global information. Gathering this information needs expensive communication.
- In the case of distributed memory machines, memory management including garbage collection may be quite costly.

* Research supported by the Deutsche Forschungsgemeinschaft, SFB 124 - VLSI-Design Methods and Parallelism

** Author's current address: Metalevel Software, Saarbrücken

- If the data communicated between processors are a graph-like linked structures, each communication may be preceded and followed by an expensive conversion, because the local representation of the graphs may not be invariant under the transport to a different processor.

In an implementation on a distributed memory machine, where communication is expensive, the overhead in communication hurts the most. Among the communication overheads listed above there are *problem inherent* overheads. These consist in the distribution of problem data and/or code over the network. Then there are the *organizational* overheads, e.g. managing distributed memory structures, gathering load information for scheduling. These overheads have to be compensated for by an exploitation of the increased computational power. Successes have only been achieved on restricted classes of problems [FWM94].

Embarrassingly parallel problems: These are problems, which admit solutions with very large grain and little communication, e.g. factorization of large numbers.

Data parallel problems: These are problems, whose solutions consist of regular computations on large sets of homogeneous data.

Large reactive systems: In some applications a large homogeneous set of processes is dynamically created on response to stimuli from the environment.

Distributed data bases: The data are spread over a set of local memories with appropriate replication and migration mechanisms to allow for parallel transactions while preserving data consistency.

Problems in NC: These are problems, which allow efficient solutions on the PRAM, the complexity peoples' favourite machine model. The algorithms typically explicitly allocate work to processors.

What are the expectations of a programmer, who writes a parallel program X?

1. X will run *not much slower* than the best corresponding sequential version.
2. X will run *faster* than the best corresponding sequential version.
3. X will run *faster with a predictable speedup* than the best corresponding sequential version.
4. X will run *faster with a reasonably sized constant fraction speedup* than the best corresponding sequential version.

Here "best sequential implementation" refers to the state-of-the-art and not to proved lower bounds. Thus, the parallel implementor aims at a moving target. Predicting the overhead involved in managing parallelism and thus predicting speedup is difficult and only possible for a small set of algorithms so far.

Usually, X will be some application, such as predicting the weather, simulating the air stream around a car, or solving some other large system of differential equations. We would then interpret the above statements as holding for all inputs to X. Note, that the program may access and use the information about the size of the problem!

In the case of the parallel implementation of a language, the challenge is considerably higher. One expects, that these statements are interpreted as holding for at least a reasonably large, not contrived set of programs and all inputs to these programs.

We should not be content with a language or language class, which doesn't even let us exploit the parallelism admitted by the problem. It would be very surprising if any implementation of such a language would exhibit any speedups given the rather restricted success in the exploitation of parallelism. In other words, if skilled algorithms people and programmers were unable to use parallelism to speed up execution of their programs, how could we expect that implementations of a rather general class of languages could do better? This would be even more true for languages, which don't support constructs responsible for the success in the above listed problem classes, e.g. large grain parallelism, higher order operators on aggregates of homogeneous data, explicit allocation of work to groups of processors.

Hence, we arrive at the following maxim for the designer and the implementor of a language.

The language should allow the programmer to formulate a solution to his problem, such that the maximal parallelism available in the solution is expressible in the program, and the implementation should exploit this parallelism to gain a constant fraction speedup.

Functional languages, says the folklore, offer a huge potential for the parallel execution of programs, because these are referentially transparent and therefore inherently parallel. Similar arguments are made in favour of attempts to execute logic languages [AB90], constraint languages [AMT93], and termrewriting systems on parallel architectures [AK96]. For reasons of programming methodology lazy functional languages have been advocated as preferable to strict languages. They offer the greater challenge for the parallel implementation, since the lazy reduction strategy is inherently sequential, and thus parallelism has first to be discovered by extremely expensive and complex analyses [Mau86,Bur90b]. Still many groups, including ours, chose a lazy source language in their attempt to develop efficient parallel implementations [RRH+88] [Bur90a] [NSMC92] [Hil95] [Tre94] [Cha94][THJ+96][NSEP91], although it now looks like a masochist approach. We take the purist's position in this paper. Source language is a purely functional language. Most of the treatment does apply to eager and lazy languages. We don't consider (course grain) functional languages, where programs would have a static number of (rather large) tasks communicating through specified channels.

Besides a few implementations of data parallel languages [FMS+95] none of the attempts have shown impressive results. This article tries to show where progress has been made, where no breakthrough has been achieved, and why this probably will not happen.

We will highlight during our discussion open questions for which no efficient solution is known so far by:

This is an open problem. ▌

2 Target architectures and fair measurements

As target architectures we consider distributed memory machines. Until PRAM-architectures become commercially available [ACC+90,AKP91], these are the favourite target architectures for reasons of scalability and availability in a rather large variety (at least until most makers went bankrupt). Virtual shared memory machines often are not scalable and expose a nonuniform memory access behaviour, which makes it hard to predict runtimes.

Processing power is still increasing faster than the communication speed in the networks. Currently sending one message through the network costs approximately as much as executing 1000 floating point instructions. This makes up the quotient t_{comm}/t_{comp}, mentioned below. Hence, a processor can compute quite a bit, until it pays to send some work it has to another processor. In addition it means, that all the algorithms, which are needed to manage parallelism, i.e. process management, scheduling, and garbage collection heavily increase the organizational overhead, when they need communication.

2.1 Grain size

[FWM94], p. 51, shows a formula for the inter-node communication part of the parallel computation overhead. This part of the overhead is said to be proportional to t_{comm}/t_{comp}, i.e. the relation between the time needed to send a word to a neighbour and the time to execute one instruction. It is claimed to also be proportional to the reciprocal of some root of the *grain size*, the unit of work executed in parallel, and to some factor derived from the difficulty to embed the problem dimension into the topology dimension. Think of which of the different parts can be influenced by an implementation. The problem dimension, i.e. the connectivity of the graph can be influenced by the decision to share or to copy common computations. The main influence on this overhead, however, will come from the grain size. Since communication overhead is the "killer" for many attempts to parallel execution, it pays to increase the grain size. However, this should be done in a honest way, see below.

In our problem domain, a grain usually is the evaluation of one closure or one function application. The size of these grains is statically not known, in general. Non-recursive and *small* expressions [Rab94] are the exceptions. However, given the usual style of functional programming they tend to have rather small evaluation times. Most of the time, it doesn't pay to send them away for a remote evaluation. We are then left with recursive expressions whose dynamic sizes, i.e. evaluation times, are unknown.

2.2 Sources of false happiness

There are several ways an enthusiastic implementor of a functional (or other) language on a DMM can cheat himself.

The first and most commonly found way is to run the parallel implementation on one processor as a comparison with the p-processor version. This usually gives nice speedups mostly due to effects discussed in the next paragraph.

The attribution of certain effects to a parallel implementation are debatable. The fact that a p-processor machine will have roughly p times the memory of a single processor machine often leads to super-linear speedups when carefully chosen problem sizes cause heavy garbage collection on the single processor machine while running without garbage collection on the p-processor machine. Similar effects can be observed due to p-fold increase in processor cache size.

One could argue, and this is often to be found, that it would be sufficient to use comparable implementation techniques in the sequential implementation and the parallel implementation in order to judge the potential for parallelisation, e.g. sequential interpretation vs. parallel interpretation. However, interpretation would increase the grain size by the slowdown factor of the interpreted implementation compared to a compiled version, thus reduce the parallel computation overhead, and therefore give the parallel implementation an unfair advantage. The requirement that the best sequential implementation be the point of comparison prevents this possible way of cheating oneself.

Here is an example showing, how one can cheat oneself and people with the same conviction:

```
pfib n == if n < n0
          then fib n
          else spawn f1 == pfib (n-1)
                     f2 == pfib (n-2)
               in f1 + f2

fib 0 == 0
fib 1 == 1
fib n == fib (n-1) + fib (n-2)
```

`pfib` generates an exponentially growing number of tasks (available parallelism!) with no communication between independent tasks. `n0` is used for granularity control. It should be determined taking the number of processors, the computing and the communication power, and even n into account to obtain an impressive speedup. It's the perfect parallel program! Of course, one should not compare it to the linear time sequential program computing Fibonacci numbers.

3 Abstract parallel machine for graph manipulation

To implement a lazy functional language one uses a parallel abstract machine [RRH+88,Joh83] which abstracts from some nasty features of real life machines such as fixed number of processors with bounded memory size. Executing a functional program will then dynamically create an a priori unknown number of incarnations of sequential abstract machines. These must at any time be mapped to the set of physical processors. This is the job of a network operating system.

Because we are here not interested in the details of compiling functional languages into abstract machine code [Pey87,WM95], we introduce another parallel machine, which is reduced to the bare minimum of functionality needed to create and delete sequential incarnations and to manipulate the storage structures they work on.

3.1 Mutator machine

The *parallel mutator machine* [Rab94] which we use forgets about most details of graph reduction. So it is possible to implement the essentially parallel aspects of any kind of parallel functional machine like parallel versions of the G-machine [Joh83], e.g. the νG-machine [Joh91], the CAM [CCM85], the MaMa [WM95] or the TIM [FW87] on this parallel mutator machine. With slight modifications it will also be possible to adapt it to a parallel WAM for a Prolog implementation. The name of the machine is adopted from the garbage collection nomenclature. A similar machine has been described by Kesseler [Kes96].

The machine has a dynamically changing number of (sequentially working) mutators which together evaluate a common global graph that can be accessed (read and written) from all mutators. It only allocates nodes and never frees a single node. A mutator has its stack, some registers and the code as private components. The graph and the data structure representing the set of currently existing mutators are common components.

It is the job of an operating system to simulate an unbounded number of mutators each with unbounded memory on a concrete limited target architecture.

Mutators may turn into *processes* of the operating system. Hence, the two major duties of the operating system are process management and memory management.

There are instructions of the sequential machine to:

manipulate the stack :
push makes a copy of a graph pointer
slide removes graph pointers

manipulate the graph :
mknode creates a node with contents taken from the stack
update overwrites a node
getlabel reads a node if evaluated; may lead to blocking
getsuccs reads the successors of a node referred to from the top of the stack

manipulate mutators :
start creates a new mutator for a reference to some unevaluated expression
stop finishes the mutator or the whole computation, resp.

These instructions reflect the graph manipulations by functional programs (almost) independently of the reduction strategy. So we can abstract from these aspects. All that is left is the functionality, which needs support by the operating system.

3.2 Operating System

The operating system consists of two parts: The *memory manager* distributes the common data (the graph) over the memory of the different processors and reclaims unused space (garbage collection). The *process manager* takes care of the mutators and schedules them to the different processors. In the next sections, we describe what their duties are, and what a minimal functionality they have to offer is. Different implementations of the operating system will implement these functions differently. This is discussed in detail in [Rab94].

Memory Management The abstract machine deals with abstract graph addresses (*references*). These references have to be mapped to real machine addresses. Accesses to graph nodes are then translated into local addresses in case of a local node, and into request messages to the remote owner in case of a remote node. Any choice of a heap representation of graphs is connected to a trade-off between costs for local accesses and costs for conversion of the representation when graph parts are communicated. Any scheme using direct local access needs expensive back and forth conversion before and after sending graph parts. Depending on the computation on the graph, there may be a different representation being both efficient in local access and in communication, cf. Kesseler's Thesis [Kes96].

Call-by-need semantics of the functional language to be implemented suggests that expressions with several "costumers" are shared, that they be evaluated by the first one to ask for the value, and that the others access the value. The meaning of a program will, however, not change, when the expression is copied to and evaluated by several remote costumers. It is a question of design whether to make copies of subgraphs to different processors, or to have only a single, possibly shared copy of each subgraph. Note, that this is the only chance to change the amount of problem inherent communication.

Assume we have n consumers of the result of a computation located at different processors. Then sharing causes one single evaluation, time e, and for each remote access one message to the owner and either one blocking message, time t, and one wake-up message including the result, time d_{result}, or one copy message with the requested value, time d_{result}. Duplication causes n evaluations and one access message to the owner, time t, and $n-1$ copy messages with the unevaluated subgraph, time d_{work}.

Summarizing we have:

	evaluations (e)	tag-messages (t)	data-messages (d_X)
Sharing	1	$2 \times (n-1)$	$n-1$
Duplication	n	$n-1$	$n-1$

which leads to the inequality

$$\underbrace{e + (n-1) \times (2 \times t + d_{result})}_{sharing} > \underbrace{n \times e + (n-1) \times (t + d_{work})}_{duplication}$$

This can be simplified (assuming $n \neq 1$) slightly to

$$t - e \times \frac{n+1}{n-1} + d_{result} > d_{work}$$

Satisfaction of the inequality favours duplication, otherwise sharing. Of course, the existence of local costumers may favour sharing as it avoids duplication of work and does not need communication.

> A decision about whether to copy or to share would need information about the relative sizes of the e, d_{work}, d_{result} which are unknown. The value of n is unknown, too.

Independently of the particular method used, the memory manager needs information about

- the structure of the graph nodes (which information is a reference to another node, and the size of objects)
- the pointers from the stack and registers of the mutators to the graph. These pointers are needed to find unused nodes and to rearrange the heap.

Additionally, one has to decide which garbage collection method to use, cf. section 5.

The minimal functionality of the memory manager needed for the implementation of mutator machines is:

alloc	creates a node of a given type and returns a new reference to it
copyref	makes a copy of a reference
delref	informs the memory subsystem that a reference is no longer in use
write	updates the information in a graph node
read	extracts information from a graph node

alloc creates references for real addresses; the other operations receive references as parameters, decode them to real addresses and take effect there.

Different implementations of the memory manager will implement these functions differently.

Process Management The decision, which computations should form a process is taken in several stages:

1. The language implementor selects the language constructs, which may potentially lead to parallel activities; either there are some explicitly parallel constructs in the language, or he selects those whose parallel execution is possible and supposedly profitable;
2. the compiler based on information about the program may decide whether a computation is worth to be executed in parallel and should become a mutator and correspondingly, whether to generate a *start* for it;

3. the operating system knowing the actual load can decide which mutators to convert into processes.

The process manager administrates the (dynamically changing number of) sequential mutators. In particular, it schedules them to the different processors. The main goal is to minimize the maximal running time of any processor; it may help to evenly distribute the work among the processors.

The process manager needs to offer at least the following functions:

fork	creates a new mutator for a subgraph; *may* result in a new process
dispatch	attempts to find a waiting process
suspend	suspends a process not able to continue evaluation
resume	resumes a process; reason of blocking disappeared
finish	terminates a process

The following table shows the relation between the mutators and the operating system. Mutator instructions on the left side are implemented using the operating system commands on the right side.

mknode	alloc, write
push	copyref
slide	delref
update	write, resume
getlabel	read, suspend
start	fork
stop	finish; dispatch

mknode calls alloc to obtain a new heap area and write to store a label and to pop a list of stack addresses into this area.

push copies a graph pointer into the stack. May call copyref depending on the kind of garbage collection used.

slide deletes a list of heap graph pointers from the stack; may have to call delref depending on the type of garbage collection used.

update overwrites a graph node using write. Calls resume if a blocked process waited for the value just written.

getlabel issues a read-command. The process trying to access a node is blocked by a suspend-command if the node isn't yet evaluated. Another process is scheduled by executing the dispatch-command.

start creates a new mutator. This mutator may be turned into a process by calling fork.

stop terminates the mutator. It calls finish to terminate the corresponding process and then *dispatch* to schedule another ready process.

4 Load balancing, scheduling

The goal of load balancing is:

Distribute work such that the maximal execution time on any processor is minimized

Global scheduling of processes to processors is in charge of achieving a good load balance. The above stated problem can in general not be solved statically, since the work is evolving dynamically. This means, that one has to deal with an online problem. It could be assumed, that an even distribution of the work among the processors guarantees satisfaction of the above goal. However, this need not be true due to the relative high costs of communication over computation. Any scheduling algorithm requiring too much communication, e.g. for gathering load information, may achieve a balanced work distribution, but will fail to minimize the overall execution time.

4.1 Scheduling

There is a whole zoo of scheduling problems, each characterised by a set of parameters [BESW94,GLLK79]. [BESW94] use three sets of together 11 parameters. They firstly concern the characteristics of the processor sets, i.e. single processor or multiple identical/uniform/dedicated and the actual number of processors. Secondly, they describe task and resource characteristics. These are the possibility of preemption, the existence of other resources, information about task processing times, i.e. uniform time, bounded times, arbitrary, but known, and dynamic, and the type of dependences between tasks. These range from no dependence over chains and forests to arbitrary dependences. The last parameter indicates the optimization criterion. There is one parameter missing, i.e. the one saying whether the scheduler works in a centralised or in a decentralised fashion. The former is assumed as default.

Most scheduling problems are NP-complete. Turning one parameter to a worse value usually makes the situation in some way more undesirable. A problem solvable in polynomial time may turn into an NP-complete problem. An NP-complete problem, for which a standard heuristics is guaranteed to nearly reach the optimum, may turn into one, for which no such good bound can be proved. Finally, an offline problem may turn into an online problem.

Our setting belongs almost to the worst in the zoo. We have a dynamically changing set of tasks, whose processing times in general are unknown. Rather general dependences evolve during the execution. In addition, we have to do with decentralised scheduling, and both the scheduling algorithm and the reallocation of work cause communication with nonnegligible costs. To the best of our knowledge,

> there is no algorithm known to solve our scheduling problem with any guaranteed performance.

There are (as always) strategical and technical questions about the scheduling method. The strategical questions are:

when should process migration be initiated?

which processes should migrate? One could decide to only migrate processes, whose results are needed. It has, however, been tried to increase the amount of parallelism by also migrating processes, whose results are not known to be needed. This is called *speculative evaluation*. Kesseler[Kes96] argues, that no proposed method should be used in managing speculative parallelism, since they are all too expensive in communication.

where, from where should a process migrate? There are two extreme answers to this this question. The first is the attempt to preserve locality by migrating processes only to neighbours. This risks a slow distribution of work. The other is to randomly distribute work [SW89]. The latter achieves provably good load balancing under realistic assumptions, but will probably be too expensive in communication.

The technical questions are:

how should process migration be executed? By *fork, resume*, or *dispatch*? The main characteristic is, whether an overloaded processor *actively* distributes work, i.e. tasks from its task queue, or whether idle (*passive*) processors ask other processors for excess work. A second design issue is, whether only newly created processes are migrated or also older processes together with their context. Hence, the following design choices are available: Actively distribute only new processes applying *fork* on the same processor, actively distribute all processes applying *dispatch* to the own task queue, or passively acquire work using *dispatch* applied to another processor's task queue.

The main disadvantages of active strategies are that idle processors may wait a long time, since they cannot influence the distribution, and that busy processors are additionally burdened with collecting load information and distributing processes.

Passive strategies have as main advantages, that only idle processors ask for work. If all processors are busy, no communication takes place.

how much should migrate with the process? This question has also to be solved under the condition, that communication should be minimized. Copying a graph from one processor to another one can take two forms. The basic techniques are *eager* copying and *full lazy* copying. The former means that the graph is copied as a whole, the latter transmits only nodes when they are needed. Advantages of the first approach are that only a single message is needed to transmit the graph which can decrease communication overheads. The latter may introduce a lot of small messages which can be costly, if the whole graph is needed, but is good if only small parts are needed. *Full lazy* copying also increases the (possible) sharing of results. Kesseler [Kes96] developed a combined technique, called *lazy* copying. It tries to avoid the copying of work, while retaining the advantage of copying multiple nodes together. It copies nodes unless it hits a redex which has a *defer attribute*. These nodes represent work, which should not be copied. Once a deferred node has been evaluated, it looses its defer attribute and may be copied. Deadlock avoidance requires an evaluation of each deferred node.

Which node should have a *defer* attribute initially?

Some schedulers base their decision on actual load information. The whole system has to be halted or an elaborate and expensive protocol to collect a snapshot has to be executed to gather exact load information. Thus, only approximate information can realistically be collected. Higher demands on the precision and the actuality of this information increase the communication costs of the computation. Kuchen and Wagener [KW90] have experimented with several frequencies of collection. Collecting load information periodically and after each change in the load turned out to be too expensive. Most promising was the strategy to collect each time a processor's state turned from idle to busy and vice versa.

Another aspect, which could be relevant for scheduling decisions is memory consumption on the different processors. This has so far not been regarded.

5 Distributed garbage collection

Naive conversions of sequential garbage collection algorithms to parallel ones often have high communication costs due to the necessary synchronization overhead. In a distributed multiprocessor system each processor is responsible for allocating and reclaiming structures residing in its local memory. Traditionally, the following three techniques are distinguished; each could be used in a parallel context.

mark/scan
: Cells are not reclaimed immediately when they become garbage. Collection works in two phases. The first (mark) phase starts from all references to heap cells in stacks and registers and marks the reachable cells. The second (scan) phase reclaims the unmarked cells (normally by a move/fix-up run). It takes several runs over the heap. During garbage collection the computation is halted. In a parallel implementation, there is substantial communication during the scan phase. To detect termination of the mark phase one needs an expensive global snapshot computation.

reference counting
: Every node x has an additional attribute, its *reference count* ($RC(x)$). It stores the number of pointers to the node. The operation **alloc** initialises the count, **delref** and **copyref** update the reference counts. Garbage is reclaimed when a count becomes zero. The additional space storing the reference counts and the inability to reclaim cycles are the main drawbacks.
: In distributed memory management, reference counting needs communication in the case of non-local references. A *non-overtaking* message system is required because garbage is reclaimed when a count becomes zero thereby possibly ignoring pending increment messages.

copying

This technique divides the heap equally into two *semi-spaces*. During computation, one semi-space contains the current data and the other obsolete data. Garbage collection is done by copying live cells to the obsolete semi-space and then swapping the roles of the two parts. In contrast to the *mark/scan* it needs only one run over the heap but twice the space.

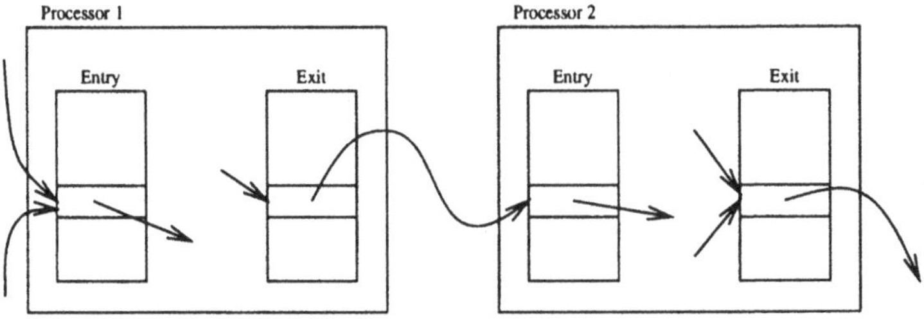

Fig. 1. Entry and exit tables

Any method used in the distributed case should avoid global synchronisation and should minimize communication. To decouple the activities of the different processors, garbage collection is split into two parts: *local* and *global* garbage collection. Pointers are divided into local and global ones. Non-local references are managed in entry and exit tables at each processor, cf. Figure 1. Global references into a heap go indirectly through the entry table of the processor, global references from a heap go indirectly through the exit table of that processor. Local garbage collection is normally done via a form of the *mark/scan* technique. A technique with a priori low communication costs is chosen for global garbage collection, namely reference counting. One has to extend this technique to be able to reclaim non-local cycles. The required non-overtaking message passing system can be realized spending additional space as follows. *Weighted reference counting* [Bev89] reduces the amount of communication needed for reference counting. It associates a weight $W(X,Y)$ with each reference from X to Y. The sum of all reference weights is equal to the reference count of the node:

$$RC(Y) = \sum_{X \to Y} W(X,Y)$$

Initially, a node created by alloc is given a sufficiently large power of two as reference count. When a reference X to Y is asked to supply a copy of the reference i.e. copyref, it splits its weight into half, keeping one half for itself and passing on the other half with the new copy. Indirection cells are needed when the weight of a reference to be copied has reached one. Thus, copying does not need communication.

Deleting a reference by delref requires a message to the owner of the node containing the weight of the reference. The owner subtracts the weight from its reference count. When the reference count falls to zero, the node is identified as garbage. Because only deletion message are needed, it can run on an *over-taking* message system. Figure 2 shows the three needed operations.

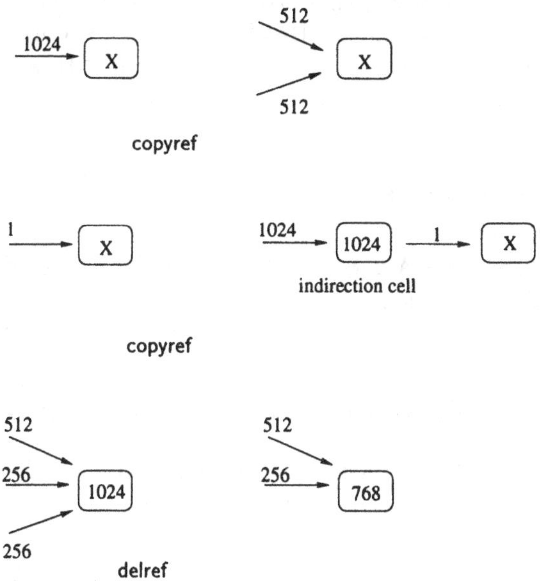

Fig. 2. Weighted reference count technique

The technique of Lins and Jones [LJ91], *cyclic weighted reference counting*, solves the problem of reclaiming cycles. They associate a second reference count (SRC, only temporary for mark phase) with each cell. A color is assigned to each cell during garbage collection: *red* for potential garbage (cyclic), *green* for live cells, and *blue* for garbage. It keeps a control queue for potential entries to garbage cycles. A node is put into the queue at a delete reference operation, if the reference count is not zero ([LV91] give a discussion of managing the control queue). At garbage collection time, a node is selected from the control queue. Then a *mark red* phases colors all reachable cells, updating additionally the SRC. In an additional run, cells are divided into green (SRC> 0) and blue cells. A further run reclaims the blue cells and removes related references from the control queue. This technique causes much synchronization communication to detect termination of the separated runs and also global synchronisations (*barrier synchronisation*).

It is still not clear how to reclaim efficiently and concurrently (non-local) garbage.

6 Conclusion

Of course, no negative results of the type "parallelism in functional program cannot be exploited" have been proved. Techniques developed in other areas may come to help. Increasing the grain size by lazy threads [GSC95], prefetching needed remote data by sampling [BAW] may lead to overlapping computation and communication and thus to reduced wait times. However, the problem doesn't seem to admit an easy solution.

7 Acknowledgements

The authors thank Susanne Albers, Yosi Ben Asher, Thomas Rauber, and Gudula Rünger for valuable discussions.

We would like to end this article in the spirit of our starting quotation.

Parallelism in functional programs is maximal (up to exploitation).

References

[AB90] V. Bafna A. Gupta, A. Banerjea, V. Jha and PCP Bhatt. Parallel implementation of logic languages. In *CONPAR 90 - VAPP IV*, pages 154–165, Berlin - Heidelberg - New York, 1990. Springer.

[ACC+90] R. Alverson, D. Callahan, D. Cummings, B. Koblenz, A. Porterfield, and B. Smith. The tera computer system. *1990 International Conf. on Supercomputing*, June 11-15 1990. Published as Computer Architecture News 18:3.

[AK96] I. Alouini and C. Kirchner. Toward the Concurrent Implementation of Computational Systems. In *Algebraic and Logic Programming*, volume 1139 of *LNCS*, pages 1–31. Springer-Verlag, September 1996.

[AKP91] F. Abolhassan, J. Keller, and W.J. Paul. On the Cost-Effectiveness of PRAMs. In *SPDP*, pages 2–9. IEEE Computer Society, 1991.

[AMT93] C. Atay, K. McAloon, and C. Tretkoff. 21p: A highly parallel constraint logic programming language. In Linda R. Petzold Richard F. Sincovec, David E. Keyes, Michael R. Leuze and Daniel A. Reed, editors, *Proceedings of the 6th SIAM Conference on Parallel Processing for Scientific Computing*, pages 822–828, Norfolk, VI, March 1993. SIAM Press.

[BAW] Y. Ben-Asher and R. Wilhelm. Compiler support for fair execution of shared memory parallel programs on networks of workstations. in preparation.

[BESW94] J. Błazewicz, K. H. Ecker, G. Schmidt, and J. Węglarz. *Scheduling in Computer and Manufacturing Systems*. Springer-Verlag, 1994. Second, Revised Edition.

[Bev89] D.I. Bevan. An efficient reference counting solution to the distributed garbage collection problem. *Parallel Computing*, 9(2):179–192, 1989.

[Bur90a] G. L. Burn. Implementing Lazy Functional Languages on Parallel Architectures. In P. C. Treleaven, editor, *Parallel Computers — Object-Oriented, Functional, Logic*, Series in Parallel Computing, chapter 5, pages 101–140. John Wiley & Sons, Chichester, 1990.

[Bur90b] G. L. Burn. Using Projection Analysis in Compiling Lazy Functional Programs. In *LISP'90, Nice, France*, pages 227–241. ACM Press, 1990.

[CCM85] G. Cousineau, P. L. Curien, and M. Mauny. The categorical abstract machine. In J.-P. Jouannaud, editor, *Functional Programming Languages and Computer Architecture*, pages 50–64. Springer-Verlag, Berlin, DE, 1985. Lecture Notes in Computer Science 201Proceedings of. Conference at Nancy.

[Cha94] M. M. T. Chakravarty. A self-scheduling, non-blocking, parallel abstract machine for lazy functional languages. Proceedings of the 6th International Workshop on the Implementation of Functional Languages, 1994.

[FMS+95] J. Feo, P. Miller, S. Skedzielewski, S. Denton, and C. Solomon. Sisal 90. In A. P. Wim Bohm and John T. Feo, editors, *High Performance Functional Computing*, pages 35–47, April 1995.

[FW87] J. Fairbairn and S. Wray. TIM: A simple, lazy abstract machine to execute supercombinators. In *Functional Programming Languages and Computer Architecture*, pages 34–45. Springer Verlag, September 1987. LNCS 274.

[FWM94] G. C. Fox, R. D. Williams, and P. C. Messina. *Parallel Computing Works!* Morgan Kaufmann, 1994.

[GLLK79] R. Graham, E. Lawler, J. Lenstra, and A. Rinnoy Kan. Optimization and approximation in deterministic sequencing and scheduling: A survey. In *Annals of Discrete Mathematics*, volume 5, pages 287–326. North-Holland, Amsterdam, 1979.

[GSC95] S. C. Goldstein, K. E. Schauser, and D. E. Culler. Lazy threads, stacklets, and synchronizers: Enabling primitives for compiling parallel languages. In *Third Workshop on Languages, Compilers, and Run-Time Systems for Scalable Computers*, 1995.

[Hil95] J. M. D. Hill. Data-parallel lazy functional programming (Phd Thesis). Technical Report QMW-DCS-1995-701, Queen Mary and Westfield College, Department of Computer Science, Mile End Road, London, E1 4NS, UK, May 1995.

[Joh83] T. Johnsson. The G-machine: An abstract machine for graph reduction. In *Proceedings of the Joint SERC/Chalmers Workshop on Declarative Programming, University College*, London, UK, 1983.

[Joh91] T. Johnsson. Parallel evaluation of functional programs: The $<\nu$,G$>$ approach (summary). In *Parallel Architectures and Languages Europe PARLE*, pages 406–422. Springer-Verlag, 1991. LNCS 505.

[Kes96] M. Kesseler. *The Implementation of Functional Languages on Parallel Machines with Distributed Memory.* PhD thesis, "Katholieke Universiteit Nijmegen, The Netherlands", April 1996.

[KW90] H. Kuchen and A. Wagener. Comparison of dynamic load balancing strategies. Technical Report 90-05, Technical University of Aachen (RWTH Aachen), 1990.

[LJ91] R. D. Lins and R. E. Jones. Cyclic weighted reference counting. Technical Report 95, University of Kent, Canterbury, United Kingdom, December 1991.

[LV91] R. D. Lins and M. A. Vasques. A comparative study of algorithms for cyclic reference counting. Technical Report No. 92, Computing Laboratory,

University of Kent, Canterbury, UK, 1991. Submitted to Software - Practice and Experience.

[Mau86] D. Maurer. Strictness Computation Using Special Lambda-Expressions. In Harald Ganzinger and Neil D. Jones, editors, *Programs as Data Objects*, volume 217 of *LNCS*, pages 136–155. Springer-Verlag, October 1986.

[NSEP91] E. G. J. M. H. Nöcker, J. E. W. Smetsers, M. C. J. D. Eekelen, and M. J. Plasmeijer. Concurrent Clean. In E. H. L. Aarts, J. van Leeuwen, and M. Rem, editors, *PARLE '91, Parallel Architectures and Languages Europe, Volume I: Parallel Architectures and Algorithms*, volume 505 of *Lecture Notes in Computer Science*, pages 202–219, Eindhoven, The Netherlands, June 10–13, 1991. Springer, Berlin.

[NSMC92] J. H. Nang, D. W. Shin, S. R. Maeng, and J. W. Cho. A parallel execution of functional logic language with lazy evaluation. In *Fifth Generation Computer Systems*. IOS Press, Amsterdam, NL, 1992.

[Pey87] S. Peyton Jones. *The Implementation of Functional Programming Languages*. Prentice-Hall, 1987.

[Rab94] M. Raber. *Parallele Implementierung funktionaler Programmiersprachen*. PhD thesis, Universität des Saarlandes, 1994.

[RRH+88] M. Raber, Th. Remmel, E. Hoffmann, D. Maurer, F. Müller, H.-G. Oberhauser, and R. Wilhelm. Compiled graph reduction on a processor network. In *'Architektur und Betrieb von Rechensystemen', 10. GI/ITG-Fachtagung*, pages 198–212, Paderborn, FRG, March 1988. *Informatik Fachberichte 168*, Springer-Verlag.

[SW89] H. Seidl and R. Wilhelm. Probabilistic load balancing for parallel graph reduction. In *Proceedings IEEE Region 10 Conference*, pages 879–884, New York, 1989. IEEE.

[THJ+96] P W Trinder, K Hammond, J S Mattson Jr, A S Partridge, and S L Peyton Jones. GUM: a portable parallel implementation of Haskell. In *Proceedings of the ACM SIGPLAN '96 Conference on Programming Language Design and Implementation*, pages 79–88, Philadelphia, Pennsylvania, 21–May 1996.

[Tre94] G. Tremblay. *Parallel implementation of lazy functional languages using abstract demand propagation*. PhD thesis, McGill University, November 1994.

[WM95] R. Wilhelm and D. Maurer. *Compiler Design*. International Computer Science Series. Addison–Wesley, 1995.

Mobile Processes with Local Clocks*

Pierpaolo Degano, Jean-Vincent Loddo and Corrado Priami

Dipartimento di Informatica, Università di Pisa
Corso Italia, 40, I-56125 Pisa, Italy
{degano,priami}@di.unipi.it

Abstract. We propose a structural operational semantics that expresses temporal aspects of mobile and distributed systems, each sequential component of which has its local clock. Since the run-time support of a programming language implements the operations of the language via some lower-level routines, the same action, put in different contexts, may have different durations. Also the network topology affects these durations, typically when messages are exchanged. We model this through a transition system labelled by actions and their costs, in a discrete time. Then, we define two performance preordings that say when the execution of a process is faster than that of another. The first preorder is similar to those presented in the literature, while the second refines it in that it considers a process faster than another if it is such from some point onwards of its execution. Finally, as an example we compare the performance of a conventional uniprocessor architecture with a prefetch pipeline architecture.

1 Introduction

We propose a timed semantics for mobile processes, in which actions do not occur instantaneously, but require some (discrete) time to be executed. Unlike other proposals, we assume that actions *do not* have a fixed duration. This is a further step towards a more accurate description of the behaviour of processes, because the time an action a consumes depends on the basic operations that the run-time support of the target architecture performs for firing a. Typically, the resolution of a choice imposes some operations on the target architecture such as checking the ready list or implementing fairness policies. Therefore, in practice an action fired after a choice costs more than the same action occurring deterministically. Note that the run-time routine implementing action a is represented in the usual SOS descriptions of processes by the context in which a occurs.

As an example, consider the process

$$(a.P|b.Q) + R$$

where ".", "|" and "+" are interpreted as prefixing, parallel and nondeterministic composition as usual. To fire action a, the run time support spends some time,

* Work partially supported by ESPRIT BRA n. 8130 - LOMAPS.

say t, to choose the sub-process $(a.P|b.Q)$. So, the time needed to complete action b must include also t, even if b is independent of a. Also, in order to tune the cost of actions with the architecture of the network, we establish that communication costs depend on the allocation of processes, on the link used and on the size of the message exchanged. Typically, a communication between processes placed on close nodes is cheaper than a communication involving extensive routing.

We define a structural operational semantics of the π-calculus that associates any sequential component of a system with its own clock, in a truly concurrent fashion. It is a conservative extension of the original semantics given in [20]. Our starting point is an enhanced version of operational semantics from which one smoothly obtains a hierarchy of specifications of concurrent systems closer and closer to implementations. In this way, it is possible to analyse both qualitative and quantitative aspects of systems on tightly related formal descriptions [11]. More precisely, we exploit proved transition systems, a parametric model used in [9, 10] to describe uniformly different qualitative aspects of processes. The transitions of these transition systems are labelled by encodings of their proofs. Then, by inspecting these richer labels we rebuild the operations needed for deducing actions and we can derive their context sensitive costs, reflecting the target architecture. Remarkably, the knowledge of the interacting processes in a communication permits to make their allocation influence costs. In the actual SOS definition of the operational semantics of the π-calculus, the cost function is parametric and can be instantiated to reflect different target architectures. In this way, the same definition can describe the behaviour of a system running on different targets. For simplicity, we consider here networks of homogeneous machines only. The extension of our proposal to heterogeneous networks is only a matter of longer definitions, especially those expressing the costs of operations.

We also define two preorders which say when a process is more efficient than another. Both relations require that the processes to be compared are bisimilar. The first preorder is similar to other proposals (see below) and requires the faster process to be such from the very beginning of its execution. The second preorder refines the first one in that it requires the faster process to perform better from a given point of its execution onwards. Our preorders compare two specifications running on the same architecture. This is the case the literature deals with, and in our framework it requires to keep fixed the function that estimates operation costs, and let only the algorithm change. As our description is parametric, we can also compare a *single* specification when it runs on *different* networks of processors, i.e., we can compare different architectures (operations have different costs) on a specific task.

A brief discussion of some work similar to ours follows. Temporal extensions of *CCS* are proposed in [1, 13, 12, 14]. In these approaches any sequential component of the system has its private clock and any action has a fixed duration expressed by a natural number. Then equivalences are defined over timed processes in the style of the interleaving bisimulation equivalence. Another extension of *CCS* is presented in [7] where the authors define a preordering to establish when a process is more efficient than another. Apart from being parametric and mobility sensitive, our first preorder is essentially that of [7]. Finally, we mention also a temporal model based on continuous time [15], where higher-order transitions and computations are given a geometric description.

Temporal extensions of process algebra not directly related to our proposal may be found in [23, 24, 3, 21, 16, 17, 18]. A survey of these approaches can be found in [22]. Many other models for timed behaviours have been proposed in the literature, e.g. those based on Kripke structures, automata, temporal logics. We do not discuss them here and we refer the interested reader to for instance the proceedings of CONCUR conferences in the LNCS series (for the last editions the volume numbers are 962 and 1119).

This paper is organized as follows. In the next section we recall π-calculus. Its proved semantics is defined in Sect. 3 and it is used to derive the timed semantics in Sect. 4. Section 5 introduces our amortized preordering. An example is discussed in Sect. 6.

2 π-Calculus

In this section we briefly recall π-calculus [20, 19], a model of concurrent communicating processes providing the notion of *naming.*

Definition 1.
Let $\mathcal{N}$ be a countably infinite set of *names* ranged over by $a, b, \ldots, x, y, \ldots$ and let $\mathcal{S} = \{\tau_0, \tau_1, \tau_2, \ldots\}$ be a countably infinite set of invisible actions ranged over by τ_i, with $\mathcal{N} \cap \mathcal{S} = \emptyset$. We also assume a set of *agent identifiers* ranged over by $A, A_1, \ldots$. *Processes* (denoted by $P, Q, R, \ldots \in \mathcal{P}$) are built from names according to the syntax

$$P ::= \mathbf{0} \mid \pi.P \mid P + P \mid P|P \mid (\nu x)P \mid [x = y]P \mid A(y_1, \ldots, y_n)$$

where π may be either $x(y)$ for *input*, or $\overline{x}y$ for *output* (where x is the *subject* and y the *object*, extracted by functions *sbj* and *obj*, respectively) or τ_i for *silent* moves. Hereafter, the trailing $\mathbf{0}$ will be omitted.

The prefix π is the first atomic action that the process $\pi.P$ can perform. The input prefix binds the name y in the prefixed process. Intuitively, some name y is received along the link named x. The output prefix does not bind the name y which is sent along x. A silent prefix τ_i denotes an action which is invisible to an external observer of the system. We use a set of silent prefixes because different internal actions will have different durations. Typically, communications require different times. Summation $(+)$ denotes nondeterministic choice. The operator $|$ describes parallel composition of processes. The operator (νx) acts as a static binder for the name x in the process P that it prefixes. In other words, x is a unique name in P which is different from all the external names. Finally, matching $[x = y]P$ is an `if-then` operator: process P is activated if $x = y$. $A(y_1, \ldots, y_n)$ is the definition of constants (hereafter, $\tilde{y}$ denotes $y_1, \ldots, y_n$).

The early operational semantics for the π-calculus is defined in the *SOS* style, and the labels of the transitions are τ for silent actions, xy for free input, $\overline{x}y$ for free output, and $\overline{x}(y)$ for bound output. We will use μ as a metavariable for the labels of transitions (it is distinct from π, the metavariable for prefixes, though it coincides in two cases). We introduce the set $\mathcal{A}$ of visible actions ranged over by α (i.e. either $\mu = \alpha$ and the action is visible or $\mu = \tau$ and is invisible). We sometimes write $(\nu x, y)P$ for $(\nu x)(\nu y)P$. We recall the notion of free names $fn(\mu)$, bound names $bn(\mu)$, and names $n(\mu) = fn(\mu) \cup bn(\mu)$ of a label μ.

μ	*Kind*	$fn(\mu)$	$bn(\mu)$
τ	Silent	$\emptyset$	$\emptyset$
$xy, \overline{x}y$	Free Input and Output	$\{x, y\}$	$\emptyset$
$\overline{x}(y)$	Bound Output	$\{x\}$	$\{y\}$

Functions fn, bn and n are extended in the obvious way to processes. Below we assume that the *structural congruence* $\equiv$ on processes is defined as the least congruence satisfying the following clauses:

- if P and Q are α-equivalent (they only differ in the choice of bound names) then $P \equiv Q$,
- $(\nu x)(\nu y)P \equiv (\nu y)(\nu x)P$, $(\nu x)(R \,|\, S) \equiv (\nu x)R \,|\, S$ if $x \notin fn(S)$, $(\nu x)(R \,|\, S) \equiv R \,|\, (\nu x)S$ if $x \notin fn(R)$, and $(\nu x)P \equiv P$ if $x \notin fn(P)$.

A *variant* of $P \xrightarrow{\mu} Q$ is a transition which only differs in that P and Q have been replaced by structurally congruent processes, and μ has been α-converted, where a name bound in μ includes Q in its scope.

The early transition system for the π-calculus is in Tab. 1. The transition in the conclusion of each rule, as well as in the axiom, stands for all its variants. The table only reports one rule for the binary operators $|$ and $+$; they also have a symmetric rule.

We end this section with the definition of the interleaving weak bisimulation.

Definition 2. A binary relation $\mathcal{R}$ on processes is a *weak simulation* if whenever $(P, Q) \in \mathcal{R}$ implies

- If $Q \xrightarrow{\mu} Q'$, with $bn(\mu) \cap fn(P, Q) = \emptyset$, then for some P', $P \overset{\mu}{\Rightarrow} P'$, and $(P', Q') \in \mathcal{R}$.

where $\overset{\mu}{\Rightarrow}$ is defined as $\overset{\tau}{\Rightarrow} = (\xrightarrow{\tau})^*$ and $\overset{\alpha}{\Rightarrow} = \overset{\tau}{\Rightarrow} \circ \xrightarrow{\alpha} \circ \overset{\tau}{\Rightarrow}$. The relation $\mathcal{R}$ is a *weak bisimulation* if $\mathcal{R}$ and $\mathcal{R}^{-1}$ are weak simulations. We say that P and Q are *weakly equivalent*, in symbols $P \approx Q$, if there exists a weak bisimulation $\mathcal{R}$ such that $(P, Q) \in \mathcal{R}$.

$$Out : \overline{x}y.P \xrightarrow{\overline{x}y} P \quad Ein : x(y).P \xrightarrow{xw} P\{w/y\} \quad Sil : \tau_i.P \xrightarrow{\tau} P$$

$$Par : \frac{P \xrightarrow{\mu} P'}{P|Q \xrightarrow{\mu} P'|Q}, bn(\mu) \cap fn(Q) = \emptyset \qquad Sum : \frac{P \xrightarrow{\mu} P'}{P+Q \xrightarrow{\mu} P'}$$

$$Res : \frac{P \xrightarrow{\mu} P'}{(\nu x)P \xrightarrow{\mu} (\nu x)P'}, x \notin n(\mu) \qquad Open : \frac{P \xrightarrow{\overline{x}y} P'}{(\nu y)P \xrightarrow{\overline{x}(y)} P'}, y \neq x$$

$$Close : \frac{P \xrightarrow{\overline{x}(y)} P', Q \xrightarrow{xy} Q'}{P|Q \xrightarrow{\tau} (\nu y)(P'|Q')}, \; y \notin fn(Q) \qquad Com : \frac{P \xrightarrow{\overline{x}y} P', Q \xrightarrow{xy} Q'}{P|Q \xrightarrow{\tau} P'|Q'}$$

$$Match : \frac{P \xrightarrow{\mu} P'}{[x=x]P \xrightarrow{\mu} P'} \qquad Ide : \frac{P\{\tilde{y}/\tilde{x}\} \xrightarrow{\mu} P'}{Q(\tilde{y}) \xrightarrow{\mu} P'}, Q(\tilde{x}) = P$$

Table 1. Early transition system for the π-calculus.

3 Proved Transition System

We enrich the labels of the standard interleaving transition system in order to encode more information, in the style of [8, 6, 9]. Essentially, the label of a transition records the inference rules used during its deduction, besides the action itself. It is then possible to derive different semantic models for the π-calculus by extracting new kinds of labels from the enriched ones. In [10] the first and the last authors studied non interleaving qualitative aspects of the π-calculus. In the next sections we apply similar techniques to derive a machine-dependent temporal model. Processes are given a non interleaving semantics, so it is possible to single out the sequential components of a system of mobile processes, or even groups of them residing on the same processor. This permits to make costs dependent on the topology of the underlying network and to associate each sequential (group of) processes with their own local clocks. We start with the definition of our *enhanced labels.* In addition, we extract only the encoding of the proof from an enhanced label, called *proof term.* Finally, we introduce a function ℓ that takes an enhanced label to the corresponding standard action label.

Definition 3. Let $\mathcal{L} = \{||_0, ||_1\}$ with $\chi \in \mathcal{L}^*$, $\mathcal{O} = \{+_0, +_1, =, ()\} \ni o$ and let $\vartheta \in (\mathcal{L} \cup \mathcal{O})^*$. Then *enhanced labels* (with metavariable θ) are defined by the following syntax

$$\theta ::= \vartheta\alpha \mid \vartheta\tau_i \mid \vartheta\langle ||_0\vartheta_0\alpha_0, ||_1\vartheta_1\alpha_1\rangle$$

with $\alpha_0 = xy$ iff α_1 is either $\overline{x}(y)$ or $\overline{x}y$, or vice versa.

The set $\mathcal{T}$ of *proof terms* is obtained from enhanced labels via the auxiliary function p defined as $p(\vartheta\alpha) = p(\vartheta\tau_i) = \vartheta$, $p(\vartheta\langle\vartheta_0\alpha_0, \vartheta_1\alpha_1\rangle) = \vartheta\langle\vartheta_0, \vartheta_1\rangle$. Function ℓ is defined as $\ell(\vartheta\alpha) = \alpha$, $\ell(\vartheta\tau_i) = \ell(\vartheta\langle\vartheta_0\alpha_0, \vartheta_1\alpha_1\rangle) = \tau$.

Our version of the early transition system for the π-calculus is in Tab. 2, where the symmetric rules for communication (Com_1 and $Close_1$) are omitted. Again, the transitions in the conclusion of each rule stand for all their variants. We call this transition system *proved*, because the labels of the transitions encode portions of their proofs.

$$Act : \pi.P \xrightarrow{\pi} P, \ \pi \text{ not input} \qquad Ein : x(y).P \xrightarrow{xw} P\{w/y\}$$

$$Par_0 : \frac{P \xrightarrow{\theta} P'}{P|Q \xrightarrow{\|_0\theta} P'|Q}, bn(\ell(\theta)) \cap fn(Q) = \emptyset \qquad Sum_0 : \frac{P \xrightarrow{\theta} P'}{P + Q \xrightarrow{+_0\theta} P'}$$

$$Par_1 : \frac{P \xrightarrow{\theta} P'}{Q|P \xrightarrow{\|_1\theta} Q|P'}, bn(\ell(\theta)) \cap fn(Q) = \emptyset \qquad Sum_1 : \frac{P \xrightarrow{\theta} P'}{Q + P \xrightarrow{+_1\theta} P'}$$

$$Res : \frac{P \xrightarrow{\theta} P'}{(\nu x)P \xrightarrow{\theta} (\nu x)P'}, x \notin n(\ell(\theta)) \qquad Match : \frac{P \xrightarrow{\theta} P'}{[x = x]P \xrightarrow{=\theta} P'}$$

$$Close_0 : \frac{P \xrightarrow{\vartheta\bar{x}(y)} P', Q \xrightarrow{\vartheta' xy} Q'}{P|Q \xrightarrow{\langle\|_0\vartheta\bar{x}(y), \|_1\vartheta' xy\rangle} (\nu y)(P'|Q')}, \ y \notin fn(Q) \qquad Open : \frac{P \xrightarrow{\vartheta\bar{x}y} P'}{(\nu y)P \xrightarrow{\vartheta\bar{x}(y)} P'}, x \neq y$$

$$Com_0 : \frac{P \xrightarrow{\vartheta\bar{x}y} P', Q \xrightarrow{\vartheta' xy} Q'}{P|Q \xrightarrow{\langle\|_0\vartheta\bar{x}y, \|_1\vartheta' xy\rangle} P'|Q'} \qquad Ide : \frac{P\{\tilde{y}/\tilde{x}\} \xrightarrow{\theta} P'}{Q(\tilde{y}) \xrightarrow{()\theta} P'}, Q(\tilde{x}) = P$$

Table 2. Early proved transition system for the π-calculus.

The proved transition system differs from the standard one only in the labels of transitions. Rule Par_0 (Par_1) adds to the label a tag $\|_0$ ($\|_1$) to record that the left (right) component is moving. A tag $+_0$ ($+_1$) means that a nondeterministic choice has been resolved in favour of its left (right) summand. The rules Com_0 and $Close_0$ have in their conclusion a pair instead of a τ to record the components which interacted (and the proof of the relevant transitions). Their symmetric version Com_1 and $Close_1$ are obvious. We record the resolution of a matching through tag $=$. Finally, the invocation of a definition enriches the label of the conclusion of rule *Ide* with the tag $()$.

Hereafter, we will write a transition $P \xrightarrow{\theta} Q$ simply as θ, when unambiguous.

The standard interleaving semantics is obtained from the proved transition system by relabelling each transition through function ℓ in Def. 3, as stated by the following proposition. Its proof is by straightforward induction.

Proposition 4. *$P \xrightarrow{\mu} P'$ is an early transition if and only if there exists θ with $\ell(\theta) = \mu$ such that $P \xrightarrow{\theta} P'$ is an early proved transition.*

4 Timed semantics

In this section we derive a temporal model of the π-calculus from the proved transition system. The new semantics takes into account the target architecture on which a system runs. Essentially, we relabel the proved transitions with new labels, consisting of a pair $\langle \alpha, t \rangle$, where α is an action whose execution is completed at time t. The label for invisible actions is simply τ, yet care is taken to record the time needed to execute it. Since our model is truly concurrent, the execution of actions on different processors may overlap in time. We give an example of overlapping actions in the conclusions. We will see below how local clocks are associated with the sequential components of a system.

As mentioned in the Introduction, we wish to reflect the different duration of actions due to the different needs of their run-time support routines. Since the structural operational semantics of a language specifies its abstract machine, the context in which an action a occurs in the program represents the operations that the target machine performs for firing a. Accordingly, a suitable linearization of the deduction of a transition represents the execution of the corresponding run-time support routines on the target machine. Following this intuition, we assign a cost (in discrete time) to each inference rule of the operational semantics via a function denoted by \$. Of course, this comprises an estimate of the duration of the actions. In other words, the occurrence of a transition receives a duration time computed according to its deduction.

As a matter of fact, we do not fix function \$, and we let it be a parameter to the definition of our timed transition system. In this way, it is possible to estimate the performance of different architectures, each with its own cost function.

More formally, function \$ has the following type

$$\$: \mathcal{A} \cup \mathcal{S} \cup \mathcal{C} \cup \mathcal{O} \rightarrow I\!N$$

where $\mathcal{C} = \mathcal{N} \times \mathcal{N} \times \mathcal{L}^* \times \mathcal{L}^*$.

When applied to a visible action $\alpha \in \mathcal{A}$, function \$ returns the time needed to perform the very basic, low-level operations corresponding to α, independently of the context in which α occurs. Similarly for the invisible actions τ_i that are not communications. Different actions in $\mathcal{S}$ are given different costs, just to model different delays a system may exhibit. This is why we introduced a set of indexed internal actions. For communications, we propose a more complex cost function. A call has the format $\$(x, y, \chi_0, \chi_1)$. The first argument is the link $x \in \mathcal{N}$, whose bandwidth affects the cost of a communication. Also the size of the datum $x \in \mathcal{N}$ does, so the message exchanged is the second argument. The last two arguments are used to record which sub-processes actually communicate, rather than the locations where they reside. Indeed, the distance between them is a relevant parameter for computing the time needed to exchange a message. Collecting the above considerations, a typical function assigning costs to communications may be as follows

$$\$(x, y, \chi_0, \chi_1) = bandwidth(x) \times size(y) \times distance(\chi_0, \chi_1).$$

For encoding locations, we use here $\chi_0, \chi_1 \in \{||_0, ||_1\}^*$. To see why, consider the binary abstract syntax tree of a process, when the parallel composition $|$ is the only syntactic operator. Then, a sequence χ can be seen as the access path from the root, i.e. from the whole process, to a leaf, i.e. to a sub-process. So, the two last arguments, together with allocation tables, can be used to determine where the two communicating processes have been actually placed. Function \$ applied to an operator $o \in \mathcal{O}$ estimates the cost needed to execute the run-time support routines implementing o. For example, a typical definition of $\$(())$ should take into account the access to the definition of the identifier P, the binding of the actual parameters $\tilde{y}$ to the formal ones $\tilde{x}$ and the operations on the control stack.

The configurations of our timed transition systems are pairs made up of a process and a function, that we call *timer*, that associates a local time to each sequential component of the process. This is analogous to the common notion of configuration used in operational semantics of imperative languages, made up of a program and a store. More precisely, a *timer* is a total function

$$\sigma : \mathcal{L}^* \rightarrow I\!N.$$

For example, $\sigma(||_0||_1) = 7$ records that the actions of the sub-process Q of $(P|Q)|R$ can only start at time 8. In a sense, $\sigma(||_0||_1)$ *is* the local clock of Q, as $||_0||_1$ uniquely identifies Q within the running process. A timer can then be seen as the collection of the local clocks associated with all the active sub-processes of a given system, plus some local clocks that however are useless and will never be used improperly, as we show later on. For example, consider again the process above, in which the location $||_0$ corresponds to no sub-process any more. However, $\sigma(||_0)$ can also have a value, because, say, $(P|Q)|R$ has been reached from $\alpha.(P|Q)|R$ after firing α. Analogously, all the locations not yet used, e.g. of the form $||_0||_1||_0\chi$, will receive a value, even if it will never be accessed. This is for technical reasons made clear below, and ensures that our timers are total.

We now define the initial timer and two further operations on timers. Since we assume that timed computations start at time 0, we define below the initial timer as the constant zero function. The other operations are needed to modify timers. The first updates timers, and is analogous to the standard one for stores, $[value/identifier]$. The second one simply adds up the values of timers on corresponding locations.

Definition 5. The set of timers Σ, ranged over by $\sigma : \mathcal{L}^* \rightarrow I\!N$, is the smallest set that contains the initial timer and is closed under the (primitive recursive) operations of update and sum defined hereafter.

The *initial* timer is the constant function $0_\sigma :\rightarrow \Sigma$, defined as

$$0_\sigma = \lambda\chi.\, 0.$$

The *update* function $\cdot[\cdot/\cdot] : \Sigma \times \mathcal{N} \times \mathcal{L}^* \rightarrow \Sigma$ is defined as

$$\sigma[t/\chi_0] = \lambda\chi.\, \texttt{if } \chi = \chi_0\chi_1 \texttt{ then } t \texttt{ else } \sigma(\chi).$$

The *sum* function $\cdot + \cdot : \Sigma \times \Sigma \rightarrow \Sigma$ is defined as

$$\sigma + \sigma' = \lambda\chi.\sigma(\chi) + \sigma'(\chi).$$

A few comments are in order. First, note that the above definition is effective. To explain the update function, consider again the process $\alpha.(P|Q)|R$ introduced above. Assume a timer such that $\sigma(||_0) = 3$, and let action α require 4 time units to occur. After firing α, P and Q become active in two different locations, namely $||_0||_0$ and $||_0||_1$. Also, their local clocks should change their value to 7. This is made by calling the update function as follows: $\sigma[7/||_0]$, where $||_0$ is the location where α actually occurred. As noted above, all the locations with prefix $||_0$ will be updated, including $||_0||_0$ and $||_0||_1$.

The following is a simple auxiliary function. Roughly, it extracts the locations $\chi \in \{||_0, ||_1\}^*$ of sub-processes involved in a proved transition from its enhanced label.

Definition 6. The function $\underline{\cdot} : \{\mathcal{L} \cup \mathcal{O}\}^* \rightarrow \mathcal{L}^*$ is inductively defined as follows.

$$\underline{\epsilon} = \epsilon, \quad \underline{||_i\vartheta} = ||_i\underline{\vartheta} \quad \underline{o\vartheta} = \underline{\vartheta}$$

We now define by induction an auxiliary function $\mathcal{F}$ that computes the time elapsed to execute the run-time support routines implementing an action. It produces a timer given a proof term and a location. Recall that a proof term encodes the context in which an action occurs, so it represents the calls to the run-time support routines needed to enable the occurrence of that action. We will shortly comment on the next definition below.

Definition 7. The function $\mathcal{F} : \mathcal{T} \times \mathcal{L}^* \rightarrow \Sigma$ is defined as

1. $\mathcal{F}(\epsilon, \chi) \;=\; 0_\sigma$
2. $\mathcal{F}(o\varsigma, \chi) \;=\; 0_\sigma[\$(o)/\chi] + \mathcal{F}(\varsigma, \chi)$,
3. $\mathcal{F}(||_i\varsigma, \chi) \;=\; \mathcal{F}(\varsigma, \chi||_i)$,
4. $\mathcal{F}(\langle\vartheta_0, \vartheta_1\rangle, \chi) \;=\; \mathcal{F}(\vartheta_0, \chi) + \mathcal{F}(\vartheta_1, \chi)$

When there is no context, function $\mathcal{F}$ returns the initial timer, as no run-time support is invoked. When the proof term begins with an operation o, say a matching or a non deterministic choice, its cost is accumulated in the timer, say σ', resulting from processing the rest of the proof term ς, at the position determined by the location χ. Argument χ singles out the (sub-)process involved in the action. Technically, the cost of the operation o is assigned in the initial timer at χ, and then added, at the same location, to σ'. Instead, if the proof term begins with a $\|_i$, then the location that has to be affected is the left component of the current one. So, in item (3), the relevant tag is added to the current location for future use, and no cost is charged to the location, because we assume that different sequential sub-processes be allocated on different processors. Finally, when the proof term is a pair recording the contexts of two partners of a communication, the costs of both contexts is computed, and the resulting timers are merged via the sum function.

We now give three examples of applications of function $\mathcal{F}$. The three timers computed here will be used in the examples after the definition of the timed operational semantics.

Example 1. The timer resulting from the application of function $\mathcal{F}$ to the proof term $= \|_0{+}_0$ and the empty location ϵ is computed as follows.

$$\begin{aligned}
&\mathcal{F}(= \|_0{+}_0, \epsilon) = \\
&\quad \mathbf{0}_\sigma[\$(=)/\epsilon] + \mathcal{F}(\|_0{+}_0, \epsilon) = \\
&\quad \mathbf{0}_\sigma[\$(=)/\epsilon] + \mathcal{F}(+_0, \|_0) = \\
&\quad \mathbf{0}_\sigma[\$(=)/\epsilon] + \mathbf{0}_\sigma[\$(+_0)/\|_0] + \mathcal{F}(\epsilon, \|_0) = \\
&\quad \mathbf{0}_\sigma[\$(=)/\epsilon] + \mathbf{0}_\sigma[\$(+_0)/\|_0] + \mathbf{0}_\sigma = \\
&\quad \mathbf{0}_\sigma[\$(=)/\epsilon] + \mathbf{0}_\sigma[\$(+_0)/\|_0] = \tilde{\sigma}
\end{aligned}$$

For instance $\tilde{\sigma}(\|_0\|_1) = \$(=) + \$(+_0)$ and $\tilde{\sigma}(\|_1) = \$(=)$.

Consider now the proof term $\langle \|_0, \|_1{+}_0 \rangle$ originated by a communication. The application of $\mathcal{F}$ to it and to ϵ yields

$$\begin{aligned}
&\mathcal{F}(\langle \|_0, \|_1{+}_0 \rangle, \epsilon) = \\
&\quad \mathcal{F}(\|_0, \epsilon) + \mathcal{F}(\|_1{+}_0, \epsilon) = \\
&\quad \mathcal{F}(\epsilon, \|_0) + \mathcal{F}(+_0, \|_1) = \\
&\quad \mathbf{0}_\sigma + \mathbf{0}_\sigma[\$(+_0)/\|_1] + \mathcal{F}(\epsilon, \|_1) = \\
&\quad \mathbf{0}_\sigma[\$(+_0)/\|_1] + \mathbf{0}_\sigma = \\
&\quad \mathbf{0}_\sigma[\$(+_0)/\|_1]
\end{aligned}$$

The third proof term we consider is $+_0\langle \|_0{+}_0, \|_1 = \rangle$ that encodes a communication within the scope of a nondeterministic choice.

$$\begin{aligned}
&\mathcal{F}(+_1\langle \|_0{+}_0, \|_1 = \rangle, \epsilon) = \\
&\quad \mathbf{0}_\sigma[\$(+_1)/\epsilon] + \mathcal{F}(\langle \|_0{+}_0, \|_1 = \rangle = \\
&\quad \mathbf{0}_\sigma[\$(+_1)/\epsilon] + \mathcal{F}(\|_0{+}_0, \epsilon) + \mathcal{F}(\|_1 =, \epsilon) = \\
&\quad \mathbf{0}_\sigma[\$(+_1)/\epsilon] + \mathcal{F}(+_0, \|_0) + \mathcal{F}(=, \|_1) = \\
&\quad \mathbf{0}_\sigma[\$(+_1)/\epsilon] + \mathbf{0}_\sigma[\$(+_0)/\|_0] + \mathcal{F}(\epsilon, \|_0) + \mathbf{0}_\sigma[\$(=)/\|_1] + \mathcal{F}(\epsilon, \|_1) = \\
&\quad \mathbf{0}_\sigma[\$(+_1)/\epsilon] + \mathbf{0}_\sigma[\$(+_0)/\|_0] + \mathbf{0}_\sigma[\$(=)/\|_1]
\end{aligned}$$

We now have all the ingredients to define our timed transition for the π-calculus. As mentioned above, its configurations, ranged over by $S, S_0, S_1, \ldots$, have the form

$$\langle P, \sigma \rangle,$$

where $P \in \mathcal{P}$ is a process and $\sigma \in \Sigma$ is a timer. A timed transition is written as

$$\langle P, \sigma \rangle \overset{\beta}{\longmapsto}_{\$} \langle P', \sigma' \rangle,$$

where the label β is either τ for invisible actions or $\langle \alpha, t \rangle$ for the visible ones ($\alpha \in \mathcal{A}$ and $t \in I\!N$). The index \$ makes explicit the dependency of the components of labels expressing time on the cost function chosen. Hereafter, we feel free to omit the index \$ when no ambiguity can arise. The timed transition relation of the π-calculus is defined by the rules in Tab. 3. Their premises use proved transitions, defined in Tab. 2.

$$Ext: \frac{P \xrightarrow{\vartheta\alpha} P'}{\langle P, \sigma \rangle \overset{\alpha, \sigma'(\vartheta)}{\longmapsto}_{\$} \langle P', \sigma' \rangle}, \quad \sigma' = \sigma + \mathcal{F}(\vartheta, \epsilon) + \mathbf{0}_\sigma[\$(\alpha)/\underline{\vartheta}]$$

$$Sil: \frac{P \xrightarrow{\vartheta\tau_i} P'}{\langle P, \sigma \rangle \overset{\tau}{\longmapsto}_{\$} \langle P', \sigma' \rangle}, \quad \sigma' = \sigma + \mathcal{F}(\vartheta, \epsilon) + \mathbf{0}_\sigma[\$(\tau_i)/\underline{\vartheta}]$$

$$Int: \frac{P \xrightarrow{\vartheta\langle\vartheta_0\alpha_0, \vartheta_1\alpha_1\rangle} P'}{\langle P, \sigma \rangle \overset{\tau}{\longmapsto}_{\$} \langle P', \sigma' \rangle}, \quad \begin{cases} \sigma'' = \sigma + \mathcal{F}(\vartheta\langle\vartheta_0, \vartheta_1\rangle, \epsilon) \\ t = max_i\ \sigma''(\underline{\vartheta\vartheta_i}) + \$(sbj(\alpha_0), obj(\alpha_0), \underline{\vartheta\vartheta_0}, \underline{\vartheta\vartheta_1}) \\ \sigma' = \sigma''[t/\underline{\vartheta\vartheta_0}, \underline{\vartheta\vartheta_1}] \end{cases}$$

Table 3. Early timed transition system for the π-calculus.

Now we briefly comment on the three inference rules of Tab. 3. Rule *Ext* is for visible actions. So, we compute two timers that express the two components of the actual cost of α, performed by the sub-process at the location $\underline{\vartheta}$. The timer $0_\sigma[\$(\alpha)/\underline{\vartheta}]$ stores the cost needed to perform action α in isolation. The other is timer $\mathcal{F}(\vartheta, \epsilon)$ and reflects the time spent in solving the constraints imposed by the context in which α occurs. Note that the correct values of time have been assigned to all the sub-processes actively involved in traversing the context, as exemplified after the definition of function $\mathcal{F}$. The two timers are then added to that of the source of the transition, which records the local clocks at the beginning of the execution of α. Rule *Sil* for internal actions is quite similar. The only difference here concerns the label, which is simply τ and carries no information on the elapsed time. However, the time spent in silent actions, both internal and communications, is recorded in the new timer σ' of the target state of the transition. The last rule is a little more complex. For readability, we introduce the intermediate timer σ''. It results from the sum of the timer at the beginning of the communication and of the timer collecting the costs of the context. Actually, the last timer is the sum of two timers, one for each the components at location $\underline{\vartheta\vartheta_i}$. Then, the selection of the time $max_i\ \sigma''(\underline{\vartheta\vartheta_i})$ of the slower process mimics that the faster process is delayed till the slower one is ready to synchronize. Finally, the actual timer σ' is obtained by adding to the above also the cost of the communication. Recall that we stipulated it dependent on the channel ($sbj(\alpha_0)$ which is equal $sbj(\alpha_1)$), the data exchanged ($obj(\alpha_0) = obj(\alpha_1)$) and the distance between the locations ($\underline{\vartheta\vartheta_i}$) where the partners reside.

The following example shows two timed computations. As usual, a computation is just a sequence of transitions, such that the source and the target of two consecutive transitions match.

Example 2. Consider the process

$$R = [x = x](((\nu y)\overline{x}y.\overline{y}z.P + P') \mid (y(w).Q + Q'))$$

It has the following proved computation

$$R \stackrel{=\|_0+_0\overline{x}(y)}{\longrightarrow} \overline{y}z.P|(y(w).Q + Q') \stackrel{\langle \|_0\overline{y}z, \|_1+_0yz\rangle}{\longrightarrow} P|Q\{z/w\}$$

The derived timed computation is

$$\langle R, \mathbf{0}_\sigma\rangle \stackrel{\overline{x}(y), \sigma'(\|_0)}{\longmapsto} \langle \overline{y}z.P|(y(w).Q + Q'), \sigma'\rangle \stackrel{\tau}{\longmapsto} \langle P|Q\{z/w\}, \sigma''\rangle$$

Using the value of $\mathcal{F}(= \|_0+_0, \epsilon)$ computed in the example above, the timer

$$\sigma' = \mathbf{0}_\sigma + \mathcal{F}(= \|_0+_0, \epsilon) + \mathbf{0}_\sigma[\$(\overline{x}(y))/\|_0]$$

becomes

$$\begin{aligned} &\mathbf{0}_\sigma[\$(=)/\epsilon] + \mathbf{0}_\sigma[\$(+_0)/\|_0] + \mathbf{0}_\sigma[\$(\overline{x}(y))/\|_0] = \\ &\mathbf{0}_\sigma[\$(=)/\epsilon] + \mathbf{0}_\sigma[\$(+_0) + \$(\overline{x}(y))/\|_0] \end{aligned}$$

Similarly,

$$\sigma'' = \sigma'''[max\ \{\sigma'''(\|_0), \sigma'''(\|_1)\} + \$(y, z, \|_0, \|_1)/\|_0, \|_1],$$

where

$$\sigma''' = \sigma' + \mathcal{F}(\langle \|_0, \|_1+_0\rangle, \epsilon) = \mathbf{0}_\sigma[\$(=)/\epsilon] + \mathbf{0}_\sigma[\$(+_0) + \$(\overline{x}(y))/\|_0] + \mathbf{0}_\sigma[\$(+_0)/\|_1].$$

Since $\sigma'''(\|_0) = \sigma'''(\|_1) + \$(\overline{x}(y))$, $max\{\sigma'''(\|_0), \sigma'''(\|_1)\} = \sigma'''(\|_0)$. Therefore

$$\sigma'' = \mathbf{0}_\sigma[\$(=)/\epsilon] + \mathbf{0}_\sigma[\$(+_0) + \$(\overline{x}(y)) + \$(y, z, \|_0, \|_1)/\|_0, \|_1].$$

We now give another example of computation. It consists of a single communication, one partner of which is within the scope of a nondeterministic choice. Consider the proved computation

$$R + ((\overline{x}y.P + P')|[x = x]x(w).Q) \xrightarrow{+_1\langle||_0+_0,||_1=\rangle} P|Q\{y/w\}$$

The derived timed computation is

$$\langle R + ((\overline{x}y.P + P')|[x = x]x(w).Q), \mathbf{0}_\sigma\rangle \overset{\tau}{\longmapsto} \langle P|Q\{y/w\}, \sigma'\rangle$$

using the value $\mathcal{F}(+_1\langle||_0+_0, ||_1 =\rangle, \epsilon)$ computed above, the auxiliary timer is

$$\sigma'' = \mathbf{0}_\sigma[\$(+_1)/\epsilon] + \mathbf{0}_\sigma[\$(+_0)/||_0] + \mathbf{0}_\sigma[\$(=)/||_1]$$

from which

$$\sigma' = \sigma''[t/||_0, ||_1],$$

where $t = \$(+_1) + max\{\$(=), \$(+_0)\} + \$(x, y, ||_0, ||_1)$.
Note that the communication has synchronized the local clocks of both P and $Q\{y/w\}$ to time t.

Above, we anticipated that a timer can be seen as the collection of the local clocks associated with the *active* sub-processes only, although it is a total function on locations. Also, we claimed that no reference is made to local clocks of sub-processes no longer there or not yet present in the whole system. A simple inspection to the rules defining the timed operational semantics justifies the above statements. In fact, in a transition $\langle P, \sigma\rangle \overset{\alpha,t}{\longmapsto} \langle P', \sigma'\rangle$, the time t is the value of timer σ' at the location where action α occurred (cfr. rule *Ext*). Similarly when a silent transition is derived via rule *Sil*. In rule *Int*, the auxiliary timer σ'' is accessed twice, at the locations where the input and the output action are performed.

We end this section with a proposition that establishes the correspondence between interleaving and timed transitions, and shows that the latter conservatively extend the former. Its proof relies on the correspondence between the above relations with the proved one. First we need a function that maps timed labels to actions.

Definition 8. The function $\ell_T(\cdot) : (\mathcal{A} \times \mathbb{N}) \cup \{\tau\} \to \mathcal{A} \cup \{\tau\}$ is defined as

$$\ell_T(\langle\alpha, t\rangle) = \alpha \;\text{ and }\; \ell_T(\tau) = \tau$$

Proposition 9. *Given a process P and a timer σ, $P \xrightarrow{\mu} P'$ is an early transition if and only if there exists β with $\ell_T(\beta) = \mu$ and $\langle P, \sigma\rangle \overset{\beta}{\longmapsto} \langle P', \sigma'\rangle$, is a timed transition.*

5 Performance preorders

In this section we introduce two preorderings between processes that express their relative efficiency and that require their behaviour to be the same from a functional point of view. More precisely, if P and P' are in a preordering relation, we say that P is faster than P'. This will provide us with the basis for choosing the specification more suited to the architecture at hand, or the architecture better suited to a given specification.

Before introducing our first preordering, we define a weak timed transition relation and the notion of viable and stuck configurations. The new relation is used to abstract from the internal actions of a system and it is quite standard. Viable (stuck) configurations may (may not) originate visible transitions.

Definition 10. Given a cost function \$ and the transition relation $\longmapsto_{\$}$ in Tab. 3, then the timed weak transition relation $\stackrel{\beta}{\Longmapsto}_{\$}$ is

$$\stackrel{\tau}{\Longmapsto}_{\$} = (\stackrel{\tau}{\longmapsto}_{\$})^* \quad \text{and} \quad \stackrel{\beta}{\Longmapsto}_{\$} = \stackrel{\tau}{\Longmapsto}_{\$} \circ \stackrel{\beta}{\longmapsto}_{\$} \circ \stackrel{\tau}{\Longmapsto}_{\$}$$

A process P is *viable* if there exists a process P' such that $P \stackrel{\alpha}{\Rightarrow} P'$. Otherwise, it is said *stuck*. A configuration $\langle P, \sigma \rangle$ is viable (stuck) if its process part is.

We define below a simulation, called *efficiency simulation*, saying that a process S_0 simulates S_1 and is faster than it. Similarly, we define an *inefficiency simulation* by imposing that S_0 simulates S_1 and is slower than it. Finally, we define the *performance preordering* that relates S_0 and S_1 if S_0 simulates efficiently S_1 and S_1 simulates inefficiently S_0. This relation turns out to be a refinement of the classical interleaving bisimulation equivalence.

Definition 11. Let $\$_0$ and $\$_1$ be two cost functions. Then, a binary relation $\mathcal{R}$ on configurations is an *efficiency simulation* if whenever $(S_0, S_1) \in \mathcal{R}$ implies either

- S_0, S_1 are stuck, or
- if $S_1 \stackrel{\beta_1}{\longmapsto}_{\$_1} S_1'$, with $bn(\beta_1) \cap fn(S_0, S_1) = \emptyset$, then for some S_0', $S_0 \stackrel{\beta_0}{\Longmapsto}_{\$_0} S_0'$, and $\beta_0 \leq \beta_1$ and $(S_0', S_1') \in \mathcal{R}$.

where $\beta_0 \leq \beta_1$ iff $\beta_0 = \beta_1 = \tau$ or $\beta_0 = \langle \alpha, t_0 \rangle$ and $\beta_1 = \langle \alpha, t_1 \rangle$ with $t_0 \leq t_1$.

Inefficiency simulation is obtained by replacing $\beta_0 \leq \beta_1$ above with $\beta_1 \leq \beta_0$.

The relation $\mathcal{R}$ is a *performance preordering* if $\mathcal{R}$ is an efficiency simulation and $\mathcal{R}^{-1}$ is an inefficiency simulation.

Finally, we say that a process P is more efficient than a process Q (written $P \preceq Q$) if there exists a performance preordering $\mathcal{R}$ such that $(\langle P, 0_\sigma \rangle, \langle Q, 0_\sigma \rangle) \in \mathcal{R}$.

When the indexing cost functions $\$_0$ and $\$_1$ are equal, preordering $\preceq$ coincides with the analogous relation defined on CCS usually called performance preordering in the literature [7]. It relates two processes running on the same target machine and on the same network if and only if one is faster than the other for any action that it can perform. In other words, the faster process must simulate more efficiently the other step by step from the very beginning.

When instead the cost functions $\$_0$ and $\$_1$ are different, the advantages of the parametricity of our timed transition system show up. For example, we can compare the same algorithm on different target machines. More precisely, let $S_0 = S_1$ in Def. 11 and define the cost functions $\$_0 \neq \$_1$ in order to express the costs of execution instructions on two different architectures.

Performance preordering gives a rough estimation of the efficiency of processes. Indeed, it may consider incomparable processes which should sensibly be comparable. Consider for instance a process P that is slower than another, say Q, in its initial steps (e.g. because it initializes complex data structures) and then performs better than Q (e.g. because its sophisticated data structures help a lot). In this case, we should say that the process P is more efficient than Q, while according to the performance preordering the two processes are simply unrelated.

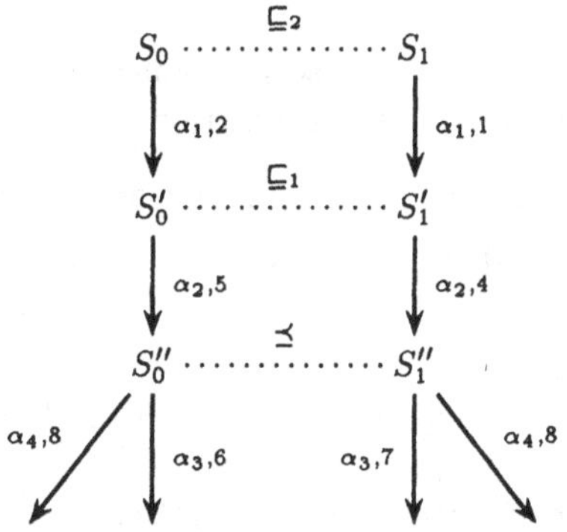

Fig. 1. Comparing performance and amortized preordering.

As an example consider the processes S_0 and S_1 depicted in Fig. 1, and assume that $S_0'' \preceq S_1''$. After an initial delay on actions α_1 and α_2, S_0 is always faster than S_1. To overcome the weakness of performance preordering and to gain the relation between the processes above we define an *amortized preordering*, in the style of amortized complexity. Essentially, it relates two processes if one is faster than the other from a given point on of the simulation. This new preordering is defined through a family of indexed relations of the form $\sqsubseteq_i$. The intuition of $P \sqsubseteq_i Q$ is that the process P will always be faster than Q after i steps.

Definition 12. Given two cost functions $\$_0$ and $\$_1$, the family of binary relations $\sqsubseteq_i$ over configurations is defined as follows

- $\sqsubseteq_0 = \preceq$
- $\sqsubseteq_{i+1}$ is the smallest relation including $\sqsubseteq_i$ such that
  - if $S_1 \stackrel{\beta_1}{\longmapsto}_{\$_1} S_1'$, with $bn(\beta_1) \cap fn(S_0, S_1) = \emptyset$, then for some S_0', $S_0 \stackrel{\beta_0}{\Longmapsto}_{\$_0} S_0'$, $\ell_T(\beta_0) = \ell_T(\beta_1)$ and $S_0' \sqsubseteq_i S_1'$;
  - if $S_0 \stackrel{\beta_0}{\longmapsto}_{\$_0} S_0'$, with $bn(\beta_0) \cap fn(S_0, S_1) = \emptyset$, then for some S_1', $S_1 \stackrel{\beta_1}{\Longmapsto}_{\$_1} S_1'$, $\ell_T(\beta_0) = \ell_T(\beta_1)$ and $S_0' \sqsubseteq_i S_1'$.

The *amortized preordering* $\sqsubseteq$ between configurations is defined as

$$S_0 \sqsubseteq S_1 \text{ if and only if } \exists i \,:\, S_0 \sqsubseteq_i S_1$$

We say that two processes P and Q are in the amortized preordering (written $P \sqsubseteq Q$) iff $\langle P, \mathbf{0}_\sigma \rangle \sqsubseteq \langle Q, \mathbf{0}_\sigma \rangle$, and we let $P \sqsubseteq_i Q$ iff $\langle P, \mathbf{0}_\sigma \rangle \sqsubseteq_i \langle Q, \mathbf{0}_\sigma \rangle$.

Consider again Fig. 1. We can establish the amortized preordering between S_0 and S_1, because $S_0 \sqsubseteq_2 S_1$ due to the assumption $S_0'' \preceq S_1''$.

We end this section by establishing the relations of our amortized preordering with the performance preordering and with the interleaving weak equivalence. We first report a useful lemma. Also, we need the following auxiliary definition.

Definition 13. Let $\mathcal{T}_c$ and $\mathcal{T}_p$ be the sets of binary relations over configurations and over processes, respectively. Then, function $\phi : \mathcal{T}_c \to \mathcal{T}_p$ is defined as

$$\begin{aligned}\phi(\mathcal{R}) = \{&(P, Q) \in \mathcal{P} \times \mathcal{P} \mid (\langle P, \sigma \rangle, \langle Q, \sigma' \rangle) \in \mathcal{R}\} \cup \\ &\{(P, Q) : P, Q \in \mathcal{P} \text{ and they are stuck}\}\end{aligned}$$

Lemma 14.

- *$\{(P, Q) : P, Q \in \mathcal{P}$ and they are stuck$\}$ is a weak bisimulation.*
- *if $\mathcal{R}$ is*
  - *an efficiency or an inefficiency simulation then $\phi(\mathcal{R})$ is a weak simulation*
  - *a performance preordering then $\phi(\mathcal{R})$ is a weak bisimulation.*
- *$\phi(\sqsubseteq_i)$ is a weak bisimulation.*

Proof. The proof of the first two items is immediate by definition. The last item follows by definition and from the preceeding items.

It is now easy to prove that our semantic model conservatively extends the original semantics of the π-calculus.

Theorem 15.

- *$P \preceq Q$ implies but is not implied by $P \approx Q$,*
- *$P \sqsubseteq_i Q$ implies but is not implied by $P \approx Q$.*

Proof. We first prove the inclusions. Let $\mathcal{R}$ be either $\preceq$ or $\sqsubseteq_i$ and $\mathcal{S}$ be either of their obvious extension to configurations. Given $(P, Q) \in \mathcal{R}$, by definition $(\langle P, 0_\sigma, Q, 0_\sigma \rangle) \in \mathcal{S}$. By Lemma 14 there exists a weak bisimulation $\phi(\mathcal{S})$ that contains (P, Q). Strictness of implication relies on lack of symmetry in preorders.

The following corollary is immediate by noting that $\sqsubseteq_0 = \preceq$ and that $\sqsubseteq_i \subset \sqsubseteq$.

Corollary 16.

- $P \preceq Q$ *implies but is not implied by* $P \sqsubseteq Q$,
- $P \sqsubseteq Q$ *implies but is not implied by* $P \approx Q$.

6 A case study

In this section we use our mathematical framework to compare the efficiency of two architectures that run sequential programs. We consider a conventional uniprocessor and a prefetch pipeline machine. For the sake of simplicity, in computing the time of the fetch-execute cycle we assume that all instructions take the same time.

We start with the specification of the uniprocessor architecture. It consists of two modules: a memory M and a processor P. The memory fetches an instruction i and sends it to the processor for execution along the channel $fetch$; then, it resumes. The processor P receives the instruction, executes it and then restarts. Their specifications are

$$M = \overline{fetch}\, i.M \quad \text{and} \quad P = fetch(x).x.P$$

The overall system hides the channel *fetch* and is

$$SYS_c = (\nu\, fetch)(M \mid P).$$

The prefetch pipeline architecture has two modules in place of P above: an instruction unit IU and a execution unit EU. The unit IU interacts with M to fetch instructions. The unit EU executes them. We specify the three units composing the system as follows.

$$M = \overline{fetch}\, i.M, \quad IU = fetch(x).\overline{exec}\, x.IU \quad \text{and} \quad EU = exec(s).s.EU.$$

The behaviour of the prefetch pipeline machine is described by

$$SYS_p = (\nu\, fetch, exec)(M \mid (IU \mid EU)).$$

Figure 2 shows the proved transition systems of the two architectures. Note that both are finite state; in passing, we remark that the proved transition system for a process has exactly the same states as the standard interleaving transition system. As we will see later, this property allows us to derive closed forms for the costs of executing the kth instruction of a program.

Assume that the cost functions of the conventional and the prefetch pipeline processors are $\$_c$ and $\$_p$, respectively. Furthermore, we assume that there is no

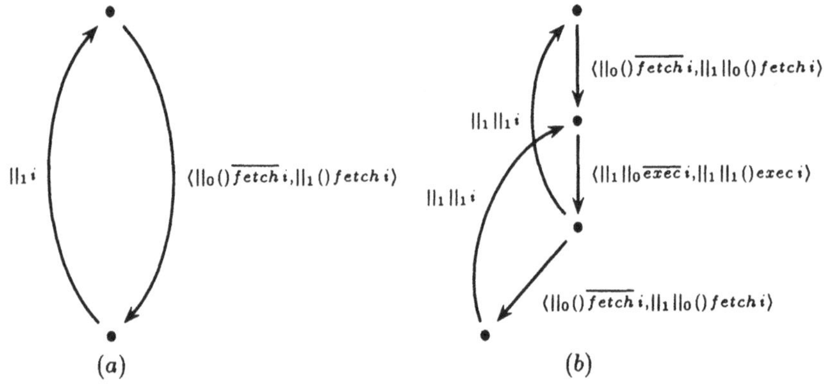

Fig. 2. Proved transition system of the conventional (a) and the prefetch pipeline uniprocessor (b).

appreciable difference between the time required by the two architectures for fetching, as well as for executing instructions. This amounts to say that

$$\$_c(fetch, i, ||_0, ||_1) = \$_p(fetch, i, ||_0, ||_1||_0) = \$(fetch) \text{ and } \$_c(i) = \$_p(i) = \$(i),$$

where the arguments $||_0$ and $||_1$ of $\$_c$ are the locations of M and P, and the arguments $||_0$ and $||_1||_0$ of $\$_p$ are the locations of M and of IU.

In any prefetch pipeline processor the cost of sending the (decoded) instruction from IU to EU is always smaller than fetching (and decoding) it. Hence

$$\$_p(exec, i, ||_1||_0, ||_1||_1) \leq \$_p(fetch),$$

where $||_1||_1$ is the location of EU.

Suppose that the machines we are comparing have to interpret a set of CISC instructions. Generally, both of them take more time in the execution of an instruction than in its fetch, so we let

$$\$(fetch) \leq \$(i).$$

Usually, the architectures we are considering have a firmware run-time support, and resolve calls to routines, in our case invocations of identifiers, through a jump instruction. Then, we neglect in what follows the cost of invoking identifiers M, P, IU and EU and let

$$\$_c(()) = \$_p(()) = 0.$$

In fact, assigning a cost different than 0 to invocations of identifiers only makes the cost function a bit more complex, but does not at all change our results.

The above assumptions reflect the features of real conventional and prefetch pipeline architectures. Under them, the cost of the execution of a single instruction i in the conventional architecture is

$$t_c = \$(fetch) + \$(i).$$

When $k-1$ instructions are executed, the timer associated with P has value $(k-1) \times t_c$. Hence, we can express the label of the transition representing the execution of the kth instruction as $\langle i, T_c(k) \rangle$, where

$$T_c(k) = k \times t_c.$$

Consider now the prefetch pipeline architecture. The cost of executing the first instruction is $\$(fetch) + t_p$, where

$$t_p = \$_p(exec, i, ||_1||_0, ||_1||_1) + \$(i).$$

The time for completing the next instruction, call it i' for a while, only involves that of the communication between IU and EU and that of the actual execution of i'. This is because the fetch of the current instruction i' can overlap in time with the execution of the preceding one. Figure 2(b) shows clearly that the transitions corresponding to a fetch of an instruction can occur independently of the execution of the previous one. In fact, the action of sending, of receiving and of executing an instruction are performed in different locations, namely in $||_0$, $||_1||_0$ and $||_1||_1$, respectively. Therefore, we can express the label of the transition representing the execution of the kth instruction as $\langle i, T_p(k) \rangle$, where

$$T_p(k) = \$(fetch) + k \times t_p.$$

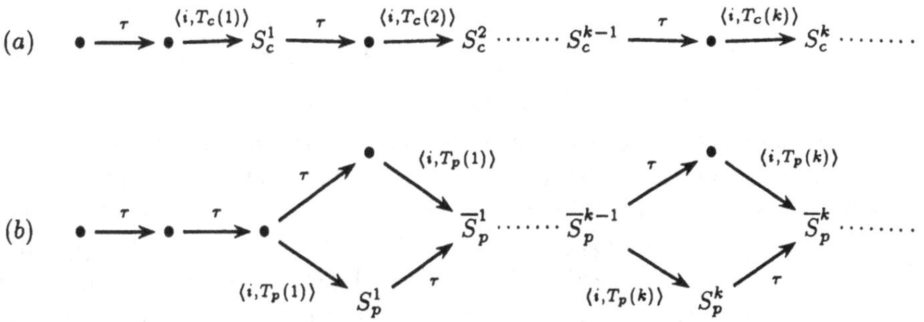

Fig. 3. Timed behaviour of the conventional (a) and the prefetch pipeline uniprocessor (b).

Now, it is easy to draw the timed transition systems for SYS_c and SYS_p, relying on functions T_c and T_p. They are depicted in Fig. 3, and have a denumerable set of states. Nevertheless, we can compare the efficiency of the two architectures. Indeed, for determining the preordering relations between SYS_c and SYS_p, we first establish a weak bisimulation $\mathcal{B}$ that relates the nodes of the two timed transition systems. Of course, $\mathcal{B}$ should only consider the actions in labels, i.e. $\ell_T(\beta)$. Determining $\mathcal{B}$ is easy, because all the nodes of one timed transition system are weakly bisimilar to those of the other one, as one can check by inspecting Fig. 2, modified by replacing the enhanced labels θ with standard actions $\ell(\theta)$. In particular, we consider below the pairs of bisimilar states (S_c^k, S_p^k) and $(S_c^k, \overline{S}_p^k)$, as we called them in Fig. 3 (index k records that k instructions have been executed).

Now, to establish a preordering relation, we only need to compare the temporal part of the labels of the transitions with target S_c^k and S_p^k, $\overline{S}_p^k$. In other words, it suffices to compare the values $T_c(k)$ and $T_p(k)$. Since

$$\langle SYS_c, \mathbf{0}_\sigma\rangle \overset{i,T_c(1)}{\Longmapsto} S_c^1 \quad \text{and} \quad \langle SYS_p, \mathbf{0}_\sigma\rangle \overset{i,T_p(1)}{\Longmapsto} S_p^1,\ \langle SYS_p, \mathbf{0}_\sigma\rangle \overset{i,T_p(1)}{\Longmapsto} \overline{S}_p^1$$

and $T_c(1) < T_p(1)$, we derive that $SYS_p \not\preceq SYS_c$. Also, $SYS_c \not\preceq SYS_p$, because after some initial steps the prefetch pipeline architecture is faster than the conventional one. In fact, there exists $\tilde{k}$ such that, for all $k \geq \tilde{k}$, the transitions

$$S_c^{k-1} \overset{i,T_c(k)}{\Longmapsto} S_c^k \quad \text{and} \quad \overline{S}_p^{k-1} \overset{i,T_p(k)}{\Longmapsto} S_p^k,\ \overline{S}_p^{k-1} \overset{i,T_p(k)}{\Longmapsto} \overline{S}_p^k$$

satisfy the inequality $T_p(k) < T_c(k)$. Hence, $SYS_c \not\preceq SYS_p$. Actually, the number $\tilde{k} \in I\!N$ is the smallest k such that

$$k \geq 1/(1 - (\$_p(exec, i, ||_1|_0, ||_1||_1)/\$(fetch))).$$

Also, for all $k \geq \tilde{k}$, the inequality $T_p(k) < T_c(k)$ implies that $S_p^k \preceq S_c^k$ and $\overline{S}_p^k \preceq S_c^k$. Therefore $SYS_p \sqsubseteq_{\tilde{k}} SYS_c$, from which $SYS_p \sqsubseteq SYS_c$.

To give an idea of the value of $\tilde{k}$, we consider the following two cases. If the internal communication between IU and EU takes 50% of the time needed for a fetch, the value of $\tilde{k}$ is 2, hence $SYS_p \sqsubseteq_2 SYS_c$. When the percentage above is 90%, $\tilde{k} = 10$ and hence $SYS_p \sqsubseteq_{10} SYS_c$. This shows that the prefetch pipeline architecture is faster than a conventional uniprocessor if the interpreted assembler program has more than 1 instruction in the first case, and more than 9 in the second one. The amortized preordering gives formal evidence that a prefetch pipeline architecture is (almost) always more efficient than the conventional uniprocessor one.

The above argument can be applied when the considered set of instructions to be interpreted by our architectures is of type RISC, rather than CISC as done above. In this case the fetch is usually slower then the execution of an instruction, so we let

$$\$(i) \leq \$(fetch).$$

Under this assumption, to get the new cost function, it is sufficient to exchange the role of $\$(i)$ and $\$(fetch)$ in the definitions above. More precisely, we define the cost of executing a single instruction as

$$t_p^R = \$_p(exec, i, ||_1||_0, ||_1||_1) + \$(fetch)$$

and that of the transition representing the execution of the kth instruction as

$$T_p^R(k) = \$(i) + k \times t_p^R.$$

Also in the RISC case, simple calculations determine a value $\tilde{k}$, from which onwards $SYS_p \sqsubseteq_k SYS_c$. Summing up, we have formally shown that the pipeline-based architecture is better.

7 Conclusions and Future Work

The basis of our work is an enhanced structural operational semantics that uniformly describes qualitative as well as quantitative aspects of mobile and distributed systems. More precisely, we use proved transition systems, whose transitions are labelled by (encodings of) their derivations. A simple relabelling then suffices for recovering the many different aspects of systems.

Taking advantage of this, here we defined a timed semantics for π-calculus that associates a local clock, with discrete values, with any sequential component of a process. Besides considering mobile processes rather than processes in calculi without value passing as done in the literature, we refined previous work on timed semantics on three aspects. First, we established a cost for any operator of the language to reflect that the run-time support executes some low-level routines to implement an operator of the language. Also, we determine the cost of communications according to the placement of processes on the underlying interconnection network, to the links used and to the size of the messages transferred. Second, we parametrized our transition relation with a cost function. In this way, one can instantiate the same semantic definition to take into account different target architectures. Finally, we extended the machinery introduced in the literature to compare the performance of processes. As usual, we required the two processes to be (interleaving) bisimilar as far as only actions are concerned. Then, we refined the known notion of efficiency pre-orderings, stipulating that a process is faster than another if it is such from a given point of its execution onwards.

The mathematical framework introduced can be used to estimate and compare the performance of two different processes when they run on a given architecture. This could provide potential benefits in the construction of optimizing compilers for concurrent and distributed systems. Due to parametricity, we can also select the architecture more suited to a specific system of mobile processes, by comparing its performance when it is executed on different architectures. In fact, the costs of the run-time support routines are machine sensible, as well as those of communications depend on the network topology and on its technology.

Our proposal is interleaving in style. Nevertheless, our timed transition systems describes, to some extent, non interleaving features. In fact, it may happen that in a computation the occurrence of two transitions overlap in time. A simple example follows. Suppose we have the process $\alpha.\beta.P \mid \gamma.Q$ and that the cost function is $\$(\alpha) = 3, \$(\beta) = 2, \$(\gamma) = 4$. Then, a possible computation, starting with the initial timer identically equal to 0, is

$$\langle \alpha.\beta.P \mid \gamma.Q, 0_\sigma \rangle \overset{\alpha,3}{\longmapsto} \langle \beta.P \mid \gamma.Q, \sigma \rangle \overset{\beta,5}{\longmapsto} \langle P \mid \gamma.Q, \sigma' \rangle \overset{\gamma,4}{\longmapsto} \langle P \mid Q, \sigma'' \rangle,$$

where $\sigma(\beta.P) = 3$, $\sigma(\gamma.Q) = \sigma'(\gamma.Q) = 0$, $\sigma'(P) = \sigma''(P) = 5$, $\sigma''(Q) = 4$ (for clarity, we are using processes in place of locations, so we write $\gamma.Q$ in place of $||_1$). In the computation above, the execution of γ starts at time 0 and ends at time 4, and during this interval α has been completed and β started. Therefore, timed computations convey some information about causality. In our example, clearly α and γ are not causally related. It would be interesting to place the timed semantics in the spectrum interleaving versus non interleaving descriptions. We already established that our semantics conservatively extends the original, interleaving semantics of π-calculus [20], but its exact relations with causal or local semantics (see, e.g. [10]) are still unknown.

Another research direction is about real time (see, e.g., [2, 15]). The extension is easy as fas as transitions are concerned. It suffices to consider cost functions that take value over the positive reals. Much work has to be done instead for studying the performance of concurrent systems in this case.

Here, we compared the idealized specifications of a traditional and of a pipeline architectures (both CISC and RISC), and show that the latter behaves more efficiently almost always. Admittedly, the size of our example is small. We feel that only an extensive testing of our proposal on real size examples can assess its validity. We plan to take examples from both the side of parallel architectures and of networks of asynchronous processors. We are confident that our techniques will scale up without major problems. In fact, the existing programming language Facile [5] has been equipped with a proved operational semantics. From this, we derived information about qualitative aspects, used then sucessfully to debug Facile programs [5]. Thus, we hope the same with quantitative descriptions. A minor point concerns the labels of the proved transitions used to derive the transitions of interest, qualitative or quantitative.. They may be long wired and difficult to deal with, but we handle them mechanically. We already experimented on this [4] in derived models that express qualitative aspects of processes, like causality and locality. Another minor problem arises from our assumption to have an unbounded number of processors available. In fact, we assign a new processor/location to a sequential sub-process as soon as needed. E.g., from one processor running process $\alpha.(P|Q)$, we pass to two processors after α has been executed. More realistically, we can allocate more than one sequential sub-process on the same processor. Technically, this is easily achieved by imposing an equivalence relation over locations.

Together with other papers on the qualitative descriptions of concurrent systems mentioned above, this work encourages us to develop further the idea of having a single detailed model from which many others can be coherently derived and fruitfully used for the analysis of systems.

References

1. L. Aceto and D. Murphy. Timing and causality in process algebra. Technical Report 9/93, University of Sussex, 1993.
2. R. Alur and D. Dill. A theory of timed automata. *Theoretical Computer Science*, 126(2):183–236, 1994.
3. J.C.M Baeten and J.A. Bergstra. Real-time process algebra. Technical Report CS-R9053, Centre for Mathematics and Computer Science, Amsterdam, 1990.
4. A. Bianchi, S. Coluccini, P. Degano, and C. Priami. An efficient verifier of truly concurrent properties. In V. Malyshkin, editor, *Proceedings of PaCT'95, LNCS 964*, pages 36–50. Springer-Verlag, 1995.
5. Roberta Borgia, Pierpaolo Degano, Corrado Priami, Lone Leth, and Bent Thomsen. Understanding mobile agents via a non-interleaving semantics for facile. Technical Report ECRC-96-4, European Computer-Industry Research Centre, 1996.
6. G. Boudol and I. Castellani. A non-interleaving semantics for CCS based on proved transitions. *Fundamenta Informaticae*, XI(4):433–452, 1988.
7. F. Corradini, R. Gorrieri, and M. Roccetti. Performance preordering: ordering processes with respect to speed. In *Proceedings of MFCS95, LNCS 969*, 1995.
8. P. Degano, R. De Nicola, and U. Montanari. Partial ordering derivations for CCS. In *Proceedings of FCT, LNCS 199*, pages 520–533. Springer-Verlag, 1985.
9. P. Degano and C. Priami. Proved trees. In *Proceedings of ICALP'92, LNCS 623*, pages 629–640. Springer-Verlag, 1992.
10. P. Degano and C. Priami. Causality for mobile processes. In *Proceedings of ICALP'95, LNCS 944*, pages 660–671. Springer-Verlag, 1995.
11. P. Degano and C. Priami. Enhanced operational semantics. *ACM Computing Surveys*, 28(2):352–354, 1996.
12. G. Ferrari and U. Montanari. Dynamic matrices. In *Proceedings of AMAST'95, LNCS 936*. Springer-Verlag, 1995.
13. R. Gorrieri and M. Roccetti. Towards performance evaluation in process algebras. In *Proceedings of AMAST'93, LNCS*. Springer Verlag, 1993.
14. R. Gorrieri, M. Roccetti, and E. Stancapiano. A theory of processes with durational actions. *Theoretical Computer Science*, (140), 1994.
15. E. Goubault. Durations for truly concurrent transitions. In *Proceedings of ESOP96, LNCS 1058*, pages 173–187, 1995.
16. M. Hennessy and T. Regan. A temporal process algebra. Technical Report 2/90, University of Sussex, 1990.
17. Andrea Maggiolo-Schettini and Adriano Peron. A graph rewriting framework for statecharts semantics. In J. Cuny, H. Ehrig, G. Engels, and G. Rozenberg, editors, *Proc. Fifth Intl. Workshop on Graph Grammars and Their Application to Comp. Sci.*, volume 1073 of *Lecture Notes in Computer Science*, pages 107–121. Springer, 1996.
18. Andrea Maggiolo-Schettini and Józef Winkowski. Towards an algebra for timed behaviours. *Theeoretical Computer Science*, 103(2):335–363, 1992.
19. R. Milner. The polyadic π-calculus: a tutorial. Technical Report ECS-LFCS-91-180, University of Edinburgh, 1991.

20. R. Milner, J. Parrow, and D. Walker. A calculus of mobile processes (I and II). *Information and Computation*, 100(1):1–77, 1992.
21. F. Moller and C. Tofts. A temporal calculus of communicating processes. In *Proceedings of CONCUR'90, LNCS 458*. Springer-Verlag, 1990.
22. X. Nicollin and J. Sifakis. An overview and synthesis on timed process algebras. In *Real Time: Theory in Practice, LNCS 600*, pages 526–548. Springer-Verlag, 1991.
23. G.M. Reed and A.W. Roscoe. A timed model for communicating sequential processes. *Theoretical Computer Science*, pages 249–261, 1988.
24. Y. Wang. Real-time behaviour of asynchronous agents. In J.C.M. Beaten and J.W. Klop, editors, *Proceedings of CONCUR'90, LNCS 458*. Springer Verlag, 1990.

Testing Semantics of Asynchronous Distributed Programs*

Rocco De Nicola and Rosario Pugliese

Dipartimento di Sistemi ed Informatica
Università di Firenze
Via Lombroso 6/17, 50134 Firenze (ITALY)

Abstract. The algebraic approach to concurrency is tuned for modelling operational semantics and supporting formal verification of distributed imperative programs with asynchronous communications. We consider an imperative process algebra, IPAL, which is obtained by embedding the Linda primitives for interprocess communication in a CSP–like process description language enriched with a construct for assignment. We setup a testing scenario and present a proof system for IPAL which is sound and complete with respect to the induced behavioural relations.

1 Introduction

Programming languages equipped with primitives for *interprogram communication* are increasingly used nowadays. Program correctness is a major problem to face when designing applications that take advantage of these primitives. Indeed, the possible interactions which can take place when two or more concurrent programs are simultaneously executed may give rise to new (unwanted) behaviours and may lead to nondeterministic behaviour.

Process Algebras (CCS [19], ACP [4], CSP [17], etc.) represent a useful tool for better understanding concurrent systems and developing methods for reasoning about concurrent programs in a rigorous and formal way. The algebraic approach has so far mainly concentrated on languages with uninterpreted action symbols that use a synchronous paradigm for program interaction. Moreover, only a few well–established formal theories there exist for process algebras which handle some kind of data values.

In this paper we use the algebraic approach to concurrency for modelling operational semantics and supporting formal verification of distributed programs which can manipulate values, can assign them to variables, and can pass them over to other programs asynchronously.

We take the Linda paradigm [12, 5] for process interaction as our starting point. Linda [12, 5] is a member of a relatively recent generation of global environment parallel languages (e.g. Concurrent Prolog [23], UNITY [6], Shared

* This work has been partially supported by EEC within the HCM Project EXPRESS, by CNR within Progetto Coordinato Comitato 12 "Metodologie e strumenti di analisi, verifica e validazione per sistemi software affidabili", and by Istituto di Elaborazione dell'Informazione.

Prolog [2]) that differ from those of previous generations because they offer, and often require, explicit control of interactions. A communication between Linda processes is obtained by accessing tuples (sequences of variables and data) in a shared memory called "tuple space" (a multiset of tuples). The communication mechanism is asynchronous (send operations always proceed whilst read operations can block) and associative (tuples are content–addressable). Linda is a coordination model rather than a complete programming language; all of its primitives are devoted to coordinate interactions among programs. However, a concurrent language can be obtained by embedding the Linda primitives in a sequential (functional, imperative, logic, etc.) programming language (see, e.g., [3, 24, 20, 25]). This renders Linda very general and leads to a family of concurrent languages based on Linda rather than to a single language.

Our main objective has been that of developing a semantic framework that supports analysis of programs written in an imperative Linda dialect obtained by embedding the Linda primitives in a language with assignments. Our language is in between process algebras and really implemented Linda imperative programming dialects (see, e.g., [25]). Testing preorders [7] are our observational machinery for abstracting away from unwanted details of the operational behaviour of programs and for comparing them with respect to a notion of "being an approximation of". Two programs are considered as equivalent whenever they reciprocally approximate.

In [11, 22] we have defined PAL, a process algebra obtained by substituting abstract action prefixes of a pure CSP-like process algebra with the Linda primitives for process interaction. The asynchronous communication mechanism has been rendered by modelling outputs as concurrent processes thus decoupling senders and receivers, without introducing any passive component which corresponds to the tuple space. A behavioural testing (must) preorder has been defined, where observers are, as for CCS, processes which can interact with the observed process and report success. The fact that a different (with respect to a synchronous setting) communication (i.e. observation) mechanism is used leads to a different observational semantics. Two other equivalent interpretations for PAL processes were given: an equational interpretation via a sound and complete proof system, useful in practice for performing process verification via symbolic manipulation, and a denotational one via a fully abstract model of double-labelled trees, AT^L (*Linda Acceptance Trees*), which are a generalization of standard Acceptance Trees of [13] used as a model for CCS.

In this paper, we present a generalization of that study to an imperative extension of PAL, that we call IPAL (Imperative PAL), with an assignment construct in the form of action prefixing. We follow the approach used by Hennessy and Ingolfsdottir in [16] for adapting the testing scenario for CCS with value–passing of [15] to an imperative extension of the language with assignment prefixes.

We model the language in such a way that each process has its own private store. Informations from or about other processes can be obtained only by communication via the tuple space. Thus, the mutual influence of processes in updating the store, which would lead to counterintuitive situations, is avoided. The operational semantics of the language is modelled as a relation over configurations, consisting of pairs of terms and stores. Compositions operators over configurations, corresponding to those over IPAL terms, are used to guarantee that each component has its own private store. We can reuse most of the theory developed for PAL. For example, we can continue using the model AT^L for IPAL too and all the equational laws it supports. Of course, specific laws for assignments are required, but, by using a suitable definition of substitution application, a single law suffices.

The rest of the paper is organized as follows. In the next section, we briefly introduce the main features of Linda. In Section 3, we define the syntax of IPAL, while in Section 4 we introduce its operational semantics in the SOS style [21]. A theory of testing [7] based on this operational semantics is described in Section 5. In Section 6, we present a proof system for IPAL which is sound and complete with respect to the behavioural preorder. In Section 7, by means of a small example, we show how the proof system works. In the last section, we discuss related work and future research.

2 A brief presentation of Linda

Linda [12, 5] is a coordination language that relies on an asynchronous and associative communication mechanism based on a shared global environment called Tuples Space (TS), a multiset of tuples. A *tuple* is a sequence of *actual fields* (value objects) and *formal fields* (variables) with the constraint that the first field be an actual field, called *logic* name (or *tag*).

The basic interaction mechanism is *pattern-matching*. It is used to select a tuple in TS that matches a given tuple t. Matching is an indivisible act which permits nondeterministically selecting one of those tuples in TS with the same tag as t and with the same number of fields and such that corresponding fields have matching values or variables. Variables match any value of the same type and two values match only if identical.

There are four operations for manipulating the tuple space: two possibly blocking operations for accessing tuples in TS and two non-blocking operations for adding tuples to TS.

- **in**(t): the process evaluates t and then looks in TS for a tuple t' matching t. If and when t' is found, it is removed from TS; the corresponding values of t' are assigned to the variables of t and the process continues. If no matching tuple is found, the process is suspended until one is available.
- **read**(t) is similar to **in**(t), but it does not require removal of the matched tuple t' from TS.
- **out**(t): the process adds to TS the tuple resulting from the evaluation of t and proceeds.
- **eval**(t) is similar to **out**(t), but rather than evaluating t, the process creates a new process that will evaluate t and then add the resulting tuple to TS.

It is worth noting that nondeterminism is inherent in the definition of Linda primitives. It arises when more **in/read** operations are suspended waiting for a tuple; when such a tuple becomes available, only one of the suspended operations is nondeterministically selected to proceed. Similarly, when an **in/read** operation has more than one matching tuple one is arbitrarily chosen.

The following example, borrowed from [5], is a very intuitive C-Linda [25] solution of the well-known dining philosophers problem. In the example, Num is the number of philosophers and % is the C notation for the remainder of an integer division.

```
phil(i)
  int i;
{
  while(1) {
    think();
    in("room ticket");
    in("chopstick", i);
    in("chopstick", (i + 1)%Num);
    eat();
    out("chopstick", i);
    out("chopstick", (i + 1)%Num);
    out("room ticket");
  }
}
```

```
initialize()
{
  int i;
  for (i = 0; i < Num; i++) {
    out("chopstick", i);
    eval(phil(i));
    if (i < (Num - 1)) out("room ticket");
  }
}
```

The use of actual fields in the argument tuple of an **in/read** instruction is known as "structured naming". It makes TS content-addressable, in the sense that processes may select from a collection of tuples that share the same tag by means of the value of any other component field. Formal fields in the argument tuples of **out/eval** instructions can be thought of as "don't care" fields: no value is associated to their variables, neither it will be by matching operations.

The Linda model is known as *Generative Communication* [12]. Indeed, once a tuple is added to TS, its life-time is independent from that of the producer process. This permits writing programs where complex data structures are distributed to allow different programs to work simultaneously on their elements. Linda's communication mechanism, somewhat similarly to "explicit message passing", makes the interactions of a program with its environment explicit. However, one can easily write Linda programs that essentially communicate via messages. Thus the simple basic Linda model can deal with parallelism of all grain sizes.

3 Syntax of IPAL

In this section we describe the syntax of IPAL. The major change with respect to PAL [11] is the introduction of assignments and, thus, that of new binding operators for value variables.

We assume a predefined syntactic category, *Exp*, of ***value expressions***, ranged over by e, which contains a set of variable symbols, Var, ranged over by x, y, z, etc., and a non empty countable set of value symbols, Val, ranged over by v. We make use of the usual notion of closed expression, i.e. one without occurrences of variables, and a notion of ***substitution***. In general, a substitution for variables is a function from Var to Exp which is almost everywhere the identity. We write $[e_1/x_1, \ldots, e_n/x_n]$ for the substitution ρ defined by $\rho(x_i) = e_i$ whose non trivial domain, denoted by $bv(\rho)$, is $\{x_1, \ldots, x_n\}$. We write $\rho[e/x]$ for denoting the substitution which is the same as ρ except that x is mapped to e. We write $e[e_1/x_1, \ldots, e_n/x_n]$ for denoting the expression which is obtained by simultaneously substituting each occurrence of x_i in e with e_i.

Furthermore, we assume existence of a predefined syntactic category, *BExp*, of ***boolean expressions***, ranged over by *be*, which contains at least the boolean values ***false*** (denoted by *ff*) and ***true*** (denoted by *tt*), the usual boolean operators $(\wedge, \vee, \ldots)$ and an operator, $=$, for testing equality of value expressions.

As usual, we assume a predefined countable set of process variables, which is denoted with $\mathcal{X}$ and ranged over by $X, Y, Z, \ldots$. Thus, the language has two kinds of variables, value and process variables and, correspondingly, two kinds of binding operators.

Free and bound process variables are defined as usual, rec$X$._ being the binding operator. Substitutions for process variables are mappings from process variables to terms and are ranged over by ξ.

The assignment construct $x := e$._ binds variable x while variables which occur in formal fields of t are bound by **in**(t)._ and **read**(t)._. If E is a term, we let $bv(E)$ denote the set of variables bound in E and $fv(E)$ denote that of variables free in E. Substitutions of value–expressions for variables are also extended to terms. If E is a term, we use $E\rho$ to denote the term resulting from simultaneously substituting in E all free occurrences of x with $\rho(x)$.

Due to the interplay between the IPAL binders for process and value variables, the application of a substitution ρ to a term of the form rec$X.E$ such that some occurrences of X lie within the scope of a binder for a value variable in $fv(E) \cap bv(\rho)$ requires the unfolding of the recursive term. Therefore, ρ is applied to the term $E[\text{rec}X.E/X]$ obtained by syntactically replacing in E all free occurrences of X with rec$X.E$.

Definition 3.1 (Syntax of IPAL) The set of terms (ranged over by E, F) is generated from the following grammar:

$$
\begin{aligned}
E &::= \mathbf{nil} \mid \Omega \mid p.E \mid \mathbf{if}\ be\ \mathbf{then}\ E_1\ \mathbf{else}\ E_2 \mid E_1\ op\ E_2 \mid X \mid \mathrm{rec}\, X.E \\
p &::= cp \mid \mathbf{eval}(E) \mid x := e \\
cp &::= \mathbf{out}(ot) \mid \mathbf{in}(it) \mid \mathbf{read}(it) \\
ot &::= e \mid !x \mid ot_1, ot_2 \\
it &::= e \mid !x \mid \star \mid it_1, it_2 \\
op &::= \oplus \mid \Box \mid \| \mid \lfloor\!\lfloor \mid \|_c
\end{aligned}
$$

Let IPAL (for *Imperative Process Algebra based on Linda*) denote the set of all terms which contain no free occurrences of value variables. We will call *processes* or *closed terms* those IPAL terms which contain no free occurrences of process variables. Let $\mathcal{P}$, ranged over by P, Q, R etc., be the set of all IPAL processes. We shall use $\equiv$ for denoting syntactic identity of terms.

The language has a few operators for building up terms from more basic ones.

nil (*inaction*) It denotes the term that cannot perform any action.

Ω (*undefined*) It denotes the term that may only compute internally.

$p.\_$ (*action prefix*) The meaning of $p.E$ depends on the prefix p: if it is not an output action, $p.E$ executes action p and then behaves like E, otherwise, $p.E$ can execute action p in parallel with E.

if *be* **then** _ **else** _ (*conditional*) The term **if** *be* **then** E_1 **else** E_2 acts like E_1 if the boolean expression *be* evaluates to true and like E_2 otherwise.

$\_[]\_$ (*external choice*) The term $E[]F$ behaves either like E or like F and the choice is controlled by the environment.

$\_\oplus\_$ (*internal choice*) The term $E\oplus F$ may autonomously decide to behave either like E or like F.

$\_|\_$ (*parallel composition*) The term $E|F$ denotes the concurrent execution of E and F.

$\_\lfloor\_$ (*left-merge*) The term $E\lfloor F$ denotes the concurrent execution of E and F but inhibits F from performing any action until E has performed a visible one.

$\_|_c\_$ (*communication-merge*) The term $E|_c F$ denotes the concurrent execution of E and F but inhibits visible actions until a synchronization between E and F has taken place.

rec$X._$ (*recursive definition*) A definition rec$X.E$ has the same meaning as the term defined by the equation $X = E$ and is used for describing recursive behaviours.

We have modified the Linda process creation primitive. The original definition permits process terms to compute values as fields of tuples, but here we only permit evaluation of process expressions. However, with our formalism, **eval**(**out**(t).**nil**) can be used to express the original **eval**(t).

We distinguish between input and output tuples. This, in connection with a slightly different pattern–matching mechanism with respect to the Linda one, permits, on one hand, to determine which tuple has been selected by pattern–matching and, on the other hand, to recover the original communication capabilities of processes (see also Section 4). We use "$!\,x$" for denoting a formal field whose variable is x, "e" for denoting an actual field which contains the value–expression e and, in the case of input tuples, "$\star$" for denoting a field which can match only with a formal field of output tuples (a rationale for its introduction will be given in Section 4).

Notation 3.2 If t is a tuple then $|t|$ denotes the number of fields of t (i.e. the length of t), t_i denotes the i-th field in t ($1 \leq i \leq |\, t \,|$), $var(t)$ the set of variables which occur in formal fields of t, $if(t)$ the set of indexes of formal fields of t and $ia(t)$ the set of indexes of actual fields of t.

If t, t' are tuples, indexes i and j are such that $1 \leq i \leq |t|$ and $1 \leq j \leq |t'|$, and $I \subseteq \{1, 2, \ldots, |t|\}$ then we will use the following notations for comparing tuples:

- $t =_{\bar{i}} t'$ if $|t| = |t'|$ and $\forall j : j \neq i$ imply $t_j = t'_j$;
- $t =_{\bar{I}} t'$ if $|t| = |t'|$ and $\forall j \notin I : t_j = t'_j$.

4 Operational Semantics

The operational rules for the language require evaluation mechanisms for expressions, boolean expressions, input tuples and output tuples. These mechanisms are similar to (i.e. obtain the same evaluations as) those for PAL but need a *store*, i.e. a (total) function from Var to Val, which keeps the bindings of variables to values. We will use σ to range over the set of stores, *Store*.

The functions $\mathcal{E}[\![\cdot]\!]\cdot : Exp \longrightarrow (Store \longrightarrow Val)$ and $\mathcal{B}[\![\cdot]\!]\cdot : BExp \longrightarrow (Store \longrightarrow \{ff, tt\})$ are the evaluation mechanisms for expressions and boolean expressions, respectively. We use $\mathcal{E}[\![e]\!]_\sigma$ and $\mathcal{B}[\![be]\!]_\sigma$ for denoting the values of the expression, e, and of the boolean expression, be, relative to store σ.

Let $OTpl$ and $ITpl$ be the sets of output tuples and input tuples, respectively. The functions $\mathcal{O}[\![\cdot]\!]\cdot : OTpl \longrightarrow (Store \longrightarrow EOT)$ and $\mathcal{I}[\![\cdot]\!]\cdot : ITpl \longrightarrow (Store \longrightarrow EIT)$ are the evaluation mechanisms for output tuples and input tuples, respectively, and are defined in Table 1. The tuples resulting from

$\mathcal{O}[\![\,!x\,]\!]_\sigma = \star$	$\mathcal{I}[\![\,!x\,]\!]_\sigma = !x$
$\mathcal{O}[\![\,e\,]\!]_\sigma = \mathcal{E}[\![\,e\,]\!]_\sigma$	$\mathcal{I}[\![\,e\,]\!]_\sigma = \mathcal{E}[\![\,e\,]\!]_\sigma$
$\mathcal{O}[\![\,(t_1, t_2)\,]\!]_\sigma = (\mathcal{O}[\![\,t_1\,]\!]_\sigma, \mathcal{O}[\![\,t_2\,]\!]_\sigma)$	$\mathcal{I}[\![\,\star\,]\!]_\sigma = \star$
	$\mathcal{I}[\![\,(t_1, t_2)\,]\!]_\sigma = (\mathcal{I}[\![\,t_1\,]\!]_\sigma, \mathcal{I}[\![\,t_2\,]\!]_\sigma)$

Table 1. Tuple Evaluation Functions

evaluation are, respectively, elements of the following two sets:

- EOT, ***evaluated output tuples***, which is generated by the following rules: $t ::= v \mid \star \mid t_1, t_2$;
- EIT, ***evaluated input tuples***, which is generated by the following rules: $t ::= v \mid !x \mid \star \mid t_1, t_2$.

Note that the evaluation mechanism for output tuples abstracts away from the formals used in tuples; all of them are represented as $\star$.

Furthermore, we will use the set $AEIT$ of ***patterns*** (***abstract evaluated input tuples***) of input tuples which is generated from the following grammar:

$$t ::= v \mid ! \mid \star \mid t_1, t_2$$

and a function $patt : EIT \longrightarrow AEIT$ which returns the pattern of an evaluated input tuple. Essentially, *patt* abstracts away from the formals used in input tuples; all of them are represented as !.

Pattern–matching between evaluated input and output tuples is checked by means of predicate *match* defined over $EIT \times EOT$ via the rules in Table 2. Observe that our pattern–matching mechanism differs slightly from that of Linda (see Section 2). We restrict matching by imposing that values in input tuples can match only with the same values in output tuples. Moreover, we impose that the symbol $\star$, which can be used as field of input tuples, can match only with a formal field of output tuples. This new mechanism permits to test which tuple has been selected by pattern–matching. So, for example, we are able to express **read**(t) in terms of **in**(t) and **out**(t). The use of $\star$ in input tuples, in connection with that of the external choice operator $[]$, makes it possible to recover the original communication capabilities of Linda input primitives and has motivated the syntactic distinction between input and output tuples. For example, the Linda primitive $\mathbf{in}(!\,x, v)$ can access each tuple of the form (v', v) or $(v', !\,y)$, where $v' \in Val$ and $y \in Var$. In IPAL we can obtain the same overall communication capability by composing the primitives $\mathbf{in}(!\,x, v)$ and $\mathbf{in}(!\,x, \star)$ by means of the operator $[]$.

$$
\begin{array}{ll}
match(v, v) & v \in Val \\
match(!\,x, v) & v \in Val \\
match(\star, \star) & \\[6pt]
\multicolumn{2}{c}{\dfrac{match(t'_1, t'_2)\,, \qquad match(t''_1, t''_2)}{match((t'_1, t''_1), (t'_2, t''_2))}}
\end{array}
$$

Table 2. Pattern-Matching Rules

The operational semantics of IPAL describes how a *configuration*, i.e. essentially a pair consisting of a term and a store, evolves to another one by either an internal or an external move. Compositions operators over configurations, corresponding to those over IPAL terms, are used for duplicating the store thus guaranteeing that each component has its own private store.

Definition 4.1 The *operational semantics of IPAL* is characterized by the extended labelled transition system $(\mathcal{C}on, \mathcal{A}ct, \longrightarrow, \rightarrowtail)$ where:

- the set of *configurations*, $\mathcal{C}on$ ranged over by γ, is defined by the following rules:

$$\gamma ::= \phi \mid cp.\phi \mid \gamma_1 \; op \; \gamma_2$$

  where $op \in \{\oplus, [], |, \lfloor, |_c\}$ and ϕ is a generic *basic* configuration, that is an element of the following set

$$\mathcal{B}\mathcal{C}on = \{<E, \sigma> \mid E \text{ is a term}, \sigma \text{ is a store}\}.$$

- $Act = \{t \mid t \in EOT\} \cup \{(t', t) \mid t' \in AEIT, t \in EOT\}$, ranged over by α, is the set of *actions* or *labels*.
- $\longrightarrow \subseteq Con \times Act \times Con$, the *action relation*, is the least relation defined by the rules in Table 3.
- $\rightarrowtail \subseteq Con \times Con$, the *internal relation*, is the least relation defined by the rules in Tables 3 and 5.

In the rules in Table 5 we make use of a complementation notation for labels. Actually, in our setting labels may have many complements. For example, both labels $((5,7),(5,7))$ and $((5,!),(5,7))$ are complement of label $(5,7)$. More formally, we can say that a complement label of α, denoted by $\overline{\alpha}$, is any element of the set $Comp(\alpha)$ defined by:

- $Comp(\alpha) = \{(t', t) \mid t' \in \text{AEIT} \wedge match(t', t)\}$, if $\alpha = t$;
- $Comp(\alpha) = \{t\}$, if $\alpha = (t', t)$.

The operational rules of IPAL are very close to those for PAL. Apart from the specific rule for assignment, the major difference is that they use configurations instead of processes. In our model, Linda Tuple Space is not a passive component (where tuples that had been produced but not yet consumed are stored), it is instead modelled as a set of elementary processes. The asynchronous nature of the communication paradigm is rendered by allowing term E of $\mathbf{out}(t).E$ to proceed before tuple t is actually accessed; that is, by transforming the configuration $<\mathbf{out}(ot).E, \sigma>$ into $(\mathbf{out}(\mathcal{O}[\![ot]\!]_\sigma).<\mathbf{nil}, \sigma>) | <E, \sigma>$ (rule IR8 in Table 5). Therefore, when tuples are used their producers are not obliged to take part in the communication.

$$\textbf{AR1}\ \ \mathbf{in}(t).<E,\sigma> \xrightarrow{(patt(t),t')} <E,\sigma[t'/t]> \qquad \text{if } match(t,t')$$

$$\textbf{AR2}\ \ \mathbf{read}(t).<E,\sigma> \xrightarrow{(patt(t),t')} (\mathbf{out}(t').<\mathbf{nil},\sigma>) | <E,\sigma[t'/t]> \qquad \text{if } match(t,t')$$

$$\textbf{AR3}\ \ \mathbf{out}(t).<E,\sigma> \xrightarrow{t} <E,\sigma>$$

$$\textbf{AR4}\ \ \frac{\gamma_1 \xrightarrow{\alpha} \gamma_1'}{\gamma_1 [\,] \gamma_2 \xrightarrow{\alpha} \gamma_1'} \qquad \textbf{AR5}\ \ \frac{\gamma_1 \xrightarrow{\alpha} \gamma_1'}{\gamma_1 | \gamma_2 \xrightarrow{\alpha} \gamma_1' | \gamma_2}$$

$$\textbf{AR6}\ \ \frac{\gamma_1 \xrightarrow{\alpha} \gamma_1'}{\gamma_1 \lfloor \gamma_2 \xrightarrow{\alpha} \gamma_1' | \gamma_2}$$

Table 3. SOS rules for the Action Relation

In Table 3, the symmetrical versions of rules AR4 and AR5 have been omitted. Rule AR1 shows that the configuration $\mathbf{in}(t).<E,\sigma>$ consumes a tuple t' matching the tuple t; this causes a store updating where the formals of t are bound to the corresponding values of t'. The visible action carries information only about the pattern used for reading and about the consumed tuple. We abstract away from the formals of tuples because they do not affect the communication capabilities of processes. Moreover, no information about the updating of the store is reported because we consider it an internal action. Rule AR2 shows that the configuration **read**$(t).<E,\sigma>$ differs from **in**$(t).<E,\sigma>$ because it makes the accessed tuple available again. The updating resulting from the actual execution of a blocking (**in**/**read**) operation is defined by the rules in Table 4.

$$
\begin{array}{|l|}
\hline
[v/v] = \lambda y.y \\
[v/!\,x] = \lambda y.[y = x] \longrightarrow v, y \\
[\star/\star] = \lambda y.y \\
[(ot_1, ot_2)/(it_1, it_2)] = [ot_1/it_1] \circ [ot_2/it_2] \\
\hline
\end{array}
$$

Table 4. Substitution resulting from a successful matching

In Table 5, the symmetrical versions of rules IR11 and IR15 have been omitted. The specific rule for assignment is IR5; it triggers an internal move that results in the updating of the store. Rule IR9 shows that **eval** is a primitive for dynamic process creation. Rules IR3 and IR4 show that the conditional term **if** *be* **then** E **else** F acts like E if the boolean expression *be* evaluates to true and like F otherwise. Rules IR13 and IR14 deal with interprocess communication. The rules for the binary operators are similar to those for TCCS presented in [14] and for ACP presented in [1], but here these operators have configurations not processes as operands. The only new rule is IR10; it splits configurations in their components, each one with its own private store.

$$
\begin{array}{|ll|}
\hline
\textbf{IR1} & <\Omega,\sigma> \rightarrowtail <\Omega,\sigma> \\
\textbf{IR2} & <\mathrm{rec}X.E,\sigma> \rightarrowtail <E[\mathrm{rec}X.E/X],\sigma> \\
\textbf{IR3} & \dfrac{\mathcal{B}[\![be]\!]_\sigma = tt}{<\textbf{if } be \textbf{ then } E \textbf{ else } F,\sigma> \rightarrowtail <E,\sigma>} \\
\textbf{IR4} & \dfrac{\mathcal{B}[\![be]\!]_\sigma = ff}{<\textbf{if } be \textbf{ then } E \textbf{ else } F,\sigma> \rightarrowtail <F,\sigma>} \\
\textbf{IR5} & <x := e.E,\sigma> \rightarrowtail <E,\sigma[\mathcal{E}[\![e]\!]_\sigma/x]> \\
\textbf{IR6} & <\textbf{in}(it).E,\sigma> \rightarrowtail \textbf{in}(\mathcal{I}[\![it]\!]_\sigma).<E,\sigma> \\
\textbf{IR7} & <\textbf{read}(it).E,\sigma> \rightarrowtail \textbf{read}(\mathcal{I}[\![it]\!]_\sigma).<E,\sigma> \\
\textbf{IR8} & <\textbf{out}(ot).E,\sigma> \rightarrowtail (\textbf{out}(\mathcal{O}[\![ot]\!]_\sigma).<\textbf{nil},\sigma>)|<E,\sigma> \\
\textbf{IR9} & <\textbf{eval}(E).F,\sigma> \rightarrowtail <E,\sigma>|<F,\sigma> \\
\textbf{IR10} & <E\ op\ F,\sigma> \rightarrowtail <E,\sigma>\ op\ <F,\sigma> \quad \text{if } op \in \{\oplus, [\,], |, \lfloor, |_c\} \\
\textbf{IR11} & \gamma_1 \oplus \gamma_2 \rightarrowtail \gamma_1 \qquad\qquad \textbf{IR12} \quad \dfrac{\gamma_1 \rightarrowtail \gamma_1'}{\gamma_1 \lfloor \gamma_2 \rightarrowtail \gamma_1' \lfloor \gamma_2} \\
\textbf{IR13} & \dfrac{\gamma_1 \xrightarrow{\alpha} \gamma_1', \quad \gamma_2 \xrightarrow{\overline{\alpha}} \gamma_2'}{\gamma_1|\gamma_2 \rightarrowtail \gamma_1'|\gamma_2'} \qquad \textbf{IR14} \quad \dfrac{\gamma_1 \xrightarrow{\alpha} \gamma_1', \quad \gamma_2 \xrightarrow{\overline{\alpha}} \gamma_2'}{\gamma_1|_c\gamma_2 \rightarrowtail \gamma_1'|\gamma_2'} \\
\textbf{IR15} & \dfrac{\gamma_1 \rightarrowtail \gamma_1'}{\gamma_1\ op\ \gamma_2 \rightarrowtail \gamma_1'\ op\ \gamma_2} \text{ if } op \in \{[\,], |, |_c\} \\
\hline
\end{array}
$$

Table 5. SOS rules for the Internal Relation

5 Testing Semantics

In this section we show how to apply the standard theory of testing to IPAL.

For defining a testing scenario for PAL [11], we assume a special action prefix, **success**, and a special label, ω, used to denote success. Thus observers are processes which can perform also the special action **success**. In the case of IPAL, observers are terms equipped with a private store which can perform also the special action **success**. We will use o to range over these special configurations.

Notice that an observer cannot access the private memory of the tested configuration, but can only gather information by communication. A different choice was made in [10] for a Linda dialect with both sequential composition and assignment. There observers are able to test the (final) store of (finite computations of) processes. This was essential for the equivalences be preserved by all the operators of the language, in particular by sequential composition.

Since IAPL observers are configurations, their operational semantics is given by the same rules used for the language with only two additional SOS rules which corresponds to the special prefix **success**:

$$\textbf{IR16} \quad <\textbf{success}.E,\sigma> \rightarrowtail \textbf{success}.<E,\sigma>,$$
$$\textbf{AR7} \quad \textbf{success}.<E,\sigma> \stackrel{\omega}{\longrightarrow} <E,\sigma> .$$

Experiments are terms of the form $\gamma|o$. To establish the result of an experiment $\gamma|o$ we must consider all of its *computations*. A computation is a *maximal sequence* of internal transitions, i.e. a sequence

$$\gamma|o \equiv \gamma_0|o_0 \rightarrowtail \gamma_1|o_1 \rightarrowtail \gamma_2|o_2 \dots \gamma_k|o_k \rightarrowtail \dots$$

which is either infinite or such that its last configuration cannot perform any internal transition.

For every configuration γ and observer o, we say γ *must* o if for each computation $\gamma|o \equiv \gamma_0|o_0 \rightarrowtail \gamma_1|o_1 \rightarrowtail \gamma_2|o_2 \dots \gamma_k|o_k \rightarrowtail \dots$ there exists some $n \geq 0$ such that $o_n \stackrel{\omega}{\longrightarrow}$.

Definition 5.1 The *testing preorder* over configurations is defined by:

$$\gamma_1 \underset{\sim}{\sqsubset}_{\mathrm{M}} \gamma_2 \text{ if for every observer } o,\ \gamma_1 \textit{ must } o \text{ implies } \gamma_2 \textit{ must } o.$$

To compare the proof-theoretic relation (defined via the proof system in Section 6) with the behavioural one, we also define the *testing preorder* over terms:

$$E \underset{\sim}{\sqsubset}_{\mathrm{M}} F \text{ if for any closed substitution } \xi \text{ and store } \sigma,\ <E\xi,\sigma> \underset{\sim}{\sqsubset}_{\mathrm{M}} <F\xi,\sigma>.$$

5.1 Alternative characterization of the testing preorder

In this subsection we shall define an alternative characterization of the preorder $\underset{\sim}{\sqsubset}_{\mathrm{M}}$, in the same spirit of [14, 15], that provides a relatively simpler, observers independent method for checking whether two configurations are behaviourally related. The specific communication mechanism, based on pattern–matching, gives rise to a number of complications and has several effects on the construction.

Definition 5.2 For $\rho \in \mathcal{A}ct^*$ we define $\gamma_1 \stackrel{\rho}{\Longrightarrow} \gamma_2$ by

1. $\gamma_1 \stackrel{\epsilon}{\Longrightarrow} \gamma_2$ if $\gamma_1 \rightarrowtail^* \gamma_2$;
2. $\gamma_1 \stackrel{\alpha \cdot \rho'}{\Longrightarrow} \gamma_2$ if $\exists \gamma_1', \gamma_1''$: $\gamma_1 \stackrel{\epsilon}{\Longrightarrow} \gamma_1'$, $\gamma_1' \stackrel{\alpha}{\longrightarrow} \gamma_1''$, $\gamma_1'' \stackrel{\rho'}{\Longrightarrow} \gamma_2$.

A first complication is that observers cannot perceive the differences among patterns which access a given tuple. Thus, to abstract away from them we introduce the notion of *abstract action*.

Definition 5.3 The set $\mathcal{A}a$ (ranged over by a) of *abstract actions* is:

$$\mathcal{A}a = \{(t, ir) \mid t \in EOT\} \cup \{(t, out) \mid t \in EOT\}.$$

We use s to range over $\mathcal{A}a^*$. The function $ab : \mathcal{A}ct^* \longrightarrow \mathcal{A}a^*$ abstracts away from the patterns used in the input actions of a sequence and is defined by:
$ab(\epsilon) = \epsilon,\ ab((t, t')) = (t', ir),\ ab(t) = (t, out),\ ab(\alpha \cdot \rho) = ab(\alpha) \cdot ab(\rho)$.

Definition 5.4 The *language* of a configuration γ is the set of all the sequences of abstract actions the configuration can perform; that is

$$L(\gamma) = \{s \in \mathcal{A}a^* \mid \exists \rho, \gamma' :\ \gamma \stackrel{\rho}{\Longrightarrow} \gamma' \ \wedge s = ab(\rho)\}.$$

The set of initial actions a configuration can perform may be infinite. In fact, the transition system is not finite branching as any configuration of the form $\mathbf{in}(t).<E, \sigma>$ (or $\mathbf{read}(t).<E, \sigma>$) can have an infinite number of derivations $\mathbf{in}(t).<E, \sigma> \xrightarrow{(patt(t), t')} <E, \sigma[t'/t]>$, where $match(t, t')$. We single out the set of patterns a configuration can use for accessing tuples by introducing the notion of *event*. This permits expressing the interaction capability of configurations in terms of a finite set, namely the set of tuples they can output and the set of patterns they can use for accessing tuples.

Definition 5.5 Let Ev (ranged over by e) be the set of *events* defined as:

$$Ev = \{(ir, t) \mid t \in AEIT\} \cup \{(out, t) \mid t \in EOT\}.$$

The function $ev : \mathcal{A}ct \longrightarrow Ev$ returns the event associated to an action and is defined by the following clauses:

$$ev((t, t')) = (ir, t), \quad ev(t) = (out, t).$$

We extend the predicate *match* to events by defining:

$$\forall (ir, t), (out, t') \in Ev\text{: } match((ir, t), (out, t')) \Longleftrightarrow match(t, t').$$

Intuitively, each event corresponds to a set of abstract actions: (out, t) corresponds to (t, out) and (ir, t) corresponds to any abstract action of the form (t', ir) such that $match(t, t')$. The set of abstract actions corresponding to an event e may be strictly contained in that corresponding to an event e'. For example, the set of abstract actions corresponding to $(ir, (!, 7))$ contains that corresponding to $(ir, (5, 7))$. Therefore, for comparing two finite sets of events we must generalize the usual subset relation. We shall write $A \lhd B$ for saying that any abstract action corresponding to an event of A also corresponds to an event of B. Intuitively, this means that B has at least the same interaction capability as A.

Now we define *convergence* along sequences of abstract actions.

Definition 5.6 For every sequence $s \in \mathcal{A}a^*$ let $\downarrow s$ be defined by

1. $\gamma \downarrow \epsilon$ if there is no infinite computation $\gamma \rightarrowtail \gamma_1 \rightarrowtail \gamma_2 \rightarrowtail \ldots$,
2. $\gamma \downarrow (t, ir) \cdot s'$ if $\gamma \downarrow \epsilon$ and for every t', γ' such that $\gamma \stackrel{(t',t)}{\Longrightarrow} \gamma'$ we have $\gamma' \downarrow s'$,
3. $\gamma \downarrow (t, out) \cdot s'$ if $\gamma \downarrow \epsilon$ and for every γ' such that $\gamma \stackrel{t}{\Longrightarrow} \gamma'$ we have $\gamma' \downarrow s'$.

Let $\gamma \uparrow s$ if $\gamma \downarrow s$ is false.

Definition 5.7 The set of *successors* (or *initial events*) of γ, $S(\gamma) \subseteq Ev$ is:

$$S(\gamma) = \{(ir, t) \mid \exists t', \gamma' : \gamma \stackrel{(t,t')}{\Longrightarrow} \gamma' \} \cup \{(out, t) \mid \exists \gamma' : \gamma \stackrel{t}{\Longrightarrow} \gamma' \}.$$

Definition 5.8 The *acceptance set of* γ *after* $s \in \mathcal{A}a^*$, $\mathcal{A}(\gamma, s)$ is:

$$\mathcal{A}(\gamma, s) = \{S(\gamma') \mid \gamma \stackrel{\rho}{\Longrightarrow} \gamma' \wedge s = ab(\rho)\}.$$

Over acceptance sets we shall use the following preorder relation:

$$\mathcal{A} \subset\subset \mathcal{B} \text{ if for all } A \in \mathcal{A} \text{ there exists } B \in \mathcal{B} \text{ such that } B \lhd A.$$

Thus, for comparing finite sets of events we use the relation $\lhd$ instead of the usual set inclusion (see, e.g., [14]).

Finally, we can define another preorder over configurations and we can prove that it coincides with the one defined in Definition 5.1.

Definition 5.9 For configurations γ_1 and γ_2, $\gamma_1 \ll_{\mathrm{M}} \gamma_2$ if for every $s \in \mathcal{A}a^*$

$$\gamma_1 \downarrow s \Longrightarrow \begin{array}{l} 1.\ \gamma_2 \downarrow s \\ 2.\ \mathcal{A}(\gamma_2, s) \subset\subset \mathcal{A}(\gamma_1, s). \end{array}$$

Proposition 5.10 For configurations γ_1 and γ_2, $\gamma_1 \sqsubseteq_{\mathrm{M}} \gamma_2$ iff $\gamma_1 \ll_{\mathrm{M}} \gamma_2$.

Proof. The structure of the proof is similar to the corresponding one for process algebras [14, 15]; due to the Linda communication paradigm, only a few additional complications have to be faced. However, we can mimic the corresponding proof for PAL in [22] by taking as special observers those used for PAL (which are closed terms) and any store σ.

The alternative characterization of $\underset{\sim}{\sqsubset}_{M}$ established above simplifies many proofs. For example, it is now easy to show that the behavioural preorder is a congruence over $\Sigma = \{\mathbf{nil}, \Omega, \mathbf{out}(t).\_, \mathbf{eval}(E).\_, \_\oplus\_, \_\Box\_, \_|\_, \_\lfloor\_, \_|_c\_\}$.

Proposition 5.11 The operators $\mathbf{nil}$, Ω, $\mathbf{out}(t).\_$, $\mathbf{eval}(E).\_$, $\_\oplus\_$, $\_\Box\_$, $\_|\_$, $\_\lfloor\_$, and $\_|_c\_$ preserve $\underset{\sim}{\sqsubset}_{M}$.

Proof. The proof can be performed by an exhaustive case analysis and relies on the coincidence of $\underset{\sim}{\sqsubset}_{M}$ and $\ll_{M}$. Whenever one of the parallel operators $\_|\_$, $\_\lfloor\_$, and $\_|_c\_$ is considered then $\underset{\sim}{\sqsubset}_{M}$ is used, in the remaining cases, $\ll_{M}$ is used instead.

For the operators $\mathbf{in}.\_$ and $\mathbf{read}.\_$, which have not been considered in the above proposition, we must take into account all the substitutions they may give rise to.

Proposition 5.12 If for each tuple $t' \in EOT$ such that $match(t, t')$ it holds that $< E, \sigma[t'/t] > \underset{\sim}{\sqsubset}_{M} < F, \sigma'[t'/t] >$ then $\mathbf{in}(t).< E, \sigma > \underset{\sim}{\sqsubset}_{M} \mathbf{in}(t).< F, \sigma' >$ and $\mathbf{read}(t).< E, \sigma > \underset{\sim}{\sqsubset}_{M} \mathbf{read}(t).< F, \sigma' >$.

Proof. Also here we take advantage of the alternative characterization $\ll_{M}$ of $\underset{\sim}{\sqsubset}_{M}$. We only consider $\mathbf{in}(t).\_$; the proof for $\mathbf{read}(t).\_$ is similar. If $s = \epsilon$ we have $\mathbf{in}(t).<E, \sigma> \downarrow \epsilon$ and $\mathbf{in}(t).<F, \sigma'> \downarrow \epsilon$. We also have that $\mathcal{A}(\mathbf{in}(t).<E, \sigma>, \epsilon) = \{\{(ir, t'')\}\} = \mathcal{A}(\mathbf{in}(t).<F, \sigma'>, \epsilon)$, where $t'' = patt(t)$. Every non–empty sequence of actions from $\mathbf{in}(t).<E, \sigma>$ or $\mathbf{in}(t).<F, \sigma'>$ is of the form $(t'', t') \cdot s$, for some $t' \in EOT$ such that $match(t'', t')$ and s sequence from $<E, \sigma[t'/t]>$ or $<F, \sigma'[t'/t]>$. Now, we can use the hypothesis $<E, \sigma[t'/t]> \ll_{M} <F, \sigma'[t'/t]>$ for comparing acceptance sets and convergence, and the thesis follows.

6 A Proof System for IPAL

Here, we define a proof system for IPAL processes; then, we will sketch the strategy used for proving its soundness and completeness with respect to the behavioural interpretation of IPAL processes.

The proof system, that we call C, is obtained by extending the one for PAL with the axiom in Table 11. It relies on some equational laws and two induction rules: one handling recursively defined processes, the other dealing with input prefixes. Each equation $X = Y$ has to be red as standing for the pairs of inequations $X \sqsubseteq Y$ and $Y \sqsubseteq X$.

The proof system for PAL contains the standard equations for testing (Table 6), the laws for establishing strictness of the operators (Table 7), the equations for expanding the derived operators (Table 8), the specific laws for the Linda operations (Table 9) and, obviously, a set of inference rules (Table 10). In particular, in rule `VI` we make use of notation E^n (where E is a value-closed term and n is an integer) for the n-th *finite syntactic approximation* of E. The

IC1	$X \oplus (Y \oplus Z) = (X \oplus Y) \oplus Z$
IC2	$X \oplus Y = Y \oplus X$
IC3	$X \oplus X = X$
IC4	$\mathbf{out}(\mathrm{t}).\mathbf{nil} \lfloor X \oplus \mathbf{out}(\mathrm{t}).\mathbf{nil} \lfloor Y = \mathbf{out}(\mathrm{t}).\mathbf{nil} \lfloor (X \oplus Y)$
IC5	$X \oplus Y \sqsubseteq X$
EC1	$X \Box (Y \Box Z) = (X \Box Y) \Box Z$
EC2	$X \Box Y = Y \Box X$
EC3	$X \Box X = X$
EC4	$X \Box \mathbf{nil} = X$
MIX1	$\mathbf{out}(\mathrm{t}).\mathbf{nil} \lfloor X \Box \mathbf{out}(\mathrm{t}).\mathbf{nil} \lfloor Y = \mathbf{out}(\mathrm{t}).\mathbf{nil} \lfloor (X \oplus Y)$
MIX2	$X \oplus (Y \Box Z) = (X \oplus Y) \Box (X \oplus Z)$
MIX3	$X \Box (Y \oplus Z) = (X \Box Y) \oplus (X \Box Z)$

Table 6. Inequations for sequential, nondeterministic processes

UND1	$\Omega \sqsubseteq X$	UND4	$\Omega \| X \sqsubseteq \Omega$
UND2	$X \Box \Omega \sqsubseteq \Omega$	UND5	$\Omega \lfloor X \sqsubseteq \Omega$
UND3	$X \| \Omega \sqsubseteq \Omega$	UND6	$X \|_c \Omega \sqsubseteq \Omega$

Table 7. Inequations for Ω

actual definition of this class of processes is standard in algebraic semantics and can be found in, e.g., [14].

The axiom in Table 11 is specific for assignment. In AS, $X[e/x]$ is used to denote the application to X of the substitution $[e/x]$ as defined in Section 3. Since stores can only be investigated by communication or by conditional choice, we do not introduce any additional inference rule for ensuring substitutivity of value expressions (rules VII and VIII in Table 10 are sufficient).

It could be proven that each axiom is *independent* from the other, in the sense that its removal would affect the relation provable in C. This is in part pointed out in the completeness proof where the specific function of each axiom is clarified.

The soundness and the completeness of the proof system C relatively to the testing preorder can be proven by using standard proof techniques (see, e.g., [7]). The proof proceeds in two steps: first a reduced proof system is considered and its soundness and completeness for finite processes is proven; then, the inference rules are used to establish soundness and completeness of C.

We call R the proof system obtained from C by deleting rules IV(a) and VI in Table 10, dealing with possibly infinite terms. We shall write $E \sqsubseteq_R F$ ($E \sqsubseteq_C F$) to indicate the fact that $E \sqsubseteq F$ can be derived within the proof system R (resp. C). We are only interested in value-closed terms. Thus, we can consider terms rather than configurations; whenever E is value-closed, the behaviour of $<E, \sigma>$ is independent of store σ.

PAR1 $(X \oplus Y)|Z = (X|Z) \oplus (Y|Z)$

PAR2 $X|(Y \oplus Z) = (X|Y) \oplus (X|Z)$

PAR3 Let $X = \sum_{i \in I} \mathbf{in}(t_i).X_i \,\Box\, \sum_{k \in K} \mathbf{out}(t_k).\mathbf{nil} \lfloor X_k$
and $Y = \sum_{j \in J} \mathbf{in}(t_j).Y_j \,\Box\, \sum_{l \in L} \mathbf{out}(t_l).\mathbf{nil} \lfloor X_l$.
Let $\mathrm{COMM}(X, Y) = \{(i, l) \mid \mathrm{match}(t_i, t_l)\} \cup \{(j, k) \mid \mathrm{match}(t_j, t_k)\}$; then:
$X|Y = ((X \lfloor Y) \Box (Y \lfloor X) \Box (X|_c Y)) \oplus (X|_c Y)$ if $\mathrm{COMM}(X, Y) \neq \emptyset$
$X|Y = (X \lfloor Y) \Box (Y \lfloor X)$ if $\mathrm{COMM}(X, Y) = \emptyset$

PAR4 $\mathbf{out}(t).X = \mathbf{out}(t).\mathbf{nil}|X$

EVAL $\mathbf{eval}(X).Y = X|Y$

LM1 $(X \Box Y) \lfloor Z = X \lfloor Z \Box Y \lfloor Z$

LM2 $(X \oplus Y) \lfloor Z = X \lfloor Z \oplus Y \lfloor Z$

LM3 $(\mathbf{in}(t).X) \lfloor Y = \mathbf{in}(t).(X|Y)$ $\quad$ $var(t)$ not free in Y

LM4 $(\mathbf{out}(t).\mathbf{nil} \lfloor X) \lfloor Y = \mathbf{out}(t).\mathbf{nil} \lfloor (X|Y)$

LM5 $\mathbf{nil} \lfloor X = \mathbf{nil}$

LM6 $X \lfloor \mathbf{nil} = X$

CM1 $(X \Box Y)|_c Z = (X|_c Z) \Box (Y|_c Z)$ if $Z = \sum_{i \in I} \mathbf{in}(t_i).Z_i \,\Box\, \sum_{k \in K} \mathbf{out}(t_k).\mathbf{nil} \lfloor X_k$

CM2 $(X \oplus Y)|_c Z = (X|_c Z) \oplus (Y|_c Z)$

CM3 $X|_c Y = Y|_c X$

CM4 $\mathbf{nil}|_c X = \mathbf{nil}$

CM5 $(\mathbf{in}(t_1).X)|_c(\mathbf{out}(t_2).\mathbf{nil} \lfloor Y) = X[t_2/t_1]|Y$ $\quad$ if $match(t_1, t_2)$

CM6 $(\mathbf{in}(t_1).X)|_c(\mathbf{out}(t_2).\mathbf{nil} \lfloor Y) = \mathbf{nil}$ $\quad$ if $\neg match(t_1, t_2)$

CM7 $(\mathbf{in}(t_1).X)|_c(\mathbf{in}(t_2).Y) = \mathbf{nil}$

CM8 $(\mathbf{out}(t_1).\mathbf{nil} \lfloor X)|_c(\mathbf{out}(t_2).\mathbf{nil} \lfloor Y) = \mathbf{nil}$

Table 8. Axioms for the derived operators

The next theorem states soundness of proof system R.

Theorem 6.1 For value-closed terms E and F, $E \sqsubseteq_{\mathrm{R}} F$ implies $E \underset{\sim}{\sqsubset}_{\mathrm{M}} F$.

Proof. The soundness proof consists in checking that the preorder $\underset{\sim}{\sqsubset}_{\mathrm{M}}$ is preserved by all of the rules and that all of the laws are satisfied by $\underset{\sim}{\sqsubset}_{\mathrm{M}}$. Rule I states that $\underset{\sim}{\sqsubset}_{\mathrm{M}}$ is a preorder and then preserves $\underset{\sim}{\sqsubset}_{\mathrm{M}}$. Soundness of rules II and III stating the substitutivity of $\underset{\sim}{\sqsubset}_{\mathrm{M}}$ into IPAL contexts is affirmed by Propositions 5.11 and 5.12. Soundness of rules IV(b), VII, VIII and IX can be easily proven by using the alternative characterization $\ll_{\mathrm{M}}$ of $\underset{\sim}{\sqsubset}_{\mathrm{M}}$. Rule V(a) is sound by definition of $\underset{\sim}{\sqsubset}_{\mathrm{M}}$ over terms which are open with respect to process variables. Therefore, soundness of the proof system for open terms is an easy consequence of soundness for closed ones. Soundness of rule V(b) reduces to that of the axioms in R. The axioms in R can be easily proven sound by using the alternative characterization $\ll_{\mathrm{M}}$ of $\underset{\sim}{\sqsubset}_{\mathrm{M}}$.

L1 $\mathbf{read}(t).X = \mathbf{in}(t).\mathbf{out}(t').X$

where $t' =_{\bar{I}} t,\ I = if(t)$ and $i \in I \wedge t_i = !x \Longrightarrow t'_i = x$

L2 $$\frac{t' =_{\bar{I}} t,\ var(t')\backslash var(t) \text{ are not free in } X}{\mathbf{in}(t).X[]\mathbf{in}(t').Y = \mathbf{in}(t').\mathbf{if}\ cond(t,t')\ \mathbf{then}\ X\oplus Y\ \mathbf{else}\ Y}$$

where $I = if(t') \cap ia(t)$ and $cond(t,t') = \wedge_{i \in I} var(t'_i) = t_i$

L3 $$\frac{t' =_{\bar{I}} t,\ var(t')\backslash var(t) \text{ are not free in } X,\ var(t)\backslash var(t') \text{ are not free in } Y}{\begin{array}{l}\mathbf{in}(t).X[]\mathbf{in}(t').Y = \mathbf{in}(t).\mathbf{if}\ cond_1(t,t')\ \mathbf{then}\ Y\rho_1\oplus X\ \mathbf{else}\ X\\ \qquad\qquad [] \ \mathbf{in}(t').\mathbf{if}\ cond_2(t,t')\ \mathbf{then}\ X\rho_2\oplus Y\ \mathbf{else}\ Y\end{array}}$$

where $I_1 = if(t) \cap ia(t') \neq \emptyset,\ I_2 = if(t') \cap ia(t) \neq \emptyset,\ I = I_1 \cup I_2$,
$cond_1(t,t') = \wedge_{i \in I_1} var(t_i) = t'_i,\ cond_2(t,t') = \wedge_{i \in I_2} var(t'_i) = t_i$,
$\rho_1 = [t_i/var(t'_i)]_{i \in I_2}$ and $\rho_2 = [t'_i/var(t_i)]_{i \in I_1}$

L4 $$\frac{t' =_{\bar{I}} t,\ var(t')\backslash var(t) \text{ are not free in } X,\ var(t)\backslash var(t') \text{ are not free in } Y}{\begin{array}{l}\mathbf{in}(t).X\oplus\mathbf{in}(t').Y = \mathbf{in}(t).\mathbf{if}\ cond_1(t,t')\ \mathbf{then}\ Y\rho_1\oplus X\ \mathbf{else}\ X\\ \qquad\qquad \oplus\ \mathbf{in}(t').\mathbf{if}\ cond_2(t,t')\ \mathbf{then}\ X\rho_2\oplus Y\ \mathbf{else}\ Y\end{array}}$$

where $I_1 = if(t) \cap ia(t'),\ I_2 = if(t') \cap ia(t),\ I = I_1 \cup I_2$,
$cond_1(t,t') = \wedge_{i \in I_1} var(t_i) = t'_i,\ cond_2(t,t') = \wedge_{i \in I_2} var(t'_i) = t_i$,
$\rho_1 = [t_i/var(t'_i)]_{i \in I_2}$ and $\rho_2 = [t'_i/var(t_i)]_{i \in I_1}$

Table 9. Linda Laws

Let us now concentrate on proving completeness for closed terms. Therefore, from now on, we shall be concerned with IPAL processes only.

The completeness proof for R rests on the existence of certain standard forms for processes called *head normal forms* (*hnfs*). Intuitively, these special forms aim at describing processes as an internal nondeterministic choice among a set of initial states. In our framework, each initial state is represented by the initial events the process can perform and their corresponding derivatives.

To define head normal forms and to provide a syntactical characterization of the preorder we introduce the notions of *closed* set of events and *saturated set.*

For defining a partial order over acceptance sets, we must adapt the standard saturation procedure since our basic preorder relation $\lhd$, used for comparing finite sets of events, is not a partial order.

Definition 6.2 Let A be a finite subset of Ev. A is *closed* if for each $e \in A$, it does not exists an $e' \in A$ such that $\{e'\} \lhd \{e\}$.

We let $cl(A)$ denote the set which represents the equivalence class of A with respect to $\lhd$.

We can now define the notion of saturated set, which in our framework applies to sets of events. If $\mathcal{A}$ is a finite collection of finite sets of events we shall use $Ev(\mathcal{A})$ for denoting the set $\bigcup\{A \mid A \in \mathcal{A}\}$ of all events in $\mathcal{A}$.

I	$\frac{}{E \sqsubseteq E}$	$\frac{E_1 \sqsubseteq E_2, \quad E_2 \sqsubseteq E_3}{E_1 \sqsubseteq E_3}$
II	$\frac{E_1 \sqsubseteq E_1', \quad E_2 \sqsubseteq E_2'}{E_1 \; op \; E_2 \sqsubseteq E_1' \; op \; E_2'}$ for every $op \in \{\oplus, [], \mid, \lfloor, \mid_c\}$	
III	$\frac{E_1[t'/t] \sqsubseteq E_2[t'/t]}{\mathbf{in}(t).E_1 \sqsubseteq \mathbf{in}(t).E_2}$ for every tuple $t' \in EOT : match(t, t')$	
IV	$\frac{E_1 \sqsubseteq E_2}{\mathrm{rec}X.E_1 \sqsubseteq \mathrm{rec}X.E_2}$	$\frac{}{\mathrm{rec}X.E = E[\mathrm{rec}X.E/X]}$
V	$\frac{E_1 \sqsubseteq E_2}{E_1\xi \sqsubseteq E_2\xi}$	$\frac{}{E_1 \sqsubseteq E_2}$ for every inequation $E_1 \sqsubseteq E_2$
VI	$\frac{\forall n \geq 0 : E_1^n \sqsubseteq E_2}{E_1 \sqsubseteq E_2}$	
VII	$\frac{\mathcal{B}[\![be]\!] = tt}{\mathbf{if}\; be \;\mathbf{then}\; E_1 \;\mathbf{else}\; E_2 = E_1}$	$\frac{\mathcal{B}[\![be]\!] = ff}{\mathbf{if}\; be \;\mathbf{then}\; E_1 \;\mathbf{else}\; E_2 = E_2}$
VIII	$\frac{\mathcal{O}[\![t]\!] = \mathcal{O}[\![t']\!]}{\mathbf{out}(t).\mathbf{nil} \lfloor E = \mathbf{out}(t').\mathbf{nil} \lfloor E}$	$\frac{\mathcal{I}[\![t]\!] = \mathcal{I}[\![t']\!]}{\mathbf{in}(t).E = \mathbf{in}(t').E}$
IX	$\frac{x \in var(t), \quad y \text{ fresh}}{\mathbf{in}(t).E = \mathbf{in}(t[y/x]).E[y/x]}$	

Table 10. Inference Rules

AS	$x := e.X \;=\; X[e/x]$

Table 11. Axiom for Assignment

Definition 6.3 A finite collection $\mathcal{A}$ of closed sets of events is *saturated*, or is a *saturated set*, if the following conditions hold:

1. $cl(Ev(\mathcal{A})) \in \mathcal{A}$;
2. $A, B \in \mathcal{A}$, C closed: $A \lhd C \lhd B$, $C \neq A$ and $C \neq B$ imply $C \notin \mathcal{A}$.

Let $sat(Ev)$, ranged over by $\mathcal{A}, \mathcal{B}$, be the set of all saturated sets over Ev.

Definition 6.4 *(Head Normal Forms)*

– A partial function $g : Ev \longrightarrow \mathcal{P}$ is a *normal function* if
  a) $(out, t) \in dom(g)$ implies $g((out, t))$ is of the form $\mathbf{out}(t).\mathbf{nil} \lfloor P$;
  b) $(ir, t) \in dom(g)$ implies $g((ir, t))$ is of the form $\mathbf{in}(t').E$ and $patt(t') = t$;
  c) $(ir, t_1), (ir, t_2) \in dom(g)$, thus there exist t and t' such that $patt(t) = t_1$, $patt(t') = t_2$, $g((ir, t_1)) = \mathbf{in}(t).E$ and $g((ir, t_2)) = \mathbf{in}(t').F$, and $t =_I t'$, where $I = I_1 \cup I_2 \neq \emptyset$, $I_1 = if(t) \cap ia(t')$ and $I_2 = if(t') \cap ia(t)$, imply $E[\rho_1] = F[\rho_2]$, where $\rho_1 = [t_i'/var(t_i)]_{i \in I_1}$ and $\rho_2 = [t_i/var(t_i')]_{i \in I_2}$.

- A process P is in (or is a) ***head normal form***, hnf for short, if one of the following conditions holds:
  - $\gamma \equiv \sum_{e \in A} g(e)$ where A is a closed set of events and g is a normal function with *domain*$(g) = A$;
  - $\gamma \equiv \sum_{A \in \mathcal{A}} \sum_{e \in A} g(e)$ where $\mathcal{A}$ is saturated and g is a normal function with *domain*$(g) = Ev(\mathcal{A})$.

By convention, we let $\sum_{e \in A} g(e) \equiv \mathbf{nil}$ if $A = \emptyset$; therefore, **nil** is a hnf. From the definition it is evident that if P is in hnf then $P \downarrow \epsilon$ (i.e. for any store σ, $<P, \sigma> \downarrow \epsilon$). In the definition of hnf we adopt a functional notation for pointing out that each event e is associated with a single term $g(e)$. Condition c) ensures that for each initial abstract action a that a hnf P can perform there exists a unique P_a such that $P \Longrightarrow \xrightarrow{a} P_a$; this P_a is called *a-derivative* of P.

The counterpart of hnfs for divergent but finite processes are ***Ω-head normal forms***.

Definition 6.5 A process P is in (or is a) ***Ω-head normal form***, $\Omega - hnf$ for short, if one of the following conditions holds:

1. **nil** and Ω are $\Omega - hnf$;
2. $\sum_{A \in \mathcal{A}} \sum_{e \in A} P_e^A$ is a $\Omega - hnf$ if $\forall A \in \mathcal{A}, \forall e \in A$ P_e^A is of the form $\mathbf{in}(t).E$ or of the form $\mathbf{out}(t).\mathbf{nil} \lfloor P$.

The following propositions will be used in the proof of the completeness theorem. Their proofs follow the same lines of the corresponding ones for CCS in [7]. In particular, the proof of Proposition 6.6 relies on a double induction on the structure of terms and on the maximal number of internal communications a convergent process P can perform (this number is finite since $P \downarrow \epsilon$). The proof of Proposition 6.7 relies on a double induction on the structure of terms and on the maximal number of communications that a process P can perform with another one (this number is finite since P is finite). In both proofs, the laws in Table 8 are used for expanding out the parallel operators in terms of the non-deterministic ones and the law in Table 11 is used for removing assignment; the laws in Tables 6, 9 and 12 are crucial for obtaining saturated sets of events.

All of the laws in Table 12 can be derived within the proof system R. Indeed, the first two laws are easily derived from laws L4 and L2, respectively. Laws D3 and D4 can be derived in exactly the same way as the corresponding ones in [14]. The last two laws can be obtained in a similar fashion as Der3 in (page 97 of) [14]; in particular, D6 is obtained if L3 and L4 are used instead of the laws which in [14] correspond to D1 and D2.

Proposition 6.6 For any process P, if $P \downarrow \epsilon$ then there exists a hnf, $h(P)$ such that: $P =_{\mathrm{R}} h(P)$.

Proposition 6.7 For any finite process P there exists a $\Omega - hnf$, $\Omega(P)$ such that $P =_{\mathrm{R}} \Omega(P)$.

D1	$\mathbf{in}(t).X \,[]\, \mathbf{in}(t).Y = \mathbf{in}(t).(X \oplus Y)$
D2	$\mathbf{in}(t).X \oplus \mathbf{in}(t).Y = \mathbf{in}(t).(X \oplus Y)$
D3	$X \oplus Y = X \oplus Y \oplus (X \,[]\, Y)$
D4	$X \oplus (X \,[]\, Y \,[]\, Z) = X \oplus (X \,[]\, Y) \oplus (X \,[]\, Y \,[]\, Z)$
D5	$((\mathbf{out}(t).\mathbf{nil} \lfloor X_1) \,[]\, Y_1) \oplus ((\mathbf{out}(t).\mathbf{nil} \lfloor X_2) \,[]\, Y_2) =$ $((\mathbf{out}(t).\mathbf{nil} \lfloor (X_1 \oplus X_2)) \,[]\, Y_1) \oplus ((\mathbf{out}(t).\mathbf{nil} \lfloor (X_1 \oplus X_2)) \,[]\, Y_2)$
D6	$\dfrac{t' =_I t,\ var(t') \backslash var(t) \text{ are not free in } X_1,\ var(t) \backslash var(t') \text{ are not free in } X_2}{\begin{array}{l}((\mathbf{in}(t).X_1) \,[]\, Y_1) \oplus ((\mathbf{in}(t').X_2) \,[]\, Y_2) = \\ \quad ((\mathbf{in}(t).\mathbf{if}\ cond_1(t,t')\ \mathbf{then}\ X_2\rho_1 \oplus X_1\ \mathbf{else}\ X_1) \,[]\, Y_1) \\ \quad \oplus ((\mathbf{in}(t').\mathbf{if}\ cond_2(t,t')\ \mathbf{then}\ X_1\rho_2 \oplus X_2\ \mathbf{else}\ X_2) \,[]\, Y_2)\end{array}}$ where $I_1 = if(t) \cap ia(t')$, $I_2 = if(t') \cap ia(t)$, $I = I_1 \cup I_2$, $cond_1(t,t') = \wedge_{i \in I_1} var(t_i) = t'_i$, $cond_2(t,t') = \wedge_{i \in I_2} var(t'_i) = t_i$, $\rho_1 = [t_i/var(t'_i)]_{i \in I_2}$ and $\rho_2 = [t'_i/var(t_i)]_{i \in I_1}$

Table 12. Derived Laws

We can now prove completeness of proof system R.

Theorem 6.8 For finite processes P and Q, P finite, $P \underset{\sim_M}{\sqsubset} Q$ implies $P \sqsubseteq_R Q$.

Proof. Propositions 6.6 and 6.7 allow us to assume that P is in $\Omega - hnf$ and Q is in hnf. If $P \uparrow \epsilon$, P is in $\Omega - hnf$ implies $P = \Omega$ and the thesis directly follows from law UND1. Otherwise, we may further assume that P is in hnf and we reason by induction on the maximal number of communications that P can perform relying on the following property of the a-derivatives of P and Q: if a is an abstract action that both P and Q can perform, $P_a \underset{\sim_M}{\sqsubset} Q_a$. By induction the previous relation still holds when we substitute $\underset{\sim_M}{\sqsubset}$ with $\sqsubseteq_R$. Then $P \sqsubseteq_R Q$ can be deduced by using rules II, III, L2, and IC1-IC3.

Now we consider the full proof system C.

Theorem 6.9 For processes P and Q, $P \sqsubseteq_C Q$ implies $P \underset{\sim_M}{\sqsubset} Q$.

Proof. We are only left to show that rules IV(a) and VI are sound. Rule IV(a) for substitutivity into a rec$X$._ operator is derivable from the other axioms and rules in C (see [7]) and therefore it is sound. Soundness of the ω-inductive rule VI easily follows from the definition of syntactic finite approximation by exploiting the following fact: for any process P and any observer o, if P *must* o then there exists a finite syntactic approximation P^n of P such that P^n *must* o. This property relies on the completeness of R and can be easily proven by structural induction by using head normal forms.

Theorem 6.10 For processes P and Q, $P \underset{\sim_M}{\sqsubset} Q$ implies $P \sqsubseteq_C Q$.

Proof. Suppose that $P \underset{\sim_M}{\sqsubset} Q$. A standard result of algebraic semantics (see, e.g., [14]) states that since $\underset{\sim_M}{\sqsubset}$ satisfies rule IV(b) and axiom UND1 then for every $n \geq 0 : P^n \underset{\sim_M}{\sqsubset} Q$. By completeness of R, we can infer that for every $n \geq 0 : P^n \sqsubseteq_R Q$, and, then, for every $n \geq 0 : P^n \sqsubseteq_C Q$. Now, we can apply rule VI and we can conclude that $P \sqsubseteq_C Q$. Therefore, the next theorem stating the soundness of proof system C is proven.

7 A small example

In this section we show how the proof system can be used for proving equivalence of two IPAL processes. Our language is parameterized on a countable set of values, Val; for the example, we require Val to be the set *Natural Numbers*.

Let us consider the following two IPAL processes that compute the factorial:

$$P \equiv \mathbf{in}(!\,x).k := 1.i := 1.P' \quad \text{and} \quad Q \equiv \mathbf{in}(!\,x).k := 1.i := x.Q'$$

where

$$P' \equiv \mathrm{rec}X.E \quad \text{and} \quad Q' \equiv \mathrm{rec}X.F$$

and

$$E \equiv \mathbf{if}\ i \leq x\ \mathbf{then}\ k := k * i.i := i + 1.X\ \mathbf{else}\ \mathbf{out}(x, k).\mathbf{nil}$$

and

$$F \equiv \mathbf{if}\ i > 1\ \mathbf{then}\ k := k * i.i := i - 1.X\ \mathbf{else}\ \mathbf{out}(x, k).\mathbf{nil}.$$

We will show that processes P and Q are testing equivalent, i.e. $P = Q$ can be deduced within C. By rule II, it suffices to show that for any n:

$$(k := 1.i := 1.P')[n/x] \;=\; (k := 1.i := x.Q')[n/x]$$

that is, by axiom AS, that for any n:

$$P'[1/k, 1/i, n/x] \;=\; Q'[1/k, n/i, n/x].$$

We will show that the equation above holds for every n.

If $n = 0$, we have:

$$\begin{aligned}
P'[1/k, 1/i, 0/x] &= \mathbf{if}\ 1 \leq 0\ \mathbf{then}\ k := 1.i := 2.P'[0/x] && \text{rule IV(b)}\\
&\qquad\qquad \mathbf{else}\ \ \mathbf{out}(0, 1).\mathbf{nil} \\
&= \mathbf{out}(0, 1).\mathbf{nil} && \text{rule VII(b)}\\
&= \mathbf{if}\ 0 > 1\ \mathbf{then}\ k := 0.i := -1.Q'[0/x] && \text{rule VII(b)}\\
&\qquad\qquad \mathbf{else}\ \ \mathbf{out}(0, 1).\mathbf{nil} \\
&= Q'[1/k, 0/i, 0/x] && \text{rule IV(b)}
\end{aligned}$$

If $n = 1$, we have:

$$\begin{array}{lll} P'[1/k,1/i,1/x] & = \textbf{if } 1 \leq 1 \textbf{ then } k := 1.i := 2.P'[1/x] & \text{rule } \mathtt{IV(b)} \\ & \qquad \textbf{else } \ \textbf{out}(1,1).\textbf{nil} & \\ & = P'[1/k,2/i,1/x] & \text{rule } \mathtt{VII(a)}\text{, axiom } \mathtt{AS} \\ & = \textbf{if } 2 \leq 1 \textbf{ then } k := 2.i := 3.P'[1/x] & \text{rule } \mathtt{IV(b)} \\ & \qquad \textbf{else } \ \textbf{out}(1,1).\textbf{nil} & \\ & = \textbf{out}(1,1).\textbf{nil} & \text{rule } \mathtt{VII(b)} \\ & = \textbf{if } 1 > 1 \textbf{ then } k := 1.i := 0.Q'[1/x] & \text{rule } \mathtt{VII(b)} \\ & \qquad \textbf{else } \ \textbf{out}(1,1).\textbf{nil} & \\ & = Q'[1/k,1/i,1/x] & \text{rule } \mathtt{IV(b)} \end{array}$$

Suppose now that $n > 1$. We split the proof into two parts:

i) $P'[1/k,1/i,n/x] \sqsubseteq Q'[1/k,n/i,n/x]$;
ii) $Q'[1/k,n/i,n/x] \sqsubseteq P'[1/k,1/i,n/x]$.

We only show part i) since part ii) is dual.

To prove that $P'[1/k,1/i,n/x] \sqsubseteq Q'[1/k,n/i,n/x]$, for any $n > 1$, we use *Recursion Induction* [7, 14], which is expressed by the following rule:

$$\mathtt{RI} \qquad \frac{E[P/X] \sqsubseteq P}{\text{rec}X.E \sqsubseteq P}.$$

It relies on the interpretation of $\text{rec}X.E$ as the least fixpoint of the equation $X = E$. The rule is sound because it can be derived, similarly to [7], from the proof system presented in Section 6.

Therefore, we are left to show that

$$(E[1/k,1/i,n/x])[Q'[1/k,n/i,n/x]/X] \sqsubseteq Q'[1/k,n/i,n/x]$$

Indeed, we show a stronger result, namely that

$$(E[1/k,1/i,n/x])[Q'[1/k,n/i,n/x]/X] = Q'[1/k,n/i,n/x]$$

In fact, we have:

$$\begin{array}{ll} (E[1/k,1/i,n/x])[Q'[1/k,n/i,n/x]/X] & \\ \equiv \textbf{if } 1 \leq n \textbf{ then } k := 1.i := 2.Q'[1/k,n/i,n/x] \textbf{ else } \textbf{out}(n,1).\textbf{nil} & \\ = Q'[1/k,n/i,n/x] & \text{rules } \mathtt{VII(b)} \text{ and } \mathtt{IV(b)} \end{array}$$

since $Q'[1/k,n/i,n/x]$ is a closed term (and then $(Q'[1/k,n/i,n/x])[1/k,2/i] = Q'[1/k,n/i,n/x]$) and $n > 1$.

8 Conclusions and Related Work

In this paper we have generalized the testing framework introduced for PAL [11, 22] to an imperative extension of the language. PAL, an applicative process algebra which allows programs to manipulate values and to asynchronously pass them over to other programs, has been obtained by substituting uninterpreted actions of a CSP–like process algebra with the Linda primitives for process interaction. Its imperative extension, IPAL, has been obtained by adding assignment to the language.

By and large, we have used methods similar to those of [15, 16, 18]. There a testing framework has been developed for applicative and imperative variants of TCCS [8, 14] with value–passing. However, tuples based asynchronous communication call for a different formal set up. Apart from the presence of non finitely branching transition systems, we had to face additional complications introduced by the inability of observers to perceive the differences among patterns which access a given tuple.

Our extension is simpler than the one of [16, 18] for CCS with value-passing and assignment. There, the new proof system is obtained by adding to the applicative one both a set of laws (one for each process operator) for rewriting assignment in the normalization procedure and an inference rule for ensuring substitutivity of expressions in assignments. Here, we show that, by using a suitable definition of substitution application, a single law suffices.

The development of a similar framework to deal with full sequential program composition rather than with action prefixing is under progress. In [10] we have already studied an imperative language, L, obtained by embedding the Linda primitives for interprocess communication in a simple imperative language with sequential composition. We succeeded in defining a testing scenario for L, by letting the observers to be able to test the (final) store of (finite computations of) programs, but we were unable to give equational characterizations of the testing preorders. Obviously, this makes it difficult to use that framework for verifying programs, such as the example in [9] shows.

The use of action prefixing instead of full sequential composition has been essential for reusing the semantical machinery introduced in [11, 22] for PAL. Indeed, since the effects of the executions of terms on their private memories are local and not visible by any external observer, equivalent processes may have different stores. Had we chosen to use sequential composition, terms could inherit a store and the equivalences could not be congruences. In our opinion, this generalization would be possible only if a different approach is taken for the $\_|\_$ operator, and the store is not considered as private to single processes. We could use the Linda **eval** operator for expressing "real" parallelism.

Additional work is needed also to deal properly with the merge operators. Their use, on the one hand, has rendered the definition of the alternative behavioural characterization and of the proof system easier; but, on the other hand, it has strictly increased the discriminating power of observers. Indeed, the merge operators permit expressing causal dependencies on output actions. Thus, our observation mechanism allows observers to determine whether a system has actually consumed a message. This may conflict with the idea that asynchronous outputs are intended to take place immediately without requiring availability of a corresponding input; in these circumstances it might be argued that observers cannot have the guarantee that a message has been consumed. We see two possibilities for weakening our behavioural relations in this respect: discarding the merge operators or modifying the observation mechanism. We are currently investigating the first possibility.

Another research direction we are following concerns the extension of the language presented in the paper with an explicit notion of locality. In this way we obtain a setting with multiple tuple spaces in which programmers are able to distribute/retrieve data and programs over/from different nodes of a net. Localities, which are essentially addresses of nodes, can be manipulated as any other data. Such a language could be used as a program notation for supporting mobile applications. Taking as a starting point the work on PAL and IPAL, we plan to develop foundations for programming logic and verification techniques for this extended language too.

Acknowledgments We are grateful to Anna Ingolfsdottir for e-mail correspondence about the subject of the paper and to the anonymous referees for stimulating comments.

References

1. L.Aceto, A.Ingolfsdottir. A Theory of Testing for ACP. *Proceedings of CONCUR 91*, J.C.M. Baeten and J.F. Groote, editors, *LNCS* 527, pages 78-95, Springer-Verlag, Berlin, 1991.
2. A. Brogi, P. Ciancarini. The concurrent language Shared Prolog. *ACM Trans. on Programming Languages and Systems*, 13(1):99-123, 1991.
3. L. Borrmann, M. Herdieckerhoff, A. Klein. Tuple Space integrated into Modula-2: Implementation of the Linda Concept on a Hierarchical Multiprocessor. Proc. of CONPAR'88, Manchester, U.K., edited by Jesshope and Reinartz, Cambridge University Press, 1988.
4. J. Bergstra, J.W. Klop. Process Algebra for Synchronous Communication. *Information and Control*, 60:109-137, 1984.
5. N. Carriero, D. Gelernter. Linda in Context. *Communications of the ACM*, 32(4):444-458, 1989.
6. K.M. Chandy, J. Misra. *Parallel Program Design: a Foundation.* Addison Wesley, Massachusetts, 1988.
7. R. De Nicola, M.C.B. Hennessy. Testing Equivalence for Processes. *Theoretical Computers Science*, 34:83-133, 1984.
8. R. De Nicola, M.C.B. Hennessy. CCS without τ's. *Proceedings of TAPSOFT'87*, *LNCS* 249, pages 138-152, 1987.
9. R. De Nicola, R. Pugliese. Testing Linda: an Observational Semantics for an Asynchronous Language. Research Report: SI/RR - 94/06, Dipartimento di Scienze dell'Informazione, Università di Roma "La Sapienza", 1994.
10. R. De Nicola, R. Pugliese. An Observational Semantics for Linda. *Proceedings of STRICT'95*, pp.129-143, Jorg Desel (ed.), Series Workshops in Computing, Springer - Verlag, Berlin, 1995.

11. R. De Nicola, R. Pugliese. A Process Algebra based on Linda. First International Conference on Coordination Models and Languages, Lectures Notes in Computer Science 1061, pp. 160-178, Springer, 1996.
12. D. Gelernter. Generative Communication in Linda. *ACM Transactions on Programming Languages and Systems*, 7(1):80-112, 1985.
13. M.C.B Hennessy. Acceptance Trees. *Journal of the ACM*, 32(4):896-928, 1985.
14. M.C.B. Hennessy. *Algebraic Theory of Processes.* The MIT Press, 1988.
15. M.C.B. Hennessy, A. Ingolfsdottir. A theory of communicating processes with value–passing. *Information and Computation*, 107(2)202-236, 1993.
16. M.C.B. Hennessy, A. Ingolfsdottir. Communicating processes with value–passing and assignment. *Journal of Formal Aspects of Computing Science*, pages 3:346-366, 1993.
17. C.A.R. Hoare. *Communicating Sequential Processes.* Prentice-Hall International, 1985.
18. A. Ingolfsdottir. Semantic Models for Communicating Processes with Value–Passing. *Ph.D. Thesis*, University of Edinburgh, 1994.
19. R. Milner. *Communication and Concurrency.* Prentice Hall International, 1989.
20. J. Pinakis, C. McDonald. The Inclusion of the Linda Tuple Space Operations in a Pascal-based Concurrent Language. Dept. of Computer Science, Univ. of Western Australia. (Presented at the 14th Australian Computer Science Conference, Sidney, Jan. 1991).
21. G.D. Plotkin. A Structural Approach to Operational Semantics. Technical Report DAIMI FN-19, Aarhus University, Dep. of Computer Science, Denmark, 1981.
22. R. Pugliese. *Semantic Theories for Asynchronous Languages.* University of Rome "La Sapienza", Dipartimento di Scienze dell'Informazione, Dottorato di Ricerca in Informatica, Collana delle tesi VIII-96-6, 1996.
23. E. Shapiro. *Concurrent Prolog: Collected Papers.* The MIT Press, 1987.
24. G. Sutcliffe, J. Pinakis, N. Lewins. Prolog-Linda: An Embedding of Linda in muProlog. Tech. Report 89/14, Dept. of Computer Science, Univ. of Western Australia, 1989.
25. *C-Linda User's Guide & Reference Manual.* Scientific Research Associates, 1992.

Analysis of Facile Programs: A Case Study*

Pierpaolo Degano[1], Corrado Priami[1], Lone Leth[2] and Bent Thomsen[2]

[1] Dipartimento di Informatica, Università di Pisa
Corso Italia, 40, I-56125 Pisa, Italy - {degano,priami}@di.unipi.it
[2] ICL, Technology Businesses, Research & Advanced Technology
Lovelace Road, Bracknell, Berks RG12 8SN, UK - {lone,bt}@sst.icl.co.uk

Abstract. Mobile agents, i.e. pieces of programs that can be sent around networks of computers, are starting to appear on the Internet. Such programs may be seen as an enrichment of traditional distributed computing. Since mobile agents may carry communication links with them as they move across the network, they create very dynamic interconnection structures that can be extremely complex to analyse. In this paper we apply a non-interleaving semantics to analyse a system based on the mobile agent principle written in the Facile programming language. This example is a scaled down version of a system demonstrated at the European IT Conference Exhibition in Brussels, 1995.
This paper further develops a non-interleaving semantics for Facile, first presented in [4]. We develop a Structural Operational Semantics (SOS) for Facile, giving a proved transition system that records encodings of the derivation trees of transitions in their labels. This information allows us to easily recover non-interleaving semantics for Facile by looking only at the labels of transitions. This semantics may be instantiated to recover both causality and locality information.

1 Introduction

Facile [9, 10, 14, 15, 16] is a multi-paradigm programming language combining functional and concurrent programming. The language is conceived for programming reactive systems and distributed systems. In particular Facile supports the construction of systems based on the emerging mobile agent principle since processes and channels naturally are treated as first class objects. Facile provides safe execution of mobile agents because they only have access to resources they have been explicitly given. Facile offers integration of different computational paradigms in a clean and well understood programming model that allows formal reasoning about program behaviour and properties.

Facile may be viewed as an extension of λ-calculus with primitives for concurrency, communication and distribution. The language has a binding operator (λ-abstraction) to define (possibly higher-order) functions. Functions, processes and channels may be either the result of the evaluation or the arguments of expressions.

* Work partially supported by ESPRIT Basic Research Action 8130 - LOMAPS

Facile handles concurrency through dynamic definition of processes, channels and virtual processing units (called nodes). Processes exchange messages with send and receive primitives along channels that are explicitly managed. Communication is synchronous.

The functional and the concurrent parts of Facile are strongly integrated: processes evaluate expressions to values while expressions may activate processes or return channels and node identifiers.

The semantics of Facile has been studied quite extensively [9, 10, 14, 11, 1], either focusing on defining the (abstract) execution of programs in terms of transition systems, reduction systems or abstract machines, or being concerned with the development of program equivalences. So far the approach to semantics for Facile has been based on the interleaving approach to modeling concurrency.

A first step towards developing a non-interleaving semantics for Facile was presented in [4]. That semantics covered the functional concurrent core of Facile. In this paper we further develop the non-interleaving semantics for Facile to capture the distributed aspects of Facile. The semantics is based on the parametric approach introduced in [7, 8]. We adopt a very concrete (SOS) transition system whose transitions are labelled by encodings of their proofs. We then instantiate it to locality semantics through relabelling functions, which maintain only the relevant information in the labels. This approach allows us to use the standard definitions and tools developed for the interleaving case.

In [4] we used the non-interleaving semantics for Facile to debug the behaviour of a mobile agent based system. The system is a scaled down version of a system of Mobile Service Agents demonstrated at the EITC'95 Exhibition. By instantiating the semantics to look at causality it is possible to see that the system exhibits a problem due to causal dependencies between higher order processes and mobile channels. However, the causal semantics does not provide much information to identify and locate which components are to blame for the problem. In this paper we revisit the system and apply the extended semantics to locate the faulty components.

We would like to point out that we address the question of analysis of "real code". Using "traditional" debugging techniques it took two weeks to track down the problem. However, even if we adopt an analysis "post mortem", we can rely on the operational semantics to simulate the system and foresee the troublesome behaviour. This results in saving time and resources of a real network.

The rest of this paper is organised as follows: Section 2 introduces the syntax of core Facile and in section 3 a Proved Transition System semantics is defined. Section 4 defines the notion of locality which may be derived from the Proved Transition System semantics and in section 5 we apply the mathematical framework to a case study derived from a larger mobile agent based application implemented in Facile. Section 6 gives some concluding remarks.

2 Facile

In this paper we consider only the core syntax of Facile, i.e. the set of constructs which is sufficient to define any Facile program. A translation from the full syntax to the core syntax is given in [9]. The core syntax consists of three parts: expressions (functions) E, behaviour expressions (processes) BE and distributed behaviour expressions (systems) DBE. Expressions are statically typed, and t ranges over types. We assume that all expressions are correctly typed. The type system is reported in [9]. Note that processes and systems have no type. See [14] for further details.

2.1 Syntax

The core syntax of Facile is given by the grammar in Tab. 1.

$$v ::= x \mid c \mid \lambda x.e \mid \mathsf{code}(be)$$

$$\begin{aligned} e ::= {} & v \mid ee \mid \mathtt{spawn}(be) \mid \mathtt{channel}(t) \mid e!e \mid e? \\ & \mathtt{r\_spawn}(e, be) \mid \mathtt{newnode} \mid \mathtt{newnode}(be) \end{aligned}$$

$$be ::= \mathtt{terminate} \mid \mathtt{activate}(e) \mid be \| be \mid be + be$$

$$dbe ::= n :: be \mid dbe \| \| dbe$$

Table 1. Core syntax of Facile.

Val, ranged over by v, denotes the set of syntactic values. Values are a subclass of expressions without free variables. Values can be passed as parameters to functions or be communicated between processes, possibly residing on different nodes in a system.

We assume a countable set of variables denoted by $x, x_i, \ldots$. Constants are ranged over by c, and these include integers, booleans, channel-valued constants, node identifiers and a distinguished value `triv`. Predefined operators such as `if-then-else` are denoted by c as well. We assume that all operations are in curried form to avoid the introduction of tuples and product types. Functions are defined and manipulated in λ-calculus style with abstractions and applications. λ is a variable binder with the usual notion of free and bound variables. The set of free variables of an expression is denoted by fn. fn is structurally extended to behaviour expressions and distributed behaviour expressions. Substituting an expression for a variable with the usual avoidance of accidental binding is denoted by $e[e'/x]$. For a formal definition of these concepts see [9]. Normally we only need to substitute values for variables. The **code** construct transforms a process into a value that can be used in the functional style. More precisely, **code**(be) is a process closure whose behaviour is described by be. A new channel on which we can transmit values of type t is generated by **channel**(t). The send operation $e_1!e_2$ sends the value resulting from the evaluation of e_2 along the channel resulting from the evaluation of e_1. The operation returns the value **triv** when the receiver gets the value. The receive operation $e?$ returns the value read on the channel resulting from the evaluation of e. The evaluation of **spawn**(be) and **r_spawn**(e, be) both return the value **triv**. The spawning operations have the effect of concurrently executing the process specified by be on the current virtual node, respectively on the virtual node identified by the evaluation of e. The expressions **newnode** and **newnode**(be) create the identifier of a new virtual node. The former expression leaves the new node empty, while the latter allocates the process be on the new node.

Unlike evaluation of expressions, the execution of behaviour expressions does not produce values. The simplest process is **terminate** which does not do anything. The process **activate**(e) activates the evaluation of the expression e. The operator $||$ describes the parallel composition of processes allocated on the same virtual node. The operator $+$ denotes non-deterministic choice.

The last syntactic category DBE describes distributed systems consisting of a collection of nodes. The construct $n :: be$ means that process be is allocated on node n. The parallel composition operator $|||$ concurrently composes processes allocated on different nodes.

$||$ has precedence over $|||$ since DBE is defined in terms of BE. Therefore, $be_1||be_2\,|||be_3$ means $(be_1||be_2)\,|||be_3$.

2.2 Operational semantics

We define the operational semantics of Facile in SOS style [12] through a labelled transition system. We start with the definition of the alphabet for the labels.

Let $\mathcal{S}$ be the set of all channels, and $\mathcal{S}_t$ be its subset consisting of channels on which we can transmit values of type t. We say that a value v is transmissible on a channel k if v has type t (for short $\emptyset \vdash v : t$) and $k \in \mathcal{S}_t$.

Definition 1. Let $\mathcal{N}$ be a countable infinite set of nodes. Then,

$$\ell \in L = \{k(v), \overline{k(v)} \mid \exists t : (k \in \mathcal{S}_t, v \in Val, \emptyset \vdash v : t)\} \;\cup\; \{\tau\} \;\cup\; \mathcal{N} \;\cup$$

$$\{\Phi(be)\ : be \in BE\} \cup \{(be \to n)\ : be \in BE, n \in \mathcal{N}\} \cup \{n(be)\ : n \in \mathcal{N}, be \in BE\}$$

is an action. We call $Comm$ the first set in the definition of labels L.

The intuitive meaning of labels is as follows. Receiving the value v on channel k is denoted by $k(v)$, and sending the value v on channel is denoted by $\overline{k(v)}$. We call $k(v)$ and $\overline{k(v)}$ complementary labels. The label τ denotes invisible actions, the labels $\Phi(be)$ and $(be \to n)$ are introduced by **spawn**(be) and **r_spawn**(n, be), respectively, and the labels n and $n(be)$ are introduced by **newnode** and **newnode**(be), respectively.

$$1.a : \frac{K,N,e_1 \xrightarrow{\mu}_e K',N',e_1'}{K,N,e_1 e_2 \xrightarrow{\mu}_e K',N',e_1' e_2} \quad 1.b : \frac{K,N,e_2 \xrightarrow{\mu}_e K',N',e_2'}{K,N,v\, e_2 \xrightarrow{\mu}_e K',N',v\, e_2'}$$

$$1.c : K,N,(\lambda x.e)v \xrightarrow{\tau}_e K,N,e[v/x]$$

$$2.a : \frac{K,N,e_1 \xrightarrow{\mu}_e K',N',e_1'}{K,N,e_1\,!\,e_2 \xrightarrow{\mu}_e K',N',e_1'\,!\,e_2} \qquad 2.b : \frac{K,N,e_2 \xrightarrow{\mu}_e K',N',e_2'}{K,N,k\,!\,e_2 \xrightarrow{\mu}_e K',N',k\,!\,e_2'}$$

$$2.c : K,N,k\,!\,v \xrightarrow{\overline{k(v)}}_e K,N,\mathtt{triv},\ k \in K \quad 3.a : \frac{K,N,e \xrightarrow{\mu}_e K',N',e'}{K,N,e\,? \xrightarrow{\mu}_e K',N',e'\,?}$$

$$3.b : K,N,k\,? \xrightarrow{k(v)}_e K,N,v,\ k \in K, k \in \mathcal{S}_t, \emptyset \vdash v : t$$

$$4. : K,N,\mathtt{channel}(t) \xrightarrow{\tau}_e K \cup \{k\},N,k,\ k \notin K, k \in \mathcal{S}_t$$

$$5. : K,N,\mathtt{spawn}(be) \xrightarrow{\Phi(be)}_e K,N,\mathtt{triv}$$

$$6.a : \frac{K,N,e \xrightarrow{\mu}_e K',N',e'}{K,N,\mathtt{r\_spawn}(e,be) \xrightarrow{\mu}_e K',N',\mathtt{r\_spawn}(e',be)}$$

$$6.b : K,N,\mathtt{r\_spawn}(n,be) \xrightarrow{(be \to n)}_e K,N,\mathtt{triv}$$

$$7. : K,N,\mathtt{newnode} \xrightarrow{n}_e K,N \cup \{n\},n \quad n \notin N$$

$$8. : K,N,\mathtt{newnode}(be) \xrightarrow{n(be)}_e K,N \cup \{n\},n \quad n \notin N$$

Table 2. Rules for function expressions.

We now define configurations of the labelled transition system of Facile. Let $2_f^{\mathcal{S}}$ (ranged over by K) and $2_f^{\mathcal{N}}$ (ranged over by N) be the set of finite subsets of $\mathcal{S}$ and $\mathcal{N}$, respectively. These sets are used to ensure uniqueness of channels and nodes. Creation of channels and nodes inserts the new name into the corresponding set in configurations if it does not already exist (see rules 4 and 8 in Tab. 2). The sets of configurations are

$$Econ \subseteq 2_f^{\mathcal{S}} \times 2_f^{\mathcal{N}} \times E \text{ for expressions}$$

$$Bcon \subseteq 2_f^{\mathcal{S}} \times 2_f^{\mathcal{N}} \times BE \text{ for processes}$$

$$DBcon \subseteq 2_f^{\mathcal{S}} \times 2_f^{\mathcal{N}} \times DBE \text{ for systems.}$$

Transition relations between configurations are defined as follows. The relation

$$\longrightarrow_e \subseteq Econ \times L \times Econ$$

evaluates expressions. For instance, we have $K, N, e \xrightarrow{\ell}_e K', N', e'$. The transition relation for processes is

$$\longrightarrow_{be} \subseteq Bcon \times L \backslash \{\Phi(be) \ : be \in BE\} \times Bcon.$$

$$9.a : \frac{K, N, e \xrightarrow{\mu}_e K', N', e'}{K, N, \texttt{activate}e \xrightarrow{\mu}_{be} K', N', \texttt{activate}e'}, \ \mu \neq \Phi(be)$$

$$9.b : \frac{K, N, e \xrightarrow{\Phi(be)}_e K', N', e'}{K, N, \texttt{activate}e \xrightarrow{\tau}_{be} K', N', \texttt{activate}e' || be}$$

$$9.c : K, N, \texttt{activatecode}(be) \xrightarrow{\tau}_{be} K, N, be$$

$$10.a : \frac{K, N, be_1 \xrightarrow{\mu}_{be} K', N', be_1'}{K, N, be_1 || be_2 \xrightarrow{\mu}_{be} K', N', be_1' || be_2}$$

$$10.b : \frac{K, N, be_2 \xrightarrow{\mu}_{be} K', N', be_2'}{K, N, be_1 || be_2 \xrightarrow{\mu}_{be} K', N', be_1 || be_2'}$$

$$11. : \frac{K, N, be_1 \xrightarrow{\mu}_{be} K', N', be_1' \quad K, N, be_2 \xrightarrow{\overline{\mu}}_{be} K', N', be_2'}{K, N, be_1 || be_2 \xrightarrow{\tau}_{be} K', N', be_1' || be_2'}$$

$$12.a : \frac{K, N, be_1 \xrightarrow{\mu}_{be} K', N', be_1'}{K, N, be_1 + be_2 \xrightarrow{\mu}_{be} K', N', be_1'}$$

$$12.b : \frac{K, N, be_2 \xrightarrow{\mu}_{be} K', N', be_2'}{K, N, be_1 + be_2 \xrightarrow{\mu}_{be} K', N', be_2'}$$

Table 3. Rules for behaviour expressions.

A derivation step is written $K, N, be \xrightarrow{\ell}_{be} K', N', be'$. Finally, transitions for systems are expressed by $\longrightarrow_{dbe} \subseteq DBcon \times (Comm \times \mathcal{N}) \cup \{\tau\} \times DBcon$. A derivation step is written $K, N, dbe \xrightarrow[n]{\ell}_{dbe} K', N', dbe'$ where $\ell \in Comm$ and $K, N, dbe \xrightarrow{\tau}_{dbe} K', N', dbe'$.

We can now define the labelled transition system for Facile.

Definition 2. The labelled transition system of Facile is

$$LTS = \langle \text{DBcon}, L, \longrightarrow_{dbe} \rangle$$

where $DBcon$ is the set of configurations of systems, L is the set of labels and $\longrightarrow_{dbe}$ is the transition relation defined by axioms and rules in Tables 2, 3, 4, 5.

$$13.a: \quad \frac{K, N, be \xrightarrow{\mu}_{be} K', N', be'}{K, N, n :: be \xrightarrow[n]{\mu}_{dbe} K', N', n :: be'}, \ \mu \neq n, n(be), (be \rightarrow n), \tau$$

$$13.b: \quad \frac{K, N, be \xrightarrow{n}_{be} K', N', be'}{K, N, n' :: be \xrightarrow{\tau}_{dbe} K', N', n' :: be' ||| n :: \mathtt{terminate}}$$

$$13.c: \quad \frac{K, N, be \xrightarrow{n(be'')}_{be} K', N', be'}{K, N, n' :: be \xrightarrow{\tau}_{dbe} K', N', n' :: be' ||| n :: be''}$$

$$13.d: \quad \frac{K, N, be \xrightarrow{(be'' \rightarrow n)}_{be} K', N', be'}{K, N, n' :: be ||| n :: be''' \xrightarrow{\tau}_{be} K', N', n' :: be' ||| n :: (be''' || be'')}$$

$$13.e: \quad \frac{K, N, be \xrightarrow{\tau}_{be} K', N', be'}{K, N, n :: be \xrightarrow{\tau}_{dbe} K', N', n :: be'}$$

Table 4. Rules for distributed behaviour expressions.

Detailed comments to the rules of Tables 2, 3 and 4, 5 are given in [14]. Here we introduce some notation that will be used later on. The core of Facile has no operator for sequentialisation of expressions or processes. The term $e_1.e_2$ is implemented in the core language as:

$$e_1.e_2 \equiv (\lambda x.e_2)e_1 \qquad if\ x \notin fn(e_2)$$

The term $e.be$ is translated as

$$e.be \equiv \mathtt{activate}((\lambda x.\mathtt{code}(be))e) \qquad if\ x \notin fn(be)$$

In the following we will use sequentialisation to simplify the representation of Facile systems. When the direction of communication is immaterial we may simply write $a.be$ and when an action is the last action of a processes, i.e. $a.$**terminate** we may drop the **terminate** behaviour expression and simply write a.

We adopt the following conventions on the representation of computations (i.e. sequences of transitions). We only visualise nodes and branches of computations that are interesting for the study at hand. Nodes which are not essential are represented as '•'. To ease the understanding of labels (always listed on the left-hand side of arcs) we write the operation corresponding to the actual transition on the right-hand side of some arcs labelled τ. Thus, we will have arcs with the format $\tau \downarrow\!\leadsto$ *'operation'*. i', i'', i''' denote the actions of process be_i when their exact nature is irrelevant. Furthermore, we write **newnode** for both **newnode** and **newnode**(be) if no confusion arises.

$$14.c: \frac{K, N, dbe_1 \xrightarrow{\tau}_{dbe} K', N', dbe_1'}{K, N, dbe_1 |||dbe_2 \xrightarrow{\tau}_{dbe} K', N', dbe_1' |||dbe_2}$$

$$14.d: \frac{K, N, dbe_2 \xrightarrow{\tau}_{dbe} K', N', dbe_2'}{K, N, dbe_1 |||dbe_2 \xrightarrow{\tau}_{dbe} K', N', dbe_1 |||dbe_2'}$$

$$15.: \frac{K, N, dbe_1 \xrightarrow[n]{\mu}_{dbe} K', N', dbe_1' \quad K, N, dbe_2 \xrightarrow[n']{\overline{\mu}}_{dbe} K', N', dbe_2'}{K, N, dbe_1 |||dbe_2 \xrightarrow{\tau}_{dbe} K', N', dbe_1' |||dbe_2'}$$

Table 5. Distributed behaviour expressions (cont.).

Creation of nodes and processes may alter the structure of systems. The creation of a new process depends on whether it is local or remote to the node that executes the operation. If it is local, i.e. created by **spawn**(be), the new process be is put in parallel with the processes that already run on the current node:

$$\ldots (n_1 :: \mathbf{spawn}(be).\alpha || be_1 || be_2) \; ||| \; (n_2 :: \ldots$$
$$\tau \downarrow\!\rightsquigarrow \; spawn(be)$$
$$\ldots (n_1 :: (\alpha || be) || be_1 || be_2) \; ||| \; (n_2 :: \ldots$$

When the new process be must be activated on a node different from the current node, i.e. **r_spawn**(n, be) is executed, the process be is placed as the last component of the parallel composition describing node n:

$$\ldots (n_1 :: \mathbf{r\_spawn}(n_2, be).\alpha || be_1) \; ||| \; (n_2 :: be_2 || be_3) \; ||| \ldots$$
$$\tau \downarrow\!\rightsquigarrow \; r\_spawn(n_2, be)$$
$$\ldots (n_1 :: \alpha || be_1) \; ||| \; (n_2 :: be_2 || be_3 || be) \; ||| \ldots$$

The creation of a new node modifies the system by inserting the new node immediately to the right of the node that executes the operation:

$$\ldots (n_1 :: be_1 || be_2) \; ||| \; (n_2 :: \mathbf{newnode}(be).\alpha || be_3) \; ||| \; (n_3 :: be_4 \ldots$$
$$\tau \downarrow\!\rightsquigarrow \; newnode(be)$$
$$\ldots (n_1 :: be_1 || be_2) \; ||| \; ((n_2 :: \alpha || be_3) \; ||| \; n_4 :: be) \; ||| \; (n_3 :: be_4 \ldots$$

3 Proved Transition System

In this section we define the proved operational semantics of Facile following [3]. First we modify the core syntax of Facile to eliminate the set N of nodes and the set K of channels from configurations. Nodes will from now on be denoted by natural numbers that identify the position of nodes within Facile systems. Nodes are ordered from left to right, starting with 1. We add a syntactic category program. A program is a distributed behaviour expression with a begin and an end guard n, with $n \in \mathbb{N}\backslash\{0\}$. The two guards denote the number of nodes in the system. To distinguish these guards from other integers we write them in boldface. The new syntax of Facile is obtained from the syntax given in Def. 1 by modifying distributed behaviour expressions as

$$dbe ::= be \mid \mathbf{n} \mid dbe|||dbe$$

and defining programs as

$$p ::= \mathbf{n}|||dbe|||\mathbf{n}.$$

Hereafter, the set of programs will be denoted by P. Static checks ensure that dbe in $\mathbf{n}|||dbe|||\mathbf{n}$ does not contain any distributed behaviour expression equal to $\mathbf{n}$. To define the semantics of **r_spawn**(e, be) we add an end guard, denoted §, to processes. Thus, behavioural expressions are extended with the following two items

$$be ::= \ldots \mid be||\S \mid \S$$

Again, static checks ensure that be in $be \,||\, \S$ does not contain §. Finally, to simplify the definition of causality and locality semantics of Facile, we assume that both $||$ and $|||$ are right associative.

3.1 Labels of transitions

We start with the definition of actions. In the following definition the set *Comm* is as in Def. 1.

Definition 3. The set *Act* of actions is:

$$Comm \cup \{\tau\} \cup \{(\tau, k) \ : k \in \mathcal{S}\} \cup \{new(be) \ : be \in BE\} \cup$$
$$\{(be \rightarrow n, i) \ : be \in BE, n \in \mathbb{N}, i \in Z\}.$$

Elements of *Act* are denoted as $\mu, \mu_i, \mu', \ldots$.

The label (τ, k) is caused by **channel**(t) and contains the name of the new channel. The label $new(be)$ denotes the creation of a new node on which be is activated. Finally, the label $(be \rightarrow n, i)$ represents the creation of a new process to be activated on node n. The value 0 is assigned to n for **spawn**(be) since be is activated on the same node as the **spawn** operation itself. The integer i denotes the number of $|||$ operators between the node n and the node performing the **r_spawn**, i.e. i is the relative address of the two nodes.

Following the developments in [7, 8], we extend actions with the parallel structure of the process which executes them.

Definition 4. Let $\mu \in Act$, $\sigma \in \{|||_0, |||_1\}^*$, and $\vartheta \in \{||_0, ||_1\}^*$. The set Θ of proof terms is:

$$\{\sigma\vartheta\mu\} \cup \{\sigma\vartheta\langle\sigma_0\vartheta_0\lambda, \sigma_1\vartheta_1\bar{\lambda}\rangle \ : \lambda \in Comm\} \cup \{\sigma_0\vartheta_0 \bullet \sigma_1\vartheta_1\tau\}$$

Elements of Θ are denoted as $\theta, \theta_i, \theta', \ldots$.

The proof term $\sigma\vartheta\mu$ is the label of a generic action μ executed by a process whose position is encoded by $\sigma\vartheta$. The synchronisation of two processes is labelled $\sigma\vartheta\langle\sigma_0\vartheta_0\lambda, \sigma_1\vartheta_1\bar{\lambda}\rangle$. The label $\sigma_0\vartheta_0 \bullet \sigma_1\vartheta_1\tau$ encodes either the creation of a new node or the allocation of a process through an **r_spawn**; its use will be clear later on.

The following example shows the intuition behind proof terms. Consider the computation in Fig. 1: The label $|||_1|||_0||_0\tau$ of the first transition says that the process at position $|||_1|||_0||_0$ performs an internal action τ. Since $|||$ and $||$ are right-associative, the transition is caused by the $\mathbf{spawn}(be_1)$ prefix.

Unlike in the standard semantics of Facile (see Sect. 2), a new node is placed immediately before the end guard (second transition). The proof part before $\bullet$ is the position of the process that performs the **newnode** without considering the node created. The proof part after $\bullet$ is the position of the node just created. Note that the proof term of a **newnode** will end with $|||_0||_0$ because of the end guards of systems and processes that impose the presence of a $|||$ at the right of each node and of a $||$ at the right of each process.

The third transition is due to **r_spawn**. The first part of its label is the address of the process that executes the operation. The proof part after $\bullet$ is the address of the process spawned which is placed immediately before the end guard of the destination node.

The last transition is a communication. Its label shows that v is transmitted along channel k. The sender and the receiver are located at $|||_1|||_0||_1||_0$ and $|||_1^2|||_0||_0$, respectively. Assume that the residual γ of the receiver is influenced by the value v. Then γ becomes γ'.

$$\mathbf{3}\,|||\,\mathbf{spawn}(be_1).\alpha||k\,!\,v.\beta||\S|||\,k\,?.\gamma||\mathbf{newnode}(be_4).\delta||\S|||\,\mathbf{r\_spawn}(2, be_5).\xi||\S|||\,\mathbf{3}$$

$$\downarrow |||_1|||_0||_0\tau$$

$$\mathbf{3}\,|||\,(\alpha||be_1)||k\,!\,v.\beta||\S|||\,k\,?.\gamma||\mathbf{newnode}(be_4).\delta||\S|||\,\mathbf{r\_spawn}(2, be_5).\xi||\S|||\,\mathbf{3}$$

$$\downarrow |||_1^2|||_0||_1||_0 \bullet |||_1^4|||_0||_0\tau$$

$$\mathbf{4}\,|||\,(\alpha||be_1)||k\,!\,v.\beta||\S|||\,k\,?.\gamma||\delta||\S|||\,\mathbf{r\_spawn}(2, be_5).\xi||\S|||\,be_4||\S|||\,\mathbf{4}$$

$$\downarrow |||_1^3|||_0||_0 \bullet |||_1^2|||_0||_1^2||_0\tau$$

$$\mathbf{4}\,|||\,(\alpha||be_1)||k\,!\,v.\beta||\S|||\,k\,?.\gamma||\delta||be_5||\S|||\,\xi||\S|||\,be_4||\S|||\,\mathbf{4}$$

$$\downarrow |||_1\langle|||_0||_1||_0\overline{k(v)}, |||_1|||_0||_0k(v)\rangle$$

$$\mathbf{4}\,|||\,(\alpha||be_1)||\beta||\S|||\,\gamma'||\delta||be_5||\S|||\,\xi||\S|||\,be_4||\S|||\,\mathbf{4}$$

Fig. 1. A computation of a Facile program.

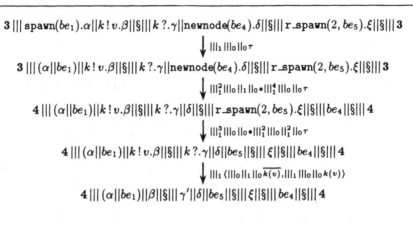

3.2 Auxiliary functions

We now introduce some auxiliary functions that are needed to define the proved semantics of Facile. The first function ℓ is used to recover the action starting from a proof term. It can also be used to obtain the interleaving semantics of Facile.

Definition 5. Let $\delta \in \{||_0, ||_1, |||_0, |||_1\}$. Then the function $\ell : \Theta \rightarrow Act$ is defined as:

$$\ell(\mu) = \mu \ ; \quad \ell(\langle \sigma_0 \vartheta_0 \lambda, \sigma_1 \vartheta_1 \bar{\lambda} \rangle) = \tau \ ; \quad \ell(\delta_0 \mu_0 \bullet \delta_1 \mu_1) = \tau \ ; \quad \ell(\delta\theta) = \ell(\theta)$$

We extend the involution $^{-}$ to ℓ as follows.

$$\overline{\ell(\theta)} = \overline{k(v)} \ \mathit{if} \ \ell(\theta) = k(v)$$

The second auxiliary function $\mathcal{C}$ returns the channel valued constants in a Facile system. When creating a new channel name, the function is used to check whether this name is already in use. The function $\mathcal{C}$ works recursively through expressions, behaviour expressions and distributed behaviour expressions.

Definition 6. The function $\mathcal{C} : E \cup BE \cup DBE \rightarrow \mathcal{S}$ is defined by structural induction as follows:

$$\mathcal{C}(x) = \emptyset \qquad \mathcal{C}(\lambda x.e) = \mathcal{C}(e)$$

$$\mathcal{C}(c) = \begin{cases} \{c\} \text{ if } c \in \mathcal{S} \\ \emptyset \ \text{ otherwise} \end{cases} \qquad \mathcal{C}(e_1 e_2) = \mathcal{C}(e_1) \cup \mathcal{C}(e_2)$$

$$\mathcal{C}(\texttt{channel}(t)) = \emptyset \qquad \mathcal{C}(e_1 ! e_2) = \mathcal{C}(e_1) \cup \mathcal{C}(e_2)$$

$$\mathcal{C}(e?) = \mathcal{C}(e) \qquad \mathcal{C}(\texttt{code}(be)) = \mathcal{C}(be)$$

$$\mathcal{C}(\S) = \emptyset \qquad \mathcal{C}(\texttt{spawn}(be)) = \mathcal{C}(be)$$

$$\mathcal{C}(\texttt{r\_spawn}(e, be)) = \mathcal{C}(e) \cup \mathcal{C}(be) \qquad \mathcal{C}(\texttt{newnode}) = \emptyset$$

$$\mathcal{C}(\texttt{newnode}(be)) = \mathcal{C}(be) \qquad \mathcal{C}(be_1 \ || \ be_2) = \mathcal{C}(be_1) \cup \mathcal{C}(be_2)$$

$$\mathcal{C}(be_1 \ + \ be_2) = \mathcal{C}(be_1) \cup \mathcal{C}(be_2) \qquad \mathcal{C}(\texttt{activate}(e)) = \mathcal{C}(e)$$

$$\mathcal{C}(\texttt{terminate}) = \emptyset \qquad \mathcal{C}(dbe_1 \ ||| \ dbe_2) = \mathcal{C}(dbe_1) \cup \mathcal{C}(dbe_2)$$

$$\mathcal{C}(\text{n}) = \emptyset$$

Recall that the set $\mathcal{S}$ in the above definition is the set of all channels (see Subsect. 2.2).

The function $\mathcal{F}$ below computes the position of the node on which a new process is activated through an **r_spawn**(be). Its parameters are the address σ of the process which performs the **r_spawn** and the number i of $|||$ between the node identified by σ and the node on which be will run. The number i is positive if the node, on which the new process is activated, is to the right of the node that performs the **r_spawn**. i is negative if the node is to the left. Note that the index i will be obtained from the labels of transitions coming from **r_spawn** operations.

Definition 7. The function $\mathcal{F}$:$\{|||_0, |||_1\}^+ \times Z \rightarrow \{|||_0, |||_1\}^+$ is defined as:

1. $\mathcal{F}(\sigma, 0) = \sigma$;

2. $\mathcal{F}(\sigma, i) = \mathcal{F}(|||_1\sigma, i-1)$ if $i > 0$;
3. $\mathcal{F}(|||_1\sigma, i) = \mathcal{F}(\sigma, i+1)$ if $i < 0$

Note that we do not use $\{|||_0, |||_1\}^*$ in the domain and codomain of $\mathcal{F}$ because of the end guard of programs. In fact, the proof term which encodes the position of nodes within a program is always of the form

$$\{|||_1\}^+|||_0$$

because $|||$ is right associative and programs have a begin and an end guard. Intuitively, the position of the node, on which the new process is activated, is obtained from the position of the node that executes the **r_spawn** by adding (if $i > 0$) or subtracting (if $i < 0$) the absolute value of i occurrences of $|||_1$.

The function $\mathcal{B}$ builds the label of a behaviour expression be allocated on a node by an **r_spawn**. It also builds the structure of the destination node. The first parameter of $\mathcal{B}$ is the process that must be put in parallel with the process to be spawned (second parameter). The last parameter is the address, computed inductively, of the process to be spawned.

Definition 8.
The function $\mathcal{B} : BE \times BE \times \{||_0, ||_1\}^+ \rightarrow BE \times \{||_0, ||_1\}^+$ is defined as:

1. $\mathcal{B}(be_1||\S, be, \vartheta) = be_1||be||\S, \vartheta||_0$; [3]
2. $\mathcal{B}(be_1||be_2, be, \vartheta) = be_1||\mathcal{B}(be_2, be, \vartheta||_1)$ if $be_2 \neq \S$

The function $\mathcal{D}$ computes the address of a node created through a **newnode**(be) and the address of the process to be activated on it. $\mathcal{D}$ computes similarly to $\mathcal{B}$.

Definition 9.
The function $\mathcal{D} : DBE \times DBE \times \{|||_0, |||_1\}^+ \rightarrow DBE \times \{|||_0, |||_1\}^+$ is defined as:

1. $\mathcal{D}(dbe|||\mathbf{n}, be, \sigma) = dbe|||be||\S|||\mathbf{n}+\mathbf{1}, \sigma|||_0||_0$;
2. $\mathcal{D}(dbe_1|||dbe_2, be, \sigma) = dbe_1|||\mathcal{D}(dbe_2, be, \sigma|||_1)$ if $dbe_2 \neq \mathbf{n}$

Note that both $\mathcal{B}$ and $\mathcal{D}$ have strings of $||_i$ and $|||_i$ of length at least one in their domains and codomains. This is because they are applied with $\vartheta = ||_1$ for $\mathcal{B}$ and $\sigma = |||_1$ for $\mathcal{D}$ (see rules 16.e, 16.m and 17.b in Tables 9, 10 and 11).

3.3 Transition relation

We now define the proved transition system of Facile.

[3] To avoid the introduction of projection functions on pairs, we avoid the pair constructors $\langle$ and $\rangle$. This allows us to build proof terms correctly without composing projections.

$$1.a: \frac{e_1 \xrightarrow{\theta}_e e_1'}{e_1 e_2 \xrightarrow{\theta}_e e_1' e_2}, \begin{cases} \ell(\theta) = (\tau, k) \Rightarrow \\ k \notin \mathcal{C}(e_2) \end{cases} \qquad 1.b: \frac{e_2 \xrightarrow{\theta}_e e_2'}{v e_2 \xrightarrow{\theta}_e v e_2'}, \begin{cases} \ell(\theta) = (\tau, k) \Rightarrow \\ k \notin \mathcal{C}(v) \end{cases}$$

$$2.a: \frac{e_1 \xrightarrow{\theta}_e e_1'}{e_1 \,!\, e_2 \xrightarrow{\theta}_e e_1' ! e_2}, \begin{cases} \ell(\theta) = (\tau, k) \Rightarrow \\ k \notin \mathcal{C}(e_2) \end{cases} \qquad 1.c: (\lambda x.e)v \xrightarrow{\tau}_e e[v/x]$$

$$2.b: \frac{e_2 \xrightarrow{\theta}_e e_2'}{k!e_2 \xrightarrow{\theta}_e k!e_2'}, \begin{cases} \ell(\theta) = (\tau, h) \Rightarrow \\ h \neq k \end{cases} \qquad 2.c: k!v \xrightarrow{\overline{k(v)}}_e \mathtt{triv}, \begin{cases} k \in \mathcal{S}_t \\ \emptyset \vdash v : t \end{cases}$$

$$3.a: \frac{e \xrightarrow{\theta}_e e'}{e? \xrightarrow{\theta}_e e'?} \qquad 3.b: k? \xrightarrow{k(v)}_e v, \begin{cases} k \in \mathcal{S}_t \\ \emptyset \vdash v : t \end{cases}$$

$$4.: \mathtt{channel}(t) \xrightarrow{(\tau,k)}_e k, \; k \in \mathcal{S}_t \qquad 5.: \mathtt{spawn}(be) \xrightarrow{(be \to 0,0)}_e \mathtt{triv}$$

$$6.a: \frac{e \xrightarrow{\theta}_e e'}{\mathtt{r\_spawn}(e, be) \xrightarrow{\theta}_e \mathtt{r\_spawn}(e', be)}, \begin{cases} \ell(\theta) = (\tau, k) \Rightarrow \\ k \notin \mathcal{C}(be) \end{cases}$$

$$6.b: \mathtt{r\_spawn}(n, be) \xrightarrow{(be \to n,0)}_e \mathtt{triv}, \; n > 0$$

$$7.: \mathtt{newnode} \xrightarrow{new(terminate)}_e \$ \quad 8.: \mathtt{newnode}(be) \xrightarrow{new(be)}_e \$$$

Table 6. Proved rules for function expressions.

Definition 10. The *proved transition system* of Facile is the triple $PTS = \langle T, \Theta, \longrightarrow_p \rangle$ where T is the set of closed Facile programs, Θ is the set of proof terms, and $\longrightarrow_p$ is the transition relation defined in Tables 6 ,..., 11.

We introduce a new transition relation for programs

$$\longrightarrow_p \subseteq Prog \times \Theta \times Prog.$$

Before discussing the rules that define the operational semantics, we state a proposition that relates the original and the proved semantics of Facile. The proof is by induction on the rules that define the transition relations.

Proposition 11.
Let $\xrightarrow{\mu}$ and $\xrightarrow{\theta}_p$ be the transition relations in Defs. 2 and 10, respectively. Then,

$$K, N, dbe \xrightarrow{\mu} K', N', dbe' \Leftrightarrow \exists \theta \,.\, dbe \xrightarrow{\theta}_p dbe' \wedge \ell(\theta) = \mu$$

Expressions Here we examine the rules of expressions (Tab. 6). As in Def. 2, the creation of a new channel returns the name of that channel. We must ensure that the new name is not already in use elsewhere in the program to avoid name confusion. Since the channel generated by **channel**(t) is recorded in the labels of transitions (see rule 4.), we perform the name clash check at each derivation step by checking the condition $\ell(\theta) = (\tau, k) \Rightarrow k \notin \mathcal{C}(-)$. The same condition is applied in the rules for parallel composition of processes and systems. Note that in rule 3.a there is not the above condition because channel names have already been checked inductively during the derivation of the premise. Instead, rule 6.a has the condition because, even if e must evaluate to a node identifier, it is possible to create channels and to export them in communications beforehand. Since we check channel names when they are created, clash of names would arise without the condition. The distributed check on channel names allows us to drop the set K of channels from configurations.

The $(be \rightarrow n, 0)$ label in rules 5 and 6.b represents the creation of a new process be by either **spawn**(be) if $n = 0$ or **r_spawn**(n, be) otherwise. The second component of the pair is 0 because we do not know the relative address of n with respect to the current node. The label is updated with this information in either rule 16.b or 16.c or 16.m. The integer allows us to apply the function $\mathcal{F}$ correctly in rule 17.c.

The $new(be)$ label in rules 7 and 8 records the process that must be activated on the new node. This process is **terminate** for the creation of an empty node and be otherwise. We distinguish nodes according to their position within the program. Each time we generate a new node, its position is determined by the guards of systems. Since we do not know the value of guards at the expression level we introduce a placeholder \$ that is instantiated at the program level in rule 17.b (Tab. 11). Identifying nodes with their position allows us to eliminate the set N of nodes from configurations.

Behaviour expressions Consider the rules of behaviour expressions. The tag $||_0$ in rule 10.a means that the left component of a parallel composition moves, the tag $||_1$ in rule 10.b means that the right component moves. When two processes be_1 and be_2, allocated on the same node, communicate (rule 11), the label on the transition is the pair of the actions performed by the two partners θ_1 and θ_2, decorated with their positions $||_0$ and $||_1$, respectively.

The non-deterministic choice + does not change the labels (rules 12.a and 12.b) because the non-interleaving relations, in which we are interested, are interpretations of the parallel structure of processes only. There is no need for checking channel names in rules 12.a-b, because the choice operator discards either summand be_2 or be_1. Assume that be_1 generates a channel k which already exists in be_2. Since the rule discards be_2, there is no name clash and the name can be re-used. The symmetric case is similar.

$$9.a : \frac{e \xrightarrow{\theta}_{e} e'}{\texttt{activatee} \xrightarrow{\theta}_{be} \texttt{activatee}'}, \ \ell(\theta) \neq (be \rightarrow 0, 0)$$

$$9.b : \frac{e \overset{\vartheta(be \rightarrow 0,0)}{\longrightarrow_{e}} e'}{\texttt{activatee} \xrightarrow{\vartheta\tau}_{be} \texttt{activatee}' || be}$$

$$9.c : \texttt{activatecode}(be) \xrightarrow{\tau}_{be} be$$

$$10.a : \frac{be_1 \xrightarrow{\theta}_{be} be_1'}{be_1 \,||\, be_2 \xrightarrow{||_0 \theta}_{be} be_1' \,||\, be_2}, \begin{cases} \ell(\theta) = (\tau, k) \Rightarrow \\ k \notin \mathcal{C}(be_2) \end{cases}$$

$$10.b : \frac{be_2 \xrightarrow{\theta}_{be} be_2'}{be_1 \,||\, be_2 \xrightarrow{||_1 \theta}_{be} be_1 \,||\, be_2'}, \begin{cases} \ell(\theta) = (\tau, k) \Rightarrow \\ k \notin \mathcal{C}(be_1) \end{cases}$$

$$11. : \frac{be_1 \xrightarrow{\theta_1}_{be} be_1' \quad be_2 \xrightarrow{\theta_2}_{be} be_2'}{be_1 \,||\, be_2 \overset{\langle ||_0 \theta_1, ||_1 \theta_2 \rangle}{\longrightarrow_{be}} be_1' \,||\, be_2'}, \ \ell(\theta_1) = \overline{\ell(\theta_2)}$$

$$12.a : \frac{be_1 \xrightarrow{\theta}_{be} be_1'}{be_1 + be_2 \xrightarrow{\theta}_{be} be_1'} \qquad 12.b : \frac{be_2 \xrightarrow{\theta}_{be} be_2'}{be_1 + be_2 \xrightarrow{\theta}_{be} be_2'}$$

Table 7. Proved rules for behaviour expressions.

$$13.a : \frac{be \xrightarrow{\theta}_{be} be'}{be \xrightarrow{\theta}_{dbe} be'}, \ \ell(\theta) \neq (be'' \rightarrow n, 0)$$

$$13.b : \frac{be \overset{\vartheta(be'' \rightarrow n,0)}{\longrightarrow_{be}} be'}{be|||dbe \overset{\vartheta(be'' \rightarrow n,0)}{\underset{1 \quad 0}{\longrightarrow}} be'|||dbe}$$

$$14.a : \frac{dbe_1 \xrightarrow{\theta}_{dbe} dbe_1'}{dbe_1 \,|||dbe_2 \xrightarrow{|||_0 \theta}_{dbe} dbe_1'|||dbe_2}, \ \ell(\theta) = (\tau, k) \ \Rightarrow \ k \notin \mathcal{C}(dbe_2)$$

$$14.b : \frac{dbe_2 \xrightarrow{\theta}_{dbe} dbe_2'}{dbe_1 \,|||dbe_2 \xrightarrow{|||_1 \theta}_{dbe} dbe_1|||dbe_2'}, \ \ell(\theta) = (\tau, k) \ \Rightarrow \ k \notin \mathcal{C}(dbe_1)$$

$$15. : \frac{dbe_1 \xrightarrow{\theta_1}_{dbe} dbe_1 \quad dbe_2 \xrightarrow{\theta_2}_{dbe} dbe_2'}{dbe_1 \,|||dbe_2 \overset{\langle |||_0 \theta_1, |||_1 \theta_2 \rangle}{\longrightarrow_{dbe}} dbe_1'|||dbe_2'}, \ \ell(\theta_1) = \overline{\ell(\theta_2)}$$

Table 8. Proved rules for distributed behaviour expressions.

Distributed behaviour expressions We now examine distributed behaviour expressions. The only difference between distributed behaviour expressions and behaviour expressions is in the rules for parallel composition and communication where we use tags $|||_i$ instead of $||_i$.

If the operation is an **r_spawn**(e, be) we must find the node n on which the process is to be activated. For this purpose we define a quite technical auxiliary relation. (Its definition can be skipped by the non-interested reader, reading can then be resumed with the rules for programs.) In rule 13.b we consider all nodes on the right of the current node. The indices 1 and 0 indicate that we move a position to the right but we do not know the name of the new node yet (there is at least the end guard). The auxiliary relation

$$\xrightarrow[i\quad j]{\theta}$$

is defined in Tables 9 and 10. The index i denotes the number of $|||$ operators between the node that performs the **r_spawn** and the node under consideration. In other words, it denotes the right shift, with respect to the address of **r_spawn**, if i is positive or the left shift if i is negative. Since parallel operators are right-associative, we move to the right until the end guard by making $|||$ left-associative through parentheses (rule 16.a).

Assume that we want to allocate a process at the right of the spawning node. When the end guard is reached (at this point we know the number of nodes in the system), we consider the nodes to the left of the end guard by recovering the right associativity of $|||$. We initialise index j to the number of nodes in the system (rule 16.c) and we move to the left until the destination node is reached, by decrementing indices i and j (rule 16.d). When the destination node is identified, we allocate the spawned process on this node, and we add its local address to the label of the transition (rule 16.e and function $\mathcal{B}$). Note that $||_1$ in the call to $\mathcal{B}$ is needed to keep track of the $||$ operator inserted in the node to allocate the new process be'' (see also Def. 8). What remains is to restore the associativity up to the node that performs the **r_spawn**. We replace the value of j with the number of steps needed to reach the spawning node $(i-1)$. The index i is no longer needed and we set it to 0 (rule 16.f). The same happens in rule 16.b, handling the case in which the destination node is the node immediately to the left of the end guard. While moving to the left and recovering right associativity, we decrement the index j until it becomes 1. Index j is 1 when we are on the node performing **r_spawn**. Now we add a $|||_0$ in the label of the transition to build the proof term correctly, and we resume the actual transition relation (rule 16.g).

If the destination node is at the left of the node performing **r_spawn**, the index i becomes 1 before j. This means that we are back on the node performing **r_spawn**, and the destination node has not been found. We add a $|||_0$ to the label of the transition, and we set the index i to 0 (rule 16.h). Rule 16.i handles the case in which the node performing **r_spawn** is immediately at the left of the end guard. We continue moving left by decrementing the indices i and j and by adding $|||_1$s in the labels to update proof terms correctly (rule 16.l). This is

$$16.a:\ \frac{dbe_1|||dbe_2|||dbe_3\ {}_{i}\!\xrightarrow{\theta}{}_{0}\ dbe'_1|||dbe_2|||dbe_3}{(dbe_1|||dbe_2)|||dbe_3\ {}_{i+1}\!\xrightarrow{\theta}{}_{0}\ (dbe'_1|||dbe_2)|||dbe_3},\ dbe_3 \neq \mathbf{n}$$

$$16.b:\ \frac{dbe_1|||be|||\mathbf{n}\ {}_{i}\!\xrightarrow{\vartheta(be''\to n,0)}{}_{0}\ dbe'_1|||be|||\mathbf{n}}{dbe_1|||be|||\mathbf{n}\ {}_{0}\!\xrightarrow{\vartheta\bullet\vartheta'(be''\to n,i)}{}_{i}\ dbe'_1|||be'|||\mathbf{n}},\ \mathcal{B}(be, be'', ||_1) = be', \vartheta'$$

$$16.c:\ \frac{dbe_1|||be|||\mathbf{n}'\ {}_{i}\!\xrightarrow{\vartheta(be''\to n,0)}{}_{0}\ dbe'_1|||be|||\mathbf{n}'}{dbe_1|||be|||\mathbf{n}'\ {}_{i}\!\xrightarrow{\vartheta(be''\to n,0)}{}_{n'-1}\ dbe'_1|||be|||\mathbf{n}'},\ n \neq \mathbf{n}'$$

$$16.d:\ \frac{(dbe_1|||be)|||dbe_3\ {}_{i}\!\xrightarrow{\vartheta(be''\to n,0)}{}_{j}\ (dbe'_1|||be)|||dbe_3}{dbe_1|||be|||dbe_3\ {}_{i-1}\!\xrightarrow{\vartheta(be''\to n,0)}{}_{j-1}\ dbe'_1|||be|||dbe_3},\ j > n, i > 1$$

$$16.e:\ \frac{(dbe_1|||be)|||dbe_3\ {}_{i}\!\xrightarrow{\vartheta(be''\to n,0)}{}_{n}\ (dbe'_1|||be)|||dbe_3}{dbe_1|||be|||dbe_3\ {}_{0}\!\xrightarrow{\vartheta\bullet\vartheta'(be''\to n,i-1)}{}_{i-1}\ dbe'_1|||be'|||dbe_3},\ \begin{cases}\mathcal{B}(be, be'', ||_1) = \\ be', \vartheta'\end{cases}$$

$$16.f:\ \frac{(dbe_1|||dbe_2)|||dbe_3\ {}_{0}\!\xrightarrow{\theta}{}_{j}\ (dbe'_1|||dbe_2)|||dbe'_3}{dbe_1|||dbe_2|||dbe_3\ {}_{0}\!\xrightarrow{\theta}{}_{j-1}\ dbe'_1|||dbe_2|||dbe'_3},\ j \neq 1$$

$$16.g:\ \frac{dbe\ {}_{0}\!\xrightarrow{\theta}{}_{1}\ dbe'}{dbe\ \xrightarrow{|||_0\theta}{}_{dbe}\ dbe'}$$

Table 9. Proved rules for distributed behaviour expressions (cont.).

the case in which the shift with respect to the node of **r_spawn** yields a negative index i. When index j becomes $n+1$, we allocate the process, we build its local address and we resume the actual transition relation (rule 16.m and function $\mathcal{B}$). The last parameter of $\mathcal{B}$ is needed for the same reason as in rule 16.e (see above). Note that we store the index $i-1$ in the label of the transition. This will be used by the function $\mathcal{F}$ in rule 17.c.

Programs Now we consider the rules of programs. Rule 17.b replaces the placeholder \$ (generated by either rule 7 or 8) with the value of the guards plus one. The function $\mathcal{D}$ allocates the new node and recovers its address. The parameter $|||_1$ keeps track of the $|||$ operator added to the program to allocate the new node. Note that the tag $||_0$ in the side condition of rule 17.b keeps track of the end guard of nodes inserted by **newnode**. At the program level, if the operation is **r_spawn**, we only need to complete the label with the function $\mathcal{F}$ (rule 17.c). We

$$16h : \frac{dbe \xrightarrow[1 \quad j]{\vartheta(be'' \to n,0)} dbe'}{dbe \xrightarrow[0 \quad j]{|||_0 \vartheta(be'' \to n,0)} dbe'}, j > 0 \quad 16.i : \frac{be|||\mathbf{n}' \xrightarrow[1 \quad 0]{\vartheta(be'' \to n,0)} be'|||\mathbf{n}'}{be|||\mathbf{n}' \xrightarrow[0 \quad n']{|||_0 \vartheta(be'' \to n,0)} be'|||\mathbf{n}'}$$

$$16.l : \frac{dbe \xrightarrow[i \quad j]{\sigma\vartheta(be'' \to n,0)} dbe'}{be|||dbe \xrightarrow[i-1 \quad j-1]{|||_1 \sigma\vartheta(be'' \to n,0)} be|||dbe'}, i \leq 0, j > n+1$$

$$16.m : \frac{dbe \xrightarrow[i \quad n+1]{\sigma\vartheta(be'' \to n,0)} dbe'}{be|||dbe \xrightarrow{|||_1 \sigma\vartheta \bullet \vartheta'(be'' \to n, i-1)}_{dbe} be'|||dbe'}, \begin{cases} \mathcal{B}(be, be'', ||_1) = be', \vartheta' \\ i \leq 0 \end{cases}$$

Table 10. Proved rules for distributed behaviour expressions (cont.).

internalise the creation of channels by transforming its label into τ (rule 17.d).

$$17.a : \frac{dbe \xrightarrow{\theta}_{dbe} dbe'}{\mathbf{n}'|||dbe \xrightarrow{|||_1 \theta}_p \mathbf{n}'|||dbe'}, \ell(\theta) \neq new(be), (be \to n, i), (\tau, k)$$

$$17.b : \frac{dbe \xrightarrow{\sigma\vartheta new(be)}_{dbe} dbe'}{\mathbf{n}'|||dbe \xrightarrow{|||_1 \sigma\vartheta \bullet \sigma' ||_0 \tau}_p \mathbf{n}' + \mathbf{1}|||dbe''\{\mathbf{n}' + \mathbf{1}/\$\}}, \begin{cases} \mathcal{D}(dbe', be, |||_1) = \\ dbe'', \sigma'||_0 \end{cases}$$

$$17.c : \frac{dbe \xrightarrow{\sigma\vartheta \bullet \vartheta'(be \to n,i)}_{dbe} dbe'}{\mathbf{n}'|||dbe \xrightarrow{|||_1 \sigma\vartheta \bullet \mathcal{F}(\sigma,i)\vartheta'\tau}_p \mathbf{n}'|||dbe'} \quad 17.d : \frac{dbe \xrightarrow{\sigma\vartheta(\tau,k)}_{dbe} dbe'}{\mathbf{n}'|||dbe \xrightarrow{|||_1 \sigma\vartheta\tau}_p \mathbf{n}'|||dbe'}$$

Table 11. Proved rules for programs.

Even if the labels of **newnode** and **r_spawn** have the same structure at the program level, we can always distinguish them. In fact, the **r_spawn** label has at least one $||_1$ between the $|||_0$ that ends the sequence of $|||_i$ after $\bullet$, and the $||_0$ that ends the sequence of $||_i$. The labels of **newnode** do not have this. The following proposition expresses this.

Proposition 12. *Let θ and θ' be the labels of a* **newnode** *and an* **r_spawn**, *respectively. Then,*

$$\theta = \{|||_1\}^+|||_0\{||_0, ||_1\}^*||_0 \bullet \{|||_1\}^+|||_0||_0\tau$$

and

$$\theta' = \{|||_1\}^+|||_0\{||_0, ||_1\}^*||_0 \bullet \{|||_1\}^+|||_0\{||_0, ||_1\}^*||_1||_0\tau$$

Proof. The proof part before • is the same for both θ and θ' because • encodes the position of the process which performs the operation. The tags $|||_0$ and $||_0$ are always present because of the end guards of programs and processes.
Now consider the proof term which follows • in θ. The tags $|||_0$ and $||_0$ are always present for the same reasons as above. Since the nodes created are placed immediately before the end guard of programs, their addresses end with $|||_0$. The process allocated on the new node is at the left of the end guard § and there is no other process on the node. Therefore, the process address is $||_0$.
Now consider the proof part after • in θ'. The same arguments as in the case above still hold for $|||_0$. Since **r_spawn** places the process on an existing node, that therefore contains at least one process apart from the end guard §, we have $\{||_0, ||_1\}^*||_1$ before the last $||_0$.

4 Locality semantics

Recently, many attention is paid to the ditribution of resources in concurrent distributed systems, both theoretically and practically. Some semantics that naturally deal with this issue have been presented in the literature (see, e.g., [8, 5]). Essentially, they associates with each process in a system a location that can vary dynamically. More precisely, when a process spawns some subprocesses, these are assigned a sublocation of their parent. These semantics can be useful to determine the load of a given node in a system and also for debugging purposes. Indeed, when a bug show up, it is easy to detect the location of the process that performed the incorrect action. In this section, we define a locality semantics for Facile in the style of [8].

Facile can express the distribution of processes on nodes. As a consequence, some notions of locality naturally arises, depending on the granularity of locations. Inter-node locality considers transitions at the node level by assuming that the internal structure of each node is sequential. This assumption corresponds to having uniprocessor nodes. Infra-node locality is an extension of inter-node locality introducing the parallel structure of processes. This is the case of multiprocessor nodes and it is the semantics that we study in this paper. Hereafter, let $\gamma \in A \cup \{\bullet\sigma\vartheta\tau\}$. Finally, recall that locality semantics studies the distribution in space of activities and thus it is insensible to silent transitions. Hence, we simply ignore communications.

Infra-node locality is obtained by considering both the parallel structure of nodes and the parallel structure of processes.

Definition 13. Let $P_0 \xrightarrow{\theta_0}_p P_1 \xrightarrow{\theta_1}_p \ldots \xrightarrow{\theta_n}_p P_{n+1}$ be a proved computation and let $\theta_n = \sigma'\vartheta'\gamma'$. Then, θ_n has a *direct infra-node locality* dependency on θ_h ($\theta_h \sqsubseteq^1_{ploc} \theta_n$) iff $\theta_h = \sigma\vartheta\gamma$ and $\sigma\vartheta$ is a prefix of $\sigma'\vartheta'$.

The *infra-node locality* dependencies of θ_n are obtained by the reflexive and transitive closure of $\sqsubseteq^1_{ploc}$, i.e., $\sqsubseteq_{ploc} = (\sqsubseteq^1_{ploc})^*$.

Note that a process may have sub-processes. Thus, the check whether the process P is placed in a sub-location of another process Q is implemented by checking if the address of Q is a prefix of the address of P. Accordingly, the actions of P will depend of the ones of Q.

5 Analysis of a Mobile File Browser Agent

The following is a scaled down version of a problem with spatial distribution of higher order processes and mobile channels. It originally arose in the code for the Mobile Service Agent demonstration given at the EITC'95 Exhibition. Using "traditional" debugging techniques it took two weeks to track down the problem.

In [4] we analysed the system using causality information. Even though the causality semantics helps to identify that there is a problem, it is not directly apparent from the analysis which components of the system cause the problem. Thus in a large system it can be difficult to identify which components have to be repaired. In this section we review the analysis and apply the extended semantic framework that we have developed in this paper.

The problem is the following. We have an agent server that can be called to deliver a client (FB) to the user and leave behind a server (FTP). There is a mistake in the overall system, namely that all client/server pairs share the same channel. Thus FB clients and FTP servers are not strictly related. Indeed an FB client may "steal" the FTP server from another FB client.

Below we give the Facile code, both for running code (typewritten) in the Facile Antigua Release [15], and a version written in core Facile (italics). We omit parts not relevant to our discussion. The system activates the two processes FBS and AC on different nodes. Process AC is busy waiting for an agent request. When the request arrives, AC creates a channel (`reqch`) and sends it to process FBS along their common channel `getch`. Now process AC is waiting for an agent from FBS. Once the process FBS has received the channel name on which AC is waiting for the agent, FBS sends process FB to AC together with the needed channels. Then it activates an FTP server on its node and restarts. Process AC activates the client FB on its node and resumes. Now the interaction is between FTP and FB as follows. The client waits for a request on channel `getinfo`, then creates the channel on which it wants to receive the service (`repch`) and sends it to FTP. Then it waits for the service. The FTP server receives the channel on which it sends the answer to FB, then prints a message to say that the connection is established and sends the answer. At this point the FTP server terminates. The FB client receives the answer, prints a message to say that the interaction is finished and reactivates itself. Since channel `reqch` is global and the client FB is a recursive process while FTP is not, the problem described at the beginning of this section may arise. Note that even if the FTP server is made recursive, there would still not be the wanted correspondence between pairs of FTP servers and file browsers FB.

```
(* Declarations *)
proc FB (getinfo,reqch) =
```

```
  let val _ = receive getinfo (* keep it waiting until asked *)
      val repch = channel ()
      val _ = send(reqch,repch)
      val _ = receive repch
      val _ = print "Got handshake from server\n"
  in activate FB (getinfo,reqch)
  end
```

$FB(getinfo,reqch)=getinfo?.(\lambda repch.reqch!repch.repch?.FB(getinfo,reqch))channel$

```
proc FTP reqch =
  let val repch = receive reqch
      val _ = print "Request from client\n"
  in send(repch,());activate FTP reqch
  end
```

$FTPreqch=(\lambda repch.repch!.activateFTPreqch)reqch?$

```
proc FBS (getch,reqch,getinfo) =
  let val fbch = receive getch
      val _ = send(fbch,FB(getinfo,reqch))
      val _ = spawn (FTP reqch)
  in activate FBS (getch,reqch,getinfo)
  end
```

$FBS(getch,reqch,getinfo)=(\lambda fbch.fbch!FB(getinfo,reqch).$

$spawn(FTPreqch).FBS(getch,reqch,getinfo))getch?$

```
proc AC (getag,getch) =
  let val _ = receive getag (* keep it waiting until asked *)
      val reqch = channel ()
      val _ = send(getch,reqch)
      val FBCagent = receive reqch
  in spawn FBCagent;
     activate AC (getag,getch)
  end
```

$AC(getag,getch)=getag?.(\lambda reqch.getch!reqch.(\lambda FBCagent.spawn(FBCagent).$

$AC(getag,getch))reqch?)channel$

```
(* Body *)
val getag = channel (): unit channel
val getinfo = channel (): unit channel

let
  val reqch = channel ()
  val getch = channel ()
in r_spawn (newnode,FBS (getch,reqch,getinfo));
  r_spawn (newnode,AC (getag,getch))
end
```

$(\lambda reqch.\lambda getch.r\_spawn(newnode,FBC(getch,reqch,getinfo)).$

$r\_spawn(newnode,AC(getag,getch)))channel)channel$

We now show how the mistake can easily be singled out by using a locality relation between transitions. With the same relation we also detect which are the faulty components. The idea is that the actions of the partners of an FTP server in the communications must be locality related. This amounts to say that an FTP server always communicates with the same FB client.

Now consider the computation in Fig. 2 extracted from the transition system of the incorrect code (begin and end guards are omitted here for the sake of readability). It is the scaled down version of one of the computations that showed up a bug during the European IT Conference Exhibition in Brussels, 1995. Assume that two FTP servers and two FB clients have been activated, and that client FB_1 steals the server of FB_2.

Infra-node locality establishes that

$$\theta_1 = ||\|_1\|_1\, reqch(repch) \not\sqsubseteq_{ploc} ||\|_1\|_0\|_1\, reqch(repch)$$

The intuitive meaning of the above relation is that two different FB clients request services from the same FTP server in transitions θ_1 and θ_2. This violates the invariant of the system that FB/FTP pairs are strictly related. From the label prefixes $||\|_0||\|_1\|_1$, $||\|_1\|_1$ and $||\|_1\|_0\|_1$ we see that the components in question are FTP_i and FB_i.

A way out is to make sure that each pair of FTP server and FB client shares a private channel. It is implemented by replacing FBS and the body by

```
proc FBS (getch,getinfo) =
  let val fbch = receive getch
      val reqch = channel ()
      val _ = send(fbch,FB(getinfo,reqch))
      val _ = spawn (FTP reqch)
  in activate FBS (getch,getinfo)
  end
```

$$
\begin{array}{c}
\texttt{r\_spawn}(\texttt{newnode}, FBS).\texttt{r\_spawn}(\texttt{newnode}, AC) \\
\downarrow \tau \\
(\texttt{r\_spawn}(\texttt{newnode}, AC) ||| FBS) \\
\downarrow |||_0 \tau \\
((\texttt{terminate} ||| AC) ||| FBS) \\
\vdots \\
((\texttt{terminate} ||| ((AC || FB_2) || FB_1)) ||| ((FBS || FTP_2) || FTP_1)) = s_0 \\
\theta_1 \downarrow \langle |||_0 |||_1 ||_1 \overline{reqch(repch)}, |||_1 ||_1 reqch(repch) \rangle \\
\bullet \\
\downarrow |||_1 ||_1 request\ client\ 1 \\
\bullet \\
\downarrow \langle |||_0 |||_1 ||_1 repch, |||_1 ||_1 \overline{repch} \rangle \\
((\texttt{terminate} ||| ((AC || FB_2) || FB_1)) ||| ((FBS || FTP_2) || FTP_1)) = s_1 \\
\theta_2 \downarrow \langle |||_0 |||_1 ||_1 \overline{reqch(repch)}, |||_1 ||_0 ||_1 reqch(repch) \rangle \\
\bullet \\
\downarrow |||_1 ||_0 ||_1 request\ client\ 2 \\
\vdots
\end{array}
$$

Fig. 2. A computation of the client-server system for mobile agents.

$$FBS(getch,getinfo)=(\lambda fbch.(\lambda reqch.fbch!FB(getinfo,reqch).spawn(FTPreqch).$$

$$FBS(getch,reqch,getinfo))channel)getch?$$

and by, respectively

```
val getag = channel (): unit channel
val getinfo = channel (): unit channel

let
  val getch = channel ()
in r_spawn (newnode,FBS (getch,getinfo));
   r_spawn (newnode,AC (getag,getch))
end
```

$$(\lambda getch.r\_spawn(newnode,FBC(getch,getinfo)).r\_spawn(newnode,AC(getag,getch)))channel$$

Now it is straightforward to prove that a client FB_i communicates with a server FTP_i along a private channel, generated by the same i^{th} activation of

FBS that creates FB_i and FTP_i. As any FTP has only one channel, it can serve only its client, and vice versa. Hence the problem has been easily detected and solved. Now is only a clerical matter going back to the original code made up of about 6K Facile Antigua lines and fix the bug.

6 Conclusion

In this paper we have further developed an operational semantics for the Facile programming language based on the notion of proved transition systems. In [4] we developed the semantics for the functional concurrent core of Facile, allowing us to derive information about causal dependencies of communications. The enrichment of the semantics to cater for the distributed aspects of Facile, developed in this paper, makes it possible to derive many different types of information. In particular, we have used the semantics to derive information that takes the distribution of processes on processors in Facile programs into account. The framework is applied to a case study derived from a successful demonstration of agent programming in Facile.

Other types of information may be derived from the proved semantics, though these were not needed for the analysis presented in this paper. Some of these are studied in [3, 13].

The proved semantics for Facile is an interesting example of what can be achieved with a programming language based on strong formal foundations since they allow formal reasoning about properties to be related directly to the running program. This tight and natural correspondence eliminates the model/running program gap that usually exists in systems with formal specifications, but implementations in traditional programming languages.

Furthermore, since the proved semantics for Facile is based on quite standard, interleaving-like transition system definitions (although the labels carry a lot more information) it is possible to (re)-use existing verifier tools like *CWB* [6] and *YAPV* [2]. In particular, the latter has been used to derive the proved computation used here, and to derive the causal [4] and locality relations by handling the long wired labels mechanically.

References

1. R. Amadio, L. Leth, and B. Thomsen. From a concurrent λ-calculus to the π-calculus. In *Proceedings of FCT'95*, 1995. Full version in technical report ECRC-95-18.
2. A. Bianchi, S. Coluccini, P. Degano, and C. Priami. An efficient verifier of truly concurrent properties. In V. Malyshkin, editor, *Proceedings of PaCT'95, LNCS 964*, pages 36–50. Springer-Verlag, 1995.
3. R. Borgia. Semantiche causali per FACILE. Master's thesis, Dipartimento di Informatica, Università di Pisa, 1995.
4. Roberta Borgia, Pierpaolo Degano, Corrado Priami, Lone Leth, and Bent Thomsen. Understanding mobile agents via a non-interleaving semantics for facile. In *Proceedings of SAS'96*, To appear in LNCS. Springer-Verlag, 1996.

5. G. Boudol, I. Castellani, M. Hennessy, and A. Kiehn. A theory of processes with localities. *Theoretical Computer Science*, 114, 1993.
6. R. Cleaveland, J. Parrow, and B. Steffen. The concurrency workbench: A semantics-based tool for the verification of concurrent systems. *ACM Transaction on Programming Languages and Systems*, pages 36–72, 1993.
7. P. Degano and C. Priami. Proved trees. In *Proceedings of ICALP'92, LNCS 623*, pages 629–640. Springer-Verlag, 1992.
8. P. Degano and C. Priami. Causality for mobile processes. In *Proceedings of ICALP'95, LNCS 944*, pages 660–671. Springer-Verlag, 1995.
9. A. Giacalone, P. Mishra, and S. Prasad. Facile: A symmetric integration of concurrent and functional programming. *International Journal of Parallel Programming*, 18:121–160, 1989.
10. A. Giacalone, P. Mishra, and S. Prasad. Operational and algebraic semantics for Facile: A symmetric integration of concurrent and functional programming. In *Proceedings ICALP'90, LNCS 443*, pages 765–780. Springer-Verlag, 1990.
11. L. Leth and B. Thomsen. Some Facile Chemistry. *Formal Aspects of Computing, Volume 7, Number 3*, pages 314–328, 1995.
12. G. Plotkin. A structural approach to operational semantics. Technical Report DAIMI FN-19, Aarhus University, Denmark, 1981.
13. C. Priami. *Enhanced Operational Semantics for Concurrency*. PhD thesis, Dipartimento di Informatica, Università di Pisa, March 1996. Available as Tech. Rep. TD-08/96.
14. B. Thomsen, L. Leth, and A. Giacalone. Some Issues in the Semantics of Facile Distributed Programming. In *Proceedings of the 1992 REX Workshop on "Semantics: Foundations and Applications"*, LNCS 666. Springer-Verlag, 1992.
15. B. Thomsen, L. Leth, S. Prasad, T.-M. Kuo, A. Kramer, F. Knabe, and A. Giacalone. Facile Antigua Release Programming Guide. Technical Report ECRC-93-20, European Computer-Industry Research Centre, 1993.
16. Bent Thomsen, Lone Leth, and Tsung-Miu Kuo. A facile tutorial. In *Proceedings of CONCUR'96, LNCS 1119*, pages 278–298. Springer-Verlag, 1996.

A Non-Standard Semantics for Generating Reduced Transition Systems

Nicoletta De Francesco, Antonella Santone, Gigliola Vaglini

Dipartimento di Ingegneria dell'Informazione Università di Pisa I-56126 Pisa, Italy

Abstract. In recent years many techniques have been developed for automatically verifying concurrent systems and most of them are based on a representation of the concurrent system by means of a finite state transition system. State explosion is one of the most serious problems of this approach: in fact often the prohibitive number of states renders the verification inefficient and, in some cases, impossible.
We propose an approach to the reduction of the state space of the transition system corresponding to a CCS process, which takes into account the deadlock freeness property. The reduced transition system is generated by means of a *non-standard operational semantics* containing a set of rules which are an abstraction, preserving deadlock freeness, of the inference rules of the standard semantics.

1 Introduction

In the recent years many techniques have been developed for automatically verifying concurrent systems; most of these techniques are based on a representation of the concurrent system given by means of a transition system. State explosion is one of the most serious problems of this approach: in fact, often, not only intrinsically complex systems, but also not very large ones are described by a transition system with a prohibitive number of states, a lot of which are in some sense equivalent. To overcome this problem, many approaches have been developed aiming at a reduction of the number of states of the transition system by means of a suitable abstraction. Since we are particularly interested in properties of concurrent systems, like deadlock freeness or fairness, which are independent from data, the abstraction we consider is not derived as a "side-effect" of data abstraction [6, 7, 11].

Our work is devoted to define an abstraction of the finite state transition system corresponding to a concurrent system, preserving *deadlock freeness*. Given a CCS term [20], we define a reduced transition system, which has in general a fewer number of states than that generated by the SOS standard semantics of CCS [20], and is deadlock free if and only if the standard transition system is deadlock free. A fundamental characteristic of the approach is that we generate the reduced transition system by means of a *non-standard operational semantics* containing a set of rules which are, in some sense, an abstraction, preserving deadlock freeness, of the inference rules of the standard semantics.

Other works can be found in the literature aiming at state space reduction for systems in which the most important part is their concurrent structure. They essentially follow either a *standard semantics* approach or a *syntactic* approach. Methods in the first category (see, for instance, [1, 24]) start from generating the standard transition system corresponding to a concurrent system, and then reduce it obtaining a transition system with fewer states. Such approach is very general, but it requires a lot of memory to store the standard transition system and effort to apply the reduction algorithm.

The works in the second category (see, for instance, [5]) are based on syntactic transformations of the concurrent system description, given by a program written in some concurrent language. The program obtained by the transformation corresponds to a transition system smaller than the standard one. The advantage of this approach is that the standard transition system needs not to be generated. Nevertheless, any syntactic approach is less general and efficient than a semantic one: in fact, being static, it cannot know in advance all the situations that can occur during program execution. Thus a reduction algorithm applied to a standard transition system can lead to a more optimized (with fewer states) transition system than that obtained by a syntactic approach.

Our approach can be seen as a compromise between the semantic and syntactic methods: since it is based on a non-standard semantics, it is more powerful, due to its flexibility, than the syntactic reduction methods. On the other hand, while it is less powerful than the semantic methods (in terms of the size of the reduced transition systems), it has the fundamental advantage of not generating the complete standard transition, thus saving memory space.

Finally, the main differences with respect to other approaches reducing state space during the generation of the transition system (see, for example, [3, 15, 16, 21, 26, 27]) are in the use of a non-standard semantics instead of defining ad hoc algorithms. Thus we gain the advantage that the correctness of the method can be easily proved and moreover the method is easily implementable.

After the preliminaries described in section 2, we define deadlock in section 3; then we define the non-standard semantics in section 4, while section 5 concludes the paper.

2 Preliminaries

We assume that the reader is familiar with the basic concepts of process algebras and CCS. We summarize the most relevant definitions below, and refer to [20] for more details.

The CCS syntax we consider is the following:

$$p ::= \mu.p \mid nil \mid p+p \mid p|p \mid p\backslash A \mid x \mid p[f]$$

We call *Terms* the *(process) terms* generated from p; moreover, we call *Const* the set of constants ranged over by x. A constant is defined by a constant definition $x \stackrel{def}{=} p_x$, (where p_x is called the *body* of x).

As usual, there is a set of visible actions $Vis = \{a, \overline{a}, b, \overline{b}, ...\}$ over which α ranges, while μ, ν range over $Act = Vis \cup \{\tau\}$, where τ denotes the so-called *internal action*. The complementary action of any action α is denoted by $\overline{\alpha}$. By *nil* we denote the empty process term.
The operators to build process terms are prefixing ($\mu.p$), summation ($p+p$), parallel composition ($p|p$), restriction ($p\backslash A$) and relabelling ($p[f]$), where $A \subseteq Vis$ and $f : Vis \rightarrow Vis$ is such that $f(\overline{\alpha}) = \overline{f(\alpha)}$. The precedence of the operators is given by the following list, in increasing order: $+$, $|$, $.$, $\backslash A$, $[f]$ (parentheses will be avoided wherever possible). We extend f to *Act* by decreeing $f(\tau) = \tau$ and we assume that *Vis* is finite. In the following, given a set A of actions, we use $\mu \in A$ as shorthand for $\mu \in (A \cup \overline{A})$.

An *operational semantics* OP is given by a set of inference rules defining a relation $\rightarrow_{OP} \subseteq Terms \times Act \times Terms$. Each rule has a *conclusion* and zero or more *hypotheses*. The relation is the least relation satisfying the rules. If $(p, \mu, q) \in \rightarrow_{OP}$, we write $p \xrightarrow{\mu}_{OP} q$. The rules defining the semantics of CCS [20], from now on referred to as SOS, are recalled in Figure 1. We have omitted the symmetric version of the rules **Sum** and **Par**.

A *(labelled) transition system* is a quadruple (S, T, R, s_0), where S is a set of states, T is a set of transition labels, $s_0 \in S$ is the initial state, and $R \subseteq S \times T \times S$ is a set of transitions. Given a transition $t = (s, u, s') \in R$, s is denoted as *source* of t.

Given a relation $\rightarrow$, if $\sigma \in Act^*$ and $\sigma = \mu_1 \ldots \mu_n, n \geq 1$, we write $p \xrightarrow{\sigma} q$ if $p \xrightarrow{\mu_1} \cdots \xrightarrow{\mu_n} q$; we also write $p \xrightarrow{\lambda} p$.
If $p \xrightarrow{\sigma} q$ for some σ, we say that q is a derivative of p by $\rightarrow$. We denote as $\mathcal{D}_{\rightarrow}(p)$ the set of the derivatives of p by $\rightarrow$.

Given a term p and an operational semantics OP, the transition system $OP(p) = (\mathcal{D}_{OP}(p), Act, \rightarrow_{OP}, p)$ is the *operational semantics of* p by OP. The *standard semantics* of a term p is $SOS(p)$.

A CCS term p is *guarded* if each constant occurring in p occurs within a sub-term of p with form $\mu.q$, it is *unguarded* otherwise. We assume that all the constant bodies are guarded. Moreover, p is said to be *finite* if $SOS(p)$ has a finite number of states. In the paper we consider only finite CCS terms. Syntactic characterizations of finite terms can be found in [2, 19].

$$\textbf{Act}\ \frac{}{\mu.p \xrightarrow{\mu} p} \qquad \textbf{Sum}\ \frac{p \xrightarrow{\mu} p'}{p+q \xrightarrow{\mu} p'} \qquad \textbf{Par}\ \frac{p \xrightarrow{\mu} p'}{p|q \xrightarrow{\mu} p'|q}$$

$$\textbf{Com}\ \frac{p \xrightarrow{\mu} p' \quad q \xrightarrow{\overline{\mu}} q'}{p|q \xrightarrow{\tau} p'|q'} \qquad \textbf{Res}\ \frac{p \xrightarrow{\mu} p'}{p\backslash A \xrightarrow{\mu} p'\backslash A}\ \mu \notin A \qquad \textbf{Rel}\ \frac{p \xrightarrow{\mu} p'}{p[f] \xrightarrow{f(\mu)} p'[f]}$$

$$\textbf{Con}\ \frac{p_x \xrightarrow{\mu} p'}{x \xrightarrow{\mu} p'}\ x \stackrel{def}{=} p_x$$

Fig. 1. The *SOS* rules

2.1 Notations

Let be given a relation $\rightarrow$ between terms. We use the following notations.
Given a term p, we write $p \not\rightarrow$, if no p', μ exist such that $p \xrightarrow{\mu} p'$; while we write $p \xrightarrow{\mu}$ (resp. $p \rightarrow$), if p' exists such that $p \xrightarrow{\mu} p'$ (resp. p' and μ exist such that $p \xrightarrow{\mu} p'$).
Given a term p, we denote by $\mathcal{M}_{\rightarrow}(p) = \{\mu \in Act | p \xrightarrow{\mu}\}$ the set of the actions that p can perform, i.e the labels of the transitions having p as source.

Given $\sigma \in Act^*$, the set of actions occurring in σ is denoted by $\mathcal{A}(\sigma) = \{\alpha | \alpha \textit{ or } \overline{\alpha} \textit{ occurs in } \sigma\}$.

3 Deadlock and deadlock freeness

Deadlock can be characterized in a parametric way with respect to a relation given by an operational semantics: given a relation $\rightarrow$, a CCS term p is $\rightarrow$ *deadlocked* if $p \not\rightarrow$. Note that by this characterization we do not distinguish between correct termination and deadlock. We now define *deadlock sensitivity* (and *deadlock freeness*) with respect to a semantic relation $\rightarrow$:

Definition 1 ($\rightarrow$ deadlock sensitivity, $\rightarrow$ deadlock freeness). Let be given a CCS term p and a relation $\rightarrow$ between terms.

1. p is $\rightarrow$ *deadlock sensitive* if and only if $q \in \mathcal{D}_{\rightarrow}(p)$ exists such that $q \not\rightarrow$;
2. p is $\rightarrow$ *deadlock free* if and only if it is not $\rightarrow$ deadlock sensitive.

Given an operational semantics OP, we say that p is OP deadlock sensitive (OP deadlock free) if it is $\rightarrow_{OP}$ deadlock sensitive ($\rightarrow_{OP}$ deadlock free). Note that, given a term p and an operational semantics OP, p is OP deadlock sensitive if and only if $OP(p)$ contains at least a state which is source of no transition (sink state). Thus, usually, algorithms for deadlock checking of CCS terms check whether, for a given term p, $SOS(p)$ contains a sink state.

In the following we use the predicate $\delta(p)$, which is true if and only if p is SOS deadlocked. Note that it is decidable whether a term is SOS deadlocked. We call δ-terms SOS deadlocked terms. The following theorem states some results on SOS deadlock sensitivity for CCS terms.

Theorem 2.

1. *nil is SOS deadlock sensitive;*
2. *$\mu.p$ is SOS deadlock sensitive if and only if p is SOS deadlock sensitive;*
3. *$p+q$ is SOS deadlock sensitive if and only if one of the following conditions holds:*
   i) $p \not\rightarrow_{SOS}$ and $q \not\rightarrow_{SOS}$;
   ii) p is SOS deadlock sensitive and $p \rightarrow_{SOS}$;
   ii) q is SOS deadlock sensitive and $q \rightarrow_{SOS}$;
4. *$p|q$ is SOS deadlock sensitive if both p and q are SOS deadlock sensitive;*
5. *$p\backslash A$ is SOS deadlock sensitive if and only if q exists, such that $\mathcal{M}_{\rightarrow_{SOS}}(q) \subseteq A$ and $p \stackrel{\sigma}{\rightarrow}_{SOS} q$ with $\mathcal{A}(\sigma) \cap A = \emptyset$;*
6. *$p[f]$ is SOS deadlock sensitive if and only if p is SOS deadlock sensitive;*
7. *if $x \stackrel{def}{=} p$, x is SOS deadlock sensitive if and only if p is SOS deadlock sensitive.*

Note that for all operators except restriction deadlock sensitivity of a term can be derived by deadlock sensitivity of the operands: $\mu.p$ has the same deadlock possibilities of p; $p|q$ has a deadlocked derivative if both p and q have one; while $p+q$ has a deadlocked derivative if either p or q has a deadlocked derivative without being a δ-term; finally, $p[f]$ has a deadlocked derivative if and only if p has one. On the contrary, we cannot derive deadlock freeness of $p\backslash A$ from deadlock freeness of p: in fact, it is possible that p has a deadlocked derivative, while $p\backslash A$ is deadlock free, and vice-versa. For example, $a.x$ with $x \stackrel{def}{=} c.x$ is deadlock free, while $(a.x)\backslash\{a\}$ is not; on the other hand, $(a.nil + c.x)\backslash\{a\}$ is deadlock free, while $a.nil+c.x$ is not. Point 5 of theorem 2 says that $p\backslash A$ can have a deadlocked derivative $q\backslash A$ only if q is reachable from p (possibly $q = p$) with a sequence of actions not belonging to A and the possible moves of q are contained in A. For example, for the deadlock free term $(a.nil + c.x)\backslash\{a\}$, no derivative of $a.nil + c.x$ exists with the required property, while for $(b.a.nil + c.x)\backslash\{a\}$ and $(a.x)\backslash\{a\}$, $a.nil$ and $a.x$ are the required derivatives, respectively.

4 Non-standard semantics

Our approach to deadlock checking of a term p consists in defining a non-standard operational semantics ABS such that $ABS(p)$ is considerably smaller than $SOS(p)$ and contains a sink state if and only if $SOS(p)$ contains one such state. In other words, $ABS(p)$ is an abstraction of $SOS(p)$ preserving deadlock freeness. As a consequence, deadlock can be checked on $ABS(p)$ by verifying whether it contains a sink state. Obviously, the advantage we gain depends both on the degree of the reduction (i.e. the ratio between the number of states of $ABS(p)$ and that of $SOS(p)$) and on the complexity of generating $ABS(p)$ with respect to the complexity of generating $SOS(p)$.

The idea underlying our semantics is that a term p having a derivative q which is SOS deadlocked is moved to q with only one transition. In order to obtain this behaviour, the rules for action-prefixing of the non-standard semantics have been designed in such a way that they look ahead until they find a derivative q which is a δ-term and, if and when they find it, they move p to q. Moreover, this transition is labelled by τ, since the name of the actions leading to a deadlock is not relevant. For example, the non-standard transition system $ABS(a.b.c.nil)$ contains the only transition $a.b.c.nil \xrightarrow{\tau}_{ABS} nil$.

On the other hand, it is obviously possible that no δ-term is reachable from p; thus, to make effective our method, we must choose a way to stop our looking ahead also in this case. We could, for example, state a limit to the length of the sequence of actions we examine; alternatively, we can stop when a term with a particular syntactic structure is reached. Our solution is of this last type: we stop when we reach a term q which is either SOS deadlocked or *unguarded* (i.e. before expanding a constant). Thus, for each term p consisting of a sequence of n actions followed by a δ-term q, we generate a transition system with only two states p and q, independently from the length of the sequence, while $SOS(p)$ has $n+1$ states.

However, the choice of looking ahead for a deadlocked or unguarded term and of labelling the transitions only by τ actions is not always safe when we consider the restriction operator. In fact we cannot hide the actions involved in a restriction (*restricted action* from now on): such actions can be either not executable (as occurs for a in $(a.b.x)\backslash\{a\}$) or able to participate in a communication, (as for a in $(a.x|\bar{a}.y)\backslash\{a\}$); in the first case, the term is deadlocked; in the second case, the communication can be executed. Thus a restricted action must always be considered and cannot miss its identity.

Another problem is caused by restriction in connection with summation. To exemplify this problem, that we call *summation+restriction anomaly*, consider the terms $(a.b.nil + c.x)\backslash\{b\}$ and $(b.nil + c.x)\backslash\{b\}$, with $x \stackrel{def}{=} c.x$. The former is deadlock sensitive, while the latter is deadlock free. Nevertheless, if a (which is not restricted) is hidden, the two terms move to the same deadlock free term x. In fact, it is the action a that leads to a sink state (i.e. the state in which b cannot be performed). In other words, while non-restricted actions can be always hidden when we are not in a summation context, when we derive a term p occurring as an operand of a summation, we must preserve its ability of performing a non-restricted action. Thus the action-prefixing rules of the non-standard semantics must be defined in such a way that

- in a summation context, an action is hidden only if it is neither restricted nor immediately preceding a restricted one;
- outside summation contexts, an action is hidden only if not restricted.

In order to manage the two cases, we define two relations (arrows) between terms: by $\Rightarrow$ we derive terms occurring in a summation context, by $\rightarrow$ we handle the other terms; thus, the initial term is derived by $\rightarrow$, while $\Rightarrow$ is introduced by the summation rules.

We have pointed out above that we need to know whether an action belongs to some restriction set in the term being derived at the top level. For example, when we examine $a.b.x$, while building the inference diagram for a move of $(a.b.x)\backslash\{a\}$, we must know that a belongs to a restriction set. But this information cannot be retrieved from $a.b.x$, because it is a global information with respect to it.
To solve this problem we enrich the relations $\rightarrow$ and $\Rightarrow$ by an *environment* $\rho \subseteq Vis$, keeping the set of actions on which some restriction holds, and define $\rightarrow_\rho$ and $\Rightarrow_\rho$ in such a way that both perform the actions in ρ and moreover $\Rightarrow_\rho$ performs also the actions preceding an action in ρ. The initial term is derived by $\rightarrow_\emptyset$. The environment is modified only by the restriction rules which add to the previous environment a new restriction set. During the proof of a term p, we derive a sub-term q with an environment which is the union of the restriction sets occurring in all terms containing q in p. For example, if the term derived at the top level is $((a.b.x)\backslash\{a\}|q)\backslash\{b\}$, we derive $a.b.x$ considering the environment $\{a,b\}$.
Formally, each rule defining the relations $\rightarrow_\rho$ and $\Rightarrow_\rho$ is intended as a set of rules, one for each environment ρ. The treatment of environments is the nucleus of our the non-standard semantics.
In the following, we explain the ABS rules case by case. In all rules the notation $p \overset{\nu \in \rho}{\rightarrow}_\rho p'$ stands for $p \overset{\nu}{\rightarrow}_\rho p'$ with side condition $\nu \in \rho$ (the same for $\nu \notin \rho$). Moreover, we use the predicate $\mathcal{G}(p)$ which is *true* if and only if p is guarded.

Action-prefixing rules

The rules in figure 2 handle action-prefixing outside summation contexts. Given the term $\mu.p$, rule $\mathbf{Act}_1$ looks ahead until a δ-term or an unguarded term q is reached, provided that the skipped actions do not belong to ρ; if such term is reached, $\mu.p$ is moved to q by $\mathbf{Act}_2$ and the transition is labelled by τ. Instead, if $\mu \in \rho$, $\mathbf{Act}_3$ is used, imposing to perform the action with its own name.

To derive $\mu.p$ in a summation context the relation $\Rightarrow_\rho$ is used instead of $\rightarrow_\rho$. The action-prefixing rules for $\Rightarrow_\rho$ are shown in Figure 3: $\mathbf{Act}_1$ is split into two rules ($\mathbf{Act}'_{11}$ and $\mathbf{Act}'_{12}$) to better observe the action ν performed by p after μ.

Act$_1$	$\dfrac{p \overset{\nu}{\rightarrow}_\rho p'}{\mu.p \overset{\nu}{\rightarrow}_\rho p'}\ \mu \notin \rho,\ \mathcal{G}(p)$
Act$_2$	$\dfrac{}{\mu.p \overset{\tau}{\rightarrow}_\rho p}\ \mu \notin \rho, (\neg\mathcal{G}(p)\ or\ \delta(p))$
Act$_3$	$\dfrac{}{\mu.p \overset{\mu}{\rightarrow}_\rho p}\ \mu \in \rho$

Fig. 2. *ABS*-**Act** rules for $\rightarrow_\rho$

Act$'_{11}$	$\dfrac{p \overset{\nu \notin \rho}{\Rightarrow}_\rho p'}{\mu.p \overset{\nu}{\Rightarrow}_\rho p'}\ \mu \notin \rho,\ \mathcal{G}(p)$
Act$'_{12}$	$\dfrac{p \overset{\nu \in \rho}{\Rightarrow}_\rho p'}{\mu.p \overset{\tau}{\Rightarrow}_\rho p}\ \mu \notin \rho,\ \mathcal{G}(p)$
Act$'_2$	$\dfrac{}{\mu.p \overset{\tau}{\Rightarrow}_\rho p}\ \mu \notin \rho, (\neg\mathcal{G}(p)\ or\ \delta(p))$
Act$'_3$	$\dfrac{}{\mu.p \overset{\mu}{\Rightarrow}_\rho p}\ \mu \in \rho$

Fig. 3. *ABS*-**Act** rules for $\Rightarrow_\rho$

In fact, when such action does not belong to the environment (**Act**$'_{11}$), it is hidden and the proof goes on; otherwise (**Act**$'_{12}$) a transition is generated, labelled by τ (for any μ). Moreover, **Act**$'_2$ and **Act**$'_3$ are similar to **Act**$_2$ and **Act**$_3$ of Figure 2, respectively.

Summation rules

Figure 4 shows the rules for summation **Sum** and **Sum**$'$, for $\rightarrow_\rho$ and $\Rightarrow_\rho$, respectively (the symmetric rules are not shown). The important point to remark is that the hypothesis of **Sum** introduces $\Rightarrow_\rho$ in order to overcome the summation+restriction anomaly.

$$\textbf{Sum}\quad \frac{p \overset{\mu}{\Rightarrow}_{\rho} p'}{p+q \overset{\mu}{\rightarrow}_{\rho} p'} \qquad \textbf{Sum}'\quad \frac{p \overset{\mu}{\Rightarrow}_{\rho} p'}{p+q \overset{\mu}{\Rightarrow}_{\rho} p'}$$

Fig. 4. *ABS*-**Sum** rules

Restriction and Relabelling rules

The restriction and relabelling rules rules handle the environment. The restriction rules for $\rightarrow_\rho$ and $\Rightarrow_\rho$ are shown in Figure 5: $p\backslash A$ produces μ, if p is able to produce $\mu \notin A$ in the environment $\rho \cup A$. Thus, if ρ is the environment occurring in the conclusion, the set A is added to ρ in the hypothesis of the rule: the restricted actions of p are those in ρ and those in A.

$$\textbf{Res}\quad \frac{p \overset{\mu}{\rightarrow}_{\rho\cup A} p'}{p\backslash A \overset{\mu}{\rightarrow}_{\rho} p'\backslash A}\ \mu \notin A \qquad \textbf{Res}'\quad \frac{p \overset{\mu}{\Rightarrow}_{\rho\cup A} p'}{p\backslash A \overset{\mu}{\Rightarrow}_{\rho} p'\backslash A}\ \mu \notin A$$

Fig. 5. *ABS*-**Res** rules

The rules for relabelling, shown in Figure 6, derive the term in the hypothesis by $\rightarrow_{f^{-1}(\rho)}$ ($\Rightarrow_{f^{-1}(\rho)}$) if $\rightarrow_\rho$ ($\Rightarrow_\rho$) occurs in the conclusion: in fact, in order to capture the actions in ρ of $p[f]$, we must capture the actions in $f^{-1}(\rho)$ of p.

$$\textbf{Rel}\quad \frac{p \overset{\mu}{\rightarrow}_{f^{-1}(\rho)} p'}{p[f] \overset{f(\mu)}{\rightarrow}_{\rho} p'[f]} \qquad \textbf{Rel}'\quad \frac{p \overset{\mu}{\Rightarrow}_{f^{-1}(\rho)} p'}{p[f] \overset{f(\mu)}{\Rightarrow}_{\rho} p'[f]}$$

Fig. 6. The *ABS*-**Rel** rules

Parallel composition and constant rules

The rules for constants and parallel composition, shown in Figure 7, are similar to the corresponding *SOS* ones (the symmetric rules of **Par** and **Par′** have been omitted). Note that only actions belonging to ρ are executed with their name and thus can communicate.

$$\textbf{Par}\quad \frac{p \stackrel{\mu}{\rightarrow}_\rho p'}{p|q \stackrel{\mu}{\rightarrow}_\rho p'|q} \qquad\qquad \textbf{Par}'\quad \frac{p \stackrel{\mu}{\Rightarrow}_\rho p'}{p|q \stackrel{\mu}{\Rightarrow}_\rho p'|q}$$

$$\textbf{Com}\quad \frac{p \stackrel{\mu}{\rightarrow}_\rho p',\ q \stackrel{\overline{\mu}}{\rightarrow}_\rho q'}{p|q \stackrel{\tau}{\rightarrow}_\rho p'|q'} \qquad\qquad \textbf{Com}'\quad \frac{p \stackrel{\mu}{\Rightarrow}_\rho p',\ q \stackrel{\overline{\mu}}{\Rightarrow}_\rho q'}{p|q \stackrel{\tau}{\Rightarrow}_\rho p'|q'}$$

$$\textbf{Con}\quad \frac{p \stackrel{\mu}{\rightarrow}_\rho p'}{x \stackrel{\mu}{\rightarrow}_\rho p'}\ x \stackrel{def}{=} p \qquad\qquad \textbf{Con}'\quad \frac{p \stackrel{\mu}{\Rightarrow}_\rho p'}{x \stackrel{\mu}{\Rightarrow}_\rho p'}\ x \stackrel{def}{=} p$$

Fig. 7. *ABS*-**Par** and **Con** rules

We now show some examples.

Example 1. Consider the deadlock sensitive term $(a.b.nil + c.x)\backslash\{b\}$, showing an example of summation+restriction anomaly. Since

$b.nil \stackrel{b}{\Rightarrow}_{\{b\}} nil$, $(\mathbf{Act}'_3)$, thus

$a.b.nil \stackrel{\tau}{\Rightarrow}_{\{b\}} b.nil(\mathbf{Act}'_{12})$, consequently,

$a.b.nil + c.x \stackrel{\tau}{\rightarrow}_{\{b\}} b.nil$ (**Sum**) and finally

$(a.b.nil + c.x)\backslash\{b\} \stackrel{\tau}{\rightarrow}_{\emptyset} (b.nil)\backslash\{b\}$ (**Res**)

and a deadlocked derivative is reached.

Example 2. Now consider the term $(b.nil + c.x)\backslash\{b\}$, with $x \stackrel{def}{=} c.x$. We have that

$b.nil \stackrel{b}{\Rightarrow}_{\{b\}} nil$ $(\mathbf{Act}'_3)$ and $c.x \stackrel{\tau}{\Rightarrow}_{\{b\}} x$ $(\mathbf{Act}'_2)$

thus the only move of $(b.nil + c.x)\backslash\{b\}$ is

$(b.nil + c.x)\backslash\{b\} \stackrel{\tau}{\rightarrow}_{\emptyset} x\backslash\{b\}$ (**Res**), and

$x\backslash\{b\} \stackrel{\tau}{\rightarrow}_{\emptyset} x\backslash\{b\}$

As a consequence, by the ABS rules, the terms of the examples 1 and 2, have (correctly) different transition systems, deadlock sensitive and deadlock free, respectively.

Note that $a.b.nil$ and $b.nil$, when derived outside summation contexts (and in the same environment $\{b\}$), exhibit the same behaviour:

$$a.b.nil \xrightarrow{b}_{\{b\}} nil \text{ and } b.nil \xrightarrow{b}_{\{b\}} nil.$$

4.1 Correctness of the *ABS* semantics

The non-standard semantics is defined as follows:

Definition 3. The non-standard semantics relation is defined as $\rightarrow_{ABS} = \rightarrow_{\emptyset}$.

Now we state some results holding for the non-standard semantics. First we state some results on the states of the abstract transition system and give some relations among the arrows we have defined. Then we state the main theorem of the paper, i.e. deadlock freeness preservation by the non-standard semantics. The proofs of the theorems can be found in [12].

The following lemma describes the behaviour of the ABS semantics. In fact it asserts that the label of each transition belonging to $\rightarrow_\rho$ or $\Rightarrow_\rho \rightarrow_\rho$ is either τ or an action belonging to ρ, i.e. no action is visible except those in ρ. Moreover, if q is reachable from p by $\rightarrow_\rho$ or $\Rightarrow_\rho$, then q is reachable from p by a non-empty sequence of transitions of $\rightarrow_{SOS}$.

Lemma 4. *Let be given a CCS term p. For each $\rho \subseteq Vis$, if $p \xrightarrow{\mu}_\rho q$ or $p \stackrel{\mu}{\Rightarrow}_\rho q$, then*

1. $\mu \in \{\tau\} \cup \rho$;
2. $p \xrightarrow{\sigma}_{SOS} q$ *for some* $\sigma \neq \lambda$;

The following theorem is a straightforward consequence of lemma 4 and characterizes the states of $ABS(p)$ as a subset of the states of $SOS(p)$.

Theorem 5. *Given a CCS term p, $q \in \mathcal{D}_{\rightarrow_{ABS}}(p)$ implies $q \in \mathcal{D}_{\rightarrow_{SOS}}(p)$.*

Note that, since $SOS(p)$ is finite, this theorem implies the finiteness of $ABS(p)$ too.

The following lemmas show some properties of $\rightarrow_\rho$ and $\Rightarrow_\rho$.

Lemma 6. *Given a CCS term p, for each $\rho \subseteq Vis$ it holds that:*

1. $p \not\rightarrow_{SOS}$ *if and only if* $p \not\Rightarrow_\rho$ *and* $p \not\rightarrow_{SOS}$ *if and only if* $p \not\rightarrow_\rho$;
2. $p \xrightarrow{\mu \notin \rho}_{SOS}$ *if and only if* $p \stackrel{\nu \notin \rho}{\Rightarrow}_\rho$;
3. $p \xrightarrow{\mu \in \rho}_{SOS}$ *if and only if* $p \stackrel{\mu \in \rho}{\Rightarrow}_\rho$.

The first point asserts that the terms not moved by $\rightarrow_{SOS}$ coincide with the terms not moved by $\rightarrow_\rho$ and $\Rightarrow_\rho$. The second and third points state a property of $\Rightarrow_\rho$ suitable to overcome the summation+restriction anomaly: the moves of a term p by $\rightarrow_{SOS}$ "correspond" to the moves of p by $\Rightarrow_\rho$, in the sense that p has the same ability by $\rightarrow_{SOS}$ and by $\Rightarrow_\rho$ of producing actions belonging to ρ and actions not belonging to ρ.

Lemma 7. *Let be given $\rho \subseteq Vis$. If $\sigma \in Act^*$, let $\sigma\downarrow_\rho$ be the sequence obtained from σ by deleting all the actions not occurring in ρ. Let $\rightsquigarrow_\rho \in \{\Rightarrow_\rho, \rightarrow_\rho\}$. Then*

$$p \xrightarrow{\sigma}_{SOS} r \text{ if and only if } p \overset{\sigma'}{\rightsquigarrow}_\rho s$$

with $\sigma\downarrow_\rho = \sigma'\downarrow_\rho$

The above lemma states that a term p is able to perform the same sequences of actions belonging to ρ by $\rightarrow_{SOS}$ and by $\rightarrow_\rho$ or $\Rightarrow_\rho$.

The following theorem assures the correctness of the *ABS* semantics: deadlock freeness is preserved.

Theorem 8 (Main theorem). *Given a CCS term p, p is SOS deadlock sensitive if and only if p is ABS deadlock sensitive.*

The proof of the theorem can be done by defining *ABS* deadlock in a structural way as well as theorem 2 does for *SOS*, and using the lemmas above.

Note that, if we derive a term using the relation $\Rightarrow_\emptyset$, the size of the corresponding transition system is in general larger than the one built exploiting also $\rightarrow_\emptyset$, but deadlock freeness is still preserved.

4.2 A complete example

We consider the classical *mutual exclusion* problem regarding n processes sharing a common *resource* by means of the operations of *acquire* and *release*. The following CCS program describes the mutual exclusion on the resource r shared by processes x, y, z.

$$p = (x|y|z|r)\backslash\{acq, rel\}$$

where:

$$x \stackrel{def}{=} a_1.acq.b_1.rel.x$$

$$y \stackrel{def}{=} a_2.acq.b_2.rel.y$$

$$z \stackrel{def}{=} a_3.acq.b_3.rel.z$$

$$r \stackrel{def}{=} \overline{acq}.\overline{rel}.r$$

While $SOS(p)$ has 32 states, $ABS(p)$, shown in Figure 8, has 4 states. In general, for n processes, the states of $SOS(p)$ are $2^n(n+1)$, while $ABS(p)$ has $n+1$ states.

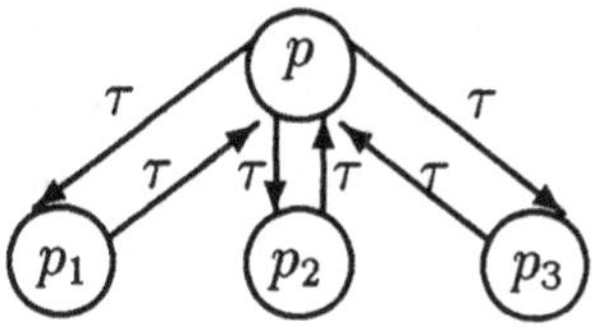

$$p = (x|y|z|r)\backslash\{acq, rel\}$$
$$p_1 = (b_1.rel.x|y|z|\overline{rel}.r)\backslash\{acq, rel\}$$
$$p_2 = (x|b_2.rel.y|z|\overline{rel}.r)\backslash\{acq, rel\}$$
$$p_3 = (x|y|b_3.rel.z|\overline{rel}.r)\backslash\{acq, rel\}$$

Fig. 8. $ABS(p)$

5 Considerations and related works

First of all we recall that static deadlock checking in concurrent systems is an intractable problem [25]: i.e., each algorithm has an exponential complexity, in the general case. Thus a method can be more efficient than another one in some cases and less efficient in some other cases.

In general, each approach aiming at reducing state space during the transition system generation is valuable on the basis of the trade-off between the number of states and the cost of a single transition. In general, the cost (in terms of memory space) of generating a single transition increases with the decreasing of the number of states of the transition system. With our approach, the states of the standard transition system we hide occur within the proof of some move and thus still need memory space to be stored. For example, the state *b.nil* of $SOS(a.b.nil)$, not included in $ABS(a.b.nil)$ occurs in the proof of the move $a.b.nil \xrightarrow{\tau}_{\emptyset} nil$. The advantage of considering these states only in the proofs is that the memory allocated for a proof can be deallocated once generated the transition and reallocated for another transition proof. But this can be considered as an advantage only as long as the proof of a single transition does not need a memory space close to the memory for storing the whole standard transition system. Our choice is to limit the depth of the proofs of the transitions by means of a syntactic criterion: if we do not reach a deadlocked term, we stop when we encounter an unguarded term. Note that our approach belongs to an intermediate level between a purely semantic and a syntactic one. In fact we prefer to stop the proof of a single transition of a term p when a syntactically well defined derivative of p is reached, without trying to go on until a possible cycle in the proof is recognized. As a consequence, terms having isomorphic SOS transition systems may have different ABS ones, as for example, the term $a.b.nil$ above and $a.y$ with $y \stackrel{def}{=} b.nil$: $SOS(a.b.nil)$ is isomorphic (up to the labels of the states) to $SOS(a.y)$, while $ABS(a.b.nil)$ has two states and $ABS(a.y)$ has three states.

A well-known approach to verification is the *on the fly* method, where, in order to verify a property, the whole transition system is not generated, but the property is checked during the generation. Roughly speaking, the idea is that a depth-first traversal of the transition system can be performed, and only the current path has to be stored, while memory is deallocated when verifying another path [8, 13, 14, 17, 18].

Our approach is better than the on the fly method, from the point of view of the number of stored states, if and only if the longest path (without repetitions) of the standard transition system for a term p has more states than $ABS(p)$. On the other hand, the two approaches do not contrast each other, and on the fly verification can be made using our non-standard semantics instead of the standard one, thus furtherly reducing the state space.

Other approaches to deadlock detection, as, for example [16, 27], reduce the state space of the transition system by exploring only one sequence (interleaving) of transitions for each possible partial ordering of transitions from a state to another one. The algorithms to do this need a set of ad hoc notions, while our method is very simple and straightforward since it is based on a non-standard semantics. Moreover it is easily implementable. A comparison of our approach with these methods, from the point of view of the memory space, can be done case by case and depends on the number of unguarded states of the transition system: our method can be better when the length of the sequence of transitions representing an interleaving of actions leading from a state p to a state q is less than the number of unguarded states between p to q.

A comparison of our method can be made with syntactic transformations which substitute unrestricted actions by τ and possibly simplify sequences of τ actions [5]. The power of our method, because of its flexibility, is greater than that of a purely syntactic approach, as can be seen the following example.

Example 3. Consider the term

$$q = (x|y)\backslash\{b\} + (x|a.b.y)\backslash\{a\}$$

where

$$x \overset{def}{=} \overline{a}.\overline{b}.x$$

$$y \overset{def}{=} c.b.y$$

We have that the constant x is used in different restriction environments: $(x|y)\backslash\{b\}$ is derived with environment $\{b\}$, while $(x|a.b.y)\backslash\{a\}$ with $\{a\}$. This allows us, for example, to ignore $\overline{a}$, occurring in the body of x, while deriving $(x|y)\backslash\{b\}$. The transition system $ABS(q)$ (shown in Figure 9) has 3 states, while $SOS(q)$ has 9 states.

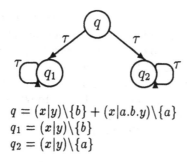

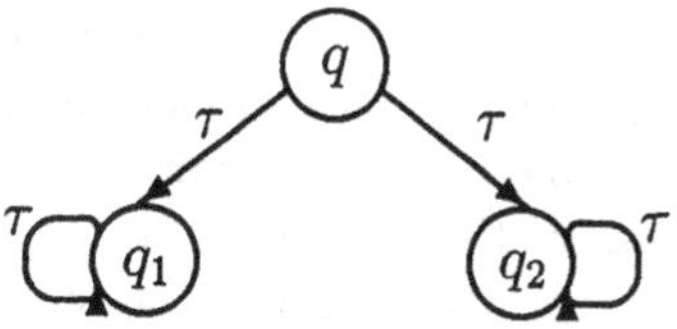

$q = (x|y)\backslash\{b\} + (x|a.b.y)\backslash\{a\}$
$q_1 = (x|y)\backslash\{b\}$
$q_2 = (x|y)\backslash\{a\}$

Fig. 9. $ABS(q)$

Note that a syntactic method, like that in [5] cannot make any simplification of the body of the constant x, since the set of the restrictions includes all actions of x (a and b), that thus cannot be substituted by τ. Nevertheless, x is used in different restriction environments ($\{a\}$ and $\{b\}$), in each of which some unrestricted action exists that we are able to dynamically skip. Our method is able to consider, for each subterm in which a constant occurs, just the local restriction environment, so obtaining a more reduced transition system.

In [23], to check deadlock freeness of a CCS term, the term is first transformed into a Petri net [22] by means of a truly concurrent semantics of CCS, then the obtained net is reduced using known reduction techniques for Petri nets, and lastly the reduced net is checked for deadlock freeness. This method does not depend at all on the syntactic structure of the terms, and thus achieves the full generality of the semantic approaches; consequently, in some cases it can be better than ours, in terms of the size of the generated transition system. Nevertheless, apart the obvious considerations on its low uniformity (a different formalism, Petri nets, is used), the approach still suffers of the drawbacks of the semantic approaches (memory must be allocated to store the whole Petri net corresponding to a CCS program), even if at a lower degree, since the Petri net corresponding to a CCS program is "smaller" than the standard transition system.

5.1 Final remarks and future work

It may be interesting to note that all theorems stated in the paper also hold for infinite terms, even if our method cannot be applied to those terms in a decision procedure, since $ABS(p)$ may be infinite.

An interesting future work can be to characterize our approach as an *abstract interpretation* one: abstract interpretation is a well-known powerful and elegant method [9] for proving program properties. A starting point can be the paper [10], where a theory of abstract interpretations for rule-based semantics is shown.

One of the most appealing features of a non-standard operational approach is modularity: improvements of the method can be achieved by substituting a subset of the rules, for example those concerning an operator, with more "efficient" ones. The correctness of the new rules can be "locally" proved, without modifying the complete correctness proof. A possible improvement is that of defining rules for parallel composition able to move with only one transition both partners; for example $a.x|b.y$ can be moved with only one action to $x|y$. Moreover, some rules can be modified in order to restrict the states of $ABS(p)$ to contain only states labelled by deadlocked and unguarded terms. Some of these improvements are shown in [12].

We are actually developing a tool written in Prolog to check deadlock freeness of CCS terms, based on the ABS semantics. The tool will be included in the JACK environment [4], which is a verification system for process algebra description languages. The environment, among other tools for model checking of CCS processes, contains a set of non-standard semantics based tools by which it is possible to prove, for instance, finiteness of CCS programs.

References

1. S. Bensalem, A. Bouajjani, C. Loiseaux, J. Sifakis. *Property Preserving Simulations.* In Proceedings of the Fourth Workshop on Computer Aided Verification, 1992.
2. T. Bolognesi, S. Smolka. *Fundamental results for the verification of observational equivalence: a survey.* In Proc. IFIP WG 6.1 7th Conference on Protocol Specification, Testing and Verification. Amsterdam: North-Holland 1987.
3. A. Bouajjani, J.C. Fernandez, N. Halbwachs, P. Raymond, C. Ratel. *Minimal state graph generation.* Science of Computer Programming, 1992. Vol. 18(3), pp. 247-271.
4. A. Bouali, S. Gnesi, S. Larosa. *The integration Project for JACK Environment.* Bulletin of EATCS, n.54, October 1994, pp. 207-223.
5. G. Bruns. *A Practical Technique for Process Abstraction.* In Proceedings of th Fourth International Conference on Concurrency Theory (CONCUR'93), Lecture Notes in Computer Science, Springer-Verlag, 1993, pp. 37-49.

6. E.M. Clarke, O.Grumberg, D.E. Long. *Model Checking and Abstraction.* ACM Transactions on Programming Languages and Systems, 1994. Vol. 16 (5), pp. 1512-1542.
7. R. Cleaveland, J. Riely. *Testing-Based Abstractions for Value-Passing Systems.* Lecture Notes in Computer Science 836 (CONCUR'94), Springer-Verlag, 1994, pp. 417-432.
8. C. Courcoubetis, M. Vardi, P. Wolper, M. Yannakakis. *Memory Efficient Algorithms for the Verification of Temporal Properties.* In Workshop on Computer Aided Verification, DIMACS 90, June 1990.
9. P. Cousot and R. Cousot. *Systematic Design of Program Analysis Frameworks.* In Proc. 6th ACM Symp. Principles of Programming Languages (1979), pp. 269-282.
10. P. Cousot and R. Cousot. *Inductive Definitions, Semantics and Abstract Interpretations.* ACM Symp. Principles of Programming Languages, Albuquerque, 1992, pp. 83-94.
11. D. Dams, R. Gerth. G. Döhmen, R. Herrmann, P. Kelb, H. Pargmann. *Model Checking Using Adaptive State and Data Abstraction.* Lecture Notes in Computer Science 818 (CAV'94), Springer-Verlag, 1994, pp. 455-467.
12. N. De Francesco, A. Santone, G. Vaglini. *Reducing State Space with Non-Standard Semantics.* Internal Report IR-3/95, Dipartimento di Ingegneria dell'Informazione, Univ. of Pisa.
13. J.C. Fernandez, L. Mounier. *Verifying bisimulation on the fly.* In Third International Conference on Formal Description Techniques, FORTE'90, Madrid, November 1990.
14. J.C. Fernandez, L. Mounier. *"On th Fly" Verification of Behavioural Equivalences and Preordes.* In Proceedings of the Third International Conference on Computer-Aided Verification, Lecture Notes in Computer Science, Springer-Verlag, vol. 575 pp. 181-191, 1991.
15. P. Godefroid, P. Wolper. *A partial approach to model checking.* In Proceedings of the Sixth Annual IEEE Symposium on Logic in Computer Science (LICS), 1991.
16. P. Godefroid, P. Wolper. *Using Partial Orders for Efficient Verification of Deadlock Freedom and Safety Properties.* In Proceedings of the Third International Conference on Computer-Aided Verification, Lecture Notes in Computer Science, Springer-Verlag, vol. 575 pp. 332-342, 1991.
17. C. Jard, T. Jéron. *On-Line Model-Checking for Finite Linear Temporal Logic Specifications.* In International Workshop on Automatic Verification Methods for Finite State Systems, Lecture Notes in Computer Science, Springer-Verlag, vol. 407 pp. 189-196, 1989.
18. C. Jard, T. Jéron. *Bounded-memory Algorithms for Verification On-the-fly.* In Proceedings of the Third International Conference on Computer-Aided Verification, Lecture Notes in Computer Science, Springer-Verlag, vol. 575 pp. 192-201, 1991.
19. E. Madelaine, D. Vergamini. *Finiteness conditions and structural construction of automata for all process algebras.* In Proceedings, 2nd Workshop on Computer-Aided Verification. DIMACS Technical report 90-31, June 1990.
20. R. Milner. *Communication and Concurrency.* Prentice-Hall, 1989.
21. D. Peled. *All from one, one for all, on model-checking using representatives.* In Proceedings of the Fifth International Conference on Computer-Aided Verification, Lecture Notes in Computer Science, Springer-Verlag, 1993, pp. 409-423.
22. W.Reisig. *Petri Nets.* EATCS Monographs on Theoretical Computer Science 4 (Springer-Verlag, New York, 1985).

23. P. Rondogiannis, M.H.M Cheng. *Petri-net-based deadlock analysis of Process Algebra programs.* Science of Computer Programming, 1994. Vol. 23 (1), pp. 55-89.
24. J. Sifakis. *Property Preserving Homomorphisms of Transition Systems.* In Logics of Programs, Springer Verlag, 1983. Lecture Notes in Computer Science, vol. 164.
25. R.N. Taylor. *Complexity of analyzing the synchronization structure of concurrent programs.* Acta Informatica, 1983. Vol. 19, pp 57-84.
26. A. Valmari. *A Stubborn Attack on State Explosion.* In Proceedings of the Second International Conference on Computer-Aided Verification, Lecture Notes in Computer Science, Springer-Verlag, vol. 531 pp. 156-165, 1990.
27. A. Valmari, M. Clegg. *Reduced Labelled Transition Systems Save Verification Effort.* In Proceedings of the Second International Conference on Concurrency Theory (CONCUR'91), Lecture Notes in Computer Science, Springer-Verlag, 1991.

A Process Language for Statecharts *

Francesca Levi

Dipartimento di Informatica, Università di Pisa
Corso Italia 40, 56100, Pisa, Italy

Abstract. We define a compositional labelled transition system semantics for statecharts via a translation into a new process language called $\mathcal{SP}$. The main novelty of the language is an operator of process refinement, which reflects the statecharts hierarchical structure. The translation agrees with Pnueli and Shalev semantics of statecharts. However, since the language is parametric in the set of basic actions and in some operations over actions, other semantics of statecharts can be obtained by suitably instantiating the actions corresponding to transitions and the operations over actions.

1 Introduction

Statecharts [4] are a visual synchronous formalism for the specification of reactive systems, which is based on the idea of enriching state-transition diagrams with notions of hierarchy, concurrency and broadcast communication. These features permit high level and succinct descriptions. The underlying assumption of synchronous languages [2, 11, 3] is that the output of the system is simultaneous with the input that causes it. This *synchrony hypothesis* is indeed an abstraction and relies on the idea that the environment is discrete and that the system is faster than the environment. The approach has the clear advantage to permit to reason in abstract time without reference to the physical reaction time. However, the definition of a formal semantics of statecharts meets some intrinsic difficulties due to the well-known causal paradoxes, such as events disabling their own causes. Since the definition of a formal semantics for statecharts is quite complicated, there is no widely accepted semantics and many approaches have been proposed in the last years [5, 8, 7, 16, 6, 10]. The semantics of Pnueli and Shalev [13] is a very convincing proposal for dealing with causality problems. The main drawback of this proposal is that the semantics is not compositional.

In this paper we propose a compositional labelled transition system semantics for statecharts via a translation into a process language called $\mathcal{SP}$. The main novelty of the language is an operator of process refinement for representing the statecharts hierarchical structure. Moreover, $\mathcal{SP}$ processes have locations as counterpart of statecharts boxes. The language is general, namely it is parametric in the set of basic actions and in some operations over actions and other process calculi such as SCCS [12] and CBS [14] can easily be expressed into $\mathcal{SP}$.

* Research partially supported by Esprit BRA 8130 LOMAPS

We define the semantics of closed $\mathcal{SP}$ processes in the SOS style and we show a translation of statecharts into closed processes, which is correct with respect to the semantics of Pnueli and Shalev. The idea is to take a process where basic actions represent transitions and the corresponding communication and locations correspond to statechart boxes. The main problem is that the semantics of Pnueli and Shalev is not modular [7]. In other words, it is not possible to obtain the semantics of the whole statechart by considering the parts of the system as black boxes and by observing only their input-output behaviour. One way of achieving compositionality is to consider structured actions corresponding to transitions, where both the input-output and the causal ordering between input and output is represented. This is not surprising as already pointed out by many authors [16, 8, 6, 7]. However, it is imporant to stress that the translation is not ad hoc for the Pnueli and Shalev semantics, since other semantics of statecharts, such as the ones of [5, 10], can be obtained by taking different actions describing transitions and a different definition of parallel composition of actions.

The definition of a process algebra for statecharts provides a formal basis for verification, since it allows us to use various techniques proposed for process algebras such as equivalences, preorders and model checking. A process algebra for statecharts has been already presented in [17]. However, the translation of Uselton and Smolka does not give a labelled transition system semantics equivalent to the one of [13].

The paper is organized as follows. In section 2 statecharts are introduced. Section 3 presents the language $\mathcal{SP}$ and its operational semantics. Sections 4 shows how statecharts can be embedded into $\mathcal{SP}$. Finally section 5 discuss the relation of our semantics with the one of [17].

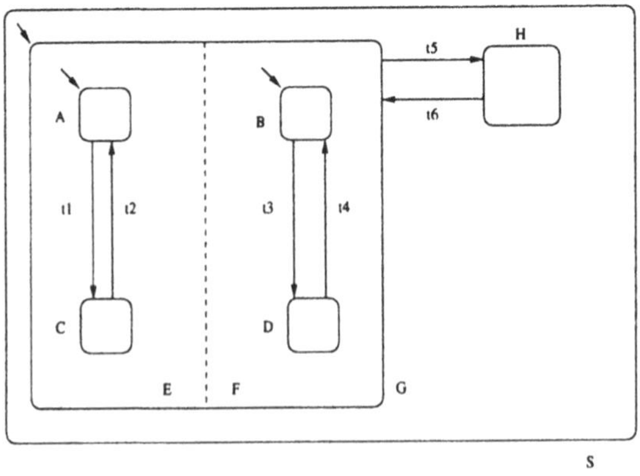

Fig. 1. A statechart

2 Introduction to Statecharts

In this section we introduce statecharts and briefly discuss the main features of the semantics proposed in [13].

A statechart specifies a reactive system, which continuously interacts with its environment by receiving and sending signals of a finite set Π of primitive events. We assume $nil \in \Pi$, where nil denotes the null event, and we denote by $\bar{\Pi} = \{\bar{e} \mid e \in \Pi\}$, where $\bar{e}$ is the negation of event e. For $\bar{e} \in \bar{\Pi}$, we denote by $\bar{\bar{e}} = e$.

In the following, we use the notation $i \in \{1, k\}$ for $i \in \{1, \ldots, k\}$.

Definition 1. A statechart over Π is defined as follows:

- a basic statechart $S : (\{S_1, \ldots, S_k\}, T, in, out, \chi, \delta)$ over Π, where
  - $\{S_1, \ldots, S_k\}$ is a set of boxes, such as $S_i \neq S$, for each $i \in \{1, k\}$. We define $boxes(S) = \{S\} \cup \{S_1, \ldots, S_k\}$.
  - T is a finite not empty set of transitions.
  - $out : T \to \{S_1, \ldots, S_k\}$, $in : T \to \{S_1, \ldots, S_k\}$ give the source and target states of transitions, respectively.
  - $\chi : T \to 2^{\Pi \cup \bar{\Pi}} \times 2^{\Pi}$ is the labelling function of transitions. We denote by $trigger(t)$ and $action(t)$ the first and second component of χ, respectively and we require $trigger(t), action(t) \neq \emptyset$ and $e, \bar{e} \notin trigger(t) \cup action(t)$.
  - $\delta : S \to \{S_1, \ldots S_k\}$ is the default function giving the default substate.

  If $k = 0$ then S is an *empty* statechart and $boxes(S) = \{S\}$.

- A refined statechart $\nabla(S, \{S_1, \ldots, S_k\})$ over Π, where
  - S is a basic non-empty statechart, where $boxes(S) = \{S\} \cup \{S_1, \ldots, S_k\}$.
  - $\{S_1, \ldots, S_k\}$ is a non-empty finite set of statecharts S_i over Π such that $\{S\} \cap boxes(S_i) = \emptyset$ and $boxes(S_i) \cap boxes(S_j) = \emptyset$, for all $i, j \in \{1, k\}$, such that $i \neq j$. Moreover, $boxes(\nabla(S, \{S_1, \ldots, S_k\})) = \{S\} \cup \bigcup_{i \in \{1,k\}} boxes(S_i)$.

- An AND statechart $S : \text{AND}(S_1, S_2)$ over Π iff
  - S_1, S_2 are a non-empty statecharts over Π, and $boxes(S) = \{S\} \cup \bigcup_{i \in \{1,2\}} boxes(S_i)$, and $\{S\} \cap boxes(S_i) = \emptyset$ and $boxes(S_i) \cap boxes(S_j) = \emptyset$, for all $i, j \in \{1, 2\}$, such that $i \neq j$.

Consider the statechart of figure 1, where transitions are labelled as follows

$$t_1 : a/b, t_2 : a/b, t_3 : b/nil, t_4 : b/nil$$
$$t_5 : d/nil, t_6 : d/nil.$$

Statecharts E and F are basic statecharts, while G : AND(E, F). Statechart of figure 1 is a refined statechart $\nabla(S, \{G, H\})$, where S is a basic statechart with boxes G and H. As shown by the picture, state G is refined by the parallel composition of E and F, while state H is refined by the empty statechart. Transitions are depicted by arrows and are labelled by a pair *trigger/action*. Intuitively, the trigger gives conditions on the input for the transition to be permorfed, while the action gives the set of generated signals. For instance t_1 requires event a from the environment and produces event b. Note that the trigger may contain negated events, where $\bar{a}$ is interpreted as "a is absent". For a basic statechart a state is distinguished as the default state by an entering arrow without source, such as state A in statechart E.

A configuration (global state) of a statechart is given by a maximal and consistent subset of boxes, where two states are consistent iff they are in two parallel components. Given $S_1, S_2 \in boxes(S)$, we denote by $LCA(S_1, S_2)$ the statechart S', such that $S' \in boxes(S)$ and $S_1, S_2 \in boxes(S')$ and, for all $S'' \in boxes(S)$, such that $S_1, S_2 \in boxes(S'')$, $S' \in boxes(S'')$.

Definition 2. The set $C(S)$ of configurations of a statechart S is given by the subsets $c \in 2^{boxes(S)}$ such that, for each $S_1, S_2 \in c$, $LCA(S_1, S_2)$ is an AND statechart and c is maximal.

A configuration $c \in C(S)$ is called a *default* configuration iff, for each $S' \in boxes(S)$, such that either S' is a basic statechart or a refined statechart, $\delta(S') \in c$. We denote by $\Delta(S)$ the default configuration of S, namely the initial configuration.

We briefly discuss the semantics of [13]. The semantics relies on the assumption that both the system and the environment can be described as discrete processes and that the reaction of the system is instantaneous. The environment prompts the system by means of a sequence of primitive events sets and the statechart reacts to each set of inputs by performing a *step*, that is a maximal set of parallel transitions taking the statechart to a new configuration and producing a set of outputs. A step satisfies some basic requirements, which can be summarized as the *synchrony hypothesis* and the principles of *causality* and *global consistency*.

By the synchrony hypothesis all the events generated by transitions taken in a step are simultaneous with inputs. Consider the statechart of figure 1 and the configuration $\{S, G, E, F, A, B\}$. If the environment communicates event a, transitions t_1 and t_3 are taken in the same step, since t_1 generates event b, which enables t_3. The reached configuration is $\{S, G, E, F, C, D\}$. On the other hand, if the environment produces d, then $\{t_5\}$ is a step and the reached configuration is $\{S, H\}$. Note that, if the environment produces both a and d, then both $\{t_1, t_3\}$ and $\{t_5\}$ are steps and there is a non deterministic choice.

The principle of causality requires the existence of a causal ordering between transitions taken in a step. Consider the statechart G of figure 1, where transitions t_1 and t_3 are labelled by a/b and b/a, respectively. If the current configuration is $\{G, E, F, A, B\}$ and if the environment communicates neither a nor b, the reaction of the system is the empty step, since each transition depends on the other.

Global consistency requires that the causes of a transition are never disallowed. Consider statechart G, where transitions t_1 and t_3, are labelled by $\bar{a}/b$ and b/a, respectively. If the current configuration is $\{G, E, F, A, B\}$ and if the environment produces neither a nor b, then no step is possible. Actually, t_1 is enabled with respect to the input and produces b which enables t_3. However, t_3 produces a which disables t_1. This is a so called causal paradox. Note that in this case the reaction of the system is not defined.

All these requirements are satisfied if a step is defined as a subset of transitions that is the fixpoint of a relation $En_{c,I}$. The idea is that $t \in En_{c,I}(T)$ iff t is enabled in configuration c with respect to input I assuming that transitions in T are taken.

We denote by $T(S)$ the set of transitions of S, namely the union of sets T, such that $S' : (\{S_1, \dots, S_k\}, T, in, out, \chi, \delta) \in boxes(S)$.

Definition 3. Let S be a statechart and $I \subseteq \Pi$.

- For $t_1, t_2 \in T(S)$, t_1 is *consistent* with t_2 iff $t_1 \in T(S_1), t_2 \in T(S_2)$, for $S_1, S_2 \in boxes(S)$, and $LCA(S_1, S_2)$ is an AND statechart.
- For $T \subseteq T(S)$, we define $con(T) = \{t \in T(S) \mid t$ is consistent with t' for all $t' \in T\}$.
- For $c \in C(S)$, we define $rel(c) = \{t \in T(S) \mid out(t) \in c\}$.
- We define $trig(I) = \{t \in T(S) \mid \forall e \in trigger(t), e \in I$ and $\forall \bar{e} \in trigger(t), e \notin I\}$.
- We define $En_{c,I}(T) = rel(c) \cap con(T) \cap trig(I \cup gen(T))$, where $gen(T) = \bigcup_{t \in T} action(t)$.

Definition 4. Given a configuration $c \in C(S)$ and a set of input signals $I \subseteq \Pi$, the set of transitions $T \subseteq T(S)$ is an *admissible step* with respect to c and I iff $En_{c,I}(T) = T$ and if T is *inseparable*, i.e. for each $T' \subset T$, $En_{c,I}(T') \cap (T - T') \neq \emptyset$.

The configuration $c' \in C(S)$ obtained from c via T is given by

$$c' = c - (\bigcup_{t \in T} boxes(out(t))) \cup (\bigcup_{t \in T} \Delta(in(t))).$$

Note that, when a step is performed, the reached configuration is the one containing the default configurations of the states that are the target of transitions in the step. The condition of inseparability guarantees the existence of a causal relation between transitions.

We use the notation $c \overset{I,O}{\Longrightarrow} c'$ to denote that there is a step from configuration c to configuration c' on input I, which produces output O.

It is important to stress that, in this approach, empty steps are admissible, while there are cases where the reaction is not defined, because of a causal paradox. These cases can be seen as run-time errors.

Different interpretations to causal paradoxes are given in the other semantics. In the original semantics of [5] a step is defined as a sequence of microsteps causally but not temporally related. The main difference is that a step is not required to be globally consistent. Consider statechart G, where transitions t_1 and t_3, are labelled by $\bar{a}/b$ and b/a, respectively. If the current configuration is $\{G, E, F, A, B\}$ and if the input is empty, then the step $\{t_1, t_3\}$ is admissible, since it is obtained by the sequence of microsteps $\{t_1\}, \{t_3\}$. Actually, t_1

is enabled with respect to the input and enables t_2. On the other hand, in the semantics of [10] a step is required to be globally consistent, but a different interpretation to negative conditions is given. For instance, in the example before $\{t_1\}$ is the only admissible step. The idea is that, even if t_3 is enabled, it is not performed since t_3 disables t_1. We believe that the semantics of Pnueli and Shalev gives the more natural interpretation to negative events so that they can be adequately used for expressing priorities and interrupts.

It is important to stress that a common feature of all the semantics for statecharts is the principle of causality. As pointed out in [7] this has the drawback that they cannot be modular.

3 The language $\mathcal{SP}$

In this section we present the process language $\mathcal{SP}$. We assume a set Act of basic actions, a set Loc of locations and a set Var of variables. Since a reactive system interacts continuously with the environment, basic actions tipically describe also the behaviour of the environment. On Act we assume an operation $\times : Act \times Act \to 2^{Act}$ of parallel composition and an operation $\# : Act \cup \{*\} \to 2^{Act}$. The idea is that actions $\#(a)$ are in conflict with action a, i.e. the environment cannot enable both a and a', if $a' \in \#(a)$. The action $\{*\}$ is used to give the semantics of the empty process. Moreover, we assume $\times$ to be associative, namely, for each $a_1, a_2, a_3 \in Act$, $a_1 \times (a_2 \times a_3) = (a_1 \times a_2) \times a_3$.

Definition 5. We define processes $\mathcal{SP}$ as follows:

$$\begin{aligned} \mathcal{B} &::= nil \mid a.t \mid b_1 + b_2 \\ \mathcal{T} &::= \ell :: b \mid rec\ x.t \mid t \bigtriangledown p \mid x \\ \mathcal{SP} &::= \ell :: t \mid \ell :: p_1 \times p_2 \end{aligned}$$

where $a \in Act$, $x \in Var$, $\ell \in Loc$.

Process $\ell :: t \in \mathcal{SP}$ denotes the process t at location ℓ and process $\ell :: p_1 \times p_2$ denotes the parallel composition of processes p_1 and p_2. As usual nil denotes the empty process, $b_1 + b_2$ denotes the choice between b_1 and b_2, while $a.t$ denotes process t prefixed by action a. Process $rec\ x.t$ is the classical recursive process and process $t \bigtriangledown p$ denotes process t refined by p. The choice for locations is motivated by the corresponding definition of boxes in statecharts.

As usual we assume $variables(p) = \{x \in Var \mid x \text{ is a subterm of } p\}$ and $free(p) = \{x \in variables(p) \mid x \text{ does not occur inside the scope of } rec\ x\}$.

Assume $p \in \mathcal{SP}$, we define the set of *current locations*, $loc(p)$ as

- $loc(\ell :: t) = \{\ell\} \cup loc(t)$;
- $loc(\ell :: p_1 \times p_2) = \{\ell\} \cup loc(p_1) \cup loc(p_2)$;
- $loc(\ell :: b) = \{\ell\}$;
- $loc(rec\ x.t) = loc(t)$;
- $loc(t \bigtriangledown p) = loc(t) \cup loc(p)$.

Intuitively, for a process p describing a statechart, $loc(p)$ will be the configuration represented by the process.

The operational semantics of the process language is given as a labelled transition system $(\mathcal{CSP}, \mathcal{S}(Act), \mapsto)$, where $\mathcal{CSP}$ is the subset of closed $\mathcal{SP}$ and $\mathcal{S}(Act)$ is the set of *semantic* actions, defined as follows.

Definition 6. Let Act be a set of basic actions. We define $\mathcal{S}(Act)$ as the set of *semantic* actions such that, for each $a \in Act$, $\tau \in \{\epsilon, \bar{\epsilon}\}$, $a : \tau \in \mathcal{S}(Act)$.

Types ϵ and $\bar{\epsilon}$ denote ***non-idle*** and ***idle*** actions, respectively. Idle actions are used to represent empty steps of statecharts, while non-idle are used to represent non-empty steps. This distinction is essential for ensuring the maximality of steps. The idea is that idle actions are taken iff no non-idle action is enabled by the environment.

We extend the operation $\times$ to semantic actions $\mathcal{S}(Act)$ as follows.

Definition 7. Assume $\alpha_i = a_i : \tau_i \in \mathcal{S}(Act)$, for $i \in \{1,2\}$. We define $\alpha_1 \times \alpha_2$ as the set $\{a : \tau \in \mathcal{S}(Act)\}$, such that

- $a \in a_1 \times a_2$;
- $\tau = \epsilon$ if $\tau_i = \epsilon$, for some $i \in \{1,2\}$, and $\tau = \bar{\epsilon}$ otherwise.

For $\alpha = a : \tau \in \mathcal{S}(Act)$, we denote by $type(\alpha) = \tau$.

Assume $p \in \mathcal{CSP}$. The transition relation is obtained by the following rules:

$$\frac{t \overset{\alpha}{\mapsto} t'}{\ell :: t \overset{\alpha}{\mapsto} \ell :: t'}$$

$$\frac{\{p_i \overset{\alpha_i}{\mapsto} p_i'\}_{i \in \{1,2\}} \quad \alpha \in \alpha_1 \times \alpha_2}{\ell :: p_1 \times p_2 \overset{\alpha}{\mapsto} \ell :: p_1' \times p_2'} \; par$$

$$\ell :: a.t \overset{a:\epsilon}{\mapsto} t \qquad\qquad \ell :: a.t \overset{b:\bar{\epsilon}}{\mapsto} \ell :: a.t \quad b \in \#(a)$$

$$\ell :: nil \overset{b:\bar{\epsilon}}{\mapsto} \ell :: nil \quad b \in \#(*)$$

$$\frac{\ell :: b_i \overset{\alpha}{\mapsto} t \quad type(\alpha) = \epsilon}{\ell :: b_1 + b_2 \overset{\alpha}{\mapsto} t} \; choice_1 \qquad \frac{\ell :: b_1 \overset{\alpha}{\mapsto} \ell :: b_1 \quad \ell :: b_2 \overset{\alpha}{\mapsto} \ell :: b_2 \quad type(\alpha) = \bar{\epsilon}}{\ell :: b_1 + b_2 \overset{\alpha}{\mapsto} \ell :: b_1 + b_2} \; choice_2$$

$$\frac{t \overset{\alpha}{\mapsto} t' \; type(\alpha) = \epsilon}{t \bigtriangledown p \overset{\alpha}{\mapsto} t'} \; \bigtriangledown_1$$

$$\frac{p \overset{\alpha}{\mapsto} p' \; type(\alpha) = \epsilon}{t \bigtriangledown p \overset{\alpha}{\mapsto} t \bigtriangledown p'} \bigtriangledown_2 \qquad \frac{\begin{array}{c} t \overset{\alpha}{\mapsto} t \\ p \overset{\alpha}{\mapsto} p \\ type(\alpha) = \bar{\epsilon} \end{array}}{t \bigtriangledown p \overset{\alpha}{\mapsto} t \bigtriangledown p} \bigtriangledown_3$$

$$\frac{t[rec\, x.t/x] \overset{\alpha}{\mapsto} t' \; type(\alpha) = \epsilon}{rec\, x.t \overset{\alpha}{\mapsto} t'} rec_1$$

$$\frac{t[rec\, x.t/x] \overset{\alpha}{\mapsto} t[rec\, x.t/x] \; type(\alpha) = \bar{\epsilon}}{rec\, x.t \overset{\alpha}{\mapsto} rec\, x.t} rec_2$$

Let us explain the rules. The rule of parallel composition is the standard rule for synchronous languages and is based on the operation of parallel composition of actions. Note that an action of the parallel composition is idle iff it results from idle actions of both the components. Consider a process $\ell :: a.t \in \mathcal{T}$. If the environment enables action a then $\ell :: a.t$ evolves into t by performing an action $a : \epsilon$ (non-idle) and location ℓ is left. On the other hand, if an action a' in conflict with a is enabled by the environment then the reached process is $\ell :: a.t$ and the action is a' of type $\bar{\epsilon}$. Actions of type ϵ and type $\bar{\epsilon}$ give a different behaviour to the operators of refinement and of choice. Consider $\ell :: b_1 + b_2 \in \mathcal{T}$. Rule $choice_1$ correspond to the classical rule for choice and is applicable iff the action is non-idle. On the other hand, b_1 and b_2 must agree on idle actions, as required by rule $choice_2$. In a similar way the semantics of $t \bigtriangledown p$ is defined. Actions $\bar{\epsilon}$ of $t \bigtriangledown p$ must be actions $\bar{\epsilon}$ of both t and p. Note that when a non-idle action of p is performed, the process t is not left. This is the basic idea of process refinement. Rule rec_1 is standard, while rule rec_2 reflects the idea that, when an idle action is performed, the process does not change.

4 The translation

In this section we define a compositional mapping α from statecharts into closed processes, such that the labelled transition system semantics of $\alpha(S)$ is equivalent to Pnueli and Shalev semantics of S.

Given a statechart S over Π, we construct a process with basic actions Act corresponding to transitions and describing their input-output and locations Loc corresponding to the boxes of S. However, since the input-output is not sufficient for compositionality, also the causal ordering between events is recorded in basic actions.

Hence, we consider actions with the following syntax.

Definition 8. Let Π a finite set of primitive events. We define $\Sigma(\Pi)$ as the set of pairs $(\ell, \prec)$ where

1. $\ell \in 2^{\Pi \cup \bar{\Pi}}$ and ℓ is *consistent*, i.e. $e, \bar{e} \notin \ell$;
2. $\prec$ is an ordering over $2^\ell \times 2^\ell$ such that:
   (a) $\prec$ is an *irreflexive* ordering relation;

(b) for each $C, C' \in 2^{\ell}$ such that $C' \subseteq C$, if $C'' \prec C'$ then $C[C''/C'] \prec C$.

The ordering reflects causality, so that $\{e, e''\} \prec \{e'\}$ means that both e and e'' are necessary for event e' to be produced. On the other hand, $\{e\} \prec \{e'\}$ and $\{e''\} \prec \{e'\}$ means that both e and e'' are sufficient for event e' to be produced. Moreover, we require labels to be *consistent* for global consistency.

For $\sigma = (\ell, \prec) \in \Sigma(\Pi)$, we define $trigger(\sigma) = \{e \in \Pi \cup \bar{\Pi} \mid \nexists C \in 2^{\Pi \cup \bar{\Pi}}$ such that $C \prec \{e\}\}$ and $action(\sigma) = \ell \setminus trigger((\ell, \leq))$. The trigger of σ is the set of events required either to be present or absent in the input for enabling the step, while its action is the set of events produced by the step.

The operation $\times$ of parallel composition over actions $\Sigma(\Pi)$ is quite complex due to the communication between parallel components. Given two orderings $\prec_1, \prec_2$, we denote by $(\prec_1 \cup \prec_2)^+$, the ordering $\prec$, such that $\prec_1 \cup \prec_2 \subseteq \prec$ and such that, if $C \prec C'$ and $C' \prec C''$, then $C \prec C''$ and such that, for each C, C', if $C' \subseteq C$ and $C'' \prec C'$, then $C[C''/C'] \prec C$.

Definition 9. Given $\sigma_1 = (\ell_1, \prec_1) \in \Sigma(\Pi)$ and $\sigma_2 = (\ell_2, \prec_2) \in \Sigma(\Pi)$, we define $\sigma_1 \times \sigma_2 = \{\sigma = (\ell, \prec)\}$ such that

- $\ell = \ell_1 \cup \ell_2$ iff $\ell_1 \cup \ell_2$ is consistent;
- $\prec \subseteq (\prec_1 \cup \prec_2)^+$ such that:
  - $(\ell, \prec) \in \Sigma(\Pi)$;
  - $\prec$ is maximal.

The idea is that the parallel composition of actions $(\ell_1, \prec_1)$ and $(\ell_2, \prec_2)$ is given by the union of events $\ell_1 \cup \ell_2$ and by the ordering, that is the maximal subset of $(\prec_1 \cup \prec_2)^+$, which is irreflexive.

Consider $\sigma_1 = (\{a, b\}, \{a\} \prec_1 \{b\})$ and $\sigma_2 = (\{b, c\}, \{b\} \prec_2 \{c\})$. We have $\sigma_1 \times \sigma_2 = \{\sigma\}$ with $\sigma = (\{a, b, c\}, \{a\} \prec \{b\}, \{b\} \prec \{c\}, \{a\} \prec \{c\})$. The communication is realized by the transitive closure of the two orderings. Actually, $trigger(\sigma) = \{a\}$ and $action(\sigma) = \{b, c\}$, while $trigger(\sigma_1) = \{a\}$, $trigger(\sigma_2) = \{b\}$, so that b is not required from the environment.

Note that $(\prec_1 \cup \prec_2)^+$ may be reflexive. Consider $\ell_1 = (\{a, b\}, \{a\} \prec_1 \{b\})$ and $\ell_2 = (\{a, b\}, \{b\} \prec_2 \{a\})$. The parallel composition of σ_1 and σ_2 cannot be $\sigma = (\{a, b\}, \{a\} \prec \{b\}, \{b\} \prec \{a\})$ since $trigger(\sigma) = \emptyset$ and this contradicts the causality principle. We have $\sigma_1 \times \sigma_2 = \{\sigma_1, \sigma_2\}$ so that either event a or event b is needed from the environment.

Definition 10. For $\sigma \in \Sigma(\Pi)$, we define $\#(\sigma) = \{(E, \emptyset) \mid E \subseteq \Pi \cup \bar{\Pi}$, such that E is consistent and $\forall e \in \Pi$, either $e \in E$ or $\bar{e} \in E$ and there exists $e \in E$, such that $\bar{e} \in trigger(\sigma)\}$. Moreover, we define $\#(*) = \{(E, \emptyset) \mid E \subseteq \Pi \cup \bar{\Pi}$, such that E is consistent and $\forall e \in \Pi$, either $e \in E$ or $\bar{e} \in E\}$.

Intuitively, $\sigma' \in \#(\sigma)$ iff for each input $I \subseteq \Pi$, if I enables σ', then I does not enable σ. Consider an action $\sigma = (\{a, b, c\}, \{a\} \prec \{c\})$. We have $\#(\sigma) = (\{\bar{a}, b, c\}, \emptyset), (\{\bar{a}, b, \bar{c}\}, \emptyset), (\{\bar{a}, \bar{b}, \bar{c}\}, \emptyset), (\{\bar{b}, a, c\}, \emptyset), (\{\bar{b}, \bar{a}, c\}, \emptyset), (\{\bar{b}, a, \bar{c}\}, \emptyset)\}$. Actually, if the environment does not produce both a and b the transition corresponding to σ cannot be performed, since $trigger(\sigma) = \{a, b\}$.

The translation $\alpha(S)$ is inductively defined over the structure of statechart S. We need the following definition for refinement.

Definition 11. Let $t \in \mathcal{T}$, $\{p_i\}_{i \in \{1,n\}} \in \mathcal{CSP}$ be closed processes and let $l_i \in Loc$. We define $ref(t, \{(l_1, p_1), \ldots, (l_n, p_n)\})$ as the term obtained by substituting in t each occurrence of a subterm $l_i :: t'$ with $l_i :: t' \bigtriangledown p_i$.

Moreover, for a transition $t \in T(S)$, we define $lab(t) = (trigger(t) \cup action(t), \{trigger(t) \prec \{e'\} \mid e' \in action(t) - \{nil \cup trigger(t)\}\})$.

Definition 12. The mapping α is inductively defined as follows.

- Let S be a basic empty statechart. Then $\alpha(S) = S :: S :: nil$.

- Let $S : (\{S_1, \ldots, S_n\}, T, in, out, \chi, \delta)$ be a basic non-empty statechart. For each $i \in \{1,n\}$, let $T_i = \{t \in T \mid out(t) = S_i\}$. Let $t_{S_i} = rec\ s_i.S_i :: (\sum_{t \in T_i} lab(t).in(t))$, if $T_i \neq \emptyset$ and $t_{S_i} = S_i :: nil$, otherwise. Process $\alpha(S)$ is obtained by repeating the following substitutions, where initially $\alpha(S) = S :: t_{\delta(S)}$:
  - If $\alpha(S)$ is closed then stop;
  - If $\alpha(S)$ is open, then for each $S_j \in free(\alpha(S))$, $\alpha(S) = \alpha(S)[t_{S_j}/S_j]$.

- Let S be a refined statechart $\bigtriangledown(S, \{S_1, \ldots, S_n\})$ and $\alpha(S) = S :: t_S$. Then $\alpha(\bigtriangledown(S, \{S_1, \ldots, S_n\}))$ is defined as

$$S :: ref((t_S, \{(S_1, \alpha(S_1)), \ldots, (S_n, \alpha(S_n))\}).$$

- Let $S : \text{AND}(S_1, S_2)$. Then $\alpha(S) = S :: \alpha(S_1) \times \alpha(S_2)$.

The definitions of $lab(t)$ and of $\times$, $\#$ are given so that the semantics of $\alpha(S)$ agrees with the Pnueli and Shalev semantics of S. We need some preliminary concepts.

Assume $I \subseteq \Pi$ and $\ell \subseteq \Pi \cup \bar{\Pi}$. We say that I *triggers* ℓ ($I \rightsquigarrow \ell$) iff, for each $e \in \ell \cap \Pi$, $e \in I$, and for each $\bar{e} \in \ell \cap \bar{\Pi}$, $e \notin I$. Moreover, for $\alpha = \sigma : \tau$, we denote by $trigger(\alpha)$ and $action(\alpha)$ the sets $trigger(\sigma)$ and $action(\sigma)$, respectively.

Assume $p \in \mathcal{CSP}$. Process p is *regular* iff it has guarded recursion and for each variable x, x does not occur free in subterms $\ell :: p_1 \times p_2$ and in process p_1, such that $\ell :: t \bigtriangledown p_1$ is a subterm of p.

Definition 13. Assume $p \in \mathcal{CSP}$. We define $\mathcal{R}_p$ as the subset of $\mathcal{CSP}$ such that

- $p \in \mathcal{R}_p$;
- if $p' \in \mathcal{R}_p$ and, if $p' \overset{\alpha}{\mapsto} p''$, then $p'' \in \mathcal{R}_p$.

For a regular process $p \in \mathcal{CSP}$, $\mathcal{R}_p$ is finite, namely the process is finite-state. It is quite obvious that the $\mathcal{SP}$ processes corresponding to statecharts are closed and regular.

Theorem 14. *Let S be a statechart over Π.*

- *For each* $c \in C(S)$*, such that* c *is reachable from* $\Delta(S)$*, there exists* $p \in \mathcal{R}_{\alpha(S)}$*, such that* $loc(p) = c$*. Moreover, for each* $I \subseteq \Pi$*, if* $c \overset{I,O}{\Longrightarrow} c'$*, then* $p \overset{\alpha}{\mapsto} p'$*, where* $loc(p') = c'$ *and* $I \rightsquigarrow trigger(\alpha)$*,* $O - trigger(\alpha) = action(\alpha)$*;*
- *For each* $p \in \mathcal{R}_{\alpha(S)}$*, if* $p \overset{\alpha}{\mapsto} p'$*, then there exist* $c, c' \in C(S)$*, where* $loc(p) = c$*,* $loc(p') = c'$ *and* $c \overset{I,O}{\Longrightarrow} c'$*, for each* $I, O \subseteq \Pi$*, such that* $I \rightsquigarrow trigger(\alpha)$ *and* $O - trigger(\alpha) = action(\alpha)$*.*

This theorem can be proved by induction on the structure of the statechart. We omit the proof for lack of space. Consistency of steps is guaranteed by the definition of actions $\Sigma(\Pi)$, while maximality is guaranteed by the definition of # and by the semantics of idle actions (rules *choice*$_2$ and ∇_3). The more complex case is that of parallel composition, since it is necessary to show that the condition of inseparability is captured by the definition of $\times$ over $\Sigma(\Pi)$. The idea is that the irreflexivity of the ordering ensures the existence of a causal ordering between transitions.

Note that by taking a different set of actions corresponding to transitions and different operations $\times$ and #, we could have a process $\alpha(S)$, which has a different semantics, for instance the ones of [5, 10].

We explain the translation for the statechart of figure 1 over primitive events $\Pi = \{a, b, d, nil\}$. For basic statecharts E and F,

$$\alpha(E) = E :: rec\ x.A :: lab(t_1).rec\ y.C :: lab(t_2).x$$
$$\alpha(F) = F :: rec\ x.B :: lab(t_3).rec\ y.D :: lab(t_4).x.$$

Note that $loc(\alpha(E)) = \{E, A\}$ and $loc(\alpha(F)) = \{F, B\}$, which are the initial configurations of E and F respectively. It is quite obvious that the semantics of $\alpha(E)$ and of $\alpha(F)$ correspond to the semantics of E and F, respectively.

By rule *rec*$_1$,

$$\alpha(E) \overset{lab(t_1):\epsilon}{\mapsto} E :: rec\ y.C :: lab(t_2).t_1$$

where $t_1 = rec\ x.A :: lab(t_1).rec\ y.C :: lab(t_2).x$. Since $trigger(lab(t_1)) = \{a\}$ and $action(lab(t_1)) = \{b\}$, this trasition corresponds to the step $\{t_1\}$ from $\{E, A\}$ to $\{E, C\}$ for inputs containing a. On the other hand, by rule *rec*$_2$,

$$\alpha(E) \overset{\sigma:\bar{\epsilon}}{\mapsto} \alpha(E)$$

for $\sigma \in \#(lab(t_1))$, i.e. $\sigma \in \{(\{\bar{a}, b, d\}, \emptyset), (\{\bar{a}, b, \bar{d}\}.\emptyset), (\{\bar{a}, \bar{b}, d\}, \emptyset), (\{\bar{a}, \bar{b}, \bar{d}\}, \emptyset)\}$. This transition corresponds to the empty step from $\{E, A\}$ with respect to inputs that do not contain a.

Since G : AND(E, F), $\alpha(G) = G :: \alpha(E) \times \alpha(F)$. Maximality and consistency of steps are obtained by the definition of $\times$ over actions. Let $p_1 = E :: rec\ y.C :: lab(t_2).t_1$ and $p_2 = F :: rec\ y.D :: lab(t_4).t_2$. By rule *par*,

$$\alpha(G) \overset{(\{a,b\}, \{a\} \prec \{b\}):\epsilon}{\mapsto} G :: p_1 \times p_2.$$

This transition corresponds to the step $\{t_1, t_3\}$ from the configuration $\{G, E, F, A, B\}$ to the configuration $\{G, E, F, C, D\}$, when the environment produces a.

Actually, $trigger((\{a,b\},\{a\} \prec \{b\})) = \{a\}$. Steps such that one component takes a transition and the other one not, are obtained by combining a non-idle arrow of one component with an idle arrow of the other. For instance, from $\alpha(E) \overset{(\{\bar{a},b,\bar{d}\},\emptyset):\bar{\epsilon}}{\mapsto} \alpha(E)$ and $\alpha(F) \overset{\{b\},\emptyset):\epsilon}{\mapsto} F :: rec\, y.D :: lab(t_4).t_2$, we have

$$G :: \alpha(E) \times \alpha(F) \overset{\{b,\bar{a},\bar{d}\},\emptyset):\epsilon}{\mapsto} G :: \alpha(E) \times F :: rec\, y.D :: lab(t_4).t_2.$$

This transition corresponds to the non-empty step $\{t_3\}$ when the environment produces b and does not produce a and d. Note that there are no steps, such that E takes a transition and F does not take a transition, since $action(t_1)$ triggers transition t_2. Finally, we have the following empty step $\alpha(G) \overset{\sigma:\bar{\epsilon}}{\mapsto} \alpha(G)$ for $\sigma \in \#(lab(t_1)) \cap \#(lab(t_3))$, i.e. $\sigma \in \{(\{\bar{a},\bar{b},d\},\emptyset), \{\bar{a},\bar{b},\bar{d}\},\emptyset)$.

Consider basic statechart S. We have

$$\alpha(S) = S :: rec\, x.G :: lab(t_5).rec\, y.H :: lab(t_6).x.$$

Hence, for the refinement of S, $\alpha(\nabla(S,\{G,H\}))$

$$S :: rec\, x.(G :: lab(t_5).rec\, y.(H :: lab(t_6).x \nabla \alpha(H))) \nabla \alpha(G)$$

where $\alpha(H) = H :: H :: nil$.

Since $\alpha(G) \overset{(\{a,b\},\{a\}\prec\{b\}):\epsilon}{\mapsto} G :: p_1 \times p_2$, by rule rec_1 and by rule ∇_2,

$$\alpha(\nabla(S,\{G,H\})) \overset{(\{a,b\},\{a\}\prec\{b\}):\epsilon}{\mapsto} S :: t_4 \nabla G :: p_1 \times p_2$$

where $t_4 = G :: lab(t_5).rec\, y.(H :: lab(t_6).t_6 \nabla \alpha(H))$.

Since $loc(G :: p_1 \times p_2) = \{G,E,F,D,C\}$, $loc(S :: t_4 \nabla G :: p_1 \times p_2) = \{S,G,E,F,D,C\}$, this arrow corresponds to the step $\{t_1,t_3\}$ when the input contains event a.

Since $S :: t_4 \overset{lab(t_5):\epsilon}{\mapsto} S :: rec\, y.\ (H :: lab(t_6).t_6 \nabla \alpha(H))$, by rule ∇_1,

$$\alpha(\nabla(S,\{G,H\})) \overset{lab(t_5):\epsilon}{\mapsto} S :: rec\, y.(H :: lab(t_6).t_6 \nabla \alpha(H)).$$

Since $loc(S :: rec\, y.(H :: lab(t_6).t_6 \nabla \alpha(H))) = \{S,H\}$, this corresponds to the step $\{t_5\}$ from configuration $\{S,G,E,F,A,B\}$ to configuration $\{S,H\}$, when the environment produces d.

Note that rules ∇_1 and ∇_2 can be applied, since the type of the action of $S :: t_4$ and $\alpha(G)$ is non-idle, respectively. On the other hand, empty steps from $\{S,G,E,F,A,B\}$ must be empty steps both of statechart G and of basic statechart S. Hence, we have an empty step iff the environment produces neither a, b nor d. This is reflected by rule ∇_3, where we require that the two parts agree on idle actions.

We have $\alpha(G) \overset{(\{\bar{a},\bar{b},\bar{d}\},\emptyset):\bar{\epsilon}}{\mapsto} \alpha(G)$ and $S :: t_4 \overset{(\{\bar{a},\bar{b},\bar{d}\},\emptyset):\bar{\epsilon}}{\mapsto} S :: t_4$, so that

$$S :: t_4 \nabla \alpha(G) \overset{(\{\bar{a},\bar{b},\bar{d}\},\emptyset):\bar{\epsilon}}{\mapsto} S :: t_4 \nabla \alpha(G).$$

By rule rec_2,

$$\alpha(\nabla(S,\{G,H\}) \overset{(\{\bar{a},\bar{b},\bar{d}\},\emptyset):\bar{\epsilon}}{\mapsto} \alpha(\nabla(S,\{G,H\}).$$

Note that $\#(lab(t_1))\cap\#(lab(t_3)) \cap \#(lab(t_5)) = (\{\bar{a},\bar{b},\bar{d}\},\emptyset)$.

5 Related works

In this section we discuss the differences between our process-algebraic semantics and the one of [17]. The process language has an operator of refinement similar to ours and the translation differs only in the actions describing transitions. However, the labelled transition system semantics of the language differs in many aspects.

The first difference arises in the definition of basic actions corresponding to transitions. In the approach of [17] transitions are represented by pairs $(\ell, \prec)$, where ℓ is a set of events and $\prec$ is an irreflexive and transitive ordering on ℓ. On the other hand, in our definition $\prec$ is an ordering over $2^{\Pi \cup \bar{\Pi}}$. This definition leads to a semantics different from the one of Pnueli and Shalev, when a transition has a set of events as trigger.

Consider statechart G of figure 1, where the labels of t_1 and t_3 are ac/b and b/c, respectively. The action corresponding to transition t_1 is $a_1 = (\{a,b,c\}, a \prec b, c \prec b)$, while that corresponding to t_2 is $a_2 = (\{b,c\}, b \prec c)$. The parallel composition of actions is defined as in our approach. However, if we combine a_1 and a_2 we obtain the set $\{(\{a,b,c\}, a \prec b, c \prec b), (\{a,b,c\}, a \prec b, b \prec c, a \prec c)\}$. The first action corresponds to take both transitions on input $\{a,c\}$. On the other hand, the action $(\{a,b,c\}, a \prec b, b \prec c, a \prec c)$ corresponds to take both transitions with respect to an input that contain $\{a\}$. In particular this is a step with respect to the input $\{a\}$. This is not correct, since event a is not suffient for enabling both transitions.

In our definition, we have considered a causal ordering between sets of events instead of single events. Hence, the action corresponding to t_1 is $a_1 = (\{a,b,c\}, \{a,c\} \prec \{b\})$, while the one corresponding to t_3 is $a_2 = (\{b,c\}, \{b\} \prec \{c\})$. The parallel composition of a_1 and a_2 is the set $\{a = (\{a,b,c\}, \{a,c\} \prec \{b\}), a' = (\{a,b,c\}, \{b\} \prec \{c\})\}$. Hence, we have $trigger(a) = \{a,c\}$ and $trigger(a') = \{a,b\}$ so that event a is not sufficient to trigger the step $\{t_1, t_3\}$.

Another drawback in the semantics of Uselton and Smolka regards the labelled transition system semantics of the process language. Actually, in their approach idle actions are not considered so that empty steps are not explicitely represented. Consider statechart G of figure 1 where t_1 and t_3 are labelled by $\bar{a}/b$ and b/a, respectively. The $\mathcal{SP}$ process corresponding to statechart G is given by $G :: p_1 \times p_2$, where $p_1 = E :: rec\, x.A :: lab(t_1).t_1$ and $p_2 = F :: rec\, y.B :: lab(t_3).t_2$ with $lab(t_1) = (\{\bar{a}, b\}, \{\bar{a}\} \prec \{b\})$ and $lab(t_2) = (\{b,a\}, \{b\} \prec \{a\})$ and t_1, t_2 the obvious processes. The process obtained by Uselton and Smolka is equivalent to this one and differs only for the notation. However, in this approach the only transition for the process corresponding to G is given by

$$G :: p_1 \times p_2 \overset{(\{b,a\}, b \prec a)}{\mapsto} G :: p_1 \times F :: t_2.$$

Actually, the step $\{t_3\}$ with respect to inputs that contain b is the only non-empty step from the configuration $\{G, E, F, A, B\}$. With respect to the empty input a causal paradox occurs, while for inputs with $\{a\}$ the empty set of transitions is an admissible reaction. However, the difference between the empty step on input

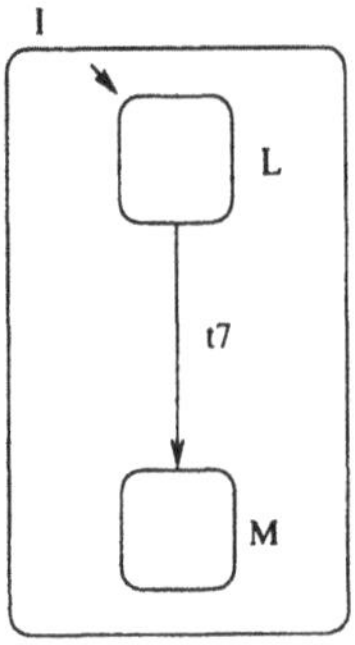

Fig. 2. The basic statechart I

$\{a\}$ and the run-time error on empty input is not reflected by the transition system semantics of Uselton and Smolka. This gives rise to non-empty steps, that are not admissible. The problem arises, when a non-empty step of the parallel composition is given by an empty step of one component and by a non-empty step of the other component. Since empty steps are not explicitly represented, Uselton and Smolka use an additional rule for parallel composition with negative premises. However, non-admissible steps and empty steps cannot be distinguished by this rule.

Consider for instance the statechart H : AND(G, I), where I is shown in figure 2 and t_7 is labelled by nil/c. The corresponding process is

$$p' = H :: G :: (p_1 \times p_2) \times p_3$$

where $p_3 = I :: rec\ z.L :: lab(t_7).M :: nil = \alpha(I)$. By applying the rule with negative premises, we would obtain the following transition

$$p' \overset{(\{\bar{b},c,\bar{a},nil\},nil \prec c)}{\longmapsto} H :: G :: (p_1 \times p_2) \times I :: M :: nil$$

where $(\{\bar{b}, c, \bar{a}, nil\}, nil \prec c) \in (\{c, nil\}, nil \prec c) \times (\{\bar{a}, \bar{b}\}, \emptyset)$.
The action $(\{c, nil\}, nil \prec c)$ is the one of the non-empty step of I, $p_3 \overset{(\{c,nil\},nil \prec c)}{\longmapsto} I :: M :: nil$, while the action $(\{\bar{a}, \bar{b}\}, \emptyset)$ represents an empty step of G. The idea is that $(\{\bar{a}, \bar{b}\}, \emptyset)$ is in conflict with the action $(\{b, a\}, b \prec a)$, namely when the environment produces neither b nor a, the only non-empty step of G is not enabled. However, since $trigger((\{\bar{b}, c, \bar{a}, nil\}, nil \prec c)) = \{nil, \bar{a}, \bar{b}\}$, this transition corresponds to the step $\{t_7\}$ with respect to inputs that contain neither a nor b. This is not an admissible step in the Pnueli and Shalev semantics, because of the causal paradox.

Therefore, the explicit representation of empty steps in the labelled transition system semantics is necessary to obtain the correct semantics. Moreover, this approach allows us to define a single rule for parallel composition rather than the complex rules of [17]. Note that the same drawbacks are present also in the labelled transition system semantics presented in [16].

6 Conclusions

In this paper we have defined the process language $\mathcal{SP}$ and we have shown a translation of statecharts into closed processes of $\mathcal{SP}$ according to the semantics of Pnueli and Shalev. The main novelty of the process language $\mathcal{SP}$ is the operator of process refinement, which is needed to represent statecharts hierarchy. In [17] a process-algebraic version of statecharts has been proposed, with the aim of finding an axiomatization of statecharts equivalence. The operator of refinement is similar to ours. However, the labelled transition system semantics of the language does not represent *idle* actions so that it is not equivalent to the one of Pnueli and Shalev, as we have discussed. Moreover, our translation has the advantage to be general, since other semantics of statecharts can be obtained by modifying the operations over actions.

Our interest for a process-algebraic semantics for statecharts is motivated by the possibility of using the semantics for studying equivalences of statecharts and for proving temporal properties by model checking [15]. Actually, the translation allows us to construct in a compositional way the labelled transition system of a statechart. This is very useful since, if we replace a component with one that is equivalent with respect to labelled transition system isomorphism, we should not redo the proofs. Moreover, this proposal is a first step towards a compositional verification technique for statecharts, where the verification that a composed statechart satisfies a formula is reduced to the verification of derived formulas for its components. The main advantage is that, when changing a part of a process, only the verification concerning that part must be redone. Moreover, compositional verfication permits to reason with partial specifications and can be applied during the process of specifications development. A compositional proof system in the style of [1] for checking whether an $\mathcal{SP}$ process satisfies a μ-calculus formula has been developed in [9].

References

1. H.R. Andersen, C. Stirling, and G. Winskel. A Compositional Proof System for the Modal mu-Calculus. In *Proc. Ninth IEEE Symp. on Logic In Computer Science*, pages 144–153, 1994.
2. G. Berry and G. Gonthier. The ESTEREL Synchronous Programming Language: Design, Semantics, Implementation. *Science of Computer Programming*, (19):87–152, 1992.
3. P. Caspi, N. Halbwachs, D. Pilaud, and J. Plaice. Lustre, a Declarative Language for Programming Synchronous Systems. In *Proccedings 14-th Symposium of Principles of Programming Languages*, pages 178–188, 1987.
4. D. Harel. Statecharts: A Visual Formalism for Complex Systems. *Science of Computer Programming*, 8:231–274, 1987.
5. D. Harel, A. Pnueli, J. P. Schmidt, and R. Sherman. On the Formal Semantics of Statecharts. In *Proc. Second IEEE Symp. on Logic In Computer Science*, pages 54–64. IEEE Computer Society Press, 1987.
6. J.J.M. Hooman, R. Ramesh, and W.P. de Roever. A Compositional Axiomatization of Statecharts. *Theoretical Computer Science*, 101:289–335, 1992.

7. C. Huizing and R. Gerth. Semantics of Reactive Systems in Abstract Time. volume 600 of *Lecture Notes in Computer Science*, pages 291–314. Springer-Verlag, Berlin, 1992.
8. C. Huizing, R. Gerth, and W.P. de Roever. Modelling Statecharts in a Fully Abstract Way. volume 299 of *Lecture Notes in Computer Science*, pages 271–294. Springer-Verlag, Berlin, 1988.
9. F. Levi. *Verification of Temporal and Real-Time Properties of Statecharts*. PhD thesis, Dipartimento di Informatica, Università di Pisa, 1997.
10. A. Maggiolo-Schettini, A. Peron, and S. Tini. Equivalences of Statecharts. In *Proc. of CONCUR 96*, volume 1119 of *Lecture Notes in Computer Science*, pages 687–702. Springer-Verlag, Berlin, 1996.
11. F. Maraninchi. Operational and Compositional Semantics of Synchronous Automaton Composition. In *Proc. of CONCUR 92*, volume 630 of *Lecture Notes in Computer Science*, pages 550–564, 1992.
12. R. Milner. Calculi for synchrony and asynchrony. *Theoretical Computer Science*, 25:267–310, 1983.
13. A. Pnueli and M. Shalev. What is in a Step. volume 525 of *Lecture Notes in Computer Science*, pages 244–464. Springer-Verlag, Berlin, 1991.
14. K.V.S. Prasad. A Calculus of Broadcast Systems. In *Proc. of TAPSOFT-CAAP'91*, volume 493 of *Lecture Notes in Computer Science*, pages 338–358, 1991.
15. C. Stirling. Modal and Temporal Logics. In S. Abramsky and D. Gabbay, editors, *Handbook of Logic in Computer Science*, volume 2, pages 477–563. Oxford University Press, 1992.
16. A.C. Uselton and S.A. Smolka. A Compositional Semantics for Statecharts using Labelled Transition Systems. In *Proc. of CONCUR 94*, volume 836 of *Lecture Notes in Computer Science*, pages 2–17, 1994.
17. A.C. Uselton and S.A. Smolka. A Process Algebraic Semantics for Statecharts. In *Proceedings of IFIP Working Conference on Programming Concepts, Methods and Calculi*, 1994.

Priorities in Statecharts*

Andrea Maggiolo-Schettini, Massimo Merro

Dipartimento di Informatica, Università di Pisa, Corso Italia 40, 56125 Pisa, Italy

Abstract. The paper examines the specification language Statecharts from the point of view of its capability to express notions of priority. First a version of Statecharts that does not support priority is introduced, then various syntactic and semantics extensions are examined and compared from the point of view of expressing a general notion of priority. Finally, a special kind of priority, interrupt, is investigated.

1 Introduction

Statecharts are a visual formalism, originally proposed in [6], for the specification of complex systems consisting of components running in parallel, reacting to prompts from an environment, and interacting with each other by broadcast. Statecharts have been successfully used to specify hardware components, communication networks, operating systems (e.g. [5, 7]).

Statecharts are state-transition diagrams enriched by a tree-like structuring of states, explicit representation of parallelism and communication among parallel components. States are either of type *AND*, *AND-states*, used to describe parallel behaviours, or of type *OR*, *OR-states*, used to describe sequential behaviours. The graphical convention is that states are represented by boxes, and the box of a substate of a state is drawn inside the area of the box of the state. The area of an AND-state is partitioned by dashed lines. Each element of the partition represents a parallel component. An OR- state has a privileged immediate substate (*default state*) that is pointed to by an arrow without source. A transition is labelled by a set of events and negated events (these to be interpreted as absence of events) enabling its performance (the *trigger*) and by a set of events that are communicated when the transition is performed (the *action*). An example of statechart is in Figure 1.

The semantics of a statechart is the following. It is assumed that the *environment* prompts the statechart by means of events that are related to a discrete time domain (for instance natural numbers). The history of the prompts of the environment is described as a sequence of sets of events $E_1, \ldots, E_i, \ldots$, and it is intended that the events in E_i are communicated at the $i-th$ instant of time. At the instant i the statechart "reacts" to the set of communicated events by performing a number of enabled transitions. The reaction (a *step*) is assumed to be immediate, namely input and corresponding output occur at the same time. This assumption has been introduced in [3] as *synchrony hypothesis*. Now, in

* Research partially supported by Esprit BRA 8130 LOMAPS.

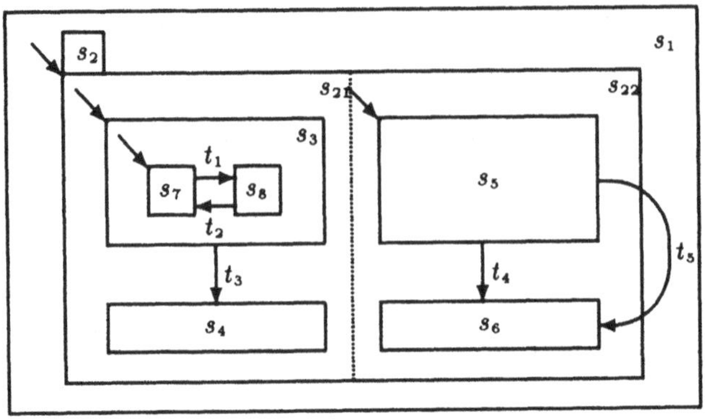

$$
\begin{array}{ll}
trigger_Z(t_1) = \{e_1\} & action_Z(t_1) = \emptyset \\
trigger_Z(t_2) = \{e_2\} & action_Z(t_2) = \{e_3\} \\
trigger_Z(t_3) = \{e_3\} & action_Z(t_3) = \emptyset \\
trigger_Z(t_4) = \{e_1\} & action_Z(t_4) = \{e_2\} \\
trigger_Z(t_5) = \{e_1\} & action_Z(t_5) = \{e_2\}
\end{array}
$$

Fig. 1.

reality no action occurs simultaneously with the input that has caused it, but the synchrony hypothesis can be justified if it is considered an abstraction from the case that a reaction takes place in time but before the next input occurs. In this paper we adopt the microstep approach proposed first in ([8]), namely we assume that a step is divided in a number of *microsteps*. If the execution of a transition enables the execution of another, these two transitions will be taken in subsequent microsteps of the same step. In order to model the synchrony hypothesis, during the execution of microsteps, within a step, it is assumed that events from the environment are not sensed. In order to avoid the execution of an infinite number of transitions in a step, two feasible possibilities exist. A *step semantics* (like that in [8]) guarantees finiteness of a step by requiring that transitions in the step affect different components of an AND-state. An *instantaneous semantics* allows a step to contain chains of transitions in the same parallel component. In this case, finiteness of the step is guaranteed by requiring either that a state is not exited twice (see the semantics proposed in [11]) or that a transition is not performed twice (see the semantics proposed in [12]), in the step. In this paper we shall consider both step and instantaneous semantics.

Now, in a language for concurrent system specification, it is useful to express priorities between operations that can be (nondeterministically) chosen at an instant. So we investigate which syntactic and semantic extensions are needed in Statecharts to model transition based priorities. It is known that priorities can be modelled by negated events, but we show that this can be done only under some restrictive conditions. Therefore we consider an alternative way to express priorities, namely that of endowing statecharts by explicit priority relations between transitions. This approach allows us to do without negated events and to express, at the same time, a more general kind of priority. We believe that specifications without negated events are also more perspicuous.

Also the hierarchical structure of states induces forms of priority. Priorities of this type are those defined by Day ([4]) and by Pnueli and Shalev ([13]). We examine how priorities of this kind may be used to model interrupts. We define a priority relation motivated by this purpose, and we show that it is equivalent to Pnueli and Shalev's priority. This holds for both step and instantaneous semantics.

2 Statecharts: Syntax and Semantics

In this section we give a syntax for Statecharts in a restricted version with respect to [8]. Then we define a step stemantics and two instantaneous semantics. These three semantics are obtained by only varying a key definition.

We shall henceforward assume an infinite set $\mathcal{S}$ of states, an infinite set $\mathcal{T}$ of transitions and an infinite set $\mathcal{E}$ of events. We shall use $s, s', s_1, s_2, \dots$ to range over $\mathcal{S}$, $t, t', t_1, t_2, \dots$ to range over $\mathcal{T}$ and $e, e', e_1, e_2, \dots$ to range over $\mathcal{E}$. Moreover we shall assume S as a general subset of $\mathcal{S}$, T as a general subset of $\mathcal{T}$ and E as a general subset of $\mathcal{E}$.

Definition 2.1 A *statechart* Z is a tuple $(S_Z, hrc_Z, type_Z, default_Z, E_Z, T_Z, lout_Z, lin_Z, hout_Z, hin_Z, label_Z)$, where:

1. $S_Z \subseteq \mathcal{S}$ is the finite non-empty set of *states*.
2. $hrc_Z : S_Z \to 2^{S_Z}$ is the *hierarchy function* that, for a state $s \in S_Z$, gives the set of immediate substates of s. A state $s \in S_Z$ is *basic* if $hrc_Z(s) = \emptyset$, *composite* otherwise. By hrc^*_Z and hrc^+_Z we denote the transitive-reflexive and the transitive-non-reflexive closure of hrc_Z, respectively, such that for $s \in S_Z$, the following predicates hold:
   (a) $s \in hrc^*_Z(s)$
   (b) $hrc_Z(s) \subseteq hrc^*_Z(s)$
   (c) $s' \in hrc_Z(s) \Rightarrow hrc_Z(s') \subseteq hrc^*_Z(s)$,
   (d) $hrc^+_Z(s) = hrc^*_Z(s) \setminus \{s\}$.
   There exists a unique state $s \in S_Z$, denoted $root_Z$, such that $hrc^*_Z(s) = S_Z$. Moreover for every $s \in S_Z$, $s \neq root_Z$, there exists a unique state $s' \in S_Z$, denoted $parent_Z(s)$, with $s \in hrc_Z(s')$, so that hrc_Z describes a tree-like structure. Finally, for a non-empty set of states $S \subseteq S_Z$, the *lowest common ancestor* (resp.: *strict lowest common ancestor*) of S, denoted $lca_Z(S)$ (resp.: $lca^+_Z(S)$), is the state $s \in S_Z$ such that:
   (a) $S \subseteq hrc^*_Z(s)$ (resp.: $S \subseteq hrc^+_Z(s)$)
   (b) $\forall s' \in S_Z \;\; S \subseteq hrc^*_Z(s') \Rightarrow s \in hrc^*_Z(s')$.
3. $type_Z : S_Z \to \{AND, OR\}$ is the *state-type function* that assigns a type to each composite state and is undefined for basic states. Immediate substates of AND-states cannot be AND-states.

4. $default_Z : S_Z \rightarrow S_Z$ is the *default function* that, for a state $s \in S_Z$ such that $hrc_Z(s) \neq \emptyset$ and $type_Z(s) = OR$, gives the default state of s, and is undefined otherwise.
5. $E_Z \subseteq \mathcal{E}$ is the finite set of *events*.
6. $T_Z \subseteq \mathcal{T}$ is the finite set of *transitions*.
7. $lout_Z : T_Z \rightarrow S_Z \setminus \{root_Z\}$ is a total function, called *lowest-source function*, s.t $lout_Z(t) = s$ iff transition t originates from state s. A transition cannot originate from an immediate substate of an AND-state, namely for every $t \in T_Z$ $type_Z(parent_Z(lout_Z(t))) = OR$.
8. $lin_Z : T_Z \rightarrow S_Z \setminus \{root_Z\}$ is a total function, called *lowest-target function*, s.t. $lin_Z(t) = s$ iff transition t ends in state s. Analogously to the lowest-source function, we have that for every $t \in T_Z$ $type_Z(parent_Z(lin_Z(t))) = OR$.
9. $hout_Z, hin_Z : T_Z \rightarrow S_Z \setminus \{root_Z\}$ are total functions, called *highest-source function* and *highest-target function* respectively, such that the following predicates hold:
   (a) $\forall t \in T_Z \; lout_Z(t) \in hrc^*_Z(hout_Z(t))$
   (b) $\forall t \in T_Z \; lin_Z(t) \in hrc^*_Z(hin_Z(t))$
   (c) $\forall t \in T_Z \; parent_Z(hout_Z(t)) = parent_Z(hin_Z(t)) = s$ with $type_Z(s) = OR$.
10. $label_Z : T_Z \rightarrow 2^{E_Z} \times 2^{E_Z}$ is the *labelling function*. The two components of $label_Z(t)$ are called $trigger_Z(t)$ and $action_Z(t)$, respectively.

Intuitively $hout_Z(t) = lout_Z(t)$ (resp.: $hin_Z(t) = lin_Z(t)$) if t does not cross the border of any state, and $hout_Z(t) = s$ (resp.: $hin_Z(t) = s$) if t crosses the border of s with $lout_Z(t) \in hrc^+_Z(s)$ (resp.: $lin_Z(t) \in hrc^+_Z(s)$) and there is no $s' \in S_Z$ s.t. t crosses the border of s' and $s \in hrc^+_Z(s')$. The assumption that functions $hout_Z$ and hin_Z are total implies that transitions never cross the dashed line of an AND-state.
With reference to statechart Z in Figure 1 we have:

1. $S_Z = \{s_1, s_2, s_{21}, s_{22}, s_3, s_4, s_5, s_6, s_7, s_8\}$
2. $hrc_Z(s_2) = \{s_{21}, s_{22}\}$, $hrc_Z(s_3) = \{s_7, s_8\}$, $hrc^*_Z(s_2) = \{s_2, s_{21}, s_{22}, s_3, s_4, s_5, s_6, s_7, s_8\}$, $hrc^+_Z(s_2) = hrc^*_Z(s_2) \setminus \{s_2\}$, $parent_Z(s_{21}) = s_2$, $lca_Z(\{s_8, s_{22}\}) = s_2$, $lca^+_Z(\{s_8, s_{22}\}) = s_2$, $lca_Z(\{s_4, s_8, s_{21}\}) = s_{21}$, $lca^+_Z(\{s_4, s_8, s_{21}\}) = s_2$
3. $type_Z(s_2) = AND$, $type_Z(s_3) = OR$
4. $default_Z(s_{21}) = s_3$, $default_Z(s_3) = s_7$
5. $E_Z = \{e_1, e_2, e_3\}$
6. $T_Z = \{t_1, t_2, t_3, t_4, t_5\}$
7. $lout_Z(t_4) = hout_Z(t_4) = s_5$, $lin_Z(t_4) = hin_Z(t_4) = s_6$, $lout_Z(t_5) = s_5$, $hout_Z(t_5) = hin_Z(t_5) = s_2$, $lin_Z(t_5) = s_6$
8. $trigger_Z(t_1) = \{e_1\}$, $action_Z(t_1) = \emptyset$, $trigger_Z(t_2) = \{e_2\}$, $action_Z(t_2) = \{e_3\}$

We call $\mathcal{Z}$ the class of statecharts as in Definition 2.1, and we shall use $Z, Z', Z_1, Z_2, \ldots$ to range over $\mathcal{Z}$.

Now we are going to present a step semantics for $\mathcal{Z}$ closely related to the semantics of [8, 13]. From now on, if not specified otherwise, we assume a statechart $Z = (S_Z, hrc_Z, type_Z, default_Z, E_Z, T_Z, lout_Z, lin_Z, hout_Z, hin_Z, label_Z) \in \mathcal{Z}$.

Definition 2.2 Given a transition $t \in T_Z$, the *arena* of t, denoted $arena_Z(t)$, is the state $s \in S_Z$ such that $s = parent_Z(hout_Z(t)) = parent_Z(hin_Z(t))$.

With reference to statechart Z of Figure 1 we have $arena_Z(t_1) = s_3$, $arena_Z(t_4) = s_{22}$, $arena_Z(t_5) = s_1$. The concept of arena was introduced (but not formalized) in [13]. In the intention of the authors it represents the minimal context containing all the changes caused by the performance of transition. Note that for every $t \in T_Z$ $type_Z(arena_Z(t)) = OR$ by definition of $hout_Z$ and hin_Z.

Definition 2.3 Two transitions $t_1, t_2 \in T_Z$ are *structurally consistent* iff $type_Z(lca_Z(\{arena_Z(t_1), arena_Z(t_2)\})) = AND$. A set of transitions $T \subseteq T_Z$ is *structurally consistent* iff any two transitions $t_1, t_2 \in T$ are structurally consistent.

Two structurally consistent transitions are in two different parallel components of the same AND-state. This definition formalizes consistency of transitions as in [13]. It is more restrictive than that of [8], which could be obtained by substituting, in the definition above, $arena_Z(t)$ with $lca_Z^+(\{lout_Z(t), lin_Z(t)\})$. As an example, transitions t_3 and t_5 in Figure 1 are structurally consistent in the semantics of [8], but not in the semantics of [13] and in our semantics.

Definition 2.4 Two states $s_1, s_2 \in S_Z$ are *consistent*, if either $s_1 \in hrc_Z^*(s_2)$ or $s_2 \in hrc_Z^*(s_1)$ or $type_Z(lca_Z(\{s_1, s_2\})) = AND$. A set of states $S \subseteq S_Z$ is *consistent* iff any two states $s_1, s_2 \in S$ are consistent. A set of states $S \subseteq S_Z$ is *maximally consistent* iff for every $s \in S_Z \setminus S$, the set $S \cup \{s\}$ is not consistent.

With reference to the statechart of Figure 1, s_3 is consistent with s_5 and s_7 but not with s_4. The set $S = \{s_1, s_2, s_{21}, s_{22}, s_3, s_6, s_7\}$ is maximally consistent, $S \setminus \{s_{21}\}$ is only consistent and $S \cup \{s_4\}$ is not consistent.

Now we introduce the concepts of microconfiguration and microstep. A microstep within a step takes from a microconfiguration to a microconfiguration. A microconfiguration records the set of states exited and the set of transitions done in previous microsteps of the step, the set of current states and the set of events currently available.

Definition 2.5 A *microconfiguration* μC is a quadruple $(S_{exit}, T_{done}, S_{curr}, E_{curr})$ where:

1. $S_{exit} \subseteq S_Z$
2. $T_{done} \subseteq T_Z$
3. $S_{curr} \subseteq S_Z$ is maximally consistent
4. $E_{curr} \subseteq E_Z$.

Definition 2.6 Given a transition $t \in T_Z$ and a microconfiguration $\mu C = (S_{exit}, T_{done}, S_{curr}, E_{curr})$, t is *relevant* in μC iff $lout_Z(t) \in S_{curr}$, *triggered* in μC iff $trigger_Z(t) \subseteq E_{curr}$, and *consistent* in μC iff $T_{done} \cup \{t\}$ is structurally consistent.

Definition 2.7 A transition $t \in T_Z$ is *enabled* in a microconfiguration $\mu C = (S_{exit}, T_{done}, S_{curr}, E_{curr})$ iff:

1. t is relevant in μC
2. t is triggered in μC
3. t is consistent in μC.

Definition 2.8 A *microstep* $\mu\Sigma$ from a microconfiguration μC is a non-empty set of transitions in T_Z satisfying the following conditions:

1. $\forall t \in \mu\Sigma \;\; t$ is enabled in μC
2. $\mu\Sigma$ is structurally consistent.

Definition 2.9 Given two states $s_1, s_2 \in S_Z$ with $s_2 \in hrc_Z^*(s_1)$, the *path* from s_1 to s_2, denoted by $path(s_1, s_2)$, is the set $\{s \in S_Z \mid s \in hrc_Z^*(s_1) \wedge s_2 \in hrc_Z^*(s)\}$.

With reference to the statechart in Figure 1, $path(s_1, s_8) = \{s_1, s_2, s_{21}, s_3, s_8\}$.

Definition 2.10 The *downward closure* of a set $S \subseteq S_Z$ denoted $downclos(S)$, is the least superset of S such that:

1. $(s \in downclos(S) \wedge type_Z(s) = AND) \;\Rightarrow\; hrc_Z(s) \subseteq downclos(S)$
2. $(s \in downclos(S) \wedge type_Z(s) = OR \wedge hrc_Z(s) \neq \emptyset \wedge hrc_Z(s) \cap S = \emptyset) \Rightarrow default_Z(s) \in downclos(S)$.

With reference to the statechart of Figure 1, $downclos(\{s_2, s_6\}) = \{s_2, s_{21}, s_{22}, s_3, s_6, s_7\}$.

Definition 2.11 Given a microconfiguration $\mu C = (S_{exit}, T_{done}, S_{curr}, E_{curr})$, a transition $t \in T_Z$ relevant in μC and a microstep $\mu\Sigma \subseteq T_Z$, we define:

1. $exited(t, S_{curr}) = \{s \in S_Z \mid s \in hrc_Z^*(hout_Z(t)) \cap S_{curr}\}$
2. $entered(t) = downclos(path(hin_Z(t), lin_Z(t)))$
3. $next\mu C(\mu\Sigma, \mu C) = (S'_{exit}, T'_{done}, S'_{curr}, E'_{curr})$ with:
   (a) $S'_{exit} = S_{exit} \cup \bigcup_{t \in \mu\Sigma} exited(t, S_{curr})$
   (b) $T'_{done} = T_{done} \cup \mu\Sigma$
   (c) $S'_{curr} = (S_{curr} \setminus \bigcup_{t \in \mu\Sigma} exited(t, S_{curr})) \cup (\bigcup_{t \in \mu\Sigma} entered(t))$
   (d) $E'_{curr} = E_{curr} \cup \bigcup_{t \in \mu\Sigma} action_Z(t)$.

So, in a microconfiguration $\mu C = (S_{exit}, T_{done}, S_{curr}, E_{curr})$, $exited(t, S_{curr})$ and $entered(t)$ give the set of states exited and entered, respectively, when transition t is executed, and $next\mu C(\mu\Sigma, \mu C)$ gives the microconfiguration reached by the execution of the microstep $\mu\Sigma$ in μC.

Now we introduce the concepts of configuration and step, and define the semantics we have previously announced.

Definition 2.12 A *configuration* is a maximally consistent set of states. The set $downclos(\{root_Z\})$ is the *default configuration*.

Definition 2.13 Given an environment $E \subseteq E_Z$, an *admissible step* (also, briefly, a *step*) Σ from a configuration C to a configuration C' is a sequence of microsteps $\langle \mu\Sigma_0, \ldots, \mu\Sigma_n \rangle$ such that:

1. $\mu C_0 = (\emptyset, \emptyset, C, E)$ is the initial microconfiguration
2. $\mu\Sigma_i$ is a microstep from $\mu C_i = (S^i_{exit}, T^i_{done}, S^i_{curr}, E^i_{curr})$, for $0 \le i \le n$
3. $\mu C_{i+1} = next\mu C(\mu\Sigma_i, \mu C_i)$, for $0 \le i \le n$
4. $\forall t \in T_Z$ t is not enabled in $\mu C_{n+1} = (S^{n+1}_{exit}, T^{n+1}_{done}, S^{n+1}_{curr}, E^{n+1}_{curr})$
5. $C' = S^{n+1}_{curr}$, denoted $nextC(\Sigma)$.

A step contains a finite number of transitions. In fact, by restriction 3 of definition 2.7, a step contains only transitions affecting different parallel components, and the number of these is finite. Furthermore, condition 4 of definition 2.13 ensures that a step is a maximal set of enabled transitions. We define now a semantic function.

Definition 2.14 The step semantic function $Sem^{step} : \mathcal{Z} \times 2^{\mathcal{S}} \times 2^{\mathcal{E}} \longrightarrow 2^{(2^{\mathcal{T}})^*}$ is such that for a statechart $Z \in \mathcal{Z}$, a configuration C for Z and an environment $E \subseteq E_Z$, $Sem^{step}[\![Z]\!]CE = \{\Sigma_1, \ldots, \Sigma_k\}$, where $\Sigma_1, \ldots \Sigma_k$ are all the admissible steps from the configuration C in the environment E.

We call this semantics *step semantics*. It differs from that of [8] only by the concept used of structural consistency of two transitions, as we have already pointed out. In a step semantics it is not possible, in a step, to exit a state entered in the same step (namely in the same instant of time). There are semantics, like those introduced in [11, 12], called instantaneous, that allow, in a step, chains of transitions inside the same parallel component. Our semantics can easily become instantaneous by weakening the condition for consistency of a transition t in a microconfiguration $\mu C = (S_{exit}, T_{done}, S_{curr}, E_{curr})$ in Definition 2.6, namely, by replacing the condition either by $exited(t, S_{curr}) \cap S_{exit} = \emptyset$ or by $t \notin T_{done}$.

Proposition 2.1 For a microconfiguration $\mu C = (S_{exit}, T_{done}, S_{curr}, E_{curr})$ of Z and a transition $t \in T_Z$ relevant in μC:

$$T_{done} \cup \{t\} \text{ structurally consistent } \Rightarrow exited(t, S_{curr}) \cap S_{exit} = \emptyset \Rightarrow t \notin T_{done}.$$

■

The converse implications does not hold.
So similarly to Sem^{step}, we can define semantic functions Sem^{ch1} and Sem^{ch2} by assuming the first and the second of the two new conditions of consistency of transitions, respectively. We call these new semantics *chain semantics of type 1* and *chain semantics of type 2*, respectively. In both the cases infinite steps are avoided, in the former because a state cannot be exited twice in a step, in the latter because a transition cannot appear twice in a step.
Now, let us consider the statechart Z of Figure 1 in the default configuration C_0 and in the environment $E = \{e_1\}$. In this case we have:

$$Sem^{step}[\![Z]\!]C_0E = \{\langle\{t_1, t_4\}\rangle, \langle\{t_1\}, \{t_4\}\rangle, \langle\{t_4\}, \{t_1\}\rangle, \langle\{t_5\}\rangle\}$$

$$Sem^{ch1}[\![Z]\!]C_0E = \{\langle\{t_1, t_4\}, \{t_2\}\rangle, \langle\{t_1\}, \{t_4\}, \{t_2\}\rangle, \langle\{t_4\}, \{t_1\}, \{t_2\}\rangle, \langle\{t_1\}, \{t_5\}\rangle, \langle\{t_5\}\rangle\}$$

$$Sem^{ch2}[\![Z]\!]C_0E = \{\langle\{t_1, t_4\}, \{t_2\}, \{t_3\}\rangle, \langle\{t_1\}, \{t_4\}, \{t_2\}, \{t_3\}\rangle, \langle\{t_4\}, \{t_1\}, \{t_2\}, \{t_3\}\rangle, \langle\{t_1\}, \{t_5\}\rangle, \langle\{t_5\}, \{t_1\}, \{t_2\}, \{t_3\}\rangle\}.$$

The step semantics allows, in a step, only transitions in parallel components. In the initial configuration, with the given environment, t_1, t_4 and t_5 are all enabled, but, while t_1 and t_4 are structurally consistent and can be performed in the same step, t_5 must be performed alone because t_5 and t_1 are not structurally consistent. Here we see that performances of t_4 and t_5, which have the same *trigger*, *action*, *lout* and *lin*, but not the same *hout* and *hin*, give rise to different behaviours. In fact, the performance of t_5, differently with respect to that of t_4, causes exiting and then reinitializing s_{21} together with exiting s_{22} and then reentering it in its substate s_6. The chain semantics of type 1 allows, in a step, chains of transitions in the same parallel component, such as t_1 and t_2 in state s_3, but it excludes the execution of transitions from states that have been reentered. In chain semantics of type 2 it is only required that a transition is not repeated in a step so that, as an example, t_3 can be performed after performing t_2.

3 Priority and negated events

Statecharts are, in general, nondeterministic descriptions. Nondeterminism arises from the fact that there may be more transitions that are contemporaneously enabled but cannot be performed contemporaneously because they are mutually exclusive, so that one of them is supposed to be chosen nondeterministically. Otherwise, a priority may be assigned to transitions to solve conflicts.

Definition 3.1 Two transitions $t_1, t_2 \in T_Z$ are *potentially conflicting* if

1. $lout_Z(t_1)$ and $lout_Z(t_2)$ are consistent
2. t_1, t_2 are not structurally consistent.

Definition 3.2 A *priority relation* on a statechart Z is a partial relation $\mathcal{R} \subseteq T_Z \times T_Z$ such that $(t_1, t_2) \in \mathcal{R}$ implies that t_1 e t_2 are potentially conflicting.

The meaning of $\mathcal{R}$ is that if transitions t_1, t_2 are both enabled and $(t_1, t_2) \in \mathcal{R}$ then t_1 has lower priority than t_2. Note that we do not assume either irreflexivity or antisymmetry or transitivity, and this may give rise to circularity. This situation is acceptable because in a configuration not all the transitions in conflict are necessarily triggered. Furthermore, note that a possible deadlock is limited to the current step.

Pnueli and Shalev ([13]) show how priority can be expressed by allowing a transition to be triggered by the absence of a specific event among the ones currently communicated. The absence of an event e is represented by its negation $\overline{e}$, and for $E \subseteq \mathcal{E}$, $\overline{E}$ denotes the set $\{\overline{e} \mid e \in E\}$. It also assumed that, for all $e \in \mathcal{E}$, $\overline{\overline{e}} = e$. So we extend the class of statecharts $\mathcal{Z}$ by assuming in definition 2.1, condition 10, $label_Z : T_Z \rightarrow 2^{E_Z \cup \overline{E_Z}} \times 2^{E_Z}$. We call the new class of statecharts $\mathcal{Z}_{neg}$. Consequently, in definition 2.6 we assume that a transition $t \in T_Z$ is triggered in $\mu C = (S_{exit}, T_{done}, S_{curr}, E_{curr})$ iff:

1. $trigger_Z(t) \cap E_Z \subseteq E_{curr}$

2. $\overline{(trigger_Z(t) \cap \overline{E_Z})} \cap E_{curr} = \emptyset$.

So, by replacing $\mathcal{Z}$ with $\mathcal{Z}_{neg}$, we can define new semantic functions Sem^{step}_{neg}, Sem^{ch1}_{neg}, Sem^{ch2}_{neg}.

Now we show how it is possible to model a priority relation by negated events.

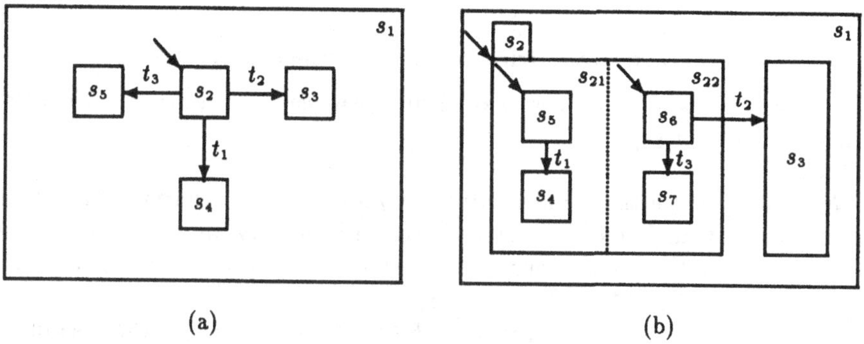

Fig. 2.

Let us consider the statechart of Figure 2(a) assuming $trigger_Z(t_1) = \{e_1\}$, $trigger_Z(t_2) = \{e_2\}$, $trigger_Z(t_3) = \{e_3\}$. Transitions t_1, t_2, t_3 are potentially conflicting with each other. Therefore if we want to model a priority relation $\mathcal{R}$ such that $(t_1, t_2) \in \mathcal{R}$ and $(t_2, t_3) \in \mathcal{R}$ but $(t_1, t_3) \notin \mathcal{R}$ (namely $\mathcal{R}$ is not transitive) we must change the triggers of transitions t_1 and t_2 in $\{e_1, \overline{e_2}\}$ and $\{e_2, \overline{e_3}\}$ respectively. So if the statechart is in configuration $\{s_1, s_2\}$ and events e_1, e_2 are supplied, then t_2 is performed, whereas if only events e_2, e_3 are supplied then transition t_3 is performed, and, finally, if only events e_1 and e_3 are supplied the choice between t_1 and t_3 is non-deterministic.
In our opinion this method does not always work. As an example, let us consider the statechart in Figure 2(b) with $trigger_Z(t_1) = \{e_1\}$ and $trigger_Z(t_2) = \{e_2\}$. Transitions t_1 and t_2 are potentially conflicting, and therefore in order to model a priority relation $\mathcal{R} = \{(t_1, t_2)\}$, we should only insert in $trigger_Z(t_1)$ the negated event $\overline{e_2}$. But, in this way, if we assume the configuration $C = \{s_1, s_2, s_{21}, s_{22}, s_5, s_7\}$ and the environment $E = \{e_1, e_2\}$, transition t_1 could not be executed because it would not be triggered, against our intention. This is due to the fact that we augment the trigger of t_1 by $\overline{e_2}$ independently of the fact that t_2 is relevant or not, whereas the priority between two transition plays a role only when both of them are relevant and triggered. So negated events can support correctly a priority relation $\mathcal{R}$ only if $(t_1, t_2) \in \mathcal{R}$ implies that, for every microconfiguration μC, if t_1 is relevant in μC also t_2 is relevant in μC.

We have seen how negated events allow us to implement a priority relation on transitions and with what limitations this can be done. On the other hand, statecharts with negated events are not always perspicuous, and one may prefer to endow a statechart directly with a relation expressing the priority wanted. So we consider statecharts $Z = (S_Z, hrc_Z, label_Z, default_Z, E_Z, T_Z, lout_Z, lin_Z, hout_Z, hin_Z, label_Z, \prec_Z)$, where S_Z, hrc_Z, $label_Z$, $default_Z$, E_Z, T_Z, $lout_Z$, lin_Z, $hout_Z$, $hin_Z, label_Z$ are as in definition 2.1, and $\prec_Z \subseteq T_Z \times T_Z$ is a priority relation where $t \prec_Z t'$ implies t and t' potentially conflicting. We call $\mathcal{Z}_{prior}$ the class of these statecharts. Moreover, if we add the following condition of enabling in definition 2.7 :

4. $\forall t' \in T_Z$ t' relevant, triggered and consistent in $\mu C \Rightarrow t \not\prec_Z t'$

by replacing $\mathcal{Z}$ with $\mathcal{Z}_{prior}$, we can define new semantic functions Sem^{step}_{prior}, Sem^{ch1}_{prior} and Sem^{ch2}_{prior}.

Now we shall see that, under suitable hypotheses, statecharts with negated events can be transformed into statecharts with priority and vice versa, while preserving semantics. To this purpose we define two transformations $TRANS1 : \mathcal{Z}_{prior} \rightarrow \mathcal{Z}_{neg}$ and $TRANS2 : \mathcal{Z}_{neg} \rightarrow \mathcal{Z}_{prior}$.

Let us see first the transformation $TRANS1$. For $Z \in \mathcal{Z}_{prior}$, the idea of the construction of $Z' = TRANS1(Z)$, inspired by [13], is the following. If we have $t_1 \prec_Z t_2^{(j)}$ for $t_1, t_2^{(j)} \in T_Z$, $1 \leq j \leq m$, transition t_1 is splitted into k transitions $t_1^{(1)}, \ldots, t_1^{(k)} \in T_{Z'}$ such that at least one of them is triggered when all transitions $t_2^{(1)}, \ldots, t_2^{(m)}$ are not triggered, and all $t_1^{(1)}, \ldots, t_1^{(k)}$ are not triggered if there is at least a transition $t_2^{(j)}$ triggered.

Given a statechart $Z \in \mathcal{Z}_{prior}$ let us assume:

1. $REM_Z = \{t_1 \in T_Z \mid \exists t_2 \in T_Z \text{ s.t. } t_1 \prec_Z t_2, trigger_Z(t_2) \subseteq trigger_Z(t_1)\}$. If we assume that, for every two transitions $t_1, t_2 \in T_Z$, $t_1 \prec_Z t_2$ always implies that for every microconfiguration μC, when t_1 is relevant in μC also t_2 is relevant in μC, then transitions in REM_Z can be never executed, and so they can be removed.
2. $REP_Z = \{t_1 \in T_Z \setminus REM_Z \mid \exists t_2 \in T_Z \text{ s. t. } t_1 \prec_Z t_2\}$, the set of transitions that must be splitted.
3. $transsplit_Z(t) : REP_Z \rightarrow 2^T$, the *transition splitting function* such that $transsplit_Z(t)$ is the set of transitions into which t is splitted.
4. $\mathcal{B}_Z$, the set of boolean expressions over E_Z constructed by means of the operators *and*, *or* and *negation*, such that, given a microconfiguration $\mu C = (S_{exit}, T_{done}, S_{curr}, E_{curr})$ and an event $e \in E_Z$, the atomic expression e is true iff $e \in E_{curr}$. We shall use $b, b', b_1, b_2, \ldots$ to range over $\mathcal{B}_Z$. Let us remember that in original Harel's statecharts triggers of transitions are boolean expressions over $\mathcal{E}$ and that in [13] Pnueli and Shalev give the equivalent representation of triggers by means of sets of events, that we have used in our syntax.
5. $lockexpr_Z(t) : REP_Z \rightarrow \mathcal{B}_Z$, the *lock expression function* such that $lock$ $expr_Z(t) = b_1 \vee \ldots \vee b_{m(t)}$ is the disjunctive normal form of the logical formula

$$\bigwedge_{t \prec_Z t_1} (\overline{\bigwedge_{e \in trigger_Z(t_1)} e}).$$

So, given a microconfiguration μC, $lockexpr_Z(t)$ has value true iff for every $t_1 \in T_Z$ such that $t \prec_Z t_1$, t_1 is not triggered in μC, false otherwise.

6. $lockexprsplit_Z : REP_Z \rightarrow 2^{2^{\overline{E_Z}}}$, the *lock expression splitting function* s.t. $lockexprsplit_Z(t) = \{\overline{E_1}, \ldots, \overline{E_{m(t)}}\}$ with $\overline{E_i} = \{\overline{e} \in \overline{E_Z} \mid \overline{e}$ is a conjunct of b_i with b_i the i-th disjunct of $lockexpr_Z(t)\}$, for $1 \leq i \leq m(t)$. For $t \in REP_Z$ the set $lockexprsplit_Z(t)$ bijectively corresponds to $transsplit_Z(t)$ with $f_Z(t) : transsplit_Z(t) \rightarrow lockexprsplit_Z(t)$ such a bijection. The intuition is that each $\overline{E_i}$ contains the negated events that, together with $trigger_Z(t)$, constitute the trigger of the i-th of the transitions into which t is splitted.

The statechart $Z' = TRANS1(Z)$ is defined as follows:

1. $S_{Z'} = S_Z$
2. $hrc_{Z'} = hrc_Z$
3. $type_{Z'} = type_Z$
4. $default_{Z'} = default_Z$
5. $E_{Z'} = E_Z$
6. $T_{Z'} = ((T_Z \setminus REP_Z) \setminus REM_Z) \cup \bigcup_{t \in REP_Z} transsplit_Z(t)$
7. $lout_{Z'}(t') = lout_Z(t')$ for $t' \in (T_Z \setminus REP_Z) \setminus REM_Z$
   $lout_{Z'}(t') = lout_Z(t)$ for $t \in REP_Z$, $t' \in transsplit_Z(t)$
8. $lin_{Z'}(t') = lin_Z(t')$ for $t' \in (T_Z \setminus REP_Z) \setminus REM_Z$
   $lin_{Z'}(t') = lin_Z(t)$ for $t \in REP_Z$, $t' \in transsplit_Z(t)$
9. $hout_{Z'}(t') = hout_Z(t')$ for $t' \in (T_Z \setminus REP_Z) \setminus REM_Z$
   $hout_{Z'}(t') = hout_Z(t)$ for $t \in REP_Z$, $t' \in transsplit_Z(t)$
10. $hin_{Z'}(t') = hin_Z(t')$ for $t' \in (T_Z \setminus REP_Z) \setminus REM_Z$
    $hin_{Z'}(t') = hin_Z(t)$ for $t \in REP_Z$, $t' \in transsplit_Z(t)$
11. $trigger_{Z'}(t') = trigger_Z(t')$ for $t' \in (T_Z \setminus REP_Z) \setminus REM_Z$
    $trigger_{Z'}(t') = trigger_Z(t) \cup f_Z(t)(t')$ for $t \in REP_Z$, $t' \in transsplit_Z(t)$
12. $action_{Z'}(t') = action_Z(t')$ for $t' \in (T_Z \setminus REP_Z) \setminus REM_Z$
    $action_{Z'}(t') = action_Z(t)$ for $t \in REP_Z$, $t' \in transsplit_Z(t)$

As an example, let us consider the statechart $Z \in \mathcal{Z}_{prior}$ of Figure 3(a) with $trigger_Z(t_1) = \{e_1\}$, $trigger_Z(t_2) = \{e_2, e_3\}$, $trigger_Z(t_3) = \{e_3, e_4\}$, $action_Z(t_i) = \emptyset$, for $1 \leq i \leq 3$, $t_1 \prec_Z t_2$, $t_1 \prec_Z t_3$. We have $REM_Z = \emptyset$, $REP_Z = \{t_1\}$, $transsplit_Z = \{(t_1, \{t_1^{(1)}, t_1^{(2)}, t_1^{(3)}, t_1^{(4)}\})\}$, $lockexpr_Z = \{(t_1, (\overline{e_2} \wedge \overline{e_3}) \vee \overline{e_3} \vee (\overline{e_2} \wedge \overline{e_4}) \vee (\overline{e_3} \wedge \overline{e_4}))\}$, $lockexprsplit_Z = \{(t_1, \{\{\overline{e_2}, \overline{e_3}\}, \{\overline{e_3}\}, \{\overline{e_2}, \overline{e_4}\}, \{\overline{e_3}, \overline{e_4}\}\})\}$, $f_Z(t_1) = \{(t_1^{(1)}, \{\overline{e_2}, \overline{e_3}\}), (t_1^{(2)}, \{\overline{e_3}\}), (t_1^{(3)}, \{\overline{e_2}, \overline{e_4}\}), (t_1^{(4)}, \{\overline{e_3}, \overline{e_4}\})\}$. So, if we apply the transformation $TRANS1$ to Z, we obtain the statechart $Z' \in \mathcal{Z}_{neg}$ of Figure 3(b) with $trigger_{Z'}(t_1^{(1)}) = \{e_1, \overline{e_2}, \overline{e_3}\}$, $trigger_{Z'}(t_1^{(2)}) = \{e_1, \overline{e_3}\}$ $trigger_{Z'}(t_1^{(3)}) = \{e_1, \overline{e_2}, \overline{e_4}\}$, $trigger_{Z'}(t_1^{(4)}) = \{e_1, \overline{e_3}, \overline{e_4}\}$, $trigger_{Z'}(t_2) = \{e_2, e_3\}$, $trigger_{Z'}(t_3) = \{e_3, e_4\}$, $action_{Z'}(t') = \emptyset$, for every $t' \in T_{Z'}$.

We want to show that, under suitable hypotheses , $TRANS1$ is a semantics preserving transformation. It is immediate to prove the following proposition.

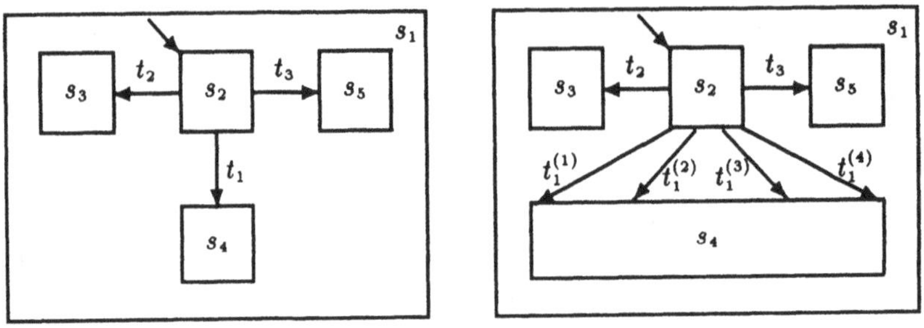

Fig. 3.

Proposition 3.1 Given transitions $t_1, t_2 \in T_Z$, for every microconfiguration μC t_1 is relevant in μC implies t_2 relevant in μC iff $lout_Z(t_1) \in hrc^*_Z(lout_Z(t_2))$. ∎

We need a notation and a lemma.

Notation. Given $Z \in \mathcal{Z}_{prior}$ and $Z' = TRANS1(Z)$, if $\mu C = (S_{exit}, T_{done}, S_{curr}, E_{curr})$ is a microconfiguration for Z and $\mu C' = (S'_{exit}, T'_{done}, S'_{curr}, E'_{curr})$ is a microconfiguration for Z', we write $\mu C \doteq \mu C'$ iff:

1. $S'_{exit} = S_{exit}$
2. there exists a bijection $h_1 : T_{done} \rightarrow T'_{done}$ such that for $t \in T_{done}$ either $h_1(t) = t$ if $t \in (T_Z \setminus REP_Z) \setminus REM_Z$ or $h_1(t) = t'$ if $t \in REP_Z$ with $t' \in transsplit_Z(t)$
3. $S'_{curr} = S_{curr}$
4. $E'_{curr} = E_{curr}$.

Lemma 3.1 Given $Z \in \mathcal{Z}_{prior}$, s.t. $t_1 \prec_Z t_2$ implies $lout_Z(t_1) \in hrc^*_Z(lout_Z(t_2))$, and $Z' = TRANS1(Z)$, let us assume either the step semantics or the chain semantics of type 1. If Z and Z' are in two microconfigurations $\mu C = (S_{exit}, T_{done}, S_{curr}, E_{curr})$ and $\mu C' = (S'_{exit}, T'_{done}, S'_{curr}, E'_{curr})$, respectively, such that $\mu C \doteq \mu C'$, for every $t \in T_Z$:

1. t enabled in $\mu C \wedge t \notin REP_Z \Leftrightarrow t \in T_{Z'} \wedge t$ enabled in $\mu C' \wedge trigger_{Z'}(t) \subseteq E_{Z'}$
2. t enabled in $\mu C \wedge t \in REP_Z \Leftrightarrow \exists t^{(j)} \in transsplit_Z(t)$ enabled in $\mu C'$.

Proof.
See appendix. ∎

Now we can enunciate the following theorem.

Theorem 3.1 Given $Z \in \mathcal{Z}_{prior}$, s.t. $t_1 \prec_Z t_2$ implies $lout_Z(t_1) \in hrc^*_Z(lout_Z(t_2))$, $Z' = TRANS1(Z)$, a configuration C and an environment E, there exists a total function $p : Sem^{step}_{prior}[\![Z]\!]CE \rightarrow 2^{Sem^{step}_{neg}[\![Z']\!]CE}$ such that:

1. $\forall \Sigma \in Sem^{step}_{prior}[\![Z]\!]CE \;\; \forall \Sigma' \in p(\Sigma) \; nextC(\Sigma) = nextC(\Sigma')$

2. $\forall \Sigma' \in Sem^{step}_{neg}[\![Z']\!]CE \; \exists \Sigma \in Sem^{step}_{prior}[\![Z]\!]CE \;\; \Sigma' \in p(\Sigma)$.

Proof.
See appendix. ∎

An analogous result can be obtained by assuming the chain semantics of type 1, but it does not hold if one assumes the chain semantics of type 2. Actually, in case of statecharts with cycles (a cycle is a sequence of transitions $t_1, \ldots, t_k$ where $lout_Z(t_{i+1}) \in entered_Z(t_i)$, $1 \le i \le k-1$, and $lout_Z(t_1) \in entered_Z(t_k)$), if a transition of the cycle is splitted by $TRANS1$ in more transitions, two or more of these might be executed in the same step and the equivalence would not hold anymore. Therefore we are able to prove equivalence for the chain semantics of type 2 only under the further assumption that, if a statechart has a cycle, any transition of the cycle has at most a transition with higher priority, and in this case such transition has at most one triggering event.
Note that when we have a statechart $Z \in \mathcal{Z}_{prior}$ with two transitions $t_1, t_2 \in T_Z$ s.t. $trigger_Z(t_2) \subseteq trigger_Z(t_1)$ and $t_1 \prec_Z t_2$ (under the hypothesis that $lout_Z(t_1) \in hrc^*_Z(lout_Z(t_2))$, t_1 will never be performed, because it will never be enabled. Correspondingly, in $Z' = TRANS1(Z)$ all the transitions in $ranssplit_Z(t_1)$ have triggers containing both e and $\overline{e}$ for some $e \in E_{Z'}$. Obviously such transitions will never be triggered and, therefore, will never be performed, as we want.

Let us see now the transformation $TRANS2$. For $Z \in \mathcal{Z}_{neg}$, the idea of the construction of $Z' = TRANS2(Z)$ is the following. We replace every transition $t \in T_Z$, with negated events in its trigger, by a transition $t' \in T_{Z'}$ that differs from t only because the negative events of the trigger are dropped. Moreover, for every negated event $\overline{e} \in trigger_Z(t)$ we add a new transition $t'' \in T_{Z'}$ with $lout_{Z'}(t'') = lin_{Z'}(t'') = hout_{Z'}(t'') = hin_{Z'}(t'') = lout_Z(t)$, $trigger_{Z'}(t'') = \{e\}$ and $action_{Z'}(t'') = \emptyset$. In order that t' is not performed when the event e is in the environment, we give t' a lower priority than that of t''. Now, in the step semantics, the execution of t'' would not allow the execution of another transition in the same parallel component in the considered step. The idea is that of giving t'' a lower priority than that of itself, so it will never be executed, but we will reach the effect that also t' is not executed.
Given a statechart $Z \in \mathcal{Z}_{neg}$ let us assume:

1. $NEG_Z = \{t \in T_Z \mid trigger_Z(t) \cap \overline{E_Z} \neq \emptyset\}$, the set of transitions that contain negated events in their trigger.
2. $NEWT_Z$ a set of new transitions bijectively corresponding to NEG_Z with $r_Z : NEG_Z \to NEWT_Z$ such bijection.
3. $negevents_Z : NEWT_Z \to 2^{E_Z}$, the *negated events function* that for a transition $t' \in NEWT_Z$ gives the set of events appearing negated in $trigger_Z(t)$ with $r_Z(t) = t'$, i.e. such that $negevents_Z(t') = \overline{trigger_Z(r_Z^{-1}(t')) \cap \overline{E_Z}}$.
4. $loop_Z : NEWT_Z \to 2^T$, the *loop function* such that for $t' \in NEWT_Z$, $loop_Z(t')$ is a set of new transitions bijectively corresponding to $negevents_Z(t')$, with $g_Z(t') : loop_Z(t') \to negevents_Z(t')$ such bijection.

The statechart $Z' = TRANS2(Z)$ is defined as follows:

1. $S_{Z'} = S_Z$
2. $hrc_{Z'} = hrc_Z$
3. $type_{Z'} = type_Z$
4. $default_{Z'} = default_Z$
5. $E_{Z'} = E_Z$
6. $T_{Z'} = (T_Z \setminus NEG_Z) \cup NEWT_Z \cup \bigcup_{t' \in NEWT_z} loop_Z(t')$
7. $lout_{Z'}(t') = lout_Z(t')$ if $t' \in T_Z \setminus NEG_Z$
   $lout_{Z'}(t') = lout_Z(t)$ if $t' \in NEWT_Z \wedge r_Z(t) = t'$
   $lout_{Z'}(t'') = lout_Z(t)$ if $t'' \in loop_Z(t') \wedge t \in NEG_Z \wedge r_Z(t) = t'$
8. $lin_{Z'}(t') = lin_Z(t')$ if $t' \in T_Z \setminus NEG_Z$
   $lin_{Z'}(t') = lin_Z(t)$ if $t' \in NEWT_Z \wedge r_Z(t) = t'$
   $lin_{Z'}(t'') = lin_Z(t)$ if $t'' \in loop_Z(t') \wedge t \in NEG_Z \wedge r_Z(t) = t'$
9. $hout_{Z'}(t') = hout_Z(t')$ if $t' \in T_Z \setminus NEG_Z$
   $hout_{Z'}(t') = hout_Z(t)$ if $t' \in NEWT_Z \wedge r_Z(t) = t'$
   $hout_{Z'}(t'') = hout_Z(t)$ if $t'' \in loop_Z(t') \wedge t \in NEG_Z \wedge r_Z(t) = t'$
10. $hin_{Z'}(t') = hin_Z(t')$ if $t' \in T_Z \setminus NEG_Z$
    $hin_{Z'}(t') = hin_Z(t)$ if $t' \in NEWT_Z \wedge r_Z(t) = t'$
    $hin_{Z'}(t'') = hin_Z(t)$ if $t'' \in loop_Z(t') \wedge t \in NEG_Z \wedge r_Z(t) = t'$
11. $trigger_{Z'}(t') = trigger_Z(t')$ if $t' \in T_Z \setminus NEG_Z$
    $trigger_{Z'}(t') = trigger_Z(t) \cap E_Z$ if $t' \in NEWT_Z \wedge r_Z(t) = t'$
    $trigger_{Z'}(t'') = \{g_Z(t')(t'')\}$ if $t'' \in loop_Z(t')$ for some $t' \in NEWT_Z$
12. $action_{Z'}(t') = action_Z(t')$ if $t' \in T_Z \setminus NEG_Z$
    $action_{Z'}(t') = action_Z(t)$ if $t' \in NEWT_Z \wedge r_Z(t) = t'$
    $action_{Z'}(t'') = \emptyset$ if $t'' \in loop_Z(t')$ for some $t' \in NEWT_Z$
13. $t' \prec_{Z'} t''$ if $t' \in NEWT_Z \wedge t'' \in loop_Z(t')$
    $t'' \prec_{Z'} t''$ if $t'' \in loop_Z(t')$ for some $t' \in NEWT_Z$.

As an example, let us consider the statechart $Z \in \mathcal{Z}_{neg}$ of Figure 4(a) with $trigger_Z(t_1) = \{\overline{e_1}, e_2\}$, $trigger_Z(t_2) = \{\overline{e_2}, \overline{e_3}\}$, $action_Z(t_i) = \emptyset$, for $1 \le i \le 2$. In this case we have $NEG_Z = \{t_1, t_2\}$, $NEWT_Z = \{t'_1, t'_2\}$, $r_Z = \{(t_1, t'_1), (t_2, t'_2)\}$, $negevents_Z = \{(t'_1, \{e_1\}), (t'_2, \{e_2, e_3\})\}$, $loop_Z = \{(t'_1, \{t_1^{(1)}\}), (t'_2, \{t_2^{(1)}, t_2^{(2)}\})\}$, $g_Z(t'_1) = \{(t_1^{(1)}, e_1)\}$, $g_Z(t'_2) = \{(t_2^{(1)}, e_2), (t_2^{(2)}, e_3).\}$. So if we apply the transformation $TRANS2$ to Z we obtain the statechart $Z' \in \mathcal{Z}_{prior}$ of Figure 4(b) with $trigger_{Z'}(t'_1) = \{e_2\}$, $trigger_{Z'}(t'_2) = \emptyset$, $trigger_{Z'}(t_1^{(1)}) = \{e_1\}$, $trigger_{Z'}(t_2^{(1)}) = \{e_2\}$, $trigger_{Z'}(t_2^{(2)}) = \{e_3\}$, $action_{Z'}(t') = \emptyset$, for every $t' \in T_{Z'}$, $t'_1 \prec_{Z'} t_1^{(1)}$, $t_1^{(1)} \prec_{Z'} t_1^{(1)}$, $t'_2 \prec_{Z'} t_2^{(1)}$, $t'_2 \prec_{Z'} t_2^{(2)}$, $t_2^{(1)} \prec_{Z'} t_2^{(1)}$, $t_2^{(2)} \prec_{Z'} t_2^{(2)}$.

Now we need a notation and a lemma.

Notation. Given $Z \in \mathcal{Z}_{neg}$ and $Z' = TRANS2(Z)$, if $\mu C = (S_{exit}, T_{done}, S_{curr}, E_{curr})$ is a microconfiguration for Z and $\mu C' = (S'_{exit}, T'_{done}, S'_{curr}, E'_{curr})$ is a microconfiguration for Z' we write $\mu C \hat{=} \mu C'$ iff:

1. $S'_{exit} = S_{exit}$

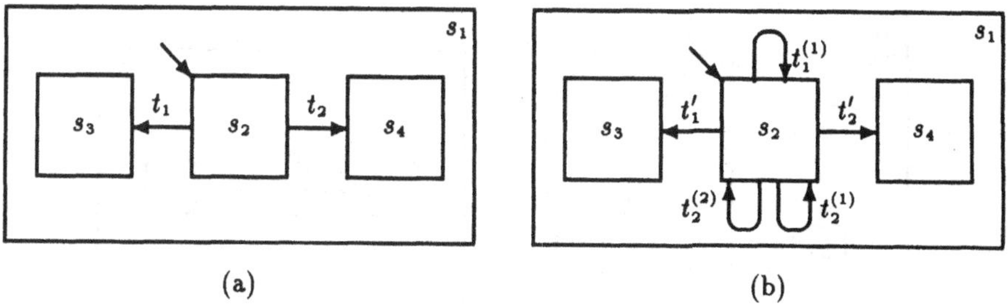

Fig. 4.

2. there exists a bijection $h_2 : T_{done} \rightarrow T'_{done}$ such that for $t \in T_{done}$ either $h_2(t) = t$ if $t \in (T_Z \setminus NEG_Z)$ or $h_2(t) = r_Z(t)$ if $t \in NEG_Z$
3. $S'_{curr} = S_{curr}$
4. $E'_{curr} = E_{curr}$.

Lemma 3.2 Given $Z \in \mathcal{Z}_{neg}$ and $Z' = TRANS2(Z)$, let us assume any of the three semantics considered. If Z and Z' are in microconfigurations $\mu C = (S_{exit}, T_{done}, S_{curr}, E_{curr})$ and $\mu C' = (S'_{exit}, T'_{done}, S'_{curr}, E'_{curr})$, respectively, such that $\mu C \hat{=} \mu C'$, for every $t \in T_Z$:

1. t enabled in $\mu C \wedge t \notin NEG_Z \Leftrightarrow t \in (T_Z \setminus NEG_Z) \wedge t$ enabled in $\mu C'$
2. t enabled in $\mu C \wedge t \in NEG_Z \Leftrightarrow r_Z(t)$ enabled in $\mu C'$.

Proof.
See appendix. ∎

Now we can enunciate the following theorem.

Theorem 3.2 Given $Z \in \mathcal{Z}_{neg}$, $Z' = TRANS2(Z)$, a configuration C and an environment E, there exists a bijective function $q : Sem^{step}_{neg}[\![Z]\!]CE \rightarrow Sem^{step}_{prior}[\![Z']\!]$ CE s.t. for every step $\Sigma \in Sem^{step}_{neg}[\![Z]\!]CE$ it holds $nextC(\Sigma) = nextC(q(\Sigma))$.

Proof.
See appendix. ∎

An analogous result can be obtained by assuming either the chain semantics of type 1 or the chain semantics of type 2.

Now for statecharts in $\mathcal{Z}_{neg}$ consistency problems may arise (see [13, 1]). As an example, let us consider the statechart $Z \in \mathcal{Z}_{neg}$ of Figure 5(a) assuming $trigger_Z(t_1) = \{\overline{e_1}\}$, $action_Z(t_1) = \{e_2\}$, $trigger_Z(t_2) = \{e_2\}$, $action_Z(t_2) = \{e_1\}$, and any of the three semantics defined for $\mathcal{Z}_{neg}$. Let us take as configuration the default configuration and $E = \emptyset$ as set of external events. In this case $\Sigma = \langle\{t_1\}, \{t_2\}\rangle$ is the only admissible step. This step is not consistent because, by the synchrony hypothesis, we have that in the instant when Σ is performed both

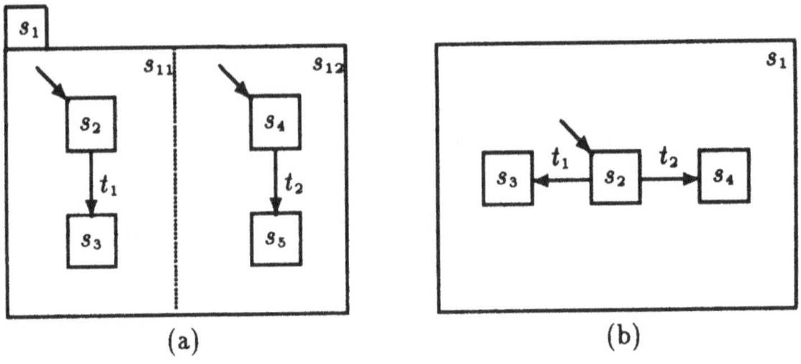

Fig. 5.

the event e_1 occurs and the transition t_1 is performed, whose triggering condition requires that e_1 does not occur in the instant. We formalize now the concept of global consistency of a step.

Definition 3.3 Given a statechart $Z \in \mathcal{Z}_{neg}$, an admissible step $\Sigma = \{\mu\Sigma_0, \ldots, \mu\Sigma_n\}$ of Z from a configuration C in an environment E is ***globally consistent*** iff it does not contain two (non-necessarily distinct) transitions $t \in \mu\Sigma_i$ and $t' \in \mu\Sigma_j$ such that $0 \leq i \leq j \leq n$, $\overline{e} \in trigger_Z(t)$ and $e \in action_Z(t')$ for some $e \in E_Z$.

A semantics for $\mathcal{Z}_{neg}$ is called globally consistent iff it only allows globally consistent admissible steps. Our semantics are not globally consistent. Two examples of globally consistent semantics are those in [13, 9].

Now one may wonder whether by replacing negated events with an explicit priority relation consistency problems of the kind seen above disappear. We shall see that this is not the case. Also for statecharts in $\mathcal{Z}_{prior}$ we may have consistency problems. As an example consider the statechart of Figure 5(b) assuming $trigger_Z(t_1) = \{e_1\}$, $action_Z(t_1) = \{e_2\}$, $trigger_Z(t_2) = \{e_2\}$, $action_Z(t_2) = \emptyset$, and $t_1 \prec_Z t_2$. Let us take as a configuration the default configuration and $E = \{e_1\}$ as environment. In this case $\Sigma = \langle\{t_1\}\rangle$ is the only admissible step. This step is not consistent because, by the synchrony hypothesis, in the instant when Σ is performed both the event e_2 occurs and transition t_1 is chosen, but, if e_2 occurs, t_2 should be chosen as $t_1 \prec_Z t_2$.

Definition 3.4 Given a statechart $Z \in \mathcal{Z}_{prior}$, an admissible step $\Sigma = \{\mu\Sigma_0, \ldots, \mu\Sigma_n\}$ of Z from a configuration C in an environment E is ***consistent w.r. to priority*** iff for every microstep $\mu\Sigma_i$ of Σ and for every transition $t \in \mu\Sigma_i$, $0 \leq i \leq n$, there is no transition $t' \in T_Z$ such that $t \prec_Z t'$, t' is relevant and consistent in μC_i and triggered in μC_j for $j > i$.

A semantics for $\mathcal{Z}_{prior}$ is called consistent w.r. to priority iff it only allows admissible steps consistent w.r. to priority. Our semantics are not consistent w.r. to priority.

Now we show that the transformations $TRANS1$ and $TRANS2$ preserve consistency in the sense that they neither introduce nor eliminate inconsistencies.

Theorem 3.3 Given $Z \in \mathcal{Z}_{prior}$, s.t. $t_1 \prec_Z t_2$ implies $lout_Z(t_1) \in hrc_Z^*(lout_Z(t_2))$, $Z' = TRANS1(Z)$, a configuration C and an environment E, for every step $\Sigma \in Sem_{prior}^{step}[\![Z]\!]CE$ it holds:

$$\Sigma \text{ consistent w.r. to priority} \Leftrightarrow \exists\, \Sigma' \in p(\Sigma)\ \ \Sigma' \text{ globally consistent.}$$

Proof.
See appendix. ∎

An analogous result can be proved by assuming chain semantics of type 1.

Theorem 3.4 Given $Z \in \mathcal{Z}_{neg}$, $Z' = TRANS2(Z) \in \mathcal{Z}_{prior}$, a configuration C and an environment E, for every step $\Sigma \in Sem_{neg}^{step}[\![Z]\!]CE$ it holds:

$$\Sigma \text{ globally consistent} \Leftrightarrow q(\Sigma) \text{ consistent w.r. to priority.}$$

Proof.
It follows easily from Theorem 3.2 along the line of the proof of Theorem 3.3. ∎

We can enunciate an analogous theorem for both the chain semantics of type 1 and the chain semantics of type 2.

4 Priority induced by the hierarchical structure of states

The hierarchical structure of states may be used to express several forms of priority. In particular, one may think of modelling interrupts, namely mechanisms to interrupt (under suitable conditions) system activities. In fact, in statecharts activities are modelled by states, and so interrupts can be modelled by transitions whose source state represents the (sequential or parallel) activity that should be interrupted. As an example, consider the statecharts Z_1 and Z_2 in Figure 6(a) and Figure 6(b), respectively. Transition t_6 may be interpreted as an interrupt for the sequential (resp. parallel) activity associated with state s_2 of Z_1 (resp. Z_2). Now, according to Harel's semantics ([8]), assuming that the statecharts are in both the case in the default configuration, with only transitions t_i, $2 \leq i \leq 6$, triggered, there would be a nondeterministic choice between transition t_6 and transitions t_2. Now, if we want that transition t_6 behaves as an interrupt, all the transitions in s_2 must have lower priority than transition t_6. In the literature there are various forms of priorities between transitions, that are induced by the hierarchical structure of states and support the concept of interrupt above.

In [4] a priority is defined that depends on the level of the source state of the transitions.

Definition 4.1 Given a statechart $Z \in \mathcal{Z}$ and two transitions $t_1, t_2 \in T_Z$, t_1 has lower priority than t_2 *à la Day*, denoted $t_1 \prec_{Day} t_2$, iff $lout_Z(t_1) \in hrc_Z^+(lout_Z(t_2))$.

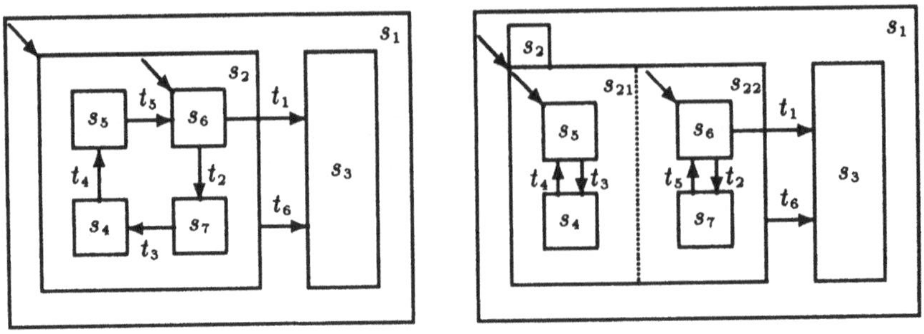

(a) (b)

Fig. 6.

So, assuming the class of statecharts $\mathcal{Z}$ we can define a semantic function Sem^{step}_{Day} (resp. Sem^{ch1}_{Day}, Sem^{ch2}_{Day}): $\mathcal{Z} \times 2^{\mathcal{S}} \times 2^{\mathcal{E}} \rightarrow 2^{(2^{\mathcal{T}})^*}$ that differs from Sem^{step} (resp. Sem^{ch1}, Sem^{ch2}) because a new enabling condition :

$$4'.\ \forall t' \in T_Z\ t' \text{ relevant, triggered and consistent in } \mu C \Rightarrow t \not\prec_{Day} t'$$

is added to the condition in definition 2.7

From [13] another form of priority can be deduced. It is based on the concept of arena.

Definition 4.2 Given a statechart $Z \in \mathcal{Z}$ and two transitions $t_1, t_2 \in T_Z$, t_1 has lower priority than t_2 *à la Pnueli and Shalev*, denoted $t_1 \prec_{P\&S} t_2$, iff

1. $arena_Z(t_1) \in hrc^+_Z(arena_Z(t_2))$
2. $lout_Z(t_1)$ and $lout_Z(t_2)$ are consistent.

Note that condition 1 and 2 together ensure that we are considering potentially conflicting transitions. Semantic functions $Sem^{step}_{P\&S}$ (resp. $Sem^{ch1}_{P\&S}$, $Sem^{ch2}_{P\&S}$) can be defined analogously to what done before for priority à la Day. Note that $Sem^{step}_{P\&S}$ does not suffer the limitations due to the use of negated events that we have discussed in the previous section.

The following proposition shows that the two concepts of priority are equivalent if we limit ourselves to statecharts without interlevel transitions.

Proposition 4.1 Given a statechart $Z \in \mathcal{Z}$ such that for every $t \in T_Z$ $hout_Z(t) = lout_Z(t)$ and $hin_Z(t) = lin_Z(t)$, and two transitions $t_1, t_2 \in T_Z$, it holds that

$$t_1 \prec_{Day} t_2 \Leftrightarrow t_1 \prec_{P\&S} t_2.$$

Proof.

$\Longrightarrow$

If in Z there are no interlevel transitions and $lout_Z(t_1) \in hrc^+_Z(lout_Z(t_2))$ then $lin_Z(t_1) \in hrc^+_Z(lout_Z(t_2))$, and then $arena_Z(t_1) \in hrc^*_Z(lout_Z(t_2))$. This implies

that $arena_Z(t_1) \in hrc_Z^+(arena_Z(t_2))$. Moreover, as $lout_Z(t_1) \in hrc_Z^+(lout_Z(t_2))$, $lout_Z(t_1)$ and $lout_Z(t_2)$ are consistent, and so we have $t_1 \prec_{P\&S} t_2$.
$\Longleftarrow$
Assume $lout_Z(t_1) \notin hrc_Z^+(lout_Z(t_2))$; as $lout_Z(t_1)$ and $lout_Z(t_2)$ are consistent, there would be three possible cases:

1. $lout_Z(t_1) = lout_Z(t_2)$. In this case, as in Z there are no interlevel transitions, $arena_Z(t_1) = arena_Z(t_2)$, against the hypothesis that $arena_Z(t_1) \in hrc_Z^+(arena_Z(t_2))$.
2. $lout_Z(t_2) \in hrc_Z^+(lout_Z(t_1))$. In this case, as in Z there are no interlevel transitions, from the first part of the proof we have just seen that $arena_Z(t_2) \in hrc_Z^+(arena_Z(t_1))$, against the hypothesis that $arena_Z(t_1) \in hrc_Z^+(arena_Z(t_2))$.
3. $type_Z(lca_Z(\{lout_Z(t_1), lout_Z(t_2)\})) = AND$ and $lout_Z(t_2) \notin hrc_Z^*(lout_Z(t_1))$. In this case, as in Z there are no interlevel transitions, in $lca_Z(\{lout_Z(t_1), lout_Z(t_2)\}) = lca_Z(\{arena_Z(t_1), arena_Z(t_2)\})$ and so $type_Z(lca_Z(\{arena_Z(t_1), arena_Z(t_2)\})) = AND$, against the hypothesis that $arena_Z(t_1) \in hrc_Z^+(arena_Z(t_2))$.

■

The equivalence does not hold in general. In the case of the statechart of Figure 7(a) we have $t_1 \prec_{Day} t_2$ and $t_1 \not\prec_{P\&S} t_2$; moreover $t_3 \prec_{P\&S} t_1$ and $t_3 \not\prec_{Day} t_1$.

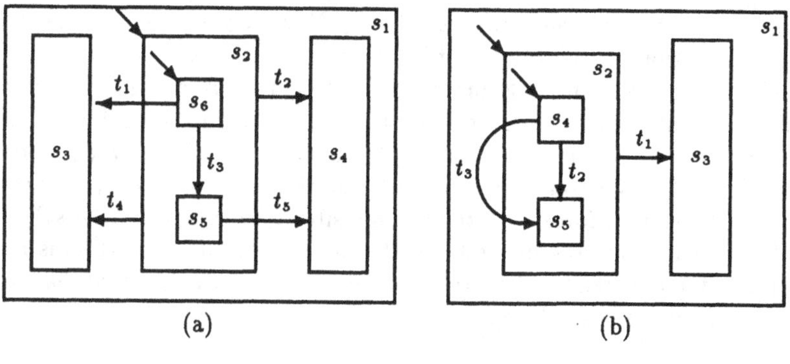

Fig. 7.

In [12] a transition is seen as an interrupt for the activity associated with its lowest source state. This is formalized by means of an implicite relation between a transition t and the transitions t_j inside $lout_Z(t)$, namely

$$t_j \prec_i t \text{ iff } lca_Z(\{lout_Z(t_j), lin_Z(t_j)\}) \in hrc_Z^*(lout_Z(t)).$$

If we consider the statechart in Figure 7(b), we see that with the definition above we would have $t_2 \prec_i t_1$ but also $t_3 \prec_i t_1$, and this is not reasonable because t_3

does not model an internal activity of state s_2. For this reason we consider now the relation

$$t_j \prec_i t \text{ iff } arena_Z(t_j) \in hrc_Z^*(lout_Z(t)).$$

Let us compare now the new relation $\prec_i$ with $\prec_{Day}$ and $\prec_{P\&S}$.

Proposition 4.2 Given a statechart $Z \in \mathcal{Z}$ and two transitions $t_1, t_2 \in T_Z$:

1. $t_1 \prec_i t_2 \Rightarrow t_1 \prec_{Day} t_2$
2. $t_1 \prec_i t_2 \Rightarrow t_1 \prec_{P\&S} t_2$.

Proof.

1. $t_1 \prec_i t_2 \Rightarrow arena_Z(t_1) \in hrc_Z^*(lout_Z(t_2)) \Rightarrow lout_Z(t_1) \in hrc_Z^+(lout_Z(t_2)) \Rightarrow t_1 \prec_{Day} t_2$. The vice versa does not hold. Consider, in fact, the statechart in Figure 7(a), for which it holds $t_5 \prec_{Day} t_4$ and $t_5 \not\prec_i t_4$.
2. $t_1 \prec_i t_2 \Rightarrow arena_Z(t_1) \in hrc_Z^*(lout_Z(t_2)) \Rightarrow arena_Z(t_1) \in hrc_Z^+(arena_Z(t_2))$ and $lout_Z(t_1)$ and $lout_Z(t_2)$ are consistent $\Rightarrow t_1 \prec_{P\&S} t_2$. The vice versa does not hold. Consider, in fact, the statechart in Figure 7(a), for which it holds $t_4 \prec_{P\&S} t_5$ and $t_4 \not\prec_i t_5$.

■

The proposition above shows that $\prec_{Day}$ and $\prec_{P\&S}$ may support a notion of interrupt more general than that supported by $\prec_i$. Now we want to investigate about a proper extension of the concept of interrupt.
Let us consider once more Figure 6. According to our concept of interrupt, in both the statecharts in figure, transition t_6 is an interrupt for transitions t_i, $2 \leq i \leq 5$, but not for transition t_1 (as $arena_Z(t_1) = arena_Z(t_6)$). In fact, transitions t_1 may be considered to be a "degenerate" interrupt, an interrupt because its execution forces to exit a composite state (namely state s_2), degenerate because its enabling depends on the internal status of s_2 (this is not the case of an interrupt like t_6). The formalization of *extended interrupt* that we give now covers also the case above.

Definition 4.3 Given a statechart $Z \in \mathcal{Z}$ and two transitions $t_1, t_2 \in T_Z$ we define $t_1 \prec_i^e t_2$ iff

1. $hout_Z(t_1) \in hrc_Z^+(hout_Z(t_2))$
2. $lout_Z(t_1)$ and $lout_Z(t_2)$ are consistent.

Obviously, given a statechart $Z \in \mathcal{Z}$, $\prec_i$ is a proper subset of $\prec_i^e$. Now we can prove that following proposition.

Proposition 4.3 Given a statechart $Z \in \mathcal{Z}$ and two transitions $t_1, t_2 \in T_Z$:

$$t_1 \prec_{P\&S} t_2 \Leftrightarrow t_1 \prec_i^e t_2.$$

Proof.

$\Longrightarrow$

We first prove that $arena_Z(t_1) \in hrc^*_Z(hout_Z(t_2))$. If $arena_Z(t_1) \notin hrc^*_Z(hout_Z(t_2))$, then, as $\forall\, t \in T_Z\ hout_Z(t) \in hrc_Z(arena_Z(t))$, there would exist a state $a \in hrc_Z(arena_Z(t_2))$, $a \neq hout_Z(t_2)$, such that $arena_Z(t_1) \in hrc^*_Z(a)$ against the hypothesis that $lout_Z(t_1)$ and $lout_Z(t_2)$ are consistent (remember that $\forall\, t \in T_Z\ type_Z(arena_Z(t)) = OR$). Finally, as it holds that for every $t \in T_Z\ hout_Z(t) \in hrc_Z(arena_Z(t))$, we have $t_1 \prec^*_i t_2$.

$\Longleftarrow$

If $hout_Z(t_1) \in hrc^+_Z(hout_Z(t_2))$, by definition of $hout_Z$ it holds $arena_Z(t_1) \in hrc^*_Z(hout_Z(t_2))$ and, as for every $t \in T_Z\ hout_Z(t) \in hrc_Z(arena_Z(t))$, we have $arena_Z(t_1) \in hrc^+_Z(arena_Z(t_2))$. ■

This shows that our formulation of extended interrupt is equivalent to Pnueli and Shalev's priority, while resembling that of Day as it is based on information regarding sources of transitions (the extra power comes from considering $hout_Z$ instead of $lout_Z$). It is immediate to see that the priorities considered in this section are transitive and therefore they are only a special case of the priorities of section 3.

5 Conclusions and future work

We have analyzed the power of the Statecharts language with respect to expressing transition based priority. Starting from the definition of a basic version of the language we have extended its syntax and semantics for expressing a general notion of priority. We have compared Statecharts with explicit priorities and Statecharts with negated events in triggers of transitions, and proved that the two formalisms can be translated one into the other under some restrictive conditions, showing that the formalism with explicit priorities is more powerful. We have also examined how a concept of interrupt can be modeled by a suitable interpretation of the hierarchical structure of states, and compared with priorities defined in terms of the structures of states by Day ([4]) and by Pnueli and Shalev ([13]).

We have assumed Statecharts with both a step semantics and instantaneous semantics that allow chain of transitions in the same component. In all the cases we have adopted a microstep approach in the definition of semantics. This gives rise to inconsistencies when basic statecharts are endowed with either negated events in triggers or explicit priorities. Among future developments, we consider to study priorities for Statecharts with consistent semantics (such as those of [13] and [9]).

The interrupts we have considered are preemptive, namely they cause immediate interruption of the activity of the subsystem associated. In the case of instantaneous semantics it would also be meaningful to study non-preemptive interrupts. Such interrupts, if enabled, only forbid the subsystem to continue its current activity at the next instant of time, while at the present instant the activity of the subsystem may be interrupted at every stage of its advancement (note that the language Esterel supports an analogous concept (see [2]).

Acknowledgement We thank two anonymous referees for constructive criticism.

References

1. von der Beeck, M.: A Comparison of Statecharts Variants, Proc. FTRTFT '94, Lecture Notes in Computer Science 863, Springer, Berlin, 1994, pp. 128–148.
2. Berry, G.: Preemption in Concurrent Systems, Proc. 13th FSTTCS Conference, Lecture Notes in Computer Science 761, Springer, Berlin, 1993, pp. 72-93.
3. Berry, G., Gonthier, G.: The ESTEREL Synchronous Programming Language: Design, Semantics, Implementation, Science of Computer Programming **19** (1992), pp. 87-152.
4. Day, N.: A Model Checker for Statecharts (Linking CASE Tools with Formal Methods), Technical Report 93-35, University of British Columbia, Vancouver, Canada, 1993.
5. Drusinsky, D., Harel, D.: Using Statecharts for Hardware Description and Synthesis, IEEE Transactions on Computer-Aided Design **8** (1989), pp. 798–807.
6. Harel, D.: Statecharts: A Visual Formalism for Complex Systems, Science of Computer Programming **8** (1987), pp. 231–274.
7. Harel, D., Lachover, H., Naamad, A., Pnueli, A., Politi, M., Sherman, R., Shtull-Trauring, A., Trakhtenbrot M.: Statemate: A Working Environment for the Development of Complex Reactive Systems, IEEE Transations on Software Engineering **16** (1990), pp. 403–414.
8. Harel, D., Pnueli, A., Schmidt, J., P., Sherman, R.: On the Formal Semantics of Statecharts, Proc. 2nd IEEE Symposium on Logic in Computer Science, IEEE CS Press, New York, 1987, pp. 54–64.
9. Maggiolo-Schettini, A., Peron, A., Tini, S.: Equivalence of Statecharts, Proc. CONCUR '96, Lecture Notes in Computer Science 1119, Springer, Berlin, 1996, pp. 687-702.
10. Maraninchi, F.: Operational and Compositional Semantics of Synchronous Automaton Composition, Proc. CONCUR '92, Lecture Notes in Computer Science 630, Springer, Berlin, 1992, pp. 550-564.
11. Peron, A.: Synchronous and Asynchronous Models for Statecharts, Dipartimento di Informatica, Università di Pisa, PhD Thesis, TD 21/93, 1993.
12. Peron, A., Maggiolo-Schettini, A.: Transitions as Interrupts: A New Semantics for Timed Statecharts, Proc. TACS '94, Lecture Notes in Computer Science 789, Springer, Berlin, 1994, pp. 806–821.
13. Pnueli, A., Shalev, M.: What is a Step: On the Semantics of Statecharts, Proc. TACS '91, Lecture Notes in Computer Science 526, Springer, Berlin, 1991, pp. 244–264.

Appendix

Proof of Lemma 3.1

1. $\Longrightarrow$

   There is no $t_1 \in T_Z$ such that $t \prec_Z t_1$. In this case it is easy to see that t is not affected by $TRANS1$ namely $t \in (T_Z \setminus REP_Z) \setminus REM_Z$. Therefore $t \in T_{Z'}$ and $trigger_{Z'}(t) = trigger_Z(t) \subseteq E_Z$. Moreover, as $\mu C \doteq \mu C'$, it is immediate to see that t is enabled in $\mu C'$.

$\Longleftarrow$

If $t \in T_{Z'}$ and $trigger_{Z'}(t) \subseteq E_Z$, t is not affected by $TRANS1$, and therefore $t \in (T_Z \setminus REP_Z) \setminus REM_Z$. Now, if t is enabled in $\mu C'$, as $\mu C \doteq \mu C'$, the enabling of t in μC follows immediately.

2. $\Longrightarrow$

For every transition $t_1 \in T_Z$ such that $t \prec_Z t_1$ (t_1 is relevant in μC by the hypothesis on $\prec_Z$) t_1 is not triggered in μC. In this case $lockexpr_Z(t)$ has value true in μC, namely there exists a disjunct b_j that is true. This implies that the corresponding transition $t^{(j)} \in transsplit_Z(t)$ is such that $f_Z(t)(t^{(j)}) \cap E'_{curr} = \emptyset$. So, as $trigger_{Z'}(t^{(j)}) = trigger_Z(t) \cup f_Z(t)(t^{(j)})$ and $E_{curr} = E'_{curr}$, $t^{(j)}$ is triggered in $\mu C'$. Moreover, as $S_{curr} = S'_{curr}$, $lout_Z(t) = lout_{Z'}(t^{(j)})$ and $hout_Z(t) = hout_{Z'}(t^{(j)})$, $t^{(j)}$ is relevant in $\mu C'$. Finally, because t and $t^{(j)}$ are in the same parallel component and have the same $lout$ and $hout$, $t^{(j)}$ is consistent in $\mu C'$, and therefore $t^{(j)}$ is enabled in $\mu C'$.

$\Longleftarrow$

If there exists a transition $t^{(j)} \in transsplit_Z(t)$ enabled in $\mu C'$, $t \in T_Z$ is relevant in μC because $S_{curr} = S'_{curr}$, $lout_Z(t) = lout_{Z'}(t^{(j)})$, $hout_Z(t) = hout_{Z'}(t^{(j)})$; in μC t is also triggered, because $E_{curr} = E'_{curr}$ and $trigger_Z(t) = trigger_{Z'}(t^{(j)}) \cap E_Z$, and consistent, because t and $t^{(j)}$ are in the same parallel component and have the same $lout$ and $hout$. Finally, if $t^{(j)}$ is triggered in $\mu C'$ the disjunct b_j of $lockexpr_Z(t)$ is true and so also $lockexpr_Z(t)$. This implies immediately there does not exist a transition $t_1 \in T_Z$, such that $t \prec_Z t_1$, triggered in μC. So $t \in T_Z$ is enabled in μC.

Proof of Theorem 3.1

1. Let us take $\Sigma = \{\mu\Sigma_0, \ldots, \mu\Sigma_n\} \in Sem^{step}_{prior}[\![Z]\!]CE$ and let $\mu\Sigma_i$ be a microstep from the microconfiguration $\mu C_i = (S^i_{exit}, T^i_{done}, S^i_{curr}, E^i_{curr})$ to $\mu C_{i+1} = (S^{i+1}_{exit}, T^{i+1}_{done}, S^{i+1}_{curr}, E^{i+1}_{curr})$, for $0 \leq i \leq n$. Let us construct a set $\Sigma' = \{\mu\Sigma'_0, \ldots, \mu\Sigma'_n\}$ where each $\mu\Sigma'_i \subseteq T_{Z'}$ is such that:
   (a) $t \in \mu\Sigma_i \wedge t \notin REP_Z \Rightarrow t \in \mu\Sigma'_i$
   (b) $t \in \mu\Sigma_i \wedge t \in REP_Z \wedge f_Z(t)(t^{(j)}) \cap E^i_{curr} = \emptyset$ for some $t^{(j)} \in transsplit_Z(t)$ $\Rightarrow t^{(j)} \in \mu\Sigma'_i$.

   If we assume the configuration C, the environment E and the microconfiguration $\mu C'_0 = (\emptyset, \emptyset, C, E)$, we have that, by Lemma 3.1, all the transitions of $\mu\Sigma'_0$ are enabled in $\mu C'_0$ and, immediately, that they are pairwise structurally consistent, and so $\mu\Sigma'_0$ is a microstep from $\mu C'_0$ ($= \mu C_0$) to $\mu C'_1$ (with $\mu C_1 \doteq \mu C'_1$). Moreover, again by Lemma 3.1, each $\mu\Sigma'_i$ is a microstep from $\mu C'_i$ to $\mu C'_{i+1}$ with $\mu C_i \doteq \mu C'_i$ and $\mu C_{i+1} \doteq \mu C'_{i+1}$, for $1 \leq i \leq n$. So Σ' is a set of microsteps. It also easy to see that Σ' is maximal. If this were not true, there would be a transition $t' \in T_{Z'}$ enabled in $\mu C'_{n+1}$. Now, either t' would be a transition not affected by $TRANS1$, and the same transition would be enabled in μC_{n+1}, or $t' \in transsplit_Z(t)$ for some $t \in REP_Z$, and in this case t would be enabled in μC_{n+1}, in both the cases against the maximality of Σ. Therefore $\Sigma' \in Sem^{step}_{neg}[\![Z']\!]CE$. Now we define p such that, given a step $\Sigma = \{\mu\Sigma_0, \ldots, \mu\Sigma_n\} \in Sem^{step}_{prior}[\![Z]\!]CE$, all steps Σ', constructed from Σ, are in $p(\Sigma)$. Finally, as, for each $\Sigma' \in p(\Sigma)$, $\mu C_{n+1} \doteq \mu C'_{n+1}$, it holds $nextC(\Sigma') = nextC(\Sigma)$.

2. Let us take $\Sigma' = \{\mu\Sigma'_0, \ldots, \mu\Sigma'_n\} \in Sem^{step}_{neg}[\![Z']\!]CE$ and let $\mu\Sigma'_i$ be a microstep from the microconfiguration $\mu C'_i$ to $\mu C'_{i+1}$, $0 \leq i \leq n$. Let us construct a set $\Sigma = \{\mu\Sigma_0, \ldots, \mu\Sigma_n\}$ where each $\mu\Sigma_i \subseteq T_Z$ is such that:
   (a) $t' \in \mu\Sigma'_i \land trigger_{Z'}(t') \cap \overline{E_{Z'}} = \emptyset \Rightarrow t' \in \mu\Sigma_i$
   (b) $t' \in \mu\Sigma'_i \land trigger_{Z'}(t') \cap \overline{E_{Z'}} \neq \emptyset \Rightarrow t \in \mu\Sigma_i$ for $t' \in transsplit_Z(t)$
   If we assume the configuration C, the environment E and the microconfiguration $\mu C_0 = (\emptyset, \emptyset, C, E)$, we have that, by Lemma 3.1, all the transitions of $\mu\Sigma_0$ are enabled in μC_0 and, immediately, that they are pairwise structurally consistent, and so $\mu\Sigma_0$ is a microstep from μC_0 ($= \mu C'_0$) to μC_1 ($\doteq \mu C'_1$). Moreover, again by Lemma 3.1, each $\mu\Sigma_i$ is a microstep from μC_i to μC_{i+1} with $\mu C_i \doteq \mu C'_i$ and $\mu C_{i+1} \doteq \mu C'_{i+1}$. So Σ is a set of microsteps. Its maximality follows immediately. Therefore, $\Sigma \in Sem^{step}_{prior}[\![Z]\!]CE$. Finally, by definition of p, $\Sigma' \in p(\Sigma)$.

Proof of Lemma 3.2

1. $\Longrightarrow$
   In this case t is not affected by $TRANS2$, and therefore $t \in (T_Z \setminus NEG_Z)$. Moreover, as $\mu C \doteq \mu C'$ and there is no $t' \in T_{Z'}$ such that $t \prec_{Z'} t'$ by definition of $TRANS2$, t is enabled in $\mu C'$.
   $\Longleftarrow$
   The proof follows a converse reasoning with respect to that of the direct implication.
2. $\Longrightarrow$
   In this case $r_Z(t) \in T_{Z'}$ and $\forall\, t'' \in loop_Z(r_Z(t))\;\; r_Z(t) \prec_{Z'} t''$. Now, as $\mu C \doteq \mu C'$, $trigger_{Z'}(r_Z(t)) = trigger_Z(t) \cap E_Z$, $lout_{Z'}(r_Z(t)) = lout_Z(t)$, $hout_{Z'}(r_Z(t)) = hout_Z(t)$, $lin_{Z'}(r_Z(t)) = lin_Z(t)$, $hin_{Z'}(r_Z(t)) = hin_Z(t)$, $r_Z(t)$ is trivially relevant, triggered and consistent in $\mu C'$. Moreover if t is triggered in μC, $negevents_Z(r_Z(t)) \cap E_{curr} = \emptyset$, and as $E_{curr} = E'_{curr}$, each $t'' \in loop_Z(r_Z(t))$ is not triggerd in $\mu C'$. Therefore there are no transitions with higher priority than $r_Z(t)$ and so $r_Z(t)$ is enabled in $\mu C'$.
   $\Longleftarrow$
   The proof follows a converse reasoning with respect to that of the direct implication.

Proof of Theorem 3.2

1. Let us take $\Sigma = \{\mu\Sigma_0, \ldots, \mu\Sigma_n\} \in Sem^{step}_{neg}[\![Z]\!]CE$ and let $\mu\Sigma_i$ be a microstep from the microconfiguration μC_i to μC_{i+1}, for $0 \leq i \leq n$. Let us construct a set $\Sigma' = \{\mu\Sigma'_0, \ldots, \mu\Sigma'_n\}$ where each $\mu\Sigma'_i \subseteq T_{Z'}$ is such that:

(a) $t \in \mu\Sigma_i \ \wedge\ t \notin NEG_Z \ \Rightarrow\ t \in \mu\Sigma'_i$

(b) $t \in \mu\Sigma_i \ \wedge\ t \in NEG_Z \ \Rightarrow\ r_Z(t) \in \mu\Sigma'_i$.

If we assume the configuration C, the environment E and the microconfiguration $\mu C'_0 = (\emptyset, \emptyset, C, E)$, we have that, by Lemma 3.2, all the transitions of $\mu\Sigma'_0$ are enabled in $\mu C'_0$ and, immediately, that they are pairwise structurally consistent, and so $\mu\Sigma'_0$ is a microstep from $\mu C'_0$ ($= \mu C_0$) to $\mu C'_1$ (with $\mu C_1 \hat{=} \mu C'_1$). Moreover, again by Lemma 3.2, each $\mu\Sigma'_i$ is a microstep from $\mu C'_i$ to $\mu C'_{i+1}$ with $\mu C_i \hat{=} \mu C'_i$ and $\mu C_{i+1} \hat{=} \mu C'_{i+1}$. So Σ' is a set of microsteps. It also easy to see that Σ' is maximal. If this were not true there would be a transition $t' \in T_{Z'}$ enabled in $\mu C'_{n+1}$. Now, either t' would be a transition not affected by $TRANS2$, and the same transition would be enabled in μC_{n+1}, or if $t' \in NEWT_Z$ and $r_Z^{-1}(t')$ would be enabled in μC_{n+1}, in both the cases against the maximality of Σ. Therefore $\Sigma' \in Sem^{step}_{prior}[\![Z']\!]CE$. Now we define q such $q(\Sigma) = \Sigma'$. As $\mu C_{n+1} \hat{=} \mu C'_{n+1}$, it holds $nextC(\Sigma) = nextC(q(\Sigma))$.

2. Let us take $\Sigma' = \{\mu\Sigma'_0, \ldots, \mu\Sigma'_n\} \in Sem^{step}_{prior}[\![Z']\!]CE$ and let $\mu\Sigma'_i$ be a microstep from the microconfiguration $\mu C'_i$ to $\mu C'_{i+1}$, $0 \le i \le n$. Let us construct a set $\Sigma = \{\mu\Sigma_0, \ldots, \mu\Sigma_n\}$ where each $\mu\Sigma_i \subseteq T_Z$ is such that:

   (a) $t' \in \mu\Sigma'_i \ \wedge\ t' \in (T_Z \backslash NEG_Z) \ \Rightarrow\ t' \in \mu\Sigma_i$

   (b) $t' \in \mu\Sigma'_i \ \wedge\ t' \in NEWT_Z \ \Rightarrow\ r_Z^{-1}(t') \in \mu\Sigma_i$.

   If we assume the configuration C, the environment E and the microconfiguration $\mu C_0 = (\emptyset, \emptyset, C, E)$, we have that, by Lemma 3.2, all the transitions of $\mu\Sigma_0$ are enabled in μC_0 and, immediately, that they are pairwise structurally consistent, and so $\mu\Sigma_0$ is a microstep from μC_0 ($= \mu C'_0$) to μC_1 ($\hat{=} \mu C'_1$). Moreover, again by Lemma 3.2, each $\mu\Sigma_i$ is a microstep from μC_i to μC_{i+1} with $\mu C_i \hat{=} \mu C'_i$ and $\mu C_{i+1} \hat{=} \mu C'_{i+1}$. So Σ is a set of microsteps. Its maximality follows immediately. Therefore, $\Sigma \in Sem^{step}_{neg}[\![Z]\!]CE$. Finally, by definition of q, $q(\Sigma) = \Sigma'$ for a unique step Σ, and hence q is a bijection.

Proof of Theorem 3.3

$\Longrightarrow$

Let us consider $\Sigma = \{\mu\Sigma_0, \ldots, \mu\Sigma_n\} \in Sem^{step}_{prior}[\![Z]\!]CE$ and let $\mu\Sigma_i$ be a μstep from the microconfiguration μC_i to μC_{i+1}, for $0 \le i \le n$. Let us assume Σ consistent w.r. to priority and let $t_1, \ldots, t_m$ be the sequence of all transitions in Σ such that:

1. $t_k \in REP_Z$ for $1 \le k \le m$
2. $t_k \in \mu\Sigma_{r_k} \Rightarrow t_l \in \mu\Sigma_{r_l}$, for $1 \le k < l \le m$, $0 \le r_k \le r_l \le n$.

Let us consider t_1 with $t_1 \in \mu\Sigma_{r_1}$, $0 \le r_1 \le n$. All steps in $p(\Sigma)$, contain in their r_1-th microstep, a transition of $transplit_Z(t_1)$. Now there is at least one $t_1^{(j_1)} \in transsplit_Z(t_1)$ such that, in all steps of $p(\Sigma)$ with $t_1^{(j_1)}$ in the r_1-th microstep, events are not generated that contradict the trigger of $t_1^{(j_1)}$. If this were not true, by definition of $TRANS1$, Σ would be not consistent w.r. to priority (t_1 should be not executed) against the hypothesis. Let us call R_1 the set of steps in $p(\Sigma)$ with $t_1^{(j_1)}$ in the r_1-th microstep. Now, by induction,

assume R_l, for $1 \leq l < m$, the set of steps with $t_h^{(j_h)}$ in the r_h-th microstep, $1 \leq h \leq l$, $t_h^{(j_h)} \in \mathit{transsplit}_Z(t_h)$ such that, in all steps of R_l events are not generated that contradict the triggers of $t_h^{(j_h)}$, for each h. Now all steps in R_l contain in their r_{l+1}-th microstep a transition of $\mathit{transsplit}_Z(t_{l+1})$ and there is at least one $t_{l+1}^{(j_l+1)} \in \mathit{transsplit}_Z(t_{l+1})$ such that, in all steps R_l with $t_{l+1}^{(j_l+1)}$ in the r_{l+1}-th microstep, events are not generated that contradict the trigger of $t_{l+1}^{(j_l+1)}$. If this were not true, by definition of $TRANS1$, Σ would be not consistent w.r. to priority. We define R_{l+1} the set of steps in R_l with $t_{l+1}^{(j_l+1)}$ in the r_{l+1}-th microstep. So we can conclude that there is a non empty set $R_m \subseteq p(\Sigma)$ of globally consistent steps.
It is easy to see that, in general, not all steps in $p(\Sigma)$ are globally consistent.

$\Longleftarrow$

Let us consider $\Sigma = \{\mu\Sigma_0, \ldots, \mu\Sigma_n\} \in Sem^{step}_{prior}[\![Z]\!]CE$ and let $\mu\Sigma_i$ be a μstep from the microconfiguration μC_i to μC_{i+1}, for $0 \leq i \leq n$. Let us assume a globally consistent step $\Sigma' \in p(\Sigma)$. Now if Σ were not consistent w.r. to priority there would be a transition $t \in \mu\Sigma_i$, for some i, and a transition $t_1 \in T_Z$ such that $t \prec_Z t_1$, t_1 relevant and consistent in μC_i but triggered in μC_j, with $j > i$. In this case, by definition of $TRANS1$, all steps in $p(\Sigma)$ should contain, in their i-th microstep, some transition of $\mathit{transsplit}_Z(t)$ whose trigger contains some negated event that is generated in the step. Therefore all the steps in $p(\Sigma)$ would not be globally consistent, against the hypothesis.

Subject Index

Author Index

Springer and the environment

At Springer we firmly believe that an international science publisher has a special obligation to the environment, and our corporate policies consistently reflect this conviction.
We also expect our business partners – paper mills, printers, packaging manufacturers, etc. – to commit themselves to using materials and production processes that do not harm the environment. The paper in this book is made from low- or no-chlorine pulp and is acid free, in conformance with international standards for paper permanency.

Springer

Lecture Notes in Computer Science

For information about Vols. 1–1112

please contact your bookseller or Springer-Verlag

Vol. 1113: W. Penczek, A. Szałas (Eds.), Mathematical Foundations of Computer Science 1996. Proceedings, 1996. X, 592 pages. 1996.

Vol. 1114: N. Foo, R. Goebel (Eds.), PRICAI'96: Topics in Artificial Intelligence. Proceedings, 1996. XXI, 658 pages. 1996. (Subseries LNAI).

Vol. 1115: P.W. Eklund, G. Ellis, G. Mann (Eds.), Conceptual Structures: Knowledge Representation as Interlingua. Proceedings, 1996. XIII, 321 pages. 1996. (Subseries LNAI).

Vol. 1116: J. Hall (Ed.), Management of Telecommunication Systems and Services. XXI, 229 pages. 1996.

Vol. 1117: A. Ferreira, J. Rolim, Y. Saad, T. Yang (Eds.), Parallel Algorithms for Irregularly Structured Problems. Proceedings, 1996. IX, 358 pages. 1996.

Vol. 1118: E.C. Freuder (Ed.), Principles and Practice of Constraint Programming — CP 96. Proceedings, 1996. XIX, 574 pages. 1996.

Vol. 1119: U. Montanari, V. Sassone (Eds.), CONCUR '96: Concurrency Theory. Proceedings, 1996. XII, 751 pages. 1996.

Vol. 1120: M. Deza. R. Euler, I. Manoussakis (Eds.), Combinatorics and Computer Science. Proceedings, 1995. IX, 415 pages. 1996.

Vol. 1121: P. Perner, P. Wang, A. Rosenfeld (Eds.), Advances in Structural and Syntactical Pattern Recognition. Proceedings, 1996. X, 393 pages. 1996.

Vol. 1122: H. Cohen (Ed.), Algorithmic Number Theory. Proceedings, 1996. IX, 405 pages. 1996.

Vol. 1123: L. Bougé, P. Fraigniaud, A. Mignotte, Y. Robert (Eds.), Euro-Par'96. Parallel Processing. Proceedings, 1996, Vol. I. XXXIII, 842 pages. 1996.

Vol. 1124: L. Bougé, P. Fraigniaud, A. Mignotte, Y. Robert (Eds.), Euro-Par'96. Parallel Processing. Proceedings, 1996, Vol. II. XXXIII, 926 pages. 1996.

Vol. 1125: J. von Wright, J. Grundy, J. Harrison (Eds.), Theorem Proving in Higher Order Logics. Proceedings, 1996. VIII, 447 pages. 1996.

Vol. 1126: J.J. Alferes, L. Moniz Pereira, E. Orlowska (Eds.), Logics in Artificial Intelligence. Proceedings, 1996. IX, 417 pages. 1996. (Subseries LNAI).

Vol. 1127: L. Böszörményi (Ed.), Parallel Computation. Proceedings, 1996. XI, 235 pages. 1996.

Vol. 1128: J. Calmet, C. Limongelli (Eds.), Design and Implementation of Symbolic Computation Systems. Proceedings, 1996. IX, 356 pages. 1996.

Vol. 1129: J. Launchbury, E. Meijer, T. Sheard (Eds.), Advanced Functional Programming. Proceedings, 1996. VII, 238 pages. 1996.

Vol. 1130: M. Haveraaen, O. Owe, O.-J. Dahl (Eds.), Recent Trends in Data Type Specification. Proceedings, 1995. VIII, 551 pages. 1996.

Vol. 1131: K.H. Höhne, R. Kikinis (Eds.), Visualization in Biomedical Computing. Proceedings, 1996. XII, 610 pages. 1996.

Vol. 1132: G.-R. Perrin, A. Darte (Eds.), The Data Parallel Programming Model. XV, 284 pages. 1996.

Vol. 1133: J.-Y. Chouinard, P. Fortier, T.A. Gulliver (Eds.), Information Theory and Applications II. Proceedings, 1995. XII, 309 pages. 1996.

Vol. 1134: R. Wagner, H. Thoma (Eds.), Database and Expert Systems Applications. Proceedings, 1996. XV, 921 pages. 1996.

Vol. 1135: B. Jonsson, J. Parrow (Eds.), Formal Techniques in Real-Time and Fault-Tolerant Systems. Proceedings, 1996. X, 479 pages. 1996.

Vol. 1136: J. Diaz, M. Serna (Eds.), Algorithms – ESA '96. Proceedings, 1996. XII, 566 pages. 1996.

Vol. 1137: G. Görz, S. Hölldobler (Eds.), KI-96: Advances in Artificial Intelligence. Proceedings, 1996. XI, 387 pages. 1996. (Subseries LNAI).

Vol. 1138: J. Calmet, J.A. Campbell, J. Pfalzgraf (Eds.), Artificial Intelligence and Symbolic Mathematical Computation. Proceedings, 1996. VIII, 381 pages. 1996.

Vol. 1139: M. Hanus, M. Rogriguez-Artalejo (Eds.), Algebraic and Logic Programming. Proceedings, 1996. VIII, 345 pages. 1996.

Vol. 1140: H. Kuchen, S. Doaitse Swierstra (Eds.), Programming Languages: Implementations, Logics, and Programs. Proceedings, 1996. XI, 479 pages. 1996.

Vol. 1141: H.-M. Voigt, W. Ebeling, I. Rechenberg, H.-P. Schwefel (Eds.), Parallel Problem Solving from Nature – PPSN IV. Proceedings, 1996. XVII, 1.050 pages. 1996.

Vol. 1142: R.W. Hartenstein, M. Glesner (Eds.), Field-Programmable Logic. Proceedings, 1996. X, 432 pages. 1996.

Vol. 1143: T.C. Fogarty (Ed.), Evolutionary Computing. Proceedings, 1996. VIII, 305 pages. 1996.

Vol. 1144: J. Ponce, A. Zisserman, M. Hebert (Eds.), Object Representation in Computer Vision. Proceedings, 1996. VIII, 403 pages. 1996.

Vol. 1145: R. Cousot, D.A. Schmidt (Eds.), Static Analysis. Proceedings, 1996. IX, 389 pages. 1996.

Vol. 1146: E. Bertino, H. Kurth, G. Martella, E. Montolivo (Eds.), Computer Security – ESORICS 96. Proceedings, 1996. X, 365 pages. 1996.

Vol. 1147: L. Miclet, C. de la Higuera (Eds.), Grammatical Inference: Learning Syntax from Sentences. Proceedings, 1996. VIII, 327 pages. 1996. (Subseries LNAI).

Vol. 1148: M.C. Lin, D. Manocha (Eds.), Applied Computational Geometry. Proceedings, 1996. VIII, 223 pages. 1996.

Vol. 1149: C. Montangero (Ed.), Software Process Technology. Proceedings, 1996. IX, 291 pages. 1996.

Vol. 1150: A. Hlawiczka, J.G. Silva, L. Simoncini (Eds.), Dependable Computing – EDCC-2. Proceedings, 1996. XVI, 440 pages. 1996.

Vol. 1151: Ö. Babaoğlu, K. Marzullo (Eds.), Distributed Algorithms. Proceedings, 1996. VIII, 381 pages. 1996.

Vol. 1152: T. Furuhashi, Y. Uchikawa (Eds.), Fuzzy Logic, Neural Networks, and Evolutionary Computation. Proceedings, 1995. VIII, 243 pages. 1996. (Subseries LNAI).

Vol. 1153: E. Burke, P. Ross (Eds.), Practice and Theory of Automated Timetabling. Proceedings, 1995. XIII, 381 pages. 1996.

Vol. 1154: D. Pedreschi, C. Zaniolo (Eds.), Logic in Databases. Proceedings, 1996. X, 497 pages. 1996.

Vol. 1155: J. Roberts, U. Mocci, J. Virtamo (Eds.), Broadbank Network Teletraffic. XXII, 584 pages. 1996.

Vol. 1156: A. Bode, J. Dongarra, T. Ludwig, V. Sunderam (Eds.), Parallel Virtual Machine – EuroPVM '96. Proceedings, 1996. XIV, 362 pages. 1996.

Vol. 1157: B. Thalheim (Ed.), Conceptual Modeling – ER '96. Proceedings, 1996. XII, 489 pages. 1996.

Vol. 1158: S. Berardi, M. Coppo (Eds.), Types for Proofs and Programs. Proceedings, 1995. X, 296 pages. 1996.

Vol. 1159: D.L. Borges, C.A.A. Kaestner (Eds.), Advances in Artificial Intelligence. Proceedings, 1996. XI, 243 pages. (Subseries LNAI).

Vol. 1160: S. Arikawa, A.K. Sharma (Eds.), Algorithmic Learning Theory. Proceedings, 1996. XVII, 337 pages. 1996. (Subseries LNAI).

Vol. 1161: O. Spaniol, C. Linnhoff-Popien, B. Meyer (Eds.), Trends in Distributed Systems. Proceedings, 1996. VIII, 289 pages. 1996.

Vol. 1162: D.G. Feitelson, L. Rudolph (Eds.), Job Scheduling Strategies for Parallel Processing. Proceedings, 1996. VIII, 291 pages. 1996.

Vol. 1163: K. Kim, T. Matsumoto (Eds.), Advances in Cryptology – ASIACRYPT '96. Proceedings, 1996. XII, 395 pages. 1996.

Vol. 1164: K. Berquist, A. Berquist (Eds.), Managing Information Highways. XIV, 417 pages. 1996.

Vol. 1165: J.-R. Abrial, E. Börger, H. Langmaack (Eds.), Formal Methods for Industrial Applications. VIII, 511 pages. 1996.

Vol. 1166: M. Srivas, A. Camilleri (Eds.), Formal Methods in Computer-Aided Design. Proceedings, 1996. IX, 470 pages. 1996.

Vol. 1167: I. Sommerville (Ed.), Software Configuration Management. VII, 291 pages. 1996.

Vol. 1168: I. Smith, B. Faltings (Eds.), Advances in Case-Based Reasoning. Proceedings, 1996. IX, 531 pages. 1996. (Subseries LNAI).

Vol. 1169: M. Broy, S. Merz, K. Spies (Eds.), Formal Systems Specification. XXIII, 541 pages. 1996.

Vol. 1170: M. Nagl (Ed.), Building Tightly Integrated Software Development Environments: The IPSEN Approach. IX, 709 pages. 1996.

Vol. 1171: A. Franz, Automatic Ambiguity Resolution in Natural Language Processing. XIX, 155 pages. 1996. (Subseries LNAI).

Vol. 1172: J. Pieprzyk, J. Seberry (Eds.), Information Security and Privacy. Proceedings, 1996. IX, 333 pages. 1996.

Vol. 1173: W. Rucklidge, Efficient Visual Recognition Using the Hausdorff Distance. XIII, 178 pages. 1996.

Vol. 1174: R. Anderson (Ed.), Information Hiding. Proceedings, 1996. VIII, 351 pages. 1996.

Vol. 1175: K.G. Jeffery, J. Král, M. Bartošek (Eds.), SOFSEM'96: Theory and Practice of Informatics. Proceedings, 1996. XII, 491 pages. 1996.

Vol. 1176: S. Miguet, A. Montanvert, S. Ubéda (Eds.), Discrete Geometry for Computer Imagery. Proceedings, 1996. XI, 349 pages. 1996.

Vol. 1177: J.P. Müller, The Design of Intelligent Agents. XV, 227 pages. 1996. (Subseries LNAI).

Vol. 1178: T. Asano, Y. Igarashi, H. Nagamochi, S. Miyano, S. Suri (Eds.), Algorithms and Computation. Proceedings, 1996. X, 448 pages. 1996.

Vol. 1179: J. Jaffar, R.H.C. Yap (Eds.), Concurrency and Parallelism, Programming, Networking, and Security. Proceedings, 1996. XIII, 394 pages. 1996.

Vol. 1180: V. Chandru, V. Vinay (Eds.), Foundations of Software Technology and Theoretical Computer Science. Proceedings, 1996. XI, 387 pages. 1996.

Vol. 1181: D. Bjørner, M. Broy, I.V. Pottosin (Eds.), Perspectives of System Informatics. Proceedings, 1996. XVII, 447 pages. 1996.

Vol. 1182: W. Hasan, Optimization of SQL Queries for Parallel Machines. XVIII, 133 pages. 1996.

Vol. 1183: A. Wierse, G.G. Grinstein, U. Lang (Eds.), Database Issues for Data Visualization. Proceedings, 1995. XIV, 219 pages. 1996.

Vol. 1184: J. Waśniewski, J. Dongarra, K. Madsen, D. Olesen (Eds.), Applied Parallel Computing. Proceedings, 1996. XIII, 722 pages. 1996.

Vol. 1185: G. Ventre, J. Domingo-Pascual, A. Danthine (Eds.), Multimedia Telecommunications and Applications. Proceedings, 1996. XII, 267 pages. 1996.

Vol. 1186: F. Afrati, P. Kolaitis (Eds.), Database Theory - ICDT'97. Proceedings, 1997. XIII, 477 pages. 1997.

Vol. 1187: K. Schlechta, Nonmonotonic Logics. IX, 243 pages. 1997. (Subseries LNAI).

Vol. 1189: : Lomas (Ed.), Cryptographic Protocols. Proceedings, 1996. VIII, 203 pages. 1997.

Vol. 1190: S. North (Ed.), Graph Drawing. Proceedings, 1996. XI, 409 pages. 1997.

Vol. 1191: V. Gaede, A. Brodsky, O. Günther, D. Srivastava, V. Vianu, M. Wallace (Eds.), Constraint Databases and Applications. Proceedings, 1996. X, 345 pages. 1996.

Vol. 1192: M. Dam (Ed.), Analysis and Verification of Multiple-Agent Languages. Proceedings, 1996. VIII, 435 pages. 1997.